NCERT SOLUTIONS

Chemistry

CLASS
11

NCERT SOLUTIONS

Chemistry

CLASS
11

with *Selected* **NCERT Exemplar** Problems

by
Purnima Sharma

✶arihant
Arihant Prakashan (School Division Series)

ꜽ **Administrative & Production Offices**

Regd. Office

'Ramchhaya' 4577/15, Agarwal Road, Darya Ganj, New Delhi -110002
Tele: 011- 47630600, 43518550

ꜽ **Head Office**

Kalindi, TP Nagar, Meerut (UP) - 250002
Tel: 0121-7156203, 7156204

ꜽ **Sales & Support Offices**

Agra, Ahmedabad, Bengaluru, Bareilly, Chennai, Delhi, Guwahati, Hyderabad, Jaipur, Jhansi, Kolkata, Lucknow, Nagpur & Pune.

ꜽ **ISBN**   978-93-27198-05-8

PO No : TXT-XX-XXXXXXX-X-XX

Published by Arihant Publications (India) Ltd.

For further information about the books published by Arihant, log on to www.arihantbooks.com or e-mail at info@arihantbooks.com

Follow us on

Preface

Feeling the immense importance and value of NCERT books, we are presenting this book, having the NCERT Exercises Solutions.

For the overall benefit of the students we have made this book unique in such a way that it presents not only solutions but also detailed explanations. Through these detailed and through explanations, students can learn the concepts which will enhance their thinking and learning abilities.

We have introduced some **Additional Features** with the solutions which are given below:

Thinking Process ( ) Before giving solutions to questions we have discussed the points that tell how to approach to solve a problem. Here we have tried to cover all those loopholes which may lead to confusion. All formulae and hints are discussed in full detail.

Note We have provided notes also to solutions in which special points are mentioned which are of great value for the students.

This book also covers Solutions to selected problems of **NCERT Exemplar Problems.**

With the hope that this book will be of great help to the students, we wish great success to our readers.

Purnima Sharma

Contents

Chapter 1

Some Basic Concepts of Chemistry

Important Results

1. Seven **basic SI units** for physical quantities are:
   Length-metre (m), mass-kilogram (kg), time-second (s), temperature-kelvin (K), electric current-Ampere (A), Luminous intensity-Candela (Cd) and amount of substance-Mole (mol).

2. **Some useful conversion factors**

   $1\ pm = 10^{-12}\ m$, $1\ Å = 10^{-10}\ m$, $1\ nm = 10^{-9}\ m$

   $1\ L = 10^{-3}\ m^3 = 1\ dm^3$; $760\ torr = 101325\ Pa = Nm^{-2}$

   $1\ atm = 1.01325\ bar$

   $1\ bar = 10^5\ Nm^{-2} = 10^5\ Pa$; $1\ atm = 760\ mm\ Hg = 760\ torr$

   $1\ Calorie = 4.184\ J$, $1\ eV = 1.6022 \times 10^{-19}\ J$

3. $Mole = \dfrac{Mass\ (g)}{Molar\ mass\ (g\ mol^{-1})}$

4. 1 mole of a substance $= N_0$ molecules $= 6.022 \times 10^{23}$ molecules
   1 mole of an element $= N_0$ atoms $= 6.022 \times 10^{23}$ atoms

5. $1\ amu\ (or\ u) = \dfrac{Atomic\ mass}{N_0}$ $(N_0 = \text{Avogadro number} = 6.022 \times 10^{23})$

6. At STP $(T = 273\ K$ and $p = 1\ atm)$ 1 mole of an ideal gas occupies volume 22.4 L.

7. Molarity $=$ concentration in $mol\ L^{-1}$.

   $$Molarity = \dfrac{Number\ of\ moles}{Volume\ in\ litres}$$

8. Normality $=$ concentration in $g\ equi.\ L^{-1}$.
   (i) Normality of an acid $=$ molarity $\times$ basicity (basicity is the number of ionisable H^+ ions.
   (ii) Normality of a base $=$ molarity $\times$ acidity (acidity is the number of ionisable OH^- ions).

9. Molality $=$ concentration in mol per kg solvent.

10. Molality $= \dfrac{\text{Number of moles}}{\text{Mass of solvent (kg)}}$

11. Mass per cent $= \dfrac{\text{Mass of solute} \times 100}{\text{Mass of solution}}$

12. **Percentage composition** Mass % of an element
$$= \dfrac{\text{Mass of that element in the compound} \times 100}{\text{Molar mass of the compound}}.$$

13. Mole fraction of the component 1 in the mixture of 1 and 2 with number of moles n_1 and n_2,
$$x_1 = \dfrac{n_1}{n_1 + n_2}; x_1 + x_2 = 1$$
So, $\qquad x_1 = 1 - x_2$

14. Empirical formula represents the simplest whole number ratio of various atoms present in a compound.

15. Molecular formula represents exact number of different types of atoms present in a molecule of a compound.

16. Molecular formula $= n \times$ empirical formula and
$$n = \dfrac{\text{Molar mass}}{\text{Empirical formula mass}}$$

17. In a reaction, when the reactants are not present in the amounts as required by a balanced chemical reaction, in this case, one reactant is in excess over the other. The reactant which is present in lesser amount gets consumed first. This reactant is known as **limiting reagent** because it limits the amount of product.

18. Average molar mass of an element
$$\overline{M} = \dfrac{\text{Sum of isotopic molar mass} \times \text{\% abundance}}{100} \text{ or } \dfrac{\Sigma A_i \times P_i}{100}$$
where, P_i is the per cent abundance of isotope with atomic mass A_i.

or $\qquad\qquad\qquad \overline{M} = \Sigma f_i \times A_i$

where, $f_i =$ fractional abundances of isotopes and $A_i =$ their corresponding mass numbers.

Exercises

Question 1. Calculate the molecular mass of the following.
  (i) H_2O (ii) CO_2 (iii) CH_4

      (i) Molecular mass of a molecule is the sum of atomic masses of all the atoms present in the molecule.
   (ii) Molecular mass of H = 1.0079
        Molecular mass of O = 16.00
        Molecular mass of C = 12.01

Solution.
(i) Molecular mass of H_2O = 2 × Atomic mass of hydrogen
+ 1 × Atomic mass of oxygen
= 2 × 1.0079 u + 1 × 16.00 u = 18.0158 u
(ii) Molecular mass of CO_2 = 1 × Atomic mass of carbon
+ 2 × Atomic mass of oxygen
= 1 × 12.01 u + 2 × 16.00 u = 44.01 u
(iii) Molecular mass of CH_4 = 1 × Atomic mass of carbon
+ 4 × Atomic mass of hydrogen
= 1 × 12.01 u + 4 × 1.0079 u = 16.0416

Question 2. Calculate the mass per cent of different elements present in sodium sulphate, Na_2SO_4.

Solution. Mass per cent of an element

$$= \frac{\text{Mass of that element in the compound} \times 100}{\text{Molar mass of the compound}}$$

Molar mass of Na_2SO_4 = (2 × 22.99) + 32.06 + (4 × 16.00) = 142.04 g

Mass per cent of sodium $= \dfrac{45.98 \times 100}{142.04} = 32.37$

Mass per cent of sulphur $= \dfrac{32.06 \times 100}{142.04} = 22.57$

Mass per cent of oxygen $= \dfrac{64 \times 100}{142.04} = 45.06$

Question 3. Determine the empirical formula of an oxide of iron which has 69.9% iron and 30.1% dioxygen by mass.

(i) Empirical formula shows the number of moles of different elements present in a molecule, so first find the relative number of moles of each element by dividing the mass percentage by respective atomic masses.
(ii) Divide the mole value obtained in above step by the smallest number, to obtain the simplest ratio.
(iii) Write the empirical formula by mentioning the numbers after writing the symbols of respective elements.

Solution.

Element	Symbol	% by mass	Atomic mass	Relative number of moles of element	Simple molar ratio	Simple whole number molar ratio
Iron	Fe	69.9	55.85	$\dfrac{69.9}{55.85} = 1.25$	$\dfrac{1.25}{1.25} = 1$	1 × 2 = 2
Oxygen	O	30.1	16.00	$\dfrac{30.1}{16.00} = 1.88$	$\dfrac{1.88}{1.25} = 1.5$	1.5 × 2 = 3

∴ Empirical formula = Fe_2O_3

Note *In case the ratios are not whole numbers, they may be converted into whole number by multiplying by the suitable coefficient.*

4   *NCERT* Class XI **Chemistry Solutions**

Question 4. Calculate the amount of carbon dioxide that could be produced when
  (i) 1 mole of carbon is burnt in air.
  (ii) 1 mole of carbon is burnt in 16 g of dioxygen.
  (iii) 2 moles of carbon are burnt in 16 g of dioxygen.

    (i) In order to find the moles of different elements/compounds taking part in the reaction, write a balanced chemical equation for combustion of carbon in dioxygen (air).
    (ii) Calculate the amount of CO_2 produced with the help of information available from the balanced chemical equation.

Solution. $C(s) + O_2(g) \longrightarrow CO_2(g)$
         1 mol 1 mol   1 mol
                32 g   44 g

  (i) According to the equation when 1 mole of carbon is burnt completely, CO_2 produced is 44 g.
  (ii) 1 mole of carbon requires 32 g dioxygen from the reaction. But we have only 16g dioxygen. Hence, dioxygen is the limiting reagent. So, the amount of CO_2 produced by 16 g dioxygen is 22 g.
  (iii) In this case again, dioxygen is the limiting reagent. 16 g dioxygen can react only with 0.5 mole of carbon and produce 22 g CO_2.

Note *Limiting reagent limits the amount of product formed because it is present in lesser amount and gets consumed first.*

Question 5. Calculate the mass of sodium acetate, CH_3COONa required to make 500 mL of 0.375 molar aqueous solution. Molar mass of sodium acetate is 82.0245 g mol^{-1}.

Solution. Molarity $= \dfrac{w \times 1000}{m \times \text{volume of solution (mL)}}$

where, w = mass of solute and m = molar mass of solute.
Given,   molarity of the solution = 0.375 M
Molar mass of solute, m = 82.0245 g mol^{-1}

Volume of solution = 500 mL
Mass of solute = ?

∴ Mass of solute, $w = \dfrac{0.375 \times 82.0245 \times 500}{1000} = 15.379 \text{ g} \approx 15.38 \text{ g}$

Question 6. Calculate the concentration of nitric acid in mol per litre in a sample which has a density, 1.41 g mL^{-1} and the mass per cent of nitric acid in it being 69%.

    (i) We know that molarity $= \dfrac{w \times 1000}{m \times V}$ so in order to calculate molarity, we require mass and molar mass of solute and volume of the solution. To calculate mass convert mass per cent into gram.

(ii) Calculate, molar mass of nitric acid by adding atomic masses of different atoms and volume of solution by using the formula, $d = \dfrac{m}{V}$.

(iii) Now put these values in the formula of molarity.

Solution. $\text{Molarity} = \dfrac{w \times 1000}{m \times \text{volume of solution (mL)}}$

Given, $d = 1.41 \text{ g mL}^{-1}$, mass % of $HNO_3 = 69\%$

69% HNO_3 means 100 g of its solution contains 69 g HNO_3 (nitric acid).
Hence, mass of HNO_3 (solute) = 69 g.

Molar mass of nitric acid,

$HNO_3 = 1.0079 + 14.0067 + (3 \times 16.00) = 63.0146 \text{ g mol}^{-1}$

$$\text{Density, } d = \dfrac{m}{V} \text{ or } V = \dfrac{m}{d} = \dfrac{100 \text{ g}}{1.41 \text{ g mL}^{-1}}$$

$$\text{Molarity} = \dfrac{w \times 1000}{m \times \text{volume of solution (mL)}}$$

$$= \dfrac{69 \times 1000 \times 1.41}{63.0146 \times 100} = 15.439 \text{ M}$$

Note *Concentration of a substance in mol per litre is known as molarity.*

Question 7. How much copper can be obtained from 100 g of copper sulphate $(CuSO_4)$?

Solution. Molar mass of $CuSO_4 = 63.54 + 32.06 + (4 \times 16)$

$$= 159.6 \text{ g mol}^{-1}$$

159.6 g $CuSO_4$ contains = 63.54 g Cu

1 g $CuSO_4$ contains $= \dfrac{63.54}{159.6}$ g Cu

∴   100 g $CuSO_4$ contains $= \dfrac{63.54 \times 100}{159.6} = 39.81$ g Cu

Question 8. Determine the molecular formula of an oxide of iron in which the mass per cent of iron and oxygen are 69.9 and 30.1 respectively. Given that molar mass of the oxide is 159.89 mol^{-1}.

(i) We know that molecular formula = (empirical formula)$_n$ so find the empirical formula.

(ii) Then, find the value of *n* by using the formula

$$n = \dfrac{\text{Molar mass}}{\text{Empirical formula mass}}$$

(iii) Multiply empirical formula by *n* to get the molecular formula.

Solution. Calculation of empirical formula (see solution of Q. 3 as similar data is given). Empirical formula mass of

$Fe_2O_3 = (2 \times 55.85) + (3 \times 16.00) = 159.7 \text{ g mol}^{-1}$

$$n = \frac{\text{Molar mass}}{\text{Empirical formula mass}} = \frac{159.8}{159.7} = 1$$

Hence, molecular formula is same as empirical formula; Fe_2O_3.

Question 9. Calculate the atomic mass (average) of chlorine using the following data.

Isotope	% natural abundance	Molar mass
^{35}Cl	75.77	34.9689
^{37}Cl	24.23	36.9659

Solution. Average atomic mass is the sum of the products of fractional abundances (f_i) of the isotopes and their corresponding mass number (A_i).

Average atomic mass, $\overline{A} = \Sigma\, f_i \cdot A_i = f_1 \times A_1 + f_2 \times A_2 + \ldots\ldots$

Isotope	% natural abundance	Fractional abundance	Molar mass
^{35}Cl	75.77	0.7577	34.9689
^{37}Cl	24.23	0.2423	36.9659

Average atomic mass,
$$\overline{A} = 0.7577 \times 34.9689 + 0.2423 \times 36.9659$$
$$= 26.4959 + 8.9568 = 35.4527$$

Question 10. In three moles of ethane (C_2H_6), calculate the following.
 (i) Number of moles of carbon atoms.
 (ii) Number of moles of hydrogen atoms.
 (iii) Number of molecule of ethane.

Solution.
 (i) 1 mole of ethane, C_2H_6 contains 2 moles of carbon atoms.
   $\therefore$ 3 moles of ethane, C_2H_6 will contain $2 \times 3 = 6$ moles of C-atoms.
 (ii) 1 mole of ethane, C_2H_6 contains 6 moles of H-atoms.
   $\therefore$ 3 moles of ethane, C_2H_6 will contain $3 \times 6 = 18$ moles of H-atoms.
 (iii) 1 mole of ethane $= 6.022 \times 10^{23}$ molecules of ethane.
   $\therefore$ 3 moles of ethane $= 3 \times 6.022 \times 10^{23} = 18.066 \times 10^{23}$ molecules of ethane.

Question 11. What is the concentration of sugar ($C_{12}H_{22}O_{11}$) in mol L^{-1} if its 20g are dissolved in enough water to make a final volume up to 2 L?

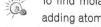 To find molar concentration, calculate the molar mass of the sugar, by adding atomic masses of different elements as molarity $= \dfrac{w}{m \times V}$.

Solution. Molar mass of the sugar, $C_{12}H_{22}O_{11}$,
$$m = (12 \times 12.01) + (22 \times 1.0079) + (11 \times 16.00)$$
$$= 342.2938 \text{ g mol}^{-1} \approx 342$$

Some Basic Concepts of Chemistry

Given, $w = 20$ g, $V = 2$ L

$$\text{Molarity} = \frac{w}{m \times V \text{ (L)}} = \frac{20}{342 \times 2} = 0.0292 \text{ mol L}^{-1}$$

$$= 0.0292 \text{ M}$$

Question 12. If the density of methanol is 0.793 kg L^{-1}, what is its volume needed for making 2.5 L of its 0.25 M solution?

(i) In case of dilution, volume is calculated by using molarity equation, $M_1V_1 = M_2V_2$, we have M_2, V_2 but not M_1, so calculate molarity of the given solution from density.

(ii) Then, find volume (V_1) needed by using molarity equation, $M_1V_1 = M_2V_2$

Solution. Given, $d = 0.793$ kg L$^{-1} = 0.793 \times 10^{3}$ g L^{-1}

Final volume, $V_2 = 2.5$ L

Final molarity, $M_2 = 0.25$ M

Molarity of initial solution $M_1 = ?$

Initial volume $V_1 = ?$

Molar mass of methanol,

$$\text{CH}_3\text{OH} = (1 \times 12.01) + (4 \times 1.0079) + 16.00 = 32.0416 \approx 32$$

$$\text{Molarity} = \frac{0.793 \times 10^{3} \text{ g L}^{-1}}{32 \text{ g mol}^{-1}} = 24.781 \text{ mol L}^{-1}$$

$$M_1V_1 = M_2V_2$$
$$24.781 \times V_1 = 0.25 \times 2.5$$
$$V_1 = \frac{0.25 \times 2.5}{24.781} = 0.02522 \text{ L} = 25.22 \text{ mL}$$

Question 13. Pressure is determined as force per unit area of the surface. The SI unit of pressure, pascal is as shown below.

$$1 \text{ Pa} = 1 \text{ Nm}^{-2}$$

If the mass of air at sea level is 1034 g cm^{-2}, calculate the pressure in pascal.

(i) The SI unit of mass is kilogram and of length is m so convert gram to kilogram and cm^2 to m^2 as pressure is to be calculated in SI units.

(ii) Write 1 kg ms^{-2} = 1 N and 1 Nm^{-2} = 1 Pa to obtain pressure in pascal.

Solution. Pressure is the force or weight per unit area.

$$\text{Pressure} = \frac{1034 \text{ g} \times 9.8 \text{ ms}^{-2}}{\text{cm}^2}$$

$$= \frac{1034 \text{ kg} \times 100 \times 100 \times 9.8 \text{ ms}^{-2}}{1000 \text{ m}^2}$$

$$= 101332.0 \text{ Nm}^{-2} \qquad (1 \text{ N} = 1 \text{ kg ms}^{-2})$$

$$= 1.01332 \times 10^5 \text{ Pa}$$

Question 14. What is the SI unit of mass? How is it defined?

Solution. SI unit of mass is kilogram (kg). It is equal to the mass of international prototype of the kilogram.

Question 15. Match the following prefixes with their multiples.

	Prefixes	Multiples
(i)	micro	10^6
(ii)	deca	10^9
(iii)	mega	10^{-6}
(iv)	giga	10^{-15}
(v)	femto	10

Solution. Micro $= 10^{-6}$, deca $= 10$, mega $= 10^6$, giga $= 10^9$ and femto $= 10^{-15}$.

Question 16. What do you mean by significant figures?

Solution. The number of significant figures in a given data is the number of all certain digits plus one uncertain digit. For example, 3.015 has four significant figures.

Note *All measured quantities are reported in such a way that only the last digit is uncertain (usually by ± 1).*

Question 17. A sample of drinking water was found to be severely contaminated with chloroform, $CHCl_3$, supposed to be carcinogenic in nature. The level of contamination was 15ppm (by mass).

(i) Express this in per cent by mass.

(ii) Determine the molarity of chloroform in the water sample.

Solution.

(i) 15 ppm means 15 parts in one million (10^6) parts.

Therefore, % by mass $= \dfrac{15 \times 100}{10^6} = 1.5 \times 10^{-3}$ %

(ii) Molar mass of $CHCl_3 = 12.01 + 1.0079 + (3 \times 35.45)$

$$M_{CHCl_3} = 119.367 \approx 119 \text{ g mol}^{-1}$$

1.5×10^{-3}% means 1.5×10^{-3} g chloroform is present in 100 g sample.

Molarity, $M = \dfrac{w \times 1000}{m \times \text{volume of sample}}$

(For water, density $= 1$ g cm^{-3}, so mass = volume)

$$M = \dfrac{1.5 \times 10^{-3} \times 1000}{119 \times 100} = 0.000126 = 1.26 \times 10^{-4} \text{ M}$$

Question 18. Express the following in scientific notation:

(i) 0.0048   (ii) 234000   (iii) 8008

(iv) 5000   (v) 6.0012

(i) To convert a digit into scientific notation ($N \times 10^n$) shift the decimal point just after a non-zero digit.

(ii) If shifting is towards right, n has negative value and if shifting is towards left, n has positive value.

Solution. (i) 4.8×10^{-3} (ii) 2.34×10^5 (iii) 8.008×10^3
(iv) 5.0×10^3 (v) 6.0012×10^0

Note *In scientific notation any number can be expressed in the form of* $N \times 10^n$. *Where n is an exponent having positive or negative values and N can vary between 1 to 10.*

Question 19. How many significant figures are present in the following?

(i) 0.0025   (ii) 208   (iii) 5005   (iv) 126000   (v) 500.0   (vi) 2.0034

   (a) All non-zero digits are significant.
   (b) Zeros present to left/right of a number are non-significant however, zeros present after decimal points are significant.
   (c) Zeros present between two non-zero digits are significant.

Solution. (i) 2   (ii) 3   (iii) 4   (iv) 3   (v) 4   (vi) 5

Question 20. Round up the following up to three significant figures :

(i) 34.216   (ii) 10.4107   (iii) 0.04597   (iv) 2808

   To round up a number, left the last digit as such, if the digit next to it is less than 5 and increase it by 1, if the next digit is greater than 5.

Solution. (i) 34.2   (ii) 10.4   (iii) 0.0460   (iv) 2810

Question 21. The following data are obtained when dinitrogen and dioxygen react together to form different compounds.

	Mass of dinitrogen	Mass of dioxygen
(i)	14 g	16 g
(ii)	14 g	32 g
(iii)	28 g	32 g
(iv)	28 g	80 g

(a) Which law of chemical combination is obeyed by the above experimental data? Give its statement.

(b) Fill in the blanks in the following conversions.
   (i) 1 km = ... mm = ... pm
   (ii) 1 mg = ... kg = ...ng
   (iii) 1 mL = ... L = ... dm^3

Solution.

(a) On fixing the mass of dinitrogen as 28 g, the masses of dioxygen combined are 32, 64, 32 and 80 in the given four oxides. These are in the simple whole number ratio *i.e.*, $2:4:2:5$. Hence, the given data obey the law of multiple proportions.

Law of multiple proportions This law was proposed by Dalton in 1803. According to this law, if two elements can combine to form more than one compound, the masses of one element that combine with a fixed mass of the other element are in the ratio of small whole numbers.

(b) (i) $1 \text{ km} = 1 \text{ km} \times \dfrac{1000 \text{ m}}{1 \text{ km}} \times \dfrac{100 \text{ cm}}{1 \text{ m}} \times \dfrac{10 \text{ mm}}{1 \text{ cm}} = 10^6 \text{mm}$

$1 \text{ km} = 1 \text{ km} \times \dfrac{1000 \text{ m}}{1 \text{ km}} \times \dfrac{1 \text{ pm}}{10^{-12} \text{ m}} = 10^{15} \text{ pm}$

$\therefore 1 \text{ km} = 10^6 \text{ mm} = 10^{15} \text{ pm}$

(ii) $1 \text{ mg} = 1 \text{ mg} \times \dfrac{1 \text{ g}}{1000 \text{ mg}} \times \dfrac{1 \text{ kg}}{1000 \text{ g}} = 10^{-6} \text{ kg}$

$1 \text{ mg} = 1 \text{ mg} \times \dfrac{1 \text{ g}}{1000 \text{ mg}} \times \dfrac{1 \text{ ng}}{10^{-9} \text{ g}} = 10^6 \text{ ng}$

$\therefore 1 \text{ mg} = 10^{-6} \text{ kg} = 10^6 \text{ ng}$

(iii) $1 \text{ mL} = 1 \text{ mL} \times \dfrac{1 \text{ L}}{1000 \text{ mL}} = 10^{-3} \text{ L}$

$1 \text{ mL} = 1 \text{ cm}^3 = 1 \text{ cm}^3 \times \dfrac{1 \text{ dm} \times 1 \text{ dm} \times 1 \text{ dm}}{10 \text{ cm} \times 10 \text{ cm} \times 10 \text{ cm}} = 10^{-3} \text{ dm}^3$

$\therefore \qquad 1 \text{ mL} = 10^{-3} \text{ L} = 10^{-3} \text{ dm}^3$

Question 22. If the speed of light is $3.0 \times 10^8 \text{ ms}^{-1}$, calculate the distance covered by light in 2.00 ns.

Solution. $\quad 2.00 \text{ ns} = 2.00 \times 10^{-9} \text{ s}$ $\hfill (1 \text{ ns} = 10^{-9} \text{ s})$

Distance covered = Speed $\times$ Time

$\qquad\qquad\qquad = 3.0 \times 10^8 \text{ ms}^{-1} \times 2.0 \times 10^{-9} \text{ s}$

$\qquad\qquad\qquad = 6.0 \times 10^{-1} \text{ m} = 0.6 \text{ m}$

Question 23. In a reaction, $A + B_2 \longrightarrow AB_2$, identify the limiting reagent, if any, in the following reaction mixtures.

   (i) **300 atoms of** A + **200 molecules of** B

  (ii) **2 moles of** A + **3 moles of** B

 (iii) **100 atoms of** A + **100 molecules of** B

 (iv) **5 moles of** A + **2.5 moles of** B

  (v) **2.5 moles of** A + **5 moles of** B

Limiting reagent is the reagent that is consumed first in the reaction, so compare the amounts of A and B to find the limiting reagent.

Solution. $\quad A + B_2 \longrightarrow AB_2$

   (i) According to the above reaction, 1 atom of A reacts with 1 molecule of B.

     $\therefore$ 200 atoms of A will react with 200 molecules of B. In this case, B is the limiting reagent, so A is in excess.

  (ii) According to the above reaction, 1 mole of A reacts with 1 mole of B.

     $\therefore$ 2 moles of A will react with 2 moles of B. In this case A is limiting reagent and B is in excess.

 (iii) No limiting reagent.

(iv) 2.5 moles of B requires only 2.5 moles of A to react. So, B is limiting reagent and A is in excess.
(v) 2.5 moles of A requires only 2.5 moles of B to react. So, A is limiting reagent and B is in excess.

Question 24. Dinitrogen and dihydrogen react with each other to produce ammonia according to the following chemical equation,

$$N_2(g) + 3H_2(g) \longrightarrow 2NH_3(g)$$

(i) Calculate the mass of ammonia produced if 2.00×10^3 g dinitrogen reacts with 1.00×10^3 g of dihydrogen.
(ii) Will any of the two reactants remain unreacted?
(iii) If yes, which one and what would be its mass?

Solution. $N_2(g) + 3H_2(g) \longrightarrow 2NH_3(g)$
       1 mol   3 mol   2 mol
       28 g   6 g   34 g

28 g N_2 reacts with 6 g H_2

1 g N_2 reacts with $\dfrac{6}{28}$ g H_2

∴ 2000 g N_2 will react with $\dfrac{2000 \times 6}{28} = 428.57$ g H_2

Hence, N_2 is the limiting reagent and H_2 is in excess. N_2 limits the amount of ammonia produced.

28 g N_2 produces 34 g NH_3

1 g N_2 produces $\dfrac{34}{28}$ g NH_3

2000 g N_2 will produce $\dfrac{34}{28} \times 2000 = 2428.57$ g NH_3

(ii) H_2 is in excess so it will remain unreacted.
(iii) Amount of H_2 remain unreacted = 1000 − 428.57 = 571.43 g

Question 25. How are 0.50 mole Na_2CO_3 and 0.50 M Na_2CO_3 different?
Solution. Molar mass of $Na_2CO_3 = (2 \times 22.99) + 12.01 + (3 \times 16)$
$$= 105.99 \approx 106 \text{ g mol}^{-1}$$
0.50 mole $Na_2CO_3 = 0.50 \times 106 = 53$ g Na_2CO_3
0.50 M Na_2CO_3 means 53 g Na_2CO_3 is present in 1 L of the solution.

Question 26. If ten volumes of dihydrogen gas react with five volumes of dioxygen gas, how many volumes of water vapour would be produced?

(i) In order to find the moles of H_2 and O_2 generally utilised to obtain water, write a balanced chemical equation for the production of water vapours from H_2 and O_2.
(ii) Apply Gay-Lussac's law of gaseous volume to calculate the volume of water vapours produced.

Solution. $2H_2(g) + O_2(g) \longrightarrow 2H_2O(g)$
          2 V   1 V   2 V

According to Gay-Lussac's law of gaseous volume, 2 volumes of dihydrogen react with 1 volume of O_2 to produce 2 volumes of water vapour. Therefore, 10 volumes of dihydrogen on reaction with 5 volumes of dioxygen will produce 10 volumes of water vapour.

Question 27. Convert the following into basic units.

(i) 28.7 pm   (ii) 15.15 μs   (iii) 25365 mg

The basic units for length is meter (m), for time is second (s) and for mass is kilogram (kg).

Solution.

(i) $28.7 \text{ pm} \times \dfrac{10^{-12} \text{ m}}{1 \text{ pm}} = 2.87 \times 10^{-11}$ m

(ii) $15.15 \text{ μs} \times \dfrac{10^{-6} \text{ s}}{1 \text{ μs}} = 1.515 \times 10^{-5}$ s

(iii) $25365 \text{ mg} \times \dfrac{1 \text{ g}}{1000 \text{ mg}} \times \dfrac{1 \text{ kg}}{1000 \text{ g}} = 2.5365 \times 10^{-2}$ kg

Question 28. Which one of the following will have the largest number of atoms?

(i) 1 g Au (s) (ii) 1 g Na (s) (iii) 1 g Li (s) (iv) 1 g of Cl_2 (g)

(i) We know that number of atoms = moles × N_A × atomicity, so first calculate the number of moles by using the formula,

$$\text{Moles of a substance} = \frac{\text{Mass of a substance } (g)}{\text{Molar mass}}$$

(ii) Then, find number of atoms from moles of the substance and compare them.
(Atomic masses : Au = 197, Na = 23, Li = 7, Cl = 35.5 u)

Solution.

(i) $1 \text{ g Au} = \dfrac{1}{197}$ mol atoms of Au $= \dfrac{1}{197} \times 6.022 \times 10^{23}$ atoms of Au.

(ii) $1 \text{ g Na} = \dfrac{1}{23}$ mole atoms of Na $= \dfrac{1}{23} \times 6.022 \times 10^{23}$ atoms of Na.

(iii) $1 \text{ g Li} = \dfrac{1}{7}$ mole atoms of Li $= \dfrac{1}{7} \times 6.022 \times 10^{23}$ molecules of Li.

(iv) $1 \text{ g Cl}_2 = \dfrac{1}{71}$ mole molecules of Cl_2

$$= \dfrac{1}{71} \times 6.022 \times 10^{23} \text{ molecules of Cl}_2.$$

$$= \frac{2}{71} \times 6.022 \times 10^{23} \text{ atoms of Cl}$$

(1 molecule of chlorine contains 2 atoms).

Therefore, 1 g of Li has largest number of atoms.

Note *If a substance exists in atomic form, it contains mole atoms and if a substance exists in molecular form, it contains mole molecules.*

Question 29. Calculate the molarity of a solution of ethanol in water in which the mole fraction of ethanol is 0.040.

(i) Molarity is the number of moles of solute present in 1 L of solution, so find moles of H_2O in 1 L solution of ethanol in water.

(ii) Then, find mole fraction of H_2O by using the formula $x_1 + x_2 = 1$ and moles of ethanol by using the formula, $x_{H_2O} = \dfrac{n_{H_2O}}{n_{C_2H_5OH} + n_{H_2O}}$

(iii) $n_{C_2H_5OH}$ gives the molarity of solution as moles of solute in 1L solution is equal to its molarity.

Solution. Molarity is defined as the moles of solute (ethanol) in 1 L of the solution.

1 L of ethanol solution (as it is diluted) = 1 L of water

Number of moles of H_2O in 1 L water $= \dfrac{1000 \text{ g}}{18} = 55.55$ moles

For a binary solution (binary solution contains two components)

$$x_1 + x_2 = 1$$

Hence,

$$x_{H_2O} = 1 - x_{C_2H_5OH}$$

$$x_{H_2O} = 1 - 0.040 = 0.96$$

$$x_{H_2O} = \frac{n_{H_2O}}{n_{H_2O} + n_{C_2H_5OH}}$$

$$0.96 = \frac{55.55}{55.55 + n_{C_2H_5OH}}$$

$$53.328 + 0.96\, n_{C_2H_5OH} = 55.55$$

$$0.96\, n_{C_2H_5OH} = 55.55 - 53.328 = 2.222$$

$$n_{C_2H_5OH} = \frac{2.222}{0.96} = 2.3145 \text{ mol}$$

Question 30. What will be the mass of one ^{12}C atom in gram?

Solution. Mass of 1 atom of $^{12}C = \dfrac{\text{Atomic mass of C}}{\text{Avogadro's number}}$

$$= \frac{12 \text{ g}}{6.022 \times 10^{23}} = 1.9927 \times 10^{-23} \text{ g}$$

Question 31. How many significant figures should be present in the answer of the following calculations?

(i) $\dfrac{0.02856 \times 298.15 \times 0.112}{0.5785}$

(ii) 5×5.364

(iii) $0.0125 + 0.7864 + 0.0215$

Solution.

(i) In multiplication and division, the least precise term 0.112 has 3 significant figures. Hence, the answer should not have more than three significant figures.

(ii) In multiplication, 5 is the exact number and the other number has 4 significant figures. Hence, the answer should have 4 significant figures.

(iii) In addition (or in subtraction), the answer cannot have more digits to the decimal point than either of the original members. Hence, the answer should have 4 significant figures.

Question 32. Use the data given in the following table to calculate the molar mass of naturally occurring argon.

Isotope	Isotopic molar mass	Abundance
^{36}Ar	35.96755 g mol^{-1}	0.337%
^{38}Ar	37.96272 g mol^{-1}	0.063%
^{40}Ar	39.9624 g mol^{-1}	99.600%

Solution. Average molar mass of

$Ar = \Sigma f_i \times A_i = (0.00337 \times 35.96755) + (0.00063 \times 37.96272)$

$+ (0.99600 \times 39.9624)$

$= 0.121 + 0.024 + 39.803 = 39.948$ g mol^{-1}

Question 33. Calculate the number of atoms in each of the following.

(i) **52 moles of Ar**   (ii) **52 u of He**   (iii) **52 g of He**

Solution.

(i) 1 mol of Ar = 6.022×10^{23} atoms.

52 moles of Ar = $52 \times 6.022 \times 10^{23}$ atoms

$= 313.144 \times 10^{23}$ atoms

$= 3.131 \times 10^{25}$ atoms

(ii) 4 u of He = 1 He atom

$\therefore$ 52 u of He $= \dfrac{52}{4}$ He atoms = 13 He atoms.

(iii) 1 mol atom of He = 4 g = 6.022×10^{23} atoms.

52 g of He $= \dfrac{52 \times 6.022 \times 10^{23}}{4}$ atoms

$= 78.286 \times 10^{23}$ atoms

$= 7.8286 \times 10^{24}$ atoms.

Question 34. A welding fuel gas contains carbon and hydrogen only. Burning a small sample of it in oxygen gives 3.38 g carbon dioxide, 0.690 g of water and no other products. A volume of 10.0 L (measured at STP) of this welding gas is found to weigh 11.6 g. Calculate (i) empirical formula (ii) molar mass of the gas and (iii) molecular formula.

(i) To find empirical formula, moles are required which are calculated by dividing the percentage of elements by their atomic mass and percentage is obtained from the mass of elements, so first calculate the amount of C and H in the given masses of CO_2 and H_2O by using the formulae $w_C\% = \dfrac{12}{44} \times$ wt. of CO_2, $w_H\% = \dfrac{2}{18} \times$ wt. of H_2O Then, calculate the per cent of C and H and empirical formula (by finding simplest ratio of moles of different elements).

(ii) At STP volume of 1 mole gas = 22.4 L thus, calculate the molar mass of the gas at STP by unitary method.

(iii) Since molecular formula = (empirical formula)$_n$, so calculate n by using the formula, $n = \dfrac{\text{Molar mass}}{\text{Empirical formula mass}}$ and then find molecular formula [by using molecular formula = (empirical formula)$_n$]

Solution.

(i)   44 g CO_2 = 12 g carbon

3.38 g CO_2 = $\dfrac{12}{44} \times 3.38$ g = 0.9218 g carbon

18 g H_2O = 2 g hydrogen

0.690 g H_2O = $\dfrac{2}{18} \times 0.690$ g = 0.0767 g hydrogen

Total mass of compound = 0.9218 + 0.0767 = 0.9985 g
(because compound contains only carbon and hydrogen).

% of C in the compound = $\dfrac{0.9218}{0.9985} \times 100 = 92.32$

% of H in the compound = $\dfrac{0.0767}{0.9985} \times 100 = 7.68$

Calculation for empirical formula

Element	Per cent by mass	Atomic mass	Relative number of moles of elements	Simplest molar ratio
C	92.32	12	$\dfrac{92.32}{12} = 7.69$	$\dfrac{7.69}{7.68} = 1$
H	7.68	1	$\dfrac{7.68}{1} = 7.68$	$\dfrac{7.69}{7.68} = 1$

Hence, empirical formula = CH

(ii) **Calculation for molar mass of the gas**
10.0 L of the given gas at STP weigh = 11.6 g
∴ 22.4 L of the given gas at STP will weigh

$$= \frac{11.6 \times 22.4}{10} = 25.984 \text{ g}$$

Molar mass = $25.984 \approx 26$ g mol^{-1}

(iii) Empirical formula mass (CH) = 12 + 1 = 13

∴ $n = \dfrac{\text{Molecular mass}}{\text{Empirical formula mass}} = \dfrac{26}{13} = 2$

Hence, molecular formula = $n \times$ CH = $2 \times$ CH = C_2H_2

Question 35. Calcium carbonate reacts with aqueous HCl to give $CaCl_2$ and CO_2 according to the reaction,

$$CaCO_3(s) + 2\,HCl(aq) \longrightarrow CaCl_2(aq) + CO_2(g) + H_2O(l)$$

What mass of $CaCO_3$ is required to react completely with 25 mL of 0.75 M HCl?

(i) To calculate the mass of $CaCO_3$ required to react completely with 25 mL of 0.75 M HCl first we will calculate the mass of HCl in 25 mL of 0.75 M HCl.

(ii) Now calculate the mass of $CaCO_3(g)$ by using the information available from a balanced chemical equation.

Solution.

(i) Calculation for mass of HCl in 25 mL of 0.75 M HCl

$$\text{Molarity} = \frac{w \times 1000}{m \times \text{vol (mL)}}$$

$$0.75 = \frac{w \times 1000}{36.5 \times 25}$$

(Molar mass of HCl = 1 + 35.5 = 36.5 g/mol)

$$w = 0.75 \times 36.5 \times 25 / 1000 = 0.6844 \text{ g}$$

(ii) Calculation for required mass of $CaCO_3$ to react completely with 0.6844 g HCl.

$$\underset{100 \text{ g}}{CaCO_3(s)} + \underset{2 \times 36.5 = 73 \text{ g}}{2HCl\,(aq)} \longrightarrow CaCl_2(aq) + CO_2(g) + H_2O(l)$$

According to balanced chemical equation,

73 g HCl completely reacts with 100 g $CaCO_3$

1 g HCl completely reacts with $\dfrac{100}{73}$ g $CaCO_3$

∴ 0.6844 g HCl will completely reacts with $\dfrac{100 \times 0.6844}{73}$

$$= 0.9375 \text{ g}$$

Note *The amount of substance present in a given volume of a solution is expressed in number of ways e.g., mass per cent, mole fraction, molarity and molality.*

Question 36. Chlorine is prepared in the laboratory by treating manganese dioxide (MnO_2) with aqueous hydrochloric acid according to the reaction,

$$4HCl(aq) + MnO_2(s) \longrightarrow 2H_2O(l) + MnCl_2(aq) + Cl_2(g)$$

How many grams of HCl reacts with 5.0 g of manganese dioxide?

Solution. $4\,HCl(aq) + MnO_2(s) \longrightarrow 2H_2O(l) + MnCl_2(aq) + Cl_2(g)$

$\qquad\quad\;\; 4 \times 36.5 \qquad\;\; 87\,g$

According to balanced chemical equation,

$\qquad$ 87 g of MnO_2 react with 4×36.5 g HCl

$\qquad$ 5 g of MnO_2 will react with $\dfrac{4 \times 36.5 \times 5}{87} = 8.39$ g HCl

Note *Amounts of one reactant required to react a particular amount of another reactant can be determined by using stoichiometric calculations.*

Selected NCERT Exemplar Problems

Short Answer Type

Question 1. How many significant figures should be present in the answer of the following calculation?

$$\frac{2.5 \times 1.25 \times 3.5}{2.01}$$

Solution. Least precise term 2.5 or 3.5 has two significant figures. Hence, the answer should have two significant figures.

$$\frac{2.5 \times 1.25 \times 3.5}{2.01} = 5.4415 \approx 5.4$$

Question 2. What is the difference between molality and molarity?

Solution. Molality It is defined as the number of moles of solute dissolved in 1 kg of solvent. It is independent of temperature.

Molarity It is defined as the number of moles of solute dissolved in 1 L of solution. It depends upon temperature (because, volume of solution $\propto$ temperature.)

Question 3. 45.4L of dinitrogen reacted with 22.7L of dioxygen and 45.4 L of nitrous oxide was formed. The reaction is given below

$$2N_2(g) + O_2(g) \longrightarrow 2N_2O(g)$$

Which law is being obeyed in this experiment? Write the statement of the law.

Solution. $2N_2(g) \;+\; O_2(g) \longrightarrow 2N_2O(g)$

$\qquad\quad$ 2 V $\qquad\;\;$ 1 V $\qquad\qquad$ 2 V

$\qquad\;\; \dfrac{45.4}{22.7} = 2 \qquad \dfrac{22.7}{22.7} = 1 \qquad \dfrac{45.4}{22.7} = 2$

Hence, the ratio between the volumes of the reactants and the product in the given question is simple *i.e.*, 2 : 1 : 2. It proves the Gay-Lussac's law of gaseous volumes.

Gay-Lussac's law of gaseous volumes   When gases combine or are produced in a chemical reaction, they do so in a simple ratio by volume provided all gases are at same temperature and pressure.

Question 4.   Hydrogen gas is prepared in the laboratory by reacting dil. HCl with granulated zinc. Following reaction takes place

$$Zn + 2HCl \longrightarrow ZnCl_2 + H_2$$

Calculate the volume of hydrogen gas liberated at STP when 32.65 g of zinc reacts with HCl. 1 mole of gas occupies 22.7 L volume at STP, atomic mass of $Zn = 65.3$ u

Solution.
$$\underset{65.3\text{ g}}{Zn} + 2HCl \longrightarrow ZnCl_2 + \underset{1 \text{ mol} = 22.7 \text{ L at STP (given)}}{H_2}$$

65.3 g Zn when reacts with HCl it produces $= 22.7$ L H_2 at STP
32.65 g Zn when reacts with HCl it will produce
$$\frac{22.7 \times 32.65}{65.3} = 11.35 \text{ L } H_2 \text{ at STP.}$$

Question 5.   The density of 3 molal solution of NaOH is 1.110 g mL^{-1}. Calculate the molarity of the solution.

Solution.   3 molal solution of NaOH means 3 moles of NaOH are dissolved in 1 kg solvent. So, the mass of solution
$$= 1000 \text{ g solvent} + 120 \text{ g NaOH} = 1120 \text{ g solution}$$
$$\text{(Molar mass of NaOH} = 23 + 16 + 1 = 40 \text{ g;}$$
$$3 \text{ moles of NaOH} = 3 \times 40 = 120 \text{ g)}$$
$$\text{Volume of solution} = \frac{\text{Mass of solution}}{\text{Density of solution}} \qquad \left(\because d = \frac{m}{V} \right)$$
$$V = \frac{1120 \text{ g}}{1.110 \text{ gmL}^{-1}} = 1009 \text{ mL}$$
$$\text{Molarity} = \frac{\text{Moles of solute} \times 1000}{\text{Volume of solution (mL)}} = \frac{3 \times 1000}{1009} = 2.973 \text{ M}$$

Question 6.   If 4 g of NaOH dissolves in 36 g of H_2O, calculate the mole fraction of each component in the solution. Also, determine the molarity of the solution (Specific gravity of solution is 1 g mL^{-1}).

Solution.   Number of moles of NaOH,
$$n_{NaOH} = \frac{4}{40} = 0.1 \text{ mol} \qquad \left\{ n = \frac{\text{Mass } (g)}{\text{Molar mass } (g \text{ mol}^{-1})} \right\}$$

Similarly, $n_{H_2O} = \dfrac{36}{18} = 2 \text{ mol}$

Mole fraction of NaOH,
$$x_{NaOH} = \frac{\text{Moles of NaOH}}{\text{Moles of NaOH} + \text{moles of } H_2O}$$

$$x_{NaOH} = \frac{0.1}{0.1+2} = 0.0476$$

Similarly, $\quad x_{H_2O} = \dfrac{n_{H_2O}}{n_{NaOH} + n_{H_2O}} = \dfrac{2}{0.1+2} = 0.9524$

Total mass of solution = mass of solute + mass of solvent

$$= 4 + 36 = 40\,g$$

$$\text{Volume of solution} = \frac{\text{Mass of solution}}{\text{Sp. gravity}} = \frac{40\,g}{1\,g\,mL^{-1}} = 40\,mL$$

$$\text{Molarity} = \frac{\text{Moles of solute} \times 1000}{\text{Volume of solution (mL)}} = \frac{0.1 \times 1000}{40} = 2.5\,M$$

Question 7. The reactant which is entirely consumed in the reaction is known as limiting reagent. In the reaction,

$$2A + 4B \longrightarrow 3C + 4D,$$

when 5 moles of A react with 6 moles of B then,

(i) which is the limiting reagent?

(ii) calculate the amount of C formed.

Solution. $2A + 4B \longrightarrow 3C + 4D$

According to the given reaction, 2 moles of A react with 4 moles of B.

Hence, 5 moles of A will react with 10 moles of $B \left(\dfrac{5 \times 4}{2} = 10 \text{ moles} \right)$

(i) It indicates that reactant B is limiting reagent as it will consume first in the reaction because we have only 6 moles of B.

(ii) Limiting reagent decide the amount of product produced.

According to the reaction,

4 moles of B produces 3 moles of C

$\therefore$ 6 moles of B will produce $\dfrac{3 \times 6}{4} = 4.5$ moles of C.

Long Answer Type

Question 8. A vessel contains 1.6 g of dioxygen at STP (273.15 K, 1 atm pressure). The gas is now transferred to another vessel at constant temperature, where pressure becomes half of the original pressure. Calculate

(i) volume of the new vessel.

(ii) number of molecules of dioxygen.

Solution.

(i) $p_1 = 1\,atm,\ p_2 = \dfrac{1}{2} = 0.5\,atm,\ T_1 = 273.15,\quad V_2 = ?,\ V_1 = ?$

32 g dioxygen occupies = 22.4 L volume at STP

$\therefore 1.6$ g dioxygen will occupy $= \dfrac{22.4\,L \times 1.6\,g}{32\,g} = 1.12\,L$

$$V_1 = 1.12\,L$$

From Boyle's law (as temperature is constant),
$$p_1V_1 = p_2V_2$$
$$V_2 = \frac{p_1V_1}{p_2} = \frac{1\,atm \times 1.12\,L}{0.5\,atm} = 2.24\,L$$

(ii) Number of moles of dioxygen $= \dfrac{\text{mass of dioxygen}}{\text{molar mass of dioxygen}}$

$$n_{O_2} = \frac{1.6}{32} = 0.05\,mol$$

1 mole molecule of dioxygen $= 6.022 \times 10^{23}$ molecules of dioxygen

$\therefore$ 0.05 mole molecules of dioxygen
$$= 6.022 \times 10^{23} \times 0.05 \text{ molecule of } O_2$$
$$= 0.3011 \times 10^{23} \text{ molecules}$$
$$= 3.011 \times 10^{22} \text{ molecules}$$

Question 9. Calcium carbonate reacts with aqueous HCl to give $CaCl_2$ and CO_2 according to the reaction,
$$CaCO_3(s) + 2HCl(aq) \longrightarrow CaCl_2(aq) + CO_2(g) + H_2O(l)$$
What mass of $CaCl_2$ will be formed when 250 mL of 0.76 M HCl reacts with 1000 g of $CaCO_3$? Name the limiting reagent. Calculate the number of moles of $CaCl_2$ formed in the reaction.

Solution. Molar mass of $CaCO_3 = 40 + 12 + 3 \times 16 = 100$ g mol^{-1}

Moles of $CaCO_3$ in 1000 g,
$$n_{CaCO_3} = \frac{\text{Mass } (g)}{\text{Molar mass}}$$
$$n_{CaCO_3} = \frac{1000\,g}{100\,g\,mol^{-1}} = 10\,mol$$
$$\text{Molarity} = \frac{\text{Moles of solute (HCl)} \times 1000}{\text{Volume of solution}}$$

(Moles of HCl in 250 mL of 0.76 M HCl $= n_{HCl}$)
$$0.76 = \frac{n_{HCl} \times 1000}{250}$$
$$n_{HCl} = \frac{0.76 \times 250}{1000} = 0.19\,mol.$$

$$CaCO_3(s) + 2HCl(aq) \longrightarrow CaCl_2(aq) + CO_2(g) + H_2O(l)$$
$$\text{1 mol} \qquad \text{2 mol}$$

According to the equation,

1 mole of $CaCO_3$ reacts with 2 moles HCl

$\therefore$ 10 moles of $CaCO_3$ will react with $\dfrac{10 \times 2}{1} = 20$ moles HCl.

But we have only 0.19 moles HCl, so HCl is limiting reagent and it limits the yield of $CaCl_2$.

2 moles of HCl produces 1 mole of $CaCl_2$

0.19 mole of HCl will produce $\dfrac{1 \times 0.19}{2} = 0.095$ mol $CaCl_2$

Molar mass of $CaCl_2 = 40 + (2 \times 35.5) = 111\,g\,mol^{-1}$

$\therefore\ 0.095$ mole of $CaCl_2 = 0.095 \times 111 = 10.54\,g$

Question 10. A box contains some identical red coloured balls, labelled as A, each weighing 2 g. Another box contains identical blue coloured balls, labelled as B, each weighing 5 g. Consider the combinations AB, AB_2, A_2B and A_2B_3 and show that law of multiple proportions is applicable.

Solution.

Combination	Mass of A (g)	Mass of B (g)
AB	2	5
AB_2	2	10
A_2B	4	5
A_2B_3	4	15

Mass of B which is combined with fixed mass of A (say 1 g) will be 2.5 g, 5 g, 1.25 g and 3.75 g. They are in the ratio 2 : 4 : 1 : 3 which is simple whole number ratio. Hence, the law of multiple proportions is applicable.

Chapter 2

Structure of Atom

Important Results

1. Relation between frequency (v) and wavelength (λ).

$$v = \frac{c}{\lambda} \quad (c = \text{velocity of light, } 3.0 \times 10^8 \text{ ms}^{-1})$$

Einstein's equation $\quad E = mc^2$

Planck's equation $\quad E = hv = \dfrac{hc}{\lambda}$

$$(h = \text{Planck's constant} = 6.626 \times 10^{-34} \text{ Js})$$

Photoelectric effect $\ hv = hv_0 + \dfrac{1}{2} mv^2$

(where, $hv =$ energy of striking photon, $hv_0 = W_0 =$ work function and $\dfrac{1}{2} mv^2 =$ kinetic energy of an ejected electron.)

Rydberg formula $\quad \bar{v} = \dfrac{1}{\lambda} = RZ^2 \left[\dfrac{1}{n_1^2} - \dfrac{1}{n_2^2} \right]; \ n_2 > n_1$

(where, $R =$ Rydberg constant $= 1.09678 \times 10^7 \text{ m}^{-1}$)

For

$n_1 = 1; n_2 = 2, 3, 4$	Lyman series (UV)	
$n_1 = 2; n_2 = 3, 4, 5$	Balmer series (visible)	
$n_1 = 3; n_2 = 4, 5, 6$	Paschen series	
$n_1 = 4; n_2 = 5, 6, 7$	Brackett series	IR
$n_1 = 5; n_2 = 6, 7, 8$	Pfund series	
$n_1 = 6; n_2 = 7, 8, 9$	Humphries series	

2. The frequency of radiation absorbed or emitted when transition occurs between two stationary states,

$$v = \frac{\Delta E}{h} = \frac{E_2 - E_1}{h}$$

(where, E_1 and E_2 are the energies of lower and higher allowed energy states respectively.)

3. Energy of the stationary states, $E_n = -R_H \left(\dfrac{1}{n^2} \right)$ where, $n = 1, 2, 3, \ldots$

4. Energy of the stationary states for H and H like species (one electron system)

$$E_n = -2.18 \times 10^{-18} \left(\frac{Z^2}{n^2} \right) J$$

5. Radius of nth orbit, $r_n = \dfrac{n^2 a_0}{Z}$

where, a_0 (Bohr's radius of H-atom) $= \dfrac{h^2}{4\pi^2 me^2 k} = 0.529 \text{ Å}$

For H like species, $r_n = \dfrac{0.529\,(n^2)}{Z} \text{ Å} = \dfrac{52.9\,(n^2)}{Z} \text{ pm}$

6. de-Broglie equation, $\lambda = \dfrac{h}{mv} = \dfrac{h}{\sqrt{2m(KE)}}$

7. Heisenberg's uncertainty principle, $\Delta x \cdot \Delta p \geq \dfrac{h}{4\pi}$ or $\Delta x \cdot \Delta v \geq \dfrac{h}{4\pi m}$

(where, Δx and Δv are uncertainty in position and velocity respectively.)

8. Angular momentum, $mvr = \dfrac{nh}{2\pi}$

9. Velocity in nth orbital, $v_n = 2.182 \times 10^6 \dfrac{Z}{n}$

10. Ionisation energy $(IE)_H = \Delta E \propto Z^2 \left[\dfrac{1}{n_1^2} - \dfrac{1}{n_2^2} \right]$

11. The position of an electron in an atom is determined by four quantum numbers (n, l, m, s)

n (principal quantum number) $= 1, 2, 3, \ldots, n$

l (angular quantum number) $= 0, 1, 2 \ldots, (n-1)$

l	0	1	2	3	4
Sub-shell	s	p	d	f	g

m (magnetic quantum number) $= -l$ to $+l$

s (spin quantum number) $= +\dfrac{1}{2}$ or $-\dfrac{1}{2}$

12. Sub-shell indicated $= nl$

e.g., $\left. \begin{array}{l} n = 3 \\ l = 2 \end{array} \right] 3d \qquad \left. \begin{array}{l} n = 1 \\ l = 0 \end{array} \right] 1s$

13. l also describes the shapes of the orbital occupied by the electron. s-spherical, p-dumb-bell and d-double dumb-bell.

14. Total values of $m = (2l + 1) =$ total number of orbitals in a sub-shell

$=$ number of spectral lines when placed in a magnetic field or electric field.

15. For a hydrogen atom wavefunction, there are $n - l - 1$ radial nodes, $(n - 1)$ total nodes
16. Electrons in various orbitals are filled on the basis of
    (i) Aufbau rule   (ii) Hund's rule   (iii) Pauli's exclusion rule
$$EC \text{ of } Cr(24) \ - \ [Ar] \ 3d^5 4s^1$$
$$EC \text{ of } Cu \ (29) \ - \ [Ar] \ 3d^{10} 4s^1$$

Exercises

Question 1. (i) Calculate the number of electrons which will together weigh one gram.

(ii) Calculate the mass and charge of one mole of electrons.

(i) 1 mole species $= 6.022 \times 10^{23}$ species

(ii) Mass of 1 e^- $= 9.11 \times 10^{-31}$ kg

(iii) Charge on 1 e^- $= 1.602 \times 10^{-19}$ C

Solution.

(i) Mass of one electron $= 9.11 \times 10^{-28}$ g (or 9.11×10^{-31} kg)

Number of electrons in $1 g = \dfrac{1}{9.11 \times 10^{-28}} = 1.0976 \times 10^{27}$ electrons

(ii) Mass of 1 electron $= 9.11 \times 10^{-31}$ kg

∴ Mass of 1 mole of electrons $= 9.11 \times 10^{-31} \times 6.022 \times 10^{23}$
$$= 54.86 \times 10^{-8} = 5.486 \times 10^{-7} \text{ kg}$$

Charge on 1 electron $= 1.602 \times 10^{-19}$ C

∴ Charge on 1 mole of electrons $= 1.602 \times 10^{-19} \times 6.022 \times 10^{23}$
$$= 9.647 \times 10^4 \text{ C}$$

Question 2. (i) Calculate the total number of electrons present in one mole of methane.

(ii) Find (a) the total number and (b) the total mass of neutrons in 7 mg of ^{14}C. (Assume that mass of a neutron $= 1.675 \times 10^{-27}$ kg)

(iii) Find (a) the total number and (b) the total mass of protons in 34 mg of NH_3 at STP. (Mass of 1 $p = 1.6726 \times 10^{-27}$ kg.)

Will the answer change if the temperature and pressure are changed?

Solution.

(i) 1 molecule of methane (CH_4) contains
$$6 + 4 = 10 \text{ electrons}$$
$$[6 \text{ from C and 1 from each H atom}]$$
∴ 1 mol molecule of methane will contain
$$6.022 \times 10^{23} \times 10 = 6.022 \times 10^{24} \text{ electrons}$$

(ii) (a) $1 \text{mol}\ {}^{14}C = 14\ g = 6.022 \times 10^{23}$ carbon atoms

Number of neutrons in 1 carbon atom

    = mass number – atomic number = $14 - 6 = 8$ neutrons

$\therefore 6.022 \times 10^{23}$ carbon atoms will contain $6.022 \times 10^{23} \times 8$ neutrons

14 g carbon-14 have $6.022 \times 10^{23} \times 8$ neutrons

$\therefore 7$ mg or 7×10^{-3} g carbon-14 will have

$$\frac{7 \times 10^{-3} \times 6.022 \times 10^{23} \times 8}{14} \text{ neutrons}$$

$$= 24.088 \times 10^{20} \text{ neutrons} = 2.4088 \times 10^{21} \text{ neutrons}$$

(b) Mass of 1 neutron $= 1.675 \times 10^{-27}$ kg

Mass of 2.4088×10^{21} neutrons

$$= 2.4088 \times 10^{21} \times 1.675 \times 10^{-27} \text{ kg} = 4.0347 \times 10^{-6} \text{ kg}$$

(iii) 1 mole of NH_3 contains protons $= 7 + 3 = 10$ moles of protons (7 in N and 1 in each H atom) $= 6.022 \times 10^{23} \times 10$ protons

(a) 1 mole of NH_3 or 17 g NH_3 contains 6.022×10^{24} protons

34 mg or 34×10^{-3} g NH_3 will contain

$$\frac{34 \times 10^{-3} \times 6.022 \times 10^{24}}{17} = 12.044 \times 10^{21} \text{ protons}$$

$$= 1.2044 \times 10^{22} \text{ protons}$$

(b) Mass of 1 proton $= 1.6726 \times 10^{-27}$ kg

$\therefore$ Mass of 1.2044×10^{22} protons

$$= 1.2044 \times 10^{22} \times 1.6726 \times 10^{-27} \text{ kg}$$

$$= 2.01447 \times 10^{-5} \text{ kg}$$

There is no effect of temperature and pressure change. The answer will remain the same.

Question 3. How many neutrons and protons are there in the following nuclei?

$$ {}^{13}_{6}C,\ {}^{16}_{8}O,\ {}^{24}_{12}Mg,\ {}^{56}_{26}Fe,\ {}^{88}_{38}Sr $$

(i) The digit written as subscript represents the atomic number (Z) and that as superscript represents the mass number (A) of the element.

(ii) Number of neutrons = $A - Z$ and number of protons = Z

Solution.

Nucleus	Atomic number (Z)	Mass number (A)	Number of protons = Z	Number of neutrons = $A - Z$
${}^{13}_{6}C$	6	13	6	$13 - 6 = 7$
${}^{16}_{8}O$	8	16	8	$16 - 8 = 8$
${}^{24}_{12}Mg$	12	24	12	$24 - 12 = 12$
${}^{56}_{26}Fe$	26	56	26	$56 - 26 = 30$
${}^{88}_{38}Sr$	38	88	38	$88 - 38 = 50$

Question 4. Write the complete symbol for the atom with the given atomic number (Z) and atomic mass (A)

    (i) $Z = 17, A = 35$ (ii) $Z = 92, A = 233$ (iii) $Z = 4, A = 9$

    See the symbols of atoms having atomic number 17, 92 and 4 respectively in the Periodic Table as the atomic number is a fundamental property of an element, *i.e.*, certain for each element.

Solution.   (i) $^{35}_{17}\text{Cl}$ (ii) $^{233}_{92}\text{U}$ (iii) $^{9}_{4}\text{Be}$

Question 5. Yellow light emitted from a sodium lamp has a wavelength (λ) of 580 nm. Calculate the frequency (ν) and wave number $(\bar{\nu})$ of the yellow light.

Solution.   Frequency, $\nu = \dfrac{c}{\lambda}$

$$1 \text{ nm} = 10^{-9} \text{ m}$$

$$580 \text{ nm} = 580 \times 10^{-9} \text{ m} = 580 \times 10^{-7} \text{ cm}$$

$$\nu = \frac{3.0 \times 10^{8} \text{ ms}^{-1}}{580 \times 10^{-9} \text{ m}} = 5.17 \times 10^{14} \text{ s}^{-1}$$

$$(\text{Velocity of light} = 3 \times 10^{8} \text{ ms}^{-1})$$

    Wave number, $\bar{\nu} = \dfrac{1}{\lambda} = \dfrac{1}{580 \times 10^{-7} \text{ cm}}$

$$= 1.724 \times 10^{4} \text{ cm}^{-1}$$

Question 6. Find energy of each of the photons which

    (i) correspond to light of frequency 3×10^{15} Hz.

    (ii) have wavelength of 0.50 Å.

Solution.

    (i) Energy, $E = h\nu$

        $[h = \text{Planck's constant} = 6.626 \times 10^{-34} \text{ Js and } \nu = 3 \times 10^{15} \text{ Hz}$

        $= 3 \times 10^{15} \text{cps}]$

      Energy, $E = 6.626 \times 10^{-34} \text{ Js} \times 3 \times 10^{15} \text{ s}^{-1}$

          $= 19.878 \times 10^{-19} \text{ J} = 1.9878 \times 10^{-18} \text{ J}$

    (ii) Energy, $E = \dfrac{hc}{\lambda}$ $\left(\because \nu = \dfrac{c}{\lambda} \right)$

        $\lambda = 0.50 \text{ Å} = 0.50 \times 10^{-10} \text{ m}$

      Energy, $E = \dfrac{6.626 \times 10^{-34} \text{ Js} \times 3 \times 10^{8} \text{ ms}^{-1}}{0.50 \times 10^{-10} \text{ m}}$

          $= 39.756 \times 10^{-16} \text{ J}$

          $= 3.975 \times 10^{-15} \text{ J}$

Question 7. Calculate the wavelength , frequency and wave number of a light wave whose period is 2.0×10^{-10}s.

Solution. Frequency, $\nu = \dfrac{1}{\text{Time period}} = \dfrac{1}{2.0 \times 10^{-10} \text{ s}} = 5 \times 10^9 \text{ s}^{-1}$

Wavelength, $\lambda = \dfrac{c}{\nu} = \dfrac{3.0 \times 10^8 \text{ ms}^{-1}}{5 \times 10^9 \text{ s}^{-1}} = 0.6 \times 10^{-1} \text{ m} = 6.0 \times 10^{-2} \text{ m}$

Wave number, $\bar{v} = \dfrac{1}{\lambda} = \dfrac{1}{6.0 \times 10^{-2} \text{ m}} = 16.66 \text{ m}^{-1}$

Question 8. What is the number of photons of light with a wavelength of 4000 pm that provide 1 J of energy?

(i) Number of photons is calculated by dividing total energy by energy of 1 photon, so first calculate the energy of 1 photon by applying,
$$E = \frac{hc}{\lambda}$$

(ii) Then, calculate the number of photons by using the formula
$$N = \frac{\text{Total energy}}{\text{Energy of one photon}}$$

Solution. Energy, $E = \dfrac{hc}{\lambda} = \dfrac{6.626 \times 10^{-34} \text{ Js} \times 3.0 \times 10^8 \text{ ms}^{-1}}{4000 \times 10^{-12} \text{ m}}$

$$(1 \text{ pm} = 10^{-12} \text{ m})$$

$$= 4.9695 \times 10^{-17} \text{ J}$$

Number of photons, $N = \dfrac{1 \text{ J}}{4.9695 \times 10^{-17} \text{ J}} = 2.0122 \times 10^{16}$ photons

Question 9. A photon of wavelength 4×10^{-7} m strikes on metal surface, the work function of the metal being 2.13 eV. Calculate

(i) the energy of the photon (eV).

(ii) the kinetic energy of the emission.

(iii) the velocity of the photoelectron ($1 \text{ eV} = 1.6020 \times 10^{-19}$ J).

Direct formula based question.

(i) Calculate the energy of a photon by using, $E = \dfrac{hc}{\lambda}$ in joule and convert it in eV.

(ii) Calculate the kinetic energy of ejected electron, $KE = h\nu - h\nu_0$ where, $E = h\nu$ and $h\nu_0 =$ work function.

(iii) Calculate the velocity of electron by using the formula, $KE = \dfrac{1}{2} mv^2$.

Solution.

(i) Energy of a photon,
$$E = \frac{hc}{\lambda} = \frac{6.626 \times 10^{-34} \text{ Js} \times 3.0 \times 10^8 \text{ ms}^{-1}}{4 \times 10^{-7} \text{ m}}$$

$$E = 4.969 \times 10^{-19} \text{ J}$$
$$(1.602 \times 10^{-19} \text{ J} = 1 \text{ eV})$$
$$4.969 \times 10^{-19} \text{ J} = \frac{4.969 \times 10^{-19}}{1.602 \times 10^{-19}} = 3.10 \text{ eV}$$

(ii) Kinetic energy of an ejected electron, $KE = h\nu - h\nu_0$

$\qquad h\nu = 3.10 \text{ eV}$ $\qquad\qquad$ (energy of striking photon)

$\qquad h\nu_0 = W_0 = 2.13 \text{ eV}$ $\qquad$ (work function of the metal)

$\qquad KE = \dfrac{1}{2} mv^2 = 3.10 - 2.13 = 0.97 \text{ eV}$

(iii) $KE = \dfrac{1}{2} mv^2 = 0.97 \text{ eV}$

$\qquad \dfrac{1}{2} mv^2 = 0.97 \times 1.602 \times 10^{-19} \text{ J}$ $\qquad (1 \text{ eV} = 1.602 \times 10^{-19} \text{ J})$

$\qquad \dfrac{1}{2} \times 9.11 \times 10^{-31} \text{ kg} \times v^2 = 0.97 \times 1.602 \times 10^{-19} \text{ J}$

$\qquad\qquad\qquad\qquad\qquad$ ($\because$ Mass of $1 e^- = 9.11 \times 10^{-31}$ kg)

$\qquad v^2 = \dfrac{0.97 \times 1.602 \times 10^{-19} \times 2 \text{ J}}{9.11 \times 10^{-31} \text{ kg}} = 0.341 \times 10^{12}$

$\qquad v^2 = 0.341 \times 10^{12} \text{ (ms}^{-1})^2$

$\qquad v = 0.584 \times 10^6 = 5.84 \times 10^5 \text{ ms}^{-1}$

Note *Minimum energy required to eject the electron is $h\nu_0$. It is also called work function, W_0.*

Question 10. Electromagnetic radiation of wavelength 242 nm is just sufficient to ionise the sodium atom. Calculate the ionisation energy of sodium in kJ mol^{-1}.

Solution. Given, wavelength, $\lambda = 242 \text{ nm} = 242 \times 10^{-9}$ m

$$\text{Energy, } E = h\nu = \frac{hc}{\lambda} = \frac{6.626 \times 10^{-34} \text{ Js} \times 3.0 \times 10^8 \text{ ms}^{-1}}{242 \times 10^{-9} \text{ m}}$$

$$E = 0.0821 \times 10^{-17} \text{ J/atom}$$

This energy is sufficient for ionization of one Na atom, so it is the ionization energy of Na.

$$E = 6.02 \times 10^{23} \times 0.0821 \times 10^{-17} \text{ J/mol}$$

$$E = 4.945 \times 10^5 \text{ J/mol} = 4.945 \times 10^2 \text{ kJ/mol}$$

Question 11. A **25** watt bulb emits monochromatic yellow light of wavelength 0.57 μm. Calculate the rate of emission of quanta per second.

Solution. $25 \text{ watt} = 25 \text{ Js}^{-1}$ $\qquad\qquad\qquad\qquad$ $(1 \text{ watt} = 1 \text{ Js}^{-1})$

Wavelength, $\lambda = 0.57 \text{ μm} = 0.57 \times 10^{-6}$ m $\qquad\qquad$ $(1 \text{ μm} = 10^{-6} \text{ m})$

Energy of one photon, $E = \dfrac{hc}{\lambda} = \dfrac{6.626 \times 10^{-34} \text{ Js} \times 3.0 \times 10^{8} \text{ ms}^{-1}}{0.57 \times 10^{-6} \text{ m}}$

$$E = 34.87 \times 10^{-20} \text{ J}$$

Number of photons emitted per second

$$= \dfrac{\text{Total energy per second}}{\text{Energy of one photon}}$$

$$= \dfrac{25 \text{ Js}^{-1}}{34.87 \times 10^{-20} \text{ J}} = 0.7169 \times 10^{20} \text{ photons per second}$$

$$= 7.169 \times 10^{19} \text{ photons per second}$$

Question 12. Electrons are emitted with zero velocity from a metal surface when it is exposed to radiation of wavelength 6800 Å. Calculate threshold frequency (v_0) and work function (W_0) of the metal.

Solution. Threshold wavelength, $\lambda_0 = 6800$ Å $= 6800 \times 10^{-10}$ m

Threshold frequency, $v_0 = \dfrac{c}{\lambda_0} = \dfrac{3.0 \times 10^{8} \text{ ms}^{-1}}{6800 \times 10^{-10} \text{ m}} = 4.41 \times 10^{14} \text{ s}^{-1}$

Work function, $W_0 = hv_0 = 6.626 \times 10^{-34} \text{ Js} \times 4.41 \times 10^{14} \text{ s}^{-1}$

$$= 29.22 \times 10^{-20} \text{ J} = 2.922 \times 10^{-19} \text{ J}$$

Note *For each metal, there is a characteristic minimum frequency, v_0 which is also know as threshold frequency below which photoelectric effect is not observed.*

Question 13. What is the wavelength of light emitted when the electron in a hydrogen atom undergoes transition from an energy level with $n = 4$ to an energy level with $n = 2$?

Solution. Wave number, $\overline{v} = \dfrac{1}{\lambda} = R\left(\dfrac{1}{n_1^2} - \dfrac{1}{n_2^2} \right)$

(Rydberg constant, $R = 109677 \text{ cm}^{-1}$)

$$\dfrac{1}{\lambda} = 109677 \left(\dfrac{1}{2^2} - \dfrac{1}{4^2} \right) \text{ cm}^{-1}$$

$$\dfrac{1}{\lambda} = 109677 \left(\dfrac{3}{16} \right) \text{ cm}^{-1}$$

$$\dfrac{1}{\lambda} = 20564.4 \text{ cm}^{-1}$$

$$\lambda = \dfrac{1}{20564.4} \text{ cm} = 486 \times 10^{-7} \text{ cm}$$

$$= 486 \times 10^{-9} \text{ m} = 486 \text{ nm}$$

The colour corresponding to this wavelength is blue.

Note n_2 *is always greater than* n_1. *If* $n_1 = 1, 2 \dots$ *then* $n_2 = n_1 + 1,$ $n_1 + 2 \dots$

Question 14. How much energy is required to ionize a H-atom if the electron occupies $n = 5$ orbit? Compare your answer with the ionization enthalpy of H-atom (energy required to remove the electron from $n = 1$ orbit).

(i) Find ΔE when $n_i = 5$ and $n_f = \infty$.
(ii) Find $\Delta E'$ when $n_i = 1$ and $n_f = \infty$ and compare them.

Solution. Energy change, $\Delta E = E_f - E_i$

$$\Delta E = 2.18 \times 10^{-18} \text{ J} \left(\frac{1}{n_i^2} - \frac{1}{n_f^2} \right)$$

When $n_i = 5$ and $n_f = \infty$, energy change,

$$\Delta E = 2.18 \times 10^{-18} \text{ J} \left(\frac{1}{5^2} - \frac{1}{\infty} \right) = 0.0872 \times 10^{-18} \text{ J}$$

When $n_i = 1$ and $n_f = \infty$, energy change,

$$\Delta E' = 2.18 \times 10^{-18} \text{ J} \left(\frac{1}{1^2} - \frac{1}{\infty} \right)$$

$$\Delta E' = 2.18 \times 10^{-18} \text{ J}$$

$$\frac{\Delta E'}{\Delta E} = \frac{2.18 \times 10^{-18}}{0.0872 \times 10^{-18}} = 25$$

Hence, energy required to remove an electron from first orbit is 25 times than that required to remove an electron from fifth orbit.

Question 15. What is the maximum number of emission lines when the excited electron of a H-atom in $n = 6$ drops to the ground state?

Solution. Number of lines produced when electron from nth shell drops to ground state $= \dfrac{n \, (n - 1)}{2}$

When $n = 6$,   number of lines produced $= \dfrac{6 \, (6 - 1)}{2} = \dfrac{6 \times 5}{2} = 15$

Question 16. (i) The energy associated with the first orbit in the hydrogen atom is $- 2.18 \times 10^{-18}$ J atom^{-1}. What is the energy associated with the fifth orbit?

(ii) Calculate the radius of Bohr's fifth orbit for hydrogen atom.

Solution.

(i) Energy in nth orbit, $E_n = \dfrac{-2.18 \times 10^{-18}}{n^2}$ J

Energy in fifth orbit, $E_5 = \dfrac{-2.18 \times 10^{-18}}{5^2}$ J $= -0.0872 \times 10^{-18}$ J

$$= -8.72 \times 10^{-20} \text{ J}$$

(ii) For H atom, radius of nth orbit, $r_n = 0.529 \times n^2$ Å

∴ Radius of 5th Bohr orbit, $r_5 = 0.529 \times 5^2 = 13.225$ Å $= 1.3225$ nm

Question 17. Calculate the wave number for the longest wavelength transition in the Balmer series of atomic hydrogen.

(i) For longest wavelength (λ), wave number ($\bar{v}$) should be minimum, *i.e.*, the difference between n_1 and n_2 is minimum.

(ii) For Balmer series, $n_1 = 2$, so $n_2 = 3$

(iii) Put the values of n_1 and n_2 in the formula, $\bar{v} = R\left[\dfrac{1}{n_1^2} - \dfrac{1}{n_2^2}\right]$ to calculate wave number for the longest wavelength in the Balmer series.

Solution. Wave number, $\bar{v} = R\left[\dfrac{1}{n_1^2} - \dfrac{1}{n_2^2}\right]$

$$\bar{v} = 109677\left(\dfrac{1}{2^2} - \dfrac{1}{3^2}\right) cm^{-1}$$

$$\bar{v} = 15232.91\, cm^{-1}$$

$$= 1.523 \times 10^4\, cm^{-1} = 1.523 \times 10^6\, m^{-1}$$

Question 18. What is the energy in joules, required to shift the electron of the hydrogen atom from the first Bohr orbit to the fifth Bohr orbit and what is the wavelength of the light emitted when the electron returns to the ground state? The ground state electron energy is -2.18×10^{-11} erg.

(i) Find energy required to shift electron from E_1 to E_5 by using the formula $\Delta E = E_5 - E_1$.

(ii) Find λ of emitted light when electron returns to E_1 (ground state) by using the formula $\Delta E = \dfrac{hc}{\lambda}$.

Solution. $\Delta E = E_5 - E_1 = 2.18 \times 10^{-11}\left(\dfrac{1}{n_i^2} - \dfrac{1}{n_f^2}\right) erg$

$$(n_i = \text{1st orbit and } n_f = \text{5th orbit})$$

$$\Delta E = 2.18 \times 10^{-11}\left(\dfrac{1}{1^2} - \dfrac{1}{5^2}\right) erg$$

$$\Delta E = 2.18 \times 10^{-11} \times \dfrac{24}{25} = 2.0928 \times 10^{-11}\, erg$$

$$= 2.0928 \times 10^{-18}\, J \qquad\qquad (1\, erg = 10^{-7}\, J)$$

When electron returns to ground state, it emits energy equals to ΔE hence,

$$\Delta E = \dfrac{hc}{\lambda}$$

$$\lambda = \dfrac{hc}{\Delta E} = \dfrac{6.626 \times 10^{-34}\, Js \times 3.0 \times 10^8\, ms^{-1}}{2.0928 \times 10^{-18}\, J}$$

$$= 9.498 \times 10^{-8}\, m = 949.8 \times 10^{-10}\, m = 949.8\, \mathring{A}$$

Question 19. The electron energy in hydrogen atom is given by $E_n = (-2.18 \times 10^{-18})/n^2$ J. Calculate the energy required to remove an electron completely from the $n = 2$ orbit. What is the longest wavelength of light in cm that can be used to cause this transition?

(i) $\Delta E = E_\infty - E_2$ (as the electron is removed completely from the orbit)

(ii) $\Delta E = \dfrac{hc}{\lambda}$ or $\lambda = \dfrac{hc}{\Delta E}$

Solution. Energy required to shift an electron from $n = 2$ to $n = \infty$.

$$\Delta E = E_\infty - E_2 = 0 - \left(-\dfrac{2.18 \times 10^{-18} \text{ J atom}^{-1}}{2^2} \right)$$

$$= 0.545 \times 10^{-18} \text{ J atom}^{-1}$$

$$= 5.45 \times 10^{-19} \text{ J atom}^{-1}$$

Wavelength, $\lambda = \dfrac{hc}{\Delta E} = \dfrac{6.626 \times 10^{-34} \text{ Js} \times 3.0 \times 10^8 \text{ ms}^{-1}}{5.45 \times 10^{-19} \text{ J}}$

$$= 3.647 \times 10^{-7} \text{ m} = 3.647 \times 10^{-5} \text{ cm}$$

Question 20. Calculate the wavelength of an electron moving with velocity of 2.05×10^7 ms^{-1}.

Solution. We know that mass of an electron, $m = 9.1 \times 10^{-31}$ kg, $h = $ Planck's constant $= 6.626 \times 10^{-34}$ Js and

$$\lambda = \dfrac{h}{mv} = \dfrac{6.626 \times 10^{-34} \text{ Js}}{9.11 \times 10^{-31} \text{ kg} \times 2.05 \times 10^7 \text{ ms}^{-1}}$$

$$\lambda = 0.35 \times 10^{-10} \text{ m} \qquad (1 \text{ J} = 1 \text{ kgm}^2\text{s}^{-2})$$

$$\lambda = 3.5 \times 10^{-11} \text{ m}$$

Question 21. The mass of an electron is 9.1×10^{-31} kg. If its KE is 3.0×10^{-25} J, calculate its wavelength.

Wavelength depends upon the mass and velocity of electron, so first calculate the velocity of electron from the formula of kinetic energy $(\text{KE} = \frac{1}{2}mv^2)$ then, calculate the wavelength by using the formula $\lambda = \dfrac{h}{mv}$.

Solution. $\text{KE} = \dfrac{1}{2}mv^2$

$$v^2 = \dfrac{2\text{KE}}{m} \text{ or } v = \sqrt{\dfrac{2\text{KE}}{m}}$$

$$v = \sqrt{\dfrac{2 \times 3.0 \times 10^{-25} \text{ J}}{9.1 \times 10^{-31} \text{ kg}}} \qquad (1 \text{ J} = 1 \text{ kg m}^2\text{s}^{-2})$$

$$v = \sqrt{0.6593 \times 10^6} = 0.8119 \times 10^3 = 812.0 \text{ ms}^{-1}$$

Wavelength, $\lambda = \dfrac{h}{mv} = \dfrac{6.626 \times 10^{-34} \text{ Js}}{9.1 \times 10^{-31} \text{ kg} \times 812.0 \text{ ms}^{-1}}$

$\lambda = 0.0008967 \times 10^{-3}$ m

$\lambda = 8967$ Å

Question 22. Which of the following are isoelectronic species, *i.e.*, those having the same number of electrons?

$$Na^+, K^+, Mg^{2+}, Ca^{2+}, S^{2-}, Ar$$

Solution. Isoelectronic species have the same number of electrons but different atomic numbers

Calculation of number of electrons have been shown below

(Number of positive charge shows, number of electrons lost and number of negative charges shows number of electrons gained by an atom).

$_{11}Na^+ = 11 - 1 = 10\ e^-$, $\qquad$ $_{19}K^+ = 19 - 1 = 18\ e^-$

$_{12}Mg^{2+} = 12 - 2 = 10\ e^-$, $\qquad$ $_{20}Ca^{2+} = 20 - 2 = 18\ e^-$

$_{16}S^{2-} = 16 + 2 = 18\ e^-$, $\qquad$ $_{18}Ar = 18\ e^-$

Hence, isoelectronic species are

(i) Na^+ and Mg^{2+} $\qquad\qquad$ (ii) K^+, Ca^{2+}, S^{2-} and Ar

Question 23. (i) Write the electronic configurations of the following ions:

(a) H^- $\qquad$ (b) Na^+ $\qquad$ (c) O^{2-} $\qquad$ (d) F^-

(ii) What are the atomic numbers of elements whose outermost electrons are represented by

(a) $3s^1$ $\qquad$ (b) $2p^3$ $\qquad$ (c) $3p^5$?

(iii) Which atoms are indicated by the following configurations?

(a) [He] $2s^1$ (b) [Ne] $3s^2 3p^3$ (c) [Ar] $4s^2\ 3d^1$

(i) First write the electronic configuration of neutral atom of the given ions and then remove or add the electrons as the ion have a charge. (If it has positive charge, remove electrons and if it has negative charge, add the electrons equal to the charge.)

(ii) To find the total number of electrons, which is equal to atomic number in case of netural atom, fill the orbitals in order of their increasing energies up to the given outer orbital configuration.

Solution.

(i) (a) $_1H = 1s^1$; $H^- = 1s^2$

(b) $_{11}Na = 1s^2 2s^2 2p^6 3s^1$; $Na^+ = 1s^2\ 2s^2\ 2p^6$

(c) $_8O = 1s^2 2s^2 2p^4$; $O^{2-} = 1s^2 2s^2 2p^6$

(d) $_9F = 1s^2 2s^2 2p^5$; $F^- = 1s^2 2s^2 2p^6$

(ii) To obtain atomic number of an element fill the orbitals in order of their increasing energies up to the given outer orbital configuration.

(a) $1s^2 2s^2 2p^6 3s^1$ (Z = 11)

(b) $1s^2 2s^2 2p^3$ (Z = 7)

(c) $1s^2 2s^2 2p^6 3s^2 3p^5$ (Z = 17)

(iii) (a) [He] $2s^1$; It represents $_3$Li (lithium)

(b) [Ne] $3s^2 3p^3$; It represents $_{15}$P (phosphorus)

(c) [Ar] $4s^2 3d^1$; It represents $_{21}$Sc (scandium)

Question 24.   What is the lowest value of n that allows g orbitals to exist?

(i) Value of $l = 0$ to $(n - 1)$

(ii) $l = 0$ means s orbital, $l = 1$ means p orbitals, $l = 2$ means d orbitals $l = 3$ means f orbitals and $l = 4$ means g orbitals

Solution.   For g subshell $l = 4$ and to have $l = 4$ minimum value of $n = 5$ [because the value of $l = 0$ to $(n - 1)$]

Question 25.   An electron is in one of the $3d$-orbitals. Give the possible values of n, l and m_l for this electron.

(i) For s, p, d and f orbitals, value of l is 0, 1, 2 and 3 respectively.

(ii) $m_l = -l$ to $+l$ including 0.

Solution.   For $3d$-electron,

$$n = 3, \qquad l = 2, \qquad\qquad m_l = -2, -1, 0, +1, +2 \text{ (any one)}$$

Question 26.   An atom of an element contains 29 electrons and 35 neutrons. Deduce

(i) the number of protons

(ii) the electronic configuration of the element.

Solution.

(i) For a neutral atom;

Number of electrons = number of protons = Z (At. no.)

29 electrons = 29 protons.

(ii) $_{29}$Z = $1s^2 2s^2 2p^6 3s^2 3p^6 3d^{10} 4s^1$ (The element is copper.)

Question 27.   Give the number of electrons in the species H_2^+, H_2 and O_2^+.

(i) Count the total number of electrons by adding electrons present in each atom of a molecule.

(ii) Then remove or add electrons according to charge (positive or negative) to count the electrons in an ion.

Solution.
$$H_2 = {}_1H + {}_1H = 1 + 1 = 2e^-$$
$$H_2^+ = 2 - 1 = 1e^-$$
$$O_2 = {}_8O + {}_8O = 8 + 8 = 16e^-$$
$$O_2^+ = 16 - 1 = 15e^-$$

Question 28. (i) An atomic orbital has $n = 3$. What are the possible values of l and m_l?

(ii) List the quantum numbers (m_l and l) of electrons for $3d$-orbital.

(iii) Which of the following orbitals are possible?

$$1p, \ 2s, \ 2p \text{ and } 3f$$

(a) l has the values 0 to $(n - 1)$
(b) m has the values $-l$ to $+l$
(c) The value of l never be equal to n or greater than it.

Solution.
(i) For $n = 3$

$$l = 0, 1, 2$$
$$l = 0; \ m_l = 0$$
$$l = 1; \ m_l = -1, 0, +1$$
$$l = 2; \ m_l = -2, -1, 0, +1, +2$$

(ii) For $3d$-orbital, $l = 2; \ m_l = -2, -1, 0, +1, +2$

(iii) $1p$ is not possible because if $n = 1$ then $l = 0$ only and for $p, l = 1$

$2s$ is possible because if $n = 2$ then $l = 0$ and 1 and for $s, l = 0$.

$2p$ is possible because if $n = 2$ then $l = 0$ and 1 and for $p, l = 1$

$3f$ is not possible because if $n = 3$ then $l = 0, 1$ and 2 for $f, l = 3$

Question 29. Using s, p, d notations, describe the orbital with the following quantum numbers,

(a) $n = 1, l = 0$ (b) $n = 3, l = 1$ (c) $n = 4, l = 2$ (d) $n = 4, l = 3$

n represents the main shell and 0, 1, 2, 3 ...... values of l represent the s, p, d, f ...... orbitals respectively.

Solution. Subshell notations

	n	l	Subshell notation
(a)	1	0	$1s$
(b)	3	1	$3p$
(c)	4	2	$4d$
(d)	4	3	$4f$

Question 30. Explain, giving reasons, which of the following sets of quantum numbers are not possible?

(a) $n = 0, l = 0, m_l = 0, m_s = +\dfrac{1}{2}$ (b) $n = 1, l = 0, m_l = 0, m_s = -\dfrac{1}{2}$

(c) $n = 1, l = 1, m_l = 0, m_s = +\dfrac{1}{2}$ (d) $n = 2, l = 1, m_l = 0, m_s = -\dfrac{1}{2}$

(e) $n = 3, l = 3, m_l = -3, m_s = +\dfrac{1}{2}$ (f) $n = 3, l = 1, m_l = 0, m_s = +\dfrac{1}{2}$

(i) n always be a positive integer.
(ii) $n \neq l$

Solution.

(a) is not possible as $n \neq 0$

(b) is possible (1s)

(c) is not possible because if $n = 1$, $l = 0$ only ($l \neq 1$)

(d) is possible (2p)

(e) is not possible because if $n = 3$, $l = 0, 1$ and 2 ($l \neq 3$)

(f) is possible (3p)

Question 31. How many electrons in an atom may have the following quantum numbers?

(a) $n = 4$, $m_s = -\dfrac{1}{2}$ (b) $n = 3$, $l = 0$

 (i) Total number of electrons in a shell (n) = $2n^2$.

(ii) Total number of electrons in an orbital = 2.

Solution.

(a) Total electrons if $n = 4 = 2n^2 = 2 \times 4^2 = 32$

Half of the total electrons, *i.e.*, 16 electrons have $m_s = -\dfrac{1}{2}$

(b) $n = 3$, $l = 0$ it is 3s-orbital and it can have two electrons.

Question 32. Show that the circumference of the Bohr orbit for the hydrogen atom is an integral multiple of the de-Broglie wavelength associated with the electron revolving around the orbit.

Solution. According to Bohr model for H-atom, the angular momentum of an electron in a given stationary state,

$$mvr = \frac{nh}{2\pi}$$

or $$2\pi r = \frac{nh}{mv}$$

From de-Broglie equation, wavelength, $\lambda = \dfrac{h}{mv}$

Hence, $$2\pi r = n\lambda$$

Therefore, the circumference ($2\pi r$) of the Bohr orbit for H-atom is an integral multiple of de-Broglie wavelength.

Question 33. What transition in the hydrogen spectrum would have the same wavelength as the Balmer transition $n = 4$ to $n = 2$ of He$^+$ spectrum?

 (i) Since, the $\bar{v}$ of He$^+$ is same as that of $\bar{v}$ of H, find the value of $\bar{v}$ of He$^+$ spectrum for Balmer transition by using the formula

$\bar{v} = RZ^2 \left(\dfrac{1}{n_1^2} - \dfrac{1}{n_2^2} \right)$.

(ii) Write the same expression for H-atom and find the value of n_1 and n_2 by putting the value of $\bar{v}$ of He$^+$ spectrum in Eq. (2).

Solution. Wave number, $\bar{v} = RZ^2\left(\dfrac{1}{n_1^2} - \dfrac{1}{n_2^2}\right)$ and $\bar{v} = \dfrac{1}{\lambda}$

For He^+ spectrum (for Balmer transition)

$$\bar{v} = R \times (2)^2 \left(\frac{1}{2^2} - \frac{1}{4^2}\right)$$

$$\bar{v} = R \times 4 \times \frac{3}{16} = \frac{3}{4}R \qquad \ldots(1)$$

For H spectrum, $\qquad \bar{v} = R \times 1^2 \left(\dfrac{1}{n_1^2} - \dfrac{1}{n_2^2}\right) \qquad \ldots(2)$

$$\frac{3}{4}R = R\left(\frac{1}{n_1^2} - \frac{1}{n_2^2}\right)$$

$$\frac{3}{4} = \frac{1}{n_1^2} - \frac{1}{n_2^2}$$

Hence, $n_1 = 1$ and $n_2 = 2$. In H-spectrum, the transition from $n = 2$ to $n = 1$ have same wavelength as the Balmer transition from $n = 3$ to $n = 2$ of He^+ spectrum.

Question 34. Calculate the energy required for the process

$$He^+(g) \longrightarrow He^{2+}(g) + e^-$$

The ionization energy for the H-atom in the ground state is 2.18×10^{-18} J atom^{-1}.

Solution. Energy of electron in unielectron atomic system,

$$E_n = \frac{-2\pi^2 mZ^2 e^4}{n^2 h^2}$$

For H-atom, ionization energy (IE) $= E_\infty - E_1$

$$IE = 0 - \left(-\frac{2\pi^2 me^4 1^2}{1^2 h^2}\right) \qquad \text{(where, } Z = 1 \text{ and } n = 1 \text{ for H-atom)}$$

$$IE = 2.18 \times 10^{-18} \text{ J atom}^{-1}$$

For He^+, $IE = E_\infty - E_1 = 0 - \left(\dfrac{-2\pi^2 me^4 2^2}{1^2 n^2}\right) = 4 \times \dfrac{2\pi^2 \, me^4}{h^2}$

$$= 4 \times 2.18 \times 10^{-18} \text{ J atom}^{-1} = 8.72 \times 10^{-18} \text{ J atom}^{-1}$$

$\therefore$ The energy required for the process $He^+ \longrightarrow He^{2+} + e^-$ is

$$8.72 \times 10^{-18} \text{ atoms}^{-1}.$$

Question 35. If the diameter of a carbon atom is 0.15 nm, calculate the number of carbon atoms which can be placed side by side in a straight line across length of scale of length 20 cm long.

Solution. Diameter of a carbon atom $= 0.15$ nm $= 0.15 \times 10^{-9}$ m

Length along which atoms are to be placed $= 20$ cm $= 0.2$ m

Number of carbon atom which can be placed in the given length

$$= \frac{0.2 \text{ m}}{0.15 \times 10^{-9} \text{ m}} = \frac{0.2 \times 10^{9}}{0.15 \text{ m}} = 1.33 \times 10^{9} \text{ atoms}$$

Question 36. 2×10^{8} atoms of carbon are arranged side by side. Calculate the radius of carbon atom if the length of this arrangement is 2.4 cm.

 Radius depends upon diameter d as $r = \dfrac{d}{2}$, so first calculate the diameter by dividing total length with number of carbon atoms present and then calculate radius.

Solution.   Total length = 2.4 cm

Number of carbon atoms along the length = 2×10^{8}

$\therefore$ Diameter of 1 carbon atom $= \dfrac{2.4 \text{ cm}}{2 \times 10^{8}} = 1.2 \times 10^{-8} \text{ cm}$

Radius of 1 carbon atom $= \dfrac{d}{2} = \dfrac{1.2 \times 10^{-8} \text{ cm}}{2}$

$$= 0.60 \times 10^{-8} \text{ cm} = 0.060 \times 10^{-7} \text{ cm}$$
$$= 0.060 \times 10^{-9} \text{ m} = 0.060 \text{ nm}$$

Question 37.   The diameter of zinc atom is 2.6 Å. Calculate (a) radius of zinc atom in pm and (b) number of atoms present in a length of 1.6 cm if the zinc atoms are arranged side by side lengthwise.

Solution.   Diameter of Zn atom = 2.6 Å = 2.6×10^{-10} m

Radius of Zn atom $= \dfrac{2.6 \times 10^{-10} \text{ m}}{2} = 1.3 \times 10^{-10} \text{ m}$

$$= 130 \times 10^{-12} \text{ m} = 130 \text{ pm}$$

Given, length = 1.6 cm = 1.6×10^{-2} m

Number of Zn atoms in 1.6×10^{-2} m

$$= \frac{1.6 \times 10^{-2} \text{ m}}{2.6 \times 10^{-10} \text{ m}} = 0.6154 \times 10^{8} \text{ atoms} = 6.154 \times 10^{7} \text{ atoms}$$

Question 38.   A certain particle carries 2.5×10^{-16} C of static electric charge. Calculate the number of electrons present in it.

Solution.   Charge on 1 electron = 1.6022×10^{-19} C

$$\text{Total charge} = 2.5 \times 10^{-16} \text{ C}$$

Number of electrons present in particle $= \dfrac{2.5 \times 10^{-16}}{1.6022 \times 10^{-19}}$

$$= 1.5603 \times 10^{3} = 1560.3 \text{ electrons}$$

Question 39. In Milikan's experiment, static electric charge on the oil drops has been obtained by shining X-rays. If the static electric charge on the oil drop is -1.282×10^{-18} C, calculate the number of electrons present on it.

Solution. Number of electrons $= \dfrac{\text{Total charge in oil drop}}{\text{Charge on 1 electron}}$

$$= \frac{-1.282 \times 10^{-18} \text{ C}}{-1.6022 \times 10^{-19} \text{ C}} = 0.800 \times 10$$

$$= 8.0 \text{ electrons}$$

Question 40. In Rutherford's experiment, generally the thin foil of heavy atoms, like gold, platinum, etc., have been used to be bombarded by the α-particles. If the thin foil of light atoms like aluminium, etc., is used, what difference would be observed from the above results?

Solution. Heavy atoms such as gold, platinum have heavy nucleus. Heavy nucleus contains large amount of positive charge. When a beam of α-particles is shot at a thin gold foil, most of them pass through without much effect. Some however, are deflected back or by small angles due to enormous repulsive force of heavy nucleus. If light aluminium foil is used, the number of α-particles deflected back or those deflected by small angles will be negligible.

Question 41. Symbols $^{79}_{35}\text{Br}$ and ^{79}Br can be written, whereas symbols $^{35}_{79}\text{Br}$ and ^{35}Br are not acceptable. Answer briefly.

Solution. The composition of any atom can be represented by using the normal element symbol (X) with superscript on the left hand side as the mass number (A) and subscript (Z) on the left hand side as the atomic number, *i.e.*, $^{A}_{Z}\text{X}$. Hence, the symbols $^{35}_{79}\text{Br}$ and ^{35}Br are not acceptable.

Question 42. An element with mass number 81 contains 31.7% more neutrons as compared to protons. Assign the atomic symbol.

Solution. We know that mass number of the element, $A = p + n = 81 \dots$(i)

Let the number of protons, $p = x$

Then, number of neutrons, $n = x + \dfrac{31.7}{100} x = 1.317 x$

(as number of neutrons are 31.7% more than the protons)

Hence, from Eq. (i) $x + 1.317x = 81$

$$2.317 x = 81 \quad \text{or} \quad x = \frac{81}{2.317} = 34.958 \approx 35$$

Therefore, number of protons = 35 and the symbol is $^{81}_{35}\text{Br}$

(Number of protons = Atomic number)

Question 43. An ion with mass number 37 possesses one unit of negative charge. If the ion contains 11.1% more neutrons than the electrons, find the symbol of the ion.

Solution. Let the number of electrons in an ion = x

$\therefore$ Number of neutrons, $n = x + \dfrac{11.1}{100} x = 1.111x$

(As the number of neutrons are 11.1% more than the number of electrons)
In the neutral atom, number of electrons, $e^- = x - 1$

(as the ion carries -1 charge)

Similarly, number of protons, $p = x - 1$
we know that, mass number $= n + p = 37$

or $\qquad 1.111 x + x - 1 = 37$
$$2.111x = 37 + 1 = 38$$
$$x = \frac{38}{2.111} = 18.0009 \approx 18$$

Number of protons = atomic number = $18 - 1 = 17$
Therefore, the symbol of the ion is $_{17}^{37}Cl^-$.

Question 44. An ion with mass number 56 contains 3 units of positive charge and 30.4% more neutrons than the electrons. Assign the symbol to this ion.

Solution. Let the number of electrons in an ion = x

$\therefore$ Number of neutrons $= x + \dfrac{30.4}{100} x = 1.304 \, x$

($\because$ Number of neutrons are 30.4% more than the number of electrons).
In the neutral atom, number of electrons $= x + 3$ ($\because$ The ion carries $+ 3$ charge.)
So, number of protons $= x + 3$
We know that, mass number $= n + p = 1.304x + x + 3 = 56$
$$2.304x = 53, \quad x = \frac{53}{2.304} = 23.003 \approx 23$$

$\therefore$ Number of protons $= 23 + 3 = 26 =$ atomic number
Therefore, the symbol of the ion is $_{26}^{56}Fe^{3+}$.

Question 45. Arrange the following type of radiations in increasing order of frequency.
  (a) Radiation from microwave oven
  (b) Amber light from traffic signal
  (c) Radiation from FM radio
  (d) Cosmic rays from outer space and
  (e) X-rays.

Solution. The order of frequency is radiation from FM radio < microwaves < amber colour < X-rays < cosmic rays.

Question 46. Nitrogen laser produces a radiation at a wavelength of 337.1 nm. If the number of photons emitted is 5.6×10^{24}, calculate the power of this laser.

 If n photons are emitted by a laser, the total energy of the photons emitted is equal to the power of the laser.

Solution. Energy of 1 photon,

$$E = \frac{hc}{\lambda}$$

$$= \frac{6.626 \times 10^{-34} \text{ Js} \times 3.0 \times 10^8 \text{ ms}^{-1}}{337.1 \times 10^{-9} \text{ m}} \quad (1 \text{ nm} = 10^{-9} \text{ m})$$

$$= 0.05896 \times 10^{-17} \text{ J}$$

Energy of 5.6×10^{24} photons $= 0.05896 \times 10^{-17} \times 5.6 \times 10^{24}$ J

$$= 0.3302 \times 10^7 \text{ J} = 3.302 \times 10^6 \text{ J}$$

Question 47. Neon gas is generally used in sign boards. If it emits strongly at 616 nm, calculate

(a) the frequency of emission.

(b) distance travelled by this radiation in 30 s.

(c) energy of quantum.

(d) number of quanta present if it produces 2 J of energy.

Solution.

(a) Frequency, $v = \dfrac{c}{\lambda}$

$$\lambda = 616 \text{ nm} = 616 \times 10^{-9} \text{ m}$$

$$v = \frac{3.0 \times 10^8 \text{ ms}^{-1}}{616 \times 10^{-9} \text{ m}} = 4.870 \times 10^{14} \text{ s}^{-1}$$

(b) Distance travelled = Speed × Time

$$= 3.0 \times 10^8 \text{ ms}^{-1} \times 30 \text{ s} = 9.0 \times 10^9 \text{ m}$$

(c) Energy of quantum (or photon),

$$E = hv = 6.626 \times 10^{-34} \text{ Js} \times 4.870 \times 10^{14} \text{ s}^{-1}$$

$$= 32.268 \times 10^{-20} \text{ J} = 32.27 \times 10^{-20} \text{ J}$$

(d) Number of quanta present $= \dfrac{\text{Total energy produced}}{\text{Energy of 1 quanta}}$

$$= \frac{2 \text{ J}}{32.27 \times 10^{-20} \text{ J}} = 6.197 \times 10^{18} \approx 6.2 \times 10^{18} \text{ quanta}$$

Question 48. In astronomical observations, signals observed from the distant stars are generally weak. If the photon detector receives a total of 3.15×10^{-18} J from the radiations of 600 nm, calculate the number of photons received by the detector.

Solution. Energy of 1 photon, $E = \dfrac{hc}{\lambda}$

Given, wavelength, $\lambda = 600$ nm $= 600 \times 10^{-9}$ m

Energy of 1 photon, $E = \dfrac{6.626 \times 10^{-34} \text{ Js} \times 3.0 \times 10^8 \text{ ms}^{-1}}{600 \times 10^{-9} \text{ m}} = 3.313 \times 10^{-19}$ J

$$\text{Number of photons} = \frac{\text{Total energy received}}{\text{Energy of 1 photon}}$$

$$= \frac{3.15 \times 10^{-18} \text{ J}}{3.313 \times 10^{-19} \text{ J}} = 0.9507 \times 10^1 \text{ photons}$$

$$\approx 10 \text{ photons}$$

Question 49. Lifetimes of the molecules in the excited states are often measured by using pulsed radiation source of duration nearly in the nanosecond range. If the radiation source has the duration of 2ns and the number of photons emitted during the pulse source is 2.5×10^{15}, calculate the energy of the source.

Solution. Frequency, $v = \dfrac{1}{\text{period}} = \dfrac{1}{2\text{ns}} = \dfrac{1}{2 \times 10^{-9} \text{ s}} = 0.5 \times 10^9 \text{ s}^{-1}$

Energy of the source = Energy of 1 photon × number of photons produced

$E_{\text{source}} = hv \times N$

$= 6.626 \times 10^{-34} \text{ Js} \times 0.5 \times 10^9 \text{ s}^{-1} \times 2.5 \times 10^{15} = 8.28 \times 10^{-10}$ J

Question 50. The longest wavelength doublet absorption transition is observed at 589 and 589.6 nm. Calculate the frequency of each transition and energy difference between two excited states.

Solution.

(i) Given, wavelength $\lambda_1 = 589$ nm $= 589 \times 10^{-9}$ m

$\lambda_2 = 589.6$ nm $= 589.6 \times 10^{-9}$ m

Frequency of wavelength 589 nm

$v_1 = \dfrac{c}{\lambda_1} = \dfrac{3.0 \times 10^8 \text{ ms}^{-1}}{589 \times 10^{-9} \text{ m}} = 5.093 \times 10^{14} \text{ s}^{-1}$

Frequency of wavelength 589.6 nm

$v_2 = \dfrac{c}{\lambda_2} = \dfrac{3.0 \times 10^8 \text{ ms}^{-1}}{589.6 \times 10^{-9} \text{ m}} = 5.088 \times 10^{14} \text{ s}^{-1}$

(ii) Energy difference between two excited states,

$\Delta E = hv_1 - hv_2 = h\,(v_1 - v_2)$

$\Delta E = 6.626 \times 10^{-34} \text{ Js}\,(5.093 \times 10^{14} \text{s}^{-1} - 5.088 \times 10^{14} \text{s}^{-1})$

$\Delta E = 6.626 \times 10^{-34} \text{ Js} \times 0.005 \times 10^{14} \text{ s}^{-1}$

$\Delta E = 3.31 \times 10^{-22}$ J

Question 51. The work function for caesium atom is 1.9 eV. Calculate
(a) the threshold wavelength.
(b) the threshold frequency of the radiation. If the caesium element is irradiated with a wavelength 500 nm, calculate the kinetic energy and the velocity of the ejected photoelectron.

(i) As we know the value of work function (W_0) and h, calculate the threshold frequency v_0 by using the formula $W_0 = hv_0$

(ii) Calculate λ_0 by using $\lambda_0 = \dfrac{c}{v_0}$

(iii) To calculate $KE = h(v - v_0)$ calculate v of the striking and then calculate v by using the formula $KE = \dfrac{1}{2}mv^2$.

Solution.

(a) Work function $W_0 = hv_0$
$$W_0 = 1.9\,eV = 1.9 \times 1.602 \times 10^{-19}\ J$$
Threshold frequency,
$$v_0 = \frac{W_0}{h} = \frac{1.9 \times 1.602 \times 10^{-19}\ J}{6.626 \times 10^{-34}\ Js}$$
$$v_0 = 4.59 \times 10^{14}\ s^{-1}$$

(b) Threshold wavelength,
$$\lambda_0 = \frac{c}{v_0} = \frac{3.0 \times 10^8\ ms^{-1}}{4.59 \times 10^{14}\ s^{-1}}$$
$$= 6.536 \times 10^{-7}\ m$$
$$= 653.6 \times 10^{-9}\ m = 653.6\ nm$$

(c) KE of ejected photoelectron $= h(v - v_0)$
λ of striking radiation $= 500\ nm = 500 \times 10^{-9}\ m$
$$v = \frac{c}{\lambda} = \frac{3.0 \times 10^8\ ms^{-1}}{500 \times 10^{-9}\ m} = 6.0 \times 10^{14}\ s^{-1}$$
$$KE = 6.626 \times 10^{-34}\ Js\,(6.0 \times 10^{14}\ s^{-1} - 4.59 \times 10^{14}\ s^{-1})$$
$$KE = 9.34 \times 10^{-20}\ J$$

(d) $KE = \dfrac{1}{2}mv^2$ (Mass of an electron $= 9.11 \times 10^{-31}\ kg$)

$$9.34 \times 10^{-20}\ J = \frac{1}{2} \times 9.11 \times 10^{-31}\ kg \times v^2$$
$$\therefore \qquad v^2 = 2.050 \times 10^{11}\ m^2 s^{-2} \qquad (\because 1\,J = 1\,kg\ m^2 s^{-2})$$
or $\qquad v = \sqrt{20.50 \times 10^{10}}\ m^2 s^{-2}$
or $\qquad v = 4.527 \times 10^5\ ms^{-1}$

Note *Minimum energy required to eject an electron is also known as work function,* W_0 ($W_0 = hv_0$).

Question 52. Following results are observed when sodium metal is irradiated with different wavelengths. Calculate

(a) threshold wavelength   (b) Planck's constant.

λ (nm)	500	450	400
$v \times 10^5$ (ms^{-1})	2.55	4.35	5.20

(i) To find the value of λ_0, v_0 is required, so first calculate the value of v for all the three experiments by using the formula, $v = \dfrac{c}{\lambda}$ and make three equation by substituting the values of v and v in the formula. $KE = h(v - v_0) = \dfrac{1}{2}mv^2$.

(ii) Divide Eq. (ii) by Eq. (i) and obtain v_0.

(iii) Find λ_0 by using the formula, $\lambda_0 = \dfrac{c}{v_0}$

(iv) Find h by putting the value of v_0 in Eq. (iii).

Solution.   Kinetic energy, $KE = h\,(v - v_0) = \dfrac{1}{2}\,mv^2$

On substituting the given results of the three experiments, we get

For Ist experiment $\lambda = 500$ nm $= 500 \times 10^{-9}$ m;

$$v = \frac{c}{\lambda} = \frac{3.0 \times 10^8 \text{ ms}^{-1}}{500 \times 10^{-9} \text{ m}} = 6 \times 10^{14}\text{s}^{-1}$$

$$h\,(6 \times 10^{14} \text{ s}^{-1} - v_0) = \frac{1}{2}\,m\,(2.55 \times 10^5 \text{ ms}^{-1})^2 \qquad \text{...(i)}$$

For 2nd experiment $\lambda = 450$ nm $= 450 \times 10^{-9}$ m;

$$v = \frac{c}{\lambda} = \frac{3.0 \times 10^8 \text{ ms}^{-1}}{450 \times 10^{-9} \text{ m}} = 6.67 \times 10^{14} \text{ s}^{-1}$$

$$h\,(6.67 \times 10^{14}\text{s}^{-1} - v_0) = \frac{1}{2}\,m\,(4.35 \times 10^5 \text{ ms}^{-1})^2 \quad \text{...(ii)}$$

For 3rd experiment $\lambda = 400$ nm $= 400 \times 10^{-9}$ m;

$$v = \frac{c}{\lambda} = \frac{3.0 \times 10^8 \text{ ms}^{-1}}{400 \times 10^{-9} \text{ m}} = 7.5 \times 10^{14} \text{ s}^{-1}$$

$$h\,(7.5 \times 10^{14} \text{ s}^{-1} - v_0) = \frac{1}{2}\,m\,(5.20 \times 10^5 \text{ ms}^{-1})^2 \quad \text{...(iii)}$$

On dividing Eq. (ii) by Eq. (i), we get

$$\frac{h\,(6.67 \times 10^{14}\text{s}^{-1} - v_0) = \dfrac{1}{2}\,m\,(4.35 \times 10^5 \text{ ms}^{-1})^2}{h\,(6 \times 10^{14} \text{ s}^{-1} - v_0) = \dfrac{1}{2}\,m\,(2.55 \times 10^5 \text{ ms}^{-1})^2}$$

$$\frac{6.67 \times 10^{14} \text{ s}^{-1} - v_0}{6 \times 10^{14} \text{ s}^{-1} - v_0} = \frac{(4.35)^2}{(2.55)^2} = 2.91$$

$$6.67 \times 10^{14} \text{ s}^{-1} - v_0 = 17.46 \times 10^{14}\text{s}^{-1} - 2.91\,v_0$$

$$2.91v_0 - v_0 = 17.46 \times 10^{14} \text{ s}^{-1} - 6.67 \times 10^{14} \text{ s}^{-1}$$
$$1.91v_0 = 10.79 \times 10^{14} \text{s}^{-1}$$
$$v_0 = \frac{10.79 \times 10^{14} \text{s}^{-1}}{1.91} = 5.649 \times 10^{14} \text{ s}^{-1}$$
$$\lambda_0 = \frac{c}{v_0} = \frac{3.0 \times 10^8 \text{ ms}^{-1}}{5.649 \times 10^{14} \text{ s}^{-1}} = 5.31 \times 10^{-7} \text{ m}$$

On substituting the value of v_0 in Eq. (iii), we get
$$h\,(7.5 \times 10^{14} \text{s}^{-1} - 5.649 \times 10^{14} \text{s}^{-1})$$
$$= \frac{1}{2} \times 9.11 \times 10^{-31} \text{ kg} \times (5.20 \times 10^5 \text{ ms}^{-1})^2$$
$$h\,(1.851 \times 10^{14} \text{s}^{-1}) \times 2 = 9.11 \times 10^{-31} \text{ kg} \times (5.20 \times 10^5 \text{ ms}^{-1})^2$$
$$h \times 3.702 \times 10^{14} \text{ s}^{-1} = 246.33 \times 10^{-21} \text{ kg m}^2\text{s}^{-2}$$
$$h = \frac{246.33 \times 10^{-21} \text{ kg m}^2\text{s}^{-2}}{3.702 \times 10^{14} \text{ s}^{-1}}$$
$$h = 6.6539 \times 10^{-34} \text{ Js} \qquad (1 \text{ J} = 1 \text{ kg m}^2\text{s}^{-2})$$

Question 53. The ejection of the photoelectron from the silver metal in the photoelectric effect experiment can be stopped by applying the voltage of 0.35 V when the radiation 256.7 nm is used. Calculate the work function for silver metal.

 We know that energy of incident radiation is related to work function as E of incident radiation = work function + KE, so first calculate E from $E = \frac{hc}{\lambda}$ and use KE of electron = potential applied (as applied potential gives the kinetic energy of electron) to calculate work function.

Solution. Energy of incident radiation, $hv = hv_0 + \text{KE}$
$$E = hv = \frac{hc}{\lambda} = \frac{6.626 \times 10^{-34} \text{ Js} \times 3.0 \times 10^8 \text{ ms}^{-1}}{256.7 \times 10^{-9} \text{ m}}$$
$$= 7.74 \times 10^{-19} \text{ J} = \frac{7.74 \times 10^{-19} \text{ eV}}{1.602 \times 10^{-19}} = 4.83 \text{ eV}$$

Applied potential gives the kinetic energy to electron, *i.e.*,
$$eV_0 = \frac{1}{2} mv_{max}^2 = \text{KE}$$
$$= \frac{1}{2} mv_{max}^2 = 1.6 \times 10^{-19} \times 0.35 = 0.56 \times 10^{19} \text{ J}$$
$$= \frac{0.56 \times 10^{-19}}{1.6 \times 10^{-19}} \text{eV} = 0.35 \text{ eV}$$

$\therefore$ $\qquad$ KE $= 0.35$ eV

Work function, W_0 or $hv_0 = hv - \text{KE}$
$$= 4.83 \text{ eV} - 0.35 \text{ eV} = 4.48 \text{ eV}$$

Question 54. If the photon of the wavelength 150 pm strikes an atom and one of its inner bound electrons is ejected out with a velocity of 1.5×10^7 ms^{-1}, calculate the energy with which it is bound to the nucleus.

 The energy ($h\nu_0$) with which an electron is bound to the nucleus is calculated by using the formula $h\nu = h\nu_0 + KE$, so first find $h\nu$ of incident radiation and KE of electron by using the formula $KE = \dfrac{1}{2} mv^2$.

Then, substitute the values of $h\nu$ and KE to find $h\nu_0$ (*i.e.*, energy with which electron is bound to the nucleus).

Solution.   Energy of incident radiation $h\nu = h\nu_0 + \dfrac{1}{2} mv^2$

$$E = h\nu = \frac{hc}{\lambda} = \frac{6.626 \times 10^{-34} \text{ Js} \times 3.0 \times 10^8 \text{ ms}^{-1}}{150 \times 10^{-12} \text{ m}} \quad (1 \text{ pm} = 10^{-12} \text{ m})$$

$$E = 13.25 \times 10^{-16} \text{ J}$$

$$KE \text{ of ejected electron} = \frac{1}{2} mv^2 = \frac{1}{2} \times 9.11 \times 10^{-31} \text{ kg} \times (1.5 \times 10^7 \text{ ms}^{-1})^2$$

$$KE = 1.025 \times 10^{-16} \text{ J}$$

$$W_0 = h\nu_0 = h\nu - \frac{1}{2} mv^2$$

$$= 13.25 \times 10^{-16} \text{ J} - 1.025 \times 10^{-16} \text{ J} = 12.225 \times 10^{-16} \text{ J}$$

$$= \frac{12.225 \times 10^{-16}}{1.602 \times 10^{-19}} \text{ eV} = 7.63 \times 10^3 \text{ eV}$$

Note   *Energy with which the electron was bound to the nucleus = work function for the metal.*

Question 55. Emission transitions in the Paschen series end at orbit $n = 3$ and start from orbit n and can be represented as $v = 3.29 \times 10^{15}$ (Hz) $\left[\dfrac{1}{3^2} - \dfrac{1}{n^2}\right]$. Calculate the value of n if the transition is observed at 1285 nm. Find the region of the spectrum.

Solution.   Frequency, $v = \dfrac{c}{\lambda} = 3.29 \times 10^{15}$ Hz $\left(\dfrac{1}{3^2} - \dfrac{1}{n^2}\right)$

$$v = \frac{3.0 \times 10^8 \text{ ms}^{-1}}{1285 \times 10^{-9} \text{ m}} = 3.29 \times 10^{15} \text{ Hz} \left(\frac{1}{9} - \frac{1}{n^2}\right)$$

$$\frac{3.0 \times 10^8 \text{ ms}^{-1}}{1285 \times 10^{-9} \text{ m} \times 3.29 \times 10^{15} \text{ Hz}} = \left(\frac{1}{9} - \frac{1}{n^2}\right)$$

$$0.0709 = 0.1111 - \frac{1}{n^2}$$

$$\frac{1}{n^2} = 0.1111 - 0.0709 = 0.0402 \approx 0.04 = \frac{1}{25}$$

$$n^2 = 25 \text{ or } n = 5$$

∴ The electrons jumps from $n = 5$ to $n = 3$ i.e., the transition occurs in Paschen series and lies in infra-red region.

Moreover the radiation 1285 nm lies in the infrared region.

Question 56. Calculate the wavelength for the emission transition if it starts from the orbit having radius 1.3225 nm and ends at 211.6 pm. Name the series to which this transition belongs and the region of the spectrum.

(i) Rydberg formula for finding λ is $\bar{v} = \dfrac{1}{\lambda} = RZ^2 \left[\dfrac{1}{n_1^2} - \dfrac{1}{n_2^2} \right]$. To calculate λ by using this formula, n_1 and n_2 are required, so first find the values of energy levels n_1 and n_2 by using the formula, $r_n = \dfrac{52.9\, n^2}{Z}$ pm, then calculate λ by using Rydberg formula.

(ii) On the basis of value of n_1, also give the name of series as for Lyman series $n_1 = 1$, for Balmer series $n_1 = 2$, for Paschen series $n_1 = 3$ and so on.

Solution. Radius of nth orbit of H like species,

$$r_n = \frac{52.9\,(n^2)}{Z} \text{ pm}$$

$$r_1 = 1.3225 \text{ nm} = 1322.5 \text{ pm}$$

$$= \frac{52.9\, n_1^2}{Z}$$

$$r_2 = 211.6 \text{ pm} = \frac{52.9\, n_2^2}{Z}$$

$$\frac{r_1}{r_2} = \frac{1322.5}{211.6} = \frac{n_1^2}{n_2^2}$$

$$\frac{n_1^2}{n_2^2} = 6.25 \text{ or } \frac{n_1}{n_2} = 2.5$$

If $n_1 = 5$, $n_2 = 2$, so, the transition (emission transition) is from 5th orbit to 2nd orbit and it belongs to Balmer series.

$$\bar{v} = \frac{1}{\lambda} = 1.09677 \times 10^7 \left(\frac{1}{n_1^2} - \frac{1}{n_2^2} \right) \text{ m}^{-1}$$

$$\frac{1}{\lambda} = 1.09677 \times 10^7 \left(\frac{1}{2^2} - \frac{1}{5^2} \right) \text{ m}^{-1}$$

$$\frac{1}{\lambda} = 1.09677 \times 10^7 \times \frac{21}{100} = 2.303 \times 10^6 \text{ m}^{-1}$$

$$\lambda = 0.434 \times 10^{-6} \text{ m} = 434 \times 10^{-9} \text{ m} = 434 \text{ nm}$$

It belongs to visible region.

Note In the above Rydberg formula if $n_1 = 1, 2, \ldots$ then $n_2 = n_1 + 1$, $n_1 + 2 \ldots$. For Balmer series, spectral region is visible.

Question 57. Dual behaviour of matter proposed by de-Broglie led to the discovery of electron microscope often used for the highly magnified images of biological molecules and other type of materials. If the velocity of the electron in this microscope is 1.6×10^6 ms^{-1}, calculate de-Broglie wavelength associated with this electron.

Solution. de-Broglie wavelength, $\lambda = \dfrac{h}{mv}$

$$\lambda = \frac{6.626 \times 10^{-34}\ \text{Js}}{9.11 \times 10^{-31}\ \text{kg} \times 1.6 \times 10^6\ \text{ms}^{-1}} \quad (1\ \text{J} = 1\ \text{kg m}^2\text{s}^{-2})$$

$$= 0.455 \times 10^{-9}\ \text{m} = 4.55 \times 10^{-10}\ \text{m} = 455\ \text{pm}.$$

Question 58. Similar to electron diffraction, neutron diffraction microscope is also used for the determination of the structure of molecules. If the wavelength used here is 800 pm, calculate the characteristic velocity associated with the neutron (mass of neutron = 1.675×10^{-27} kg).

Solution. Wavelength, $\lambda = \dfrac{h}{mv}$

Mass of neutron, $m = 1.675 \times 10^{-27}$ kg

$$\lambda = 800\ \text{pm} = 800 \times 10^{-12}\ \text{m} = \frac{6.626 \times 10^{-34}\ \text{kg m}^2\text{s}^{-1}}{1.675 \times 10^{-27}\ \text{kg} \times v}$$

$$v = \frac{6.626 \times 10^{-34}\ \text{kg m}^2\text{s}^{-1}}{1.675 \times 10^{-27}\ \text{kg} \times 800 \times 10^{-12}\ \text{m}}$$

$$= 0.494 \times 10^3\ \text{ms}^{-1} = 4.94 \times 10^2\ \text{ms}^{-1}$$

Question 59. If the velocity of the electron in Bohr's first orbit is 2.19×10^6 ms^{-1}, calculate the de-Broglie wavelength associated with it.

Solution. We know that, mass of electron $= 9.11 \times 10^{-31}$ kg

$$h = 6.626 \times 10^{-34}\ \text{J-s}$$

Wavelength, $\lambda = \dfrac{h}{mv} = \dfrac{6.626 \times 10^{-34}\ \text{kg m}^2\text{s}^{-1}}{9.11 \times 10^{-31}\ \text{kg} \times 2.19 \times 10^6\ \text{m s}^{-1}}$

$$\lambda = 3.32 \times 10^{-10}\ \text{m} = 332\ \text{pm}$$

Question 60. The velocity associated with a proton moving in a potential difference of 1000 V is 4.37×10^5 ms^{-1}. If the hockey ball of mass 0.1 kg is moving with this velocity, calculate the wavelength associated with this velocity.

Solution. Wavelength associated with the velocity of hockey ball

$$\lambda = \frac{h}{mv} = \frac{6.626 \times 10^{-34}\ \text{kg m}^2\text{s}^{-1}}{0.1\ \text{kg} \times 4.37 \times 10^5\ \text{m s}^{-1}}$$

$$= 15.16 \times 10^{-39}\ \text{m} = 1.516 \times 10^{-38}\ \text{m}$$

Question 61. If the position of the electron is measured within an accuracy of $\pm$ 0.002 nm, calculate the uncertainty in the momentum of the electron. Suppose the momentum of the electron is $\dfrac{h}{4\pi_m \times 0.05 \text{ nm}}$, is there any problem in defining this value.

Solution. $\Delta x = 0.002$ nm $= 0.002 \times 10^{-9}$ m $= 2.00 \times 10^{-12}$ m

From Heisenberg's uncertainty principle,

$$\Delta x \times \Delta p \geq \frac{h}{4\pi}$$

$$\Delta p = \frac{h}{4\pi \,\Delta x} = \frac{6.626 \times 10^{-34} \text{ kg m}^2\text{s}^{-1}}{4 \times 3.14 \times 2.00 \times 10^{-12} \text{ m}}$$

$$\Delta p = 2.638 \times 10^{-23} \text{ kg m s}^{-1}$$

$$\text{Actual momentum} = \frac{h}{4\pi \times 0.05 \text{ nm}} = \frac{6.626 \times 10^{-34} \text{ kg m}^2\text{s}^{-1}}{4 \times 3.14 \times 0.05 \times 10^{-9} \text{ m}}$$

$$= 1.055 \times 10^{-24} \text{ kg m s}^{-1}$$

It cannot be defined as the actual value of momentum is smaller than uncertainty.

Question 62. The quantum numbers of six electrons are given below. Arrange them in order of increasing energies. If any of these combination(s) has/have the same energy lists :

1. $n = 4, l = 2, m_l = -2, m_s = -\dfrac{1}{2}$ 2. $n = 3, l = 2, m_l = 1, m_s = +\dfrac{1}{2}$

3. $n = 4, l = 1, m_l = 0, m_s = +\dfrac{1}{2}$ 4. $n = 3, l = 2, m_l = -2, m_s = -\dfrac{1}{2}$

5. $n = 3, l = 1, m_l = -1, m_s = +\dfrac{1}{2}$ 6. $n = 4, l = 1, m_l = 0, m_s = +\dfrac{1}{2}$

 Energy of the orbitals in multielectron atom depends upon the values of n and l The lower the value of $(n + l)$ for an orbital, the lower is its energy. If two orbitals have the same $(n + l)$ value, the orbital with lower value of n, has the lower energy.

Solution.

	Subshell notation	$n + l$
1. $n = 4, l = 2, m_l = -2, m_s = -\dfrac{1}{2}$	4d	$4 + 2 = 6$
2. $n = 3, l = 2, m_l = 1, m_s = +\dfrac{1}{2}$	3d	$3 + 2 = 5$
3. $n = 4, l = 1, m_l = 0, m_s = +\dfrac{1}{2}$	4p	$4 + 1 = 5$
4. $n = 3, l = 2, m_l = -2, m_s = -\dfrac{1}{2}$	3d	$3 + 2 = 5$
5. $n = 3, l = 1, m_l = -1, m_s = +\dfrac{1}{2}$	3p	$3 + 1 = 4$
6. $n = 4, l = 1, m_l = 0, m_s = +\dfrac{1}{2}$	4p	$4 + 1 = 5$

$$5 < 2 = 4 < 3 = 6 < 1$$
$$3p < 3d = 3d < 4p = 4p < 4d$$
(Arrangement of orbitals in order of their increasing energies.)

Question 63. The bromine atom possesses 35 electrons. It contains 6 electrons in $2p$-orbital, 6 electrons in $3p$-orbital and 5 electron in $4p$-orbital. Which of these electron experiences the lowest effective nuclear charge?

Solution. Effective nuclear charge decreases as the distance of the orbitals increases from the nucleus. Hence, $4p$ electrons experience the lowest effective nuclear charge.

Question 64. Among the following pairs of orbitals which orbital will experience the larger effective nuclear charge?
(i) $2s$ and $3s$, (ii) $4d$ and $4f$, (iii) $3d$ and $3p$

As the distance between the nucleus and orbital increases, effective nuclear charge decreases.

Solution.
(i) $2s$-orbital experiences larger effective nuclear charge than $3s$ because $2s$ is closer to nucleus than $3s$.
(ii) Similarly $4d$-orbital experiences larger effective nuclear charge than $4f$-orbital.
(iii) In $3d$ and $3p$-orbitals, $3p$-orbital experiences larger effective nuclear charge.

Question 65. The unpaired electrons in Al and Si are present in $3p$-orbital. Which electrons will experience more effective nuclear charge from the nucleus?

Solution. $_{13}Al = 1s^2, 2s^2, 2p^6, 3s^2, 3p^1$
$_{14}Si = 1s^2, 2s^2, 2p^6, 3s^2, 3p^2$

Si (+4) has greater nuclear charge than aluminium (+3). Hence, $3p$ unpaired electrons of Si experience greater effective nuclear charge than Al.

Question 66. Indicate the number of unpaired electrons in
(a) P (b) Si (c) Cr (d) Fe (e) Kr

Solution.
(a) $_{15}P = 1s^2, 2s^2, 2p^6, 3s^2, 3p^3$ 3 unpaired electrons
(b) $_{14}Si = 1s^2, 2s^2, 2p^6, 3s^2, 3p^2$ 2 unpaired electrons
(c) $_{24}Cr = 1s^2, 2s^2, 2p^6, 3s^2, 3p^6, 3d^5, 4s^1$ 6 unpaired electrons
(d) $_{26}Fe = 1s^2, 2s^2, 2p^6, 3s^2, 3p^6, 3d^6, 4s^2$ 4 unpaired electrons
(e) $_{36}Kr = 1s^2, 2s^2, 2p^6, 3s^2, 3p^6, 3d^{10}, 4s^2, 4p^6$ No unpaired electron

Note *Either exactly half-filled or fully filled orbitals are more stable due to symmetrical distribution of electrons and maximum exchange energy.*

Question 67. (a) How many subshells are associated with $n = 4$?

(b) How many electrons will be present in the subshells having m_s value of $-\dfrac{1}{2}$ for $n = 4$?

Solution.
(a) $n = 4$, $l = 0, 1, 2, 3$, s p d f (4 subshells)
(b) Number of orbitals in 4th shell $= n^2 = 4^2 = 16$

The maximum number of electrons present in any orbital is two and each orbital has one electron with $m_s = -\dfrac{1}{2}$. Hence, there are 16 electrons with $m_s = -\dfrac{1}{2}$.

Selected NCERT Exemplar Problems

Short Answer Type

Question 1. Arrange s, p and d-subshells of a shell in the increasing order of effective nuclear charge (Z_{eff}) experienced by the electron present in them.

Solution. s-orbital is spherical in shape, it shields the electrons from the nucleus more effectively than p-orbital which in turn shields more effectively than d-orbital. Therefore, the effective nuclear charge (Z_{eff}) experienced by electrons present in them is $d < p < s$.

Question 2. Show the distribution of electrons in oxygen atom (atomic number 8) using orbital diagram.

Solution. $\quad _8O = 1s^2 \quad 2s^2 \qquad 2p^4$

⇅		⇅		⇅	↑	↑

Question 3. Nickel atom can lose two electrons to form Ni^{2+} ion. The atomic number of Ni is 28. From which orbital will nickel lose two electrons?

Solution. $_{28}Ni = 1s^2, 2s^2, 2p^6, 3s^2, 3p^6, 3d^8, 4s^2$; Nickel will lose 2 electrons from $4s$ (outer most shell) to form Ni^{2+} ion.

Question 4. Which of the following orbitals are degenerate?

$$3d_{xy}, 4d_{xy}, 3d_{z^2}, 3d_{yz} \; 4d_{z^2}$$

Solution. The orbitals which belongs to same subshell and same shell are called degenerate orbitals. $(3d_{xy}, 3d_{z^2}, 3d_{yz})$ and $(4d_{xy}, 4d_{yz}, 4d_{z^2})$ are the two sets of degenerate orbitals.

Question 5. Calculate the total number of angular nodes and radial nodes present in $3p$-orbital.

Solution. For $3p$-orbital, principal quantum number, $n = 3$ and azimuthal quantum number, $l = 1$

Number of angular nodes $= l = 1$
Number of radial nodes $= n - l - 1 = 3 - 1 - 1 = 1$

Question 6. Wavelengths of different radiations are given below.

$$\lambda(A) = 300 \text{ nm}, \lambda(B) = 300 \text{ μm}, \lambda(C) = 3 \text{ nm}, \lambda(D) = 30 \text{ Å}$$

Arrange these radiations in the increasing order of their energies.

Solution.

(A) $\lambda = 300 \text{ nm} = 300 \times 10^{-9} \text{ m}$
(B) $\lambda = 300 \text{ μm} = 300 \times 10^{-6} \text{ m}$
(C) $\lambda = 3 \text{ nm} = 3 \times 10^{-9} \text{ m}$
(D) $\lambda = 30 \text{ Å} = 30 \times 10^{-10} \text{ m} = 3 \times 10^{-9} \text{ m}$

$$\text{Energy, } E = \frac{hc}{\lambda}$$

$$\text{Therefore, } E \propto \frac{1}{\lambda}$$

Increasing order of energy is $B < A < C = D$

Question 7. The Balmer series in the hydrogen spectrum corresponds to the transition from $n_1 = 2$ to $n_2 = 3, 4 \dots$. This series lies in the visible region. Calculate the wave number of line associated with the transition in Balmer series when the electron moves to $n = 4$ orbit. ($R_H = 109677 \text{ cm}^{-1}$)

Solution. From Rydberg formula,

$$\text{Wave number, } \bar{v} = 109677 \left[\frac{1}{n_i^2} - \frac{1}{n_f^2} \right] \text{cm}^{-1}$$

Given $n_i = 2$ and $n_f = 4$ (Transition in Balmer series)

$$\bar{v} = 109677 \left[\frac{1}{2^2} - \frac{1}{4^2} \right] \text{cm}^{-1}$$

$$\bar{v} = 109677 \left[\frac{1}{4} - \frac{1}{16} \right] \text{cm}^{-1}$$

$$\bar{v} = 109677 \times \left[\frac{4-1}{16} \right] \text{cm}^{-1}$$

$$\bar{v} = 20564.44 \text{ cm}^{-1}$$

Question 8. According to de-Broglie, matter should exhibit dual behaviour, that is both particle and wave like properties. However, a cricket ball of mass 100 g does not move like a wave when it is thrown by a bowler at a speed of 100 km/h. Calculate the wavelength of the ball and explain why it does not show wave nature?

Solution. Given, $m = 100 \text{ g} = 0.1 \text{ kg}$

$$v = 100 \text{ km/h} = \frac{100 \times 1000}{60 \times 60} = \frac{1000}{36} \text{ ms}^{-1}$$

From de-Broglie equation, wavelength, $\lambda = \dfrac{h}{mv}$

$$\lambda = \frac{6.626 \times 10^{-34} \text{ kg m}^2 \text{ s}^{-1}}{0.1 \text{ kg} \times \dfrac{1000}{36} \text{ ms}^{-1}} = 238.5 \times 10^{-36} \text{ m}$$

As the wavelength is very small so wave nature cannot be detected.

Question 9. Out of electron and proton which one will have, a higher velocity to produce matter waves of the same wavelength? Explain it.

Solution. From de-Broglie equation, wavelength, $\lambda = \dfrac{h}{mv}$

For same wavelength for two different particles, *i.e.,* electron and proton, $m_1 v_1 = m_2 v_2$ (h is constant). Lesser the mass of the particle, greater will be the velocity. Hence, electron will have higher velocity.

Question 10. A hypothetical electromagnetic wave is shown in Fig. Find out the wavelength of the radiation.

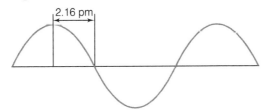

2.16 pm

Solution. **Wavelength** It is the distance between two successive peaks or two successive troughs of a wave.
Therefore, $\lambda = 4 \times 2.16 \text{ pm} = 8.64 \text{ pm}$

Question 11. Table-Tennis ball has a mass 10 g and a speed of 90 m/s. If speed can be measured within an accuracy of 4% what will be the uncertainty in speed and position?

Solution. $m = 10 \text{ g} = 10 \times 10^{-3} \text{ kg}$

Uncertainty in speed $(\Delta v) = 4\%$ of $90 \text{ ms}^{-1} = \dfrac{4 \times 90}{100} = 3.6 \text{ ms}^{-1}$

From Heisenberg uncertainty principle,

$$\Delta x \cdot \Delta v = \frac{h}{4\pi\, m} \text{ or } \Delta x = \frac{h}{4\pi\, m\, \Delta v}$$

Uncertainty in position,

$$\Delta x = \frac{6.626 \times 10^{-34} \text{ kgm}^2 \text{s}^{-1}}{4 \times 3.14 \times 10 \times 10^{-3} \text{ kg} \times 3.6 \text{ ms}^{-1}} = 1.46 \times 10^{-33} \text{ m}$$

Question 12. The effect of uncertainty principle is significant only for motion of microscopic particles and is negligible for the macroscopic particles. Justify the statement with the help of a suitable example.

Solution. If uncertainty principle is applied to an object of mass, say about a milligram $(10^{-6}$ kg), then

$$\Delta v \cdot \Delta x = \frac{h}{4\pi\,m}$$

$$\Delta v \cdot \Delta x = \frac{6.626 \times 10^{-34}\ \mathrm{kg\,m^2 s^{-1}}}{4 \times 3.14 \times 10^{-6}\ \mathrm{kg}}$$

$$= 0.52 \times 10^{-28}\ \mathrm{m^2 s^{-1}}$$

The value of $\Delta v \cdot \Delta x$ obtained is extremely small and is insignificant. Therefore, for milligram-sized or heavier objects, the associated uncertainties are hardly of any real consequence.

Question 13. Hydrogen atom has only one electron, so mutual repulsion between electrons is absent. However, in multielectron atoms mutual repulsion between the electrons is significant. How does this affect the energy of an electron in the orbitals of the same principal quantum number in multielectron atoms?

Solution. In hydrogen atom, the energy of an electron is determined by the value of n and in multielectron atom, it is determined by $n + l$. Hence, for a given principal quantum, electrons of s, p, d and f-orbitals have different energy (for s, p, d and f, $l = 0, 1, 2$ and 3 respectively.)

Long Answer Type

Question 14. Threshold frequency, v_0 is the minimum frequency which a photon must possess to eject an electron from a metal. It is different for different metals. When a photon of frequency $1.0 \times 10^{15}\ \mathrm{s^{-1}}$ was allowed to hit a metal surface, an electron having 1.988×10^{-19} J of kinetic energy was emitted. Calculate the threshold frequency of this metal. Show that an electron will not be emitted if a photon with a wavelength equal to 600 nm hits the metal surface.

Solution. We know that $hv = hv_0 + \mathrm{KE}$

or $hv - \mathrm{KE} = hv_0 = (6.626 \times 10^{-34}\ \mathrm{Js} \times 1 \times 10^{15}\ \mathrm{s^{-1}}) - 1.988 \times 10^{-19}$ J

$$hv_0 = 6.626 \times 10^{-19} - 1.988 \times 10^{-19}\ \mathrm{J}$$

$$hv_0 = 4.638 \times 10^{-19}\ \mathrm{J}$$

$$v_0 = \frac{4.638 \times 10^{-19}\ \mathrm{J}}{6.626 \times 10^{-34}\ \mathrm{Js}} = 0.699 \times 10^{15}\ \mathrm{s^{-1}}$$

When, $\lambda = 600\ \mathrm{nm} = 600 \times 10^{-9}\ \mathrm{m}$

$$v = \frac{c}{\lambda} = \frac{3.0 \times 10^8\ \mathrm{ms^{-1}}}{6.0 \times 10^{-7}\ \mathrm{m}} = 0.5 \times 10^{15}\ \mathrm{s^{-1}}$$

Thus, $v < v_0$. Hence, no electron will be emitted.

Question 15. When an electric discharge is passed through hydrogen gas, the hydrogen molecules dissociate to produce excited hydrogen atoms. These excited atoms emit electromagnetic radiation of discrete frequencies which can be given by the general formula

$$\bar{v} = 109677 \left[\frac{1}{n_i^2} - \frac{1}{n_f^2} \right]$$

What points of Bohr's model of an atom can be used to arrive at this formula? Based on these points derive the above formula giving description of each step and each term.

Solution. The two important points of Bohr's model that can be used to derive the given formula are as follows

(i) Electrons revolve around the nucleus in a circular path of fixed radius and energy. These paths are called orbits, stationary states or allowed energy states.

(ii) Energy is emitted or absorbed when an electron moves from higher stationary state to lower stationary state or from lower stationary state to higher stationary state respectively.

Derivation The energy of the electron in the nth stationary state is given by the expression,

$$E_n = -R_H \left(\frac{1}{n^2} \right) \qquad n = 1, 2, 3 \ldots \qquad \ldots(\text{i})$$

where R_H is called Rydberg constant and its value is 2.18×10^{-18} J.

The energy of the lowest state, also called the ground state, is

$$E_1 = -2.18 \times 10^{-18} \left(\frac{1}{1^2} \right) = -2.18 \times 10^{-18} \text{ J} \qquad \ldots(\text{ii})$$

The energy gap between the two orbits is given by the equation,

$$\Delta E = E_f - E_i \qquad \ldots(\text{iii})$$

On combining equations (i) and (iii)

$$\Delta E = \left(-\frac{R_H}{n_f^2} \right) - \left(-\frac{R_H}{n_i^2} \right)$$

where, n_i and n_f stand for initial orbit and final orbit.

$$\Delta E = R_H \left[\frac{1}{n_i^2} - \frac{1}{n_f^2} \right] = 2.18 \times 10^{-18} \text{ J} \left[\frac{1}{n_i^2} - \frac{1}{n_f^2} \right]$$

Frequency, v associated with the absorption and emission of the photon can be calculated as follows

$$v = \frac{\Delta E}{h} = \frac{R_H}{h} \left[\frac{1}{n_i^2} - \frac{1}{n_f^2} \right]$$

$$v = \frac{2.18 \times 10^{-18} \text{ J}}{6.626 \times 10^{-34} \text{ Js}} \left[\frac{1}{n_i^2} - \frac{1}{n_f^2} \right]$$

$$v = 3.29 \times 10^{15} \left[\frac{1}{n_i^2} - \frac{1}{n_f^2} \right] \text{Hz}$$

$$\bar{v} = \frac{v}{c} = \frac{3.29 \times 10^{15}}{3 \times 10^8 \text{ ms}^{-1}} \left[\frac{1}{n_i^2} - \frac{1}{n_f^2} \right]$$

$$\bar{v} = 1.09677 \times 10^7 \left[\frac{1}{n_i^2} - \frac{1}{n_f^2} \right] \text{m}^{-1}$$

$$\bar{v} = 109677 \left[\frac{1}{n_i^2} - \frac{1}{n_f^2} \right] \text{cm}^{-1}$$

Question 16. Calculate the energy and frequency of the radiation emitted when an electron jumps from $n = 3$ to $n = 2$ in a hydrogen atom.

Solution.   Wave number, $\bar{v} = 109677 \text{ cm}^{-1} \left(\frac{1}{2^2} - \frac{1}{3^2} \right)$

$$\bar{v} = 109677 \times \frac{5}{36} = 15232.9 \text{ cm}^{-1}$$

$$\bar{v} = \frac{1}{\lambda} \text{ or } \lambda = \frac{1}{\bar{v}} = \frac{1}{15232.9} = 6.564 \times 10^{-5} \text{ cm}$$

Wavelength, $\lambda = 6.564 \times 10^{-7}$ m

Energy, $E = \dfrac{hc}{\lambda} = \dfrac{6.626 \times 10^{-34} \text{ Js} \times 3.0 \times 10^8 \text{ ms}^{-1}}{6.564 \times 10^{-7} \text{ m}} = 3.028 \times 10^{-19}$ J

Frequency, $v = \dfrac{c}{\lambda} = \dfrac{3.0 \times 10^8 \text{ ms}^{-1}}{6.564 \times 10^{-7} \text{ m}} = 0.457 \times 10^{15} \text{ s}^{-1}$

$$v = 4.57 \times 10^{14} \text{ s}^{-1}$$

Question 17. Why was a change in the Bohr model of atom required, due to which important development(s), concept of movement of an electron in an orbit was replaced by the concept of probability of finding electron in an orbital? What is the name given to the changed model of atom?

Solution. In Bohr model, an electron is regarded as a charged particle moving in well defined circular orbits about the nucleus. An orbit can completely be defined only if both the position and the velocity of the electron are known exactly at the same time. This is not possible according to the Heisenberg uncertainty principal. Further more, the wave character of the electron is not considered in Bohr model. Therefore, concept of movement of an electron in an orbit was replaced by the concept of probability of finding electron in an orbital due to de-Broglie concept of dual nature of electron and Heisenberg's uncertainty principle. The changed model is called quantum mechanical model of the atom.

Chapter 3

Classification of Elements & Periodicity in Properties

Important Results

1. Periodic Table is an arrangement of elements with similar properties placed together.

2. Earlier attempts to classify elements :

(i) **Dobereiner's Triads** Dobereiner (1829) classified the elements into groups of three elements having similarity in physical and chemical properties. He also noticed that atomic mass of central element was the arithmetic mean of other two elements.

(ii) **Newland's Law of Octaves** Newland arranged the elements in such a manner that the eighth element starting from a given one has properties which are a repetition of those of the first, if arranged in order of increasing atomic weight.

(iii) **Mendeleev's Periodic Table** (1869) Mendeleev arranged the elements known at that time on the basis of his famous periodic law given as

(a) Atomic weight is the fundamental property of elements.

(b) The physical and chemical properties of elements are periodic function of their atomic weight.

3. **Modern Periodic Law** (1972) Moseley modified Mendeleev's periodic law and proposed modern periodic law as "the physical and chemical properties of the elements are periodic functions of their atomic numbers".

4. **Long form of Periodic Table** It was based on Bohr-Bury concept of electronic configuration. It contains 7 periods and 18 groups. Each period starts with filling of electrons in new principal quantum number and completes after the outermost shell is completely filled. Four types of elements can be recognized in the Periodic Table on the basis of their electronic configurations. These are s-block, p-block, d-block and f-block elements. Hydrogen with one electron in the s-orbital occupies a unique position in the Periodic Table.

5. Metals comprise more than 78% of the known elements. Non-metals, which are located at the extreme right of the Periodic Table, are less than twenty in number. Elements which lie at the border line between metals and non-metals are called metalloids or semi-metals.

6. Metallic character increases with increasing atomic number in a group whereas decreases from left to right in a period. The physical and chemical properties of elements vary periodically with their atomic numbers.

7. Periodic trends are observed in atomic sizes, ionization enthalpies, electron gain enthalpies, electronegativity and valence.

8. The atomic radii decreases while going from left to right in a period and increases with atomic number in a group. The size of isoelectronic species decreases with increase in the nuclear charge.

9. Ionization enthalpies generally increase across a period and decrease down a group. However, the elements having extra stable configuration have extra ordinarily high ionization enthalpies. Electronegativity also shows a similar trend.

10. Electron gain enthalpies in general, become more negative across a period and less negative down a group.

11. There is some periodicity in valence, for example, among representative elements, the valence is either equal to the number of electrons in the outermost shell or eight minus this number.

12. Chemical reactivity is the highest at the two extremes of a period and is lowest in the centre. The reactivity on the left extreme of a period is because of the ease of electron loss (or low ionization enthalpy) and reactivity on the right extreme of a period is because of the ease of gain of electron.

13. Oxides of the elements on the left are basic and of the elements on the right are acidic in nature. Oxides of elements in the centre are amphoteric or neutral.

Exercises

Question 1. What is the basic theme of organisation in the Periodic Table?

Solution. The basic theme of organisation in the Periodic Table is to simplify and systematise the study of physical and chemical properties of all the elements and their innumerable compounds.

Question 2. Which important property did Mendeleev use to classify the elements in his Periodic Table and did he stick to that?

Solution. Mendeleev used atomic weight as the basis of classification of elements in the Periodic Table. He arranged 63 elements known at that time in the Periodic Table on the basis of the order of their increasing atomic weights and he placed elements with similar nature in same group.

He stuck to this basis sincerely as some places were left vacant for new elements which were not discovered at that time. For example Ga (gallium) and Ge (germanium) were not known at that time. He left vacant space for them and named them as eka-aluminium and eka-silicon. He predicted not only the existence of these two elements but also described some of their general physical properties. These elements were discovered later.

However, he also found some elements that did not fit in his scheme of classification on the basis of atomic weight. In such cases, he ignored the order of atomic weights e.g., iodine is placed after tellurium due to its similarity in properties with other halogens although its atomic weight is lower (= 126.9) than that of tellurium (= 127.6).

Question 3. What is the basic difference in approach between the Mendeleev's periodic law and the modern periodic law?

Solution. Mendeleev periodic law It states that the properties of the elements are a periodic function of their atomic weights.

Modern periodic law It states that the properties of the elements are a periodic function of their atomic numbers.

Thus, change in the base of classification of elements from atomic weight to atomic number is the basic difference between Mendeleev's periodic law and the modern periodic law.

Question 4. On the basis of quantum numbers, justify that sixth period of the Periodic Table should have 32 elements.

Solution. In the modern Periodic Table, each period starts with the filling of a new principal energy level. Sixth period begins with filling of principal quantum number, $n = 6$. According to **Aufbau principle**, in the ground state of the atoms, the orbitals are filled in order of their increasing energies. Therefore, in sixth period, electrons enter in $6s, 4f, 5d$ and $6p$ subshells. Total 16 orbitals $(2 + 7 + 5 + 3$ respectively) are present in these subshells. According to Pauli's exclusion principle each orbital can accomodate maximum two electrons, therefore 16 orbitals can have 32 electrons and hence, 6th period have 32 elements.

Question 5. In terms of period and group where would you locate the element with $Z = 114$?

 First write electronic configuration of the given element. Highest value of n shows the period of element and group number $= 10 +$ number of electrons in ns and np shells.

Solution. $_{114}Z = {}_{86}[Rn]\, 7s^2, 5f^{14}, 6d^{10}, 7p^2$

In the Periodic Table, the element with $Z = 114$ is located in

Block – p-block (as last electron enters in p-subshell).

Period – 7th (as $n = 7$ for valence shell)

Group – 14th (for p-block elements, group number $= 10 +$ number of electrons in the valence shell).

Question 6. Write the atomic number of the element present in the third period and seventeenth group of the Periodic Table.

Solution. General configuration for 17th group elements is ns^2np^5. In the third period, the principal quantum number for valence shell is three, so the electronic configuration of valence shell for the given element is $3s^2, 3p^5$. Third period starts from atomic number, $Z = 11$ and end at $Z = 18$. Hence, the atomic number of the given element is $10 + 7 = 17$.

Question 7. Which element do you think would have been named by
 (i) Lawrence Berkeley laboratory   (ii) Seaborg's group?
Solution.
  (i) Lawrencium $(Z = 103)$ and Berkelium $(Z = 97)$.
  (ii) Seaborgium $(Z = 106)$.

Question 8. Why do elements in the same group have similar physical and chemical properties?

Solution. Same group elements have similar electronic configuration therefore, have similar physical and chemical properties.

Question 9. What does atomic radius or ionic radius mean to you?

Solution. **Atomic radius** Atomic radius means size of the atom. It can be measured by X-ray or other spectroscopic methods. In case of non-metals, it is called covalent radius and if the element is metal, it is called metallic radius.

Covalent radius is defined as one half the distance between the nuclei of two covalently bonded atoms of the same element in a molecule. For example, the bond distance in the Cl_2 molecule is 198 pm and half of this distance, 99 pm is taken as the atomic radius of chlorine.

Metallic radius is defined as one half the distance between the two adjacent atoms in the metallic lattice. For example, the distance between two adjacent copper atoms in solid copper is 256 pm; hence, the metallic radius of Cu is 128 pm.

Ionic radius Ionic radius means size of the ion (cation or anion). It can be estimated by measuring the distances between cations and anions in ionic crystal. A cation is always smaller than its parent atom because effective nuclear charge increases as a result of loss of one or more electrons. An anion is always larger than its parent atom because effective nuclear charge decreases as a result of addition of one or more electrons. For example; ionic radius of fluoride ion $(F^- = 136$ pm$)$ is greater than atomic radius of fluorine atom $(F = 72$ pm$)$. On the other hand, the atomic radius of sodium (186 pm) is larger than ionic radius of Na^+ ion (95 pm).

Question 10. How do atomic radius vary in a period and in a group? How do you explain the variation?

Solution. Atomic size decreases as we move from left to right in a period. It is because within a period the electrons enter in the same valence shell and the effective nuclear charge increases with increase in atomic number. As a result of this increased effective nuclear charge, the attraction of the nucleus for outer electrons increases and hence, the atomic size decreases.

Within a group atomic size of the elements increases regularly with increase in atomic number. As we move down a group, number of shells increases by one and the valence shell electrons are farther and farther away from the nucleus. Due to this, nuclear attraction for valence electrons decreases and hence, the size increases.

Question 11. What do you understand by isoelectronic species? Name a species that will be isoelectronic with each of the following atoms or ions.

(i) F^- (ii) Ar   (iii) Mg^{2+} (iv) Rb^+

Solution. Isoelectronic species have the same number of electrons but different nuclear charges. In case of isoelectronic species as the nuclear charge increases, their size decreases.

(i) F^- has 10 electrons (9 + 1).

(ii) Ar has 18 electrons.

(iii) Mg^{2+} has 10 electrons (12–2) and (iv) Rb^+ has 36 electrons (37–1).

N^{3-}, O^{2-}, Ne, Na^+ and Al^{3+} are some species which are isoelectronic with F^- and Mg^{2+}.

$P^{3-}, S^{2-}, Cl^-, K^+$ and Ca^{2+} are some species which are isoelectronic to Ar.

Similarly, Br^-, Kr and Sr^{2+} are isoelectronic with Rb^+.

Question 12. Consider the following species :

$$N^{3-}, O^{2-}, F^-, Na^+, Mg^{2+} \text{ and } Al^{3+}$$

(a) What is common in them?

(b) Arrange them in the order of increasing ionic radii.

  (i) Find number of electrons in each ion. For each positive charge remove one electron and for each negative charge add one electron.

(ii) Ionic radii of isoelectronic species varies inversely with atomic number.

Solution.

(i) All the given species have same number of electrons $(10\,e^-)$. Therefore, all are isoelectronic.

(ii) The ionic radii of isoelectronic species decreases with increase in atomic number (as magnitude of the nuclear charge increases with increase in atomic number). Therefore, their ionic radii increase in the order

Isoelectronic ions $= Al^{3+} < Mg^{2+} < Na^+ < F^- < O^{2-} < N^{3-}$

Atomic number, Z = 13   12   11   9   8   7

Question 13. Explain why cations are smaller and anions larger in radii than their parent atoms?

Solution. Cations are always smaller in radii than their parent atoms because by the loss of one or two electrons effective nuclear charge increases. Due to this forces of attraction of nucleus for electrons increases and hence, ionic radii decreases. On the other hand, anions are always larger in radii than their parent atoms because by the addition of one or two electrons effective nuclear charge decreases. Due to this, forces of attraction between nucleus and valence shell electrons decreases and hence, ionic radii of anion increases.

Question 14. What is the significance of the terms – 'isolated gaseous atom' and 'ground state' while defining the ionization enthalpy and electron gain enthalpy?

Hint Requirements for comparison purposes.

Solution. **Ionization enthalpy** It is the minimum amount of energy required to remove an electron from an isolated gaseous atom (X) in its ground state.

$$X(g) \longrightarrow X^+(g) + e^-$$

The force by which an electron is attracted by nucleus is also affected by the presence of other atoms within its molecule or in the neighbourhood. Therefore, ionization enthalpy is determined in gaseous state because in gaseous state interatomic distances are larger and interatomic forces of attractions are minimum. Further more, ionization enthalpy is determined at a low pressure because it is not possible to isolate a single atom but interatomic attractions can be further reduced by reducing pressure. Due to these reasons, the term isolated gaseous atom in ground state has been included in definition of ionization enthalpy.

Electron gain enthalpy It is the energy released when an isolated gaseous atom (X) in ground state gains an electron to form gaseous anion.

$$X(g) + e^- \longrightarrow X^-(g)$$

The most stable state of an atom is ground state. If isolated gaseous atom is in excited state, comparatively lesser energy will be released on addition of an electron. So, electron gain enthalpies of gaseous atoms must be determined in their ground states. Therefore, the terms ground state and isolated gaseous atom (explained above) has been also included in the definition of electron gain enthalpy.

Question 15. Energy of an electron in the ground state of the hydrogen atom is $- 2.18 \times 10^{-18}$ J. Calculate the ionization enthalpy of atomic hydrogen in terms of J mol^{-1}.

Hint Apply the idea of mole concept to derive the answer.

(i) We know that the amount of energy required to remove an electron from the ground state (E_1) to infinity (E_∞) is called ionization energy, so IE is calculated by using $\Delta E = E_\infty - E_1$. Calculate the ionization enthalpy per hydrogen atom.

(ii) Since, the energy is obtained in J, convert it into per mole of hydrogen atoms by applying mole concept.

Solution. Ionization energy is the amount of energy required to remove the electron from the ground state (E_1) to infinity (E_∞).

$$E_1 = -2.18 \times 10^{-18} \text{ J}$$

$$E_\infty = 0$$

$$\Delta E = E_\infty - E_1 = 0 - (-2.18 \times 10^{-18} \text{ J}) = 2.18 \times 10^{-18} \text{ J}$$

Ionization enthalpy per hydrogen atom $= 2.18 \times 10^{-18}$ J

$\therefore$ Ionization enthalpy per mole of hydrogen atoms

$$= 2.18 \times 10^{-18} \times 6.022 \times 10^{23} \text{ J mol}^{-1}$$

$$= 13.12 \times 10^5 \text{ J mol}^{-1}$$

Note   *Energy of an electron at infinity = 0.*

Question 16.   Among the second period elements the actual ionization enthalpies are in the order

$$\text{Li} < \text{B} < \text{Be} < \text{C} < \text{O} < \text{N} < \text{F} < \text{Ne}$$

Explain why

(i) Be has higher $\Delta_i H$ than B?

(ii) O has lower $\Delta_i H$ than N and F?

Solution.

(i) Be has higher $\Delta_i H$ (ionization enthalpy) than boron. In both the cases, the electron to be removed belongs to the same principal shell. In $_4\text{Be} = (1s^2, 2s^2)$, it is $2s$-electron while in boron $_5\text{B} = (1s^2, 2s^2, 2p^1)$ it is $2p$-electron. The penetration of a $2s$-electron to the nucleus is more than that of a $2p$-electron. It means $2s$-electrons are more strongly attracted by the nucleus than $2p$-electrons. Therefore, higher amount of energy is required to remove a $2s$-electron than a $2p$-electron. Hence, Be has higher $\Delta_i H$ than B.

(ii) O has lower $\Delta_i H$ than N and F

$$_7\text{N} = 1s^2, 2s^2, 2p_x^1, 2p_y^1, 2p_z^1;$$

$$_8\text{O} = 1s^2, 2s^2, 2p_x^2, 2p_y^1, 2p_z^1;$$

$$_9\text{F} = 1s^2, 2s^2, 2p_x^2, 2p_y^2, 2p_z^1$$

Across a period ionization enthalpy increases as we move from left to right due to decrease in atomic size. But $\Delta_i H$ of nitrogen is greater than oxygen. It is becasue of the more stable electronic configuration (exactly half filled orbitals are more stable) of nitrogen, so it is difficult to remove an electron from nitrogen than from oxygen. That's why oxygen has lower ionization enthalpy than nitrogen and fluorine.

Question 17. How would you explain the fact that the first ionization enthalpy of sodium is lower than that of magnesium but its second ionization enthalpy is higher than that of magnesium?

Solution. First ionization enthalpy of sodium (Na = $1s^2, 2s^2, 2p^6, 3s^1$) is lower than that of magnesium (Mg = $1s^2, 2s^2\ 2p^6, 3s^2$) because the electron to be removed in both the cases is from 3s-orbital but the nuclear charge is lower in Na than that of magnesium $\left(\text{IE} \propto \dfrac{1}{\text{atomic size}} \right)$.

After the removal of first electron Na^+ acquires inert gas (Ne) configuration ($Na^+ = 1s^2, 2s^2, 2p^6$) and hence, removal of second electron from sodium is difficult. While in case of magnesium, after the removal of first electron, the electronic configuration of Mg^+ is $1s^2, 2s^2, 2p^6, 3s^1$. In this case $3s^1$ electron is easy to remove in comparison to remove an electron from inert gas configuration. Therefore, IE_2 of Na is higher than that of magnesium.

Note *The species having exactly half-filled or fully filled orbitals have extra ordinarily high ionization enthalpies.*

Question 18. What are the various factors due to which the ionization enthalpy of the main group elements tends to decrease down a group?

Solution. The ionization enthalpy of the main group elements decreases regularly on moving down the group due to the following two factors:

(i) **Atomic size** On moving down the group, atomic size increases due to addition of new higher energy shell. As a result of this forces of attraction of nucleus for valence electrons decreases and ionization enthalpy also decreases.

(ii) **Screening effect** On moving down the group, screening effect or shielding effect increases, so ionization enthalpy decreases (because forces of attraction between nucleus and electrons decreases).

Question 19. The first ionization enthalpy values (in kJ mol^{-1}) of group 13 elements are

B	Al	Ga	In	Tl
801	577	579	558	589

How would you explain this deviation from the general trend?

Solution. In general on moving down the group (13th group) from B to Al, the ionization enthalpy decreases with increase in atomic size and screening effect as expected. But IE_1 of Ga is slightly higher (only 2 kJ mol^{-1}) than IE_1 of Al. It is due to imperfect shielding of the valence electrons by 3d-electrons. As a result of this effective nuclear charge in Ga is slightly more than that of Al. That's why (IE_1) $\Delta_i H_1$ of Ga is slightly more than that of Al.

On moving from In to Tl, $\Delta_i H_1$ of Tl is larger than that of In. It is due to the fact that effective nuclear charge outweighs the shielding effect of all the electrons present in 4f and 5d-electrons.

Note   *d- and f-electrons shield the valence shell electrons from nucleus less effectively than s- and p- electrons.*

Question 20. Which of the following pairs of elements would have a more negative electron gain enthalpy?

(i) O or F   (ii) F or Cl

Solution.
  (i) Oxygen and fluorine both belong to second period. Electron gain enthalpy generally becomes more negative across a period as we move from left to right. On moving from oxygen to fluorine, the effective nuclear charge increases and atomic size decreases with increase in atomic number. Due to this, forces of attraction of the nucleus increases for the incoming electron. That's why electron gain enthalpy becomes more negative for fluorine than that of oxygen. Furthermore fluorine attain stable gas configuration by picking up an electron.

$$F(g) + e^- \longrightarrow F^-(g)$$
$$\quad 2,7 \qquad\qquad 2,8$$

Therefore, electron gain enthalpy of fluorine is much more negative (-328 kJ mol^{-1}) than that of oxygen (-141 kJ mol^{-1}).

  (ii) Within a group, electron gain enthalpy becomes less negative down a group. But electron gain enthalpy of chlorine is more negative (-349 kJ mol^{-1}) than that of the fluorine (-328 kJ mol^{-1}). This is due to small size of fluorine as the electron–electron repulsions in relatively compact 2p-orbital is greater than that in   the larger 3p-orbital and hence, the incoming electron feels greater repulsion in fluorine than in the chlorine. That's why chlorine have more negative electron gain enthalpy than that of fluorine.

Question 21. Would you expect the second electron gain enthalpy of O as positive, more negative or less negative than the first? Justify you answer.

Solution. $O(g) + e^-(g) \longrightarrow O^-(g);$ $\Delta_{eg} H = -141$ kJ mol^{-1}

$\qquad\qquad O^-(g) + e^-(g) \longrightarrow O^{2-}(g);$ $\Delta_{eg} H = +780$ kJ mol^{-1}

When an electron is added to oxygen atom to form O^- ion, energy is released. Hence, first electron gain enthalpy of oxygen is negative.
But when another electron is added to O^- ion to form O^{2-} ion, it feels stronger electrostatic repulsion. Hence, addition of second electron takes place with absorption of energy. That's why the second electron gain enthalpy of oxygen is positive.

Question 22. What is the basic difference between the terms electron gain enthalpy and electronegativity?

Solution. Electron gain enthalpy is the tendency of an isolated gaseous atom to accept an extra electron to form a gaseous anion while electronegativity is the tendency of an atom of an element to attract the shared pair of electrons towards itself in a covalent bond. Unlike electron gain enthalpy, electronegativity is not a measurable quantity.

Question 23. How would you react to the statement that the electronegativity of N on Pauling scale is 3.0 in all the nitrogen compounds?

Solution. The statement that electronegativity of N on Pauling scale is 3.0 in all the nitrogen compounds is wrong because electronegativity of any given element is not constant. It varies depending on the element to which it is bound. It increases as the oxidation state of the element increases or percentage of s-character of hybrid orbital increases.

Question 24. Describe the theory associated with the radius of an atom as it

(a) gains an electron   (b) loses an electron

Solution.

(a) When an atom gains an electron to form anion, its radius increases. In an anion per electron nuclear forces decreases due to increase in number of electrons and as a result of decrease in effective nuclear charge, radius of an anion increases. For example, ionic radius of Cl^- ion is greater than the radius of its parent atom Cl.

$$Cl + e^- \longrightarrow Cl^-$$

Electrons	17	18
Nuclear charge	17	17

(b) When an atom loses an electron to form cation, its radius decreases. In a cation per electron nuclear forces increases due to decrease in number of electrons. As a result of this, effective nuclear charge increases and the radius of cation decreases. For example, ionic radius of Na^+ is smaller than the radius of its parent atom Na.

$$Na \longrightarrow Na^+ + 1e^-$$

Electrons	11	10
Nuclear charge	11	11

Question 25. Would you expect the first ionization enthalpies for two isotopes of the same element to be the same or different? Justify your answer.

Solution. First ionization enthalpies of two isotopes of the same element are expected to be same because ionization enthalpy depends upon the electronic configuration and effective nuclear charge. Isotopes of an element have same electronic configuration and thus, the same nuclear charge.

Question 26. What are the major differences between metals and non-metals?

Solution. Metals are usually solids at room temperature (mercury is an exception, Gallium and caesium also have very low melting points). Metals usually have very high melting and boiling points. They are good conductors of heat and electricity. They are malleable and ductile. They are electropositive in nature (having a tendency to form cations by the lose of 1, 2 or 3 electrons). Metals have low ionization enthalpies, less electronegativity, less negative electron gain enthalpies. They act as strong reducing agent, form basic and amphoteric oxides. Their compounds are usually ionic in nature.

Non-metals are usually solids or gases at room temperature with low melting and boiling points (boron and carbon are exceptions). They are poor conductors of heat and electricity. Most non-metallic solids are brittle. They are electronegative in nature, have high ionization enthalpies and high negative electron gain enthalpies. They act as strong oxidising agent, form acidic or neutral oxides. Their compounds are usually covalent in nature.

Question 27. Use the Periodic Table to answer the following questions.

(a) Identify an element with five electrons in the outer subshell.
(b) Identify an element that would tend to lose two electrons.
(c) Identify an element that would tend to gain two electrons.
(d) Identify the group having metal, non-metal, liquid as well as gas at the room temperature.

Solution.

(a) General electronic configuration of elements having five electrons in the outer sub shell is ns^2np^5. This configuration belongs to halogen family, *i.e.*, F, Cl, Br, I, At.

(b) Elements of second group are known as alkaline earth metals (Mg, Ca, Sr, Ba, etc). Their general electronic configuration for valence shell is ns^2. These elements form dipositive cations by the lose of two electrons easily.

(c) 16th group elements such as O, S, Se, etc., have a tendency to accept two electrons because by the gain of two electrons they attain noble gas configuration. Their general electronic configuration for valence shell is ns^2np^4.

(d) Group 1 or 17 of the Periodic Table contains metal, non-metal, liquid as well as gas at the room temperature, *e.g.*, H_2 is a non-metal and in gaseous state at room temperature. All other elements of this group are metals. Cs is a liquid metal.
Similary, Br_2 is a liquid non-metal while other elements of this group are gaseous non-metals. Iodine can form I^+ so it has some what metallic properties.

Question 28. The increasing order of reactivity among group 1 elements is Li < Na < K < Rb < Cs whereas that among group 17 elements is F > Cl > Br > I. Explain.

Solution. Chemical reactivity of alkali metals is exhibited by the loss of an electron leading to the formation of cation. The tendency to lose an electron depends upon the ionization enthalpy and ionization enthalpy decreases down the group. Hence, the reactivity increases down the group (Li < Na < K < Rb < Cs).

On the other hand, chemical reactivity of halogens is shown by the gain of an electron leading to the formation of anion. The tendency to gain an electron depends upon their electrode potentials. Their electrode potentials decrease from fluorine to iodine. Therefore, reactivity decreases down the group (F > Cl > Br > I). Furthermore, the tendency to gain an electron is also related to electron gain enthalpy. Electron gain enthalpy becomes less and less negative as we move from chlorine to iodine. Hence, reactivity decreases from chlorine to iodine. Fluorine has less electron gain enthalpy but it is the most reactive due to its low bond dissociation enthalpy.

Group-17	F	Cl	Br	I	At
$\Delta_{eq}H$ (kJ mol^{-1})	–328	–349	–325	–245	–270

$\longrightarrow$ Reactivity decreases

Question 29. Write the general outer electronic configuration of s-, p-, d- and f-block elements.

Solution. s-block elements – ns^{1-2} $(n = 2 - 7)$

p-block elements – ns^2np^{1-6} $(n = 2 - 7)$

d-block elements – $(n-1)d^{1-10}ns^{0-2}$ $(n = 3 - 7)$

f-block elements – $(n-2)f^{1-14}(n-1)d^{0-1}ns^2$ $(n = 6 - 7)$

Question 30.   Assign the position of the element having outer electronic configuration.

(i) ns^2np^4 for $n = 3$

(ii) $(n-1)d^2ns^2$ for $n = 4$, and

(iii) $(n-2)f^7(n-1)d^1ns^2$ for $n = 6$, in the Periodic Table.

Solution.

(i) ns^2np^4 for $n = 3$

$n = 3$ means element belongs to third period. Since, last electron enters in the p-orbital, it belongs to p-block. For p-block elements, the group number = 10 + valence shell electrons = 10 + (2 + 4) = 16 Hence, the element belongs to 16th group.

The complete electronic configuration of the element is as follows,
$$1s^2, 2s^2, 2p^6, 3s^2, 3p^4$$

Thus, the element is sulphur.

(ii) $(n-1)d^2\,ns^2$ for $n = 4$

$n = 4$ means the element belongs to fourth period. Since, last electron enters in d-orbital, the given element belongs to d-block. For d-block elements, group number = number of d-electrons + number of ns electrons $= 2 + 2 = 4$

Hence, the element belongs to 4th group.

The complete electronic configuration of the element is as follows,
$$1s^2, 2s^2, 2p^6, 3s^2, 3p^6, 3d^2, 4s^2$$

Thus, the element is titanium.

(iii) $(n-2)f^7\,(n-1)d^1\,ns^2$ for $n = 6$

$n = 6$ means the element belongs to sixth period. Since, last electron enters in f-orbital, the given element belongs to f-block and all f-block elements are the members of third group. Hence, the element belongs to third group.

The complete configuration of the element is as follows,
$$1s^2, 2s^2, 2p^6, 3s^2, 3p^6, 3d^{10}, 4s^2, 4p^6, 4d^{10}, 5s^2, 5p^6, 4f^7, 5d^1, 6s^2$$

Thus, the element is gadolinium (Gd).

Question 31. The first $(\Delta_i H_1)$ and the second $(\Delta_i H_2)$ ionization enthalpies (in kJ mol^{-1}) and the $(\Delta e_g H)$ electron gain enthalpy (in kJ mol^{-1}) of a few elements are given below :

Elements	ΔH_1	ΔH_2	$\Delta e_g H$
I	520	7300	– 60
II	419	3051	– 48
III	1681	3374	– 328
IV	1008	1846	– 295
V	2372	5251	+48
VI	738	1451	– 40

Which of the above elements is likely to be
(a) the least reactive element
(b) the most reactive metal
(c) the most reactive non-metal
(d) the least reactive non-metal
(e) the metal which can form a stable binary halide of the formula $MX_2 (X = \text{halogen})$
(f) the metal which can form a predominantly stable covalent halide of the formula MX $(X = \text{halogen})$?

Solution.

(a) The least reactive element is element (V) because it has highest $\Delta_i H_1$ (first ionization enthalpy) and positive electron gain enthalpy $(\Delta e_g H)$. The element (V) is an inert gas because inert gases have positive electron gain enthalpy. The given values for element (V) match with He.

(b) The most reactive metal is element (II) because it has the least $\Delta_i H_1$ (first ionization enthalpy) and low negative electron gain enthalpy ($\Delta e_g H$). The given values for element II match with K.

(c) The most reactive non-metal is element (III) because it has high $\Delta_i H_1$ (first ionization enthalpy) and a very high negative electron gain enthalpy ($\Delta e_g H$). The given values for element III match with F.

(d) The least reactive non-metal is element IV. The element IV has not so high $\Delta_i H_1$ but it has high negative electron gain enthalpy ($\Delta e_g H$). The given values for element IV match with I, (iodine).

(e) The metal which can form a stable binary halide of the formula MX_2 is element (VI). Element VI is alkaline earth metal because it has low $\Delta_i H_1$ but higher than that of alkali metals. Moreover, the difference between $\Delta_i H_1$ and $\Delta_i H_2$ is very less. The given values for element VI match with Mg.

(f) Element I has low $\Delta_i H_1$ but a very high $\Delta_i H_2$. It has less negative electron gain enthalpy. So, element (I) is alkali metal. The given values for element I match with Li. Lithium forms predominantly stable covalent halide of the formula MX.

Question 32. Predict the formulas of the stable binary compounds that would be formed by the combination of the following pairs of elements.

(a) Lithium and oxygen   (b) Magnesium and nitrogen
(c) Aluminium and iodine   (d) Silicon and oxygen
(e) Phosphorus and fluorine   (f) Element 71 and fluorine
Solution.

	Element	Group number	Electrons in valence shell	Valency	Formulae of binary compound
(a)	Lithium	Group-1	1	1	Li_2O
	Oxygen	Group-16	6	$8 - 6 = 2$	
(b)	Magnesium	Group-2	2	2	Mg_3N_2
	Nitrogen	Group-15	5	$8 - 5 = 3$	
(c)	Aluminium	Group-13	3	3	AlI_3
	Iodine	Group-17	7	$8 - 7 = 1$	
(d)	Silicon	Group-14	4	4	SiO_2
	Oxygen	Group-16	6	$8 - 6 = 2$	
(e)	Phosphorus	Group-15	5	3 or 5	PF_3 or PF_5
	Fluorine	Group-17	7	$8 - 7 = 1$	
(f)	Element 71, (Lutetium)	Group-3	3	3	LuF_3
	Fluorine	Group-17	7	$8 - 7 = 1$	

Note (i) *In case of s- and p-block elements (representative elements), the valency of an atom is generally equal to either the number of valence electrons or equal to eight minus the number of valence electrons.*

(ii) *In case of lathanoids (inner-transition elements) there is involvement of d- and f-electrons with valence shell electrons in bond formation. Common valence for lanthanoids is 3.*

(iii) *Electronic configuration of* $_{71}Lu = [Xe] 4f^{14}, 5d^1, 6s^2;$ *(Valency = 3).*

Question 33. In the modern Periodic Table, the period indicates the value of

(a) atomic number   (b) atomic mass
(c) principal quantum number   (d) azimuthal quantum number

Solution. (c) In the modern Periodic Table, the period indicates the value of principal quantum number.

Question 34. Which of the following statements related to the modern Periodic Table is incorrect?

(a) The *p*-block has 6 columns, because a maximum of 6 electrons can occupy all the orbitals in a *p*-shell.
(b) The *d*-block has 8 columns because a maximum of 8 electrons can occupy all the orbitals in a *d*-subshell.
(c) Each block contains a number of columns equal to the number of electrons that can occupy that subshell.
(d) The block indicates value of azimuthal quantum number (*l*) for the last subshell that received electrons in building up the electronic configuration.

Solution. Statement (b) is incorrect. The correct statement (b) is; the *d*-block has 10 columns, because a maximum of 10 electrons can occupy all the orbitals in a *d*-subshell.
All other given statements are correct.

Question 35. Anything that influences the valence electrons will affect the chemistry of the element. Which one of the following factors does not affect the valence shell?

(a) Valence principal quantum number (*n*)
(b) Nuclear charge (*Z*)
(c) Nuclear mass
(d) Number of core electrons

Solution. (c) Nuclear mass (protons + neutrons) does not affect the valence shell, only protons, *i.e.,* nuclear charge affects the valence shell.

Question 36. The size of isoelectronic species; F^-, Ne and Na^+ is affected by

(a) nuclear charge (*Z*)
(b) valence principal quantum number (*n*)
(c) electron-electron interaction in the outer orbitals
(d) none of the factors because their size is the same.

Solution. (a) The size of isoelectronic species; F^-, Ne and Na^+ is affected by nuclear charge (Z). With increase in nuclear charge (atomic number), the size of the isoelectronic species decreases.

Question 37. Which one of the following statements is incorrect in relation to ionization enthalpy?

(a) Ionization enthalpy increases for each successive electron.

(b) The greatest increase in ionization enthalpy is experienced on removal of electron from core noble gas configuration.

(c) End of valence electrons is marked by a big jump in ionization enthalpy.

(d) Removal of electron from orbitals bearing lower n value is easier than from orbital having higher n value.

Solution. Correct statement (d) is; removal of electron from orbitals bearing lower n value is difficult than from orbital having higher n value, due to decrease in effective nuclear charge with increase in the value of n.

Question 38. Considering the elements B, Al, Mg and K, the correct order of their metallic character is

(a) B > Al > Mg > K   (b) Al > Mg > B > K

(c) Mg > Al > K > B   (d) K > Mg > Al > B

Solution. (d) In a group, metallic character increases from top to bottom as ionisation energy decreases and in a period metallic character decreases from left to right as tendency to lose electron decreases. Therefore, the correct order is K > Mg > Al > B.

Question 39. Considering the elements B, C, N, F and Si, the correct order of their non-metallic character is

(a) B > C > Si > N > F   (b) Si > C > B > N > F

(c) F > N > C > B > Si   (d) F > N > C > Si > B

Solution. (c) Non-metallic character in a group decreases from top to bottom but it increases in a period when we move from left to right. This is because ionisation energy increases in a period and decreases in a group. Therefore, among B, C, N, F and Si, the non-metallic character decreases in the order F > N > C > B > Si.

Question 40. Considering the elements F, Cl, O and N, the correct order of their chemical reactivity in terms of oxidizing property is

(a) F > Cl > O > N   (b) F > O > Cl > N

(c) Cl > F > O > N   (d) O > F > N > Cl

Solution. (b) In a group oxidising power (*i.e.*, tendency to gain electron) decreases from top to bottom as the size increases but when we move left to right in a period it increases because size decreases. Therefore, among F, Cl, O and N, the oxidising power decreases in the order

$$F > O > Cl > N$$

Note *Oxygen is more electronegative than chlorine. Hence, O is stronger oxidising agent than Cl.*

Selected NCERT Exemplar Problems

Short Answer Type

Question 1. Explain why the electron gain enthalpy of fluorine is less negative than that of chlorine?

Solution. Electron gain enthalpy of F is less negative than that of Cl because when an electron is added to F, the added electron goes to the smaller $n = 2$ quantum level and suffers repulsion from other electrons present in this level. In case of Cl, the added electron goes to the larger $n = 3$ quantum level and suffers much less repulsion from other electrons.

Question 2. All transition elements are d-block elements, but all d-block elements are not transition elements. Explain.

Solution. Elements in which the last electron enters in the d-orbitals, are called d-block elements or transition elements. These elements have the general outer electronic configuration $(n-1)d^{1-10}ns^{0-2}$. Zn, Cd and Hg having the electronic configuration, $(n-1)d^{10}ns^2$ do not show most of the properties of transition elements. The d-orbitals in these elements are completely filled in the ground state as well as in their common oxidation states. Therefore, they are not regarded as transition elements. Thus, on the basis of properties, all transition elements are d-block elements but on the basis of electronic configuration, all d-block elements are not transition elements.

Question 3. Among the elements B, Al, C and Si,

(i) Which element has the highest first ionization enthalpy?
(ii) Which element has the most metallic character? Justify your answer in each case.

Solution.

Period	Group-13	Group-14
2nd period	Boron	Carbon
3rd period	Aluminium	Silicon

(i) Ionization enthalpy increases along a period (as we move from left to right in a period) with decrease in atomic size and decreases down the group with increase in atomic size. Hence, carbon has the highest first ionization enthalpy.
(ii) Metallic character decreases across a period but increases on moving down the group. Hence, aluminium has the most metallic character.

Question 4. Choose the correct order of atomic radii of fluorine and neon (in pm) out of the options given below and justify your answer.

(i) 72, 160   (ii) 160, 160   (iii) 72, 72   (iv) 160, 72

Solution. Atomic radius of F is expressed in terms of covalent radius while atomic radius of neon is usually expressed in terms of van der Waals' radius. van der Waals' radius of an element is always larger than its covalent radius. Therefore, atomic radius of F is smaller than atomic radius of Ne (F = 72 pm, Ne = 160 pm).

Question 5. Illustrate by taking examples of transition elements and non-transition elements that oxidation states of elements are largely based on electronic configuration.

Solution. Oxidation state of an element depends upon the electrons present in the outer most shell or eight minus the number of valence shell electrons (outermost shell electrons). For example,

Alkali metals (Group 1 elements) General valence shell electronic configuration —ns^1; Oxidation state = + 1.

Alkaline earth metals (Group 2 elements) General valence shell electronic configuration —ns^2; Oxidation state = + 2.

Alkali metals and alkaline earth metals belong to s-block elements. Elements of group 13 to group 18 are known as p-block elements.

Group 13 elements General valence shell electronic configuration — $ns^2\,np^1$; Oxidation states = + 3 and + 1.

Group 14 elements General valence shell electronic configuration — $ns^2\,np^2$; Oxidation states = + 4 and + 2.

Group 15 elements General valence shell electronic configuration — $ns^2\,np^3$; Oxidation states = – 3, + 3 and + 5. Nitrogen shows + 1, + 2, + 4 oxidation states also.

Group 16 elements General valence shell electronic configuration — $ns^2\,np^4$; Oxidation states = – 2, + 2, + 4 and + 6.

Group 17 elements General valence shell electronic configuration — ns^2np^5; Oxidation states = – 1. Cl, Br and I also show + 1, + 3, + 5 and + 7 oxidation states.

Group 18 elements General valence shell configuration —ns^2np^6. Oxidation state = zero.

Transition elements or d-block elements General electronic configuration $- (n-1)\,d^{1-10}\,ns^{1-2}$. These elements show variable oxidation states due to involvement of not only ns electrons but d- or f-electrons (inner-transition elements) as well. Their most common oxidation states are + 2 and + 3.

Question 6. Nitrogen has positive electron gain enthalpy whereas oxygen has negative. However, oxygen has lower ionization enthalpy than nitrogen. Explain.

Solution. EC of $_7N = 1s^2, 2s^2, 2p_x^1, 2p_y^1, 2p_z^1$. Nitrogen has stable configuration because p-orbital is half-filled. Therefore, addition of extra electron to any of the p-orbital requires energy.

EC of $_8O = 1s^2, 2s^2, 2p_x^2, 2p_y^1, 2p_z^1$. Oxygen has $2p^4$ electrons, so process of adding an electron to the p-orbital is exothermic.

Oxygen has lower ionization enthalpy than nitrogen because by removing one electron from $2p$-orbital, oxygen acquires stable configuration, i.e., $2p^3$. On the other hand, in case of nitrogen it is not easy to remove one of the three $2p$-electrons due to its stable configuration.

Question 7. First member of each group of representative elements (*i.e.*, *s*- and *p*-block elements) shows anomalous behaviour. Illustrate with two examples.

Solution. First member of each group of representative elements (*i.e.*, *s*- and *p*-block elements) shows anomalous behaviour due to (i) small size (ii) high ionization enthalpy (iii) high electronegativity and (iv) absence of *d*- orbitals. For example in *s*- block elements, Lithium shows anomalous behaviour from rest of the alkali metals.

(i) Compounds of lithium have significant covalent character. While compounds of other alkali metals are predominantly ionic.

(ii) Lithium reacts with nitrogen to form lithium nitride while other alkali metals do not form nitrides.

In *p*-block elements, first member of each group has four orbitals, one 2*s*- and three 2*p*-orbitals in their valence shell. So, these elements show a maximum covalency of four while other members of the same group or different group show a maximum covalency beyond four due to availability of vacant *d*- orbitals.

Question 8. *p*-block elements form acidic, basic and amphoteric oxides. Explain each property by giving two examples and also write the reactions of these oxides with water.

Solution. In *p*-block, when we move from left to right in a period, the acidic character of the oxides increases due to increase in electronegativity. For example,

(i) **2nd period** $B_2O_3 < CO_2 < N_2O_3$ acidic nature increases.

(ii) **3rd period** $Al_2O_3 < SiO_2 < P_4O_{10} < SO_3 < Cl_2O_7$ acidic character increases.

On moving down the group, acidic character decreases and basic character increases. For example

(i) **Nature of oxides of 13 group elements**

$$\underset{\text{Weakly acidic}}{B_2O_3} \quad \underbrace{Al_2O_3 \quad Ga_2O_3}_{\text{Amphoteric}} \quad \underset{\text{Basic}}{In_2O_3} \quad \underset{\substack{\text{Strongly}\\\text{basic}}}{Tl_2O}$$

(ii) **Nature of oxides of 15 group elements**

$$\underset{\substack{\text{Strongly}\\\text{acidic}}}{N_2O_5} \quad \underset{\substack{\text{Moderately}\\\text{acidic}}}{P_4O_{10}} \quad \underset{\text{Amphoteric}}{As_4O_{10}} \quad \underset{\text{Amphoteric}}{Sb_4O_{10}} \quad \underset{\text{Basic}}{Bi_2O_3}$$

Among the oxides of same element, higher the oxidation state of the element, stronger is the acid. For example, SO_3 is a stronger acid than SO_2.

B_2O_3 is weakly acidic and on dissolution in water, it forms orthoboric acid. Orthoboric acid does not act as a protonic acid (it does not ionize) but acts as a weak Lewis acid.

$$\underset{\text{Boron trioxide}}{B_2O_3} + 3H_2O \rightleftharpoons \underset{\text{Orthoboric acid}}{2H_3BO_3}$$

$$B(OH)_3 + H\!-\!OH \longrightarrow [B(OH)_4]^- + H^+$$

Al_2O_3 is amphoteric in nature. It is insoluble in water but dissolves in alkalies and reacts with acids.

$$\underset{\text{Aluminium trioxide}}{Al_2O_3} + 2NaOH \xrightarrow{\Delta} \underset{\text{Sodium meta aluminate}}{2NaAlO_2} + H_2O$$

$$Al_2O_3 + 6HCl \xrightarrow{\Delta} \underset{\text{Aluminium chloride}}{2AlCl_3} + 3H_2O$$

Tl_2O is as basic as NaOH due to its lower oxidation state (+ 1).
$$Tl_2O + 2HCl \longrightarrow 2TlCl + H_2O$$
P_4O_{10} on reaction with water gives orthophosphoric acid
$$\underset{\text{Phosphorus pentoxide}}{P_4O_{10}} + 6H_2O \longrightarrow \underset{\text{Orthophosphoric acid}}{4H_3PO_4}$$

Cl_2O_7 is strongly acidic in nature, and on dissolution in water, it gives perchloric acid.
$$\underset{\text{Dichlorine heptoxide}}{Cl_2O_7} + H_2O \longrightarrow \underset{\text{Perchloric acid}}{2HClO_4}$$

Question 9. Arrange the elements N, P, O and S in the order of
(i) increasing first ionization enthalpy.
(ii) increasing non-metallic character.
Give reason for the arrangement assigned.

Solution.

	Group 15	Group 16
2nd period	N	O
3rd period	P	S

(i) Ionization enthalpy of nitrogen $(_7N = 1s^2, 2s^2, 2p^3)$ is greater than oxygen $(_8O = 1s^2, 2s^2, 2p^4)$ due to extra stable exactly half-filled 2p-orbitals. Similarly, ionization enthalpy of phosphorus $(_{15}P = 1s^2, 2s^2, 2p^6, 3s^2, 3p^3)$ is greater than sulphur $(_{16}S = 1s^2, 2s^2, 2p^6, 3s^2, 3p^4)$.
On moving down the group, ionization enthalpy decreases with increasing atomic size. So, the order is
$S < P < O < N \rightarrow$ First ionization enthalpy increases.
(ii) Non-metallic character across a period (left to right) increases but on moving down the group it decreases. So, the order is
$P < S < N < O \rightarrow$ Non-metallic character increases.

Question 10. How does the metallic and non-metallic character vary on moving from left to right in a period?
Solution. As we move from left to right in a period, the number of valence electrons increases by one at each succeeding element but the number of shells remains same. Due to this effective nuclear charge increases. More is the effective nuclear charge, more is the attraction

between nuclei and electron. Hence, the tendency of the element to lose electrons decreases, this results in decrease in metallic character. Furthermore, the tendency of an element to gain electrons increases with increase in effective nuclear charge, so non-metallic character increases on moving from left to right in a period.

Question 11. Among alkali metals which element do you expect to be least electronegative and why?

Solution. On moving down the group, electronegativity decreases because atomic size increases. Fr has the largest size, therefore it is least electronegative.

Long Answer Type

Question 12. Discuss the factors affecting electron gain enthalpy and the trend in its variation in the Periodic Table.

Solution. Electron gain enthalpy of an element is equal to the energy released when an electron is added to valence shell of an isolated gaseous atom.

$$A(g) + e^- \longrightarrow A^-(g); \qquad \Delta e_g \; II - \text{negative}$$

Factors Affecting Electron Gain Enthalpy

(i) **Effective nuclear charge** Electron gain enthalpy increases with increase in effective nuclear charge because attraction of nucleus towards test electron (incoming electron) increases.

(ii) **Size of an atom** Electron gain enthalpy decreases with increase in the size of valence shell.

(iii) **Type of subshell** More closer is the subshell to the nucleus, easier is the addition of electron in that subshell.
Electron gain enthalpy (in decreasing order) for addition of electron in different subshell (n-same) is
$$s > p > d > f$$

(iv) **Nature of configuration** Half-filled and completely-filled subshell have stable configuration, so addition of electron in them is not energetically favourable.
Variation in the Periodic Table As a general rule, electron gain enthalpy becomes more and more negative with increase in the atomic number across a period. The effective nuclear charge increases from left to right across a period and consequently it will be easier to add an electron to a smaller atom.
Electron gain enthalpy becomes less negative as we go down a group because the size of the atom increases and the added electron would be farther from the nucleus.
Electron gain enthalpy of O or F is less than that of the succeeding element (S or Cl) because the added electron goes to the smaller $n = 2$ level and suffers repulsion from other electrons present in this

level. For the $n = 3$ level (S or Cl), the added electron occupies a larger region of space and suffers much less repulsion from electrons present in this level.

Question 13. Justify the given statement with suitable examples–"the properties of the elements are a periodic function of their atomic numbers".

Solution. There are numerous physical properties of elements such as melting points, boiling points, heats of fusion and vaporization, energy of atomization, etc., which show periodic variations. The cause of periodicity in properties is the repetition of similar outer electronic configurations after certain regular intervals. For example, all the elements of 1st group (alkali metals) have similar outer electronic configuration, *i.e.*, ns^1.

$$_3Li = 1s^2, 2s^1$$
$$_{11}Na = 1s^2, 2s^2, 2p^6, 3s^1$$
$$_{19}K = 1s^2, 2s^2, 2p^6, 3s^2, 3p^6, 4s^1$$
$$_{37}Rb = 1s^2, 2s^2, 2p^6, 3s^2, 3p^6, 3d^{10}, 4s^2, 4p^6, 5s^1$$
$$_{55}Cs = 1s^2, 2s^2, 2p^6, 3s^2, 3p^6, 3d^{10}, 4s^2, 4p^6, 4d^{10}, 5s^2, 5p^6, 6s^1$$
$$_{87}Fr = 1s^2, 2s^2, 2p^6, 3s^2, 3p^6, 3d^{10}, 4s^2, 4p^6, 4d^{10}, 4f^{14}$$
$$5s^2, 5p^6, 5d^{10}, 6s^2, 6p^6, 7s^1$$

Therefore, due to similar outermost shell electronic configuration all alkali metals have similar properties. For example sodium and potassium both are soft and reactive metals. They all form basic oxides and their basic character increases down the group. They all form unipositive ion by the lose of one electron.

Similarly, all the elements of 17th group (halogens) have similar outermost shell electronic configuration, *i.e.*, ns^2np^5 and thus possess similar properties.

$$_9F = 1s^2, 2s^2, 2p^5$$
$$_{17}Cl = 1s^2, 2s^2, 2p^6, 3s^2, 3p^5$$
$$_{35}Br = 1s^2, 2s^2, 2p^6, 3s^2, 3p^6, 3d^{10}, 4s^2, 4p^5$$
$$_{53}I = 1s^2, 2s^2, 2p^6, 3s^2, 3p^6, 3d^{10}, 4s^2, 4p^6, 4d^{10}, 5s^2, 5p^5$$
$$_{85}At = 1s^2, 2s^2, 2p^6, 3s^2, 3p^6, 3d^{10}, 4s^2, 4p^6, 4d^{10}$$
$$4f^{14}, 5s^2, 5p^6, 5d^{10}, 6s^2, 6p^5$$

Question 14. Write the drawbacks in Mendeleev's Periodic Table that led to its modification.

Solution. The main drawbacks of Mendeleev's Periodic Table are
(i) Some elements having similar properties were placed in different groups whereas some elements having dissimilar properties were placed in the same group. For example alkali metals such as Li, Na, K, etc., (IA group) are grouped together with coinage metals such

as Cu, Ag, Au (IB group) though their properties are quite different. Chemically similar elements such as Cu(IB group) and Hg (IIB group) have been placed in different groups.

(ii) Some elements with higher atomic weights are placed before the elements with lower atomic weights in order to maintain the similar chemical nature of elements. For example,
$$_{18}^{39.9}\text{Ar and } _{19}^{39.1}\text{K}; \ _{27}^{58.9}\text{Co and } _{28}^{58.7}\text{Ni, etc.}$$

(iii) Isotopes did not find any place in the Periodic Table. However, according to Mendeleev's classification, these should be placed at different places in the Periodic Table.
(All the above three defects were however removed when modern periodic law based on atomic number was given.)

(iv) Position of hydrogen in the Periodic Table is not fixed but is controversial.

(v) Position of elements of group VIII could not be made clear which have been arranged in three triads without any justification.

(vi) It could not explain the even and odd series in IV, V and VI long periods.

(vii) Lanthanides and actinides which were discovered later on have not been given proper positions in the main frame of Periodic Table.

Chapter **4**

Chemical Bonding and Molecular Structures

Important Results

1. The attractive force which holds various constituents (atoms, ions, etc.) together in different chemical species is called a chemical bond.

2. The atoms of different elements combine with each other in order to complete their respective octets (*i.e.*, 8 electrons in their outermost shell) or duplet (*i.e.*, outermost shell containing 2 electrons) in case of hydrogen, lithium and beryllium (**Octet rule**).

3. Lewis symbols are the simple symbols to denote the valence shell electrons in an atom. The valence shell electrons are shown as dots surrounding the symbol of the atom.

4. An ionic bond is formed when a metal atom transfers one or more electrons to a non-metal atom. As a result of this transfer, the metal atom converts into cation and non-metal into anion.

5. Ionic solids are good conductor of electricity in fused state and in aqueous state. These are soluble in polar solvents, insoluble in non-polar solvents and have high melting and boiling point due to strong electrostatic forces of attraction.

6. The energy given off when gaseous positive and negative ions come together to form 1 mole of the solid ionic compound is called lattice energy (U). It can be calculated using **Born-Haber cycle.**

7. If duplet (2) or octet (8) is completed by sharing of electrons between two electronegative elements, the bond formed is known as covalent bond. In single, double and triple covalent bonds, the number of shared pair of electrons between the two atoms are one, two and three.

8. Formal charge (F.C.) on an atom in a Lewis structure

   = (total number of valence electrons in the free atom)

   – [total number of non-bonding (lone pairs) electrons]

   $- \dfrac{1}{2}$ [total number of bonding (shared) electrons]

9. Bond length is defined as the equilibrium distance between the nuclei of two bonded atoms in a molecule.

10. Bond angle is defined as the angle between the orbitals containing bonding electron pairs around the central atom in a molecule/complex ion.

11. Bond enthalpy is defined as the amount of energy required to break one mole of bonds of a particular type between two atoms in the gaseous state. The unit of bond enthalpy is $kJ\,mol^{-1}$.

12. **Bond order** In the Lewis representation of a molecule or ion, the number of bonds present between two atoms is called bond order. Isoelectronic molecules and ions have identical bond orders, e.g., F_2 and O_2^{2-} have bond order 1. N_2, CO and NO^+ have bond order 3. With increase in bond order, bond enthalpy increases, bond length decreases and stability increases.

13. Whenever, a single Lewis structure cannot describe a molecule accurately, a number of structures with similar energy, positions of nuclei, bonding and non-bonding pairs of electrons are written. These structures are called canonical structures. The phenomenon is called resonance.

14. The actual structure is in between of all these contributing structures and is called resonance hybrid. The difference in the energy of the resonance hybrid and the most stable contributing structure (having least energy) is called **resonance energy**.

15. Non-polar covalent bond is formed between the two similar atoms. In this bond the electron cloud is completely symmetrical. Polar covalent bond is formed between two dissimilar atoms having different electronegativities, e.g., in HCl, HBr, etc. In this bond, electron cloud is unsymmetrical (more towards more electronegative atom). Due to this, more electronegative atom acquires slightly negative charge and less electronegative atom acquires slightly positive charge $(\overset{\delta+}{H} - \overset{\delta-}{Cl})$.

16. As a result of polarisation, the molecule possesses the dipole moment, which can be defined as the product of the magnitude of the charge and the distance between the centres of positive and negative charge.

    Dipole moment, μ = charge (Q) × distance of separation (r)

17. It is usually expressed in Debye unit. $1D = 3.33564 \times 10^{-30}$ Cm (where, C is coulomb and m is meter.)

18. **Fajan's rule**
    (i) The smaller the size of the cation and the larger the size of the anion, the greater is the polarizing power and hence, greater the covalent character of an ionic bond. That's why LiCl is more covalent than KCl and LiI is more covalent than LiCl.
    (ii) If two cations have same size and charge then the one with 18 electrons in outermost shell has greater polarizing power than the other with 8 electrons in outermost shell. That's why CuCl is more covalent than NaCl.

(iii) Larger the charge on the cation, greater is its polarizing power. Similarly, greater the charge on the anion, more easily it gets polarized.

19. **The Valence Shell Electron Pair Repulsion (VSEPR) theory**–The VSEPR theory used for predicting the geometrical shapes of the molecules is based on the assumption that electron pairs repel each other and therefore, tend to remain as far apart as possible. According to this model, molecular geometry is determined by repulsions between lone pairs-lone pairs, lone pairs – bond pairs and bond pairs – bond pairs.

20. The valence bond (VB) approach to covalent bonding is basically concerned with the energetics of covalent bond formation and discusses bond formation in terms of overlap of orbitals.

21. For explaining the characteristic shapes of polyatomic molecules, Pauling introduced the concept of hybridization of atomic orbitals. sp, sp^2, sp^3 hybridizations of atomic orbitals of Be, B, C, N and O are used to explain the formation and geometrical shapes of molecules like $BeCl_2$, BCl_3, CH_4, C_2H_2, C_2H_4, NH_3 and H_2O.

22. The molecular orbital (MO) theory describes bonding in terms of the combination and arrangement of atomic orbitals to form molecular orbitals associated with molecule. The number of molecular orbitals are always equal to the number of atomic orbitals from which they are formed.

23. Bonding molecular orbitals increase electron density between the nuclei and are lower in energy than the individual atomic orbitals. Similarly, antibonding molecular orbitals have a region of zero electron density between the nuclei and have more energy than the individual atomic orbitals.

24. The increasing order of energies of various molecular orbitals for B_2, C_2, N_2, etc., is

$$\sigma 1s < \overset{*}{\sigma} 1s < \sigma 2s < \overset{*}{\sigma} 2s < (\pi\, 2p_x \approx \pi 2p_y) < \sigma 2p_z < (\overset{*}{\pi} 2p_x \approx \overset{*}{\pi} 2p_y) < \overset{*}{\sigma} 2p_z$$

The increasing order of energies of various molecular orbitals for O_2 and F_2 is

$$\sigma 1s < \overset{*}{\sigma} 1s < \sigma 2s < \overset{*}{\sigma} 2s < \sigma 2p_z < (\pi\, 2p_x \approx \pi 2p_y) < (\overset{*}{\pi} 2p_x \approx \overset{*}{\pi} 2p_y) < \overset{*}{\sigma} 2p_z$$

25. Hydrogen bond is formed when a hydrogen atom finds itself between two highly electronegative atoms such as F, O or N. It may be intermolecular (existing between two or more molecules) or intramolecular (within the same molecule). H-bonds have a powerful effect on the structure and properties of many compounds.

Exercises

Question 1.   Explain the formation of a chemical bond.

Solution.   Kossel and Lewis approach to chemical bonding was based on the inertness of noble gases. Inertness of noble gases is due to the presence of 8 electrons in their outermost shell (called octet) except He (2 electrons in its outermost shell). Atoms of all other elements have less than eight electrons in their outermost shell, hence they are reactive chemically.

Lewis postulated that atoms achieve the stable octet when they are linked by chemical bonds. Atoms combine with one another in a number of different ways, *i.e.*, by transference of electrons (ionic bond) or by sharing of electrons (covalent bond), etc. For example, in case of sodium and chlorine, a chemical bond is formed by the transfer of an electron from sodium to chlorine.

Question 2. Write Lewis dot symbols for atoms of the following elements : **Mg, Na, B, O, N, Br.**

  (i) Write the electronic configuration of each element to find the number of valence electrons *i.e.*, electrons present in the outer shell.
  (ii) Represent the valence electrons by dots around the symbols of the element to write Lewis dot symbols.

Solution. $_{12}Mg = 2, 8, 2$;   Lewis symbol $= \overset{..}{Mg}$

$_{11}Na = 2, 8, 1$;   Lewis symbol $= \overset{.}{Na}$

$_{5}B = 2, 3$;   Lewis symbol $= \cdot \overset{.}{B} \cdot$

$_{8}O = 2, 6$;   Lewis symbol $= \overset{..}{\underset{}{:}O:}$

$_{35}Br = 2, 8, 18, 7$;   Lewis symbol $= \cdot \overset{..}{\underset{..}{Br}:}$

(Lewis symbols are simple notations to represent valence electrons in an atom.)

Question 3. Write the Lewis structure for the following atoms and ions S and S^{2-}; Al and Al^{3+}; H and H^{-}.

  (i) Write the electronic configuration of each element to find the number of valence electrons *i.e.*, electrons present in the outer shell.
  (ii) Represent the valence electrons by dots around the symbols of the element to write Lewis dot symbols.

Solution. $_{16}S = 2, 8, 6;$ Lewis symbol = $\overset{..}{\underset{..}{:S:}}$

        $S^{2-} = (16 + 2)$ electrons;   Lewis symbol = $[\overset{..}{\underset{..}{:S:}}]^{2-}$

        $_{13}Al = 2, 8, 3;$ Lewis symbol = $Al\cdot$

        $Al^{3+} = (13 - 3) = 10$ electrons;   Lewis symbol = $[Al]^{3+}$

        $_1H = 1;$ Lewis symbol = $\overset{.}{H}$

        $H^- = (1 + 1) = 2$ electrons;   Lewis symbol = $[\overset{..}{H}]^-$

Question 4. Draw the Lewis structures for the following molecules and ions.

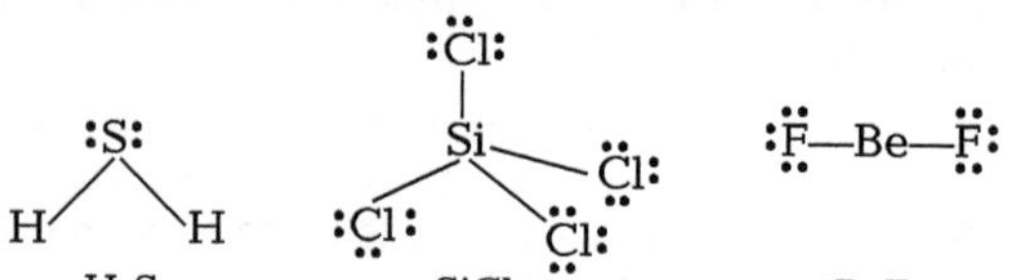

$$H_2S, \ SiCl_4, \ BeF_2, \ CO_3^{2-}, \ HCOOH$$

In Lewis structures, all the elements (except H) have 8 electrons in their outer shell. H has only 2 electrons.

Solution.

Question 5. Define octet rule. Write its significance and limitations.

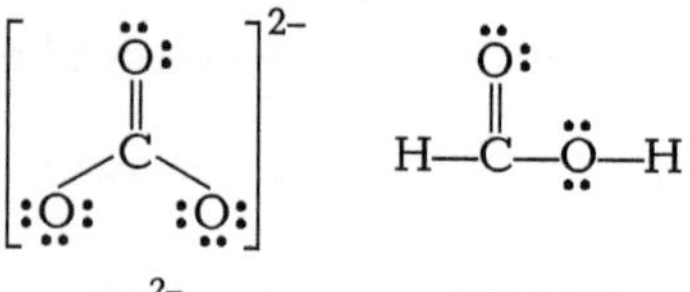

Solution.   **Octet rule** Atoms can combine either by transfer of valence electrons from one atom to another (gaining or losing) or by sharing of valence electrons in order to have an octet in their valence shell.

Significance of octet rule It helps to explain why different atoms combine with each other to form ionic or covalent compounds.

Limitations of octet rule It is quite useful for understanding the structures of most of the organic compounds and applies mainly to second period elements of the Periodic Table. Some exceptions to the octet rule are

(a) In some compounds, there are less than eight valence electrons around the central atom, *e.g.*, Li:Cl, H:Be:H; Cl $\overset{\overset{\textstyle Cl}{..}}{:B:}$ Cl. In LiCl, BeH_2 and BCl_3, central atoms Li, Be and B have only 2, 4 and 6 electrons respectively.

(b) In some compounds there are more than eight valence electrons around the central atom, $e.g.$,

In PF_5, SF_6 and H_2SO_4, central atoms P, S and S have 10, 12 and 12 electrons respectively.

(c) In molecules with an odd number of electrons like NO (nitric oxide) and NO_2 (nitrogen dioxide), the octet rule is not satisfied for all the atoms.

(d) Octet rule is based upon the chemical inertness of noble gases. However, some noble gases such as Xe and Kr also form a number of compounds, $e.g.$, XeF_2, XeF_4, XeF_6, KrF_2, $XeOF_2$, etc.

(e) It does not explain the shape of the molecules.

(f) It does not explain about the energy of a molecule and the relative stability of the molecules.

Question 6. Write the favourable factors for the formation of ionic bond.

Ionic bond is formed between ions $i.e.$, cation and anion. Thus, factors which favour the formation of these ions, also favour the formation of ionic bond.

Solution. The favourable conditions for forming stable ionic bond are

(i) Low ionization enthalpy of element forming cation.

(ii) More negative electron gain enthalpy of element forming anion.

(iii) High lattice enthalpy of the ionic compound formed.

Question 7. Discuss the shape of the following molecules using the VSEPR model.

$$BeCl_2, \ BCl_3, \ SiCl_4, \ AsF_5, \ H_2S, \ PH_3$$

(i) Find the number of bonds formed ($i.e.$, bond pairs of electrons) and lone pairs ($i.e.$, non bonding pairs) around the central atom.

(ii) If lone pairs are absent and the number of bond pairs is 2, the molecule is linear, if 3, the molecule is trigonal planar, if 4, the molecule is tetrahedral and if 5, it is trigonal bipyramidal.

(iii) If there is 1 lone pair and 3 bond pairs, the molecule is pyramidal and if there is 2 lone pairs and two bond pairs, the molecule has angular or V shape.

Solution. According to VSEPR theory, the shape of a molecule depends upon the number of valence shell electron pairs (bonded or non-bonded) around the central atom. Pairs of electrons in the valence shell repel each other. The order of their repulsions is as follows

$$lp - lp > lp - bp > bp - bp$$

(i) **BeCl$_2$** : Cl $\vdots$ Be $\vdots$ Cl; The central atom Be has only 2 valence electrons which are bonded to Cl, so there are only 2 bond pairs and no lone pairs. It is of the type AB_2 and hence, the shape is linear.

(ii) **BCl$_3$** : Cl—B$\begin{smallmatrix} \diagup Cl \\ \diagdown Cl \end{smallmatrix}$ or   Cl $\vdots$ B $\begin{smallmatrix} \ddot{}Cl \\ \\ \ddot{}Cl \end{smallmatrix}$;

The central atom B has only 3 valence electrons which are bonded with three Cl atoms, so it contains only 3 bond pairs and no lone pair. It is of the type AB_3 and hence, the shape is trigonal planar.

(iii) **SiCl$_4$** : $\begin{smallmatrix} Cl \\ | \\ Si \\ Cl \diagup | \diagdown Cl \\ Cl \end{smallmatrix}$ or $\begin{smallmatrix} Cl \\ \cdot\cdot \\ Si \quad \cdot\cdot \\ Cl\vdots \quad \cdot\cdot \quad Cl \\ Cl \end{smallmatrix}$

Similarly, the central atom Si has only 4 bond pairs and no lone pair. It is of the type AB_4 and hence, the shape is tetrahedral.

(iv) **AsF$_5$** : $\begin{smallmatrix} F \\ F\diagdown | \\ \quad >As—F \\ F\diagup | \\ F \end{smallmatrix}$ or $\begin{smallmatrix} F\vdots \quad \cdot\cdot \\ As \vdots F \\ F\vdots \quad \cdot\cdot \\ F \end{smallmatrix}$

The central atom As has only 5 bond pairs and no lone pair. It is of the type AB_5 and hence, the shape is trigonal bipyramidal.

(v) **H$_2$S** : $\begin{smallmatrix} \text{(lone pairs)} \\ S \\ H\diagup \quad \diagdown H \end{smallmatrix}$ or $\ddot{S}\ddot{}$ H$\cdot\cdot$H

The central atom S has 6 valence electrons. Out of these, only two are used in bond formation with two H atoms while four (two pairs) remains as non-bonding electrons (*i.e.,* lone pairs). So it contains 2 bond pairs and 2 lone pairs. It is of the type AB_2L_2 and hence, the shape is bent or V shaped.

(vi) **PH$_3$** : $\begin{smallmatrix} \ddot{} \\ P \\ H\diagup \quad \diagdown H \\ H \end{smallmatrix}$ or $\ddot{P}$ H$\cdot\cdot$H$\,$H

The central atom P has 5 valence electrons. Out of which three are utilized in bonding with H atoms and one pair remains as lone pair. So, it contains 3 bond pairs and 1 lone pair. It is of the type AB_3L and hence, the shape is pyramidal.

Question 8. Although geometries of NH$_3$ and H$_2$O molecules are distorted tetrahedral, bond angle in water is less than that of ammonia. Discuss.

The size of lone pair is larger than the bond pair, so more the number of lone pairs of electrons, lesser is the bond angle.

Solution.

NH₃
bp = 3
lp = 1

H₂O
bp = 2
lp = 2

In H_2O molecule there is lone pair-lone pair repulsion due the presence of two lone pairs of electrons while in NH_3 molecule there found only lone pair-bond pair repulsion. According to VSEPR theory, the former one is more stronger and hence, the bond angle in water is less than that of ammonia (NH_3).

Question 9. How do you express the bond strength in terms of bond order?

Solution. With increase in bond order, bond enthalpy increases. Therefore, greater the bond order, higher is the bond strength, *i.e.*, bond strength ∝ bond order.

Question 10. Define the bond length.

Solution. **Bond length** It is defined as the equilibrium distance between the nuclei of two bonded atoms in a molecule. It is measured by spectroscopic, X-ray diffraction and electron diffraction techniques. In an ionic compound, the bond length is the sum of their ionic radii, $d = r_+ + r_-$ and in a covalent molecule, it is the sum of their covalent radii, *e.g.*, for HBr, $d = r_{H^+} + r_{Br^-}$.

Question 11. Explain the important aspects of resonance with reference to the CO_3^{2-} ion.

Solution. When a single Lewis structure of a molecule cannot describe its all properties, a number of structures, called canonical structures, are written. The actual structure, known as resonance hybrid, is in between of all these canonical forms. This phenomenon is called resonance. According to experimental findings, all carbon to oxygen bonds in CO_3^{2-} are equivalent, while in a single Lewis structure, there are two single bonds and one double bond between carbon and oxygen. So, a single Lewis structure is inadequate for the representation of CO_3^{2-} ion. The carbonate ion is best described as a hybrid of the canonical or resonance forms I, II and III.

Resonance in CO_3^{2-} ion

All canonical forms have similar energy, same positions of atoms and same number of bonded and non-bonded pairs of electrons.

Question 12. H_3PO_3 can be represented by structures 1 and 2 shown below. Can these two structures be taken as the canonical forms of the resonance hybrid representing H_3PO_3? If not, give reasons for the same.

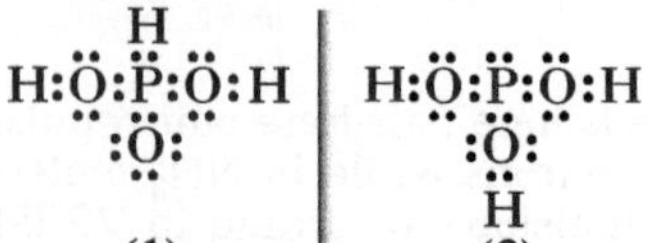

$$
\begin{array}{cc}
\text{H} & \\
\text{H:}\ddot{\text{O}}\text{:}\dot{\text{P}}\text{:}\ddot{\text{O}}\text{:H} & \text{H:}\ddot{\text{O}}\text{:}\ddot{\text{P}}\text{:}\ddot{\text{O}}\text{:H} \\
\text{:}\ddot{\text{O}}\text{:} & \text{:}\ddot{\text{O}}\text{:} \\
& \text{H} \\
(1) & (2)
\end{array}
$$

 Resonating structures or canonical forms differ only in the arrangement of electrons, but not in the positions of atoms.

Solution. No. These two structures cannot be taken as the canonical forms of the resonance hybrid because positions of the atoms have been changed.

Question 13. Write the resonance structures for SO_3, NO_2 and NO_3^-.

 Draw the possible structures in which octet (duplet in case of H) of all the atoms is complete and which differ only in the positions of electrons, but not in the position of atoms or nuclei.

Solution. **Sulphur trioxide, SO_3**

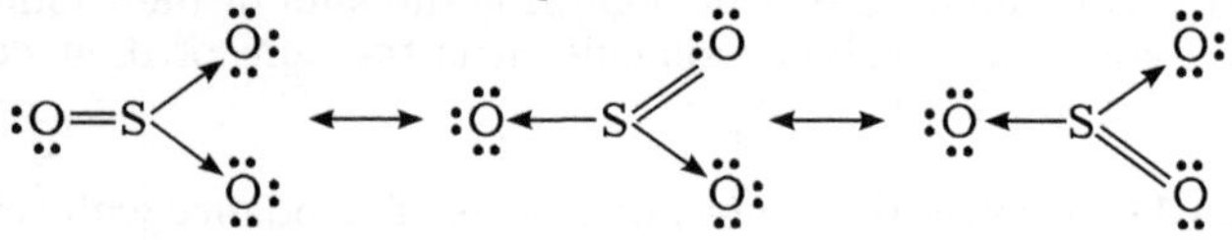

Nitrogen dioxide, NO_2

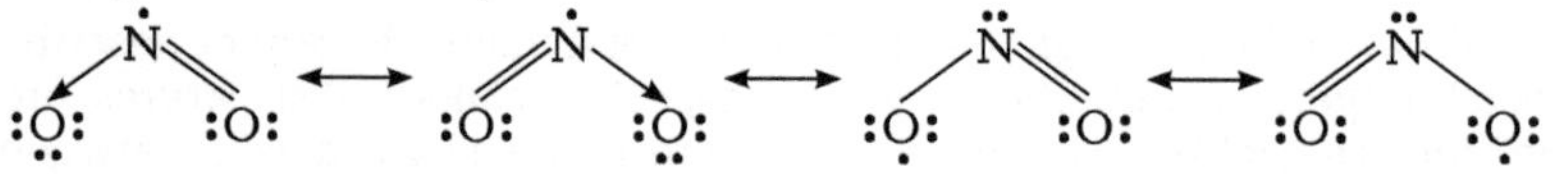

Nitrate ion, NO_3^-

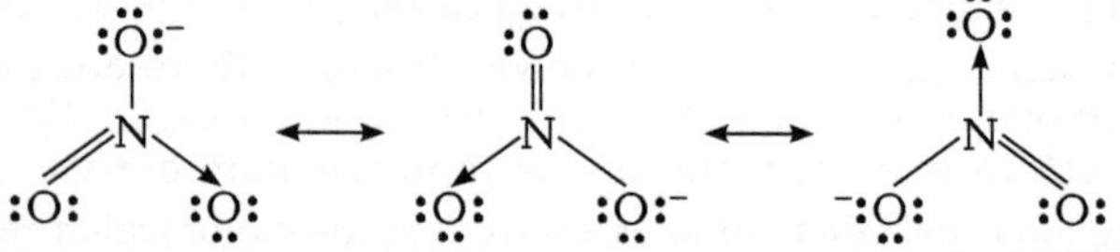

Question 14. Use Lewis symbols to show electron transfer between the following atoms to form cations and anions :

(a) K and S   (b) Ca and O   (c) Al and N

 Metals lose electrons to complete their octet while non-metals gain electrons to complete octet. So write the Lewis symbol *i.e.*, symbols with valence electrons to show the transfer of electron from metal to non-metal.

Solution.

(a) $2 \underset{2,\,8,\,8,\,1}{K^{\bullet}} + \underset{2,\,8,\,6}{\ddot{\underset{\bullet\bullet}{S}}} \longrightarrow 2K^+ [\ddot{\underset{\bullet\bullet}{S}}]^{2-}; K_2S$

(b) $\underset{2,\,8,\,8,\,2}{Ca\!\!:} + \underset{2,\,6}{\ddot{\underset{\bullet\bullet}{O}}} \longrightarrow Ca^{2+} [\ddot{\underset{\bullet\bullet}{O}}]^{2-}; CaO$

(c) $\dot{\underset{\bullet\bullet}{Al}}\!\!: + \dot{\underset{\bullet\bullet}{N}}\!\!: \longrightarrow Al^{3+} [\ddot{\underset{\bullet\bullet}{N}}]^{3-}; AlN$

Question 15. Although both CO_2 and H_2O are triatomic molecules, the shape of the H_2O molecule is bent while that of CO_2 is linear. Explain this on the basis of dipole moment.

For symmetrical or regular structures dipole moment is zero. Unsymmetrical structures have some dipole moment.

Solution. The net dipole moment of CO_2 is zero. This is because the two equal bond dipoles ($\overset{\delta^+}{C}$—$\overset{\delta^-}{O}$) point in opposite directions and cancel the effect of each other. Hence, CO_2 is linear. On the other hand, H_2O molecule is found to have a net dipole moment (1.84 D) which suggests that the two O—H dipoles are not in a straight line opposing each other, *i.e.*, H_2O does not have linear structure, but they (O—H) must be inclined to each other at certain angle. Thus, H_2O molecule has a bent structure in which the two O—H bonds are oriented at an angle of 104.5°.

$$\underset{H}{\overset{H}{\diagdown}}\!\!\!\!\overset{104.5°}{\diagup}\ddot{\underset{\bullet\bullet}{O}} \qquad O\!\!=\!\!C\!\!=\!\!O$$

Question 16. Write the significance/applications of dipole moment.

Solution. The applications of dipole moment are :

(i) The dipole moment helps to predict whether a molecule is polar or non-polar. As $\mu = q \times d$, greater is the magnitude of dipole moment, higher will be the polarity of the bond. For non-polar molecules, the dipole moment is zero.

(ii) The percentage of ionic character can be calculated as

$$\text{Percentage of ionic character} = \frac{\mu_{\text{observed}}}{\mu_{\text{ionic}}} \times 100$$

(iii) Symmetrical molecules have zero dipole moment although they have two or more polar bonds. (In determination of symmetry).

(iv) It helps to distinguish between *cis-* and *trans-*isomers. Usually *cis-*isomer has higher dipole moment than *trans-*isomer.

(v) It helps to distinguish between *ortho, meta* and *para* isomers. Dipole moment of *para* isomer is zero. Dipole moment of *ortho* isomer is greater than that of *meta* isomer.

Question 17. Define electronegativity. How does it differ from electron gain enthalpy?

Solution. Electronegativity of an element is the tendency of its atom to attract the shared pair of electrons towards itself in a covalent bond.
Electron gain enthalpy of an element may be defined as the energy released when a neutral isolated gaseous atom accepts an extra electron to form the gaseous negative ion, *i.e.,* anion.

$$X(g) \quad + \quad e^- \longrightarrow \quad X^-(g); \quad \Delta H = \Delta e_g H$$
$$\text{Neutral gaseous atom} \qquad\qquad \text{Anion}$$

Greater the amount of energy released in the above process, higher is the electron gain enthalpy of the element.
Electronegativity differs from electron gain enthalpy because electronegativity is a property of an atom in the bonded state while electron gain enthalpy relates to atoms in their isolated gaseous states.

Question 18. Explain with the help of suitable example polar covalent bond.

Solution. When covalent bond is formed between two dissimilar atoms, for example, HF (heteronuclear molecule), the shared pair of electrons between the two atoms gets displaced more towards more electronegative atom, fluorine. As a result, hydrogen atom becomes slightly positively charged and fluorine becomes slightly negatively charged. This type of bond is called polar covalent bond.

$$\text{H :F:}, \quad \overset{\delta+}{\text{H}} - \overset{\delta-}{\text{F}}$$

attracted more towards fluorine

Question 19. Arrange the bonds in order of increasing ionic character in the molecules; LiF, K_2O, N_2, SO_2 and ClF_3.

    (i) Ionic character $\propto$ lattice energy $\propto \dfrac{1}{\text{size of ion}} \propto$ charge on ion.

(ii) A non-polar molecule like N_2 has almost negligible ionic character.
Solution. $N_2 < SO_2 < ClF_3 < K_2O < LiF$

Question 20. The skeletal structure of CH_3COOH as shown below is correct, but some of the bonds are shown incorrectly. Write the correct Lewis structure for acetic acid.

$$\text{H} = \underset{\underset{\text{H}}{|}}{\overset{\overset{\text{H :O:}}{|}}{\text{C}}} - \overset{|}{\text{C}} - \text{O} - \text{H}$$

    Complete the octet (or duplet in case of H) of all the atoms to correct the structure.

Solution. The correct Lewis structure for acetic acid is

$$
\begin{array}{ccc}
\text{H} & \ddot{:}\text{O}\ddot{:} & \\
| & \| & \\
\text{H}-\text{C}-\text{C}-\ddot{\text{O}}-\text{H} \\
| & \ddot{} \\
\text{H} &
\end{array}
$$

Question 21. Apart from tetrahedral geometry, another possible geometry for CH_4 is square planar with the four H-atoms at the corners of the square and the C atom at its centre. Explain, why CH_4 is not square planar?

Solution. Electronic configuration of carbon

In ground state : $_6C- 1s^2, 2s^2, 2p_x^1, 2p_y^1$

In excited state : $\underbrace{1s^2, 2s^1, 2p_x^1, 2p_y^1, 2p_z^1}_{sp^3 \text{ hybridized}}$

In CH_4 molecule, carbon is sp^3 hybridized, so it is tetrahedral in shape. For square planar dsp^2 hybridization is required which is not possible in carbon due to absence of d-orbitals. Furthermore according to VSEPR theory, the four bonded electron pairs around carbon atom arranged themselves in a regular tetrahedron geometry. For tetrahedral structure, the bond angle is 109°28′ while in square planar structure, the bond angle is 90°. Therefore, in tetrahedral structure repulsions between bonded electron pairs is less than that of the square planar.

Question 22. Explain why BeH_2 molecule has a zero dipole moment although the Be—H bonds are polar?

 Dipole moment is the vector sum of all the bond dipoles.

Solution. BeH_2 molecule is linear. The two equal bond dipoles point in opposite directions and cancel the effect of each other. That's why its dipole moment is zero.

$$
\overset{180°}{\text{H}\underset{\leftarrow}{\overset{}{-}}\text{Be}\underset{\rightarrow}{\overset{}{-}}\text{H}}
$$
BeH_2 molecule, $\mu = 0$

Question 23. Which out of NH_3 and NF_3 has higher dipole moment and why?

Solution. NH_3 has higher dipole moment than NF_3, although both the molecules are pyramidal in shape. In NH_3, the orbital dipole due to lone pair is in the same direction as the resultant dipole moment of the three N—H bonds, while in NF_3, the orbital dipole due to lone pair is in the direction opposite to the resultant dipole moment of three N—F bonds. Hence, resultant dipole in NF_3 decreases.

NH_3, ($\mu = 4.90 \times 10^{-30}$ cm) NF_3, ($\mu = 0.80 \times 10^{-30}$ cm)

Note *Dipole moment is represented by an arrow pointing towards the more electronegative atom.*

Question 24.   What is meant by hybridization of atomic orbitals? Describe the shapes of *sp*, sp^2 and sp^3 hybrid orbitals.

Solution. **Hybridization** To explain the shape of polyatomic molecules like CH_4, H_2O, etc., Pauling introduced the concept of hybridization. It is defined as the mixing of atomic orbitals of nearly same energy, resulting in the formation of new set of orbitals of equal energies and identical shapes. The new orbitals thus, formed are known as hybrid orbitals. The number of hybrid orbitals is equal to the number of atomic orbitals mixed.

sp-hybridization   It involves the mixing of one *s* and one *p* (p_z) orbital resulting in the formation of two *sp* hybridized orbitals. These two *sp* hybridized orbitals are oriented in opposite direction (linear arrangement) and make an angle of 180° with one another. Examples, in BeH_2, BeF_2 and C_2H_2, Be and C are *sp*-hybridized.

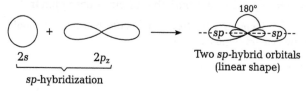

sp hybridization is also called diagonal hybridization.
sp^2-**hybridization**   It involves the mixing of one *s* and two *p*-orbitals resulting in the formation of three sp^2 hybridized orbitals. These three sp^2 hybridized orbitals are oriented in trigonal planar arrangement and make an angle of 120° with one another. Examples, in BH_3 and BF_3 boron is sp^2 hybridized and in C_2H_4, carbon is sp^2-hybridized.

Chemical Bonding and Molecular Structures 93

sp^3-hybridization It involves the mixing of one s and three p-orbitals resulting in the formation of four sp^3-hybridized orbitals. These four sp^3-hybridized orbitals are oriented towards the four corners of a regular tetrahedron and make an angle of 109°28′ with one another. Examples In methane (CH_4), ethane (C_2H_6) and all compounds of carbon containing C—C single bonds, carbon is sp^3 hybridized.

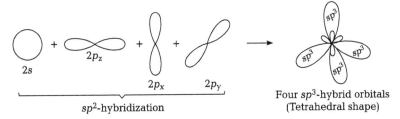

sp^2-hybridization

Four sp^3-hybrid orbitals
(Tetrahedral shape)

Question 25. Describe the change in hybridization (if any) of the Al atom in the following reaction.

$$AlCl_3 + Cl^- \longrightarrow AlCl_4^-$$

Solution. Electronic configuration of Al

In ground state $_{13}Al = 1s^2, 2s^2, 2p^6, 3s^2, 3p_x^1$

In excited state $= 1s^2, 2s^2, 2p^6, 3s^1, 3p_x^1, 3p_y^1$

In the formation of $AlCl_3$, Al undergoes sp^2-hybridization and it is trigonal planar in shape. While in the formation of $AlCl_4^-$, Al undergoes sp^3-hybridization. It means empty $3p_z$-orbital also involved in hybridization. Thus, the shape of $AlCl_4^-$ ion is tetrahedral.

Question 26. Is there any change in the hybridization of B and N atoms as a result of the reaction?

$$BF_3 + NH_3 \longrightarrow F_3B \cdot NH_3$$

Find the number of lone pairs and bond pairs on the central atom to find hybridization.

Solution. In BF_3, there are 3 bond pairs and 0 lone pairs, so boron is sp^2 hybridized and in NH_3, there are 3 bond pairs and 1 lone pair, so nitrogen is sp^3 hybridized. After the reaction, hybridization of boron changes to sp^3 but hybridization of nitrogen remains the same because N shares its lone pair with electron deficient B.

Question 27. Draw diagrams showing the formation of a double bond and a triple bond between the carbon atoms in C_2H_4 and C_2H_2.

Solution. **Formation of C_2H_4 (ethylene)**

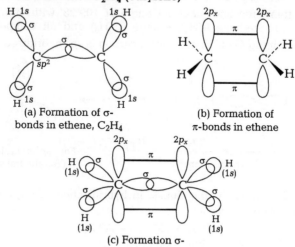

(a) Formation of σ-bonds in ethene, C_2H_4

(b) Formation of π-bonds in ethene

(c) Formation σ- and π-bonds in ethene (5σ, 1π)

Formation of C_2H_2 (acetylene)

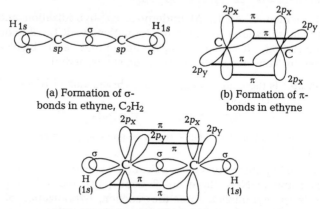

(a) Formation of σ-bonds in ethyne, C_2H_2

(b) Formation of π-bonds in ethyne

(c) Formation of σ- and π bonds in ethyne (3σ, 2π)

Question 28. What is the total number of sigma and pi bonds in the following molecules?

(a) C_2H_2 (b) C_2H_4

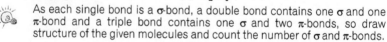
As each single bond is a σ-bond, a double bond contains one σ and one π-bond and a triple bond contains one σ and two π-bonds, so draw structure of the given molecules and count the number of σ and π-bonds.

Solution. (a) C_2H_2 $H\underset{\sigma}{-}C\equiv C\underset{\sigma}{-}H$ (b) C_2H_4

$$\underset{2\pi}{\underset{1\sigma}{\big\vert}}$$

$(3\sigma \text{ and } 2\pi)$

For (b): C_2H_4
$$\begin{array}{c}H\\ {}^{\sigma}\searrow\end{array}C\overset{\pi}{\underset{\sigma}{=}}C\begin{array}{c}\nearrow H\\ \end{array}$$
$H\diagup{}_{\sigma}\qquad {}_{\sigma}\diagdown H$
$(5\sigma \text{ and } 1\pi)$

Question 29. Considering x-axis as the internuclear axis, which out of the following will not form a sigma bond and why?

(a) $1s$ and $1s$ (b) $1s$ and $2p_x$ (c) $2p_y$ and $2p_y$ (d) $1s$ and $2s$

Axial overlapping results in the formation of σ bonds.

Solution. Only (c) will not form a σ-bond. Because on taking x-axis as the internuclear axis, $2p_y$ and $2p_y$ orbitals overlap sideway (lateral overlapping) resulting in the formation of a π-bond.

Question 30.   Which hybrid orbitals are used by carbon atoms in the following molecules?

(a) CH_3-CH_3 (b) $CH_3CH=CH_2$
(c) CH_3CH_2OH (d) CH_3CHO
(e) CH_3COOH

Find number of σ-bonds and find hybridization as $4\sigma \Rightarrow sp^3$-hybridization, $3\sigma \Rightarrow sp^2$-hybridization, $2\sigma \Rightarrow sp$-hybridization.

Solution.

(a)
$(C_2H_6)\,(4\sigma)$ — sp^3 (4σ), sp^3

(b)
$(CH_3CH=CH_2)$ — $sp^2\,(3\sigma)$, $sp^2\,(3\sigma)$, $sp^3\,(4\sigma)$

(c)
(CH_3CH_2OH) — $sp^3\,(4\sigma)$, $sp^3\,(4\sigma)$

(d)
(CH_3CHO) — $sp^2\,(3\sigma)$, $sp^3\,(4\sigma)$

(e)
(CH_3CHO) — $sp^2\,(3\sigma)$, $sp^3\,(4\sigma)$

(If a carbon atom is bonded by only single bonds, it is sp^3 hybridized, if it is bonded by double bond, it is sp^2 hybridized and if it is bonded by one triple bond, it is sp hybridized.)

Question 31. What do you understand by bond pairs and lone pairs of electrons? Illustrate by giving one example of each type.

Solution. Covalent bond is formed by mutual sharing of electrons. The shared pair of electrons present between the bonded atoms are called

are called lone pairs of electrons. For example, ammonia, NH_3 contains 3 bond pairs and 1 lone pair of electrons, water H_2O contains 2 bond pairs and 2 lone pairs of electrons and CH_4 contains only 4 bond pairs.

H
H:C:H
H
$(CH_4 - 4bp)$

H:N:H ——Lone pair
H ——Bond pair
$(NH_3 - 1\,lp\;and\;3bp)$

H:O:H
$(H_2O - 2lp\;and\;2bp)$

Question 32. Distinguish between a sigma and a pi bond.

Solution.

S. No.	Sigma (σ) bond	Pi (π) bond
1.	It is formed by the axial overlapping (end to end overlapping) of atomic orbitals.	It is formed by the sideways overlapping (lateral overlapping) of atomic orbitals.
2.	It involves overlapping of s-s, s-p and p-p atomic orbitals.	It involves overlapping of p-p atomic orbitals.
3.	In σ-bond, the overlapping of orbitals takes place to a larger extent, so, it is a stronger bond.	In π-bond, the overlapping of orbitals takes place to a smaller extent, so, it is a weaker bond.
4.	Free rotation about a σ-bond is possible.	Free rotation about a π-bond is not possible.
5.	A σ-bond may exist either alone or along with π-bonds.	It is always present along with a sigma bond.
6.	Electron cloud of sigma bond is symmetrical about internuclear axis.	Electron cloud of π-bond is unsymmetrical. It consists of electron clouds below and above the internuclear axis.
7.	In the formation of σ-bond, hybridized orbitals or unhybridised orbitals are involved.	In the formation of π-bond, only unhybridized orbitals are involved.

Question 33. Explain the formation of H_2 molecule on the basis of valence bond theory.

Solution. **Formation of H_2 molecule** Consider two hydrogen atoms A and B, each containing one electron in its 1s-subshell. When the two atoms are at large distance from each other, there is no interaction between them. As these two atoms approach each other, new attractive forces and repulsive forces begin to operate.

(i) Attractive forces arises between nucleus of A and electron of B and vice-versa, i.e., $N_A - e_B$, $N_B - e_A$.

(ii) Repulsive forces arises between nuclei of two atoms A and B, i.e., $N_A - N_B$.

(iii) Repulsive forces arises between electrons of two atoms A and B, i.e., $e_A - e_B$.

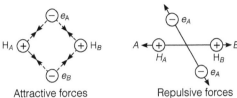

| Attractive forces | Repulsive forces |

Repulsive forces tend to push them apart while attractive forces tend to bring the two atoms close to each other . As the two atoms start to come closer to each other from infinite distance, the energy of the system starts decreasing as the forces of attraction exceed the forces of repulsion. Ultimately at a certain equilibrium distance, the net force of attraction balances the force of repulsion and system acquires minimum energy. At this stage, the two H-atoms are said to be bonded together to form a stable molecule having the bond length of 74 pm. In the formation of H_2 molecule, the released energy is called bond enthalpy. The energy changes taking place during the formation of H_2 molecule are shown graphically in the following figure.

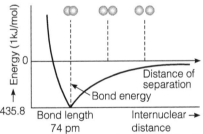

The potential energy curve for the formation of H_2 molecule as a function of internuclear distance of the H-atoms. The minimum in the curve corresponds to the most stable state of H_2.

Question 34. Write the important conditions required for the linear combination of atomic orbitals to form molecular orbitals.

Solution. Conditions for the combination of atomic orbitals :

(i) **The combining atomic orbitals must have comparable energies.** For example 1s-orbital can combine with another 1s-orbital but not with 2s-orbital because 2s-orbital have higher energy than that of 1s-orbital. Such combinations are possible if the atoms are different (heteronuclear diatomic molecules).

(ii) **The combining atomic orbitals must have the same symmetry about the molecular axis.** For example $2p_z$-orbital of one atom can combine with $2p_z$-orbital of another atom. It cannot combine with the $2p_x$ or $2p_y$ orbitals because of their different symmetries.

(iii) **The combining atomic orbitals must overlap to the maximum extent.** Greater the extent of overlapping, the greater will be the electron density between the nuclei.

Proper orientation for overlap
(same symmetry)

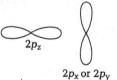

$2p_x$ or $2p_y$

Improper orientation
(no overlapping)

$2p_y$ $2p_x$

Improper orientation
(no overlapping)

Question 35. Use molecular orbital theory to explain why the Be_2 molecule does not exist?

 A positive bond order means a stable molecule (*i.e.*, it exists) while a negative or zero bond order means an unstable molecule (*i.e.*, it does not exist). Write MO electronic configuration of Be_2 to find its bond order from the formula

$$BO = \frac{1}{2}[N_b - N_a]$$

where, N_b = number of electrons in bonding molecular orbitals and N_a = number of electrons in antibonding molecular orbitals. (represented by*)

Solution. Electronic configuration of $_4Be$—$1s^2, 2s^2$

Electronic configuration of Be_2 molecule (4 + 4 = 8),

$$\sigma 1s^2, \overset{*}{\sigma} 1s^2, \sigma 2s^2, \overset{*}{\sigma} 2s^2$$

Bond order $= \frac{1}{2}[N_b - N_a] = \frac{1}{2}(4 - 4) = 0$

Hence, Be_2 does not exist.

Question 36. Compare the relative stability of the following species and indicate their magnetic properties.

$$O_2, O_2^+, O_2^- \text{ (superoxide)}, O_2^{2-} \text{ (peroxide)}.$$

 (i) Bond order is directly proportional to stability so calculate bond order by writing MO configuration and using the formula $BO = \frac{1}{2}(N_b - N_a)$. Now compare the stability by comparing bond order.

(ii) Also find whether all the electrons are paired (*i.e.*, it is diamagnetic) or not (*i.e.* it is paramagnetic).

Solution. Electronic configurations of O_2, O_2^+, O_2^- and O_2^{2-} species are as follows

$O_2 (16e^-)$ — $\sigma 1s^2, \overset{*}{\sigma} 1s^2, \sigma 2s^2, \overset{*}{\sigma} 2s^2, \sigma 2p_z^2, (\pi 2p_x^2 \approx \pi 2p_y^2)(\overset{*}{\pi} 2p_x^1 \approx \overset{*}{\pi} 2p_y^1)$

Bond order $= \frac{1}{2}(N_b - N_a) = \frac{1}{2}(10 - 6) = 2$

O_2 is paramagnetic because it has two unpaired electrons.

O_2^+ ion is formed by the lose of one electron by O_2 molecule.

O_2^+ (15e⁻) — $\sigma1s^2, \overset{*}{\sigma}1s^2, \sigma2s^2, \overset{*}{\sigma}2s^2, \sigma2p_z^2, (\pi\,2p_x^2 \approx \pi\,2p_y^2)\,(\overset{*}{\pi}2p_x^1 \approx \overset{*}{\pi}2p_y)$

Bond order $= \dfrac{1}{2}(N_b - N_a) = \dfrac{1}{2}(10 - 5) = 2.5$

O_2^+ is paramagnetic because it has one unpaired electron.

O_2^- ion is formed by the gain of one electron by O_2 molecule.

O_2^- (17e⁻) — $\sigma1s^2, \overset{*}{\sigma}1s^2, \sigma2s^2, \overset{*}{\sigma}2s^2, \sigma2p_z^2, (\pi\,2p_x^2 \approx \pi\,2p_y^2), (\overset{*}{\pi}2p_x^2 \approx \overset{*}{\pi}2p_y^1)$

Bond order $= \dfrac{1}{2}(N_b - N_a) = \dfrac{1}{2}(10 - 7) = 1.5$

O_2^- is paramagnetic because it has one unpaired electron.

O_2^{2-} ion is formed by the gain of 2 electrons by O_2 molecule.

O_2^{2-} (18e⁻) — $\sigma1s^2, \overset{*}{\sigma}1s^2, \sigma2s^2, \overset{*}{\sigma}2s^2, \sigma2p_z^2, (\pi\,2p_x^2 \approx \pi\,2p_y^2), (\overset{*}{\pi}2p_x^2 \approx \overset{*}{\pi}2p_y^2)$

Bond order $= \dfrac{1}{2}(N_b - N_a) = \dfrac{1}{2}(10 - 8) = 1$

O_2^{2-} is diamagnetic because all electrons are paired.

Relative stability of the above species in decreasing order

$$O_2^+ > O_2 > O_2^- > O_2^{2-}$$

Question 37. Write the significance of a plus and a minus sign shown in representing the orbitals.

Solution. Orbitals are represented by wave functions. A plus sign in an orbital represents a positive wave function and a minus sign represents a negative wave function. Combination of two wave functions having similar sign gave bonding molecular orbital while that having opposite sign, gave antibonding molecular orbital.

Question 38. Describe the hybridization in case of PCl_5. Why are the axial bonds longer as compared to the equatorial bonds?

 Find the number of unpaired electrons present in excited state in P atom from its electronic configuration and give hybridization on this basis.

Solution. Electronic configuration of phosphorus
In ground state, $_{15}P = 1s^2, 2s^2, 2p^6, 3s^2, 3p^3$

	$3s^2$	$3p^3$			$3d$				
	⇅	↑	↑	↑					

In excited state $_{15}P =$ 　↑　|　↑　↑　↑　|　↑

Formation of $PCl_5 =$ 　⇅　|　⇅　⇅　⇅　|　⇅

sp^3d hybrid orbitals (filled by electrons donated by 5 Cl atoms)

In the formation of PCl_5 molecule, the five orbitals, *i.e.,* one s, three p and one d-orbitals, are available for hybridization to yield five sp^3d hybridized orbitals. These five sp^3d hybridized orbitals are directed towards the five corners of a trigonal bipyramidal.

$$\underset{\underset{\displaystyle Cl}{|}}{\overset{\overset{\displaystyle Cl}{|}}{Cl-P}} \diagup^{\displaystyle Cl}_{\displaystyle Cl}$$

In PCl_5, three P—Cl bonds lie in one plane and make an angle of 120° with each other. These bonds are known as equatorial bonds. The remaining two P—Cl bonds, one lying above and other lying below the equatorial plane make an angle of 90° with the plane. These bonds are known as axial bonds. Axial P—Cl bonds are longer than equatorial P—Cl bonds because of the greater repulsion on axial bond pair electrons by equatorial bond pair electrons.

Question 39.   Define hydrogen bond. Is it weaker or stronger than the van der Waals' forces?

Solution.   Whenever in a molecule H-atom is linked with an atom of electronegative element like F, O or N, the shared pair electrons of the covalent bond are shifted towards the more electronegative atom. Due to this H-atom acquires partial positive charge and more electronegative atom acquires partial negative charge. This partially positively charged hydrogen of one molecule forms a bond with the other partially negatively charged more electronegative atom. This bond is known as hydrogen bond, *e.g.,* in HF molecule hydrogen acquires partial positive charge and F acquires partial negative charge due to the shifting of shared pair of electrons towards F. This partial positive charged H-atom of one molecule forms a hydrogen bond with partial negative charged F atom of another molecule.

$$\overset{+\delta}{H}-\overset{-\delta}{F}\cdots\overset{+\delta}{H}-\overset{-\delta}{F}\cdots\cdots\overset{+\delta}{H}-\overset{-\delta}{F}$$
Hydrogen bond

Thus, H-bond can be defined as the attractive force which binds H-atom of one molecule with the electronegative atom like F, O or N of another molecule.

Hydrogen bond is stronger than van der Waals' forces.

Question 40.   What is meant by the term bond order? Calculate the bond order of N_2, O_2, O_2^+ and O_2^-.

Solution.   **Bond order** is defined as one half the difference between the number of electrons present in the bonding and antibonding orbitals, *i.e.,*

$$\text{Bond order (B.O.)} = \frac{1}{2}(N_b - N_A)$$

A positive bond order means a stable molecule while a negative or zero bond order means an unstable molecule.

Stability of a molecule $\propto$ bond order

$$\text{Bond length} \propto \frac{1}{\text{bond order}}$$

Bond order values 1,2 or 3 correspond to single, double or triple bonds respectively.

Calculation of the bond order of N_2, O_2, O_2^+ and O_2^-

Electronic configuration of N_2 (14 electrons)

$$\sigma 1s^2, \overset{*}{\sigma} 1s^2, \sigma 2s^2, \overset{*}{\sigma} 2s^2, (\pi 2p_x^2 \approx \pi 2p_y^2), \sigma 2p_z^2$$

$$\text{Bond order} = \frac{1}{2}[N_b - N_a] = \frac{1}{2} \times (10 - 4) = 3$$

E.C. of O_2 (16 electrons)

$$= \sigma 1s^2, \overset{*}{\sigma} 1s^2, \sigma 2s^2, \overset{*}{\sigma} 2s^2, \sigma 2p_z^2, (\pi 2p_x^2 \approx \pi 2p_y^2), (\overset{*}{\pi} 2p_x^1 \approx \overset{*}{\pi} 2p_y^1)$$

$$\text{Bond order} = \frac{1}{2}(N_b - N_a) = \frac{1}{2}(10 - 6) = 2$$

E.C. of O_2^+ (15 electrons)

$$= \sigma 1s^2, \overset{*}{\sigma} 1s^2, \sigma 2s^2, \overset{*}{\sigma} 2s^2, \sigma 2p_z^2, (\pi 2p_x^2 \approx \pi 2p_y^2), (\overset{*}{\pi} 2p_x^1 \approx \overset{*}{\pi} 2p_y)$$

$$\text{Bond order} = \frac{1}{2}(N_b - N_a) = \frac{1}{2}(10 - 5) = 2.5$$

E.C. of O_2^- (17 electrons)

$$= \sigma 1s^2, \overset{*}{\sigma} 1s^2, \sigma 2s^2, \overset{*}{\sigma} 2s^2, \sigma 2p_z^2, (\pi 2p_x^2 \approx \pi 2p_y^2), (\overset{*}{\pi} 2p_x^2 \approx \overset{*}{\pi} 2p_y^1)$$

$$\text{Bond order} = \frac{1}{2}(N_b - N_a) = \frac{1}{2}(10 - 7) = 1.5$$

Selected NCERT Exemplar Problems

Short Answer Type

Question 1. Explain the non-linear shape of H_2S and non-planar shape of PCl_3 using valence shell electron pair repulsion theory.

Solution. **H_2S**—Central atom is sulphur. There are 6 electrons in its valence shell ($_{16}S = 2, 8, 6$). Two electrons are shared with two H-atoms and the remaining four electrons are present as two lone pairs. Hence, total pairs of electrons are four (2 bond pairs and 2 lone pairs). Due to the presence of 2 lone pairs the shape becomes distorted tetrahedral or angular or bent (non-linear).

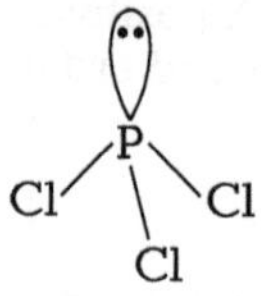

PCl_3—Central atom is phosphorus. There are 5 electrons in its valence shell ($_{15}P = 2, 8, 5$). Three electrons are shared with three Cl-atoms and the remaining two electrons are present as one lone pair. Hence, total pairs of electrons are four (1 lone pair and 3 bond pairs). Due to the presence of one lone pair, the shape becomes pyramidal (non-planar).

Question 2. Explain the shape of BrF_5^-.

Solution. The central atom Br has seven electrons in the valence shell. Five of these will form bonds with five fluorine atoms and the remaining two electrons are present as one lone pair. Hence, total pairs of electrons are six (5 bond pairs and 1 lone pair). To minimize repulsion between lone pairs and bond pairs, the shape becomes square pyramidal.

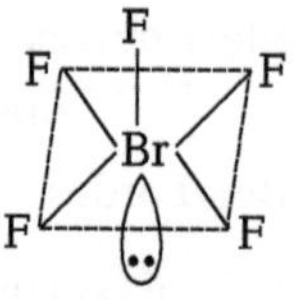

Question 3. Structures of molecules of two compounds are given below.

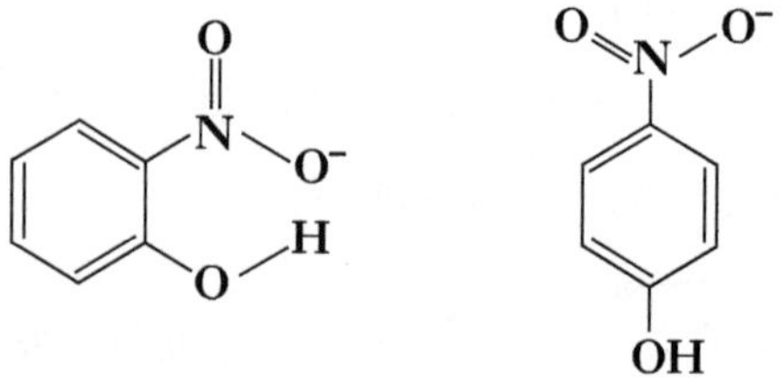

(I)   (II)

(a) Which of the two compounds will have intermolecular hydrogen bonding and which compound is expected to show intramolecular hydrogen bonding ?
(b) The melting point of a compound depends on, among other things, the extent of hydrogen bonding. On this basis explain which of the above two compounds will show higher melting point ?
(c) Solubility of compounds in water depends on power to form hydrogen bonds with water. Which of the above compounds will form hydrogen bond with water easily and be more soluble in it ?

Solution.
(a) Compound (I) will form intramolecular H-bonding. Intramolecular H-bonding is formed when H-atom, in between the two highly electronegative atoms, is present within the same molecule. In *ortho*-nitrophenol (compound I), H-atom is in between the two oxygen atoms.

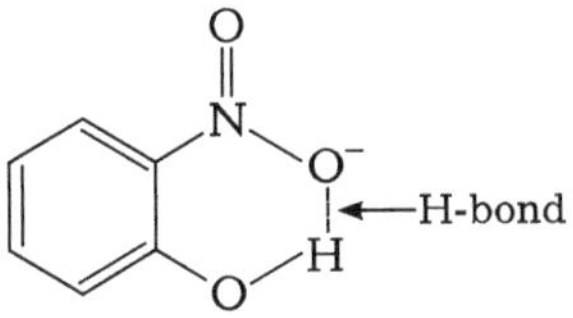

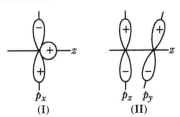

(I)

Compound (II) forms intermolecular H-bonding. In *para*-nitrophenol (II) there is a gap between NO_2 and OH group. So, H-bond exists between H-atom of one molecule and O-atom of another molecule as depicted below.

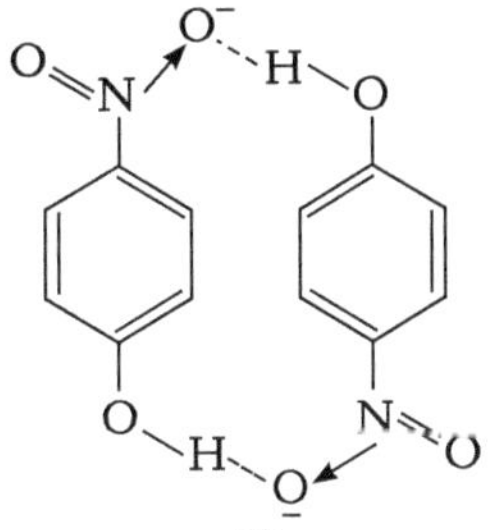

(II)

(b) Compound (II) will have higher melting point because large number of molecules are joined together by H-bonds.

(c) Due to intramolecular H-bonding compound (I) is not able to form H-bond with water, so it is less soluble in water. While molecules of compound II form H-bonding with H_2O easily, so it is soluble in water.

Question 4. Why does the type of overlap given in the following figure not result in bond formation?

p_x
(I)

p_z p_y
(II)

Solution. In the figure (I) area of ++ overlap is equal to +− overlap, so net overlap is zero, while in figure II there is no overlap due to different symmetry.

Question 5. Explain why PCl_5 is trigonal bipyramidal whereas IF_5 is square pyramidal?

Solution. PCl_5—The ground state and the excited state outer electronic configurations of phosphorus $(Z = 15)$ are represented below:

P(ground state)

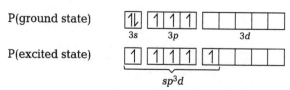

In PCl_5, P is sp^3d hybridized, therefore, its shape is trigonal bipyramidal. IF_5—The ground state and the excited state outer electronic configurations of iodine (Z = 53) are represented below.

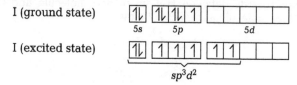

In IF_5, I is sp^3d^2 hybridized, therefore, shape of IF_5 is square pyramidal.

Question 6. In both water and dimethyl ether $(CH_3 - \overset{..}{\underset{..}{O}} - CH_3)$, oxygen atom is central atom, and has the same hybridization, yet they have different bond angles. Which one has the greater bond angle? Give reason.

Solution. Dimethyl ether has greater bond angle than that of water, however in both the molecules central atom oxygen is sp^3 hybridized with two lone pairs. In dimethyl ether, bond angle is greater (111.7°) due to the greater repulsive interaction between the two bulky alkyl (methyl) groups than that between two H-atoms.

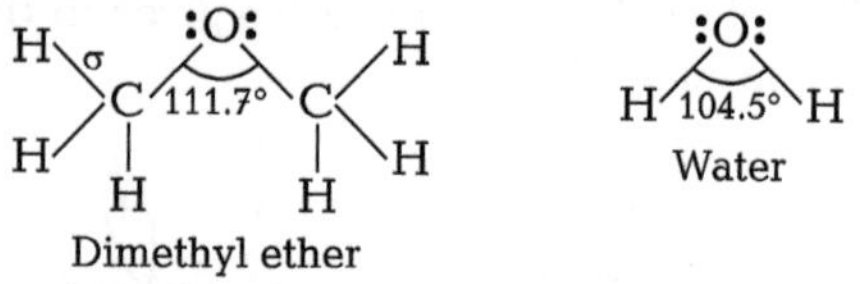

Dimethyl ether

Water

Actually C of CH_3 group is attached to three H-atoms through σ-bonds. These three C—H bond pair of electrons increases the electronic charge density on carbon atom.

Question 7. Write Lewis structure of the following compounds and show formal charge on each atom :

$$HNO_3, NO_2, H_2SO_4$$

Solution. (a) HNO_3 :

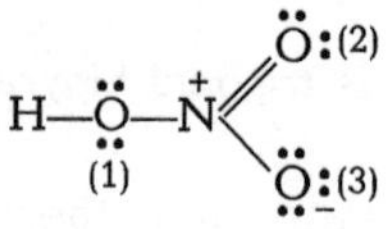

Formal charge on an atom in a Lewis structure
= [total number of valence electrons in free atom]
    – [total number of non-bonding (lone pairs) electrons]
    $-\dfrac{1}{2}$ [total number of bonding or shared electrons]

Formal charge on $H = 1 - 0 - \dfrac{1}{2} \times 2 = 0$

Formal charge on $N = 5 - 0 - \dfrac{1}{2} \times 8 = 1$

Formal charge on $O(1) = 6 - 4 - \dfrac{1}{2} \times 4 = 0$

Formal charge on $O(2) = 6 - 4 - \dfrac{1}{2} \times 4 = 0$

Formal charge on $O(3) = 6 - 6 - \dfrac{1}{2} \times 2 = -1$

NO_2 :

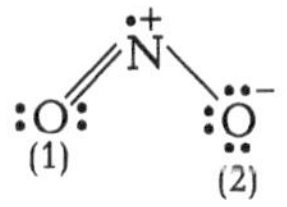

Formal charge on $O(1) = 6 - 4 - \dfrac{1}{2} \times 4 = 0$

Formal charge on $N = 5 - 1 - \dfrac{1}{2} \times 6 = +1$

Formal charge on $O(2) = 6 - 6 - \dfrac{1}{2} \times 2 = -1$

H_2SO_4 :

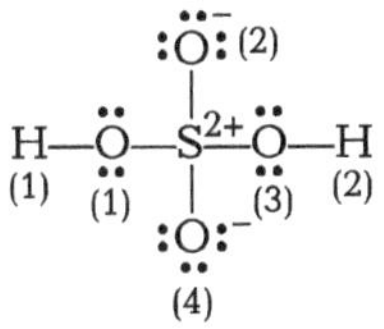

Formal charge on $H(1)$ or $H(2) = 1 - 0 - \dfrac{1}{2} \times 2 = 0$

Formal charge on $O(1)$ or $O(3) = 6 - 4 - \dfrac{1}{2} \times 4 = 0$

Formal charge on $O(2)$ or $O(4) = 6 - 6 - \dfrac{1}{2} \times 2 = -1$

Formal charge on $S = 6 - 0 - \dfrac{1}{2} \times 8 = +2$

Question 8. What is the effect of the following processes on the bond order in N_2 and O_2 ?

(i) $N_2 \longrightarrow N_2^+ + e^-$ (ii) $O_2 \longrightarrow O_2^+ + e^-$

Solution. According to molecular orbital theory, electronic configurations and bond order of N_2, N_2^+, O_2 and O_2^+ species are as follows:

$N_2 \ (14e^-) = \sigma 1s^2, \overset{*}{\sigma} 1s^2, \sigma 2s^2, \overset{*}{\sigma} 2s^2, \ (\pi \, 2p_x^2 \approx \pi 2p_y^2), \sigma 2p_z^2$

$$\text{Bond order} = \frac{1}{2}[N_b - N_a] = \frac{1}{2}(10 - 4) = 3$$

$N_2^+ \ (13e^-) = \sigma 1s^2, \overset{*}{\sigma} 1s^2, \sigma 2s^2, \overset{*}{\sigma} 2s^2, \ (\pi \, 2p_x^2 \approx \pi 2p_y^2) \, \sigma 2p_z^1$

$$\text{Bond order} = \frac{1}{2}[N_b - N_a] = \frac{1}{2}(9 - 4) = 2.5$$

$O_2 \ (16e^-) = \sigma 1s^2, \overset{*}{\sigma} 1s^2, \sigma 2s^2, \overset{*}{\sigma} 2s^2, \sigma 2p_z^2, (\pi 2p_x^2 \approx \pi 2p_y^2), (\overset{*}{\pi} 2p_x^1 \approx \overset{*}{\pi} 2p_y^1)$

$$\text{Bond order} = \frac{1}{2}[N_b - N_a] = \frac{1}{2}(10 - 6) = 2$$

$O_2^+ \ (15e^-) = \sigma 1s^2, \overset{*}{\sigma} 1s^2, \sigma 2s^2, \overset{*}{\sigma} 2s^2, \sigma 2p_z^2, (\pi 2p_x^2 \approx \pi 2p_y^2), \ (\overset{*}{\pi} 2p_x^1 \approx \overset{*}{\pi} 2p_y)$

$$\text{Bond order} = \frac{1}{2}[N_b - N_a] = \frac{1}{2}(10 - 5) = 2.5$$

(i) $N_2 \longrightarrow N_2^+ + e^-$
    B.O. = 3   B.O. = 2.5

Thus, bond order decreases.

(ii) $O_2 \longrightarrow O_2^+ + e^-$
    B.O = 2   B.O = 2.5

Thus, bond order increases.

Question 9. Give reasons for the following.

   (i) Covalent bond are directional bonds while ionic bonds are non-directional.

   (ii) Water molecule has bent structure whereas carbon dioxide molecule is linear.

   (iii) Ethyne molecule is linear.

Solution.

   (i) A covalent bond is formed by the overlap of atomic orbitals. The direction of overlapping gives the direction of bond. In ionic bond, the electrostatic field of an ion is non-directional. Each positive ion is surrounded by a number of anions in any direction depending upon its size and *vice-versa*. That's why covalent bonds are directional bonds while ionic bonds are non-directional.

   (ii) In H_2O, oxygen atom is sp^3 hybridised with two lone pairs. The four sp^3 hybridised orbitals acquire a tetrahedral geometry with two corners occupied by hydrogen atoms while other two by the lone pairs. The bond angle is reduced to 104.5° from 109.5° due to greater repulsive forces between $lp - lp$ and the molecule thus acquires a V-shape or bent structure (angular structure).

H $\overset{}{\underset{104.5°}{}}$ H

In CO_2 molecule, carbon atom is sp-hybridised. The two sp hybrid orbitals are oriented in opposite direction forming an angle of $180°$.

$$O \overset{\pi}{\underset{\sigma}{=}} C \overset{\pi}{\underset{\sigma}{=}} O$$

That's why H_2O molecule has bent structure whereas CO_2 molecule is linear.

(iii) In ethyne molecule, both the carbon atoms are sp hybridised, having two unhybridised orbitals, i.e., $2p_x$ and $2p_y$. The two sp hybrid orbitals of both the carbon atoms are oriented in opposite direction forming an angle of $180°$.

$$H—C \overset{\sigma}{\equiv} C—H$$
$$\text{2}\pi\text{-bond}$$

That's why ethyne molecule is linear.

Question 10. Arrange the following bonds in order of increasing ionic character giving reason.

$$N—H, \quad F—H, \quad C—H \quad \text{and} \quad O—H$$

Solution. Greater is the electronegativity difference between the two bonded atoms, greater is the ionic character.

	N—H	F—H	C—H	and	O—H
Electronegativity difference	$(3.0 - 2.1) =$ 0.9	$(4.0 - 2.1) =$ 1.9	$(2.5 - 2.1) =$ 0.4		$(3.5 - 2.1) =$ 1.4

Therefore, increasing order of ionic character of the given bonds is as follows :

$$C—H < N—H < O—H < F—H$$

Question 11. Predict the hybridization of each carbon in the molecule of organic compound given below. Also indicate the total number of sigma and pi-bonds in this molecule.

$$CH \equiv C—\overset{\overset{O}{\|}}{C}—CH_2—C \overset{\diagup O}{\diagdown OH}$$

Solution.

$$H \overset{\sigma}{—} C \overset{\pi}{\underset{\pi \sigma}{\equiv}} C \overset{\sigma}{—} \overset{\overset{O}{\|\sigma \| \pi}}{C} \overset{\sigma}{—} \overset{\overset{H}{|\sigma \sigma}}{C} \overset{\sigma}{—} \overset{\overset{O}{\|\sigma \|\pi}}{C} \overset{\sigma}{—} O \overset{\sigma}{—} H$$

$sp \quad sp \quad sp^2 \quad \underset{sp^3}{H} \quad sp^2$

σ-bonds = 11

π-bonds = 4

Question 12. Group the given molecules as linear and non-linear molecules.

$$H_2O, HOCl, BeCl_2, Cl_2O$$

Solution.

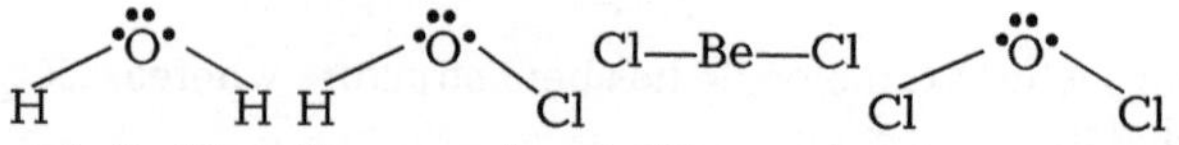

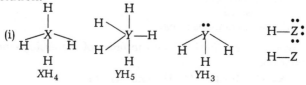

Therefore, only $BeCl_2$ is linear and rest of the molecules are non-linear.

Question 13. (i) X, Y and Z elements have 4, 5 and 7 valence electrons. Draw the structure of XH_4, YH_5, YH_3 and H—Z.

(ii) Which of these compounds has the highest dipole moment?

Solution.

(i)

XH_4 YH_5 YH_3

(ii) Z has seven electrons in its valence shell. It is the most electronegative element .Therefore, HZ will have the highest dipole moment.

Question 14. What is meant by the term average bond enthalpy? Why is there difference in bond enthalpy of O—H bond in ethanol (C_2H_5OH) and water?

Solution. All the similar bonds in a molecule do not have the same bond enthalpies. For example in H_2O(H—O—H) molecule after the breaking of first O—H bond the second O—H bond undergoes some change because of changed chemical environment. Therefore, in polyatomic molecules the term mean or average bond enthalpy is used. It is obtained by dividing total bond dissociation enthalpy by the number of bonds broken. For example,

$$H_2O(g) \longrightarrow H(g) + OH(g); \qquad \Delta_a H_1^\circ = 502 \text{ kJ mol}^{-1}$$

$$OH(g) \longrightarrow H + O(g); \qquad \Delta_a H_2^\circ = 427 \text{ kJ mol}^{-1}$$

Average O—H bond enthalpy $= \dfrac{502 + 427}{2} = 464.5 \text{ kJ mol}^{-1}$

The bond enthalpies of O—H bond in C_2H_5OH and H_2O are different because of the different chemical (electronic) environment around oxygen atom.

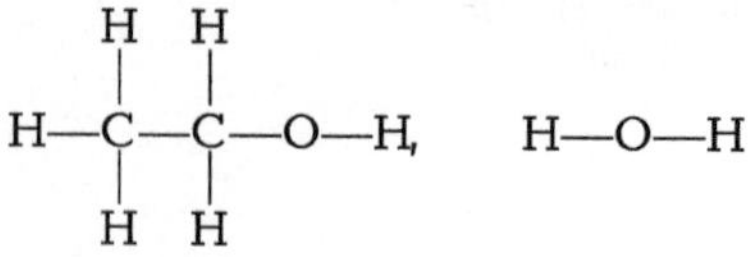

H   H
| |
H—C—C—O—H,   H—O—H
| |
H   H
(C_2H_5OH)   (H_2O)

Long Answer Type

Question 15. (i) Discuss the significance/applications of dipole moment.

  (ii) Represent diagrammatically the bond moments and the resultant dipole moment in CO_2, NF_3 and $CHCl_3$.

Solution.

  (i) Refer Q. 16 of Exercises.

  (ii)

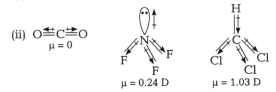

$O \overset{\longleftarrow}{=} C \overset{\longrightarrow}{=} O$
$\mu = 0$

$\mu = 0.24$ D

$\mu = 1.03$ D

Question 16. Use the molecular orbital energy level diagram to show that N_2 would be expected to have a triple bond; F_2, a single bond and Ne_2, no bond.

Solution. **Formation of N_2 molecule,** $_7N = 1s^2, 2s^2, 2p_x^1, 2p_y^1, 2p_z^1$

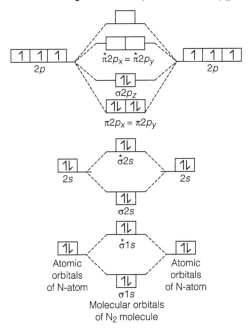

Molecular orbitals of N_2 molecule

Bond order $= \dfrac{1}{2}[N_b - N_a] = \dfrac{1}{2}(10 - 4) = 3$

Bond order value of 3 means that N_2 contains a triple bond.

Formation of F_2 molecule, $_9F = 1s^2, 2s^2, 2p_x^2, 2p_y^2, 2p_z^1$

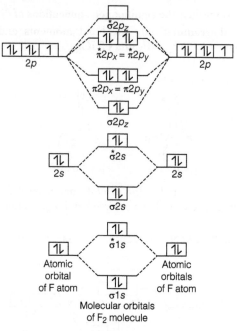

Bond order $= \dfrac{1}{2}[N_b - N_a] = \dfrac{1}{2}(10 - 8) = 1$

Bond order value 1 means that F_2 contains single bond.

Formation of Ne_2 molecule $_{10}Ne = 1s^2, 2s^2, 2p_x^2, 2p_y^2, 2p_z^2$

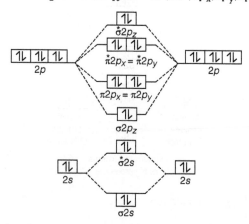

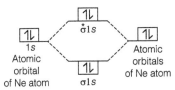

Molecular orbitals of Ne_2 molecule

Bond order $= \dfrac{1}{2}[N_b - N_a] = \dfrac{1}{2}(10 - 10) = 0$

Bond order value zero means that there is no formation of bond between two Ne atoms. Hence, Ne_2 molecule does not exist.

Question 17. Describe the hybridization in the case of PCl_5 and SF_6. The axial bonds are longer as compared to equatorial bonds in PCl_5 whereas in SF_6 both axial bonds and equatorial bonds have the same bond length. Explain.

Solution. **Formation of PCl_5**

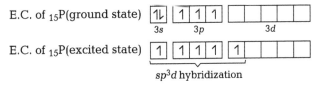

sp^3d hybridization

In PCl_5, phosphorus is sp^3d hybridized to produce a set of five sp^3d hybrid orbitals which are directed towards the five corners of a trigonal bipyramidal. These five sp^3d hybrid orbitals overlap with singly occupied p-orbitals of Cl atoms to form five P—Cl sigma bonds.

$$Cl \diagdown \atop Cl \diagup \overset{\textstyle Cl}{\underset{\textstyle Cl}{P}}{-}Cl$$

(Trigonal bipyramidal)
PCl_5

Three P—Cl bonds lie in one plane and make an angle of 120° with each other. These bonds are called equatorial bonds. The remaining two P—Cl bonds one lying above and other lying below the plane make an angle of 90° with the equatorial plane. These bonds are called axial bonds. Axial bonds are slightly longer than equatorial bonds because axial bond pairs suffer more repulsive interaction from the equatorial bond pairs.

Formation of SF_6

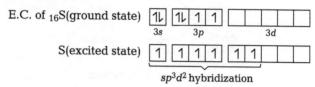

sp^3d^2 hybridization

In SF_6, sulphur is sp^3d^2 hybridized to produce a set of six sp^3d^2 hybrid orbitals which are directed towards the six corners of a regular octahedron. These six sp^3d^2 hybrid orbitals overlap with singly occupied orbitals of fluorine atoms to form six S—F sigma bonds. Thus, SF_6 molecule has a regular octahedral geometry and all S—F bonds have same bond length.

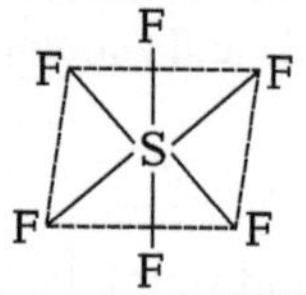

Octahedral geometry of SF_6 molecule.

Question 18.   (i) Discuss the concept of hybridization. What are its different types in a carbon atom?

(ii) What is the type of hybridization of carbon atoms marked with star?

(a) $\overset{*}{C}H_2 = CH - \overset{*}{\underset{\displaystyle \|}{C}} - O - H$ (with O double bonded to C*)

(b) $CH_3 - \overset{*}{C}H_2 - OH$

(c) $CH_3 - CH_2 - \overset{*}{\underset{\displaystyle \|}{C}} - H$ (with O double bonded to C*)

(d) $\overset{*}{C}H_3 - CH = CH - CH_3$

(e) $CH_3 - \overset{*}{C} \equiv CH$

Solution. **Hybridization** It can be defined as the process of intermixing of the orbitals of slightly different energy or of same energy to produce entirely new orbitals of equivalent energy, identical shapes and symmetrically disposed in plane. New orbitals formed are called hybrid orbitals.

Only the orbitals of an isolated single atom can undergo hybridization. The hybrid orbitals generated are equal in number to that of the pure atomic orbitals which mix up.

Hybrid orbitals do not make π, pi-bonds. If there are π-bonds, equal number of atomic orbitals must be left unhybridised for π-bonding.

Like atomic orbitals, hybrid orbitals cannot have more than two electrons of opposite spins.

Types of hybridization in carbon atoms

(i) (a) Diagonal or sp-hybridization—All compounds of carbon containing $C\equiv C$ triple bond like ethyne (C_2H_2).

(b) Trigonal or sp^2-hybridization—All compounds of carbon containing $C=C$ (double bond) like ethene (C_2H_4).

(c) Tetrahedral or sp^3-hybridization—All compounds of carbon containing C—C single bonds only like ethane (C_2H_6).

(ii) (a) $\overset{*}{C}H_2 = CH - \overset{O}{\overset{\|}{\underset{sp^2}{C^*}}} - O - H$ (b) $CH_3 \overset{*}{\underset{sp^3}{C}}H_2OH$

$\underset{(3\sigma)}{sp^2}$ $\underset{(3\sigma)}{sp^2}$ $\underset{(4\sigma)}{sp^3}$

(c) $CH_3 - CH_2 - \overset{O}{\overset{\|}{\underset{\underset{(3\sigma)}{sp^2}}{C^*}}} - H$ (d) $\overset{*}{C}H_3 - CH=CH-CH_3$

$\underset{(4\sigma)}{sp^3}$

(e) $CH_3 - \overset{*}{\underset{\underset{(2\sigma)}{sp}}{C}} \equiv CH$

Chapter 5

States of Matter

Important Results

1. At STP/NTP, $T = 273.15\,\text{K}$; $p = 1\,\text{atm} = 101.325\,\text{kPa}$; $V = 22.4\,\text{L mol}^{-1}$.

2. $1\,\text{Pa} = 1\,\text{Nm}^{-2}$; $1\,\text{atm} = 1.01325 \times 10^5\,\text{Nm}^{-2}$ (SI)

3. Boyle's law $p_1V_1 = p_2V_2$ (at constant T)

    Charles' law $\dfrac{V_1}{T_1} = \dfrac{V_2}{T_2}$ (at constant p)

4. Gay Lussac's law $p \propto T$ (at constant V)

5. Avogadro law $V \propto n$ (at constant T and p)

6. Ideal gas equation $pV = nRT$ or $p = \dfrac{nRT}{V} = \dfrac{mRT}{MV} = \dfrac{dRT}{M}$

    where, d = density in gL^{-1}.

7. Dalton's law of partial pressure

$$p_{\text{total}} = p_1 + p_2 + p_3 + \ldots..$$

    where, $p_1, p_2 \ldots..$ are partial pressures.

$$p_1 = p_{\text{total}} \cdot x_1 \text{ etc. } x_1 = \text{mole fraction.}$$
$$p_{\text{dry gas}} = p_{\text{total}} - \text{aqueous tension}$$

8. Graham's law

$$\frac{r_1}{r_2} = \sqrt{\frac{d_2}{d_1}} = \sqrt{\frac{M_2}{M_1}} = \frac{V_1 t_2}{V_2 t_1}$$

    where, d = vapour density; V_1 = volume of gas-1 diffusing in time t_1 and V_2 = volume of gas-2 diffusing in time t_2.

    If two gases diffuse under different pressures then

$$\frac{r_1}{r_2} = \frac{p_1}{p_2}\sqrt{\frac{M_2}{M_1}} = \frac{p_1}{p_2}\sqrt{\frac{d_2}{d_1}}$$

9. Kinetic theory

$$pV = \frac{1}{3}Mu^2 \qquad \text{where, } u = \text{root mean square velocity}$$

$$KE = \frac{3}{2}n\,RT$$

$$\text{Average KE} = \frac{3}{2}\frac{RT}{N_0} = \frac{3}{2}KT \text{ where, } K = \frac{R}{N_0} = \text{Boltzmann's constant}$$

10. van der Waals' equation

$$\left[p + \frac{n^2a}{V^2} \right] [V - nb] = nRT$$

where, a and b are van der Waals' constants.

11. $\frac{n^2a}{V^2}$ = internal pressure and is called pressure correction. It is a measure of force of attraction between gas molecules. Gases which can be liquified easily have high value of a.

nb is the volume correction due to finite size of the molecules; b is called excluded volume. ($b \approx 4V$, where, V is the volume of a spherical molecule).

12. Units of a = atm L^2 mol^{-2}; units of b = L mol^{-1}.

13. Compressibility factor $Z = \dfrac{pV}{nRT}$

$Z = 1$ for ideal gas, $Z \neq 1$ for real (non-ideal) gas.

14. Boyle's temperature is a temperature at which real gas obeys the gas laws over a wide range of pressure.

15. Surface tension (γ) Surface tension of a liquid is defined as the work (energy) required to expand the surface of a liquid by unit area.

$$\gamma = \text{force/length}; \ \text{dyne/cm}, \ \text{Nm}^{-1}$$

16. Surface tension is due to intermolecular attractive forces. It decreases with rise in temperature.

17. Viscosity It is defined as the resistance in flow of liquid and decreases with increase in temperature.

$$F = \eta A \frac{du}{dz};$$

where, η is the proportionality constant and is called coefficient of viscosity, F = force required to maintain the flow of layers, A = area of contact and du/dz is velocity gradient.

It is expressed in poise (dynes/cm^2 s)

$$1 \ \text{poise} = 10^{-1} \text{kg} \ \text{m}^{-1} \text{s}^{-1}$$

Exercises

Question 1. What will be the minimum pressure required to compress 500 dm^3 of air at 1 bar to 200 dm^3 at 30°C?

 Apply Boyle's law, $p_1 V_1 = p_2 V_2$ to calculate p_2 as temperature remains constant.

Solution. $p_1 = 1$ bar, $p_2 = ?$, $V_1 = 500$ dm^3, $V_2 = 200$ dm^3

$$p_1V_1 = p_2V_2$$

$$p_2 = \frac{p_1V_1}{V_2} = \frac{1 \text{ bar} \times 500 \text{ dm}^3}{200 \text{ dm}^3} = 2.5 \text{ bar}$$

Question 2. A vessel of 120 mL capacity contains a certain amount of gas at 35° C and 1.2 bar pressure. The gas is transferred to another vessel of volume 180 mL at 35℃. What would be its pressure ?

 Apply Boyle's law, $p_1V_1 = p_2V_2$ to calculate p_2 as temperature remains constant.

Solution. $p_1 = 1.2$ bar, $p_2 = ?$, $V_1 = 120$ mL, $V_2 = 180$ mL

From Boyle's law, $p_1V_1 = p_2V_2$

$$p_2 = \frac{p_1V_1}{V_2} = \frac{1.2 \text{ bar} \times 120 \text{ mL}}{180 \text{ mL}}$$

$$p_2 = 0.8 \text{ bar.}$$

Question 3. Using the equation of state $pV = nRT$; show that at a given temperature, density of a gas is proportional to gas pressure p.

Solution.

$$pV = nRT$$

$$pV = \frac{m}{M} RT \qquad \left\{ n = \frac{m}{M} = \frac{\text{Mass of gas } (g)}{\text{Molar mass of gas}} \right\}$$

or

$$p = \frac{mRT}{VM} \quad \text{or} \quad p = \frac{dRT}{M} \qquad \left(\because \text{Density}, d = \frac{m}{V} \right)$$

or

$$d = \frac{pM}{RT}; \text{If } T = \text{constant}, d \propto p$$

Question 4. At 0° C, the density of a certain oxide of a gas at 2 bar is same as that of dinitrogen at 5 bar. What is the molecular mass of the oxide ?

 Molar mass is related to the density by the formula, $d = \dfrac{Mp}{RT}$. Since, d is same and R and T are constant, $M_1p_1 = M_2p_2$. As M_2p_2 and p_1 are given, calculate M_1 (mass of gaseous oxide).

Solution. Density, $d = \dfrac{Mp}{RT}$

When T and d are same and R is constant,

then p_1M_1 (gaseous oxide) $= p_2M_2$ (nitrogen).

$$2 \text{ bar} \times M_1 = 5 \text{ bar} \times 28 \text{ u} \qquad \text{(Molar mass of N}_2 = 28 \text{ u)}$$

Molecular mass of unknown oxide, $M_1 = \dfrac{5 \text{ bar} \times 28}{2 \text{ bar}} = 70 \text{ u}$

Question 5. Pressure of 1 g of an ideal gas A at 27°C is found to be 2 bar. When 2 g of another ideal gas B is introduced in the same flask at same temperature, the pressure becomes 3 bar. Find a relationship between their molecular masses.

(i) In order to compare the molecular masses of gas A and B, write two equations for A and B gases by using the relation, $pV = nRT$.
(ii) Find the moles of A and B from their masses and pressure of B by subtracting pressure of A from total pressure.
(iii) Now, find the relation between M_A and M_B by comparing the two equations.

Solution. $pV = nRT$

For A gas, $\qquad\qquad p_A V = n_A RT$ $\qquad\qquad\qquad$ ...(i)
Similarly for B gas, $\qquad p_B V = n_B RT$ $\qquad\qquad\qquad$ ...(ii)

Number of moles of A gas; $n_A = \dfrac{1}{M_A}$ $\qquad$ (M_A = molar mass of gas A)

Number of moles of B gas; $n_B = \dfrac{2}{M_B}$ $\qquad$ (M_B = molar mass of gas B)

Pressure of gas A, $\qquad\qquad p_A = 2\,\text{bar}$

Total pressure, $\qquad\qquad p_{\text{total}} = p_A + p_B = 3\,\text{bar}$
Pressure of gas B, $\qquad\qquad p_B = p_{\text{total}} - p_A = 3 - 2 = 1\,\text{bar}$

V, R and T are same for both the gases.
Hence, from Eqs. (i) and (ii),

$$\frac{p_A}{p_B} = \frac{n_A}{n_B} = \frac{1 \times M_B}{M_A \times 2}$$

$$\frac{M_B}{M_A} = \frac{2 p_A}{p_B}$$

$$\frac{M_B}{M_A} = \frac{2 \times 2}{1}$$

$$M_B = 4\,M_A$$

Question 6. The drain cleaner, Drainex contains small bits of aluminium which react with caustic soda to produce dihydrogen. What volume of dihydrogen at 20°C and 1 bar will be released when 0.15 g of aluminium reacts ?

(i) To find the volume of dihydrogen, by using the equation $pV = nRT$, number of moles of hydrogen produced are required, so write a balanced chemical reaction between Al and NaOH and find the number of moles of H_2 produced from 0.15 g Al.
(ii) Find V_{H_2} by using the relation $pV = nRT$.

Solution. $\quad 2\text{Al} + 2\text{NaOH} + 2\text{H}_2\text{O} \longrightarrow 2\text{NaAlO}_2 + \quad 3\text{H}_2$

$\qquad\quad 2 \times 27\,\text{g}$ $\qquad\qquad\qquad\qquad\qquad\qquad\qquad\qquad\quad$ 3 mol

$\qquad\quad 0.15\,\text{g}$ $\qquad\qquad\qquad\qquad\qquad\qquad\quad \dfrac{0.15 \times 3}{2 \times 27} = 0.00833\,\text{mol}$

$$pV = nRT$$

$$V_{H_2} = \frac{0.00833\ \text{mol} \times 0.0821\ \text{dm}^3\ \text{atm K}^{-1}\ \text{mol}^{-1} \times 293\ \text{K}}{1 \times 0.987\ \text{atm}}$$

(1 bar = 0.987 atm)

$$V_{H_2} = 0.203\ \text{dm}^3$$

$$V_{H_2} = 203\ \text{mL}$$

Note *Temperature must be in kelvin. If it is given in* °C, *convert it into* K.

Question 7. What will be the pressure exerted by a mixture of 3.2 g of methane and 4.4 g of carbon dioxide contained in a 9 dm^3 flask at 27°C ?

Solution. Moles of CH_4,

$$n_{CH_4} = \frac{\text{Mass of } CH_4}{\text{Molar mass of } CH_4} \qquad [\text{Molar mass of } CH_4 = 12 + 4 \times 1 = 16]$$

$$= \frac{3.2}{16} = 0.2\ \text{mol}$$

Similarly, moles of CO_2,

$$n_{CO_2} = \frac{4.4}{44} = 0.1\ \text{mol} \qquad [\text{Molar mass of } CO_2 = 12 + 2 \times 16 = 44]$$

Total moles = 0.2 + 0.1 = 0.3 mol

$$pV = nRT$$

Pressure, $p = \dfrac{nRT}{V}$

$$= \frac{0.3\ \text{mol} \times 0.0821\ \text{dm}^3\ \text{atm K}^{-1}\ \text{mol}^{-1} \times 300\ \text{K}}{9\ \text{dm}^3} = 0.821\ \text{atm}$$

In terms of SI units :

Pressure, $p = \dfrac{0.3\ \text{mol} \times 8.314\ \text{Pa m}^3\ \text{K}^{-1}\ \text{mol}^{-1} \times 300}{9 \times 10^{-3}\ \text{m}^3}$

$$p = 8.314 \times 10^4\ \text{Pa}$$

Question 8. What will be the pressure of the gaseous mixture when 0.5 L of H_2 at 0.8 bar and 2.0 L of dioxygen at 0.7 bar are introduced in a 1L vessel at 27° C ?

(i) Calculate the total number of moles of H_2 and O_2 by using the relation $pV = nRT$.

(ii) Calculate the total pressure exerted by mixture of gas again by applying $pV = nRT$.

Solution. $pV = nRT$

Moles of H_2, $n_{H_2} = \dfrac{pV}{RT} = \dfrac{0.8 \times 0.5}{RT} = \dfrac{0.40}{RT}$

Similarly, moles of O_2, $n_{O_2} = \dfrac{pV}{RT} = \dfrac{0.7 \times 2}{RT} = \dfrac{1.4}{RT}$

$$\text{Total number of moles} = \frac{0.40}{RT} + \frac{1.4}{RT} = \frac{1.8}{RT}$$

$$\text{Total pressure, } p_{total} = \frac{nRT}{V} = \frac{1.8 \times RT}{RT \times 1} = 1.8 \text{ atm}$$

Question 9. Density of a gas is found to be 5.46 g/dm^3 at 27°C and 2 bar pressure. What will be its density at STP ?

STP mean at 1 bar and 273 K so compare the density at 27°C and 2 bar with the density at STP by using the relation $d = \frac{pM}{RT}$.

Solution. Density, $d = \frac{pM}{RT}$

For same gas at different temperatures and pressures :

$$\frac{d_2}{d_1} = \frac{p_2 T_1}{p_1 T_2}$$

$d_1 = 5.46 \text{ g / dm}^3, d_2 = ?$

$T_1 = 27°C = 300K, T_2 = 0°C = 273 \text{ K}$

$p_1 = 2 \text{ bar, } p_2 = 1 \text{ bar}$

$$d_2 = \frac{p_2 T_1 d_1}{p_1 T_2} = \frac{1 \times 300 \times 5.46}{2 \times 273} = 3 \text{ g dm}^{-3}$$

Question 10. 34.05 mL of phosphorus vapour weighs 0.0625 g at 546°C and 0.1 bar pressure. What is the molar mass of phosphorus ?

Solution. $pV = nRT$

$$pV = \frac{mRT}{M} \qquad (m = \text{mass of phosphorus } (g) \text{ and}$$

$$M = \text{molar mass of phosphorus})$$

$$M = \frac{mRT}{pV}$$

$$M = \frac{0.0625 \text{ g} \times 0.0821 \text{ L atm K}^{-1} \text{ mol}^{-1} \times 819 \text{ K}}{0.1 \times 0.987 \text{ atm} \times 0.03405 \text{ L}}$$

$$M = 1250.4 \text{ g mol}^{-1}$$

Question 11. A student forgot to add the reaction mixture to the round bottomed flask at 27°C but instead he/she placed the flask on the flame. After a lapse of time, he realized his mistake, and using a pyrometer he found the temperature of the flask was 477°C. What fraction of air would have been expelled out ?

Apply Charles' law as pressure remains constant, $\frac{V_1}{T_1} = \frac{V_2}{T_2}$ to find a relation between V_1 and V_2 and then calculate the fraction of air expelled by using the formula,

$$\text{Fraction of air expelled} = \frac{\text{Volume expelled}}{\text{Total volume}}$$

Solution. Suppose volume of the air in flask $= V\,cm^3$ at $27°C = 300\,K$

$$V_1 = V\,cm^3, \quad V_2 = ?, T_1 = 300\,K, T_2 = 750\,K$$

$$\frac{V_1}{T_1} = \frac{V_2}{T_2}$$

$$\frac{V}{300} = \frac{V_2}{750} \quad \text{or} \quad 300\,V_2 = 750\,V$$

$$V_2 = 2.5\,V \qquad\qquad \text{(final volume)}$$

Volume expelled $= 2.5\,V - V = 1.5\,V$

$$\text{Fraction of air expelled} = \frac{1.5\,V}{2.5\,V} = 0.6$$

Alternatively, using $pV = nRT$

$$n \propto \frac{1}{T}$$

$$\frac{n_2}{n_1} = \frac{T_1}{T_2} = \frac{300}{750}$$

$$\frac{n_2}{n_1} = 0.4$$

∴ Fraction of air expelled $= 0.6$

Question 12. Calculate the temperature of 4.0 mole of a gas occupying 5 dm^3 at 3.32 bar. ($R = 0.083$ bar dm^3 K^{-1} mol^{-1}).

Solution. Apply ideal gas equation, $pV = nRT$

Pressure, $\quad\quad\quad p = 3.32\,bar$

Volume, $\quad\quad\quad V = 5\,dm^3$

Number of moles, $n = 4\,mol$

Gas constant, $\quad R = 0.083$ bar dm^3 K^{-1} mol^{-1}

Temperature, $\quad T = ?$

$$T = \frac{pV}{Rn} = \frac{3.32\,bar \times 5\,dm^3}{0.083\,bar\,dm^3\,K^{-1}\,mol^{-1} \times 4\,mol}$$

$$T = 50\,K$$

Question 13. Calculate the number of electrons present in 1.4 g of dinitrogen gas.

　　(i) Convert the given mass into mole with the help of the formula,

$$\text{Moles} = \frac{\text{Mass}}{\text{Molecular mass}}$$

　　(ii) 1 mol $= 6.022 \times 10^{23}$ molecule

Solution. $n_{N_2} = \dfrac{1.4}{28} = 0.05\,mol$

$$1\,mol = 6.022 \times 10^{23} \text{ molecules}$$

$$0.05\,mol = 0.05 \times 6.022 \times 10^{23} = 0.3011 \times 10^{23} \text{ molecules}$$

1 molecule of N_2 contains $= 14$ electrons

∴ 0.3011×10^{23} molecules will contain

$$= 0.3011 \times 10^{23} \times 14 = 4.2154 \times 10^{23} \text{ electrons}$$

Question 14. How much time would it take to distribute one Avogadro number of wheat grains if 10^{10} grains are distributed each second ?

(i) $1 N_A = 6.022 \times 10^{23}$ where, N_A = Avogadro's number.

(ii) Convert time into yr.

Solution. Time required $= \dfrac{\text{Total grains}}{\text{Grains distributed}}$

$$= \frac{6.022 \times 10^{23}}{10^{10}} = 6.022 \times 10^{13} \text{ s}$$

$$= \frac{6.022 \times 10^{13}}{365 \times 24 \times 60 \times 60} = 1.909 \times 10^6 \text{ yr}$$

Question 15. Calculate the total pressure in a mixture of 8g of dioxygen and 4 g of dihydrogen confined in a vessel of 1 dm^3 at 27°C. $R = 0.083$ bar dm^3 K^{-1} mol^{-1}.

To calculate the total pressure exerted by a mixture of gases first find total number of moles of gas and then apply the relation, $pV = nRT$.

Solution. Moles of O_2, $n_{O_2} = \dfrac{\text{Mass}}{\text{Mol. wt.}} = \dfrac{8}{32} = 0.25$ mol

[mol. wt. of $O_2 = 16 + 16 = 32$]

Moles of H_2, $n_{H_2} = \dfrac{4}{2} = 2.0$ mol   [mol. wt. of $H_2 = 1 + 1 = 2$]

Total number of moles $= 0.25 + 2.0 = 2.25$ mol

$p = ?$; $n = 2.25$ mol; $V = 1 dm^3$; $R = 0.083$ bar dm^3 K^{-1} mol^{-1}

$T = 27° C = 300 K$

$pV = nRT$

Pressure, $p = \dfrac{nRT}{V} = \dfrac{2.25 \text{ mol} \times 0.083 \text{ bar } dm^3 \text{ } K^{-1} \text{ } mol^{-1} \times 300 \text{ K}}{1 dm^3}$

$p = 56.025$ bar

Question 16. Pay load is defined as the difference between the mass of displaced air and the mass of the balloon. Calculate the pay load when a balloon of radius 10 m, mass 100 kg is filled with helium at 1.66 bar at 27° C. (Density of air $= 1.2$ kg m^{-3} and $R = 0.083$ bar dm^3 K^{-1} mol^{-1}).

(i) To calculate the pay load, mass of displaced air, and mass of balloon with He are required, so calculate mass of air displaced by using the formula,

Mass of air displaced $= V \times d$

and V = volume of air displaced = volume of balloon $= \dfrac{4}{3} \pi r^3$.

∴ Mass of air displaced $= \dfrac{4}{3} \pi r^3 \cdot d$

(ii) Then, calculate the mass of helium filled in the balloon by using the relation, $pV = \dfrac{m}{M} RT$ and use the relation,

Pay load = Mass of displaced air–Mass of balloon with He (to calculate pay load.)

Solution. Radius, $R_{balloon}$ = 10 m

$$V_{balloon} = \frac{4}{3}\pi r^3 = \frac{4}{3} \times \frac{22}{7} \times (10)^3 = 4190.476 \ m^3.$$

$V_{balloon} = V_{displaced\ air\ (by\ balloon)}$

∴ Mass of displaced air = $V_{displaced\ air}$ × density of air

$$m_{displaced\ air} = 4190.476 \ m^3 \times 1.2 \ kg \ m^{-3}$$

$$m = 5028.57 \ kg$$

Mass of He filled in balloon, $m_{He} = \dfrac{pVM}{RT}$ $\left(pV = \dfrac{mRT}{M} \right)$

$$m_{He} = \frac{1.66 \ bar \times 4190.476 \times 10^3 \ dm^3 \times 4 \times 10^{-3} \ kg \ mol^{-1}}{0.083 \ bar \ dm^3 \ K^{-1} \ mol^{-1} \times 300 \ K}$$

$m_{He} = 1117.46 \ kg$

Total mass of filled balloon, $m_{balloon}$

= mass of balloon + mass of He filled in the balloon

$m_{balloon} = 100 \ kg + 1117.46 \ kg = 1217.46 \ kg$

Pay load = mass of displaced air – mass of balloon

= 5028.57 kg – 1217.46 kg = 3811.11 kg

Question 17. Calculate the volume occupied by 8.8 g of CO_2 at 31.1° C and 1 bar pressure. $R = 0.083 \ bar \ LK^{-1} \ mol^{-1}$.

Solution. $pV = nRT$

$$pV = \frac{m}{M} RT$$

$$p = 1 \ bar, \ V = ?, \ m = 8.8 \ g$$

$$M = 44 \ g \ mol^{-1} \ (CO_2)$$

$$R = 0.083 \ bar \ LK^{-1} \ mol^{-1} \quad and \quad T = 304.1 \ K$$

Volume occupied by 8.8 g of CO_2,

$$V = \frac{mRT}{pM} = \frac{8.8 \ g \times 0.083 \ bar \ LK^{-1} \ mol^{-1} \times 304.1 \ K}{1 \ bar \times 44 \ g \ mol^{-1}}$$

$$V = 5.048 \ L$$

Question 18. 2.9 g of a gas at 95° C occupied the same volume as 0.184 g of dihydrogen at 17° C, at the same pressure. What is the molar mass of the gas?

(i) Since, two gases are given write two separate equations (for unknown gas and for H_2) by using the relation, $pV = \dfrac{m}{M} RT$.

(ii) To calculate the molar mass of unknown gas compare both the equations at the same volume and pressure.

Solution. $pV = nRT$

$$pV = \frac{mRT}{M}$$

Unknown gas;   H$_2$ gas

$$p_1V_1 = \frac{m_1RT_1}{M_1}; \quad p_2V_2 = \frac{m_2RT_2}{M_2}$$

$$p_1V_1 = p_2V_2$$

Hence,
$$\frac{m_1RT_1}{M_1} = \frac{m_2RT_2}{M_2}$$

$$\frac{2.9 \text{ g} \times R \times 368 \text{ K}}{M_1} = \frac{0.184 \text{ g} \times R \times 290 \text{ K}}{2 \text{ g mol}^{-1}}$$

Molar mass of unknown gas, $M_1 = \dfrac{2.9 \text{ g} \times 368 \text{ K} \times 2 \text{ g mol}^{-1}}{0.184 \text{ g} \times 290 \text{ K}} = 40 \text{ g mol}^{-1}$

Question 19. A mixture of dihydrogen and dioxygen at one bar pressure contains 20% by weight of dihydrogen. Calculate the partial pressure of dihydrogen.

(i) To calculate the partial pressure, total pressure and mole fraction of hydrogen is required, so first calculate number of moles of H$_2$ and O$_2$ in the given mixture and mole fraction of hydrogen.

(ii) Then, calculate p_{H_2} by using the formula $p_A = p_{total} \times x_A$.

Solution. A mixture of H$_2$ and O$_2$ contains 20% by weight of H$_2$ means H$_2$ = 20 g and O$_2$ = 80 g

Moles of hydrogen, $n_{H_2} = \dfrac{20}{2} = 10 \text{ mol}$

Moles of oxygen, $n_{O_2} = \dfrac{80}{32} = 2.5 \text{ mol}$

Mole fraction of hydrogen, $x_{H_2} = \dfrac{n_{H_2}}{n_{H_2} + n_{O_2}} = \dfrac{10}{10 + 2.5} = 0.8$

Partial pressure of H$_2$, $p_{H_2} = p_{total} \times x_{H_2}$

$$p_{H_2} = 1 \text{ bar} \times 0.8$$

$$p_{H_2} = 0.8 \text{ bar.}$$

Question 20. What would be the SI unit for the quantity pV^2T^2 / n?

Solution. $\dfrac{pV^2T^2}{n} = \dfrac{(\text{Nm}^{-2}) \, (\text{m}^3)^2 \, (\text{K})^2}{\text{mol}} = \text{Nm}^4 \, \text{K}^2 \, \text{mol}^{-1}$

Question 21. In terms of Charles' law explain why $-273°C$ is the lowest possible temperature?

Solution. According to Charles' law, $V_t = V_0 \left[1 + \dfrac{t}{273} \right]$

At $t = -273°C,$ $V_t = V_0 \left[1 - \dfrac{273}{273} \right] = 0$

Thus, at $-273°C$, volume of a gas becomes equal to zero and below this the volume become negative which is meaningless.

Question 22. Critical temperature for carbon dioxide and methane are $31.1°C$ and $-81.9°C$ respectively. Which of these has stronger intermolecular forces and why ?

Solution. Critical temperature is the temperature above which the gas cannot be liquified, how so ever high pressure we may apply. Higher the critical temperature, more easily the gas can be liquified, *i.e.,* stronger are the intermolecular forces. Hence, CO_2 has stronger intermolecular forces than CH_4.

Question 23. Explain the physical significance of van der Waals' parameters.

Solution. a is a measure of magnitude of intermolecular forces of attraction while *b* is a measure of the effective volume of the gas molecules. Value of *a* and *b* depends upon the characteristics of a gas.

Selected NCERT Exemplar Problems

Short Answer Type

Question 1. If 1 g of each of the following gases are taken at STP, which of the gases will occupy (a) greatest volume and (b) smallest volume?

$$CO, H_2O, CH_4, NO$$

Solution. Volume of 1 mole of the gas $= 22.4$ L at STP

Volume occupied by 28 g CO (1 mol CO) $= 22.4$ L at STP

$$(\because \text{Molar mass of } CO = 12 + 16 = 28 \text{ g mol}^{-1})$$

$\therefore$ Volume occupied by 1 g CO $= \dfrac{22.4}{28}$ L at STP

Similarly, volume occupied by 1 g $H_2O = \dfrac{22.4}{18}$ L at STP

$$(\because \text{Molar mass of } H_2O = (2 \times 1) + 16 = 18 \text{ g mol}^{-1})$$

Volume occupied by 1 g $CH_4 = \dfrac{22.4}{16}$ L at STP

$$(\because \text{Molar mass of } CH_4 = 12 + (4 \times 1) = 16 \text{ g mol}^{-1})$$

Volume occupied by 1 g NO $= \dfrac{22.4}{30}$ L at STP

$$(\because \text{Molar mass of } NO = 14 + 16 = 30 \text{ g mol}^{-1})$$

Thus, 1 g CH_4 will occupy maximum volume and 1 g of NO will occupy minimum volume at STP.

Question 2. The behaviour of matter in different states is governed by various physical laws. According to you what are the factors that determine the state of matter?

Solution. Temperature, pressure, mass and volume are some factors which determine the state of matter.

Question 3. What will be the molar volume of nitrogen and argon at 273.15 K and 1 atm?

Solution. Every gas has 22.4 L molar volume at 273.15 K and 1atm pressure (STP).

Question 4. A gas that follows Boyle's law, Charles' law and Avogadro's law is called an ideal gas. Under what conditions a real gas would behave ideally?

Solution. At low pressure and high temperature, a real gas behaves as an ideal gas.

Question 5. Two different gases 'A' and 'B' are filled in separate containers of equal capacity under the same conditions of temperature and pressure. On increasing the pressure slightly the gas 'A' liquefies but gas B does not liquify even on applying high pressure until it is cooled. Explain this phenomenon.

Solution. A gas cannot be liquified above critical temperature. So, gas 'A' is below its critical temperature whereas gas 'B' is above its critical temperature.

Question 6. One of the assumptions of kinetic theory of gases states that "there is no force of attraction between the molecules of a gas." How far is this statement correct? Is it possible to liquefy an ideal gas? Explain.

Solution. This statement is correct only for ideal gases. It is not possible to liquefy an ideal gas because there is no intermolecular forces of attractions between the molecules of an ideal gas.

Question 7. The magnitude of surface tension of liquid depends on the attractive forces between the molecules. Arrange the following in increasing order of surface tension :
water, alcohol (C_2H_5OH) and hexane [$CH_3(CH_2)_4CH_3$].

Solution. In hexane, there are only London forces between the molecules. These forces are very weak. H-bondng is stronger in H_2O in comparison to C_2H_5OH. Hence, the increasing order of surface tension is
Hexane < alcohol < water

Question 8. Name the energy which arises due to motion of atoms or molecules in a body. How is this energy affected when the temperature is increased?

Solution. The energy which arises due to motion of atoms or molecules in a body is know as thermal energy. It is a measure of average kinetic energy of the particles. It increases with increase in temperature.

Question 9. Name two intermolecular forces that exist between HF molecules in liquid state.

Solution. HF are polar covalent molecules. In liquid state, there are dipole-dipole interactions and H-bonding.

Question 10. Compressibility factor, Z of a gas is given as $Z = \dfrac{pV}{nRT}$

(i) What is the value of Z for an ideal gas?

(ii) For real gas what will be the effect on value of Z above Boyle's temperature?

Solution.

(i) For ideal gas, compressibility factor, Z = 1.

(ii) Above Boyle's temperature, real gases show positive deviation.
So,   Z > 1

Question 11. For real gases the relation between p, V and T is given by van der Waals' equation

$$\left(p + \frac{an^2}{V^2}\right)(V - nb) = nRT$$

where, 'a' and 'b' are van der Waals' constants, 'nb' is approximately equal to the total volume of the molecules of a gas. 'a' is the measure of magnitude of intermolecular attraction.

(i) Arrange the following gases in the increasing order of 'b'. Give reason.

$$O_2, CO_2, H_2, He$$

(ii) Arrange the following gases in the decreasing order of magnitude of 'a'. Give reason.

$$CH_4, O_2, H_2$$

Solution.

(i) Molar volume occupied by the gas molecules $\propto$ size of the molecules and van der Waals' constant 'b' represents molar volume of the gas molecules. Hence, value of 'b' increases in the following order

$$H_2 < He < O_2 < CO_2$$

(ii) van der Waals' constant 'a' is the measure of magnitude of intermolecular attraction. The magnitude of intermolecular attractions increases with increase in size of electron cloud in a molecule. Hence, for the given gases magnitude of 'a' decreases in the following order:

$$CH_4 > O_2 > H_2$$

Greater the size of electron cloud, greater is the polarisability of the molecule and greater is the dispersion forces or London forces.

Question 12. The relation between pressure exerted by an ideal gas (p_{ideal}) and observed pressure (p_{real}) is given by the equation,

$$p_{ideal} = p_{real} + \frac{an^2}{V^2}$$

(i) If pressure is taken in Nm^{-2}, number of moles in mol and volume in m^3, calculate the unit of 'a'.

(ii) What will be the unit of 'a' when pressure is in atmosphere and volume in dm^3?

Solution. $p_{ideal} = p_{real} + \frac{an^2}{V^2}$

(i) $a = \frac{pV^2}{n^2}$

If units of $p = Nm^{-2}$, units of $V = m^3$, units of $n = mol$

then, units of $a = \frac{Nm^{-2}\,(m^3)^2}{(mol)^2} = Nm^4\,mol^{-2}$

(ii) If units of $p = atm$, units of $V = dm^3$, units of $n = mol$

then, units of $a = \frac{pV^2}{n^2} = \frac{atm.\,(dm^3)^2}{(mol)^2} = atm\,dm^6\,mol^{-2}$

Question 13. Explain the effect of increasing the temperature of a liquid, on intermolecular forces operating between its particles. What will happen to the viscosity of a liquid if its temperature is increased?

Solution. As the temperature of a liquid increases, kinetic energy of the molecules increases which can overcome intermolecular forces. So, the liquid can flow more easily, this results in decrease in viscosity of the liquid.

Question 14. The variation of pressure with volume of the gas at different temperatures can be graphically represented as shown in figure. On the basis of this graph answer the following questions:

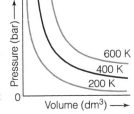

(i) How will the volume of a gas change if its pressure is increased at constant temperature?

(ii) At a constant pressure, how will the volume of a gas change if the temperature is increased from 200 K to 400 K?

Solution.

(i) The volume of a gas will decrease if the pressure on the gas is increased keeping the temperature constant. For example at 200 K when pressure increases from p_1 to p_2, volume of the gas decreases, $V_2 < V_1$.

(ii) On increasing temperature, the volume of a gas will increase if

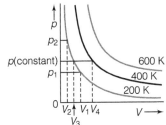

pressure is kept constant. At constant p when we increase the temperature from 200 K to 400 K, the volume of the gas increases, $V_4 > V_3$.

Question 15. Pressure *versus* volume graph for a real gas and an ideal gas are shown in figure. Answer the following questions on the basis of this graph.

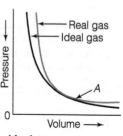

  (i) Interpret the behaviour of real gas with respect to ideal gas at low pressure.
 (ii) Interpret the behaviour of real gas with respect to ideal gas at high pressure.
(iii) Mark the pressure and volume by drawing a line at the point where real gas behaves as an ideal gas.

Solution.

  (i) At low pressure, the real gas shows very small deviation from ideal behaviour because the two curves almost coincide at low pressure.
 (ii) At high pressure, the real gas show large deviations from ideal behaviour as the curves are far apart.
(iii) At point 'A', both the curves intersect each other. At this point real gas behaves as an ideal gas. p_1 and V_1 are the pressure and volume which corresponds to this point A.

Long Answer Type

Question 16. Isotherms of carbon dioxide at various temperatures are represented in figure.

Answer the following questions based on this figure.

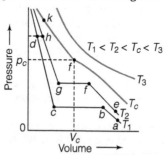

  (i) In which state will CO_2 exist between the points a and b at temperature T_1?
 (ii) At what point will CO_2 start liquefying when temperature is T_1?
(iii) At what point will CO_2 be completely liquefied when temperature is T_2?
(iv) Will condensation take place when the temperature is T_3?
 (v) What portion of the isotherm at T_1 represent liquid and gaseous CO_2 at equilibrium?

Solution.
(i) Gaseous state
(ii) At point b, the plot becomes linear, this shows the phase transition, *i.e.*, liquification of CO_2 starts and at point c, it gets completely liquified.
(iii) Similarly, at temperature T_2, g is the point at which CO_2 will be completely liquified.
(iv) Condensation will not take place at T_3 temperature because $T_3 > T_c$ (critical temperature).
(v) Between b and c, liquid and gaseous CO_2 are in equilibrium.

Question 17. Why does sharp glass edge become smooth on heating it up to its melting point in a flame? Explain which property of liquids is responsible for this phenomenon?

Solution. Sharp glass edges are heated to make them smooth. Because on heating glass melts and the surface of the liquid tends to take the rounded shape at the edges which has minimum surface area. This is called fire polishing of glass.

Question 18. Explain the term 'Laminar flow'. Is the velocity of molecules same in all the layers in laminar flow? Explain your answer.

Solution. When a liquid flows over a fixed surface, the layer of molecules in the immediate contact of surface is stationary. The velocity of the upper layers increases as the distance of layers from the fixed layer increases. This type of flow in which there is a regular gradation of velocity in passing from one layer to the next is called laminar flow. In laminar flow, the velocity of molecules is not same in all the layers because every layer offers some resistance or friction to the layer immediately below it.

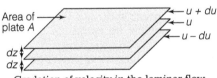

Gradation of velocity in the laminar flow

Chapter 6

Thermodynamics

Important Results

1. A part of the universe which is under investigation is called system and everything else in the universe except system is called surroundings.

2. In an open system, there is exchange of energy and matter between system and surrounding. In a closed system, there is no exchange of matter, but exchange of energy between system and surrounding. In an isolated system, there is no exchange of energy or matter between the system and the surrounding.

3. The state of a system is described by its measurable properties such as T, V, p etc., of the system. These properties of the system are called state variables.

4. A physical quantity is said to be a state function if its value depends only upon the initial state and final state of the system and does not depend upon the path by which this state has been attained. p, T, V, internal energy (U), enthalpy (H), entropy (S) and free energy (G) etc., are some examples of state functions.

5. **Thermodynamic processes**—Isothermal process is carried out at constant temperature, isobaric process is carried out at constant pressure, isochoric process is carried out at constant volume and in adiabatic process, there is no exchange of heat between system and surroundings.

6. Heat absorbed by the system = + ve, heat lost by the system = –ve.

   Work done on the system = +ve and work done by the system = –ve

   Mechanical work, $W = -p_{ex} \Delta V$; where, ΔV is the change in volume of the system by the application of external pressure.

7. Internal energy, U is the energy associated with every substance, depending on the chemical nature, temperature, pressure and volume. It is a state function.

8. First law of thermodynamics is also called law of conservation of energy.

$$\Delta U = q + W$$

   For reversible change under constant temperature, $\Delta U = 0$

$$W_{max} = q = p\Delta V = 2.303 \, nRT \log \frac{V_2}{V_1}$$

For isochoric process, $\Delta V = 0, p\Delta V = 0, \Delta U = q$

For adiabatic change, $q = 0, \Delta U = W_{ad}$

9. The thermodynamic quantity $U + pV$ is called the heat content or enthalpy of the system. Enthalpy change of a system is equal to the heat absorbed or evolved by the system at constant pressure.

$$\Delta H = \Delta U + p\Delta V$$

$$\Delta H = \Delta U + \Delta n_g RT \quad (\Delta n_g = n_{products} - n_{reactants})$$

10. Heat capacity of a system is defined as the amount of heat required to raise the temperature of the system through $1°C$.

Heat capacity of the system, $C = \dfrac{q}{\Delta T}$ (where, q is the heat supplied to a system and ΔT rise in temperature).

11. Specific heat capacity or specific heat c, of a substance is defined as the amount of heat required to raise the temperature of 1 g of the substance through $1°C$.

$$q = mc\Delta T \text{ or } q = C \Delta T$$

12. Molar heat capacity of a substance is defined as the amount of heat required to raise the temperature of one mole of the substance through $1°C$.

$$C_m = \dfrac{C}{n}$$

13. Relationship between C_p and C_V for an ideal gas

For 1 mole of an ideal gas, $C_p - C_V = R$

For n mole of an ideal gas, $C_p - C_V = nR$

14. Enthalpy of reaction, $\Delta_r H$ = sum of enthalpies of products – sum of enthalpies of reactants $= \Sigma a_i H$ (products) $- \Sigma b_i H$ (reactants)

(where, Σ (sigma) represents summation, a_i and b_i represents coefficients of the products and reactants.)

15. Standard enthalpies of formation,

$\Delta_r H° =$ (sum of the standard enthalpies of formation of products) – (sum of the standard enthalpies of formation of reactants)

$$\Delta_r H° = \Sigma a_i \Delta_f H° \text{ (products)} - \Sigma b_i \Delta_f H° \text{ (reactants)}$$

16. **Hess's law of constant heat summation :** If a reaction takes place in several steps then its standard reaction enthalpy is the sum of the standard enthalpies of the intermediate reactions into which the overall reaction may be divided at the same temperature.

$$\Delta_r H = \Delta_r H_1 + \Delta_r H_2 + \Delta_r H_3 \ldots\ldots$$

17. The standard enthalpy of reaction, $\Delta_r H°$ is related to bond enthalpies of the reactants and products in gas phase reaction as:

$\Delta_r H° = \Sigma$ bond enthalpies (reactants) $- \Sigma$ bond enthalpies (products)

18. Entropy is a measure of disorder or randomness. For a spontaneous change, total entropy change is positive. Therefore, for an isolated

system, $\Delta U = 0$, $\Delta S > 0$. Change in entropy, $\Delta S = \frac{q_{rev}}{T}$ for a reversible process. $\frac{q_{rev}}{T}$ is independent of path.

19. Gibbs energy, G is related to entropy and enthalpy changes of the system by the equation;

$$\Delta_r G = \Delta_r H - T\Delta_r S$$

For a spontaneous change, $\Delta G_{sys} < 0$ and at equilibrium, $\Delta G_{sys} = 0$.

20. Relation between Gibbs energy and equilibrium constant,

$$\Delta_r G^\circ = -RT \ln K$$
$$\Delta_r G^\circ = -2.303 \, RT \log K_c$$
$$\Delta_r G^\circ \text{ can be calculated from } \Delta_r G^\circ = \Delta_r H^\circ - T\Delta_r S^\circ$$

Exercises

Question 1. Choose the correct answer. A thermodynamic state function is a quantity

(i) used to determine heat changes.

(ii) whose value is independent of path.

(iii) used to determine pressure-volume work.

(iv) whose value depends on temperature only.

Solution. (ii) A thermodynamic state function is a quantity whose value is independent of path. Its value depends only upon the state of the system.

Question 2. For the process to occur under adiabatic conditions, the correct condition is

(i) $\Delta T = 0$ (ii) $\Delta p = 0$ (iii) $q = 0$ (iv) $w = 0$

Solution. (iii) For the process to occur under adiabatic conditions, $q = 0$, *i.e.*, heat cannot flow from system to surroundings or *vice-versa*.

Question 3. The enthalpies of all the elements in their standard states are

(i) unity   (ii) zero   (iii) < 0   (iv) different for each element.

Solution. (ii) The enthalpies of all elements in their standard states are taken as zero. The standard state of an elementary substance means the most stable form of that substance at 298 K temperature and 1 bar pressure.

Question 4. ΔU° of combustion of methane is $-X$ kJ mol^{-1}. The value of ΔH° is

(i) $= \Delta U^\circ$ (ii) $> \Delta U^\circ$ (iii) $< \Delta U^\circ$ (iv) $= 0$

(i) ΔH° (enthalpy change) is related to ΔU° (internal energy change) by the following relation;

$$\Delta H^\circ = \Delta U^\circ + \Delta n_g RT$$

So, first find Δn_g by writing a balanced chemical equation for the combustion of methane and using the formula Δn_g = total moles of gaseous products – total moles of gaseous reactants.

    (ii) If $\Delta n_g = 0$, then $\Delta H = \Delta U$; If $\Delta n_g > 0$, then $\Delta H > \Delta U$: similarly if $\Delta n_g < 0$ then $\Delta H < \Delta U$

Solution. $CH_4\ (g) + 2O_2\ (g) \longrightarrow CO_2\ (g) + 2H_2O\ (l)$

$$\Delta n_g = (n_p - n_r) = 1 - 3 = -2$$
$$\Delta H^\circ = \Delta U^\circ + \Delta n_g RT$$
$$\Delta H^\circ = -X - 2RT$$

Hence, $\Delta H^\circ < \Delta U^\circ$ [option (iii) is correct]

Question 5. The enthalpy of combustion of methane, graphite and dihydrogen at 298 K are, -890.3 kJ mol^{-1}, -393.5 kJ mol^{-1} and -285.8 kJ mol^{-1} respectively. Enthalpy of formation of $CH_4(g)$ will be

  (i) -74.8 kJ mol^{-1} (ii) -52.27 kJ mol^{-1}
  (iii) $+74.8$ kJ mol^{-1} (iv) $+52.26$ kJ mol ^{1}

    (i) Write the required equation for the formation of 1 mole of methane.

    (ii) Apply Hess's law to calculate $\Delta_f H^\circ$ for methane.

Solution. Required equation for the formation of 1 mole of methane, CH_4 is given by :

$$C(s) + 2H_2\ (g) \longrightarrow CH_4(g); \qquad\qquad \Delta_f H^\circ = ?$$

Given, the enthalpy of combustion of 1 mole of methane is

  (i) $CH_4\ (g) + 2O_2\ (g) \longrightarrow CO_2\ (g) + 2H_2O\ (l);$ $\Delta H = -890.3$ kJ mol^{-1}

the enthalpy of combustion of 1 mole of graphite is

  (ii) $C(s) + O_2\ (g) \longrightarrow CO_2\ (g);$ $\Delta H = -393.5$ kJ mol^{-1}

The enthalpy of combustion of 1 mole of dihydrogen is

  (iii) $H_2\ (g) + \dfrac{1}{2}O_2\ (g) \longrightarrow H_2O\ (l);$ $\Delta H = -285.8$ kJ mol^{-1}

Multiplying Eq. (iii) by 2, we get

  (iv) $2H_2\ (g) + O_2\ (g) \longrightarrow 2H_2O\ (l);$ $\Delta H = -571.6$ kJ mol^{-1}

Adding Eqs. (ii) and (iv), we get

  (v) $C(s) + 2H_2(g) + 2O_2(g) \longrightarrow CO_2(g) + 2H_2O(l);$ $\Delta H = -965.1$ kJ mol^{-1}

Reversing Eqs. (i),

  (vi) $CO_2(g) + 2H_2O(l) \longrightarrow CH_4(g) + 2O_2(g);$ $\Delta H = +890.3$ kJ mol^{-1}

Adding Eqs. (v) and (vi), we get required equation

    $C(s) + 2H_2(g) \longrightarrow CH_4(g);$ $\Delta H = -74.8$ kJ mol^{-1}

Hence, option (i) is correct.

Question 6. A reaction, $A + B \longrightarrow C + D + q$ is found to have a positive entropy change. The reaction will be

(i) possible at high temperature.
(ii) possible only at low temperature.
(iii) not possible at any temperature.
(iv) possible at any temperature.

 For a reaction to be spontaneous, ΔG must be negative.

Solution. (iv) $\Delta G = \Delta H - T\Delta S$

For the given reaction, $\Delta H =$ –ve as it is exothermic, $\Delta S =$ +ve then $\Delta G =$ –ve. So, the reaction will be spontaneous at all temperatures.

Question 7. In a process, 701 J of heat is absorbed by a system and 394 J of work is done by the system. What is the change in internal energy for the process ?

Solution.   Given, $q = +$ 701 J (heat is absorbed, hence q is positive.)

$W = -$ 394 J (work is done by the system, hence W is negative.)
By first law of thermodynamics;
Internal energy change, $\Delta U = q + W$
$$= + 701 \text{ J} + (- 394 \text{ J}) = + 307 \text{ J}.$$
Hence, internal energy of the system increases by 307 J.

Question 8. The reaction of cyanamide, NH_2CN (s), with dioxygen was carried out in a bomb calorimeter, and ΔU was found to be $-$ 742.7 kJ mol^{-1} at 298 K. Calculate the enthalpy change for the reaction at 298 K $(R = 8.314 \times 10^{-3} \text{ kJ K}^{-1} \text{ mol}^{-1})$

$$NH_2CN(s) + \frac{3}{2}O_2(g) \longrightarrow N_2(g) + CO_2(g) + H_2O(l)$$

(i) Enthalpy change ΔH is related to internal energy ΔU as $\Delta H = \Delta U + \Delta n_g RT$
(ii) We have ΔU, R and T, so first calculate Δn_g and then ΔH from all other values.

Solution. $NH_2CN(s) + \frac{3}{2}O_2(g) \longrightarrow N_2(g) + CO_2(g) + H_2O(l)$

Difference of moles of gaseous products and reactants,
$$\Delta n_g = n_p - n_r = 2 - \frac{3}{2} = \frac{1}{2} = 0.5 \text{ mol}$$
$$\Delta H = \Delta U + \Delta n_g RT$$
$$\Delta H = - 742.7 \text{ kJ mol}^{-1} + (0.5 \text{ mol} \times 8.314 \times 10^{-3} \text{ kJ mol}^{-1} \times 298 \text{ K})$$
$$\Delta H = (- 742.7 \text{ kJ} + 1238.786 \times 10^{-3} \text{ kJ}) \text{ mol}^{-1}$$
$$= - 741.46 \text{ kJ mol}^{-1}$$

Question 9. Calculate the number of kJ of heat necessary to raise the temperature of 60.0 g of aluminium from 35°C to 55°C. Molar heat capacity of Al is 24 J mol^{-1} K^{-1}. Molar mass of Al = 27 g mol^{-1}.

Thermodynamics

Solution. Given, mass of Al = 60.0g

Molar mass of Al = $27\,g\,mol^{-1}$

Molar heat capacity, $C = 24\,J\,mol^{-1}\,K^{-1}$

$$\Delta T = 55°C - 35°C = 20°C \text{ or } 20K$$
$$\text{Heat, } q = n.C.\Delta T$$
$$q = \frac{60}{27} \times 24\,J\,mol^{-1}\,K^{-1} \times 20K \qquad \left(n = \frac{60}{27}\,mol\right)$$
$$= 1066.66\,J = 1.067\,kJ$$

Question 10. Calculate the enthalpy change on freezing of 1.0 mole of water at $10.0°C$ to ice at $-10.0°C$. $\Delta_{fus}H = 6.03\,kJ\,mol^{-1}$ at $0°C$.

$$C_p[H_2O(l)] = 75.3\,J\,mol^{-1}\,K^{-1}$$
$$C_p[H_2O(s)] = 36.8\,J\,mol^{-1}\,K^{-1}$$

Conversion of 1 mole of water at 10°C to ice at −10°C involves the following steps:

1 mol $H_2O(l)$ at 10°C ⟶ 1 mol $H_2O(l)$ at 0°C $\Delta H_1 = C_p H_2O(l) \times \Delta T$

1 mol $H_2O(l)$ at 0°C ⟶ 1 mol $H_2O(s)$ at 0°C $\Delta H_2 = \Delta H_{freezing}$

1 mol $H_2O(s)$ at 0°C ⟶1 mol $H_2O(s)$ at 10°C $\Delta H_3 = C_p H_2O(s) \times \Delta T$;

$\Delta T = 10K$ and we know that according to Hess's law, total enthalpy change, $\Delta H = H_1 + H_2 + H_3$ so first calculate $\Delta H_1, \Delta H_2, \Delta H_3$ and then ΔH.

Solution. Enthalpy change for the conversion of 1 mole liquid water at 10°C into 1 mole liquid water at 0°C,

$$\Delta H_1 = C_p H_2O(l) \times \Delta T$$
$$= -75.3\,J\,mol^{-1}\,K^{-1} \times 10K = -753\,J\,mol^{-1}$$

Enthalpy of fusion,

$$\Delta H_2 = \Delta H_{freezing} = -\Delta H_{fusion} = -6.03\,kJ\,mol^{-1}$$

Enthalpy change for the conversion of 1 mole of ice at 0°C to 1 mole of ice at 10°C,

$$\Delta H_3 = C_p H_2O(s) \times \Delta T = -36.8\,J\,mol^{-1}\,K^{-1} \times 10K$$
$$= -368\,J\,mol^{-1}$$
$$\Delta H_{total} = -(0.753 + 6.03 + 0.368)\,kJ\,mol^{-1} = -7.151\,kJ\,mol^{-1}$$

Note *Heat is evolved in the process of cooling (freezing) so each step will have a negative sign with ΔH.*

Question 11. Enthalpy of combustion of carbon to CO_2 is $-393.5\,kJ\,mol^{-1}$. Calculate the heat released upon formation of 35.2 g of CO_2 from carbon and dioxygen gas. (Molar mass of $CO_2 = 44\,g\,mol^{-1}$).

Solution. The reaction for the combustion of carbon into CO_2 is

$$C(s) + O_2(g) \longrightarrow CO_2(g); \Delta H = -393.5\,kJ\,mol^{-1}$$
$$44\,g$$

Heat released in the formation of 44 g $CO_2 = 393.5\,kJ$

$\therefore$ Heat released in the formation of 35.2 g CO_2

$$= \frac{393.5 \text{ kJ} \times 35.2g}{44g} = 314.8 \text{ kJ}.$$

Question 12. Enthalpies of formation of $CO(g)$, $CO_2(g)$, $N_2O(g)$ and $N_2O_4(g)$ are $-110, -393, 81$ and 9.7 kJ mol^{-1} respectively. Find the value of $\Delta_r H$ for the reaction,

$$N_2O_4(g) + 3CO(g) \longrightarrow N_2O(g) + 3CO_2(g)$$

Solution. Heat of reaction, $\Delta_r H° = \Sigma \Delta_f H°_{products} - \Sigma \Delta_f H°_{reactants}$

$= [\Delta_f H° (N_2O) + 3\Delta_f H° (CO_2)] - [\Delta_f H° (N_2O_4) + 3\Delta_f H° (CO)]$
$= [81 + (3 \times -393)] - [9.7 + (3 \times -110)]$ kJ
$= -777.7 \text{ kJ} \approx -778 \text{ kJ}.$

Question 13. Given, $N_2(g) + 3H_2(g) \longrightarrow 2NH_3(g)$;

$$\Delta_r H° = -92.4 \text{ kJ mol}^{-1}$$

What is the standard enthalpy of formation of NH_3 gas ?

Standard enthalpy of formation means heat released in the formation of 1 mole of substance.

Solution. Given, $N_2(g) + 3H_2(g) \longrightarrow 2NH_3(g)$ $\Delta_r H° = -92.4$ kJ mol^{-1}
Chemical reaction for the enthalpy of formation of $NH_3(g)$ is as follows :

$$\frac{1}{2}N_2(g) + \frac{3}{2}H_2(g) \longrightarrow NH_3(g)$$

Therefore, $\Delta_f H° = \dfrac{-92.4}{2} = -46.2$ kJ mol^{-1}

Question 14. Calculate the standard enthalpy of formation of $CH_3OH(l)$ from the following data :

$$CH_3OH(l) + \frac{3}{2}O_2(g) \longrightarrow CO_2(g) + 2H_2O(l); \ \Delta_r H° = -726 \text{ kJ mol}^{-1}$$

$$C_{(graphite)} + O_2(g) \longrightarrow CO_2(g); \qquad \Delta_c H° = -393 \text{ kJ mol}^{-1}$$

$$H_2(g) + \frac{1}{2}O_2(g) \longrightarrow H_2O(l) ; \qquad \Delta_f H° = -286 \text{ kJ mol}^{-1}$$

Firstly write the required chemical equation for the formation of 1 mole of methanol (*l*) and then calculate $\Delta_f H°$ for the formation of methanol by adding all the equation in such a way so that it give the required equation (*i.e.*, apply Hess's Law)

Solution. Required reaction for the formation of methanol is as follows

$$C(s) + 2H_2(g) + \frac{1}{2}O_2(g) \longrightarrow CH_3OH(l); \qquad \Delta_f H° = ?$$

Given, enthalpy for the combustion of methanol;
(i) $CH_3OH(l) + \frac{3}{2}O_2(g) \longrightarrow CO_2(g) + 2H_2O(l); \ \Delta_r H° = -726$ kJ mol^{-1}

Enthalpy for the formation of 1 mole of $CO_2(g)$;
(ii) $C(s) + O_2(g) \longrightarrow CO_2(g)$; $\qquad\qquad \Delta_f H° = -393$ kJ mol^{-1}

Enthalpy for the formation of 2 moles of $H_2O(l)$;

(iii) $H_2(g) + \dfrac{1}{2}O_2(g) \longrightarrow H_2O(l)$; $\Delta_f H° = -286$ kJ mol^{-1}

Multiplying Eq. (iii) by 2 [because 2 moles $H_2O(l)$ are formed in equation (i)] we get,

(iv) $2H_2(g) + O_2(g) \longrightarrow 2H_2O(l)$; $\Delta_f H° = -572$ kJ mol^{-1}

Summing up the Eqs. (ii) and (iv), we get

(v) $C(s) + 2H_2(g) + 2O_2(g) \longrightarrow CO_2(g) + 2H_2O(l)$; $\Delta_f H° = -965$ kJ mol^{-1}

Reversing Eq. (i), we get

(vi) $CO_2(g) + 2H_2O(l) \longrightarrow CH_3OH(l) + \dfrac{3}{2}O_2(g)$; $\Delta_f H° = +726$ kJ mol^{-1}

Adding Eqs. (v) and (vi) we get required equation :

$C(s) + 2H_2(g) + \dfrac{1}{2}O_2(g) \longrightarrow CH_3OH(l)$; $\Delta_f H° = -239$ kJ mol^{-1}

Question 15. Calculate the enthalpy change for the process :
$$CCl_4(g) \longrightarrow C(g) + 4Cl(g)$$
and calculate the bond enthalpy of C—Cl in $CCl_4(g)$.
$$\Delta_{vap} H°(CCl_4) = 30.5 \text{ kJ mol}^{-1}.$$
$$\Delta_f H°(CCl_4) = -135.5 \text{ kJ mol}^{-1}.$$
$$\Delta_a H°(C) = 715.0 \text{ kJ mol}^{-1},$$
where, $\Delta_a H°$ is enthalpy of atomisation, $\Delta_a H°(Cl_2) = 242$ kJ mol^{-1}.

Solution. Given,

(i) $CCl_4(l) \longrightarrow CCl_4(g)$; $\Delta_{vap} H° = +30.5$ kJ mol^{-1}

(ii) $C(s) + 2Cl_2(g) \longrightarrow CCl_4(l)$; $\Delta_f H° = -135.5$ kJ mol^{-1}

(iii) $C(s) \longrightarrow C(g)$; $\Delta_a H° = 715.0$ kJ mol^{-1}

(iv) $Cl_2(g) \longrightarrow 2Cl(g)$; $\Delta_a H° = 242$ kJ mol^{-1}

Multiplying Eq. (iv) by 2, we get

(v) $2Cl_2(g) \longrightarrow 4Cl(g)$; $\Delta_a H° = 484.0$ kJ mol^{-1}

Adding Eqs. (iii) and (v), we get

(vi) $C(s) + 2Cl_2(g) \longrightarrow C(g) + 4Cl(g)$; $\Delta H = 1199$ kJ mol^{-1}

Reversing Eqs. (i) and (ii), we get

(vii) $CCl_4(g) \longrightarrow CCl_4(l)$; $\Delta H = -30.5$ kJ mol^{-1}

(viii) $CCl_4(l) \longrightarrow C(s) + 2Cl_2(g)$; $\Delta H = +135.5$ kJ mol^{-1}

Adding Eqs. (vi), (vii) and (viii), we get

$CCl_4(g) \longrightarrow C(g) + 4Cl(g)$; $\Delta H = 1304$ kJ mol^{-1}

Bond enthalpy of C—Cl bond in $CCl_4 = \dfrac{1304}{4} = 326$ kJ mol^{-1}.

$$(\because \text{ There are four C—Cl bonds in } CCl_4, \; Cl-\underset{\underset{Cl}{|}}{\overset{\overset{Cl}{|}}{C}}-Cl)$$

Question 16. For an isolated system, $\Delta U = 0$, what will be ΔS ?

Solution. For an isolated system, $\Delta U = 0$ and for a spontaneous process, total entropy change must be positive. For example, consider the diffusion of two gases A and B into each other in a closed container which is isolated from the surroundings. The two gases A and B are separated by a movable partition. When partition is removed, the gases begin to diffuse into each other and the system becomes more disordered. It shows that $\Delta S > 0$ and $\Delta U = 0$ for this process.

Moreover, $\qquad \Delta S = \dfrac{q_{rev}}{T} = \dfrac{\Delta H}{T} = \dfrac{\Delta U + p\Delta V}{T} = \dfrac{p\Delta V}{T} \qquad (\because \Delta U = 0)$

i.e., $\qquad\qquad T\Delta S$ or $\Delta S > 0$

Question 17. For the reaction at 298 K,

$$2A + B \longrightarrow C$$

$\Delta H = 400$ kJ mol^{-1} and $\Delta S = 0.2$ kJ K^{-1} mol^{-1}

At what temperature will the reaction become spontaneous considering ΔH and ΔS to be constant over the temperature range ?

 For a reaction to be spontaneous, $\Delta G \leq 0$. So, calculate the temperature at which $\Delta G = 0$ by using the relation, $\Delta G = \Delta H - T\Delta S$

Solution. Given, $\Delta H = 400$ kJ mol^{-1}, $\Delta S = 0.2$ kJ K^{-1}mol^{-1},

Gibbs free energy, $\Delta G = \Delta H - T\Delta S$

$$0 = 400 \text{ kJ mol}^{-1} - T \times 0.2 \text{ kJ K}^{-1} \text{ mol}^{-1}$$

Temperature, $T = \dfrac{400 \text{ kJ mol}^{-1}}{0.2 \text{ kJ K}^{-1} \text{ mol}^{-1}} = 2000 \text{ K}$

Therefore, above 2000K, the reaction will become spontaneous.

Note *If $\Delta G < 0$, the process is spontaneous and if $\Delta G > 0$, the process is non-spontaneous.*

Question 18. For the reaction, $2Cl(g) \longrightarrow Cl_2(g)$, what are the signs of ΔH and ΔS ?

Solution. In the given reaction, a molecule of Cl_2 is formed from its two gaseous atoms and the energy is released with the formation of bond. Hence, ΔH is –ve. In this reaction, randomness (entropy) also decreases because 2 mol atoms of Cl have more randomness than one mole molecules of chlorine. Hence, ΔS is –ve.

Question 19. For the reaction,

$$2A(g) + B(g) \longrightarrow 2D(g); \quad \Delta U° = - 10.5 \text{ kJ and } \Delta S° = - 44.1 \text{ JK}^{-1}.$$

Calculate $\Delta G°$ for the reaction, and predict whether the reaction may occur spontaneously.

$(R = 8.314 \times 10^{-3} \text{ kJ K}^{-1} \text{ mol}^{-1}, T = 298 \text{ K})$

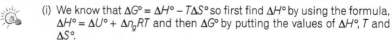
(i) We know that $\Delta G° = \Delta H° - T\Delta S°$ so first find $\Delta H°$ by using the formula, $\Delta H° = \Delta U° + \Delta n_g RT$ and then $\Delta G°$ by putting the values of $\Delta H°$, T and $\Delta S°$.
(ii) For a spontaneous reaction $\Delta G° \leq 0$

Thermodynamics 139

Solution. $2A(g) + B(g) \longrightarrow 2D(g); \Delta n_g = n_p - n_r = 2 - 3 = -1$

$\Delta H° = \Delta U° + \Delta n_g RT$

$\Delta H° = -10.5 \text{ kJ} + (-1 \times 8.314 \times 10^{-3} \text{ kJ K}^{-1} \text{ mol}^{-1} \times 298\text{K})$

$\Delta H° = -10.5 + (-2.477) \text{ kJ mol}^{-1}$

$\Delta H° = -12.977 \text{ kJ mol}^{-1}$

$\Delta G° = \Delta H° - T\Delta S°$

$\Delta G° = -12.977 \text{ kJ mol}^{-1} - (298 \text{ K} \times -44.1 \times 10^{-3} \text{ kJ K}^{-1} \text{ mol}^{-1})$

$\Delta G° = -12.977 \text{ kJ mol}^{-1} + 13.14 \text{ kJ mol}^{-1} = +0.165 \text{ kJ mol}^{-1}$

The reaction will not occur spontaneously because $\Delta G°$ is positive.

Question 20. The equilibrium constant for a reaction is 10. What will be the value of $\Delta G°$? $R = 8.314 \text{ JK}^{-1} \text{ mol}^{-1}, T = 300$ K.

Solution. $\Delta G° = -2.303 \, RT \log K_c$

Given, $R = 8.314 \text{ JK}^{-1} \text{ mol}^{-1}, T = 300 \text{ K}, K_c = 10$

$\Delta G° = -2.303 \times 8.314 \text{ JK}^{-1} \text{ mol}^{-1} \times 300 \text{ K} \times \log 10$ $(\log 10 = 1)$

$= -5744.14 \text{ J mol}^{-1}$

Question 21. Comment on the thermodynamic stability of $NO(g)$, given

$$\frac{1}{2} N_2(g) + \frac{1}{2} O_2(g) \longrightarrow NO(g); \quad \Delta_r H° = 90 \text{ kJ mol}^{-1}$$

$$NO(g) + \frac{1}{2} O_2(g) \longrightarrow NO_2(g); \Delta_r H° = -74 \text{ kJ mol}^{-1}$$

Solution. $NO(g)$ is unstable because formation of NO is endothermic (energy is absorbed), but $NO_2(g)$ is formed because its formation is exothermic (energy is released). Therefore, unstable $NO(g)$ converts into stable $NO_2(g)$.

Question 22. Calculate the entropy change in surroundings when 1.00 mole of $H_2O(l)$ is formed under standard conditions. $\Delta_f H° = -286 \text{ kJ mol}^{-1}$.

Solution. Enthalpy change for the formation of 1 mole of $H_2O(l)$,

$$H_2(g) + \frac{1}{2} O_2(g) \longrightarrow H_2O(l); \quad \Delta_f H° = -286 \text{ kJ mol}^{-1}$$

Energy released in the above reaction, is absorbed by the surroundings. It means $q_{surr} = +286 \text{ kJ mol}^{-1}$.

$$\Delta S = \frac{q_{surr}}{T} = \frac{+286 \text{ kJ mol}^{-1}}{298 \text{ K}}$$

$$= 0.9597 \text{ kJ K}^{-1}\text{mol}^{-1} = 959.7 \text{ JK}^{-1}\text{mol}^{-1}$$

Selected NCERT Exemplar Problems

Short Answer Type

Question 1. 18.0 g water completely vaporises at 100°C and 1 bar pressure and the enthalpy change in the process is 40.79 kJ mol^{-1}. What will be the enthalpy change for vaporising two moles of water under the same conditions? What is the standard enthalpy of vaporisation for water?

Solution. 18.0 g H_2O = 1 mol H_2O

Enthalpy change for vaporising 1 mole of H_2O = 40.79 kJ

∴ Enthalpy change for vaporising 2 moles of H_2O = 2 × 40.79 kJ

$$= 81.58 \text{ kJ}$$

Standard enthalpy of vaporisation at 100°C and 1 bar pressure,

$$\Delta_{vap}H° = + 40.79 \text{ kJ mol}^{-1}$$

Question 2. Standard molar enthalpy of formation, $\Delta_f H°$ is just a special case of enthalpy of reaction, $\Delta_r H°$. Is the $\Delta_r H°$ for the following reaction same as $\Delta_f H°$? Give reason for your answer.

$$CaO(s) + CO_2(g) \longrightarrow CaCO_3(s); \qquad \Delta_f H° = -178.3 \text{ kJ mol}^{-1}$$

Solution. The standard enthalpy change for the formation of one mole of a compound from its elements in their most stable states (reference states) is called standard molar enthalpy of formation, $\Delta_f H°$.

$$Ca(s) + C(s) + \frac{3}{2}O_2(g) \longrightarrow CaCO_3(s); \quad \Delta_f H°$$

This reaction is different from the given reaction.

Hence, $\Delta_r H° \neq \Delta_f H°$

Question 3. The value of $\Delta_f H°$ for NH_3 is – 91.8 kJ mol^{-1}. Calculate the enthalpy change for the following reaction,

$$2NH_3(g) \longrightarrow N_2(g) + 3H_2(g)$$

Solution. Given, $\frac{1}{2}N_2(g) + \frac{3}{2}H_2(g) \longrightarrow NH_3(g); \Delta_f H° = -91.8 \text{ kJ mol}^{-1}$

($\Delta_f H°$ means enthalpy of formation of 1 mole of NH_3)

∴ Enthalpy change for the formation of 2 moles of NH_3

$$N_2(g) + 3H_2(g) \longrightarrow 2NH_3(g); \quad \Delta_r H° = 2 \times -91.8 = -183.6 \text{ kJ mol}^{-1}$$

and for the reverse reaction,

$$2NH_3(g) \longrightarrow N_2(g) + 3H_2(g); \qquad \Delta_r H° = + 183.6 \text{ kJ mol}^{-1}$$

Thermodynamics

Question 4. The enthalpy of atomisation for the reaction, $CH_4(g) \longrightarrow C(g) + 4H(g)$ is 1665 kJ mol^{-1}. What is the bond energy of C—H bond?

Solution. In CH_4, there are four C—H bonds. The enthalpy of atomisation of 1 mole of CH_4 means dissociation of four moles of C—H bond.

$\therefore$ C—H bond energy per mol $= \dfrac{1665 \text{ kJ}}{4 \text{ mol}} = 416.25$ kJ mol^{-1}

Question 5. Use the following data to calculate $\Delta_{lattice}H°$ for NaBr.

$\Delta_{sub}H°$ for sodium metal = 108.4 kJ mol^{-1}
Ionization enthalpy of sodium = 496 kJ mol^{-1}
Electron gain enthalpy of bromine = $-$ 325 kJ mol^{-1}
Bond dissociation enthalpy of bromine = 192 kJ mol^{-1}
$\Delta_f H°$ for NaBr(s) = $-$ 360.1 kJ mol^{-1}

Solution. Born Haber cycle for the formation of NaBr is as

Na(s) $\qquad\qquad + \dfrac{1}{2}Br_2(g)$ $\xrightarrow{\Delta_f H° = -360.1 \text{ kJ}}$ NaBr(s)

$\downarrow \Delta_{sub}H° = 108.4$ kJ mol^{-1} $\qquad \downarrow \Delta_{diss}H° = 192/2$ kJ

Na(g) $\qquad\qquad\qquad\qquad$ Br(g)

$\downarrow$ IE = 496 kJ mol^{-1} $\qquad\qquad \downarrow \Delta_{eg}H° = -325$ kJ mol^{-1}

Na$^+(g)$ $\qquad\qquad\qquad\qquad$ Br$^-(g)$

$\qquad\qquad\qquad -U$ (Lattice enthalpy)

By applying Hess's law,
$$\Delta_f H° = \Delta_{sub}H° + IE + \Delta_{diss}H° + \Delta_{eq}H° + U$$
$$- 360.1 = 108.4 + 496 + 96 + (- 325) - U$$
$$U = + 735.5 \text{ kJ mol}^{-1}$$

Question 6. At 298 K, K_p for the reaction, $N_2O_4(g) \rightleftharpoons 2NO_2(g)$ is 0.98. Predict whether the reaction is spontaneous or not.

Solution. $\Delta_r G° = - 2.303 \, RT \log K_p$

Here $K_p = 0.98$, *i.e.*, $K_p < 1$ therefore, $\Delta_r G°$ is positive. Hence, the reaction is non-spontaneous.

Question 7. A sample of 1.0 mole of a monoatomic ideal gas is taken through a cyclic process of expansion and compression as shown in figure. What will be the value of ΔH for the cycle as a whole?

Solution. The net enthalpy change, ΔH for a cyclic process is zero as enthalpy change is a state function.

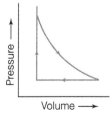

Question 8. Which quantity out of $\Delta_r G$ and $\Delta_r G^\circ$ will be zero at equilibrium?

Solution. $\Delta_r G = \Delta_r G^\circ + RT \ln K$

At equilibrium, $0 = \Delta_r G^\circ + RT \ln K$ ($\because \Delta_r G = 0$)

or $\Delta_r G^\circ = -RT \ln K$

$\Delta_r G^\circ = 0$ when $K = 1$

For all other values of K, $\Delta_r G^\circ$ will be non-zero.

Question 9. Predict the change in internal energy for an isolated system at constant volume.

Solution. For isolated system there is no transfer of energy as heat or work, so according to the first law of thermodynamics,

$$\Delta U = q + W$$
$$\Delta U = 0 + 0 = 0$$

Question 10. Expansion of a gas in vacuum is called free-expansion. Calculate the work done and the change in internal energy when 1 L of ideal gas expands isothermally into vacuum until its total volume is 5 L?

Solution. Workdone, $W = -p_{ext} (V_2 - V_1)$

As $p_{ext} = 0$, so $W = -0 (5 - 1) = 0$

For isothermal expansion, $\Delta U = 0$ as $\Delta T = 0$

Question 11. Heat capacity (C_p) is an extensive property but specific heat (C) is an intensive property. What will be the relation between C_p and C for 1 mole of water?

Solution. For water, molar heat capacity, $C_p = 18 \times$ specific heat, C

Specific heat, $C = 4.18$ $Jg^{-1}K^{-1}$ (for water)

Heat capacity, $C_p = 18 \times 4.18$ $JK^{-1} = 75.3$ JK^{-1}

Question 12. If the combustion of 1 g of graphite produces 20.7 kJ of heat, what will be molar enthalpy change? Give the significance of sign also.

Solution. Molar enthalpy change for the combustion of graphite, ΔH

= enthalpy of combustion of 1 g graphite $\times$ molar mass

$$\Delta H = -20.7 \text{ kJ g}^{-1} \times 12 \text{ g mol}^{-1}$$
$$\Delta H = -2.48 \times 10^2 \text{ kJ mol}^{-1}$$

Negative sign in the value of ΔH indicates that the reaction is exothermic.

Question 13. The enthalpy of vaporisation of CCl_4 is 30.5 kJ mol^{-1}. Calculate the heat required for the vaporisation of 284 g of CCl_4 at constant pressure (molar mass of $CCl_4 = 154$ g mol^{-1})

Solution. 1 mol of $CCl_4 = 154$ g

$\Delta_{vap} H$ for 154 g $CCl_4 = 30.5$ kJ

$\therefore$ $\Delta_{vap} H$ for 284 g $CCl_4 = \dfrac{30.5 \times 284}{154}$ kJ $= 56.25$ kJ

Thermodynamics

Question 14. What will be the work done on an ideal gas enclosed in a cylinder, when it is compressed by a constant external pressure, p_{ext} in a single step as shown in figure ? Explain graphically.

Solution. Suppose total volume of the gas is V_i and pressure of the gas inside cylinder is p. After compression by constant external pressure, (p_{ext}) in a single step, final volume of the gas becomes V_f.

Then, volume change, $\Delta V = (V_f - V_i)$

If W is the work done on the system by movement of the piston, then

$$W = p_{ext} (-\Delta V)$$
$$W = -p_{ext} (V_f - V_i)$$

This can be calculated from p-V graph as shown in the side figure. Work done is equal to the shaded area ABV_fV_i.

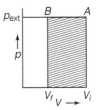

The negative sign in this expression is required to obtain conventional sign for W, which will be positive, Because in case of compression work is done on the system, so ΔV will be negative.

Question 15. How will you calculate the work done on an ideal gas in a compression, when change in pressure is carried out in infinite steps?

Solution. When compression is carried out in infinite steps with change in pressure, it is a reversible process. Work done on the gas is represented by the shaded area.

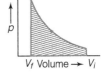

Question 16. Enthalpy diagram for a particular reaction is given in figure. Is it possible to decide spontaneity of a reaction from given diagram. Explain.

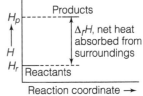

Solution. No, enthalpy is one of the contributing factors in deciding spontaneity but it is not the only factor. Another contributory factor, entropy factor has also to be taken into consideration.

Question 17. 1.0 mole of a monoatomic ideal gas is expanded from state (1) to state (2) as shown in figure. Calculate the work done for the expansion of gas from state (1) to state (2) at 298 K.

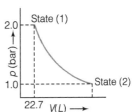

Solution. The given diagram represents that the process is carried out in infinite steps, hence it is isothermal reversible expansion of the ideal gas from pressure 2.0 atm to 1.0 atm at 298 K.

$$W = -2.303 \, nRT \, \log \frac{p_1}{p_2}$$

$$W = -2.303 \times 1 \, mol \times 8.314 \, JK^{-1}mol^{-1} \times 298 \, K \, \log 2 \qquad \left(\because \frac{p_1}{p_2} = \frac{2}{1} \right)$$

$$W = -2.303 \times 1 \times 8.314 \times 298 \times 0.3010 \, J$$
$$W = -1717.46 \, J$$

Long Answer Type

Question 18. Extensive properties depend on the quantity of matter but intensive properties do not. Explain whether the following properties are extensive or intensive. Mass, internal energy, pressure, heat capacity, molar heat capacity, density, mole fraction, specific heat, temperature and molarity.

Solution. Extensive properties—mass, internal energy, heat capacity. Intensive properties—pressure, molar heat capacity, density, mole fraction, specific heat, temperature and molarity.

Ratio of two extensive properties is always intensive.

$$\frac{\text{Extensive}}{\text{Extensive}} = \text{Intensive}$$

So, mole fraction and molarity are intensive properties.

Question 19. Graphically show the total work done in an expansion when the state of an ideal gas is changed reversibly and isothermally from (p_i, V_i) to $(p_f \cdot V_f)$. With the help of a pV plot compare the work done in the above case with that carried out against a constant external pressure p_f.

Solution.
(i) Reversible work is represented by the combined areas ABC and BCV_iV_f.

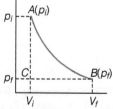

(ii) Work against constant pressure, p_f is represented by the area BCV_iV_f

Work (i) > work (ii)

Chapter 7

Equilibrium

Important Results

1. Equilibrium is a dynamic process. It is established in a system when reactants combine to form products at the same rate at which products combine to form reactants.
2. Chemical equilibrium can be approached from either sides. A catalyst can hasten the approach of equilibrium but does not alter the state of equilibrium.
3. Systems can be homogeneous or heterogeneous.
4. For a reaction in equilibrium,

$$aA + bB \rightleftharpoons cC + dD$$

$$K_c = \frac{[C]^c[D]^d}{[A]^a[B]^b} \qquad \text{(in terms of active masses)}$$

$$K_p = \frac{p_C^c p_D^d}{p_A^a p_B^b} \qquad \text{(in terms of partial pressures)}$$

5. Partial pressure of solid is taken as unity and in the calculation of partial pressure of solids, their number of moles are not considered. Molar concentration of pure solid or pure liquid is constant.

6. $K_p = K_c (RT)^{\Delta n_g}$ and $\Delta n_g = (c + d) - (a + b)$

   While calculating Δn_g, take only gaseous species

7. For,

$$A + B \rightleftharpoons C + D; \qquad\qquad K_c = K$$

$$C + D \rightleftharpoons A + B; \qquad\qquad K_c' = \frac{1}{K}$$

$$2A + 2B \rightleftharpoons 2C + 2D; \qquad\qquad K_c'' = K^2$$

$$\frac{A}{2} + \frac{B}{2} \rightleftharpoons \frac{C}{2} + \frac{D}{2}; \qquad\qquad K_c''' = \sqrt{K}$$

8. Reaction quotient, Q_c for reversible reaction,

$$A + B \rightleftharpoons C + D; \qquad Q_c = \frac{[C][D]}{[A][B]}$$

   Q is taken before equilibrium is attained.
   If $Q_c = K_c$ then system is in equilibrium.

If $Q_c > K_c$ then system proceeds in backward side to attain equilibrium.

If $Q_c < K_c$ then system proceeds in forward side to attain equilibrium.

9. Relationship between equilibrium constant (K_c), reaction quotient (Q_c) and Gibbs energy (G),

$$\Delta G = \Delta G° + RT \ln Q_c$$

At equilibrium when $\Delta G = 0$ and $Q_c = K_c$ then, $\Delta G° = -RT \ln K_c$

$$\Delta G° = -2.303 \, RT \log K_c$$

10. $\Delta G° = -nFE°_{cell}$ (where $E°_{cell}$ = standard emf and n is the number of electrons.)

and $E°_{cell} = \dfrac{2.303RT}{nF} \log K_c$

11. **Le-Chatelier's principle** It states that a change in any of the factors that determine the equilibrium conditions of a system will cause the system to change in such a manner so as to reduce or to counteract the effect of the change.

Or

If a stress is applied to a reaction mixture at equilibrium, reaction occurs in that direction that relieves the stress.

12. **Acid-Base Theory**

(i) **Arrhenius concept** Acid ionises in water to give H_3O^+ ion while base ionises to give OH^- ion.

(ii) **Bronsted-Lowry's protonic concept** Acid is H^+ ion donor and base is H^+ ion acceptor. HCl and Cl^- is a conjugate acid-base pair. If acid is weak, its conjugate base is strong and *vice-versa*.

A substance that can accept H^+ ion as well as can donate H^+ ion is called amphiprotic.

$$H_3O^+ \underset{+H^+}{\overset{-H^+}{\rightleftharpoons}} \underset{\text{Amphiprotic}}{H_2O} \rightleftharpoons H^+ + OH^-$$

(iii) **Lewis concept** Lewis acid is an electron pair acceptor, and Lewis base is an electron pair donor. All Lewis bases are Bronsted-Lowry bases and *vice-versa*.

13. Ionic product of water, $K_w = [H_3O^+][OH^-] = 1 \times 10^{-14}$ at 298 K.

14. In a mixture of acid and base, resultant is

(a) acidic mixture if N_1V_1 (acid) $> N_2V_2$ (base)

$$[H_3O^+] = \frac{N_1V_1 - N_2V_2}{V_1 + V_2}$$

(b) basic mixture if N_2V_2 (base) $> N_1V_1$ (acid)

$$[OH^-] = \frac{N_2V_2 - N_1V_1}{V_1 + V_2}$$

(c) neutral mixture if $N_1 V_1$ (acid) $= N_2 V_2$ (base)
$$K_a \cdot K_b = K_w = 1 \times 10^{-14}$$
where, K_a is the ionization constant of acid and K_b is the ionization constant of base.

$$HA + H_2O \rightleftharpoons H_3O^+ + A^-; K_a \quad (A^- + H_2O \rightleftharpoons HA + OH^-; K_b)$$

15. $pK_a + pK_b = pK_w = 14$
$$pH = -\log[H_3O^+]$$
$$pOH = -\log[OH^-]$$
$$pK_a = -\log K_a \quad \text{and} \quad pK_b = -\log K_b$$
$$pH + pOH = 14 = pK_w$$

16. Acidic solution has $pH < 7$, basic solution has $pH > 7$ and neutral solution has $pH = 7$.

17. For a weak acid by Ostwald dilution law,
$$K_a = \frac{C\alpha^2}{(1-\alpha)} = C\alpha^2$$
and for a weak base, $K_b = \dfrac{C\alpha^2}{(1-\alpha)} = C\alpha^2$
$$[H^+] = \sqrt{K_a C}, \ pH = \frac{1}{2}[pK_a - \log C]$$
$$[OH^-] = \sqrt{K_b C}, \ pOH = \frac{1}{2}[pK_b - \log C]$$

18. Hydrolysis of salts and pH of their solutions
(i) **Salt of strong acid and weak base**, e.g., NH_4Cl, its aqueous solution is acidic due to hydrolysis of cation.
$$NH_4^+ + H_2O \rightleftharpoons NH_4OH + H^+$$
Degree of hydrolysis, $h = \sqrt{\dfrac{K_w}{K_b C}}$

Hydrolysis constant, $K_h = \dfrac{K_w}{K_b}$
$$pH = 7 - \frac{pK_b}{2} - \frac{\log C}{2}$$

(ii) **Salt of weak acid and strong base**, e.g., CH_3COONa, its aqueous solution is basic due to anionic hydrolysis.
$$CH_3COO^- + H_2O \rightleftharpoons CH_3COOH + OH^-$$
Degree of hydrolysis, $h = \sqrt{\dfrac{K_w}{K_a \cdot C}}$
$$K_h = K_w / K_a$$
$$pH = 7 + \frac{pK_a}{2} + \frac{\log C}{2}$$

(iii) **Salt of weak acid and weak base,** *e.g.,* CH_3COONH_4, its aqueous solution may be neutral or weakly acidic or basic depending upon the nature of acid and base.

$$CH_3COO^- + NH_4^+ + H_2O \rightleftharpoons CH_3COOH + NH_4OH$$

Degree of hydrolysis, $h = \sqrt{\dfrac{K_w}{K_a \cdot K_b}}$

$$K_h = \frac{K_w}{K_a \cdot K_b}$$

$$pH = 7 + \left(\frac{pK_a - pK_b}{2}\right)$$

$pH = 7$ if $pK_a = pK_b$
$pH < 7$ if $pK_a < pK_b$
$pH > 7$ if $pK_a > pK_b$

For amphiprotic anion (as HCO_3^-)

$$pH = \frac{pK_1 + pK_2}{2}$$

19. **Buffer solution** The solutions which resist the change in pH on dilution or with the addition of small amounts of acid or alkali are called buffer solutions.

20. Solubility product of the sparingly soluble salt, A_xB_y with solubility $(s\ mol\ L^{-1})$ in saturated solution,

$$A_xB_y \rightleftharpoons xA^{y+} + yB^{x-}$$

$$K_{sp} = x^x \cdot y^y (s)^{x+y}$$

$$s = (K_{sp} / x^x \cdot y^y)^{1/x+y}$$

21. **Common-ion effect** Ionization of weak electrolyte is decreased in the presence of common-ion.

22. Salt analysis of inorganic mixture depends on common-ion effect and values of solubility products. Solute AB is precipitated if $[A^+][B^-] > K_{sp}$.

Exercises

Question 1. A liquid is in equilibrium with its vapour in a sealed container at a fixed temperature. The volume of the container is suddenly increased.

(a) What is the initial effect of change on vapour pressure ?
(b) How do rates of evaporation and condensation change initially ?
(c) What happens when equilibrium is restored finally and what will be the final vapour pressure ?

Solution.
$$A(l) \longrightarrow A(g)$$
$$\text{Low pressure} \qquad \text{High pressure}$$

If volume is increased at constant temperature, pressure decreases, since, $p \propto \dfrac{1}{V}$ at constant temperature.

(a) Decrease in pressure shift the equilibrium in the direction of high pressure *i.e.*, more vapours are formed hence vapour pressure increases.

(b) Rate of evaporation increases and rate of condensation decreases.

(c) When equilibrium is restored finally the rate of evaporation again becomes equal to the rate of condensation and the final vapour pressure becomes equal to the vapour pressure that was before the sudden increase in the volume of the container.

Question 2. What is K_c for the following equilibrium when the equilibrium concentration of each substance is

$$[SO_2] = 0.60 \text{ M}, [O_2] = 0.82 \text{ M and } [SO_3] = 1.90 \text{ M ?}$$

$$2SO_2(g) + O_2(g) \rightleftharpoons 2SO_3(g)$$

Solution. $2SO_2(g) + O_2(g) \rightleftharpoons 2SO_3(g)$

Given, $[SO_2] = 0.60 \text{ M}, \ [O_2] = 0.82 \text{ M}, [SO_3] = 1.90 \text{ M}$

Equilibrium constant, $\quad K_c = \dfrac{[SO_3]^2}{[SO_2]^2 \cdot [O_2]} = \dfrac{(1.90 \text{ M})^2}{(0.60 \text{ M})^2 \, (0.82 \text{ M})}$

$$= 12.2289 \text{ M}^{-1} \approx 12.23 \text{ M}^{-1}$$

Question 3. At a certain temperature and total pressure of 10^5 Pa, iodine vapour contains 40% by volume of I atoms.

$$I_2(g) \rightleftharpoons 2I(g)$$

Calculate K_p for the equilibrium.

 K_p depends upon the partial pressures of reactants and products so find their partial pressures from the percentage given and then, calculate K_p.

Solution. Given, $I_2(g) \rightleftharpoons 2I(g)$

I atoms in iodine vapours = 40% by volume

So, iodine vapours of I_2 molecules = 60% by volume

Partial pressure of iodine atoms, $p_1 = \dfrac{40}{100} \times 10^5 = 0.40 \times 10^5$ Pa

Similarly, partial pressure of iodine molecules (I_2),

$$p_2 = \dfrac{60}{100} \times 10^5 = 0.60 \times 10^5 \text{ Pa}$$

According to equation,

$$K_p = \dfrac{p_I^2}{p_{I_2}} = \dfrac{(0.40 \times 10^5 \text{ Pa})^2}{(0.60 \times 10^5 \text{ Pa})} = 0.2666 \times 10^5 \text{ Pa} \approx 2.67 \times 10^4 \text{ Pa}$$

Question 4. Write the expression for the equilibrium constant, K_c for each of the following reactions.

(i) $2NOCl(g) \rightleftharpoons 2NO(g) + Cl_2(g)$

(ii) $2Cu(NO_3)_2(s) \rightleftharpoons 2CuO(s) + 4NO_2(g) + O_2(g)$

(iii) $CH_3COOC_2H_5(aq) + H_2O(l) \rightleftharpoons CH_3COOH(aq) + C_2H_5OH(aq)$

(iv) $Fe^{3+}(aq) + 3OH^-(aq) \rightleftharpoons Fe(OH)_3(s)$

(v) $I_2(s) + 5F_2 \rightleftharpoons 2IF_5$

☼ K_c shows the ratio of the product of concentrations of the products to the product of concentrations of the reactants, each raised to a power equal to the corresponding stoichiometric coefficient.

Solution. (i) $K_c = \dfrac{[NO]^2\,[Cl_2]}{[NOCl]^2}$

(ii) $K_c = [NO_2]^4[O_2]$

(because molar concentrations of pure solids are constant)

(iii) $K_c = \dfrac{[CH_3COOH(aq)]\,[C_2H_5OH(aq)]}{[CH_3COOC_2H_5(aq)]\,[H_2O(l)]}$

(iv) $K_c = \dfrac{1}{[Fe^{3+}(aq)] \cdot [OH^-(aq)]^3}$ (because $[Fe(OH)_3(s)] = 1$)

(v) $K_c = \dfrac{[IF_5]^2}{[F_2]^5}$ (because $[I_2(s)] = 1$)

Question 5. Find out the value of K_c for each of the following equilibria from the value of K_p:

(i) $2NOCl(g) \rightleftharpoons 2NO(g) + Cl_2(g)$; $K_p = 1.8 \times 10^{-2}$ at 500 K

(ii) $CaCO_3(s) \rightleftharpoons CaO(s) + CO_2(g)$; $K_p = 167$ at 1073 K

☼ (a) First find Δn_g by subtracting the moles of gaseous reactants from the moles of gaseous products for each equation, as K_p and K_c are related as $K_p = K_c\,(RT)^{\Delta n_g}$

(b) Then, calculate K_c in each case.

Solution. (i) $2NOCl(g) \rightleftharpoons 2NO(g) + Cl_2(g)$; $K_p = 1.8 \times 10^{-2}$ at 500 K

$$\Delta n_g = n_p - n_r = 3 - 2 = 1$$

$$K_c = \frac{K_p}{(RT)^{\Delta n_g}} = \frac{1.8 \times 10^{-2}}{0.0821 \times 500} = 4.38 \times 10^{-4}$$

(ii) $CaCO_3(s) \rightleftharpoons CaO(s) + CO_2\,(g)$; $K_p = 167$ at 1073 K

$$\Delta n_g = n_p - n_r = 1$$

$$K_c = \frac{K_p}{(RT)^{\Delta n_g}} = \frac{167}{0.0821 \times 1073} = 1.89$$

Question 6. For the following equilibrium, $K_c = 6.3 \times 10^{14}$ at 1000 K

$$NO(g) + O_3(g) \rightleftharpoons NO_2(g) + O_2(g)$$

Both the forward and reverse reactions in the equilibrium are elementary bimolecular reactions. What is K_c for the reverse reaction ?

Solution. For the reaction, $NO(g) + O_3(g) \rightleftharpoons NO_2(g) + O_2(g)$;

$$K_c = 6.3 \times 10^{14} \text{ at } 1000 \text{ K}$$

$$K_c = \frac{[NO_2][O_2]}{[NO][O_3]} = 6.3 \times 10^{14} \qquad \ldots(i)$$

For reverse reaction,

$$NO_2(g) + O_2(g) \rightleftharpoons NO(g) + O_3(g)$$

$$K_c' = \frac{[NO][O_3]}{[NO_2][O_2]} \qquad \ldots(ii)$$

From Eqs. (i) and (ii), we get

$$K_c' = \frac{1}{K_c} = \frac{1}{6.3 \times 10^{14}} = 1.587 \times 10^{-15}$$

Question 7. Explain, why pure liquids and solids can be ignored while writing the equilibrium constant expression ?

Solution. Molar concentration of a pure solid or liquid (if in excess) is constant (*i.e.*, independent of the amount present) . That's why pure liquids and solids can be ignored while writing the equilibrium constant expression.

Question 8. Reaction between N_2 and O_2 takes place as follows :

$$2N_2(g) + O_2(g) \rightleftharpoons 2N_2O(g)$$

If a mixture of 0.482 mol N_2 and 0.933 mol O_2 is placed in a 10 L reaction vessel and allowed to form N_2O at a temperature for which $K_c = 2.0 \times 10^{-37}$, determine the composition of equilibrium mixture.

(i) Find the equilibrium concentrations of reactants and products in the given equation by assuming $2x$ mol of N_2 and x mol of O_2 are disappeared and $2x$ mol of N_2O are appeared.

(ii) Find the value of x to determine the concentration of reaction mixture.

Solution.

	$2N_2(g)$	$+$	$O_2(g)$	$\rightleftharpoons$	$2N_2O(g)$
Initial conc.	0.482		0.933		0
Equilibrium conc.	$(0.482 - 2x)$		$(0.933 - x)$		$2x$
Active mass	$\left(\dfrac{0.482 - 2x}{10}\right)$		$\left(\dfrac{0.933 - x}{10}\right)$		$\left(\dfrac{2x}{10}\right)$

$$K_c = 2.0 \times 10^{-37}$$

K_c is very-very small, which means negligible amounts of N_2 and O_2 react.

$$[N_2]_{eq} = \frac{0.482 - 2x}{10} = \frac{0.482}{10} = 0.0482$$

Similarly,

$$[O_2]_{eq} = \frac{0.933 - x}{10} = \frac{0.933}{10} = 0.0933$$

$$K_c = \frac{[N_2O]^2}{[N_2]^2[O_2]}$$

$$K_c = 2.0 \times 10^{-37} = \frac{[4x^2/100]}{(0.0482)^2(0.0933)}$$

$$x^2 = 10.837 \times 10^{-40} \quad \text{or} \quad x = 3.292 \times 10^{-20}$$

$$[N_2O] = \frac{2x}{10} = \frac{2 \times 3.292 \times 10^{-20}}{10} = 6.58 \times 10^{-21} \text{ mol L}^{-1}$$

Question 9. Nitric oxide reacts with Br_2 and gives nitrosyl bromide as per reaction given below :

$$2NO(g) + Br_2(g) \rightleftharpoons 2NOBr(g)$$

When 0.087 mole of NO and 0.0437 mole of Br_2 are mixed in a closed container at constant temperature, 0.0518 mole of NOBr is obtained at equilibrium. Calculate the equilibrium amount of NO and Br_2.

Find the value of x as in the previous Q. and then, substitute the value of x to calculate the equilibrium concentration of NO and Br_2.

Solution.

	2NO	+	Br_2	$\longrightarrow$	2NOBr
Initial conc.	0.087		0.0437		0
Equilibrium conc.	(0.087 − 2x)		(0.0437 − x)		2x

Given, 2x = 0.0518 = moles of NOBr formed

$$x = 0.0259 \text{ mol}$$

Moles of NO at equilibrium = (0.087 − 2x)
$$= 0.087 - 0.0518 = 0.0352 \text{ mol}$$

Moles of Br_2 at equilibrium = (0.0437 − x)
$$= 0.0437 - 0.0259 = 0.0178 \text{ mol}$$

Question 10. At 450 K, $K_p = 2.0 \times 10^{10}$/bar for the given reaction at equilibrium,

$$2SO_2(g) + O_2(g) \rightleftharpoons 2SO_3(g)$$

What is K_c at this temperature?

K_p and K_c are related as $K_p = K_c(RT)^{\Delta n_g}$ so calculate Δn_g by subtracting moles of gaseous reactants from the moles of gaseous products and then, calculate K_c.

Solution.
$$2SO_2(g) + O_2(g) \rightleftharpoons 2SO_3(g)$$
$$K_p = K_c(RT)^{\Delta n_g}$$
$$\Delta n_g = 2 - 3 = -1$$

$K_p = 2.0 \times 10^{10}$ bar^{-1}, $R = 0.0831$ L bar K^{-1}mol^{-1} and $T = 450$ K

$$K_c = \frac{K_p}{(RT)^{\Delta n_g}} = \frac{K_p}{(RT)^{-1}} \qquad (\because \Delta n_g = -1)$$

$K_c = K_p \times RT = 2.0 \times 10^{10}$ bar^{-1} $\times 0.0831$ L bar K^{-1} mol^{-1} $\times 450$ K

$K_c = 7.479 \times 10^{11}$L mol^{-1}

Question 11. A sample of HI(g) is placed in flask at a pressure of 0.2 atm. At equilibrium, the partial pressure of HI(g) is 0.04 atm. What is K_p for the given equilibrium ?

$$2HI(g) \rightleftharpoons H_2(g) + I_2(g)$$

Solution.

$$2HI(g) \rightleftharpoons H_2(g) + I_2(g)$$

Initial pressure	0.2 atm	0	0
Equili. pressure	0.04 atm	0.08 atm	0.08 atm

(Decrease in pressure of HI = 0.2 − 0.04 = 0.16 atm; so equilibrium pressure of H$_2$ is $\dfrac{0.16}{2}$ = 0.08 atm, and for I$_2$ is $\dfrac{0.16}{2}$ = 0.08 atm as two moles of HI on dissociation gives 1 mol H$_2$ and 1 mol I$_2$)

$$K_p = \frac{p_{H_2} \cdot p_{I_2}}{p_{HI}^2} = \frac{0.08 \text{ atm} \times 0.08 \text{ atm}}{(0.04 \text{ atm})^2} = 4.0$$

Question 12. A mixture of 1.57 moles of N$_2$, 1.92 moles of H$_2$ and 8.13 moles of NH$_3$ is introduced into a 20 L reaction vessel at 500 K. At this temperature, the equilibrium constant, K_c for the reaction, N$_2(g) + 3H_2(g) \rightleftharpoons 2NH_3(g)$ is 1.7×10^2. Is the reaction mixture at equilibrium? If not, what is the direction of the net reaction ?

 To predict the direction of a reaction calculate Q_c, reaction quotient. If $Q_c = K_c$, the reaction mixture is at equilibrium ;If $Q_c > K_c$ the reaction will proceed in the direction of reactants; If $Q_c < K_c$, the reaction will proceed in the direction of the products.

Solution. $N_2(g) + 3H_2(g) \rightleftharpoons 2NH_3(g)$

$$Q_c = \frac{[NH_3]^2}{[N_2][H_2]^3}$$

Given, $[NH_3] = \dfrac{8.13}{20}$ M = 0.4065 M; $[N_2] = \dfrac{1.57}{20}$ M = 0.0785 M

$[H_2] = \dfrac{1.92}{20}$ M = 0.096 M

$$Q_c = \frac{[0.4065 \text{ M}]^2}{[0.0785 \text{ M}][0.096 \text{ M}]^3} = 2.379 \times 10^3 \text{ M}^{-2}$$

$Q_c \neq K_c$, so the reaction mixture is not in equilibrium. $Q_c > K_c$, it indicates that the reaction will proceed in the direction of reactants.

Question 13. The equilibrium constant expression for a gas reaction is,

$$K_c = \frac{[NH_3]^4 \, [O_2]^5}{[NO]^4 \, [H_2O]^6}$$

Write the balanced chemical equation corresponding to this expression.

Solution. The expression shows that $4NO$ and $6H_2O$ are reactants and $4NH_3$ and $5O_2$ are products. Thus, the balanced chemical equation is

$$4NO + 6H_2O \longrightarrow 4NH_3 + 5O_2$$

Question 14. One mole of H_2O and one mole of CO are taken in 10 L vessel and heated to 725 K. At equilibrium, 40% of water (by mass) reacts with CO according to the equation,

$$H_2O(g) + CO(g) \rightleftharpoons H_2(g) + CO_2(g)$$

Calculate the equilibrium constant for the reaction.

Solution. $H_2O(g) \; + \; CO(g) \; \rightleftharpoons \; H_2(g) + CO_2(g)$

Initial conc.   1   1   0   0

Equili. conc. $(1-x)$ $(1-x)$ x x

$$H_2O \text{ reacted} = 40\% \text{ of } 1 \text{ mol of } H_2O = 0.4 \text{ mol}$$
$$x = 0.4 \text{ mol}$$
$$(1-x) = 1 - 0.4 = 0.6 \text{ mol}$$
$$K_c = \frac{[H_2]\,[CO_2]}{[H_2O]\,[CO]} = \frac{0.4 \times 0.4}{0.6 \times 0.6} = 0.444$$

Question 15. At 700 K, equilibrium constant for the reaction,

$$H_2(g) + I_2(g) \rightleftharpoons 2HI(g)$$

is 54.8. If 0.5 mol L^{-1} of $HI(g)$ is present at equilibrium at 700 K, what are the concentration of $H_2(g)$ and $I_2(g)$ assuming that we initially started with $HI(g)$ and allowed it to reach equilibrium at 700 K ?

     (i) As we started the reaction with HI, so equilibrium constant for the dissociation of HI ($2HI \rightleftharpoons H_2 + I_2$) is required. Thus, calculate equilibrium constant for backward reaction $(K_c')\left(K_c' = \dfrac{1}{K_c} \right)$

     (ii) and then calculate $[H_2]$ and $[I_2]$.

Solution. $H_2(g) + I_2(g) \rightleftharpoons 2HI(g);$ $K_c = 54.8$

$$2HI(g) \rightleftharpoons H_2(g) + I_2(g) \; ; \qquad K_c' = \frac{1}{K_c} = \frac{1}{54.8}$$

$$K_c' = \frac{[H_2]\,[I_2]}{[HI]^2} = \frac{1}{54.8}$$

Given, $[HI] = 0.5 \text{ mol } L^{-1}$

According to equation, $[H_2] = [I_2] = [x]$

$$\frac{x \cdot x}{[0.5]^2} = \frac{1}{54.8}$$

$$x^2 = \frac{[0.5]^2}{54.8} = 0.00456$$

$$x = 0.0675 \text{ M}$$

$$[H_2] = [I_2] = x = 0.0675 \text{ M}$$

Question 16. What is the equilibrium concentration of each of the substances in the equilibrium when the initial concentration of ICl was 0.78 M ?

$$2ICl(g) \rightleftharpoons I_2(g) + Cl_2(g) ; \qquad\qquad K_c = 0.14$$

Solution. $\qquad\qquad$ $2ICl(g) \rightleftharpoons I_2(g) + Cl_2(g)$

Initial conc. $\qquad\quad$ 0.78 M $\qquad$ 0 $\qquad$ 0

Equili conc. $\qquad\quad$ 0.78 – 2x $\qquad$ x $\qquad$ x

$$K_c = \frac{[I_2][Cl_2]}{[ICl]^2} = \frac{x \cdot x}{(0.78 - 2x)^2} = 0.14$$

or $\qquad\qquad$ $\dfrac{x}{(0.78 - 2x)} = \sqrt{0.14} = 0.374$ $\quad$ or $\quad$ $x = 0.29172 - 0.748x$

or $\qquad\qquad$ $1.748x = 0.29172$ $\quad$ or $\quad$ $x = \dfrac{0.29172}{1.748} = 0.1668$

$$[ICl]_{equili} = 0.45$$

Question 17. $K_p = 0.04$ atm at 899 K for the equilibrium shown below. What is the equilibrium concentration of C_2H_6 when it is placed in a flask at 4.0 atm pressure and allowed to come to equilibrium ?

$$C_2H_6(g) \rightleftharpoons C_2H_4(g) + H_2(g)$$

(i) Find the equilibrium concentration of all reactants and products in the given equation by assuming decrease in pressure of C_2H_6 is p and increase in pressure of C_2H_4 equal to H_2 is p.

(ii) Find the value of p to calculate $p_{C_2H_6}$.

Solution. $\qquad\qquad$ $C_2H_6(g) \rightleftharpoons C_2H_4(g) + H_2(g)$

Initial pressure $\qquad\qquad$ 4.0 atm $\qquad$ 0 $\qquad$ 0

Equili. pressure $\qquad\qquad$ (4.0 – p) atm $\qquad$ p $\qquad$ p

$$K_p = \frac{p_{C_2H_4} \cdot p_{H_2}}{p_{C_2H_6}} = \frac{p \cdot p}{4.0 - p}$$

$$0.04 = \frac{p^2}{4.0 - p} \quad \text{or} \quad 0.16 - 0.04p = p^2$$

$$p = \frac{-0.04 \pm \sqrt{0.0016 - 4(-0.16)}}{2}$$

$$p = \frac{-0.04 \pm 0.80}{2}$$

$$p = 0.38 \qquad\qquad \text{(by taking positive value)}$$

Hence, $\qquad\qquad$ $p_{C_2H_6} = 4.0 - 0.38 = 3.62$ atm

Question 18. Ethyl acetate is formed by the reaction between ethanol and acetic acid and the equilibrium is represented as

$$CH_3COOH(l) + C_2H_5OH(l) \rightleftharpoons CH_3COOC_2H_5(l) + H_2O(l)$$

(i) Write the concentration ratio (reaction quotient), Q_c, for this reaction (Note : Water is not in excess and is not a solvent in this reaction.)

(ii) At 293 K, if one starts with 1.00 mole of acetic acid and 0.18 mole of ethanol, there is 0.171 mole of ethyl acetate in the final equilibrium mixture. Calculate the equilibrium constant.

(iii) Starting with 0.5 mole of ethanol and 1.0 mole of acetic acid and maintaining it at 293 K, 0.214 mole of ethyl acetate is found after sometime. Has equilibrium been reached?

Solution. $CH_3COOH(l) + C_2H_5OH(l) \rightleftharpoons CH_3COOC_2H_5(l) + H_2O(l)$

(i) $Q_c = \dfrac{[CH_3COOC_2H_5][H_2O]}{[CH_3COOH][C_2H_5OH]}$

    Here, H_2O is not in excess that's why its concentration is not constant.

(ii) $CH_3COOH(l) + C_2H_5OH(l) \rightleftharpoons CH_3COOC_2H_5(l) + H_2O(l)$

Initial conc.	1.00 mol	0.180 mol	0	0
Equili. conc.	(1 − x) mol	(0.180 − x) mol	x mol	x mol

Given, $[CH_3COOC_2H_5]_{equili.} = 0.171\,mol = x$

$$K_c = \frac{[CH_3COOC_2H_5][H_2O]}{[CH_3COOH][C_2H_5OH]}$$

$$K_c = \frac{0.171 \times 0.171}{(1 - 0.171) \times (0.180 - 0.171)}$$

$$K_c = \frac{0.171 \times 0.171}{0.829 \times 0.009} = 3.919 \approx 3.92$$

(iii) $CH_3COOH(l) + C_2H_5OH(l) \rightleftharpoons CH_3COOC_2H_5(l) + H_2O(l)$

Initial conc.	1.0 mol	0.5 mol	0	0
After t time, conc.	(1.0 − 0.214) = 0.786 mol	(0.5 − 0.214) = 0.286 mol	0.214 mol	0.214 mol

$$Q_c = \frac{[CH_3COOC_2H_5][H_2O]}{[CH_3COOH][C_2H_5OH]}$$

$$Q_c = \frac{0.214 \times 0.214}{0.786 \times 0.286} = 0.2037 \approx 0.204$$

$Q_c \neq K_c$, hence, equilibrium has not been reached.

Question 19. A sample of pure PCl_5 was introduced into an evacuated vessel at 473 K. After equilibrium was attained, concentration of PCl_5 was found to be 0.5×10^{-1} mol L^{-1}. If value of K_c is 8.3×10^{-3}, what are the concentration of PCl_3 and Cl_2 at equilibrium?

$$PCl_5(g) \rightleftharpoons PCl_3(g) + Cl_2(g)$$

Solution. $\quad PCl_5(g) \rightleftharpoons PCl_3(g) + Cl_2(g)$

At equili. $\qquad$ 0.05 M $\qquad$ x $\qquad$ x

Given, $\quad [PCl_5]_{equili.} = 0.5 \times 10^{-1}$ mol L^{-1} $(= 0.05$ mol $L^{-1})$

$$K_c = 8.3 \times 10^{-3}$$

$$K_c = 8.3 \times 10^{-3} = \frac{[PCl_3][Cl_2]}{[PCl_5]}$$

$$8.3 \times 10^{-3} = \frac{x^2}{0.05} \quad \text{(because } [PCl_3] = [Cl_2])$$

$$x^2 = 0.415 \times 10^{-3} = 4.15 \times 10^{-4}$$

$$x = 2.037 \times 10^{-2} \approx 2.04 \times 10^{-2} \text{ mol } L^{-1}$$

Hence, $\qquad [PCl_3] = [Cl_2] = 2.04 \times 10^{-2}$ mol L^{-1}

Question 20. One of the reaction that takes place in producing steel from iron ore is the reduction of iron(II) oxide by carbon monoxide to give iron metal and CO_2.

$$FeO(s) + CO(g) \rightleftharpoons Fe(s) + CO_2(g) ;$$

$$K_p = 0.265 \text{ atm at } 1050 \text{ K}$$

What are the equilibrium partial pressures of CO and CO_2 at 1050 K if the initial partial pressures are; $p_{CO} = 1.4$ atm and $p_{CO_2} = 0.80$ atm ?

(i) First find Q_p by the given initial partial pressures of [CO] and [CO$_2$].

(ii) Compare Q_p and K_c to find the equilibrium partial pressure of [CO] and [CO$_2$].

Solution. $\quad FeO(s) + CO(g) \rightleftharpoons Fe(s) + CO_2(g) ; K_p = 0.265$ at 1050 K

Initial pressure $\qquad$ 1.4 atm $\qquad$ 0.80 atm

$$Q_p = \frac{p_{CO_2}}{p_{CO}} = \frac{0.80}{1.4} = 0.571 \qquad [\because \text{Fe and FeO are solids.}]$$

$Q_p > K_p$, the reaction will go in reverse direction. Due to this pressure of CO_2 will decrease and that of CO will increase to attain equilibrium. Hence, $p_{CO_2} = (0.80 - p)$ and $p_{CO} = (1.4 + p)$

(Suppose p is the decrease in pressure of CO_2 and p is the increase in pressure of CO).

$$K_p = \frac{p_{CO_2}}{p_{CO}} = 0.265 = \frac{(0.80 - p)}{(1.4 + p)}$$

$$1.265\,p = 0.80 - 0.371$$

$$1.265\,p = 0.429$$

$$p = \frac{0.429}{1.265} = 0.339 \text{ atm}$$

Hence, at equilibium,

$$p_{CO_2} = 0.80 - 0.339 = 0.461 \text{ atm}$$

and $\qquad p_{CO} = 1.4 + 0.339 = 1.739$ atm.

Question 21. Equilibrium constant, K_c for the reaction,
$$N_2(g) + 3H_2(g) \rightleftharpoons 2NH_3(g) \text{ at 500 K is 0.061}$$
At a particular time, the analysis shows that composition of the reaction mixture is 3.0 mol L^{-1} N_2, 2.0 mol L^{-1} H_2 and 0.5 mol L^{-1} NH_3. Is the reaction at equilibrium ? If not in which direction does the reaction tend to proceed to reach equilibrium ?

Find Q_c and compare it with K_c. If $Q_c = K_c$, the reaction is in equilibrium, if $Q_c < K_c$, the reaction will go in forward direction and if $Q_c > K_c$, the reaction will go in backward direction.

Solution. $N_2(g) + 3H_2(g) \rightleftharpoons 2NH_3(g)$; $K_c = 0.061$ at 500 K

Given, $[N_2] = 3.0$ mol L^{-1}, $[H_2] = 2.0$ mol L^{-1}

and $[NH_3] = 0.5$ mol L^{-1} at time t

So, $Q_c = \dfrac{[NH_3]^2}{[N_2][H_2]^3} = \dfrac{[0.5]^2}{[3.0][2.0]^3}$

$Q_c = 0.0104$

Because $Q_c \neq K_c$, equilibrium has not been attained.
Because $Q_c < K_c$ (0.0104 < 0.061), the reaction will proceed from left to right, *i.e.*, towards formation of more products.

Question 22. Bromine monochloride, BrCl decomposes into bromine and chlorine and reaches the equilibrium,
$$2BrCl(g) \rightleftharpoons Br_2(g) + Cl_2(g)$$
for which $K_c = 32$ at 500 K. If initially pure BrCl is present at a concentration of 3.3×10^{-3} mol L^{-1}, what is its molar concentration in the mixture at equilibrium?

(i) First find equilibrium concentration for all reactants and products given in the equation by assuming x mole of BrCl decomposes.
(ii) Find x by the expression of K_c and then find $[BrCl]_{equilibrium}$.

Solution. $2BrCl(g) \rightleftharpoons Br_2(g) + Cl_2(g)$; $K_c = 32$ at 500 K

Initial conc. 3.30×10^{-3} mol L^{-1} 0 0

Equili. conc. $(3.30 \times 10^{-3} - x)$ mol L^{-1} $\dfrac{x}{2}$ mol L^{-1} $\dfrac{x}{2}$ mol L^{-1}

$$K_c = \frac{[Br_2][Cl_2]}{[BrCl]^2} = \frac{x/2 \times x/2}{(3.30 \times 10^{-3} - x)^2} = 32$$

$$\frac{x^2}{4 \times (3.30 \times 10^{-3} - x)^2} = 32$$

$$\frac{x}{2 \times (3.30 \times 10^{-3} - x)} = \sqrt{32} = 5.656$$

$$\frac{x}{3.30 \times 10^{-3} - x} = 2 \times 5.656 = 11.312$$

$$x = 11.312(3.30 \times 10^{-3} - x)$$

$$x = 0.03732 - 11.312x$$
$$x + 11.312\,x = 0.03732$$
$$x = \frac{0.03732}{12.312} = 3.032 \times 10^{-3} \text{ mol L}^{-1}$$

$[BrCl]_{equili.} = (3.30 \times 10^{-3} - 3.032 \times 10^{-3})\,\text{mol L}^{-1} = 2.68 \times 10^{-4}\,\text{mol L}^{-1}$

Question 23. At 1127 K and 1 atm pressure, a gaseous mixture of CO and CO_2 in equilibrium with solid carbon has 90.55% CO by mass.

$$C(s) + CO_2(g) \rightleftharpoons 2CO(g)$$

Calculate K_c for this reaction at the above temperature.

(i) Since, the percentage by mass is given, so calculate the number of moles of CO and CO_2 to calculate their mole fractions.

(ii) Then, calculate the partial pressures of CO and CO_2 by using the formula $p_A = x_A \cdot p_{total}$

(iii) Calculate K_p by using the formula, $K_p = \dfrac{p_{CO}^2}{p_{CO_2}}$ and K_c by using the formula, $K_p = K_c(RT)^{\Delta n_g}$

Solution. 90.55% CO by mass means 90.55 g CO and 9.45 g CO_2 are present in 100 g mixture.

No. of moles of CO, $n_{CO} = \dfrac{90.55}{28} = 3.234$ mol

(Molar mass of CO = 28 g mol^{-1})

No. of moles of CO_2, $n_{CO_2} = \dfrac{9.45}{44} = 0.215$ mol

(Molar mass of CO_2 = 44 g mol^{-1})

Partial pressure of CO, $p_{CO} = x_{CO} \cdot p_{total}$ $\left(x_{CO} = \dfrac{3.234}{3.234 + 0.215} = 0.938 \right)$

$p_{CO} = 0.938 \times 1$ atm = 0.938 atm

Similarly, $p_{CO_2} = x_{CO_2} \cdot p_{total}$ $\left(x_{CO_2} = \dfrac{0.215}{3.234 + 0.215} = 0.062 \right)$

$p_{CO_2} = 0.062 \times 1$ atm = 0.062 atm

$$C(s) + CO_2(g) \rightleftharpoons 2CO(g)$$

$$K_p = \frac{p_{CO}^2}{p_{CO_2}} = \frac{(0.938)^2}{0.062} = 14.19$$

$$\Delta n_g = 2 - 1 = 1$$
$$K_p = K_c(RT)^{\Delta n_g}$$
$$K_c = \frac{K_p}{RT} \qquad (\because \Delta n_g = 1)$$
$$K_c = \frac{14.19}{0.0821 \times 1127} = 0.15336 \approx 0.153$$

Question 24. Calculate (a) $\Delta G°$ and (b) the equilibrium constant for the formation of the NO_2 from NO and O_2 at 298 K.

$$NO(g) + \frac{1}{2} O_2(g) \rightleftharpoons NO_2(g)$$

where, $\Delta_f G°(NO_2) = 52.0$ kJ/mol,

$\Delta_f G°(NO) = 87.0$ kJ/mol, $\Delta_f G°(O_2) = 0$ kJ/mol

(i) Calculate the $\Delta_r G°$ by using the formula $\Delta_r G° = \Sigma \Delta_f G°_p - \Sigma \Delta_f G°_r$
(p = products and r = reactants.)

(ii) Calculate the equilibrium constant, K_c by using the formula,
$\Delta G° = -2.303 RT \log K_c$.

Solution. (a) $NO(g) + \frac{1}{2} O_2(g) \rightleftharpoons NO_2(g)$;

$$\Delta_r G° = \Sigma \Delta_f G°_{products} - \Sigma \Delta_f G°_{reactants}$$

$$\Delta_r G° = \Delta_f G°(NO_2) - \left[\Delta_f G°(NO) + \frac{1}{2} \Delta_f G°(O_2)\right]$$

$$\Delta_r G° = 52.0 - \left(87.0 + \frac{1}{2} \times 0\right) \text{ kJ mol}^{-1}$$

$$\Delta_r G° = -35.0 \text{ kJ mol}^{-1}$$

(b) $\Delta_r G° = -2.303 \, RT \log K_c$

$-35000 \, \text{J mol}^{-1} = -2.303 \times 8.314 \, \text{J mol}^{-1} \text{K}^{-1} \times 298 \, \text{K} \times \log K_c$

$$\log K_c = \frac{35000}{5705.85} = 6.134$$

$$K_c = \text{antilog } 6.134$$

$$K_c = 1.361 \times 10^6$$

Question 25. Does the number of moles of reaction products increase, decrease or remain same when each of the following equilibria is subjected to a decrease in pressure by increasing the volume ?

(a) $PCl_5(g) \rightleftharpoons PCl_3(g) + Cl_2(g)$

(b) $CaO(s) + CO_2(g) \rightleftharpoons CaCO_3(s)$

(c) $3Fe(s) + 4H_2O(g) \rightleftharpoons Fe_3O_4(s) + 4H_2(g)$

Solution. According to Le-Chatelier's principle, on decreasing pressure equilibrium shifts in that direction where pressure increases (*i.e.*, number of moles in gaseous state are more). Therefore, number of moles of reaction products in (a) increases (b) decreases (c) remains the same. (If $\Delta n_g = 0$, there is no effect of change in pressure).

Question 26. Which of the following reactions will get affected by increasing the pressure? Also, mention whether change will cause the reaction to go into forward or backward direction.

(i) $COCl_2(g) \rightleftharpoons CO(g) + Cl_2(g)$

(ii) $CH_4(g) + 2S_2(g) \rightleftharpoons CS_2(g) + 2H_2S(g)$

(iii) $CO_2(g) + C(s) \rightleftharpoons 2CO(g)$

(iv) $2H_2(g) + CO(g) \rightleftharpoons CH_3OH(g)$

(v) $CaCO_3(s) \rightleftharpoons CaO(s) + CO_2(g)$

(vi) $4NH_3(g) + 5O_2(g) \rightleftharpoons 4NO(g) + 6H_2O(g)$

According to Le-Chatelier's principle, increase in pressure shifts the equilibrium in the direction where pressure decreases (*i.e.*, number of moles are less), Furthermore, if $n_p \neq n_r$, the change in pressure affects the equilibrium.

Solution. (i) $n_p > n_r$, the reaction will go in backward direction.

(ii) $n_p = n_r$, the reaction will not be affected by increasing pressure.

(iii) $n_p > n_r$, the reaction will go in backward direction.

(iv) $n_p < n_r$, the reaction will go in forward direction.

(v) $n_p > n_r$, the reaction will go in backward direction.

(vi) $n_p > n_r$, the reaction will go in backward direction.

Question 27. The equilibrium constant for the following reaction is 1.6×10^5 at 1024 K

$$H_2(g) + Br_2(g) \rightleftharpoons 2HBr(g)$$

Find the equilibrium pressure of all gases if 10.0 bar of HBr is introduced into a sealed container at 1024 K.

Solution. $H_2(g) + Br_2(g) \rightleftharpoons 2HBr(g);$ $\qquad K_p = 1.6 \times 10^5$ at 1024 K

$\therefore$ $\qquad 2HBr(g) \rightleftharpoons H_2(g) + Br_2(g) ; \; K'_p = \dfrac{1}{1.6 \times 10^5}$ at 1024 K

Initial pressure	10.0 bar	0	0
Equili. pressure	(10 − x)	$\dfrac{x}{2}$	$\dfrac{x}{2}$

$$K_p = \frac{p_{H_2} \cdot p_{Br_2}}{p_{HBr}^2} = \frac{\dfrac{x}{2} \cdot \dfrac{x}{2}}{(10-x)^2}$$

$$\frac{1}{1.6 \times 10^5} = 0.625 \times 10^{-5} = \frac{\dfrac{x}{2} \cdot \dfrac{x}{2}}{10 \times 10}$$

[(10 − x) ≈ 10 because magnitude of K_p is small.)]

$$2 \times 2 \times 10 \times 10 \times 0.625 \times 10^{-5} = x^2 \quad \text{or} \quad x = 0.050$$

$$p_{H_2} = p_{Br_2} = \frac{x}{2} = \frac{0.050}{2} = 0.025 \text{ bar} = 2.5 \times 10^{-2} \text{ bar}$$

$$p_{HBr} = 10 - 0.050 = 9.95 \approx 10 \text{ bar}$$

Question 28. Dihydrogen gas is obtained from natural gas by partial oxidation with steam as per following endothermic reaction,

$$CH_4(g) + H_2O(g) \rightleftharpoons CO(g) + 3H_2(g)$$

(a) Write an expression of K_p for the above reaction.

(b) How will the values of K_p and composition of equilibrium mixture be affected by

   (i) increasing the pressure
   (ii) increasing the temperature
   (iii) using a catalyst?

Solution. $CH_4(g) + H_2O(g) \rightleftharpoons CO(g) + 3H_2(g)$

(a) $K_p = \dfrac{P_{CO} \cdot P_{H_2}^3}{P_{CH_4} \cdot P_{H_2O}}$

(b)(i) Increase in pressure shifts the equilibrium in the direction where pressure decreases (*i.e.*, number of moles are less). This is backward direction. K_p remains unaffected from pressure change.

   (ii) Since, ΔH = +ve (endothermic reaction), reaction takes place with absorption of heat. Hence, increase in temperature shifts the equilibrium in the direction where heat is absorbed (*i.e.*, forward). It also increases the value of K_p.

   (iii) No effect, since catalyst affects rate of both directions equally.

Question 29. Describe the effect of

   (a) addition of H_2 (b) addition of CH_3OH
   (c) removal of CO   (d) removal of CH_3OH
   on the equilibrium of the reaction,

$$2H_2(g) + CO(g) \rightleftharpoons CH_3OH(g)$$

Solution. $2H_2(g) + CO(g) \rightleftharpoons CH_3OH(g)$

According to Le-Chatelier's principle,

(a) Addition of H_2 (increase in concentration of reactants) shifts the equilibrium in forward direction (more product is formed).

(b) Addition of CH_3OH (increase in concentration of product) shifts the equilibrium in backward direction.

(c) Removal of CO also shifts the equilibrium in backward direction.

(d) Removal of CH_3OH shifts the equilibrium in forward direction.

Question 30. At 473K, equilibrium constant K_c for decomposition of phosphorus pentachloride, PCl_5 is 8.3×10^{-3}. If decomposition is depicted as,

$$PCl_5(g) \rightleftharpoons PCl_3(g) + Cl_2(g); \qquad \Delta H° = 124.0 \text{ kJ mol}^{-1}$$

(a) Write an expression for K_c for the reaction.

Equilibrium

(b) What is the value of K_c for the reverse reaction at the same temperature?

(c) What would be the effect on K_c if (i) more PCl_5 is added (ii) pressure is increased (iii) the temperature is increased ?

Solution. $PCl_5(g) \rightleftharpoons PCl_3(g) + Cl_2(g)$; $K_c = 8.3 \times 10^{-3}$

(a) $K_c = \dfrac{[PCl_3][Cl_2]}{[PCl_5]}$

(b) For the reverse reaction, $K_c' = \dfrac{1}{K_c} = \dfrac{1}{8.3 \times 10^{-3}} = 120.48$

(c)(i) Addition of PCl_5 have no effect on K_c because K_c is constant at constant temperature.

(ii) K_c does not change with pressure.

(iii) The given reaction is endothermic, hence on increasing the temperature, K_f will increase, this results in increase in K_c

$\left(K_c = \dfrac{K_f}{K_b} \right).$

Question 31. Dihydrogen gas used in Haber's process is produced by reacting methane from natural gas with high temperature steam. The first stage of two stage reaction involves the formation of CO and H_2. In second stage, CO formed in first stage is reacted with more steam in water gas shift reaction,

$$CO(g) + H_2O(g) \rightleftharpoons CO_2(g) + H_2(g)$$

If a reaction vessel at 400°C is charged with an equimolar mixture of CO and steam such that $p_{CO} = p_{H_2O} = 4.0$ bar, what will be the partial pressure of H_2 at equilibrium? $K_p = 10.1$ at 400°C.

Solution. $CO(g) + H_2O(g) \rightleftharpoons CO_2(g) + H_2(g)$

Initial pressure 4.0 bar 4.0 bar 0 0
At equili. $(4.0 - p)$ $(4.0 - p)$ p p

$$K_p = \dfrac{p_{CO_2} \cdot p_{H_2}}{p_{CO} \cdot p_{H_2O}} = \dfrac{p \cdot p}{(4-p) \cdot (4-p)}$$

$$10.1 = \dfrac{p^2}{(4-p)^2}$$

$$\sqrt{10.1} = \dfrac{p}{(4-p)}$$

$$3.17 = \dfrac{p}{(4-p)}$$

$$p = 12.71 - 3.17p$$
$$4.17p = 12.71$$

$$p = \frac{12.71}{4.17} = 3.04 \text{ bar}$$

Hence,　　　　　　$p_{H_2} = 3.04 \text{ bar}$

Question 32. Predict which of the following reaction will have appreciable concentration of reactants and products ?

(a) $Cl_2(g) \rightleftharpoons 2Cl(g)$;　　　　　　　　　$K_c = 5 \times 10^{-39}$

(b) $Cl_2(g) + 2NO(g) \rightleftharpoons 2NOCl(g)$;　　$K_c = 3.7 \times 10^8$

(c) $Cl_2(g) + 2NO_2(g) \rightleftharpoons 2NO_2Cl(g)$;　$K_c = 1.8$

 When the value of K_c is greater than 10^3, only product predominates. If $K_c < 10^{-3}$, only reactant predominates, and if the value of K_c lies between 10^{-3} to 10^3, both reactants and products are present in appreciable concentration.

Solution. For the reaction (c) equilibrium constant, K_c is neither high nor very low so the reactants and products will be present in appreciable concentrations.

Question 33. The value of K_c for the reaction,

$$3O_2(g) \rightleftharpoons 2O_3(g)$$

is 2.0×10^{-50} at 25°C. If the equilibrium concentration of O_2 in air at 25°C is 1.6×10^{-2}, what is the concentration of O_3?

Solution.　　　　　　　　$3O_2(g) \rightleftharpoons 2O_3(g)$

Equili. conc.　　　　　　1.6×10^{-2}　　　　?

$$K_c = \frac{[O_3]^2}{[O_2]^3}$$

$$2.0 \times 10^{-50} = \frac{[O_3]^2}{[1.6 \times 10^{-2}]^3}$$

$$[O_3]^2 = 2.0 \times 10^{-50} \times [1.6 \times 10^{-2}]^3$$

$$[O_3]^2 = 8.192 \times 10^{-56}$$

$$[O_3] = 2.86 \times 10^{-28} \text{ mol L}^{-1}$$

Question 34. The reaction,

$$CO(g) + 3H_2(g) \rightleftharpoons CH_4(g) + H_2O(g)$$

is at equilibrium at 1300 K in a 1L flask. It also contains 0.30 mole of CO, 0.10 mole of H_2 and 0.02 mole of H_2O and an unknown amount of CH_4 in the flask. Determine the concentration of CH_4 in the mixture. The equilibrium constant, K_c for the reaction at the given temperature is 3.90.

Solution.　$CO(g) + 3H_2(g) \rightleftharpoons CH_4(g) + H_2O(g)$; $K_c = 3.90$ at 1300 K.

$$K_c = \frac{[CH_4] \cdot [H_2O]}{[CO] [H_2]^3}$$

$$3.90 = \frac{[CH_4] \, [0.02]}{[0.30] \, [0.10]^3}$$

(Molar concentration means number of moles present in 1 L and volume of the flask is 1 L.)

$$[CH_4] = \frac{3.90 \times 0.30 \times (0.10)^3}{0.02} = 0.0585 \, M$$

$$[CH_4]_{eq} = 5.85 \times 10^{-2} M$$

Question 35. What is meant by the conjugate acid-base pair? Find the conjugate acid/base for the following species.

$$HNO_2, \, CN^-, \, HClO_4, \, F^-, \, OH^-, \, CO_3^{2-} \text{ and } S^{2-}$$

Acid − H⁺ ⟶ Conjugate base

Base + H⁺ ⟶ Conjugate acid.

Solution. An acid-base pair differ by a proton is known as conjugate acid-base pair.

$$HNO_2 \rightleftharpoons NO_2^- + H^+$$
Acid   Conjugate base

$$CN^- + H^+ \rightleftharpoons HCN$$
Base   Conjugate acid

$$HClO_4 \rightleftharpoons ClO_4^- + H^+$$
Acid   Conjugate base

$$F^- + H^+ \rightleftharpoons HF$$
Base   Conjugate acid

$$OH^- + H^+ \rightleftharpoons H_2O$$
Base   Conjugate acid

$$OH^- \rightleftharpoons O^{2-} + H^+$$
Acid   Conjugate base

$$CO_3^{2-} + H^+ \rightleftharpoons HCO_3^-$$
Base   Conjugate acid

$$S^{2-} + H^+ \rightleftharpoons HS^-$$
Base   Conjugate acid

Question 36. Which of the following are Lewis acids ?

$$H_2O, \, BF_3, \, H^+, \, NH_4^+$$

Lewis acids have a tendency to accept electrons. Electron deficient or positively charged species have such tendency.

Solution. BF_3, H^+ and NH_4^+ act as Lewis acids.

Question 37. What will be the conjugate bases for the Bronsted acids: HF, H_2SO_4 and HCO_3^-?

 Acid ⇌ Conjugate base + H⁺

Solution.

$$HF \rightleftharpoons F^- + H^+$$

$$H_2SO_4 \rightleftharpoons HSO_4^- + H^+$$

$$HCO_3^- \rightleftharpoons CO_3^{2-} + H^+$$

Question 38. Write the conjugate acids for the Bronsted bases NH_2^-, NH_3 and $HCOO^-$.

Base $+ H^+ \rightleftharpoons$ Conjugate acid

Solution.

$$NH_2^- + H^+ \rightleftharpoons NH_3$$

$$NH_3 + H^+ \rightleftharpoons NH_4^+$$

$$HCOO^- + H^+ \rightleftharpoons HCOOH$$

Question 39. The species, H_2O, HCO_3^-, HSO_4^- and NH_3 can act both as Bronsted acids and bases. For each case give the corresponding conjugate acid and base.

Solution.

Species	Conjugate acid	Conjugate base
H_2O	H_3O^+	OH^-
HCO_3^-	H_2CO_3	CO_3^{2-}
HSO_4^-	H_2SO_4	SO_4^{2-}
NH_3	NH_4^+	NH_2^-

Question 40. Classify the following species into Lewis acids and Lewis bases and show how these act as Lewis acid/base?

(a) OH^- (b) F^-

(c) H^+ (d) BCl_3

 Lewis acids have a tendency to accept electrons and Lewis bases have a tendency to donate electrons.

Solution. OH^- and F^- are electron rich species and can donate electron pair. Hence, these act as Lewis base.

$$:\!\overset{\cdot\cdot}{O}H^- + H^+ \longrightarrow H_2O$$

$$:\!\overset{\cdot\cdot}{F}\!:^- + BF_3 \longrightarrow [BF_4^-]$$

Equilibrium

H^+ and BCl_3 are electron deficient species and can accept electron pair. Hence, these act as Lewis acid.

$$H_3N\colon + H^+ \longrightarrow NH_4^+$$
$$H_3N\colon + BCl_3 \longrightarrow H_3N \to BCl_3$$

Question 41. The concentration of hydrogen ion in a sample of soft drink is 3.8×10^{-3} M. What is its pH?

Solution.
$$pH = -\log[H^+]$$
$$pH = -\log[3.8 \times 10^{-3}]$$
$$pH = -(-3\log 10 + \log 3.8)$$
$$pH = +3 - 0.5798 = 2.4202 \approx 2.42$$

Question 42. The pH of a sample of vinegar is 3.76. Calculate the concentration of hydrogen ion in it.

Solution.
$$pH = 3.76 = -\log[H^+]$$
$$\log[H^+] = -3.76$$

[Before taking antilog add -1 in characteristic (-3) and $+1$ in mantissa (0.76), *i.e.*, $-3.76 - 1 + 1 = \overline{4}.24$]
$$\log[H^+] = \overline{4}.24 \text{ or } [H^+] = \text{antilog } \overline{4}.24$$
$$[H^+] = 1.738 \times 10^{-4} \text{ M}$$

Question 43. The ionization constant of HF, HCOOH and HCN at 298 K are 6.8×10^{-4}, 1.8×10^{-4} and 4.8×10^{-9} respectively. Calculate the ionization constants of the corresponding conjugate base.

To find K_b of a conjugate base, use the formula $K_a \cdot K_b = K_w = 1 \times 10^{-14}$.

Solution. If K_a is the ionization constant of a weak acid (HA) and K_b is the ionization constant of its conjugate base (A^-) then $K_a \cdot K_b = K_w$

$$K_b\,(F^-) = \frac{1 \times 10^{-14}}{K_a\,(HF)} = \frac{1 \times 10^{-14}}{6.8 \times 10^{-4}} = 1.47 \times 10^{-11}$$

$$K_b\,(HCOO^-) = \frac{1 \times 10^{-14}}{K_a\,(HCOOH)} = \frac{1 \times 10^{-14}}{1.8 \times 10^{-4}} = 5.56 \times 10^{-11}$$

$$K_b\,(CN^-) = \frac{1 \times 10^{-14}}{K_a\,(HCN)} = \frac{1 \times 10^{-14}}{4.8 \times 10^{-9}} = 2.08 \times 10^{-6}$$

Question 44. The ionization constant of phenol is 1.0×10^{-10}. What is the concentration of phenolate ion in 0.05 M solution of phenol ? What will be its degree of ionization if the solution is also 0.01 M in sodium phenolate?

Solution.
$$\underset{\text{phenol}}{C_6H_5OH} + H_2O \rightleftharpoons \underset{\text{phenolate}}{C_6H_5O^-} + H_3O^+$$

$$K_a = \frac{[C_6H_5O^-][H_3O^+]}{[C_6H_5OH]}$$

By Ostwald dilution law,
$$[C_6H_5O^-] = [H_3O^+] = \sqrt{K_a \cdot C}$$
$$= \sqrt{1.0 \times 10^{-10} \times 0.05} = 2.24 \times 10^{-6} \text{ M}$$

When mixture contains 0.05 M phenol and 0.01 M phenolate ion (from sodium phenolate) then

$$K_a = \frac{[C_6H_5O^-][H_3O^+]}{[C_6H_5OH]}$$

$$1.0 \times 10^{-10} = \frac{[0.01] \times [H_3O^+]}{[0.05]}$$

$$[H_3O^+] = \frac{0.05 \times 1.0 \times 10^{-10}}{0.01} = 5 \times 10^{-10} \text{ M}$$

$$[H_3O^+] = C \cdot \alpha = 5 \times 10^{-10} \quad \text{or} \quad \alpha = \frac{5 \times 10^{-10}}{C}$$

$$\alpha = \frac{5 \times 10^{-10}}{0.05} = 1 \times 10^{-8}$$

Question 45. The first ionization constant of H_2S is 9.1×10^{-8}. Calculate the concentration of HS^- ion in its 0.1 M solution. How will this concentration be affected if the solution is 0.1 M in HCl also? If the second dissociation constant of H_2S is 1.2×10^{-13}, calculate the concentration of S^{2-} under both conditions.

(i) H_2S, being a weak acid, dissociates as $H_2S + H_2O \rightleftharpoons H_3O^+ + HS^-$
so, calculate $[HS^-]$ by using the formula, $K_a = \dfrac{[H_3O^+][HS^-]}{[H_2S]}$

(ii) HCl being a strong acid dissociates completely, so calculate $[HS^-]$ in the presence of 0.1 M HCl by taking $[H^+]$ concentration as 0.1 M.

(iii) Calculate $[S^{2-}]$ ion concentration by using the equation,
$$HS^- + H_2O \rightleftharpoons H_3O^+ + S^{2-}$$

(iv) Calculate $[S^{2-}]$ ion concentration in the presence of 0.1 M HCl.

Solution. (i) $H_2S + H_2O \rightleftharpoons H_3O^+ + HS^-$

$$K_a = \frac{[H_3O^+][HS^-]}{[H_2S]}$$

$$[H_3O^+] = [HS^-] = \sqrt{K_{a_1} \cdot C}$$

$$= \sqrt{9.1 \times 10^{-8} \times 0.1} = 9.54 \times 10^{-5} \text{ M}$$

(ii) In the presence of 0.1 M HCl, $[H_3O^+] = 0.1$ M

$$K_{a_1} = \frac{[H_3O^+][HS^-]}{[H_2S]}$$

$$9.1 \times 10^{-8} = \frac{[0.1] \ [HS^-]}{[0.1]}$$

$$[HS^-] = 9.1 \times 10^{-8} \ M$$

Hence, concentration of $[HS^-]$ is decreased in the presence of 0.1 M HCl due to common-ion effect.

(iii) For second dissociation constant,

$$HS^- + H_2O \rightleftharpoons H_3O^+ + S^{2-} \quad \text{(In absence of HCl)}$$

$$[HS^-] = 9.54 \times 10^{-5} \ M$$

$$K_{a_2} = \frac{[H_3O^+] \ [S^{2-}]}{[HS^-]}$$

$$[H_3O^+] = [S^{2-}] = \sqrt{K_{a_2} \cdot C}$$

$$= \sqrt{1.2 \times 10^{-13} \times 9.54 \times 10^{-5}} = 3.38 \times 10^{-9} M$$

(iv) In the presence of 0.1 M HCl,

$$K_{a_2} = \frac{[H_3O^+] \ [S^{2-}]}{[HS^-]} = 1.2 \times 10^{-13} = \frac{[0.1] \ [S^{2-}]}{[9.1 \times 10^{-8}]}$$

$$[S^{2-}] = 1.092 \times 10^{-19} M$$

Question 46. The ionization constant of acetic acid is 1.74×10^{-5}. Calculate the degree of dissociation of acetic acid in its 0.05 M solution. Calculate the concentration of acetate ion in the solution and its pH.

Solution.

$$\begin{array}{cccc} CH_3COOH + H_2O & \rightleftharpoons & CH_3COO^- & + H_3O^+ \\ C & & 0 & 0 \quad \text{Initially} \\ C-C\alpha & & C\alpha & C\alpha \quad \text{At time } t \end{array}$$

$$K_a = \frac{[CH_3COO^-] \ [H_3O^+]}{[CH_3COOH]}$$

Given, $K_a = 1.74 \times 10^{-5}$, $[CH_3COOH] = 0.05 \ M$

$$[CH_3COO^-] = [H_3O^+] = \sqrt{K_a \cdot [CH_3COOH]}$$

$$[CH_3COO^-] = [H_3O^+] = \sqrt{1.74 \times 10^{-5} \times 0.05}$$

$$[CH_3COO^-] = [H_3O^+] = \sqrt{17.4 \times 10^{-6} \times 5.0 \times 10^{-2}}$$

$$= 9.33 \times 10^{-4} \ M$$

$$[CH_3COO^-] = [H_3O^+] = C \cdot \alpha$$

Degree of dissociation, $\alpha = \dfrac{[H_3O^+]}{C} = \dfrac{9.33 \times 10^{-4}}{0.05} = 1.86 \times 10^{-2}$

$$pH = -\log [H_3O^+]$$

$$pH = -\log [9.33 \times 10^{-4}]$$

$$pH = 4 - 0.9699 = 3.0301$$

Question 47. It has been found that the pH of a 0.01 M solution of an organic acid is 4.15. Calculate the concentration of the anion, the ionization constant of the acid and its pK_a.

(i) Organic acids are weak acids, so dissociate as $HA \rightleftharpoons H^+ + A^-$ and their K_a is calculated as, $K_a = \dfrac{[H^+][A^-]}{[HA]}$.

(ii) To calculate K_a, $[H^+]$ and $[A^-]$ are required. Calculate $[H^+]$ by using the formula, $pH = -\log[H^+]$ and calculate $[A^-]$ by using the equation $HA \rightleftharpoons H^+ + A^-$

(iii) Then, calculate K_a by using the formula, $K_a = \dfrac{[H^+][A^-]}{[HA]}$

(iv) Calculate pK_a by using the formula $pK_a = -\log K_a$

Solution. $HA \rightleftharpoons H^+ + A^-$

$$pH = 4.15 = -\log[H^+]$$

$$\log[H^+] = -4.15$$

$$\log[H^+] = \overline{5}.85 \text{ or } [H^+] = \text{antilog } \overline{5}.85 = 7.079 \times 10^{-5}$$

$$[H^+] = [A^-] = 7.079 \times 10^{-5} \text{ M}$$

$$K_a = \frac{[H^+][A^-]}{[HA]} = \frac{(7.079 \times 10^{-5})(7.079 \times 10^{-5})}{0.01}$$

$$K_a = 5011.22 \times 10^{-10} = 5.0 \times 10^{-7}$$

$$pK_a = -\log K_a = -\log[5.0 \times 10^{-7}]$$

$$pK_a = 7 - 0.699 = 6.301$$

Question 48. Assuming complete dissociation, calculate the pH of the following solutions :

(a) 0.003 M HCl   (b) 0.005 M NaOH
(c) 0.002 M HBr   (d) 0.002 M KOH

$$pH = -\log[H_3O^+]$$
$$pOH = -\log[OH^-]$$
$$pH + pOH = 14$$

Solution.   (a) 0.003 M HCl = 0.003 M $[H_3O^+]$

$$pH = -\log[H_3O^+]$$
$$pH = -\log[0.003] = -\log[3.0 \times 10^{-3}]$$
$$pH = 3 + (-0.4771) = 2.52$$

(b) 0.005 M NaOH = 0.005 M $[OH^-]$

$$pOH = -\log[OH^-] = -\log[0.005]$$
$$pOH = -\log[5.0 \times 10^{-3}] = 3 + (-0.6990)$$

$$\text{pOH} = 2.30$$
$$\text{pH} + \text{pOH} = 14 \quad \text{or} \quad \text{pH} = 14 - 2.30 = 11.70$$

(c) 0.002 M HBr

$$\text{pH} = -\log [H_3O^+] = -\log [0.002]$$
$$\text{pH} = 3 + (-0.3010) = 2.699 \approx 2.70$$

(d) 0.002 M KOH

$$\text{pOH} = -\log [0.002] = 2.70$$
$$\text{pH} + \text{pOH} = 14 \quad \text{or} \quad \text{pH} = 14 - 2.70 = 11.30$$

Question 49. Calculate the pH of the following solutions :
   (a) 2 g of TlOH dissolved in water to give 2 L of solution.
   (b) 0.3 g of $Ca(OH)_2$ dissolved in water to give 500 mL solution.
   (c) 0.3 g of NaOH dissolved in water to give 200 mL of solution.
   (d) 1 mL of 13.6 M HCl is diluted with water to give 1 L of solution.

   (i) To find pH of the given solution, first find concentration of solution in mol L^{-1}.
   (ii) To find pH of the given acidic solution use the formula
        pH $= -\log [H_3O^+]$.
   (iii) To find pH of the given basic solution, first find pOH of the solution by using the formula pOH $= -\log [OH^-]$ and then find pH by using the formula pH + pOH = 14.

Solution.   (a) Molecular mass of TlOH $= 204 + 16 + 1 = 221$ g mol^{-1}

Conc. in mol L^{-1} (molarity)

$$= \frac{\text{Mass of TlOH (g)}}{\text{Molar mass of TlOH} \times \text{Volume of solution (L)}}$$

$$= \frac{2}{221 \times 2} = 0.00452 = 4.52 \times 10^{-3} \text{ M}$$

$$\text{pH} = -\log [OH^-] = -\log [4.52 \times 10^{-3}]$$
$$\text{pOH} = 3 + (-0.6551) = 2.344$$
$$\text{pH} + \text{pOH} = 14 \quad \text{or} \quad \text{pH} = 14 - 2.334 = 11.656 \approx 11.66$$

   (b) Molecular mass of $Ca(OH)_2 = 40 + [(16 + 1) \times 2] = 74$ g mol^{-1}

$$\text{Molarity, } M = \frac{\text{Mass of } Ca(OH)_2 (g) \times 1000}{\text{Molar mass of } Ca(OH)_2 \times \text{Volume of solution (mL)}}$$

$$M = \frac{0.3 \times 1000}{74 \times 500} = 0.0081$$

One mole of $Ca(OH)_2$ gives 2 moles of OH^-. So

$$[OH^-] = 2 \times 0.0081 = 0.0162 \text{ M}$$

$$\text{pOH} = -\log [OH^-] = -\log [0.0162]$$
$$\text{pOH} = -\log [1.62 \times 10^{-2}] = 2 + (-0.2095) = 1.7905 \approx 1.79$$
$$\text{pH} + \text{pOH} = 14 \quad \text{or pH} = 14 - 1.79 = 12.21$$

(c) Molecular mass of $NaOH = 23 + 16 + 1 = 40$

$$M = \frac{\text{Mass of NaOH (g)} \times 1000}{\text{Molar mass of NaOH} \times \text{Volume of solution (mL)}}$$

$$= \frac{0.3 \times 1000}{40 \times 200} = 0.0375$$

$$pOH = -\log [0.0375] = -\log [3.75 \times 10^{-2}]$$

$$pOH = 2 + (-0.5740) = 1.426 \approx 1.43$$

$$pH + pOH = 14 \quad \text{or} \quad pH = 14 - 1.43 = 12.57$$

(d) In case of dilution $M_1 V_1 = M_2 V_2$

$$13.6 \times 1 \,(\text{mL}) = M_2 \times 1000 \,(\text{mL})$$

$$M_2 = \frac{13.6 \times 1}{1000} = 0.0136 = 1.36 \times 10^{-2} M$$

$$pH = -\log [1.36 \times 10^{-2}] = 2 + (-0.1335) = 1.8665$$

$$pH = 1.87$$

Question 50. The degree of ionization of a 0.1 M bromoacetic acid solution is 0.132. Calculate the pH of the solution and the pK_a of bromoacetic acid.

    (i) Find K_a by using the formula $K_a = C \cdot \alpha^2$ (for weak acid).

    (ii) Find pK_a by using the formula p$K_a = -\log K_a$.

    (iii) To find pH of the solution, find $[H_3O^+]$ concentration, by using the relation $[H_3O^+] = C\alpha$.

Solution. $CH_2(Br)COOH + H_2O \rightleftharpoons CH_2(Br)COO^- + H_3O^+$

Initial conc. C 0 0

Equili. conc. $C - C\alpha$ $C\alpha$ $C\alpha$

              $C\,(1-\alpha)$

$$K_a = \frac{C\alpha \cdot C\alpha}{C(1-\alpha)} = \frac{C\alpha^2}{(1-\alpha)}$$

$$K_a = C\alpha^2 \qquad [\text{For weak acid } (1-\alpha) \approx 1]$$

$$K_a = 0.1 \times (0.132)^2 = 0.00174 \approx 1.74 \times 10^{-3}$$

$$pK_a = -\log K_a$$

or $$pK_a = -\log [1.74 \times 10^{-3}]$$

$$pK_a = 3 + (-0.2405) = 2.7595$$

$$pH = -\log [H_3O^+]$$

$$pH = -\log [1.32 \times 10^{-2}]$$

$$(\text{because } [H_3O^+] = C\alpha = 0.1 \times 0.132 = 0.0132)$$

$$pH = 2 + (-0.1206) = 1.8794 \approx 1.88$$

Question 51. The pH of 0.005 M codeine ($C_{18}H_{21}NO_3$) solution is 9.95. Calculate its ionization constant and pK_b.

(i) As codeine is a weak base, its ionization constant is related to OH^- as
$$K_b = \frac{[OH^-]^2}{[\text{Codeine}]}$$

(ii) Calculate $[OH^-]$ from pOH with the help of the formula
$$pOH = -\log[OH^-]$$

(iii) $pK_b = -\log K_b$

Solution. Codeine ($C_{18}H_{21}NO_3$) + H_2O $\rightleftharpoons$ Codeine H^+ + OH^-
$$pH = 9.95 \text{ or } pOH = 14 - 9.95 = 4.05$$
$$pOH = -\log[OH^-]$$
$$\log[OH^-] = -4.05 = \overline{5}.95$$
$$[OH^-] = \text{antilog } \overline{5}.95 = 8.913 \times 10^{-5}$$
$$K_b = \frac{[\text{codeine } H^+][OH^-]}{[\text{codeine}]} = \frac{[OH^-]^2}{[\text{codeine}]} \quad (\text{because } [\text{codein } H^+] = [OH^-])$$
$$K_b = \frac{(8.913 \times 10^{-5})^2}{0.005} = 1.588 \times 10^{-6}$$
$$pK_b = -\log[K_b] = -\log[1.588 \times 10^{-6}]$$
$$pK_b = 6 + (-0.2009) = 5.7991 \approx 5.80$$

Question 52. What is the pH of 0.001 M aniline solution? The ionization constant of aniline is 4.27×10^{-10}. Calculate the degree of ionization of aniline in the solution. Also calculate the ionization constant of the conjugate acid of aniline.

(i) Find $[OH^-]$ ion concentration by using the formula $[OH^-] = \sqrt{K_b C}$.

(ii) To find pH of the solution first find pOH and then pH ($pH + pOH = 14$).

(iii) Find α by using the formula $\alpha = \sqrt{K_b / C}$ (for weak base).

(iv) Find K_a by using the formula $K_a \cdot K_b = K_w = 10^{-14}$.

Solution. $C_6H_5NH_2 + H_2O \rightleftharpoons C_6H_5NH_3^+ + OH^-$
$$K_b = \frac{[C_6H_5NH_3^+][OH^-]}{[C_6H_5NH_2]} = \frac{[OH^-]^2}{[C_6H_5NH_2]}$$
$$[OH^-] = \sqrt{K_b \cdot C} = \sqrt{4.27 \times 10^{-10} \times 0.001}$$
$$[OH^-] = 6.534 \times 10^{-7}$$
$$pOH = -\log[6.534 \times 10^{-7}]$$
$$pOH = 7 + (-0.8152) = 6.18$$
$$pH + pOH = 14$$
or
$$pH = 14 - 6.18 = 7.82$$

$$C_6H_5NH_2 + H_2O \rightleftharpoons C_6H_5NH_3^+ + OH^-$$

Initial conc.	C	0	0
Equili. conc.	$C - C\alpha$	$C\alpha$	$C\alpha$

$$K_b = \frac{C\alpha \cdot C\alpha}{C(1-\alpha)} \qquad [(1-\alpha) \approx 1 \text{ for weak base}]$$

$$K_b = C\alpha^2 \quad \text{or} \quad \alpha = \sqrt{K_b / C}$$

Degree of ionization, $\alpha = \sqrt{\dfrac{4.27 \times 10^{-10}}{0.001}} = 6.53 \times 10^{-4}$

K_a of conjugate acid of aniline,

$$K_a = \frac{K_w}{K_b} = \frac{10^{-14}}{4.27 \times 10^{-10}} = 2.34 \times 10^{-5}$$

Question 53. Calculate the degree of ionization of 0.05 M acetic acid if its pK_a value is 4.74. How is the degree of dissociation affected when its solution also contains (a) 0.01 M (b) 0.1 M in HCl ?

(i) α is related to K_a as $\alpha = \sqrt{K_a / C}$, so first find K_a from pK_a as $pK_a = -\log(K_a)$ and then calculate α.

(ii) To find α in the presence of 0.01 M HCl or 0.1 M HCl, calculate $C\alpha$ for acetate ions by taking $[H^+]$ ion concentrations 0.01 M or 0.1 M.

Solution.
$$pK_a = -\log K_a,$$
$$4.74 = -\log K_a$$
$$\log K_a = -4.74 = \overline{5} \cdot 26$$
$$K_a = \text{antilog } \overline{5}.26 = 1.82 \times 10^{-5}$$

$$\alpha = \sqrt{K_a / C} \quad \text{or} \quad \alpha = \sqrt{\frac{1.82 \times 10^{-5}}{0.05}} \qquad (C = 0.05 \text{ given})$$

$$\alpha = \sqrt{\frac{1.82 \times 10^{-5}}{5.0 \times 10^{-2}}} = \sqrt{0.364 \times 10^{-3}} = \sqrt{3.64 \times 10^{-4}}$$

$$\alpha = 1.908 \times 10^{-2}$$

(a) In the presence of 0.01 M H^+

$$CH_3COOH \rightleftharpoons CH_3COO^- + H^+$$

Initial conc.	0.05 M	0	0
Equili. conc.	0.05 – $C\alpha$	$C\alpha$	$(C\alpha + 0.01)$
	≈ 0.05		≈ 0.01

[CH_3COOH is a weak acid and HCl is a strong acid, so we can assume that $(C\alpha + 0.01) \approx 0.01$]

$$\therefore \qquad K_a = \frac{[CH_3COO^-][H^+]}{[CH_3COOH]}$$

$$1.82 \times 10^{-5} = \frac{C\alpha \times 0.01}{0.05}$$

or $\quad C\alpha = \dfrac{1.82 \times 10^{-5} \times 0.05}{0.01} = 9.1 \times 10^{-5}$

$\quad C\alpha = 9.1 \times 10^{-5} \quad$ or $\quad \alpha = \dfrac{9.1 \times 10^{-5}}{0.05} = 1.82 \times 10^{-3}$

(b) **In the presence of 0.1 M HCl** similarly, $K_a = \dfrac{[CH_3COO^-][H^+]}{[CH_3COOH]}$

$\quad 1.82 \times 10^{-5} = \dfrac{C\alpha \times 0.1}{0.05} \quad ([H^+] = (C\alpha + 0.1\,M) \approx 0.1\,M)$

$$\text{(because } 0.1\,M\ HCl = 0.1\,M\,H^+ \text{ ions)}$$

$\quad C\alpha = \dfrac{1.82 \times 10^{-5} \times 0.05}{0.1} = 0.91 \times 10^{-5}$

$\quad \alpha = \dfrac{0.91 \times 10^{-5}}{0.05} = 1.82 \times 10^{-4}$

In the presence of strong acid, dissociation of weak acid *i.e.*, CH_3COOH decreases due to common ion effect.

Question 54. The ionization constant of dimethylamine is 5.4×10^{-4}. Calculate its degree of ionization in its 0.02 M solution. What percentage of dimethylamine is ionized if the solution is also 0.1 M in NaOH?

Solution. Given, K_b for dimethylamine $= 5.4 \times 10^{-4}$

C for dimethylamine $= 0.02\,M$

$$\alpha = \sqrt{K_b / C} = \sqrt{\dfrac{5.4 \times 10^{-4}}{0.02}} = 1.64 \times 10^{-1} = 0.164$$

In the presence of 0.1 M NaOH,

$$(CH_3)_2 NH + H_2O \rightleftharpoons (CH_3)_2 \overset{+}{N}H_2 + OH^-$$

Initial conc.	0.02 M	0	0
Equili. conc.	(0.02 − Cα)	Cα	Cα + 0.1
	≈ 0.02		≈ 0.1
			(0.1 from 0.1 M NaOH)

$$K_b = \dfrac{[(CH_3)_2 \overset{+}{N}H_2]\,[OH^-]}{[(CH_3)_2 NH]}$$

or $\qquad 5.4 \times 10^{-4} = \dfrac{C\alpha \times 0.1}{0.02}$

$\qquad C\alpha = \dfrac{5.4 \times 10^{-4} \times 0.02}{0.1} = 108 \times 10^{-6}$

$\qquad \alpha = \dfrac{108 \times 10^{-6}}{0.02} = 54 \times 10^{-4} = 5.4 \times 10^{-3}$

$\qquad \alpha = 0.54\%$

Question 55. Calculate the hydrogen ion concentration in the following biological fluids whose pH are given below :

    (a) Human muscle-fluid, 6.83   (b) Human stomach fluid, 1.2

    (c) Human blood, 7.38   (d) Human saliva, 6.4

Solution.   (a) **pH of human muscle fluid** $= 6.83$

$$pH = -\log [H^+]$$

or $\log [H^+] = -6.83 = \overline{7}.17$

or $[H^+] = \text{antilog } \overline{7}.17 = 1.479 \times 10^{-7} M$

(b) **pH of human stomach fluid** $= 1.2$

      $\log [H^+] = -1.2 = \overline{2}.80$ or $[H^+] = \text{antilog } \overline{2}.80$

$\therefore$ $[H^+] = 6.31 \times 10^{-2} M$

(c) **pH of human blood** $= 7.38$

      $\log [H^+] = -7.38 = \overline{8}.62$

or $[H^+] = \text{antilog } \overline{8}.62 = 4.169 \times 10^{-8} M$

(d) **pH of human saliva** $= 6.4$

      $\log [H^+] = -6.4 = \overline{7}.60$

        $[H^+] = \text{antilog } \overline{7}.60 = 3.981 \times 10^{-7} M$

Question 56. The pH of milk, black coffee, tomato juice, lemon juice and egg white are 6.8, 5.0, 4.2, 2.2 and 7.8 respectively. Calculate the corresponding hydrogen ion concentration in each.

Solution.   (a) **pH of milk** $= 6.8$

      $\log [H^+] = -6.8 = \overline{7}.20$

        $[H^+] = \text{antilog } \overline{7}.20 = 1.585 \times 10^{-7} M$

(b) **pH of black coffee** $= 5.0$

      $\log [H^+] = -5.0$

      $[H^+] = 10^{-5} M$

(c) **pH of lemon juice** $= 2.2$

      $\log [H^+] = -2.2 = \overline{3}.8$

        $[H^+] = \text{antilog } \overline{3}.8 = 6.310 \times 10^{-3} M$

(d) **pH of tomato juice** $= 4.2$

      $\log [H^+] = -4.2 = \overline{5}.80$

        $[H^+] = \text{antilog } \overline{5}.80 = 6.310 \times 10^{-5} M$

(e) **pH of egg white** $= 7.8$

      $\log [H^+] = -7.8 = \overline{8}.20$

        $[H^+] = \text{antilog } \overline{8}.20 = 1.585 \times 10^{-8} M$

Question 57. If 0.561 g of KOH is dissolved in water to give 200mL of solution at 298 K, calculate the concentrations of potassium, hydrogen and hydroxyl ions. What is its pH?

Solution. Concentration of aq. KOH in mol L^{-1}, *i.e.*,

Molarity, $M = \dfrac{\text{Mass of KOH (g)} \times 1000}{\text{Molar mass (KOH)} \times \text{Volume of solution (mL)}}$

$M = \dfrac{0.561 \times 1000}{56 \times 200}$

(Molar mass of KOH = 39 + 16 + 1 = 56 g mol^{-1})

$M = 0.05 \text{ mol } L^{-1}$

$$KOH \rightleftharpoons K^+ + OH^-$$
$$0.05\,M \qquad 0.05\,M \quad 0.05\,M$$

$\therefore$ $[K^+] = 0.05$ M and $[OH^-] = 0.05$ M

$[H^+] \cdot [OH^-] = K_w = 1.0 \times 10^{-14}$

$[H^+] = \dfrac{1.0 \times 10^{-14}}{0.05} = 20 \times 10^{-14}$ M = 2.0×10^{-13}M

$pH = - \log[H^+] = - \log[2.0 \times 10^{-13}]$

$\qquad = - \log 2 - \log 10^{-13}$

$\qquad = - 0.3010 + 13 = 12.7$

Question 58. The solubility of $Sr(OH)_2$ at 298 K is 19.23 g/L of solution. Calculate the concentrations of strontium and hydroxyl ions and the pH of the solution.

(i) First find concentration of $Sr(OH)_2$ solution in mol per litre as concentration is given in g/L.

(ii) We have the $[OH^-]$, so find $[H^+]$ ion concentration, with the help of $[H^+][OH^-] = 10^{-14}$

(iii) Find pH of the solution from $[H^+]$.

Solution. Solubility of $Sr(OH)_2$ = 19.23 g/L at 298 K

Molarity, $M = \dfrac{19.23 \text{ (g)}}{121.6 \text{ g mol}^{-1} \times 1L}$

(Molar mass of $Sr(OH)_2$ = 87.6 + 2 (16 + 1) = 121.6 g mol^{-1})

$M = 0.1581 \text{ mol } L^{-1}$

$$Sr(OH)_2 \longrightarrow Sr^{2+} + 2OH^-$$
$$0.1581\,M \qquad 0.1581\,M \quad 2 \times 0.1581\,M$$

$[Sr^{2+}] = 0.1581$ M

$[OH^-] = 0.3162$ M

$$[H^+] \cdot [OH^-] = 10^{-14} \quad (K_w = 10^{-14} = [H^+] \cdot [OH^-])$$

$$[H^+] = \frac{10^{-14}}{0.3162} = 3.16 \times 10^{-14}$$

$$pH = -\log[H^+] = -\log[3.16 \times 10^{-14}]$$

$$pH = 14 - 0.4997 = 13.5003 \approx 13.5$$

Question 59. The ionization constant of propanoic acid is 1.32×10^{-5}. Calculate the degree of ionization of the acid in its 0.05 M solution and also its pH. What will be its degree of ionization if the solution is 0.01 M in HCl also ?

Solution.

$$\underset{\substack{\text{Propanoic acid} \\ (0.05 - C\alpha)}}{CH_3CH_2COOH} + H_2O \rightleftharpoons \underset{C\alpha}{CH_3CH_2COO^-} + \underset{C\alpha}{H_3O^+}; \ K_a = 1.32 \times 10^{-5}$$

From Ostwald's dilution law,

$$\alpha = \sqrt{K_a / C} = \sqrt{\frac{1.32 \times 10^{-5}}{0.05}}$$

$$\alpha = 0.016248$$

$$[H_3O^+] = C\alpha = 0.05 \times 0.016248$$

$$[H_3O^+] = 0.0008124 = 8.124 \times 10^{-4}$$

$$pH = -\log[H_3O^+] = -\log(8.124 \times 10^{-4})$$

$$pH = 4 - 0.9098 = 3.0902 \approx 3.09$$

When the solution contains 0.01 M HCl

$$K_a = \frac{[CH_3CH_2COO^-][H_3O^+]}{CH_3CH_2COOH}$$

$$1.32 \times 10^{-5} = \frac{C\alpha \times 0.01}{(0.05 - C\alpha)}$$

([H_3O^+] = 0.01 M from HCl. In the presence of 0.01 M HCl dissociation of propanoic acid decreases.)

$$C\alpha = \frac{1.32 \times 10^{-5} \times (0.05 - C\alpha)}{0.01} \quad \text{[as } (0.05 - C\alpha) \approx 0.05]$$

$$C\alpha = 6.60 \times 10^{-5}$$

Degree of ionization, $\alpha = \dfrac{6.60 \times 10^{-5}}{0.05} = 1.32 \times 10^{-3}$

Question 60. The pH of 0.1M solution of cyanic acid (HCNO) is 2.34. Calculate the ionization constant of the acid and its degree of ionization in the solution.

 As we have pH, find $[H_3O^+]$ to calculate K_a and α.

$$\alpha = \frac{[H_3O^+]}{C}$$

Solution. $HCNO + H_2O \rightleftharpoons H_3O^+ + CNO^-$

$$pH = 2.34$$
$$pH = -\log[H_3O^+]$$
$$\log[H_3O^+] = -2.34 = \overline{3}.66$$
$$[H_3O^+] = \text{antilog } \overline{3}.66 = 4.571 \times 10^{-3} M$$
$$[H_3O^+] = C\alpha = 4.571 \times 10^{-3}$$

Degree of ionization, $\alpha = \dfrac{4.571 \times 10^{-3}}{0.1} = 4.571 \times 10^{-2}$

Ionization constant, $K_a = \dfrac{[H_3O^+][CNO^-]}{[HCNO]}$

$$= \dfrac{4.571 \times 10^{-3} \times 4.571 \times 10^{-3}}{0.1} = 2.089 \times 10^{-4}$$

Question 61. The ionization constant of nitrous acid is 4.5×10^{-4}. Calculate the pH of 0.04 M sodium nitrite solution and also its degree of hydrolysis.

(i) Sodium nitrite is a salt of weak acid and strong base. Hence, to calculate pH of its aqueous solution use the formula
$$pH = 7 + \dfrac{pK_a + \log C}{2},$$

(ii) Degree of hydrolysis, $h = \sqrt{\dfrac{K_w}{K_a C}}$ (for a salt of weak acid + strong base)

Solution. Given, $[NaNO_2] = 0.04 \text{ M}$

$$K_a \text{ of } HNO_2 = 4.5 \times 10^{-4}$$

$\therefore$

$$pK_a = -\log K_a = -\log(4.5 \times 10^{-4})$$
$$pK_a = 4 - 0.6532 = 3.3468 \approx 3.35$$
$$pH = 7 + \dfrac{pK_a + \log C}{2}$$
$$pH = 7 + \dfrac{3.35 + \log 0.04}{2} = 7.98$$
$$pH = 7.98$$

Degree of hydrolysis, $h = \sqrt{\dfrac{K_w}{K_a C}} = \sqrt{\dfrac{10^{-14}}{4.5 \times 10^{-4} \times 0.04}}$

$$h = 2.36 \times 10^{-5}$$

Alternatively, $\qquad NO_2^- + H_2O \rightleftharpoons HNO_2 + OH^-$

Initial conc.	C	0	0
After hydrolysis conc.	$(C - Ch)$	Ch	Ch

$$[OH^-] = Ch = 0.04 \times 2.36 \times 10^{-5}$$
$$[OH^-] = 9.44 \times 10^{-7}$$

$$pOH = -\log [9.44 \times 10^{-7}]$$
$$pOH = 7 - 0.9750 = 6.03$$
$$pH + pOH = 14 \quad \text{or} \quad pH = 14 - 6.03 = 7.97$$

Question 62. A 0.02 M solution of pyridinium hydrochloride has pH = 3.44. Calculate the ionization constant of pyridine.

(i) Pyridinium hydrochloride is a salt of weak base (pyridine) and strong acid (hydrochloric acid). Therefore, to calculate K_b first calculate pK_b by using the formula,

$$pH = 7 - \frac{pK_b}{2} - \frac{\log C}{2}$$

(ii) Calculate K_b by using the formula $pK_b = -\log K_b$

Solution. $C_6H_5N^+HCl^- + H_2O \rightleftharpoons C_6H_5N^+HOH^- + HCl$

(Solution is acidic due to hydrolysis)

$$pH = 7 - \frac{pK_b}{2} - \frac{\log C}{2}$$
$$3.44 = 7 - \frac{pK_b}{2} - \frac{\log 0.02}{2}$$
$$pK_b = 8.82$$
$$pK_b = 8.82 = -\log pK_b$$
$$\log K_b = -8.82 = \overline{9}.18$$
$$K_b = \text{antilog } \overline{9}.18 = 1.5 \times 10^{-9}$$

Alternatively,

(i) Find $[H_3O^+]$ ion conc. by using the formula $pH = -\log [H_3O^+]$.

(ii) Calculate K_a by using the formula, $K_a = \frac{[C_6H_5N^+Cl^-][H_3O^+]}{[C_6H_5N \cdot HCl]}$.

(iii) Calculate pK_a from K_a and then pK_b by using the formula $pK_a + pK_b = 14$.

(iv) Calculate K_b from pK_b.

$$C_6H_5N \cdot HCl + H_2O \rightleftharpoons C_6H_5N^+Cl^- + H_3O^+$$

$$K_a = \frac{[C_6H_5N^+Cl^-][H_3O^+]}{[C_6H_5N \cdot HCl]}$$

$$pH = 3.44 = -\log [H_3O^+]$$
$$\log [H_3O^+] = -3.44 = \overline{4}.56$$
$$[H_3O^+] = \text{antilog } \overline{4}.56 = 3.63 \times 10^{-4} M$$
$$[H_3O^+] = [C_6H_5N^+Cl^-] = 3.63 \times 10^{-4}$$

Hence, $$K_a = \frac{3.63 \times 10^{-4} \times 3.63 \times 10^{-4}}{0.02} = 6.588 \times 10^{-6}$$

$$pK_a = -\log K_a = -\log 6.588 \times 10^{-6}$$
$$pK_a = 6 + (-0.8187) = 5.18$$
$$pK_a + pK_b = 14$$
$$pK_b = 14 - 5.18 = 8.82$$

Equilibrium

or
$$-\log K_b = -8.82$$
$$\log K_b = -8.82 = \overline{9}.18$$
$$K_b = \text{antilog } \overline{9}.18 = 1.5 \times 10^{-9}$$

Question 63. Predict if the solutions of the following salts are neutral, acidic or basic :

$$\text{NaCl, KBr, NaCN, NH}_4\text{NO}_3, \text{NaNO}_2 \text{ and KF}$$

 The solution of a salt of strong acid and strong base is neutral while that of weak acid and strong base is basic. A solution of salt of strong acid and weak base is acidic.

Solution.

	Salt	Acid	Base	Hydrolysis reaction	Nature of solution
(i)	NaCl	HCl	NaOH	$H_2O \rightleftharpoons H^+ + OH^-$	Neutral
(ii)	KBr	HBr	KOH	No hydrolysis No hydrolysis	Neutral
(iii)	NaCN	HCN	NaOH	$CN^- + H_2O \rightleftharpoons HCN + OH^-$	Basic
(iv)	NH_4NO_3	HNO_3	NH_4OH	$NH_4^+ + H_2O \rightleftharpoons NH_4OH + H^+$	Acidic
(v)	$NaNO_2$	HNO_2	NaOH	$NO_2^- + H_2O \rightleftharpoons HNO_2 + OH^-$	Basic
(vi)	KF	HF	KOH	$F^- + H_2O \rightleftharpoons HF + OH^-$	Basic

Question 64. The ionization constant of chloroacetic acid is 1.35×10^{-3}. What will be the pH of 0.1 M acid and its 0.1 M sodium salt solution ?

 (i) To calculate pH of the solution first find $[H_3O^+]$ ion concentration by using the formula, $[H_3O^+] = \sqrt{K_a C}$.
(ii) Calculate pH by using the formula, $pH = -\log [H_3O^+]$.
(iii) Sodium chloroacetate is a salt of strong base and weak acid therefore,
$$pH = 7 + \frac{pK_a + \log C}{2}$$

Solution. $CH_2ClCOOH + H_2O \rightleftharpoons CH_2ClCOO^- + H_3O^+$
$$K_a = 1.35 \times 10^{-3} \qquad \text{(given)}$$
$$pK_a = -\log K_a = -\log [1.35 \times 10^{-3}]$$
$$= 3 - 0.13 = 2.87$$

By Oswald's dilution law,
$$[H_3O^+] = \sqrt{K_a \cdot C} = \sqrt{1.35 \times 10^{-3} \times 0.1}$$
$$[H_3O^+] = 1.16 \times 10^{-2}M$$
$$\text{pH of acid} = -\log [H_3O^+] = -\log (1.16 \times 10^{-2}) M$$
$$pH = 2 - 0.06 = 1.94$$

0.1 M $CH_2ClCOONa$ (sod. chloroacetate) is basic due to hydrolysis.

$$CH_2ClCOO^- + H_2O \rightleftharpoons CH_2ClCOOH + OH^-$$

For a salt of strong base + weak acid,

$$pH = 7 + \frac{pK_a + \log C}{2} = 7 + \frac{2.87 + \log 0.1}{2}$$

$$pH = 7 + \frac{2.87 + (-1)}{2} = 7 + \frac{1.87}{2} = 7 + 0.935 \approx 7.94$$

$$pH = 7.94$$

Alternatively   To find pH of 0.1 M sodium salt solution use the formula,

$$pH = -\frac{1}{2}[\log K_w + \log K_a - \log C]$$

$$pH = -\frac{1}{2}[\log 10^{-14} + \log(1.35 \times 10^{-3}) - \log 0.1]$$

$$pH = -\frac{1}{2}[-14 + (-3 + 0.1303) - (-1)]$$

$$pH = -\frac{1}{2}[-15.8697] = 7.93485 \approx 7.94$$

Question 65. Ionic product of water at 310 K is 2.7×10^{-14}. What is the pH of neutral water at this temperature?

Solution. $K_w = [H_3O^+] \cdot [OH^-] = 2.7 \times 10^{-14}$ at 310 K

$$H_2O + H_2O \rightleftharpoons [H_3O^+][OH^-]$$

$$[H_3O^+] = [OH^-]$$

Therefore, $[H_3O^+] = \sqrt{2.7 \times 10^{-14}} = 1.643 \times 10^{-7} M$

$$pH = -\log[H_3O^+] = -\log 1.643 \times 10^{-7}$$

$$pH = 7 + (-0.2156) = 6.7844$$

Question 66. Calculate the pH of the resultant mixtures :

(a) 10 mL of 0.2 M $Ca(OH)_2$ + 25 mL of 0.1 M HCl

(b) 10 mL of 0.01 M H_2SO_4 + 10 mL of 0.01 M $Ca(OH)_2$

(c) 10 mL of 0.1 M H_2SO_4 + 10 mL of 0.1 M KOH

  Compare millimoles (MV) of acid and base, to find the nature of solution.

    (i) If millimoles of acid are more, the resultant mixture is acidic.

    (ii) If millimoles of base are more, the resultant mixture is basic.

    (iii) If millimoles of acid and base are equal, the resultant mixture, is neutral. Then calculate the pH.

Solution.   (a) Base, $Ca(OH)_2$ = Acid, HCl

$$M_1V_1 = M_2V_2$$

Given, $M_1 = [OH^-] = 2 \times 0.2 = 0.4\ M$

$$V_1 = 10\ mL, M_2 = 0.1\ M, V_2 = 25\ mL$$

$$M_1V_1 = M_2V_2$$
$$0.4 \times 10 = 0.1 \times 25$$
$$4 > 2.5$$

$M_1V_1 > M_2V_2$ hence, solution is basic.

$$[OH^-] = \frac{M_1V_1 - M_2V_2}{V_1 + V_2} = \frac{4 - 2.5}{10 + 25} = 0.043 \text{ M}$$

$$pOH = -\log[4.3 \times 10^{-2}] = 2 - 0.6335 = 1.3665$$
$$pH = 14 - pOH = 14 - 1.3665 = 12.6335 \approx 12.63$$

(b) Similarly, base, $Ca(OH)_2$ = Acid, H_2SO_4

$$M_1V_1 = M_2V_2$$
$$(2 \times 0.01) \times 10 = (2 \times 0.01) \times 10$$

Because $M_1V_1 = M_2V_2$, hence solution is neutral.

∴ $\qquad$ pH = 7

(c) Acid, H_2SO_4 = Base, KOH

$$M_1V_1 = M_2V_2$$
$$(2 \times 0.1) \, 10 = 0.1 \times 10$$

Because $M_1V_1 > M_2V_2$, hence solution is acidic,

$$[H^+] = \frac{M_1V_1 - M_2V_2}{V_1 + V_2}$$
$$= \frac{(0.2 \times 10) - (0.1 \times 10)}{10 + 10} = \frac{2 - 1}{20} = 0.05 \text{ M}$$

$$pH = -\log[0.05] = -\log[5.0 \times 10^{-2}]$$
$$pH = 2 - 0.6990 = 1.301 \approx 1.30$$
$$pH = 1.30$$

Question 67. Determine the solubilities of silver chromate, barium chromate, ferric hydroxide, lead chloride and mercurous iodide at 298 K from their solubility product constants.

$$[K_{sp}(Ag_2CrO_4) = 1.1 \times 10^{-12}, \, K_{sp}(BaCrO_4) = 1.2 \times 10^{-10},$$
$$K_{sp}[Fe(OH)_3] = 1.0 \times 10^{-38}, \, K_{sp}(PbCl_2) = 1.6 \times 10^{-5}$$
$$K_{sp}(Hg_2I_2) = 4.5 \times 10^{-29}]$$

Determine also the molarities of individual ions.

Solution. (a) $Ag_2CrO_4 \rightleftharpoons 2Ag^+ + CrO_4^{2-}; \, K_{sp} = 1.1 \times 10^{-12}$

$$\qquad s \qquad\qquad 2s \qquad\quad s$$

$$K_{sp} = [Ag^+]^2 \cdot [CrO_4^{2-}]$$
$$K_{sp} = [2s]^2 \cdot [s] = 4s^3$$
$$s^3 = \frac{K_{sp}}{4}$$

or $\qquad\qquad s^3 = \frac{1.1 \times 10^{-12}}{4} = 0.275 \times 10^{-12}$

$$3 \log s = \log 2.75 \times 10^{-13}$$
$$3 \log s = -13 + 0.4393 = -12.5607$$
$$\log s = \frac{-12.5607}{3} = -4.1869 = \bar{5}.8131$$
$$s = \text{antilog } \bar{5}.8131 = 6.503 \times 10^{-5} \text{ M}$$
$$[Ag^+] = 2s = 2 \times 6.503 \times 10^{-5}$$
$$= 13.006 \times 10^{-5} \approx 1.3 \times 10^{-4} \text{ M}$$
$$[CrO_4^{2-}] = s = 6.503 \times 10^{-5} \text{ M}$$

(b) $BaCrO_4 \rightleftharpoons Ba^{2+} + CrO_4^{2-}$; $K_{sp} = 1.2 \times 10^{-10}$

          s s s (Solubility of $BaCrO_4$ is s mol L^{-1})

$$K_{sp} = 1.2 \times 10^{-10} = [Ba^{2+}] \cdot [CrO_4^{2-}] = s^2$$
$$s = \sqrt{1.2 \times 10^{-10}} = 1.1 \times 10^{-5} \text{ M}$$
$$[Ba^{2+}] = [CrO_4^{2-}] = 1.1 \times 10^{-5} \text{ M}$$

(c) $Fe(OH)_3 \rightleftharpoons Fe^{3+} + 3OH^-$; $K_{sp} = 1.0 \times 10^{-38}$

       s s $3s$ (Solubility of $Fe(OH)_3$ is s mol L^{-1})

$$K_{sp} = [Fe^{3+}][OH^-]^3$$
$$K_{sp} = s \cdot (3s)^3 = 27s^4 \quad \text{or} \quad s^4 = \frac{K_{sp}}{27}$$
$$s^4 = \frac{1.0 \times 10^{-38}}{27} = 0.037 \times 10^{-38}$$
$$4 \log s = \log 3.7 \times 10^{-40}$$
$$4 \log s = -40 + 0.5682 = -39.4318$$
$$\log s = \frac{-39.4318}{4} = -9.8579 = \overline{10}.1421$$
$$s = \text{antilog } \overline{10}.1421 = 1.387 \times 10^{-10}$$
$$s \approx 1.39 \times 10^{-10}$$
$$[Fe^{3+}] = 1.39 \times 10^{-10} \text{ M}$$
$$[OH^-] = 3s = 3 \times 1.39 \times 10^{-10} = 4.17 \times 10^{-10} \text{ M}$$

(d) $PbCl_2 \rightleftharpoons Pb^{2+} + 2Cl^-$; $K_{sp} = 1.6 \times 10^{-5}$

      s s $2s$ (Solubility of $PbCl_2$ is s mol L^{-1})

$$K_{sp} = [Pb^{2+}][Cl^-]^2$$
$$K_{sp} = s \cdot (2s)^2 = 4s^3$$
$$s^3 = \frac{K_{sp}}{4} = \frac{1.6 \times 10^{-5}}{4} = 0.4 \times 10^{-5}$$
$$3 \log s = \log 0.4 \times 10^{-5} = \log 4.0 \times 10^{-6}$$

$$3 \log s = -6 + 0.6021 = -5.3979$$
$$\log s = \frac{-5.3979}{3} = -1.7993 = \overline{2}.2007$$
$$s = \text{antilog } \overline{2}.2007 = 1.585 \times 10^{-2}$$
$$\approx 1.59 \times 10^{-2} \text{ M}$$
$\therefore$ Solubility of $PbCl_2 = 1.59 \times 10^{-2}$ M
$$[Pb^{2+}] = 1.59 \times 10^{-2} \text{ M}$$
$$[Cl^-] = 2 \times 1.59 \times 10^{-2} \text{ M} = 3.18 \times 10^{-2} \text{ M}$$

(e) $\quad Hg_2I_2 \rightleftharpoons Hg_2^{2+} + 2I^-$; $K_{sp} = 4.5 \times 10^{-29}$
$\quad\quad s \quad\quad s \quad\quad 2s \quad\quad$ (Solubility of Hg_2I_2 is s mol L^{-1})
$$K_{sp} = [Hg_2^{2+}][I^-]^2$$
$$K_{sp} = s.(2s)^2 = 4s^3$$
$$s^3 = \frac{K_{sp}}{4} = \frac{4.5 \times 10^{-29}}{4} = 1.125 \times 10^{-29}$$
$$3 \log s = \log (1.125 \times 10^{-29})$$
$$3 \log s = -29 + 0.0512 = -28.9488$$
$$\log s = \frac{-28.9488}{3} = -9.6496$$
$$\log s = -9.6496 = \overline{10}.3504$$
$$s = \text{antilog } \overline{10}.3504 = 2.241 \times 10^{-10} \text{ M}$$
Solubility of $Hg_2I_2 = 2.241 \times 10^{-10}$ M
$$[Hg_2^{2+}] = 2.241 \times 10^{-10} \text{M}$$
$$[I^-] = 2 \times 2.241 \times 10^{-10} \text{ M} = 4.482 \times 10^{-10} \text{M}$$

Question 68. The solubility product constant of Ag_2CrO_4 and $AgBr$ are 1.1×10^{-12} and 5.0×10^{-13} respectively. Calculate the ratio of the molarities of their saturated solutions.

Solution. $\quad Ag_2CrO_4 \rightleftharpoons 2Ag^+ + CrO_4^{2-}$; $\quad K_{sp} = 1.1 \times 10^{-12}$
$\quad\quad\quad s \quad\quad\quad 2s \quad\quad s$
$\quad\quad\quad\quad\quad\quad$ (Solubility of Ag_2CrO_4 is s mol L^{-1})
$$K_{sp} = [Ag^+]^2[CrO_4^{2-}]$$
$$K_{sp} = (2s)^2 \cdot s = 4s^3$$
or
$$s^3 = \frac{K_{sp}}{4} = \frac{1.1 \times 10^{-12}}{4} = 0.275 \times 10^{-12}$$
$$s^3 = 2.75 \times 10^{-13}$$
$$3 \log s = \log 2.75 \times 10^{-13}$$
$$3 \log s = -13 + 0.4393 = -12.5607$$

$$\log s = \frac{-12.5607}{3} = -4.1869 = \overline{5}.8131$$

$$s = \text{antilog } \overline{5}.8131 = 6.503 \times 10^{-5} \text{ M}$$

Solubility of $[Ag_2CrO_4] = 6.503 \times 10^{-5}$ M

$$AgBr \rightleftharpoons Ag^+ + Br^-; \ K_{sp} = 5.0 \times 10^{-13}$$
$$ s \quad\quad s \quad\; s$$

(Solubility of AgBr is s mol L^{-1})

$$K_{sp} = [Ag^+][Br^-] = s \cdot s = s^2$$

or

$$s = \sqrt{K_{sp}} = \sqrt{5.0 \times 10^{-13}} = \sqrt{50 \times 10^{-14}}$$

$$s = 7.07 \times 10^{-7} \text{ M}$$

Ratio of their solubilities

$$\frac{s\,(Ag_2CrO_4)}{s\,(AgBr)} = \frac{6.50 \times 10^{-5} \text{ M}}{7.07 \times 10^{-7} \text{ M}} = 91.93 \approx 92$$

Ag_2CrO_4 is 92 times more soluble than AgBr.

Question 69. Equal volumes of 0.002 M solutions of sodium iodate and cupric chlorate are mixed together. Will it lead precipitation of copper iodate? (For cupric iodate $K_{sp} = 7.4 \times 10^{-8}$)

(i) For precipitation, ionic product $> K_{sp}$, so first find concentration, (mol L^{-1}) of Cu^{2+} ions and IO_3^- ions in mixture and then ionic product of $[Cu^{2+}]$ and $[IO_3^-]$.

(ii) If ionic product $> K_{sp}$, precipitation of $Cu(IO_3)_2$ will take place, otherwise not.

Solution. $2NaIO_3 + Cu(ClO_3)_2 \longrightarrow 2NaClO_3 + Cu(IO_3)_2$

$$ \text{copper iodate}$$

$$[Cu^{2+}]_{mix} = \frac{0.002}{2} = 0.001 \text{ M}$$

$$[IO_3^-]_{mix} = \frac{0.002}{2} = 0.001 \text{ M}$$

(Due to mixing of equal volumes, molar concentrations of each species is halved.)

$$Cu(IO_3)_2 \rightleftharpoons Cu^{2+} + 2IO_3^-$$

$Cu(IO_3)_2$ is precipitated if $[Cu^{2+}] \cdot [IO_3^-]^2 > K_{sp}$

$$[Cu^{2+}].[IO_3^-]^2 = (1.0 \times 10^{-3}) \times (1.0 \times 10^{-3})^2 = 1 \times 10^{-9}$$

It is less than K_{sp} of $Cu(IO_3)_2$ (7.4×10^{-8}). Hence, there will be no precipitation.

Question 70. The ionization constant of benzoic acid is 6.46×10^{-5} and K_{sp} for silver benzoate is 2.5×10^{-13}. How many times is silver benzoate more soluble in a buffer of pH 3.19 compared to its solubility in pure water?

(i) In order to find the hydrolysis constant of silver benzoate, first write the equation of ionization of benzoic acid and ionization of silver benzoate and find a relation of K_3 (hydrolysis constant) with $K_1(K_{sp})$ and K_a.

(ii) Find $[H^+]$ concentration to find s (solubility of silver benzoate) in buffer.

(iii) Find solubility of silver benzoate in aqueous solution and compare them.

Solution.

$$C_6H_5COOAg(s) \rightleftharpoons C_6H_5COO^- + Ag^+; \quad K_1 = K_{sp}$$

$$C_6H_5COO^- + H^+ \rightleftharpoons C_6H_5COOH; \quad K_2 = \frac{1}{K_a}$$

$$C_6H_5COOAg\ (s) + H^+ \rightleftharpoons C_6H_5COOH + Ag^+; \quad K_3 = \frac{K_{sp}}{K_a}$$

$$K_3 = \frac{[C_6H_5COOH][Ag^+]}{[H^+]} = \frac{s \cdot s}{[H^+]} = \frac{s^2}{[H^+]} = \frac{K_{sp}}{K_a}$$

where, s is the solubility of C_6H_5COOAg.

In a buffer of pH = 3.19

$$\log [H^+] = -3.19 = \overline{4}.81$$

$$[H^+] = \text{antilog } \overline{4}.81 = 6.46 \times 10^{-4}$$

$$\frac{s^2}{[H^+]} = \frac{K_{sp}}{K_a} \text{ or } s^2 = \frac{K_{sp} \times [H^+]}{K_a}$$

$$s = \sqrt{\frac{2.5 \times 10^{-13} \times 6.46 \times 10^{-4}}{6.46 \times 10^{-5}}}$$

$$s = \sqrt{2.5 \times 10^{-13} \times 10}$$

$$s = 1.6 \times 10^{-6} \text{ M (in buffer)}$$

In aqueous solution, solubility of C_6H_5COOAg :

$$K_{sp} = [C_6H_5COO^-][Ag^+] = s \cdot s = s^2$$

$$s = \sqrt{K_{sp}} = \sqrt{2.5 \times 10^{-13}} = 5 \times 10^{-7} \text{M}$$

$$\frac{s_{(C_6H_5COOAg)} \text{ in buffer}}{s_{(C_6H_5COOAg)} \text{ in aqueous solution}} = \frac{1.6 \times 10^{-6}}{5.0 \times 10^{-7}} = 3.2$$

C_6H_5COOAg is 3.2 times more soluble in buffer than in pure water.

Question 71. What is the maximum concentration of equimolar solutions of ferrous sulphate and sodium sulphide so that when mixed in equal volumes, there is no precipitation of iron sulphide ? (For iron sulphide, $K_{sp} = 6.3 \times 10^{-18}$)

Solution. FeS is at the point of precipitation when

$$[Fe^{2+}][S^{2-}] = K_{sp}$$

$$[Fe^{2+}] = [S^{2-}] = \sqrt{K_{sp}} = \sqrt{6.3 \times 10^{-18}}$$
$$[Fe^{2+}] = [S^{2-}] = 2.51 \times 10^{-9} \text{ M}$$

Since, equimolar solutions are to be mixed, hence on mixing concentration is halved. Thus, in original solution

$$[FeSO_4] = [Na_2S] = 2 \times 2.51 \times 10^{-9} \text{ M} = 5.02 \times 10^{-9} \text{M}$$

Question 72. What is the minimum volume of water required to dissolved 1g of calcium sulphate at 298 K ? (For calcium sulphate, K_{sp} is 9.1×10^{-6}).

Solution. $CaSO_4 \rightleftharpoons Ca^{2+} + SO_4^{2-}; K_{sp} = 9.1 \times 10^{-6}$

     s s s

where s is the solubility of $CaSO_4$.

$$K_{sp} = [Ca^{2+}][SO_4^{2-}] = s \cdot s = s^2$$
$$s = \sqrt{K_{sp}} = \sqrt{9.1 \times 10^{-6}}$$
$$s = 3.017 \times 10^{-3} \text{ M}$$

$\therefore$ $CaSO_4$ solubility $= 3.017 \times 10^{-3} \text{mol L}^{-1}$

$$= 3.017 \times 10^{-3} \times 136 \text{ gL}^{-1}$$

(Molar mass of $CaSO_4$ = 136 g mol^{-1})

$$= 410.3 \times 10^{-3} \text{gL}^{-1}$$

410.3×10^{-3} g $CaSO_4$ is dissolved in 1 L.

Therefore, 1 g $CaSO_4$ is dissolved in $\dfrac{1 \times 1}{410.3 \times 10^{-3}} = 2.437 \text{ L}$

Question 73. The concentration of sulphide ion in 0.1 M HCl solution saturated with hydrogen sulphide is 1.0×10^{-19} M. If 10 mL of this is added to 5 mL of 0.04 M solution of the following : $FeSO_4$, $MnCl_2$, $ZnCl_2$ and $CdCl_2$, in which of these solutions precipitation will take place ?
(Given, K_{sp} of FeS = 6.3×10^{-18}, K_{sp} of MnS = 2.5×10^{-13}
K_{sp} of ZnS = 1.6×10^{-24}, K_{sp} of CdS = 8.0×10^{-27})

For precipitation, ionic product > solubility product, so calculate ionic product of each salt and compare it with solubility product.

Solution. $[S^{2-}] = 1 \times 10^{-19}$ M

10 mL of S^{2-} is mixed with 5 mL of 0.04 M solution of different solutes so that final volume of solution is 15 mL.

$\therefore$ $[S^{2-}]_{mix} = \dfrac{10 \times 10^{-19}}{15} = 6.67 \times 10^{-20}$ M

$$[M^{2+}] = \dfrac{5 \times 0.04}{15} = 1.33 \times 10^{-2} \text{ M}$$

where, $[M^{2+}] = Fe^{2+}, Mn^{2+}, Zn^{2+}$ or Cd^{2+}

Equilibrium

$$[M^{2+}][S^{2-}] = 1.33 \times 10^{-2} \times 6.67 \times 10^{-20}$$

Ionic product of $[M^{2+}][S^{2-}] = 8.87 \times 10^{-22}$

IP of $[M^{2+}][S^{2-}] > K_{sp}$ of ZnS and CdS

So, these ($CdCl_2$ and $ZnCl_2$) are precipitated as CdS and ZnS.

Selected NCERT Exemplar Problems

Short Answer Type

Question 1. The ionization of hydrogen chloride in water is given below

$$HCl(aq) + H_2O(l) \rightleftharpoons H_3O^+(aq) + Cl^-(aq)$$

Label two conjugate acid-base pairs in this ionization.

Solution.

$$\overset{\displaystyle\ulcorner\text{Adds proton}\urcorner\downarrow}{\underset{\text{Acid}\qquad\text{Base}\qquad\qquad\text{Conjugate acid}\quad\text{Conjugate base}}{HCl(aq) + H_2O(l) \rightleftharpoons H_3O^+(aq) + Cl^-(aq)}}$$

└──── Loses proton ─────────────────↑

Question 2. Ionization constant of a weak base MOH, is given by the expression

$$K_b = \frac{[M^+][OH^-]}{[MOH]}$$

Values of ionization constant of some weak bases at a particular temperature are given below :

Base	Dimethyl amine	Urea	Pyridine	Ammonia
K_b	5.4×10^{-4}	1.3×10^{-14}	1.77×10^{-9}	1.77×10^{-5}

Arrange the bases in decreasing order of the extent of their ionization at equilibrium. Which of the above base is the strongest?

Solution. Greater the ionization constant (K_b) of a base, greater is its ionization. Hence, dimethyl amine is the strongest base.

Dimethyl amine > ammonia > pyridine > urea

K_b $\quad5.4 \times 10^{-4} \qquad 1.77 \times 10^{-5}\quad 1.77 \times 10^{-9}\quad 1.3 \times 10^{-14}$

Question 3. Conjugate acid of a weak base is always stronger. What will be the decreasing order of basic strength of the following conjugate bases?

$$OH^-, RO^-, CH_3COO^-, Cl^-$$

Solution. Conjugate acids of the given bases are, H_2O, ROH, CH_3COOH and HCl. Order of acidic strength is

$$HCl > CH_3COOH > H_2O > ROH$$

Hence, order of basic strength of their conjugate bases is

$$\bar{RO} > \bar{OH} > CH_3\bar{COO} > Cl^-$$

Question 4. Arrange the following in increasing order of pH.

$$KNO_3(aq),\ CH_3COONa(aq),\ NH_4Cl(aq),\ C_6H_5COONH_4(aq)$$

Solution. (i) KNO_3 is a salt of strong acid-strong base, hence its aqueous solution is neutral; $pH = 7$

(ii) CH_3COONa is a salt of weak acid and strong base, hence, its aqueous solution is basic; $pH > 7$.

(iii) NH_4Cl is a salt of strong acid and weak base, hence its aqueous solution is acidic; $pH < 7$.

(iv) $C_6H_5COONH_4$ is a salt of weak acid, C_6H_5COOH and weak base, NH_4OH. But NH_4OH is slightly stronger than C_6H_5COOH. Hence, pH is slightly > 7.

Therefore, increasing order of pH of the given salts is,

$$NH_4Cl < KNO_3 < C_6H_5COONH_4 < CH_3COONa$$

Question 5. On the basis of the equation $pH = -\log[H^+]$, the pH of 10^{-8} mol dm^{-3} solution of HCl should be 8. However, it is observed to be less than 7.0. Explain the reason.

Solution. Concentration 10^{-8} mol dm^{-3} indicates that the solution is very dilute. So, we cannot neglect the contribution of H_3O^+ ions produced from H_2O in the solution. Total $[H_3O^+] = 10^{-8} + 10^{-7}$ M. From this we get the value of pH close to 7 but less than 7 because the solution is acidic.

Question 6. pH of a solution of a strong acid is 5.0. What will be the pH of the solution obtained after diluting the given solution 100 times?

Solution. $pH = 5$

$$[H^+] = 10^{-5} \text{ mol L}^{-1}$$

On diluting the solution 100 times, $[H^+] = \dfrac{10^{-5}}{100} = 10^{-7}$ mol L^{-1}

Total H$^+$ ion concentration = H$^+$ ions from acid + H$^+$ ion from water

$$[H^+] = 10^{-7} + 10^{-7} = 2 \times 10^{-7} \text{ M}$$
$$pH = -\log[2 \times 10^{-7}]$$
$$pH = 7 - 0.3010 = 6.699$$

Question 7. A sparingly soluble salt gets precipitated only when the product of concentration of its ions in the solution (K_{sp}) becomes greater than its solubility product. If the solubility of $BaSO_4$ in water is 8×10^{-4} mol dm^{-3}, calculate its solubility in 0.01 mol dm^{-3} of H_2SO_4.

Solution. $\qquad\qquad BaSO_4(s) \rightleftharpoons Ba^{2+}(aq) + SO_4^{2-}(aq)$

At equili. $\quad (1-s) \qquad\qquad\quad s \qquad\qquad s$

K_{sp} for $BaSO_4 = [Ba^{2+}][SO_4^{2-}] = s \times s = s^2$

But $\qquad s = 8 \times 10^{-4} \text{ mol dm}^{-3}$

∴ $\qquad K_{sp} = (8 \times 10^{-4})^2 = 64 \times 10^{-8}$

In the presence of 0.01 M H_2SO_4, the expression for K_{sp} will be

$$K_{sp} = [Ba^{2+}][SO_4^{2-}]$$

$$K_{sp} = (s) \cdot (s + 0.01)$$

(0.01 M SO_4^{2-} ions from 0.01 M H_2SO_4)

$$64 \times 10^{-8} = s \cdot (s + 0.01)$$

$$s^2 + 0.01 \, s - 64 \times 10^{-8} = 0$$

$$s = \frac{-0.01 \pm \sqrt{(0.01)^2 + (4 \times 64 \times 10^{-8})}}{2}$$

$$= \frac{-0.01 \pm \sqrt{10^{-4} + (256 \times 10^{-8})}}{2}$$

$$= \frac{-0.01 \pm \sqrt{10^{-4}(1 + 256 \times 10^{-4})}}{2}$$

$$= \frac{-0.01 \pm 10^{-2}\sqrt{1 + 0.0256}}{2} = \frac{10^{-2}(-1 \pm 1.012719)}{2}$$

$$= 5 \times 10^{-3} \, (-1 + 1.012719) = 6.4 \times 10^{-5} \text{ mol dm}^{-3}$$

Note $\quad s \lll 0.01$, so, $s + 0.01 \approx 0.01$ and $64 \times 10^{-8} = s \times 0.01$

$$s = \frac{64 \times 10^{-8}}{0.01} = 6.4 \times 10^{-5}$$

Question 8. Calculate the pH of a solution formed by mixing equal volumes of two solutions, A and B of a strong acid having pH= 6 and pH=4 respectively.

Solution. pH of solution $A = 6$. Hence, $[H^+] = 10^{-6} \text{ mol L}^{-1}$

pH of solution $B = 4$. Hence, $[H^+] = 10^{-4} \text{ mol L}^{-1}$

On mixing 1 L of each solution, molar concentration of total H^+ is halved.

Total, $[H^+] = \dfrac{10^{-6} + 10^{-4}}{2} \text{ mol L}^{-1}$

$$[H^+] = \frac{1.01 \times 10^{-4}}{2} = 5.05 \times 10^{-5} \text{ mol L}^{-1}$$

$$[H^+] = 5.0 \times 10^{-5} \text{ mol L}^{-1}$$

$$pH = -\log [H^+]$$

$$pH = -\log (5.0 \times 10^{-5})$$

$$pH = -[\log 5 + (-5 \log 10)]$$

$$pH = -\log 5 + 5$$

$$pH = 5 - \log 5 = 5 - 0.6990$$

$$pH = 4.3010 \approx 4.3$$

Question 9. Calculate the volume of water required to dissolve 0.1 g lead (II) chloride to get a saturated solution (K_{sp} of $PbCl_2 = 3.2 \times 10^{-8}$, atomic mass of Pb = 207 u).

Solution. Suppose solubility of $PbCl_2$ in water is s mol L^{-1}.

$$PbCl_2(s) \rightleftharpoons Pb^{2+}(aq) + 2Cl^-(aq)$$
$$(1-s) \qquad\qquad s \qquad\quad 2s$$

$$K_{sp} = [Pb^{2+}] \cdot [Cl^-]^2$$

$$K_{sp} = [s][2s]^2 = 4s^3$$

$$3.2 \times 10^{-8} = 4s^3$$

$$s^3 = \frac{3.2 \times 10^{-8}}{4} = 0.8 \times 10^{-8}$$

$$s^3 = 8.0 \times 10^{-9}$$

Solubility of $PbCl_2$, $s = 2 \times 10^{-3}$ mol L^{-1}

Solubility of $PbCl_2$ in g $L^{-1} = 278 \times 2 \times 10^{-3} = 0.556$ g L^{-1}

$$(\because \text{Molar mass of } PbCl_2 = 207 + (2 \times 35.5) = 278)$$

0.556 g of $PbCl_2$ dissolve in 1 L of water.

$\therefore$ 0.1 g of $PbCl_2$ will dissolve in $\dfrac{1 \times 0.1}{0.556}$ L of water

$$= 0.1798 \text{ L} = 179.8 \text{ mL}$$

Question 10. Following data is given for the reaction,

$$CaCO_3(s) \longrightarrow CaO(s) + CO_2(g); \quad \Delta_f H^\circ[CaO(s)] = -635.1 \text{ kJ mol}^{-1}$$
$$\Delta_f H^\circ[CO_2(g)] = -393.5 \text{ kJ mol}^{-1}$$
$$\Delta_f H^\circ[CaCO_3(s)] = -1206.9 \text{ kJ mol}^{-1}$$

Predict the effect of temperature on the equilibrium constant of the above reaction.

Solution. $CaCO_3(s) \rightleftharpoons CaO(s) + CO_2(g)$

$$\Delta_f H^\circ = \Delta_f H^\circ[CaO(s)] + \Delta_f H^\circ[CO_2(g)] - \Delta_f H^\circ[CaCO_3(s)]$$
$$\therefore \quad \Delta_r H^\circ = -635.1 + (-393.5) - (-1206.9) = 178.3 \text{ kJ mol}^{-1}$$

Because ΔH value is positive, so the reaction is endothermic. Hence, according to Le-Chatelier's principle, reaction will proceed in forward direction on increasing temperature.

Long Answer Type

Question 11. How can you predict the following stages of a reaction by comparing the value of K_c and Q_c?

   (i) Net reaction proceeds in the forward direction.

   (ii) Net reaction proceeds in the backward direction.

   (iii) No net reaction occurs.

Solution. (i) If $Q_c < K_c$, the reaction will proceed in the direction of the products (forward reaction).

(ii) $Q_c > K_c$, the reaction will proceed in the direction of reactants (reverse reaction).

(iii) If $Q_c = K_c$, the reaction mixture is already at equilibrium.

Question 12. On the basis of Le-Chatelier's principle, explain how temperature and pressure can be adjusted to increase the yield of ammonia in the following reaction?

$$N_2(g) + 3H_2(g) \rightleftharpoons 2NH_3(g); \quad \Delta H = -92.38 \text{ kJ mol}^{-1}$$

What will be the effect of addition of argon to the above reaction mixture at constant volume?

Solution. $N_2(g) + 3H_2(g) \rightleftharpoons 2NH_3(g); \Delta H = -92.38 \text{ kJ mol}^{-1}$

It is an exothermic process. According to Le-Chatelier's principle, low temperature is favourable for high yield of ammonia, but practically very low temperatures slow down the reaction. So, optimum temperature, 700 K is favourable in attainment of equilibrium.

Similarly, high pressure about 200 atm is favourable for high yield of ammonia. On increasing pressure, reaction goes in the forward direction because the number of moles decreases in the forward direction.

At constant volume addition of argon does not affect the equilibrium because it does not change the partial pressures of the reactants or products involved in the reaction and the equilibrium remains undisturbed.

Question 13. Write a relation between ΔG and Q and define the meaning of each term and answer the following :

(a) Why a reaction proceeds forward when $Q < K$ and no net reaction occurs when $Q = K$?

(b) Explain the effect of increase in pressure in terms of reaction quotient Q for the reaction.

$$CO(g) + 3H_2(g) \rightleftharpoons CH_4(g) + H_2O(g)$$

Solution. $\Delta G = \Delta G° + RT \ln Q$

$\Delta G°$ = change in free energy as the reaction proceeds

ΔG = standard free energy

Q = reaction quotient

R = gas constant

T = absolute temperature

(a) Since, $\Delta G° = -RT \ln K$

$\therefore$
$$\Delta G = -RT \ln K + RT \ln Q$$
$$\Delta G = RT \ln \frac{Q}{K}$$

If $Q < K$, ΔG will be negative and the reaction proceeds in the forward direction.

If $Q = K$, $\Delta G = 0$ reaction is in equilibrium and there is no net reaction.

(b) $CO(g) + 3H_2(g) \rightleftharpoons CH_4(g) + H_2O(g)$

$$K_c = \frac{[CH_4]\,[H_2O]}{[CO]\,[H_2]^3}$$

On increasing pressure, volume decreases. If we doubled the pressure, volume will be halved but the molar concentrations will be doubled. Then

$$Q_c = \frac{2\,[CH_4] \cdot 2[H_2O]}{2\,[CO]\,\{2\,[H_2]\}^3} = \frac{1}{4}\,\frac{[CH_4]\,[H_2O]}{[CO]\,[H_2]^3} = \frac{1}{4}\,K_c$$

Therefore, Q_c is less than K_c, so Q_c will tend to increase to reestablish equilibrium and the reaction will go in forward direction.

Chapter 8

Redox Reactions

Important Results

1. Oxidation is defined as addition of oxygen or electronegative element to a substance; removal of hydrogen or electropositive element from a substance.

2. Reduction is defined as removal of oxygen or electronegative element from a substance; addition of hydrogen or electropositive element to a substance.

3. In redox reactions, oxidation and reduction occur simultaneously. Oxidation involves loss of electrons (deelectronation) while reduction involves gain of electrons (electronation). Redox reactions are classified into four categories. Combination, decomposition, displacement and disproportionation reactions.

4. The species which gets oxidised is called **reducing agent** and the species which gets reduced is called **oxidising agent.**

5. **Disproportionation reactions** It is a special type of redox reaction in which the same species is simultaneously oxidised as well as reduced, *e.g.,*

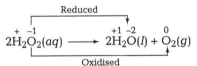

$$2\overset{+\ -1}{H_2O_2}(aq) \longrightarrow 2\overset{+1\ -2}{H_2O}(l) + \overset{0}{O_2}(g)$$

For such redox reactions to occur the reacting species must contain an element which has at least three oxidation states.

6. The **oxidation number** (ON) of an atom in a molecule or in a polyatomic ion is a hypothetical charge that the atom would have if the electrons in each bond were located on the more electronegative atom. Increase in oxidation number is oxidation and decrease in oxidation number is reduction.

7. Some rules for finding oxidation number are :
   (i) Oxidation number of elements in their elementary state is 0.
   (ii) Oxidation number of I A and II A group elements = their group number.

(iii) Fluorine always has – 1 oxidation state.

(iv) Oxidation number of oxygen = – 2 (usually), in peroxides – 1, in superoxides – $\frac{1}{2}$ and in OF_2 = + 2.

(v) Oxidation number of H is + 1 when combined with non-metals and – 1 when combined with metals.

(vi) In a compound, the more electronegative atom will have negative oxidation number where as the less electronegative atom will have positive oxidation number.

(vii) Algebraic sum of oxidation number of all the atoms in a neutral molecule is zero and in an ion is equal to charge on the ion.

8. Oxidation number of any element never exceeds its group number.

9. **Electrochemical cell** It is a device in which oxidation and reduction half reactions are carried indirectly and loss of chemical energy during the reaction appear as electrical energy.

10. **Electrolytic cell** It is a device in which electrical energy is supplied from external source to bring about chemical reaction. Electrolysis occur in same electrolyte solution.

11. **Potential difference** between the metal electrode and the metal ion in which electrode is dipped is called **electrode potential (E).**

12. At 1 atm pressure and 1 M concentration of electrolyte, electrode potential is also known as **standard electrode potential ($E°$).** Smaller the value of $E°$, stronger is the reducing agent and larger the value of $E°$, stronger is the oxidising agent.

13. If on combining an electrode A with the normal hydrogen electrode (NHE), a reduction process (*i.e.*, gain of electrons) occurs at the electrode, the potential of the electrode is known as **reduction potential.**

14. The arrangement of elements in order of increasing reduction potential values is called **electrochemical series.**

15. The difference in potentials of the two half-cells of a cell is known as **electromotive force** (emf) or **cell potential.**

$$E°_{cell} = E°_{cathode} - E°_{anode}$$

If E_{cell} is positive, reaction occurs spontaneously in forward direction.

If E_{cell} is negative, reaction occurs spontaneously in backward direction.

16. **Redox couple** is defined as the couple having together the oxidised and reduced forms of a substance taking part in oxidation or reduction half reactions.

Exercises

Question 1. Assign oxidation number to the underlined elements in each of the following species.

(a) $NaH_2\underline{P}O_4$ (b) $NaH\underline{S}O_4$ (c) $H_4\underline{P}_2O_7$

(d) $K_2\underline{Mn}O_4$ (e) $Ca\underline{O}_2$ (f) $NaB\underline{H}_4$

(g) $H_2\underline{S}_2O_7$ (h) $KAl(\underline{S}O_4)_2 \cdot 12H_2O$

Solution. (a) $NaH_2\underline{P}O_4$

Let the oxidation number of P be x. Writing the oxidation number of each atom above its symbol, we get $\overset{+1}{Na}\overset{+1}{H_2}\overset{x}{P}\overset{-2}{O_4}$

In neutral compounds, the sum of the oxidation numbers of all the atoms is zero.

$\therefore$ $\qquad 1(+1) + 2(+1) + x + 4(-2) = 0$
$$3 + x + (-8) = 0$$
$$x = 8 - 3 = 5$$

Hence, the oxidation number of P in NaH_2PO_4 is + 5.

(b) $NaH\underline{S}O_4$; Let the oxidation number of S be x.
$$\overset{+1}{Na}\overset{+1}{H}\overset{x}{S}\overset{-2}{O_4}$$
$$1(+1) + 1(+1) + x + 4(-2) = 0$$
$$2 + x + (-8) = 0$$
$$x = +6$$

Hence, the oxidation number of S in $NaHSO_4$ is + 6.

(c) $H_4\underline{P}_2O_7$; Let the oxidation number of P in $H_4P_2O_7$ be x.
$$\overset{+1}{H_4}\overset{x}{P_2}\overset{-2}{O_7}$$
$$4(+1) + 2(x) + 7(-2) = 0$$
$$4 + 2x + (-14) = 0$$
$$2x = +10 \text{ or } x = +\frac{10}{2} = +5$$

Hence, the oxidation number of P in $H_4P_2O_7$ is + 5.

(d) $K_2\underline{Mn}O_4$; Let the oxidation number of Mn in K_2MnO_4 be x.
$$\overset{+1}{K_2}\overset{x}{Mn}\overset{-2}{O_4}$$
$$2(+1) + x + 4(-2) = 0$$
$$2 + x - 8 = 0 \text{ or } x = +6$$

(e) $Ca\underline{O}_2$; Let the oxidation number of O be x.
$$\overset{+2}{Ca}\overset{x}{O_2} \text{ (Ca is an alkaline earth metal, so its O.N. is + 2)}$$
$$1(+2) + 2x = 0$$
$$2x = -2 \text{ or } x = -1$$

Hence, the oxidation number of O in CaO_2 is − 1.

(f) $NaBH_4$; Let the oxidation number of B be x.

$\underset{+1\ \ \ x\ \ -1}{Na B H_4}$ (In $NaBH_4$, H exists as hydride ion, H^-, so its oxidation number is -1)

$$1(+1) + x + 4(-1) = 0$$
$$1 + x - 4 = 0 \text{ or } x = +3$$

Hence, the oxidation number of B in $NaBH_4$ is $+3$.

(g) $H_2\underline{S}_2O_7$; Let the oxidation number of S be x.

$$\underset{+1\ \ \ x\ \ -2}{H_2\ S_2\ O_7}$$

$$2(+1) + 2x + 7(-2) = 0$$
$$2 + 2x - 14 = 0$$
$$2x = +12 \text{ or } x = +6$$

Hence, the oxidation number of S in $H_2S_2O_7$ is $+6$.

(h) $KAl(\underline{S}O_4)_2 \cdot 12H_2O$; Let the oxidation number of S in $KAl(SO_4)_2 \cdot 12H_2O$ be x.

$$\underset{+1\ +3\ \ x\ -2 \qquad +1\ -2}{K\ Al\ (S\,O_4)_2 \cdot 12H_2\ O}$$

$$1(+1) + 1(+3) + 2x + 8(-2) + 12(2 \times 1 + (-2)) = 0$$
$$4 + 2x - 16 = 0$$
$$2x = +12 \text{ or } x = +6$$

Note H_2O *is a neutral molecule, therefore sum of oxidation numbers of all atoms in* H_2O *is zero.*

Hence, the oxidation number of S in $KAl(SO_4)_2 \cdot 12H_2O$ is $+6$.

Question 2. What are the oxidation numbers of the underlined elements in each of the following and how do you rationalise your results?

(a) $K\underline{I}_3$ (b) $H_2\underline{S}_4O_6$ (c) $\underline{Fe}_3O_4$

(d) $CH_3\underline{C}H_2OH$ (e) $\underline{C}H_3\underline{C}OOH$

Solution. (a) $K\underline{I}_3$

$$\underset{+1\ \ x}{K\ I_3}; 1(+1) + 3x = 0 \text{ or } x = -\frac{1}{3}$$

Therefore, the average oxidation number of I is $-\frac{1}{3}$. It is wrong because oxidation number cannot be fractional. Let us consider the structure of KI_3.

$\overset{+}{K}(I - I \leftarrow I)^{-1}$, In this structure, a coordinate bond is formed between I_2 molecule and I^- ion. Hence, the oxidation number of three I atoms in KI_3 are 0, 0 (in I_2) and -1 respectively.

(b) $H_2S_4O_6$

Let the oxidation number of S be x.

$$\underset{+1\ \ x\ \ -2}{H_2\ S_4\ O_6}$$

$$2(+1) + 4x + 6(-2) = 0$$

$$4x = +10 \text{ or } x = +\frac{10}{4} = +2.5$$

Let us consider the structure of $H_2S_4O_6$

$$H-O \overset{+5}{-}\underset{\underset{O}{\|}}{\overset{\overset{O}{\|}}{S}} -\overset{0}{S}-\overset{0}{S}- \overset{+5}{\underset{\underset{O}{\|}}{\overset{\overset{O}{\|}}{S}}} -OH$$

In $H_2S_4O_6$, the oxidation number of each of two S-atoms which are linked with each other by a single bond (in the centre) is zero, and each of remaining two S-atoms is + 5. Hence, the oxidation number of 4 S-atoms in $H_2S_4O_6$ are + 5, 0, 0 and + 5 respectively.

(c) Fe_3O_4; Let the oxidation number of Fe be x.

$$\overset{x}{Fe}_3 \overset{-2}{O}_4$$

$$3x + 4(-2) = 0 \text{ or } x = +\frac{8}{3}$$

Therefore, the average oxidation number of Fe is $\frac{8}{3}$. But stoichiometrically, Fe_3O_4 is an equimolar mixture of FeO and Fe_2O_3. The oxidation number of Fe in Fe_3O_4 ($\equiv FeO \cdot Fe_2O_3$) is + 2 and + 3 respectively.

(d) $\underline{C}H_3\underline{C}H_2OH$

$$\overset{x}{C}_2 \overset{+1}{H}_6 \overset{-2}{O}$$

$$2x + 6(+1) + 1(-2) = 0$$

$$2x = -4 \text{ or } x = -2$$

Therefore, the average oxidation number of C is – 2.

Let us consider the structure of CH_3CH_2OH

$$H-\overset{\overset{\displaystyle H}{|}}{\underset{\underset{\displaystyle H}{|}}{C}}{}^2-\overset{\overset{\displaystyle H}{|}}{\underset{\underset{\displaystyle H}{|}}{C}}{}^1-OH$$

Oxidation number of C_1 atom = 1 (+ 1) + 2 (+ 1) + x + 1 (– 1) = 0
[C_1 atom is attached to one CH_3 group (Ox. no. = + 1), two H atoms and one —OH group (Ox. no. = – 1)]

$$x = -2$$

Oxidation number of C_2 atom = 3 (+ 1) + x + 1 (– 1) = 0
[C_2 atom is attached to three H-atoms and one —CH_2OH group (Ox. no. = – 1)]

$$x = -2$$

(e) $\underline{C}H_3\underline{C}OOH$

$$\overset{x}{C}_2 \overset{+1}{H}_4 \overset{-2}{O}_2$$

$$2x + 4(+1) + 2(-2) = 0$$

$$2x + 4 + (-4) = 0 \text{ or } x = 0$$

Therefore, the average oxidation number of C is zero.
Let us consider the structure of CH_3COOH

$$H-\underset{\underset{H}{\overset{\displaystyle |}{\underset{2}{C}}}}{\overset{\overset{\displaystyle H}{\overset{\displaystyle |}{}}}{}}-\underset{1}{\overset{\overset{\displaystyle O}{\overset{\displaystyle \|}{}}}{C}}-O-H$$

Oxidation number of C_1 atom $= 1(+1) + x + 1(-2) + 1(-1) = 0$
[C_1atom is attached to one —CH_3 group (Ox. no. $= +1$), one oxygen atom and one —OH group (oxidation number -1)]

$$x = +2$$

Similarly, oxidation number of C_2 atom

$$3(+1) + x + 1(-1) = 0$$
$$x = -2$$

Question 3.   Justify that the following reactions are redox reactions :

(a) $CuO(s) + H_2(g) \longrightarrow Cu(s) + H_2O(g)$

(b) $Fe_2O_3(s) + 3CO(g) \longrightarrow 2Fe(s) + 3CO_2(g)$

(c) $4BCl_3(g) + 3LiAlH_4(s) \longrightarrow 2B_2H_6(g) + 3LiCl(s) + 3AlCl_3(s)$

(d) $2K(s) + F_2(g) \longrightarrow 2K^+F^-(s)$

(e) $4NH_3(g) + 5O_2(g) \longrightarrow 4NO(g) + 6H_2O(g)$

Redox reactions are those reactions in which one reactant is oxidised while the other is reduced. So, first find the oxidation state of each element to find the substance undergoing oxidation or reduction, and then tell is it redox reaction or not.

Solution.   (a) $CuO(s) + H_2(g) \longrightarrow Cu(s) + H_2O(g)$

Assign oxidation numbers of each atom above its symbol.

$$\overset{+2 \ -2}{CuO}(s) + \overset{0}{H_2}(g) \longrightarrow \overset{0}{Cu}(s) + \overset{+1 \ -2}{H_2O}(g)$$

Oxidation number of Cu in CuO is $+2$. It decreases from $+2$ to zero in Cu. While oxidation number of hydrogen increases from 0 (in H_2) to $+1$ (in H_2O). This shows that CuO is reduced to Cu but H_2 is oxidised to H_2O. Hence, it is an example of redox reaction.

(b) $\overset{+3 \ -2}{Fe_2O_3}(s) + 3\overset{+2 \ -2}{CO}(g) \longrightarrow 2\overset{0}{Fe}(s) + 3\overset{+4 \ -2}{CO_2}(g)$

Oxidation number of Fe decreases from $+3$ (in Fe_2O_3) to zero (in Fe) and oxidation number of C increases from $+2$ (in CO) to $+4$ (in CO_2). This shows that Fe_2O_3 is reduced to Fe and CO is oxidised to CO_2. Hence, it is a redox reaction.

(c) $4\overset{+3 \ -1}{BCl_3}(g) + 3\overset{+1 \ +3 \ -1}{LiAlH_4}(s) \longrightarrow 2\overset{-3 \ +1}{B_2H_6}(g) + 3\overset{+1 \ -1}{LiCl}(s) + 3\overset{+3 \ -1}{AlCl_3}(s)$

Oxidation number of B decreases from $+3$ (in BCl_3) to -3 (in B_2H_6) and oxidation number of H increases from -1 (in $LiAlH_4$) to $+1$ (in B_2H_6). This shows that BCl_3 is reduced to B_2H_6 and $LiAlH_4$ is oxidised. Hence, it is a redox reaction.

(d) $\overset{0}{2K}(s) + \overset{0}{F_2}(g) \longrightarrow \overset{+1-1}{2KF}(s)$

Oxidation number of K increases from zero (in K) to +1 (in KF) and oxidation number of F reduces from zero (in F_2) to − 1 (in KF). This shows that K is oxidised and F_2 is reduced. Hence, it is a redox reaction.

(e) $\overset{-3+1}{4NH_3}(g) + \overset{0}{5O_2}(g) \longrightarrow \overset{+2-2}{4NO}(g) + \overset{+1\ -2}{6H_2O}(g)$

Oxidation number of N increases from − 3 (in NH_3) to +2 (in NO) and oxidation number of O decreases from zero (in O_2) to − 2 (in NO and H_2O). This shows that NH_3 is oxidised and O_2 is reduced. Hence, it is a redox reaction.

Question 4. Fluorine reacts with ice and results in the change :

$$H_2O(s) + F_2(g) \longrightarrow HF(g) + HOF(g)$$

Justify that this reaction is a redox reaction.

 Redox reactions involve oxidation and reduction as its two half reactions. So, find the oxidation state of each element given in the equation to find which substance is oxidizing and which is reducing, then tell, is the given reaction a redox reaction?

Solution. $\overset{+1\ -2}{H_2O}(s) + \overset{0}{F_2}(g) \longrightarrow \overset{+1\ -1}{HF}(g) + \overset{+1\ -2+1}{HOF}(g) \longrightarrow \overset{+1\ -1}{HF} + \overset{+1\ -2}{H_2O} + \overset{+2+1}{OF_2}$

Oxidation number of F decreases from zero (in F_2) to − 1 (in HF) and of O increases from −2 to + 2 (in OF_2). This shows that F_2 is reduced. It is not a disproportionation reaction, but only a redox reaction. In a disproportionation reaction, an element in one oxidation state is simultaneously reduced and oxidised.

Question 5. Calculate the oxidation number of sulphur, chromium and nitrogen in H_2SO_5, $Cr_2O_7^{2-}$ and NO_3^-. Suggest the structure of these compounds. Count for the fallacy.

Solution.

(i) Oxidation number of S in H_2SO_5 is

$$2(+1) + x + 5(-2) = 0 \text{ or } x = +8.$$

But oxidation number of 'S' cannot be more than 8 because S has only 6 valence electrons. This fallacy is removed by calculating oxidation number of S by chemical bonding method. Let us consider the structure of H_2SO_5.

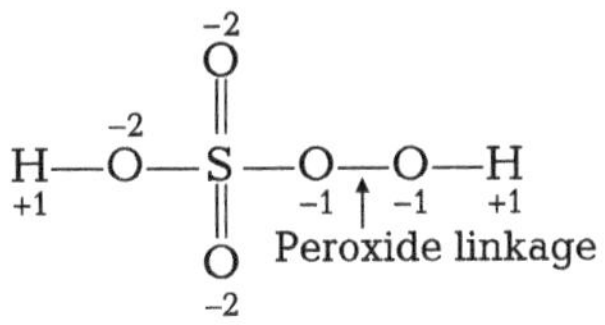

$$\overset{+1}{H}\!-\!\overset{-2}{O}\!-\!\overset{}{\underset{\underset{-2}{O}}{\overset{\overset{-2}{O}}{S}}}\!-\!\overset{-1}{O}\!\underset{\uparrow}{}\!\overset{-1}{O}\!-\!\overset{+1}{H}$$

Peroxide linkage

In H_2SO_5 two oxygen atoms are in − 1 oxidation state.

Let the oxidation number of S be x.

$$2 (+ 1) + 3 (- 2) + x + 2 (- 1) = 0$$
$$\text{(for H)} \quad \text{(for three O)} \quad \text{(for O—O)}$$
$$2 + (- 6) + x + (- 2) = 0$$
$$x = + 6$$

Therefore, the oxidation number of S in H_2SO_5 is + 6.

(ii) Oxidation number of Cr in $Cr_2O_7^{2-}$ is

$$2x + (- 2) \, 7 = - 2$$
$$2x = + 12$$
$$x = + 6$$

Let us consider the structure of $Cr_2O_7^{2-}$ ion

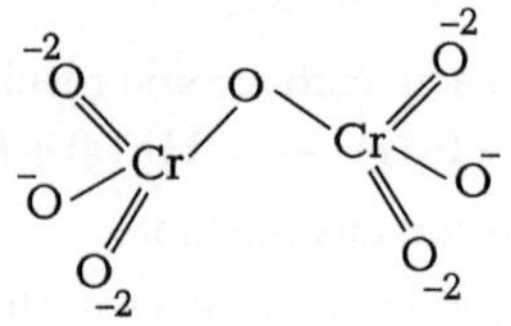

Let the oxidation number of each Cr atom be x.

$$4(- 2) + (- 2) + 1(- 2) + 2x = 0$$
$$- 8 - 2 - 2 + 2x = 0$$
$$2x = + 12$$
$$x = + 6$$

Oxidation number of Cr in $Cr_2O_7^{2-}$ is same, *i.e.*, + 6 whether it is calculated by conventional method or by chemical bonding method. Hence, there is no fallacy.

(iii) Oxidation number of N in NO_3^- is + 5 [$x + 3 (- 2) = - 1$ or $x = + 5$].

Let us consider the structure of NO_3^- ion

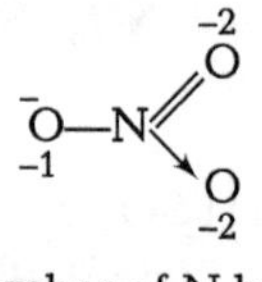

Let the oxidation number of N be x

$$1 (- 1) + x + 1 (- 2) + 1 (- 2) = 0$$
$$\text{(for } \bar{O}) \qquad \text{(for } = O) \, \text{(for} \to O)$$
$$x = + 5$$

Oxidation number of N in NO_3^- ion is same, *i.e.*, + 5 whether it is calculated by conventional method or by chemical bonding method. Hence, there is no fallacy.

Question 6. Write formulas for the following compounds :

(a) Mercury (II) chloride   (b) Nickel(II) sulphate

(c) Tin(IV) oxide   (d) Thallium(I) sulphate

(e) Iron(III) sulphate   (f) Chromium(III) oxide

(i) While writing the formula of a compound, oxidation state (or valency) of cation is written as the subscript of anion and valency of anion is written as the subscript of cation.

(ii) Valency of chloride (Cl^-), sulphate (SO_4^{2-}) and oxide (O^{2-}) are $-1, -2$ and -2 respectively. Valencies of metals are given in brackets.

Solution. (a) $Hg(II)Cl_2$ (b) $Ni(II)SO_4$ (c) $Sn(IV)O_2$
(d) $Th_2(I)SO_4$ (e) $Fe_2(III)(SO_4)_3$ (f) $Cr_2(III)O_3$

Question 7. Suggest a list of the substances where carbon can exhibit oxidation states from -4 to $+4$ and nitrogen from -3 to $+5$.

Solution.

Substance	O.N. of C	Substance	O.N. of N
CH_4	-4	NH_3	-3
C_2H_6	-3	N_2H_4	-2
C_2H_4 or CH_3Cl	-2	N_2H_2	-1
C_2H_2	-1	N_2	0
CH_2Cl_2 or $C_6H_{12}O_6$	0	N_2O	$+1$
C_6Cl_6 or C_2Cl_2	$+1$	NO	$+2$
$CHCl_3$ or CO	$+2$	N_2O_3	$+3$
$(COOH)_2$	$+3$	N_2O_4	$+4$
CCl_4 or CO_2	$+4$	N_2O_5	$+5$

Question 8. While sulphur dioxide and hydrogen peroxide can act as oxidising as well as reducing agents in their reactions, ozone and nitric acid act only as oxidants. Why?

 An element, in its lowest oxidation state, can behave only as reductant while in its highest oxidation state can behave only as oxidants. In intermediate oxidation states, elements can behave as oxidant as well as reductant.

Solution. (i) In SO_2, S is in $+4$ oxidation state. It can have minimum oxidation number -2 and maximum oxidation number $+6$. Therefore, S in SO_2 can either decrease or increase its oxidation number. So, SO_2 can act both as oxidising as well as reducing agent.

(ii) In H_2O_2, O is in -1 oxidation state. It can have minimum oxidation number -2 and maximum oxidation number zero ($+1$ and $+2$ also possible in O_2F_2 and OF_2 respectively). Therefore, 'O' in H_2O_2 can either decrease or increase its oxidation number. So, H_2O_2 can act both as oxidising as well as reducing agent.

(iii) In O_3, O is in zero oxidation state. It cannot increase its oxidation number, it can only decrease its oxidation number from zero to -1 or -2. So, ozone can act only as an oxidising agent.

(iv) In HNO_3, the oxidation number of N is $+5$. It is maximum. So, N in HNO_3 can only decrease its oxidation number. So, it can act as an oxidising agent only.

Question 9. Consider the reactions,

(a) $6CO_2(g) + 6H_2O(l) \longrightarrow C_6H_{12}O_6(aq) + 6O_2(g)$

(b) $O_3(g) + H_2O_2(l) \longrightarrow H_2O(l) + 2O_2(g)$

Why it is more appropriate to write these reactions as :

(a) $6CO_2(g) + 12H_2O(l) \longrightarrow C_6H_{12}O_6(aq) + 6H_2O(l) + 6O_2(g)$

(b) $O_3(g) + H_2O_2(l) \longrightarrow H_2O(l) + O_2(g) + O_2(g)$

Also suggest a technique to investigate the path of the above (a) and (b) redox reactions.

Solution. (a) Mechanism of photosynthesis

Step I $12H_2O(l) \longrightarrow 12H_2(g) + 6O_2(g)$ (decomposition of water)

Step II $6CO_2(g) + 12H_2(g) \longrightarrow C_6H_{12}O_6(s) + 6H_2O(l)$

(H_2 formed in step first reduces CO_2 to $C_6H_{12}O_6$ in second step). Hence, it is more appropriate to write the equation for photosynthesis as follows. (By adding step I and step II).

$6CO_2(g) + 12H_2O(l) \longrightarrow C_6H_{12}O_6(s) + 6H_2O(l) + 6O_2(g)$

Actually in the process of photosynthesis, $12H_2O$ are used up in first step and $6H_2O$ are formed per molecule of glucose (carbohydrate).

(b) Mechanism of reaction of ozone with H_2O_2

Step I $O_3(g) \longrightarrow O_2(g) + O(g)$

Step II $H_2O_2 + O(g) \longrightarrow H_2O(l) + O_2(g)$

In first step ozone liberates nascent oxygen, it oxidises H_2O_2 in step II. Therefore, overall reaction is as follows

$H_2O_2 + O_3 \longrightarrow H_2O + O_2 + O_2$

In overall reaction, O_2 is written by two times because it is released in each of the two steps.

Question 10. The compound AgF_2 is unstable compound. However, if formed, the compound acts as a very strong oxidising agent. Why?

(i) Ag^+ because of the presence of completely filled configuration is more stable than Ag^{2+}.

(ii) An oxidising agent has a great tendency of accepting electron.

Solution. In AgF_2, Ag is in +2 oxidation state. It is highly unstable so it readily accepts an electron to attain + 1 oxidation state which is more stable.

$Ag^{2+} + e^- \longrightarrow Ag^+$

That's why AgF_2 acts as a strong oxidising agent.

Question 11. Whenever a reaction between an oxidising agent and a reducing agent is carried out, a compound of lower oxidation state is formed if the reducing agent is in excess and a compound of higher oxidation state is formed if the oxidising agent is in excess. Justify this statement giving three illustrations.

Solution. (a) P_4 is a reducing agent and Cl_2 is an oxidising agent.

(i) $\overset{0}{P_4}(s) + 6Cl_2(g) \longrightarrow \overset{+3}{4PCl_3}$
Excess   Lower oxidation state of P

(ii) $\overset{0}{P_4}(s) + 10Cl_2 \longrightarrow \overset{+5}{4PCl_5}$
Excess   Higher oxidation state of P

Therefore, when P_4 (reducing agent) is in excess, PCl_3 is formed in which oxidation state of P is + 3 and if Cl_2 (oxidising agent) is in excess, PCl_5 is formed in which oxidation state of P is + 5. Other two examples are

(b) C is a reducing agent while O_2 is an oxidising agent.

(i) $\overset{0}{2C}(s) + O_2(g) \longrightarrow \overset{+2}{2CO}(g)$
Excess

(ii) $\overset{0}{C}(s) + \underset{\text{Excess}}{O_2} \longrightarrow \overset{+4}{CO_2}(g)$

When reducing agent C is in excess, a compound CO of lower oxidation state is formed, if oxidising agent O_2 is in excess, a compound CO_2 of higher oxidation state is formed.

(c) Na is a reducing agent while O_2 is an oxidising agent.

(i) $4Na(s) + O_2(g) \longrightarrow Na_2\overset{-2}{O}(s)$ (lower oxidation state)
Excess

(ii) $2Na(s) + 2O_2(g) \longrightarrow Na_2\overset{-1}{O_2}(s)$ (higher oxidation state)
Excess

Question 12. How do you account for the following observations?

(a) Though alkaline potassium permanganate and acidic potassium permanganate both are used as oxidants, yet in the manufacture of benzoic acid from toluene we use alcoholic potassium permanganate as an oxidant. Why? Write a balance redox equation for the reaction.

(b) When concentrated sulphuric acid is added to an inorganic mixture containing chloride, we get colourless pungent smelling gas HCl, but if the mixture contains bromide then we get red vapour of bromine. Why?

(i) Like dissolves like, *i.e.*, benzoic acid and toluene being covalent readily dissolve in alcohol and form homogeneous solution.
(ii) HBr is a stonger reducing agent than HCl, so reduces H_2SO_4 to SO_2.

Solution. (a) Oxidation of toluene to benzoic acid in acidic medium

5 [CH₃–benzene ring] + $6MnO_4^-(aq) + 18H^+(aq) \longrightarrow 5$ [COOH–benzene ring]
Toluene (*l*)   Benzoic acid

$+ 6Mn^{2+}(aq) + 14H_2O(l)$

(b) Oxidation of toluene to benzoic acid in basic and neutral medium

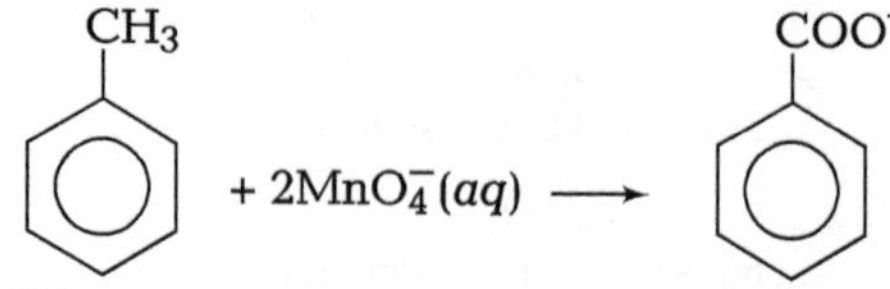

CH$_3$ + 2MnO$_4^-$(aq) ⟶ COO$^-$

Toluene   Benzoate ion

$$+ 2MnO_2(s) + H_2O(l) + OH^-(aq)$$

On industrial scale, alcoholic potassium permanganate is preferred to acidic or alkaline potassium permanganate because in the presence of alcohol both the reactants KMnO$_4$ and C$_6$H$_5$CH$_3$ are mixed very well and form homogeneous solution and in homogeneous medium reaction takes place faster than in heterogeneous medium. Further more in neutral medium OH$^-$ ions are produced in the reaction itself.

(b)   2NaCl   + 2H$_2$SO$_4$ ⟶ 2NaHSO$_4$ + 2HCl
Sodium chloride
(from inorganic mixture)

HCl is a weak reducing agent. It cannot reduce H$_2$SO$_4$ to SO$_2$, that's why pungent smelling gas HCl is obtained.

    2NaBr   + 2H$_2$SO$_4$ ⟶ 2NaHSO$_4$ + 2HBr
Sodium bromide
(from inorganic mixture)

    2HBr + H$_2$SO$_4$ ⟶   Br$_2$↑   + SO$_2$↑ + 2H$_2$O
                            Red vapours

HBr is a strong reducing agent, it reduces H$_2$SO$_4$ to SO$_2$ and is itself oxidised to Br$_2$. That's why we get red vapours of bromine when conc. H$_2$SO$_4$ reacts with inorganic mixture containing bromide salt.

Question 13. Identify the substance oxidised, reduced, oxidising agent and reducing agent for each of the following reactions.

(a) $2AgBr(s) + C_6H_6O_2(aq) \longrightarrow 2Ag(s) + 2HBr(aq) + C_6H_4O_2(aq)$

(b) $HCHO(l) + 2[Ag(NH_3)_2]^+(aq) + 3OH^-(aq) \longrightarrow$
$$2Ag(s) + HCOO^-(aq) + 4NH_3(aq) + 2H_2O(l)$$

(c) $HCHO(l) + 2Cu^{2+}(aq) + 5OH^-(aq) \longrightarrow$
$$Cu_2O(s) + HCOO^-(aq) + 3H_2O(l)$$

(d) $N_2H_4(l) + 2H_2O_2(l) \longrightarrow N_2(g) + 4H_2O(l)$

(e) $Pb(s) + PbO_2(s) + 2H_2SO_4(aq) \longrightarrow 2PbSO_4(s) + 2H_2O(l)$

To identify which substance is oxidised, reduced or act as oxidant or reductant, find the oxidation state of each element. The substance in which oxidation state of an element is increasing, is oxidised, *i.e.,* acts as reducing agent while that in which oxidation state decreases, is reduced, *i.e.,* acts as oxidising agent.

Solution.		Substance oxidised (reducing agent)	Substance reduced (oxidising agent)
	(a)	$C_6H_6O_2(aq)$	$AgBr(s)$
	(b)	$HCHO\ (l)$	$[Ag(NH_3)_2]^+(aq)$
	(c)	$HCHO\ (l)$	$Cu^{2+}(aq)$
	(d)	$N_2H_4\ (l)$	$H_2O_2(l)$
	(e)	$Pb\ (s)$	$PbO_2(s)$

Question 14. Consider the reactions :

$$2S_2O_3^{2-}(aq) + I_2(s) \longrightarrow S_4O_6^{2-}(aq) + 2I^-(aq)$$

$$S_2O_3^{2-}(aq) + 2Br_2(l) + 5H_2O(l) \longrightarrow 2SO_4^{2-}(aq) + 4Br^-(aq) + 10H^+(aq)$$

Why does the same reductant, thiosulphate react differently with iodine and bromine?

 Bromine is a stronger oxidising agent than iodine.

Solution. $2\overset{+2}{S_2}\overset{2-}{O_3}{}^{2-}(aq) + \overset{0}{I_2}(s) \longrightarrow \overset{2.5}{S_4}\overset{2-}{O_6}{}^{2-}(aq) + 2I^-(aq)$

$\overset{+2}{S_2}\overset{2-}{O_3}{}^{2-}(aq) + 2\overset{0}{Br_2}(l) + 5H_2O(l) \longrightarrow 2\overset{+6}{S}\overset{2-}{O_4}{}^{2-}(aq) + 4Br^-(aq) + 10H^+(aq)$

Bromine is a stronger oxidising agent in comparison to I_2. It oxidises S of $S_2O_3^{2-}$ to a higher oxidation state + 6 in SO_4^{2-}. While I_2 oxidises S of $S_2O_3^{2-}$ to a lower oxidation state 2.5 in $S_4O_6^{2-}$. That's why same reductant, thiosulphate react differently with bromine and iodine.

Question 15. Justify giving reactions that among halogens fluorine is the best oxidant and among hydrohalic compounds, hydroiodic acid is the best reductant.

 (i) Higher the standard electrode potential, higher is the oxidising power.

(ii) In case of halogens, standard reduction potential decreases from fluorine to iodine while in case of halide ions, the order is reverse.

Solution.	Element	F	Cl	Br	I
	Standard reduction potential $(E°\,V)$	+ 2.87	+ 1.36	+ 1.09	+ 0.54

Standard reduction potentials of halogens are positive and decrease from fluorine to iodine. Thus, halogens act as strong oxidising agents and their oxidising power decreases from fluorine to iodine. Fluorine is the strongest oxidising agent, it oxidises other halide ions to halogens in solution or when they are dry.

$$F_2 + 2X^- \longrightarrow 2F^- + X_2 \qquad (X^- = Cl^-, Br^- \text{ or } I^-)$$

In general, a halogen of low atomic number oxidises the halide ion of higher atomic number.

Halide ion, X^- or HX molecule when reacts with an oxidising agent, it reduces the oxidising agent and is itself oxidised to X_2 molecule. The tendency of X^- ions to lose electrons to form X_2 molecule increases from F^- to I^- ions. Due to this reducing power of X^- ions or HX molecules increases from F^- to I^- or HF to HI molecules.

Halide ions	I^-	Br^-	Cl^-	F^-
Electrode potentials	– 0.54 V	– 1.09 V	– 1.36 V	– 2.87 V

$$HI > HBr > HCl > HF \quad \text{(reducing power decreases)}$$
strongest reducing agent   weakest reducing agent
$$2HF + H_2SO_4 \longrightarrow \text{No reaction}$$
(HCl also does not react with H_2SO_4)
$$2HI + H_2SO_4 \longrightarrow SO_2 + 2H_2O + I_2$$
(HBr also react in the same manner)

HF or F^- is a weak reducing agent. It is so weak as a reducing agent that it does not reduce even very strong oxidising agent such as H_2SO_4 while HI or I^- reduces strong oxidising agent and is itself oxidised to I_2. That's why HI is the best reductant.

Question 16. Why does the following reaction occur?
$$XeO_6^{4-}(aq) + 2F^-(aq) + 6H^+(aq) \longrightarrow XeO_3(g) + F_2(g) + 3H_2O(l)$$
What conclusion about the compound Na_4XeO_6 (of which XeO_6^{4-} is a part) can be drawn from the reaction?

 In order to find which substance is oxidising or reducing, find the oxidation state of each element. The substance, in which oxidation number of the element increases, acts as reducing agent while the other in which oxidation number decreases, acts as oxidising agent. On this basis comment on the nature of Na_2XeO_6.

Solution. $\overset{+8}{Xe}O_6^{4-}(aq) + 2\overset{-1}{F}^-(aq) + 6H^+(aq) \longrightarrow \overset{+6}{Xe}O_3(g) + \overset{0}{F}_2 + 3H_2O(l)$

In the above reaction, oxidation number of Xe in XeO_6^{4-} decreases from + 8 to + 6 in XeO_3 and oxidation number of F increases from – 1 (in F^-) to zero (in F_2). Hence, XeO_6^{4-} or Na_4XeO_6 is reduced and F^- is oxidised. This reaction occurs because Na_4XeO_6 or XeO_6^{4-} is a stronger oxidising agent than fluorine.

Question 17. Consider the reactions,

(a) $H_3PO_2(aq) + 4AgNO_3(aq) + 2H_2O(l) \longrightarrow$
$$H_3PO_4(aq) + 4Ag(s) + 4HNO_3(aq)$$

(b) $H_3PO_2(aq) + 2CuSO_4(aq) + 2H_2O(l) \longrightarrow$
$$H_3PO_4(aq) + 2Cu(s) + H_2SO_4(aq)$$

(c) $C_6H_5CHO(l) + 2[Ag(NH_3)_2]^+(aq) + 3OH^-(aq) \longrightarrow$
$$C_6H_5COO^-(aq) + 2Ag(s) + 4NH_3(aq) + 2H_2O(l)$$

(d) $C_6H_5CHO(l) + 2Cu^{2+}(aq) + 5OH^-(aq) \longrightarrow$ No change observed.

What inference do you draw about the behaviour of Ag^+ and Cu^{2+} from these reactions?

To find the behaviour of Ag^+ and Cu^{2+} in the given reactions, find how their oxidation state changes. If it is increasing, Ag^+ or Cu^{2+} act as reducing agent (or reductant) and if decreasing, they act as oxidant.

Solution. In (a) and (b) reactions, $AgNO_3$ and $CuSO_4$ act as oxidising agents respectively. They oxidise H_3PO_2 (hypophosphorus acid) to H_3PO_4 (orthophosphoric acid). In reaction (c) $[Ag(NH_3)_2]^+(aq)$ oxidises benzaldehyde to benzoic acid but in reaction (d) Cu^{2+} do not oxidise benzaldehyde (C_6H_5CHO) to benzoic acid. This indicates that Ag^+ is a stronger oxidising agent than Cu^{2+}.

Question 18. Balance the following redox reactions by ion – electron method.

(a) $MnO_4^-(aq) + I^-(aq) \longrightarrow MnO_2(s) + I_2(s)$ (in basic medium)

(b) $MnO_4^-(aq) + SO_2(g) \longrightarrow Mn^{2+}(aq) + HSO_4^-(aq)$ (in acidic solution)

(c) $H_2O_2(aq) + Fe^{2+}(aq) \longrightarrow Fe^{3+}(aq) + H_2O(l)$ (in acidic solution)

(d) $Cr_2O_7^{2-}(aq) + SO_2(g) \longrightarrow Cr^{3+}(aq) + SO_4^{2-}(aq)$ (in acidic solution)

Solution. (a) $\overset{+7}{Mn}O_4^-(aq) + I^-(aq) \longrightarrow \overset{+4}{Mn}O_2(s) + \overset{0}{I_2}(s)$ (in basic medium)

(A) Separate the equation into oxidation half reaction and reduction half reaction.

Oxidation half reaction,

$$I^-(aq) \longrightarrow I_2(s) \qquad\qquad ...(i)$$

Reduction half reaction,

$$MnO_4^-(aq) \longrightarrow MnO_2(s) \qquad\qquad ...(ii)$$

(B) To balance I atoms in the oxidation half reaction, we write it as

$$2I^-(aq) \longrightarrow I_2(s) \qquad\qquad ...(iii)$$

and to balance oxidation number add $2e^-$ to RHS

$$2I^-(aq) \longrightarrow I_2 + 2e^- \qquad\qquad ...(iv)$$

There is no need to balance the charge (charge on either side of equation is balanced).

(C) To balance reduction half reaction first balance oxidation number by writing required number of electrons to LHS and then balance charge by adding OH^- ions because reaction occurs in basic medium.

$$MnO_4^-(aq) + 3e^- \longrightarrow MnO_2(s) \qquad\qquad ...(v)$$

$$MnO_4^-(aq) + 3e^- \longrightarrow MnO_2 + 4OH^- \qquad\qquad ...(vi)$$

(D) Balance oxygen atoms by adding H_2O

$$MnO_4^- + 3e^- + 2H_2O \longrightarrow MnO_2 + 4OH^- \qquad\qquad ...(vii)$$

By doing so H atoms are automatically balanced.

(E) Now to equalise number of electrons we multiply oxidation half reaction (iv) by 3 and reduction half reaction (vii) by 2 respectively

$$6I^-(aq) \longrightarrow 3I_2(s) + 6e^- \qquad \ldots(viii)$$

$$2MnO_4^-(aq) + 6e^- + 4H_2O(l) \longrightarrow 2MnO_2(s) + 8OH^-(aq) \qquad \ldots(ix)$$

(F) Add two half reactions to obtain net reactions after cancelling electrons on both sides.

$$2MnO_4^-(aq) + 6I^-(aq) + 4H_2O(l) \longrightarrow 2MnO_2(s) + 3I_2(s) + 8OH^-(aq)$$

This represents the final balanced redox reaction.

(b) $MnO_4^-(aq) + SO_2(g) \longrightarrow Mn^{2+}(aq) + HSO_4^-$ (in acidic medium)

Reduction half reaction

$$MnO_4^-(aq) + 8H^+(aq) + 5e^- \longrightarrow Mn^{2+}(aq) + 4H_2O(l) \qquad \ldots(i)$$

Oxidation half reaction

$$SO_2(g) + 2H_2O(l) \longrightarrow HSO_4^-(aq) + 3H^+(aq) + 2e^- \qquad \ldots(ii)$$

(Balance the oxidation number as in reaction (a) After balancing the oxidation number, charge is balanced on either side of equation by adding H^+ ions because the reaction occurs in acidic medium).

Multiply equation (i) by 2 and equation (ii) by 5 we get

$$2MnO_4^-(aq) + H^+(aq) + 5SO_2(g) + 2H_2O(l) \longrightarrow 2Mn^{2+}(aq) + 5HSO_4^-(aq)$$

(c) $H_2O_2(aq) + Fe^{2+}(aq) \longrightarrow Fe^{3+}(aq) + H_2O(l)$ (in acidic medium)

Reduction half reaction

$$H_2O_2(aq) + 2H^+(aq) + 2e^- \longrightarrow 2H_2O(l) \qquad \ldots(i)$$

Oxidatioin half reaction

$$Fe^{2+}(aq) \longrightarrow Fe^{3+}(aq) + e^-] \times 2 \qquad \ldots(ii)$$

Add equation (i) and (ii) to get final balanced redox reaction

$$H_2O_2(aq) + 2Fe^{2+}(aq) + 2H^+(aq) \longrightarrow 2H_2O(l) + 2Fe^{3+}(aq)$$

(d) $Cr_2O_7^{2-}(aq) + SO_2(g) \longrightarrow Cr^{3+}(aq) + SO_4^{2-}(aq)$ (in acidic medium)

Reduction half reaction

$$Cr_2O_7^{2-}(aq) + 14H^+(aq) + 6e^- \longrightarrow 2Cr^{3+}(aq) + 7H_2O(l) \quad \ldots(i)$$

Oxidation half reaction

$$SO_2(g) + 2H_2O(l) \longrightarrow SO_4^{2-}(aq) + 4H^+(aq) + 2e^- \qquad \ldots(ii)$$

First multiply equation (ii) by 3 (no. of loss of electrons = no. of gain of electrons) and then add it to equation (i) to get

$$Cr_2O_7^{2-}(aq) + 2H^+(aq) + 3SO_2(g) \longrightarrow 2Cr^{3+}(aq) + 3SO_4^{2-}(aq) + H_2O(l)$$

Question 19. Balance the following equations in basic medium by ion-electron method and oxidation number methods and identify the oxidising agent and the reducing agent.

(a) $P_4(s) + OH^-(aq) \longrightarrow PH_3(g) + H_2PO_2^-(aq)$

(b) $N_2H_4(l) + ClO_3^-(aq) \longrightarrow NO(g) + Cl^-(g)$

(c) $Cl_2O_7(g) + H_2O_2(aq) \longrightarrow ClO_2^-(aq) + O_2(g)$

Solution. (a) $P_4(s) + OH^-(aq) \longrightarrow PH_3(g) + H_2PO_2^-(aq)$

Ion electron method

Reduction half reaction

$$\overset{0}{P}_4(s) \longrightarrow \overset{-3}{P} H_3(g) \qquad \qquad ...(i)$$

Balance P atoms $P_4(s) \longrightarrow 4PH_3(g)$ ...(ii)

Balance oxidation number by adding electrons,

$$P_4(s) + 12e^- \longrightarrow 4PH_3(g) \qquad \qquad ...(iii)$$

Balance charge by adding OH^- ions,

$$P_4(s) + 12e^- \longrightarrow 4PH_3(g) + 12OH^-(aq) \qquad ...(iv)$$

Balance 'O' atoms by adding H_2O

$$12H_2O + P_4(s) + 12e^- \longrightarrow 4PH_3(g) + 12OH^-(aq) \qquad ...(v)$$

Oxidation half reaction

$$P_4(s) \longrightarrow H_2PO_2^-(aq) \qquad \qquad ...(vi)$$

Balance P atoms,

$$\overset{0}{P}_4(s) \longrightarrow 4H_2\overset{+1}{P} O_2^-(aq) \qquad \qquad ...(vii)$$

Balance oxidation number by adding electrons,

$$P_4(s) \longrightarrow 4H_2PO_2^-(aq) + 4e^- \qquad ...(viii)$$

Balance charge by adding OH^- ions

$$P_4(s) + 8OH^-(aq) \longrightarrow 4H_2PO_2^-(aq) + 4e^- \qquad ...(ix)$$

Oxygen and hydrogen are balanced automatically.

First multiply equation (ix) by 3 to equalise number of electrons gain and lose and add it to equation (v), we get,

$$4P_4(s) + 12OH^-(aq) + 12H_2O(l) \longrightarrow 4PH_3(g) + 12H_2PO_2^-(aq)$$

or $P_4(s) + 3OH^-(aq) + 3H_2O(l) \longrightarrow PH_3(g) + 3H_2PO_2^-(aq)$

Oxidation number method

$$\overset{0}{P}_4(s) + OH^-(aq) \longrightarrow \overset{-3+1}{PH_3}(g) + \overset{+1 +1-2}{H_2PO_2^-}(aq)$$

> O.N. decreases by 3 per P atom
> (3 electron gain)

O.N. increases by 1 per P atom (1 electron loss)

In a balanced chemical reaction loss of electrons = gain of electrons so multiply $H_2PO_2^-$ by 3 and we get

$$P_4(s) + OH^-(aq) \longrightarrow PH_3(g) + 3H_2PO_2^-$$

Multiply OH^- by 3 to balance the charge

$$P_4(s) + 3OH^-(aq) \longrightarrow PH_3(g) + 3H_2PO_2^-(aq)$$

Balance H by adding $3H_2O$ to LHS

$$P_4(s) + 3H_2O(l) + 3OH^-(aq) \longrightarrow PH_3(g) + 3H_2PO_2^-(aq)$$

In this equation P_4 acts both as an oxidising agent as well as a reducing agent.

(b) $N_2H_4(l) + ClO_3^-(aq) \longrightarrow NO(g) + Cl^-(g)$

Ion electron method

Oxidation half reaction,

$$\overset{-2}{N_2}H_4(l) \longrightarrow \overset{+2}{N}O(g)$$

Balance N atoms,

$$N_2H_4(l) \longrightarrow 2NO(g)$$

By adding electrons balance ON,

$$N_2H_4(l) \longrightarrow 2NO(g) + 8e^-$$

By adding OH$^-$ ions balance charge,

$$N_2H_4(l) + 8OH^-(aq) \longrightarrow 2NO(g) + 8e^-$$

By adding H_2O balance 'O' atoms

$$N_2H_4(l) + 8OH^-(aq) \longrightarrow 2NO(g) + 6H_2O + 8e^- \quad ...(i)$$

Reduction half reaction

$$\overset{+5}{Cl}O_3^-(aq) \longrightarrow \overset{-1}{Cl}^-(aq)$$

Balance O.N. $ClO_3^-(aq) + 6e^- \longrightarrow Cl^-$

By adding OH$^-$ ions balance charge

$$ClO_3^-(aq) + 6e^- \longrightarrow Cl^-(aq) + 6OH^-(aq)$$

By adding H_2O balance 'O' atoms

$$ClO_3^-(aq) + 3H_2O(l) + 6e^- \longrightarrow Cl^-(aq) + 6OH^-(aq) \qquad ...(ii)$$

To equalise electrons lost or gained multiply equation (i) by 3 and (ii) by 4 respectively and add to get

$$3N_2H_4(l) + 4ClO_3^-(aq) \longrightarrow 6NO(g) + 4Cl^-(aq) + 6H_2O(l)$$

This represents the final balance redox reaction.

Oxidation number method

$$\overset{-2}{N_2}H_4(l) + \overset{+5}{Cl}O_3^-(aq) \longrightarrow \overset{+2}{N}O(g) + \overset{-1}{Cl}^-(aq)$$

O.N. increases by 4 per N atom

O.N. decreases by 6 per Cl atom

Multiply NO by 2 because in N_2H_4 there are 2 N atoms

$$N_2H_4(l) + ClO_3^-(aq) \longrightarrow 2NO(g) + Cl^-(aq)$$

Total increase in oxidation number of $N = 2 \times 4 = 8$ ($8e^-$ lost)

Total decrease in oxidation number of $Cl = 1 \times 6 = 6$ ($6e^-$ gain)

Therefore, to balance increase or decrease in O.N. multiply N_2H_4 by 3, 2NO by 3 and ClO_3^-, Cl^- by 4.

$$3N_2H_4(l) + 4ClO_3^-(aq) \longrightarrow 6NO(g) + 4Cl^-(aq)$$

Balance O and H atoms by adding $6H_2O$ to RHS

$$3N_2H_4(l) + 4ClO_3^-(aq) \longrightarrow 6NO(g) + 4Cl^-(aq) + 6H_2O(l)$$

In this reaction, N_2H_4 acts as a reducing agent and ClO_3^- acts as an oxidising agent.

(c) $Cl_2O_7(g) + H_2O_2(aq) \longrightarrow ClO_2^-(g) + O_2(g)$

Ion electron method

Reduction half reaction,

Multiply ClO_2^- by 2 because in Cl_2O_7 there is 2Cl atoms.

$$\overset{+7}{Cl_2}O_7(g) \longrightarrow 2\overset{+3}{Cl}O_2^-(aq)$$

Balance O.N. by adding electrons,

$$Cl_2O_7(g) + 8e^- \longrightarrow 2ClO_2^-(aq)$$

Balance charge by adding OH^- ions,

$$Cl_2O_7(g) + 8e^- \longrightarrow 2ClO_2^-(aq) + 6OH^-$$

Balance O atoms by adding H_2O to LHS,

$$Cl_2O_7(g) + 3H_2O(l) + 8e^- \longrightarrow 2ClO_2^-(aq) + 6OH^- \qquad \ldots(i)$$

Oxidation half reaction,

$$\overset{-1}{H_2O_2}(aq) \longrightarrow \overset{0}{O_2}(g)$$

Balance O.N. by adding electrons,

$$H_2O_2(aq) \longrightarrow O_2(g) + 2e^-$$

Balance charge by adding OH^- ions,

$$H_2O_2(aq) + 2OH^-(aq) \longrightarrow O_2(g) + 2e^-$$

Balance H atoms by H_2O,

$$H_2O_2(aq) + 2OH^-(aq) \longrightarrow O_2(g) + 2H_2O(l) + 2e^- \qquad \ldots(ii)$$

Multiply equation (ii) by 4 to equalise electrons gained and lost

$$4H_2O_2(aq) + 8OH^-(aq) \longrightarrow 4O_2(g) + 8H_2O + 8e^- \qquad \ldots(iii)$$

Add equation (i) and (iii) we get

$$Cl_2O_7(g) + 4H_2O_2(aq) + 2OH^-(aq) \longrightarrow 2ClO_2^-(aq) + 5H_2O(l) + 4O_2(g)$$

Oxidation number method

$$\overset{+7 \ -2}{Cl_2O_7}(g) + \overset{+1 \ -1}{H_2O_2}(aq) \longrightarrow \overset{+3 \ -2}{ClO_2^-}(g) + \overset{0}{O_2}(g)$$

O.N. increases by 1 per O atom

O.N. decreases by 4 per Cl atom

Multiply ClO_2 by 2 because in Cl_2O_7, two Cl atoms are present.

$$Cl_2O_7(g) + H_2O_2(aq) \longrightarrow 2ClO_2^-(g) + O_2(g)$$

Total decrease in oxidation number of Cl = $2 \times 4 = 8$ ($8e^-$ gain)

Total increase in oxidation number of O = $1 \times 2 = 2$ ($2e^-$ lost)

Therefore, to balance increase or decrease in oxidation number, multiply H_2O and O_2 by 4

$$Cl_2O_7(g) + 4H_2O_2(aq) \longrightarrow 2ClO_2^-(aq) + 4O_2(g)$$

Balance charge by adding 2OH⁻ to LHS

$$Cl_2O_7(g) + 4H_2O_2(aq) + 2OH^-(aq) \longrightarrow 2ClO_2^-(g) + 4O_2(g)$$

Balance H and O by adding 5H₂O to RHS

$$Cl_2O_7(g) + 4H_2O_2(aq) + 2OH^-(aq) \longrightarrow 2ClO_2^-(g) + 4O_2(g) + 5H_2O(l)$$

In this reaction, Cl_2O_7 acts as oxidising agent and H_2O_2 as reducing agent.

Question 20. What short of informations can you draw from the following reaction?

$$(CN)_2(g) + 2OH^-(aq) \longrightarrow CN^-(aq) + CNO^-(aq) + H_2O(l)$$

Solution. $(CN)_2(g) + 2OH^-(aq) \longrightarrow CN^-(aq) + CNO^-(aq) + H_2O(l)$

(i) Let the oxidation number of C in $(CN)_2$ be x.
$$2x + 2(-3) = 0 \text{ or } x = +3$$

(ii) Let the oxidation number of C in CN⁻ be x.
$$x + (-3) = -1 \text{ or } x = +2$$

(iii) Let the oxidation number of C in CNO⁻ be x.
$$x + (-3) + (-2) = -1 \text{ or } x = +4$$

$$\overset{+3}{(CN)_2}(g) + 2OH^-(aq) \longrightarrow \overset{+2}{CN}^-(aq) + \overset{+4}{CNO}^-(aq) + H_2O(l)$$

O.N. decreases

O.N. increases

The following information we can drawn from the above reaction.

(i) Decomposition of cyanogen in the cyanide ion (CN⁻) and cyanate ion (CNO⁻) occurs in basic medium.

(ii) Cyanogen $(CN)_2$ acts as both reducing agent as well as oxidising agent.

(iii) The reaction is an example of disproportionation reaction (a special type of redox reaction).

(iv) Cyanogen $(CN)_2$ is called pseudohalogen while CN⁻, CNO⁻ ions are called pseudohalide ions.

Question 21. The Mn^{3+} ion is unstable in solution and undergoes disproportionation to give Mn^{2+}, MnO_2 and H^+ ion. Write a balanced ionic equation for the reaction.

Solution. The skeletal equation is,
$$Mn^{3+}(aq) \longrightarrow Mn^{2+}(aq) + MnO_2(s) + H^+(aq)$$

Reduction half reaction
$$Mn^{3+}(aq) + e^- \longrightarrow Mn^{2+} \qquad ...(i)$$

Oxidation half reaction
$$Mn^{3+}(aq) \longrightarrow \overset{+4}{Mn}O_2 + e^- \qquad ...(ii)$$

Balance charge by adding 4H⁺ to RHS and then balance O atoms by adding 2H₂O to LHS
$$Mn^{3+}(aq) + 2H_2O(l) \longrightarrow MnO_2(s) + e^- + 4H^+(aq) \qquad ...(iii)$$

By adding (i) and (iii) we get

$$2Mn^{3+}(aq) + 2H_2O(l) \longrightarrow Mn^{2+} + MnO_2(s) + 4H^+(aq)$$

This represents the final balanced redox reaction (disproportionation reaction).

Question 22. Consider the elements : Cs, Ne, I and F

  (a) Identify the element that exhibits only negative oxidation state.

  (b) Identify the element that exhibits only positive oxidation state.

  (c) Identify the element that exhibits both positive and negative oxidation states.

  (d) Identify the element which exhibits neither the negative nor does the positive oxidation state.

Solution.

  (a) F exhibits only negative oxidation state because it is the most electronegative element.

  (b) Cs exhibits only positive oxidation state because it is the most electropositive element.

  (c) I exhibits both positive and negative oxidation states. Iodine exhibits $-1, 0, +1, +3, +5$ and $+7$ oxidation states ($+3, +5$ and $+7$ oxidation states are exhibited by I due to the presence of vacant d-orbitals).

  (d) Ne is an inert gas, so it neither exhibits negative nor positive oxidation states.

Question 23. Chlorine is used to purify drinking water. Excess of chlorine is harmful. The excess of chlorine is removed by treating with sulphur dioxide. Present a balanced equation for this redox change taking place in water.

Solution.
$$\overset{0}{Cl_2}(aq) + \overset{+4}{S}O_2(aq) + H_2O(l) \longrightarrow \overset{-1}{Cl^-}(aq) + \overset{+6}{S}\overset{2-}{O_4^{2-}}(aq)$$

O.N. decreases by 1 per Cl atom

O.N. increases by 2 per S atom

Multiply Cl^- by 2 because in Cl_2 there are two chlorine atoms.

$$Cl_2(aq) + SO_2(aq) + H_2O(l) \longrightarrow 2Cl^-(aq) + SO_4^{2-}(aq)$$

Balance first charge by adding $4H^+$ to RHS and then multiply H_2O by 2.

$$Cl_2(aq) + SO_2(aq) + 2H_2O(l) \longrightarrow 2Cl^-(aq) + SO_4^{2-} + 4H^+$$

This represents the balanced redox reaction.

Question 24. Refer to the Periodic Table given in your book and answer the following questions :

  (a) Select the possible non-metals that can show disproportionation reaction.

  (b) Select three metals that can show disproportionation reaction.

Solution. (a) Phosphorus, chlorine and sulphur can show disproportionation reaction.

(i) $P_4(s) + 3OH^-(aq) + 3H_2O(l) \longrightarrow PH_3(g) + 3H_2PO_2^-(aq)$

(ii) $Cl_2(g) + 2OH^-(aq) \longrightarrow Cl^-(aq) + ClO^-(aq) + H_2O(l)$ (cold)

$3Cl_2(g) + 6OH^-(aq) \longrightarrow 5Cl^-(aq) + ClO_3^-(aq) + 3H_2O(l)$ (cold)

(iii) $S_8(s) + 12OH^- \longrightarrow 4S^{2-}(aq) + 2S_2O_3^{2-}(aq) + 6H_2O(l)$

(b) Manganese, copper, gallium and indium can show disproportionation reaction.

(i) $2\overset{3+}{Mn}(aq) + 2H_2O(l) \longrightarrow \overset{4+}{Mn}O_2(s) + Mn^{2+}(aq) + 4H^+$

(ii) $2\overset{+}{Cu}(aq) \longrightarrow Cu^{2+}(aq) + \overset{0}{C}u(s)$

(iii) $3\overset{+}{Ga}(aq) \longrightarrow Ga^{3+}(aq) + 2\overset{0}{G}a(s)$

(iv) $3\overset{+}{In}(aq) \longrightarrow In^{3+}(aq) + 2\overset{0}{I}n(s)$

Question 25. In Ostwald's process for the manufacture of nitric acid, the first step involves the oxidation of ammonia gas by oxygen gas to give nitric oxide gas and steam. What is the maximum weight of nitric oxide that can be obtained starting only with 10.00 g of ammonia and 20.00 g of oxygen?

(i) The amount of NO produced is decided by the amount of limiting reagent. So first find limiting reagent by writing a balanced chemical reaction and applying unitary method.

(ii) Then, find the amount of NO produced from the limiting reagent.

Solution. $4NH_3(g) + 5O_2(g) \xrightarrow[\text{Pt}]{1100K} 4NO(g) + 6H_2O(g)$

$$\begin{array}{ccc} 4 \times 17 & 5 \times 32 & 4 \times 30 \\ = 68 \text{ g} & = 160 \text{ g} & = 120 \text{ g} \end{array}$$

68 g NH_3 reacts with = 160 g O_2

1 g NH_3 reacts with $= \dfrac{160 \times 1}{68}$ g O_2

∴   10 g NH_3 reacts with $= \dfrac{160 \times 10}{68} = 23.5$ g O_2

But available amount of O_2 is 20.0 g which is less than the amount which is required to react with 10 g NH_3. So, O_2 is the limiting reagent and it limits the amount of NO produced. From the above balanced equation,

160 g of O_2 produces 120 g NO

1 g of O_2 produces $\dfrac{120 \times 1}{160}$ g NO

∴   20 g of O_2 will produce $\dfrac{120 \times 1 \times 20}{160} = 15$ g NO

Question 26. Using the standard electrode potentials given below, predict if the reaction between the following is feasible.

(a) $Fe^{3+}(aq)$ and $I^-(aq)$ (b) $Ag^+(aq)$ and $Cu(s)$
(c) $Fe^{3+}(aq)$ and $Cu(s)$ (d) $Ag(s)$ and $Fe^{3+}(aq)$
(e) $Br_2(aq)$ and $Fe^{2+}(aq)$

Given, $E^\circ_{I_2/I^-} = 0.54\,V$, $E^\circ_{Fe^{3+}/Fe^{2+}} = 0.77\,V$, $E^\circ_{Cu^{2+}/Cu} = 0.34\,V$

$E^\circ_{Ag^+/Ag} = 0.80V$ $E^\circ_{Br_2/Br^-} = 1.09V$

 For a reaction to be feasible, E°_{cell} must be positive and $E^\circ_{cell} = E^\circ_{oxi} + E^\circ_{red}$

or $E^\circ_{cell} = E^\circ_{cathode} - E^\circ_{anode}.$

Solution. (a) $Fe^{3+}(aq)$ and $I^-(aq)$

Possible reaction between $Fe^{3+}(aq)$ and $I^-(aq)$ is as follows

$$2Fe^{3+}(aq) + 2I^-(aq) \longrightarrow 2Fe^{2+}(aq) + I_2(s)$$

Oxidation half reaction

$$2I^-(aq) \longrightarrow I_2(s) + 2e^-; \qquad E^\circ = -0.54\,V$$

Reduction half reaction

$$2Fe^{3+}(aq) + 2e^- \longrightarrow 2Fe^{2+}(aq); \qquad E^\circ = +0.77\,V$$

Overall reaction;

$$2Fe^{3+}(aq) + 2I^-(aq) \longrightarrow 2Fe^{2+}(aq) + I_2(s); \; E^\circ = +0.23\,V$$

Positive emf indicates that the reaction is feasible.

(It may be noted that whenever any half reaction equation is multiplied by any integer, its E° is not multiplied by that integer.)

(b) The possible reaction between $Ag^+(aq)$ and $Cu(s)$ is as follows

$$2Ag^+(aq) + Cu(s) \longrightarrow Cu^{2+}(aq) + 2Ag(aq)$$

Separate the equation into two half reactions and write electrode potential for each half reaction.

Oxidation half reaction;

$$Cu(s) \longrightarrow Cu^{2+}(aq) + 2e^-; \qquad E^\circ = -0.34\,V$$

Reduction half reaction;

$$2Ag^+(aq) + 2e^- \longrightarrow 2Ag(s); \qquad E^\circ = +0.80\,V$$

Overall reaction,

$$Cu(s) + 2Ag^+(aq) \longrightarrow Cu^{2+}(aq) + 2Ag; \qquad E^\circ = +0.46\,V$$

Positive emf indicates that the reaction is feasible.

(c) Possible reaction between $Fe^{3+}(aq)$ and $Cu(s)$ occurs according to the following equation

$$Fe^{3+}(aq) + Cu(s) \longrightarrow Fe^{2+} + Cu^{2+}$$

Oxidation half reaction;

$$Cu(s) \longrightarrow Cu^{2+} + 2e^-; \qquad E^\circ = -0.34\,V$$

Reduction half reaction;
$$Fe^{3+}(aq) + e^- \longrightarrow Fe^{2+}(aq)] \times 2; \qquad E° = +0.77\,V$$
Overall reaction;
$$Cu(s) + 2\,Fe^{3+}(aq) \longrightarrow Cu^{2+}(aq) + 2\,Fe^{2+}(aq); \quad E° = +0.43\,V$$
Positive emf indicates that the reaction is feasible.

(d) Possible reaction between $Fe^{3+}(aq)$ and $Ag(s)$ occurs according to the following equation
$$Ag(s) + Fe^{3+}(aq) \longrightarrow Ag^+(aq) + Fe^{2+}(aq)$$
Oxidation half reaction;
$$Ag(s) \longrightarrow Ag^+(aq) + e^-; \qquad E° = -0.80\,V$$
Reduction half reaction;
$$Fe^{3+}(aq) + e^- \longrightarrow Fe^{2+}(aq); \qquad E° = +0.77\,V$$
Overall reaction;
$$Ag(s) + Fe^{3+}(aq) \longrightarrow Ag^+(aq) + Fe^{2+}(aq); \qquad E° = -0.03\,V$$
Negative emf indicates that the reaction is not feasible.

(e) Possible reaction between $Br_2(aq)$ and $Fe^{2+}(aq)$ occurs according to the following equation.
$$Br_2(aq) + 2\,Fe^{2+}(aq) \longrightarrow 2\,Br^- + 2\,Fe^{3+}(aq)$$
Oxidation half reaction
$$Fe^{2+}(aq) \longrightarrow Fe^{3+}(aq) + e^-] \times 2; \qquad E° = -0.77\,V$$
Reduction half reaction;
$$Br_2(aq) + 2e^- \longrightarrow 2\,Br^-(aq); \qquad E° = +1.09\,V$$
Overall reaction;
$$2\,Fe^{2+}(aq) + Br_2(aq) \longrightarrow 2Fe^{3+}(aq) + 2\,Br^-(aq); \qquad E° = +0.32\,V$$
Positive emf indicates that the reaction is feasible.

Question 27. Predict the products of electrolysis in each of the following.
  (i) An aqueous solution of $AgNO_3$ with silver electrodes.
 (ii) An aqueous solution of $AgNO_3$ with platinum electrodes.
(iii) A dilute solution of H_2SO_4 with platinum electrodes.
(iv) An aqueous solution of $CuCl_2$ with platinum electrodes.

  (i) Higher the oxidation potential of an element, more readily it gets oxidised.
 (ii) In case of aqueous solution, H^+ and OH^- ions are also present, so compare the oxidation potential of the elements/ions with that of the H^+ and OH^- to decide the product.

Solution. (i) **An aqueous solution of $AgNO_3$ with silver electrodes.**
Two oxidation and two reduction half reactions must be considered.
Oxidation (at anode)
$$(A)\ Ag(s) \longrightarrow Ag^+(aq) + e^-; \qquad E° = -0.80\,V$$
$$(B)\ 2H_2O(l) \longrightarrow O_2(g) + 4H^+(aq) + 4e^-; \qquad E° = -1.23\,V$$

Reduction (at cathode)

(C) $Ag^+(aq) + e^- \longrightarrow Ag(s)$; $\qquad\qquad E° = +0.80$ V

(D) $2H_2O(l) + 2e^- \longrightarrow H_2(g) + 2OH^-(aq)$; $\qquad E° = -0.83$ V

By $E°$ values of (A) and (B), it appears that **at anode** silver of silver anode gets oxidised more readily because oxidation potential of Ag is greater than that of H_2O molecule. Similarly by $E°$ values of (C) and (D), it appears that **at cathode** reduction potential of Ag^+ ions is higher than that of H_2O molecules.

Therefore, on electrolysis of aqueous $AgNO_3$ solution with silver electrodes, Ag from silver anode dissolves while $Ag^+(aq)$ ions present in the solution get reduced and deposited at cathode.

(ii) **An aqueous solution of $AgNO_3$ with platinum electrodes.**

Platinum is an inert electrode so at anode oxidation of water takes place. As a result of this O_2 is released at anode according to equation (B) [as in (i)]. At cathode reduction of Ag^+ ions takes place.

Therefore, on electrolysis of aqueous $AgNO_3$ solution with platinum electrodes, O_2 is released at anode and Ag^+ ions from solution get deposited at cathode.

(iii) **A dilute solution of H_2SO_4 with platinum electrodes.**

$$H_2SO_4(aq) \rightleftharpoons 2H^+ + SO_4^{2-}$$

When current is passed, either H^+ ions or H_2O molecules are reduced at cathode.

$2H^+(aq) + 2e^- \longrightarrow H_2(g)$; $\qquad\qquad E° = 0.0$ V

$2H_2O(aq) + 2e^- \longrightarrow H_2(g) + 2OH^-(aq)$; $\qquad E° = -0.83$ V

At cathode H^+ ions get reduced first because reduction potential of H^+ ions is greater than H_2O molecules.

Similarly on passing current either SO_4^{2-} ions or H_2O molecules are oxidised at anode. SO_4^{2-} ions are resistant to oxidation and are not discharged at anode. So, at anode H_2O molecules are oxidised to release O_2 gas.

$2H_2O(l) \longrightarrow O_2(g) + 4H^+(aq) + 4e^-$; $\qquad E° = -1.23$ V

Therefore, on electrolysis of an aqueous solution of H_2SO_4, only electrolysis of water occurs releasing H_2 at cathode and O_2 at anode.

(iv) **An aqueous solution of $CuCl_2$ with platinum electrodes**

$CuCl_2(aq) \rightleftharpoons Cu^{2+}(aq) + 2Cl^-(aq)$; (ionisation of $CuCl_2$ in water)

Two oxidation and two reduction half reactions must be considered.

Oxidation (at anode)

$$2Cl^-(aq) \longrightarrow Cl_2(g) + 2e^-; \qquad\qquad E° = -1.36\ V$$

$$2H_2O(l) \longrightarrow O_2(g) + 4H^+(aq) + 4e^-; \qquad E° = -1.23\ V$$

Reduction (at cathode)

$$Cu^{2+}(aq) + 2e^- \longrightarrow Cu(s); \qquad\qquad E° = 0.34\ V$$

$$2H_2O(l) + 2e^- \longrightarrow H_2(g) + 2OH^-; \qquad E° = -0.83\ V$$

Although oxidation potential of H_2O molecule is greater than that of Cl^- ions, oxidation of Cl^- ions takes place in preference to H_2O. It is because of the overvoltage of O_2. Much lower potential than –1.36 V is required for oxidation of H_2O molecules.

Since, the reduction potential of Cu^{2+} is much higher than the reduction potential of H_2O molecules, therefore Cu^{2+} ions are reduced at cathode.

Therefore, on electrolysis of an aqueous solution of $CuCl_2$, Cu metal is released at the cathode while Cl_2 gas is evolved at the anode.

Question 28. Arrange the following metals in the order in which they displace each other from the solution of their salts.

Al, Cu, Fe, Mg and Zn.

Solution. $E°_{Al^{3+}/Al} = -1.66\ V, \qquad E°_{Cu^{2+}/Cu} = +0.34\ V$

$E°_{Fe^{2+}/Fe} = -0.44\ V, \qquad E°_{Mg^{2+}/Mg} = -2.36\ V$ and $E°_{Zn^{2+}/Zn} = -0.66\ V$

A metal with more negative value of $E°_{red}$ is a stronger reducing agent than those which have less negative or positive value of $E°_{red}$. Therefore, Mg can displace all the given metals from their aqueous salt solutions. Al can displace all metals except Mg from their aqueous salt solutions. Zinc can displace Fe and Cu from their aqueous salt solutions and Fe can only displace Cu from its aqueous salt solution.

Hence, the order in which they can displace each other from the solution of their salts is as follows

Mg, Al, Zn, Fe, Cu

Question 29. Given the standard electrode potentials,

$$K^+ / K = -2.93\ V,\ Ag^+ / Ag = 0.80\ V,\ \ Hg^{2+} / Hg = 0.79\ V$$

$$Mg^{2+} / Mg = -2.37\ V,\ \ Cr^{3+} / Cr = -0.74\ V$$

Arrange these metals in their increasing order of reducing power.

 Lower the electrode potential ($E°_{red}$), stronger is the reducing agent.

Solution. The arrangement of metals in their increasing order of reducing power is as follows

Ag < Hg < Cr < Mg < K

Question 30. Depict the galvanic cell in which the reaction,

$$Zn(s) + 2Ag^+(aq) \longrightarrow Zn^{2+}(aq) + 2Ag(s)$$

takes place, Further show

(i) which of the electrode is negatively charged?

(ii) the carriers of the current in the cell.

(iii) individual reaction at each electrode.

Solution. The given redox reaction for the galvanic cell is

$$Zn(s) + 2Ag^+(aq) \longrightarrow Zn^{2+}(aq) + 2Ag(s)$$

At anode Zn is oxidised to Zn^{2+} ions and at cathode Ag^+ ions are reduced to Ag metal. Thus, galvanic cell for the above redox reaction may be depicted as $Zn \mid Zn^{2+}(aq) \parallel Ag^+(aq) \mid Ag$

(i) Zn electrode is negatively charged because of the oxidation of Zn to Zn^{2+} ions, electrons are accumulated on zinc electrode.

(ii) The ions carry current in the cell. Current flows from Ag electrode to Zn electrode. While electrons flow from Zn electrode to Ag electrode.

(iii) Individual reaction at each electrodes

Anode : $\qquad Zn \longrightarrow Zn^{2+} + 2e^-$

Cathode : $Ag^+(aq) + e^- \longrightarrow Ag(s)$

Selected NCERT Exemplar Problems

Short Answer Type

Question 1. The reaction,

$$Cl_2(g) + 2OH^-(aq) \longrightarrow ClO^-(aq) + Cl^-(aq) + H_2O(l)$$

represents the process of bleaching. Identify and name the species that bleaches the substances due to its oxidising action.

Solution. Write the O.N. of each element above its symbol.

$$\overset{0}{Cl_2}(g) + 2\overset{-2\,+1}{OH^-}(aq) \longrightarrow \overset{+1\,-2}{ClO^-}(aq) + \overset{-1}{Cl^-}(aq) + \overset{+1\,-2}{H_2O}(l)$$

In this reaction, O.N. of Cl increases from 0 (in Cl_2) to 1 (in ClO^-) as well as decreases from 0 (in Cl_2) to – 1 (in Cl^-). So, it acts both reducing agent as well as oxidising agent. This is an example of disproportionation reaction. In this reaction, ClO^- species bleaches the substances due to its oxidising action. [In hypochlorite ion (ClO^-) Cl can decrease its oxidation number from +1 to 0 or – 1.]

Question 2. MnO_4^{2-} undergoes disproportionation reaction in acidic medium but MnO_4^- does not. Give reason.

Solution. In MnO_4^{2-}, the oxidation number of Mn is $+6$. It can increase its oxidation number (to $+7$) or decrease its oxidation number (to $+4, +3, +2, 0$). Hence, it undergoes disproportionation reaction in acidic medium.

$$\overset{+6}{3MnO_4^{2-}} + 4H^+ \longrightarrow \overset{+7}{2MnO_4^-} + \overset{+4}{MnO_2} + 2H_2O$$

O.N. increases by 1 per atom

O.N. decreases by 2 per atom

In MnO_4^-, Mn is in its highest oxidation state, i.e., $+7$. It can only decrease its oxidation number. Hence, it cannot undergo disproportionation reaction.

Question 3. PbO and PbO_2 react with HCl according to the following chemical equations :

$$2PbO + 4HCl \longrightarrow 2PbCl_2 + 2H_2O$$

$$PbO_2 + 4HCl \longrightarrow PbCl_2 + Cl_2 + 2H_2O$$

Why do these compounds differ in their reactivity?

Solution.   (i) $\overset{+2\,-2}{2PbO} + \overset{+1\,-1}{4HCl} \longrightarrow \overset{+2\,-1}{2PbCl_2} + \overset{+1\,-2}{2H_2O}$
                     Basic oxide   Acid

In this reaction, oxidation number of each element remain same hence, it is not a redox reaction. In fact, it is an example of **acid-base reaction**.

(ii) $\overset{+4\,-2}{PbO_2} + \overset{+1\,-1}{4HCl} \longrightarrow \overset{+2\,-1}{PbCl_2} + \overset{0}{Cl_2} + \overset{+1\,-2}{2H_2O}$

In PbO_2, Pb is in $+4$ oxidation state. Due to inert pair effect Pb in $+2$ oxidation state is more stable. So, Pb in $+4$ oxidation state (PbO_2) acts as an oxidising agent. It oxidises Cl^- to Cl_2 and itself gets reduced to Pb^{2+}.

$$\overset{+4\,-2}{PbO_2} + \overset{+1\,-1}{4HCl} \longrightarrow \overset{+2\,-1}{PbCl_2} + \overset{0}{Cl_2} + \overset{+1\,-2}{2H_2O}$$
$\quad$ O.A $\qquad$ R.A

O.N. decreases by 2 per atom

O.N. increases by 1 per atom

Question 4.   Nitric acid is an oxidising agent and reacts with PbO but it does not react with PbO_2. Explain why?

Solution. PbO is a base. It reacts with nitric acid and forms soluble lead nitrate.

$$PbO + 2HNO_3 \longrightarrow Pb(NO_3)_2 + H_2O \qquad \text{(acid base reaction)}$$
$$\text{soluble}$$

Nitric acid does not reacts with PbO_2. Both of them are strong oxidising agents. In HNO_3, nitrogen is in its maximum oxidation state (+ 5) and in PbO_2, lead is in its maximum oxidation state (+ 4). Therefore, no reaction takes place.

Question 5. Calculate the oxidation number of each sulphur atom in the following compounds :

(a) $Na_2S_2O_3$ (b) $Na_2S_4O_6$

(c) Na_2SO_3 (d) Na_2SO_4

Solution. (a) $Na_2S_2O_3$: Let us consider the structure of $Na_2S_2O_3$.

$$Na^+O^- \!-\!\underset{\underset{O}{\|}}{\overset{\overset{S}{\uparrow}}{S}}\!-\!O^-Na^+$$

There is a coordinate bond between two sulphur atoms. The oxidation number of acceptor S atom is –2. Let the oxidation number of other S atom be x.

$$\underset{\text{for Na}}{2(+1)} + \underset{\text{for O atoms}}{3\times(2)} + x + \underset{\text{for coordinate S atom}}{1(-2)} = 0$$

$$x = +6$$

Therefore, the two sulphur atoms in $Na_2S_2O_3$ have -2 and $+6$ oxidation number.

(b) $Na_2S_4O_6$: Let us consider the structure of $Na_2S_4O_6$.

$$Na^+O^- \!-\!\underset{\underset{O}{\|}}{\overset{\overset{O}{\|}}{S}}\!-\!\overset{0}{S}\!-\!\overset{0}{S}\!-\!\underset{\underset{O}{\|}}{\overset{\overset{O}{\|}}{S}}\!-\!O^-Na^+$$

In this structure, two central sulphur atoms have zero oxidation number because electron pair forming the S—S bond remain in the centre. Let the oxidation number of (remaining S atoms) S atom be x.

$$\underset{\text{for Na}}{2(+1)} + \underset{\text{for O}}{6(-2)} + 2x + 2(0) = 0$$

$$2 - 12 + 2x = 0 \text{ or } x = +\frac{10}{2} = +5$$

Therefore, the two central S atoms have zero oxidation state and two terminal S atoms have + 5 oxidation state each.

(c) Na_2SO_3 : Let the oxidation number of S in Na_2SO_3 be x.
$$2(+1) + x + 3(-2) = 0 \text{ or } x = +4$$

(d) Na_2SO_4 : Let the oxidation number of S be x.
$$2(+1) + x + 4(-2) = 0 \text{ or } x = +6$$

Question 6. Balance the following equations by the oxidation number method.

$$\text{(i) } Fe^{2+} + H^+ + Cr_2O_7^{2-} \longrightarrow Cr^{3+} + Fe^{3+} + H_2O$$

$$\text{(ii) } I_2 + NO_3^- \longrightarrow NO_2 + IO_3^-$$

$$\text{(iii) } I_2 + S_2O_3^{2-} \longrightarrow I^- + S_4O_6^{2-}$$

$$\text{(iv) } MnO_2 + C_2O_4^{2-} \longrightarrow Mn^{2+} + CO_2$$

Solution. **Oxidation number method**

(i)
$$\overset{+2}{Fe^{2+}} + H^+ + \overset{+6}{Cr_2}\overset{-2}{O_7^{2-}} \longrightarrow 2\overset{+3}{Cr^{3+}} + \overset{+3}{Fe^{3+}} + H_2O$$

O.N. decreases by 3 per Cr atom
$(3 \times 2 = 6 \, e^-$ gain)

O.N. increases by 1 per Fe atom (1 e^- lose)

(Multiply Cr^{3+} by 2 because there are 2Cr atoms in $Cr_2O_7^{2-}$ ion.)

Balance increase and decrease in oxidation number.

$$6Fe^{2+} + H^+ + Cr_2O_7^{2-} \longrightarrow 2Cr^{3+} + 6Fe^{3+} + H_2O$$

Balance charge by multiplying H^+ by 14.

$$6Fe^{2+} + 14H^+ + Cr_2O_7^{2-} \longrightarrow 2Cr^{3+} + 6Fe^{3+} + H_2O$$

Balance H and O atoms by multiplying H_2O by 7.

$$6Fe^{2+} + 14H^+ + Cr_2O_7^{2-} \longrightarrow 2Cr^{3+} + 6Fe^{3+} + 7H_2O$$

This represents a balanced redox reaction.

(ii)
$$\overset{0}{I_2} + \overset{+5}{NO_3^-} \longrightarrow \overset{+4}{NO_2} + 2\overset{+5}{IO_3^-}$$

O.N. decreases by 1 per N atom
(1 e^- gain)

O.N. increases by 5 per I atom
(2×5 electrons lose)

Balance increase and decrease in oxidation number

$$I_2 + 10NO_3^- \longrightarrow 10NO_2 + 2IO_3^-$$

Balance charge by writing $8H^+$ in LHS of the equation.

$$I_2 + 10NO_3^- + 8H^+ \longrightarrow 10NO_2 + 2IO_3^-$$

Balance H-atoms by writing $4H_2O$ in RHS of the equation.

$$I_2 + 10NO_3^- + 8H^+ \longrightarrow 10NO_2 + 2IO_3^- + 4H_2O$$

Oxygen atoms are automatically balanced.
This represents a balanced redox reaction.

(iii)
$$\overset{0}{I_2} + 2\overset{+2}{S_2}O_3^{2-} \longrightarrow 2\overset{-1}{I^-} + \overset{2.5}{S_4}O_6^{2-}$$

O.N. decreases by 1 per I atom
($2 \times 1 \, e^-$ gain)

O.N. increases by 0.5 per S atom
($4 \times 0.5 = 2 \, e^-$ lose)

(Multiply $S_2O_3^{2-}$ by 2 because there are 4 S atoms in $S_4O_6^{2-}$ ion.)

Increase and decrease in oxidation number is already balanced. Charge and oxygen atoms are also balanced.

This represents a balanced redox reaction.

(iv) $\overset{+4}{Mn}O_2 + \overset{+3}{C_2}O_4^{2-} \longrightarrow \overset{+4}{Mn}^{2+} + 2\overset{+4}{C}O_2$

O.N. decreases by 2 per Mn atom
(2 e⁻ gain)

O.N. increases by 1 per C atom
(2 × 1 = 2 e⁻ lose)

Increase and decrease in oxidation number is already balanced.
Add $4H^+$ towards LHS of the equation to balance charge.

$$MnO_2 + C_2O_4^{2-} + 4H^+ \longrightarrow Mn^{2+} + 2CO_2$$

Add $2H_2O$ towards RHS of the equation to balance H-atoms

$$MnO_2 + C_2O_4^{2-} + 4H^+ \longrightarrow Mn^{2+} + 2CO_2 + 2H_2O$$

This represents a balanced redox reaction.

Long Answer Type

Question 7. On the basis of standard electrode potential values, suggest which of the following reactions would take place?

$$E^\circ_{Cu^{2+} \mid Cu} = 0.34 \text{ V}, \quad E^\circ_{Zn^{2+} \mid Zn} = -0.76 \text{ V},$$

$$E^\circ_{Mg^{2+} \mid Mg} = -2.37 \text{ V}, \quad E^\circ_{Fe^{2+} \mid Fe} = -0.74 \text{ V},$$

$$E^\circ_{Br_2 \mid Br^-} = +1.08 \text{ V}, \quad E^\circ_{Cl_2 \mid Cl^-} = +1.36 \text{ V}$$

$$E^\circ_{Cd^{2+} \mid Cd} = -0.44 \text{ V}$$

(i) $Cu + Zn^{2+} \longrightarrow Cu^{2+} + Zn$
(ii) $Mg + Fe^{2+} \longrightarrow Mg^{2+} + Fe$
(iii) $Br_2 + 2Cl^- \longrightarrow Cl_2 + 2Br^-$
(iv) $Fe + Cd^{2+} \longrightarrow Cd + Fe^{2+}$

Solution. (i) $E^\circ_{Cu^{2+} \mid Cu} = +0.34$ and $E^\circ_{Zn^{2+} \mid Zn} = -0.76 \text{ V}$

$$Cu + Zn^{2+} \longrightarrow Cu^{2+} + Zn$$

In the given cell reaction, Cu is oxidised to Cu^{2+}, therefore, Cu^{2+}/Cu couple acts as anode and Zn^{2+} is reduced to Zn, therefore, Zn^{2+}/Zn couple acts as cathode.

$$E^\circ_{cell} = E^\circ_{cathode} - E^\circ_{anode}$$
$$E^\circ_{cell} = -0.76 - (+0.34) = -1.10 \text{ V}$$

Negative value of E°_{cell} indicates that the reaction will not occur.

(ii) $Mg + Fe^{2+} \longrightarrow Mg^{2+} + Fe$

$$E^{\circ}_{Mg^{2+}/Mg} = -2.37\,V \text{ and } E^{\circ}_{Fe^{2+}/Fe} = -0.74\,V$$

In the given cell reaction, Mg is oxidised to Mg^{2+} hence, Mg^{2+}/Mg couple acts as anode and Fe^{2+} is reduced to Fe hence, Fe^{2+}/Fe couple acts as cathode.

$$E^{\circ}_{cell} = E^{\circ}_{cathode} - E^{\circ}_{anode}$$

$$E^{\circ}_{cell} = -0.74 - (-2.37) = +1.63\,V$$

Positive value of E°_{cell} indicates that the reaction will occur.

(iii) $Br_2 + 2Cl^- \longrightarrow 2Br^- + Cl_2$

$$E^{\circ}_{Br^-/Br_2} = +1.08\,V \text{ and } E^{\circ}_{Cl^-/Cl_2} = +1.36\,V$$

In the given cell reaction, Cl^- is oxidised to Cl_2 hence, Cl^-/Cl_2 couple acts as anode and Br_2 is reduced to Br^- hence, Br^-/Br_2 couple acts as cathode.

$$E^{\circ}_{cell} = E^{\circ}_{cathode} - E^{\circ}_{anode}$$

$$E^{\circ}_{cell} = +1.08 - (+1.36) = -0.28\,V$$

Negative value of E°_{cell} indicates that the reaction will not occur.

(iv) $Fe + Cd^{2+} \longrightarrow Cd + Fe^{2+}$

$$E^{\circ}_{Fe^{2+}/Fe} = -0.74\,V \text{ and } E^{\circ}_{Cd^{2+}/Cd} = -0.44\,V$$

In the given cell reaction. Fe is oxidised to Fe^{2+} hence Fe^{2+}/Fe couple acts as anode and Cd^{2+} is reduced to Cd hence, Cd^{2+}/Cd couple acts as cathode.

$$E^{\circ}_{cell} = E^{\circ}_{cathode} - E^{\circ}_{anode}$$

$$E^{\circ}_{cell} = -0.44 - (-0.74) = +0.30\,V$$

Positive value of E°_{cell} indicates that the reaction will occur.

Question 8. Why does fluorine not show disproportionation reaction?

Solution. In a disproportionation reaction, the same species is simultaneously oxidised as well as reduced. Therefore, for such a redox reaction to occur, the reacting species must contain an element which has atleast three oxidation states. The element, in reacting species, is present in an intermediate state while lower and higher oxidation states are available for reduction and oxidation to occur (respectively).

Fluorine is the strongest oxidising agent. It does not show positive oxidation state. That's why fluorine does not show disproportionation reaction.

Redox Reactions

227

Question 9. Write redox couples involved in the reactions (i) to (iv) given in question 7.

Solution. (i) Cu^{2+}/Cu and Zn^{2+}/Zn (ii) Mg^{2+}/Mg and Fe^{2+}/Fe
(iii) Br_2/Br^- and Cl_2/Cl^- (iv) Fe^{2+}/Fe and Cd^{2+}/Cd

Question 10. Which method can be used to find out strength of reductant/oxidant in a solution? Explain with an example.

Solution. Measure the electrode potential of the given species by connecting the redox couple of the given species with standard hydrogen electrode. If it is positive, the electrode of the given species acts as reductant and if it is negative, it acts as an oxidant. Find the electrode potentials of the other given species in the same way, compare the values and determine their comparative strength as an reductant or oxidant.

Examples Measurement of standard electrode potential of Zn^{2+}/Zn electrode using SHE as a reference electrode.

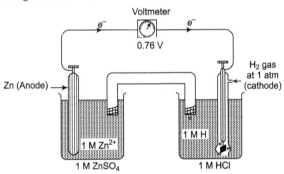

The EMF of the cell comes out to be 0.76 V. (reading of voltmeter is 0.76 V). Zn^{2+}/Zn couple acts as anode and SHE acts as cathode.

∴

$$E^o_{cell} = 0.76 = E_{cathode} - E_{anode}$$

$$0.76 = 0 - E_{anode}$$

$$E^o_{anode} = -0.76\ V$$

$$E^o_{Zn^{2+}/Zn} = -0.76\ V$$

Chapter 9

Hydrogen

Important Results

1. Hydrogen is the lightest element. It has only one electron in its atom. Loss of this electron results in an elementary particle, the proton. Thus, it is unique in properties. It has three isotopes, namely protium ($_1^1H$), deuterium (D or $_1^2H$) and tritium (T or $_1^3H$). Tritium is radioactive in nature and emits low energy β^--particles ($t_{1/2} - 12.33$ yr).

2. Inspite of resemblance both with alkali metals and halogens, it occupies a separate position in the Periodic Table because of its unique properties.

3. In laboratory dihydrogen is usually prepared by the reaction of granulated zinc with dilute hydrochloric acid or by the reaction of zinc with aqueous alkali.

4. On industrial scale dihydrogen is prepared by the water gas shift reaction from petrochemicals. It is obtained as a by-product by the electrolysis of brine.

5. The H—H bond enthalpy of dihydrogen is the highest (435.88 kJ mol^{-1}) for a single bond between two atoms of any elements. Due to the high H—H bond enthalpy it is relatively inert.

6. It combines with almost all the elements to form hydrides. Hydrides can be classified into three categories. Ionic or saline hydrides, covalent or molecular hydrides and metallic or non-stoichiometric hydrides. Metallic hydrides are useful for ultrapurification of dihydrogen and as dihydrogen storage media.

7. Dihydrogen is used in the synthesis of ammonia which is used in the manufacture of nitric acid and nitrogenous fertilizers. It is used in the manufacture of vanaspati ghee by the hydrogenation of polyunsaturated vegetable oils. It is used in metallurgical processes to reduce metal oxides. In space programmes, it is used as a rocket fuel.

8. The basic principle of hydrogen economy is the transportation and storage of energy in the form of liquid or gaseous dihydrogen. Advantage of hydrogen economy is that energy is transmitted in the form of dihydrogen. Now a days it is also used in fuel cells for generation of electric power.

9. Water is a crucial compound for the survival of all life forms. The unusual properties of water in the liquid states and solid states are due to the presence of extensive hydrogen bonding between water molecules. The high heat of vaporisation and heat capacity are responsible for moderation of the climate and body temperature of livinig beings.

10. Water is an excellent solvent for transportation of ions and molecules required for plant and animal metabolism. Due to hydrogen bonding with polar molecules, even covalent compounds like alcohol and carbohydrates dissolve in water.

11. Water molecule is highly polar in nature due to its bent structure. This property leads to hydrogen bonding which is the maximum in ice and least in water vapour. Density of ice is less than that of water. Therefore, an ice cube floats on water.

12. Water that lathers with soap is called soft and which that does not, is called hard. The hardness of water may be of two types :
    (i) Temporary hardness, due to the presence of calcium and magnesium bicarbonates.
    (ii) Permanent hardness due to the presence of chlorides and sulphates of calcium and magnesium.

13. Temporary hardness of water is removed by just boiling while permanent hardness is removed by sodalime method, Calgon's or ion exchange method or by synthetic resin method.

14. Pure and demineralised water free from all soluble mineral salts is obtained by passing water successively through a cation exchange (in the H^+ form) and an anion-exchange (in the OH^- form) resins.

15. Hydrogen peroxide is manufactured by the electrolysis of 50% H_2SO_4 or by the auto-oxidation of 2-alkyl anthraquinols. 30% solution of H_2O_2 is called per hydrol and is used as germicide and antiseptic.

16. "20 volume H_2O_2" means 1 mL of this solution on decomposition liberates, 20 mL of oxygen at NTP.

17. Hydrogen peroxide can act as oxidising agent, reducing agent and as a bleaching agent. Bleaching action of H_2O_2 is due to oxidation.

18. H_2O_2 decomposes slowly on exposure to light. In the presence of metal surfaces or traces of alkali its decomposition reaction is catalysed. Therefore, it is stored in wax-lined glass or plastic vessels in dark.

19. H_2O_2 is widely used as an industrial bleach and in pharmaceutical and pollution control treatment of industrial and domestic effluents.

20. Heavy water, D_2O is another important compound which is manufactured by the electrolytic enrichment of normal water. It is essentially used as a moderator in nuclear reactors.

Exercises

Question 1. Justify the position of hydrogen in the Periodic Table on the basis of its electronic configuration.

 Hydrogen resembles with alkali metals as well as halogens in some of its properties. However, its some properties are quite different from alkali metals and halogens. Justify its position in the Periodic Table on the basis of these properties.

Solution. Hydrogen is the first element in the Periodic Table. It has electronic configuration $1s^1$. It may donate one electron forming H^+ like alkali metals or may accept one electron forming H^- like halogens. Like alkali metals, hydrogen forms oxides, halides and sulphides. However, unlike alkali metals, it has a very high ionization enthalpy and does not possess metallic characteristics under normal conditions. Actually in terms of ionization enthalpy, hydrogen resembles more with halogens. Like halogens, it forms a diatomic molecule, reacts with elements to form hydrides and a large number of covalent compounds. However, its reactivity is very low as compared to halogens.

Therefore, on the basis of above properties, hydrogen may be placed with alkali metals in group-I and first period or with halogens in group-17 and first period. Although, the properties, which exhibit the resemblance of hydrogen with alkali metals and halogens, some properties of hydrogen are unique and with respect to these properties, it differs from both alkali metals and halogens and is therefore, best placed separately in the Periodic Table.

Question 2. Write the names of isotopes of hydrogen. What is the mass ratio of these isotopes?

Solution. Protium ^1_1H, Deuterium ^2_1H or D, Tritium ^3_1H or T. The mass ratio of protium : deuterium : tritium $= 1 : 2 : 3$.

Question 3. Why does hydrogen occur in a diatomic form rather than in a monoatomic form under normal conditions?

 Every atom has a tendency to achieve the configuration of its nearest inert gas.

Solution. Hydrogen atom has only one electron in its 1s-orbital. So, to achieve stable inert gas configuration of helium, it exists as diatomic molecule and is called dihydrogen.

Question 4. How can the production of dihydrogen, obtained from coal gasification, be increased?

Solution. The process of producing syn gas or synthesis gas from coal is called 'coal gasification'.

$$\underset{\text{Coal}}{C(s)} + \underset{\text{Stream}}{H_2O(g)} \xrightarrow[\text{Ni}]{1270 \text{ K}} \underbrace{CO(g) + H_2(g)}_{Syn\,gas}$$

The production of hydrogen can be increased by reacting carbon monoxide of *syn* gas with steam in the presence of iron chromate as catalyst at 673 K.

$$CO(g) + H_2O(g) \xrightarrow{\text{FeCrO}_4, 673 \text{ K}} CO_2(g) + H_2(g)$$

CO_2 is removed by scrubbing with a solution of sodium arsenite.

Question 5. Describe the bulk preparation of hydrogen by electrolytic method. What is the role of an electrolyte in this process?

Solution. Electrolysis of acidified water using platinum electrodes gives hydrogen.

$$2H_2O(l) \xrightarrow[\text{Traces of acid/base}]{\text{Electrolysis}} 2H_2(g) + O_2(g)$$

The role of an electrolyte is to make water conducting.

Question 6. Complete the following reactions,

(i) $H_2(g) + M_mO_o(s) \xrightarrow{\Delta}$

(ii) $CO(g) + H_2(g) \xrightarrow[\text{Catalyst}]{\Delta}$

(iii) $C_3H_8(g) + 3H_2O(g) \xrightarrow[\text{Catalyst}]{\Delta}$

(iv) $Zn(s) + NaOH(aq) \xrightarrow{\text{Heat}}$

Solution. (i) $H_2(g) + M_mO_o(s) \xrightarrow{\Delta} mM(s) + o\,H_2O(l)$

(ii) $CO(g) + 2H_2(g) \xrightarrow[\text{Catalyst}]{\Delta} \underset{\text{Methanol}}{CH_3OH(l)}$

(iii) $C_3H_8(g) + 3H_2O(g) \xrightarrow{\text{Ni, 1270 K}} 3CO(g) + 7H_2(g)$

(iv) $Zn(s) + 2NaOH(aq) \xrightarrow{\text{Heat}} \underset{\text{Sod. zincate}}{Na_2ZnO_2(aq)} + H_2(g)$

Question 7. Discuss the consequences of high enthalpy of H—H bond in terms of chemical reactivity of dihydrogen.

Solution. Due to high bond dissociation enthalpy of H—H bond, hydrogen is relatively unreactive at room temperature. However, at high temperatures or in the presence of catalysts, it combines with many metals and non-metals to form hydrides.

Question 8. What do you understand by (i) electron-deficient, (ii) electron-precise, and (iii) electron-rich compounds of hydrogen? Provide justification with suitable examples.

Solution.

(i) **Electron-deficient hydrides** These type of hydrides contain central atom with incomplete octet. These are formed by 13 group elements, *e.g.*, BH_3, AlH_3, etc. To make up their electron deficiency, they generally exist in polymeric forms such as B_2H_6, B_4H_{10}, $(AlH_3)_n$ etc. These hydrides act as Lewis acids.

(ii) **Electron-precise hydrides** These hydrides have exact number of electrons required to form normal covalent bonds. These are formed by 14 group elements, *e.g.*, CH_4, SiH_4, etc. These are tetrahedral in shape.

(iii) **Electron-rich hydrides** These hydrides contain central atom with excess electron, *i.e.*, lone pair than required. These are formed by 15, 16 and 17 group elements, *e.g.*, NH_3, H_2O, HF, etc. These hydrides act as Lewis bases.

Question 9. What characteristics do you expect from an electron-deficient hydride with resepct to its structure and chemical reactions?

Solution. These hydrides do not have sufficient number of electrons to form normal covalent bonds, *e.g.*, B in BF_3 (F ⦂ B ⦂ F) has 6 electrons in its valence shell. These hydrides are trigonal planar in shape.

$$F-B\big\langle{{F}\atop{F}}$$
Trigonal planar

(BF_3)

These hydrides act as Lewis acids, *i.e.*, electron pair acceptor *e.g.*,

$$\underset{\text{Lewis acid}}{F-\underset{|}{\overset{|}{B}}-F} \ + \ \underset{\text{Lewis base}}{:\underset{|}{\overset{|}{N}}-H} \ \longrightarrow \ F-\underset{|}{\overset{|}{B}}\leftarrow\underset{|}{\overset{|}{N}}-H$$

To make up the deficiency of electrons, these hydrides exist in polymeric forms, *e.g.*, B_2H_6, B_4H_{10}, etc. Electron deficient hydrides are very reactive. These react with metals and non-metals and their compounds readily, *e.g.*, $B_2H_6(g) + 3O_2(g) \longrightarrow B_2O_3(s) + 3H_2O(g)$

Question 10. Do you expect the carbon hydrides of the type (C_nH_{2n+2}) to act as Lewis acid or base? Justify your answer.

(i) Carbon contains four valence electrons.
(ii) Lewis acids are electron deficient species and lewis bases are electron rich species.

Solution. Carbon hydrides of the type (C_nH_{2n+2}) are electron-precise hydrides. They have exact number of electrons required to form covalent bonds. Therefore, they neither act as Lewis acids nor Lewis bases.

Question 11. What do you understand by the term "non-stoichiometric hydrides"? Do you expect this type of the hydrides to be formed by alkali metals? Justify your answer.

Solution. These hydrides are formed by many d-block (except metals of 7, 8 and 9 group) and f-block elements. These hydrides are always non-stoichiometric, *i.e.*, deficient in hydrogen. In these hydrides hydrogen atom occupies interstitial sites, *e.g.*, $LaH_{2.87}$, $YbH_{2.55}$, $TiH_{1.5-1.8}$, $PdH_{0.6-0.8}$, etc.

This type of the hydrides are not formed by alkali metals. Alkali metals form ionic or saline hydrides. Saline hydrides are stoichiometric. Alkali metals are highly electropositive, they transfer their electron to the H-atom, thereby forming H^- ions. These H^- ions occupy holes in the lattice.

Question 12. How do you expect the metallic hydrides to be useful for hydrogen storage? Explain.

Solution. In metallic hydrides, hydrogen is adsorbed as H-atoms. This property of adsorption of hydrogen on transition metals is widely used as its storage media. Some of the metals such as Pd, Pt can accomodate a very large volume of hydrogen. This property has high potential for hydrogen storage and as a source of energy. Metallic hydrides on heating decompose to form hydrogen and very finely divided metal.

Question 13. How does the atomic hydrogen or oxy-hydrogen torch function for cutting and welding purposes? Explain.

Solution. Atomic hydrogen atoms, produced by dissociation of dihydrogen with the help of an electric arc, are allowed to recombine on the surface to be welded. In this process a large amount of energy is liberated which is used to generate a tempearature of 4000 K for cutting and welding purpose in the form of atomic hydrogen or oxy-hydrogen torches.

Question 14. Among NH_3, H_2O and HF, which would you expect to have highest magnitude of hydrogen bonding and why?

 A small and highly electronegative element form a stronger hydrogen bond. The order of size of N, O and F is $F^- < O^{2-} < N^{3-}$ and the order of electronegativity is $F^- > O^{2-} > N^{3-}$.

Solution. Since, electronegativity of F is the highest, therefore, magnitude of the positive charge on hydrogen and negative charge on F is the highest in HF and hence electrostatic attraction of the H-bonding is the strongest in H—F.

Question 15. Saline hydrides are known to react with water violently producing fire. Can CO_2, a well known fire extinguisher, be used in this case? Explain.

Solution. Saline hydrides (such as NaH, CaH_2, etc.), react with water violently to form the corresponding metal hydroxides with the evolution of dihydrogen.

$$NaH(s) + H_2O(l) \longrightarrow NaOH(aq) + H_2(g)$$
$$CaH_2(s) + 2H_2O(l) \longrightarrow Ca(OH)_2(aq) + 2H_2(g)$$

These reactions are so much exothermic that the evolved H_2 catches fire. This type of fire cannot be extinguished by CO_2 because it gets reduced by the hot metal hydride to form sodium formate.

$$NaH + CO_2 \longrightarrow HCOONa$$

Question 16. Arrange the following.

(i) CaH_2, BeH_2 and TiH_2 in the order of increasing electrical conductance.

(ii) LiH, NaH and CsH in the order of increasing ionic character.

(iii) H—H, D—D and F—F in the order of increasing bond dissociation enthalpy.

(iv) NaH, MgH_2 and H_2O in order of increasing reducing property.

(i) More the ionic character, higher is the electrical conductance.
(ii) Ionic character $\propto$ size of cation.
(iii) Shorter the bond length, higher is the bond dissociation energy.
(iv) Metal hydrides are stronger reducing agents than non-metal hydrides.

Solution. (i) $BeH_2 < CaH_2 < TiH_2$ (ii) $LiH < NaH < CsH$

(iii) $F—F < H—H < D—D$ (iv) $H_2O < MgH_2 < NaH$

Question 17. Compare the structure of H_2O and H_2O_2.

Solution. In water, oxygen is sp^3-hybridized. Due to stronger lone pair-lone pair repulsions than bond pair-bond pair repulsions, the HOH bond angle decreases from 109.5° to 104.5°. Thus, water is a bent molecule as shown in figure.

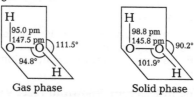

It is a highly polar molecule.

Hydrogen peroxide has a non-planar structure. Dipole moment value of H_2O_2 suggests that all the four atoms in H_2O_2 do not lie in a plane. The structure of H_2O_2 can be compared with a book open at angle 94°. The H—O—O bond angle is 97°.

H 95.0 pm 147.5 pm) 111.5° O—O 94.8° H	H 98.8 pm 145.8 pm) 90.2° O—O 101.9° H
Gas phase	Solid phase

Structure of H_2O_2

Question 18. What do you understand by the term 'auto-protolysis' of water? What is its significance?

Solution. Auto-protolysis means self ionization of water.

$$\underset{\text{Acid}_1}{H_2O(l)} + \underset{\text{Base}_2}{H_2O(l)} \rightleftharpoons \underset{\text{Acid}_2}{H_3O^+(aq)} + \underset{\text{Base}_1}{OH^-(aq)}$$

Due to auto-protolysis, water is amphoteric in nature. It reacts with both acids and bases.

For examples,

$$H_2O(l) + NH_3(aq) \longrightarrow NH_4^+(aq) + OH^-(aq)$$
$$\underset{Acid_1}{} \quad \underset{Base_2}{} \quad \quad \underset{Acid_2}{} \quad \underset{Base_1}{}$$

$$H_2O(l) + H_2S(aq) \longrightarrow H_3O^+(aq) + HS^-(aq)$$
$$\underset{Base_1}{} \quad \underset{Acid_2}{} \quad \quad \underset{Acid_1}{} \quad \underset{Base_2}{}$$

Question 19. Consider the reaction of water with F_2 and suggest, in terms of oxidation and reduction, which species are oxidised/reduced?

 Fluorine being more electronegative removes oxygen from water and itself gets reduced to fluoride ion.

Solution.
$$2F_2(g) + 2H_2O(l) \longrightarrow O_2(g) + 4H^+(aq) + 4F^-(aq)$$
$$\underset{Oxidant}{} \quad \underset{Reductant}{}$$

$$3F_2(g) + 3H_2O(l) \longrightarrow O_3(g) + 6H^+(aq) + 6F^-(aq)$$
$$\underset{Oxidant}{} \quad \underset{Reductant}{}$$

In these reactions, water acts as a reducing agent and hence itself gets oxidised to either oxygen or ozone. Fluorine acts as an oxidising agent and hence is itself reduced to F^- ion.

Question 20. Complete the following chemical reactions.

(i) $PbS(s) + H_2O_2(aq) \longrightarrow$

(ii) $MnO_4^-(aq) + H_2O_2(aq) \longrightarrow$

(iii) $CaO(s) + H_2O(g) \longrightarrow$

(iv) $AlCl_3(g) + H_2O(l) \longrightarrow$

(v) $Ca_3N_2(s) + H_2O(l) \longrightarrow$

Classify the above into (a) hydrolysis, (b) redox and (c) hydration reactions.

(i) In redox reactions, one substance is oxidised and the other is reduced.
(ii) Addition of water to form hydroxide is generally called hydrolysis.

Solution. (i) $PbS(s) + 4H_2O_2(aq) \longrightarrow PbSO_4(s) + 4H_2O(l)$ (Redox reaction)

(ii) $2MnO_4^-(aq) + 5H_2O_2(l) + 6H^+(aq) \longrightarrow 2Mn^{2+}(aq) + 8H_2O(l) + 5O_2(g)$
(Redox reaction)

(iii) $CaO(s) + H_2O(g) \longrightarrow Ca(OH)_2(aq)$ (Hydrolysis reaction)

(iv) $AlCl_3(g) + 6H_2O(l) \longrightarrow [Al(OH_2)_6]^{3+}(aq) + 3Cl^-(aq)$
(Hydration reaction)

(v) $Ca_3N_2(s) + 6H_2O(l) \longrightarrow 3Ca(OH)_2(aq) + 2NH_3(aq)$
(Hydrolysis reaction)

Question 21. Describe the structure of common form of ice.

Solution. Ice has a highly ordered three dimensional hydrogen bonded structure. Each oxygen atom is surrounded tetrahedrally by four other oxygen atoms at a distance of 276 pm. H-bonding gives ice a rather open type structure with wide holes.

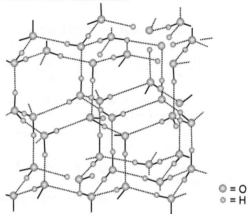

$O = O$
$\circ = H$

Question 22. What causes the temporary and permanent hardness of water?

Solution. Presence of calcium bicarbonates and magnesium bicarbonates in water causes temporary hardness of water. Presence of soluble calcium chloride, magnesium chloride, calcium sulphate and magnesium sulphate in water causes permanent hardness.

Question 23. Discuss the principle and method of softening of hard water by synthetic ion exchange resins.

Solution. Synthetic ion exchange resins are of two types.

Cation exchange resins Cation exchange resins contain large organic molecule with SO_3H group and are water soluble. It is changed to RNa by treating it with NaCl. The resin RNa exchanges Mg^{2+} and Ca^{2+} ions present in hard water to make the water soft.

$$2R\text{Na}(s) + M^{2+}(aq) \longrightarrow R_2M(s) + 2\text{Na}^+(aq) \quad (M = Ca^{2+} \text{ or } Mg^{2+})$$

The resin can be regenerated by passing NaCl (aqueous solution) in it.

Pure demineralised (deionized) water is obtained by passing water successively through a cation exchange and anion exchange resins. In the cation exchange process,

$$2R\text{H}(s) + M^{2+}(aq) \rightleftharpoons MR_2(s) + 2\text{H}^+(aq)$$
(cation exchange resin in the H^+ form)

H^+ exchanges for Ca^{2+}, Mg^{2+} and other cations present in water.

This process results in proton release and thus, makes the water acidic. In the anion exchange process,

$$R\text{NH}_2(s) + H_2O(l) \rightleftharpoons R\overset{+}{\text{NH}}_3 \cdot OH^-(s)$$

$R\overset{+}{\text{NH}}_3 \cdot OH^-$ is substituted ammonium hydroxide anion exchange resin.

$$R\overset{+}{\text{NH}}_3 \cdot OH^-(s) + X^-(aq) \rightleftharpoons R\overset{+}{\text{NH}}_3 \cdot X^-(s) + OH^-(aq)$$

OH^- exchanges for anions like Cl^-, HCO_3^-, SO_4^{2-}, etc., present in water. OH^- ions neutralise the H^+ ions. The exhausted cation and anion exchange resin are regenerated by passing dilute acid in cation exchange resin and alkali solution in anion exchange resin respectively.

Question 24. Write chemical reactions to show the amphoteric nature of water.

Solution. Water is amphoteric in character. It behaves both as an acid as well as a base. With acids stronger than itself, it behaves as a base and with bases stronger than itself, it acts as an acid.

$$\underset{Base_1}{H_2O(l)} + \underset{Acid_2}{H_2S(aq)} \longrightarrow \underset{Acid_1}{H_3O^+(aq)} + \underset{Base_2}{HS^-(aq)}$$

$$\underset{Acid_1}{H_2O(l)} + \underset{Base_2}{NH_3(aq)} \longrightarrow \underset{Acid_2}{NH_4^+(aq)} + \underset{Base_1}{OH^-(aq)}$$

Question 25. Write chemical reactions to justify that hydrogen peroxide can function as an oxidising as well as reducing agent.

Solution. H_2O_2 can act as an oxidising as well as a reducing agent both in acidic and basic media, *e.g.*,

(i) Oxidising agent in acidic medium
$$2Fe^{2+}(aq) + 2H^+(aq) + H_2O_2(aq) \longrightarrow 2Fe^{3+}(aq) + 2H_2O(l)$$

(ii) Oxidising agent in basic medium
$$Mn^{2+}(aq) + H_2O_2(aq) \longrightarrow Mn^{4+} + 2OH^-(aq)$$

(iii) Reducing agent in acidic medium
$$2MnO_4^-(aq) + 6H^+(aq) + 5H_2O_2(aq) \longrightarrow 2Mn^{2+}(aq) + 8H_2O(l) + 5O_2(g)$$

(iv) Reducing agent in basic medium
$$I_2(s) + H_2O_2(aq) + 2OH^-(aq) \longrightarrow 2I^-(aq) + 2H_2O(l) + O_2(g)$$

Question 26. What is meant by 'demineralised water' and how can it be obtained?

Solution. Water which is free from all soluble minerals salts is called demineralised water. Demineralised water is obtained by passing water successively through a cation exchange and an anion exchange resins. In cation exchanger, Ca^{2+}, Mg^{2+}, Na^+ and other cations present in water are removed by exchanging them with H^+ ions while in anion exchanger, Cl^-, HCO_3^-, SO_4^{2-}, etc., present in water are removed by exchanging them with OH^- ions.

$$\underset{\text{(released in cation exchanger)}}{H^+} + \underset{\text{(released in anion exchanger)}}{OH^-} \longrightarrow H_2O$$

Question 27. Is demineralised or distilled water useful for drinking purposes? If not, how can it be made useful?

Solution. Demineralised or distilled water is not useful for drinking purposes. It can be made useful by adding useful minerals in proper amount in it.

Question 28. Describe the usefullness of water in biosphere and biological systems.

Solution. A major part of all living organisms is made up of water. Human body has about 65% water and some plants have as much as 95% water. It is an essential compound for the survival of all life forms.

In comparison to other liquids, water has a high specific heat, thermal conductivity, surface tension, dipole moment, dielectric constant, etc. These properties allow water to play a key role in biosphere. The high heat of vaporisation and heat capacity are responsible for moderation of the climate and body temperature of living beings. It is an excellent solvent for transportation of minerals and other nutrients for plant and animal metabolism. Water is also required for photosynthesis in plants which releases O_2 into the atmosphere.

$$6CO_2(g) + 6H_2O(l) \xrightarrow[\text{Photosynthesis}]{(hv, \text{chlorophyll})} C_6H_{12}O_6 + 6O_2$$

Question 29. What properties of water make it useful as a solvent? What type of compounds can it (i) dissolve (ii) hydrolyse?

Solution. High dipole moment and high dielectric constant, these are the two properties of water which make it useful as a solvent.
 (i) It can dissolve both ionic compounds as well as those covalent compounds which can form hydrogen bonds with water such as ethyl alcohol, sugar, glucose, etc.
 (ii) Water can hydrolyse many metallic and non-metallic oxides, hydrides, carbides, phosphides and other salts, *e.g.,*

$$P_4O_{10}(s) + 6H_2O(l) \longrightarrow 4H_3PO_4(aq)$$
$$CaH_2(s) + 2H_2O(l) \longrightarrow Ca(OH)_2(aq) + 2H_2(g)$$
$$Al_4C_3(s) + 12H_2O(l) \longrightarrow 4Al(OH)_3 + 3CH_4$$

Question 30. Knowing the properties of H_2O and D_2O, do you think that D_2O can be used for drinking purposes?

Solution. Heavy water is injurious to human beings because rate of biochemical reactions decreases in heavy water.

Question 31. What is the difference between the terms 'hydrolysis' and 'hydration'?

Solution. Interaction of H^+ and OH^- ions of H_2O with the anion and the cation of a salt respectively to yield the original acid and the original base is called hydrolysis, *e.g.,*

$$\underset{\text{Salt}}{Na_2CO_3} + 2H_2O \longrightarrow \underset{\text{Base}}{2NaOH} + \underset{\text{Acid}}{H_2CO_3}$$

Hydration, on the other hand, means addition of H_2O to ions or molecules to form hydrated ions or hydrated salts. For example,

$$\underset{\text{Salt}}{KCl(s)} + H_2O(l) \longrightarrow K^+(aq) + Cl^-(aq)$$

$$\underset{\text{(Colourless)}}{CuSO_4(s)} + 5H_2O(l) \longrightarrow \underset{\text{(Blue)}}{CuSO_4 \cdot 5H_2O(s)}$$

Question 32. How can saline hydrides remove traces of water from organic compounds?

Solution. Saline hydrides such as NaH, CaH$_2$, etc., react with traces of water present in organic compounds and form their corresponding metal hydroxides with the evolution of hydrogen gas.

$$\underset{\text{Organic compound}}{NaH(s) + \quad H_2O(aq)} \longrightarrow NaOH(aq) + H_2(g)$$

Infact in saline hydrides M^+H^-, the H^- ion is a strong Bronsted base and thus, it reacts with water easily.

Question 33. What do you expect the nature of hydrides is, if formed by elements of atomic numbers 15, 19, 23, 44 with dry dihydrogen? Compare their behaviour towards water.

 Find the block of the elements to give the nature as s-block elements form ionic hydrides, p-block elements form covalent hydrides and d-block elements may form either non-stoichiometric hydrides, or no hydride.

Solution.

(i) Element with $Z = 15$, belongs to p-block. It forms covalent hydride, PH$_3$.

(ii) Element with $Z = 19$ belongs to s-block. It forms ionic or saline hydride, KH.

(iii) Element with $Z = 23$ belongs to d-block and Vth group elements. It forms interstitial hydride, VH$_{1.6}$. It is non-stoichiometric hydride.

(iv) Element with $Z = 44$ belongs to d-block and 8th group elements. It is ruthinium. It does not form any hydride because metals of group 7, 8 and 9 do not form hydride (hydride gap).
Only ionic hydride, KH reacts violently with water producing dihydrogen gas.

$$KH(s) + H_2O(aq) \longrightarrow KOH(aq) + H_2(g)$$

Question 34. Do you expect different products in solution when aluminium(III)chloride and potassium chloride are treated separately with (i) normal water (ii) acidified water, and (iii) alkaline water? Write equations wherever necessary.

Solution. AlCl$_3$ is a salt of weak base, Al(OH)$_3$ and a strong acid, HCl. Therefore, in normal water, it undergoes hydrolysis.

$$AlCl_3(s) + 3H_2O(l) \longrightarrow Al(OH)_3(s) + 3H^+(aq) + 3Cl^-(aq)$$

Its aqueous solution is acidic in nature.
In acidified water, H^+ ions react with Al(OH)$_3$ to produce Al$^{3+}(aq)$ ions and H$_2$O. Therefore, in acidified water AlCl$_3$ exists as Al$^{3+}(aq)$ and Cl$^-(aq)$ ions.
In alkaline water AlCl$_3$ yields following products

$$AlCl_3(s) \xrightarrow{\text{Alk. water}} Al[OH]_4^-(aq) + 3Cl^-(aq)$$

$$Al[OH]_4^- \longrightarrow AlO_2^-(aq) + 2H_2O(l)$$

KCl is the salt of a strong acid and a strong base. It does not undergo hydrolysis in normal water. It only dissociates in water to give $K^+(aq)$ and $Cl^-(aq)$ ion.

$$KCl(s) \xrightarrow{\text{Water}} K^+(aq) + Cl^-(aq)$$

Aqueous solution of KCl is neutral. Hence, in acidified water or in alkaline water, the ions do not react further.

Question 35. How does H_2O_2 behave as a bleaching agent?

Solution. H_2O_2 acts as a bleaching agent due to the nascent oxygen.

$$H_2O_2 \longrightarrow H_2O + O$$
$$\text{Coloured matter} + [O] \longrightarrow \text{colourless matter}$$

It bleaches materials like silk, hair, ivory, cotton, wool, etc.

Question 36. What do you understand by the terms :

(i) hydrogen economy   (ii) hydrogenation
(iii) '*syn* gas'   (iv) water-gas shift reaction and
(v) fuel cell?

Solution.

  (i) **Hydrogen economy** Hydrogen has promising potential for use as a non polluting (clean) fuel of near future. The basic principle of hydrogen economy is the transportation and storage of energy in the form of liquid or gaseous dihydrogen.

 (ii) **Hydrogenation** Addition of dihydrogen to the organic compounds containing double or triple bonds in the presence of a catalyst is known as hydrogenation. Hydrogenation of vegetable oils using nickel as catalyst gives edible fats (margarine and vanaspati ghee).

$$\text{Vegetable oil} + H_2 \xrightarrow{\text{Ni, 473 K}} \text{vegetable ghee}$$

(iii) *Syn gas* Mixture of CO and H_2, is known as synthesis gas or *syn* gas. Reaction of steam on hydrocarbons or coke at high temperatures in the presence of catalyst yields *syn* gas, *e.g.*,

$$CH_4(g) + H_2O(g) \xrightarrow[\text{Ni}]{1270\ K} CO(g) + 3H_2(g)$$

Now a days *syn* gas is produced from sewage, saw dust, scrapwood, news papers, etc. The process of production of *syn* gas from coal is called coal gasification.

$$C(s) + H_2O(g) \xrightarrow{1270\ K} CO(g) + H_2(g)$$

(iv) **Water gas shift reaction** The amount of dihydrogen in water gas can be increased by mixing it with steam and then passing the mixture over heated (500°C) catalyst (iron chromate or Fe_2O_3 / Cr_2O_3).

$$CO(g) + H_2(g) + H_2O(g) \xrightarrow{\text{Catalyst, } \Delta} CO_2(g) + 2H_2(g)$$
Water gas

The above reaction is known as water gas shift reaction.

(v) **Fuel cell** It is a device which converts the energy produced during the combustion of a fuel directly into electrical energy. One such fuel cell is hydrogen-oxygen fuel cell. It does not cause any pollution. Fuel cells generated electricity with conversion efficiency of 70-85%.

Selected NCERT Exemplar Problems

Short Answer Type

Question 1. Name the classes of hydrides to which H_2O, B_2H_6 and NaH belong.

Solution. H_2O—Covalent or molecular hydride (electron rich hydride).

B_2H_6—Covalent or molecular hydride (electron deficient hydride).

NaH—Ionic or saline hydride.

Question 2. If same mass of liquid water and a piece of ice is taken, then why is the density of ice less than that of liquid water?

Solution. In ice, molecules of H_2O are not packed so closely as in liquid water. There exists vacant spaces in the crystal lattice. This results in larger volume and lower density (density = mass/volume).

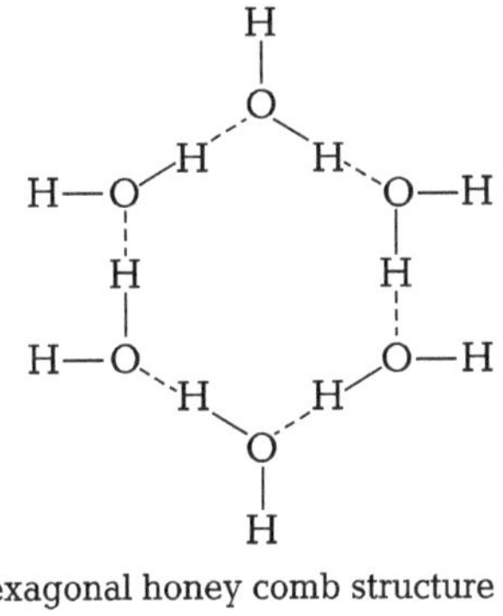

Hexagonal honey comb structure of ice

Question 3. Complete the following equations

(i) $PbS(s) + H_2O_2(aq) \longrightarrow$

(ii) $CO(g) + 2H_2(g) \xrightarrow{\text{Cobalt} \atop \text{catalyst}}$

Solution.   (i) $PbS(s) + 4H_2O_2(aq) \longrightarrow PbSO_4 + 4H_2O$

(ii) $CO(g) + 2H_2(g) \xrightarrow[\text{catalyst}]{\text{Cobalt}} CH_3OH(l)$

Question 4.   Give reasons

(i) Lakes freeze from top towards bottom.

(ii) Ice floats on water.

Solution.

(i) Density of ice is less than that of liquid water. During severe winter, the temperature of lake water keeps on decreasing. Since, cold water is heavier, therefore, it moves towards bottom of the lake and warm water from the bottom moves towards surface. This process continues. The density of water is maximum at 277 K. Therefore, any further decrease in temperature of the surface water will decrease in density. The temperature of surface water keeps on decreasing and ultimately it freezes. Thus, the ice layer at lower temperature floats over the water below it. Due to this freezing of water into ice takes place continuously from top towards bottom.

(ii) Density of ice is less than that of liquid water, so it floats over water.

Question 5.   How is heavy water prepared? Compare its physical properties with those of ordinary water.

Solution.   Heavy water is prepared by prolonged electrolysis of water. Comparison of physical properties of heavy water with those of ordinary water is as follows

Property	H_2O	D_2O
Molecular mass (g mol^{-1})	18.0151	20.0276
Melting point (K)	273.0	276.8
Boiling point (K)	373.0	374.4
Enthalpy of formation (kJ mol^{-1})	-285.9	-294.6
Enthalpy of vaporisation -373 K (kJ mol^{-1})	40.66	41.61
Enthalpy of fusion kJ mol^{-1})	6.01	—
Temp. of max. density (K)	276.98	284.2
Density at 298 K (g cm^{-3})	1.0000	1.1059
Viscosity (centipoise)	0.8903	1.107
Dielectric constant (c^2 /Nm^2)	78.39	78.06
Electrical conductivity at 298 K (ohm^{-1} cm^{-1})	5.7×10^{-8}	—

Question 6.   Write one chemical reaction for the preparation of D_2O_2.

Solution.   By the action of D_2SO_4 dissolved in water over BaO_2.

$$BaO_2 + D_2SO_4 \longrightarrow BaSO_4 + D_2O_2$$

Question 7. Calculate the strength of 5 volumes H_2O_2 solution.

Solution. 5 volumes H_2O_2 solution means that 1 L of 5 volumes H_2O_2 solution on decomposition produces 5 L of O_2 at NTP.

$$2H_2O_2 \longrightarrow 2H_2O + O_2$$
$$2 \times 34\ g \longrightarrow 22.7\ L\ at\ NTP$$

22.7 L O_2 at NTP will be obtained from $H_2O_2 = 68$ g.

$\therefore$ 5 L of O_2 at NTP will be obtained from $H_2O_2 = \dfrac{68 \times 5}{22.7}\ g = 14.98 = 15\ g$

But 5 L of O_2 at NTP is produced from 1 L of 5 volumes H_2O_2

$\therefore$ Strength of H_2O_2 solution $= 15\ g\ L^{-1}$

or percentage strength of H_2O_2 solution $= \dfrac{15}{1000} \times 100 = 1.5\%$

Question 8. Melting point, enthalpy of vaporization and viscosity data of H_2O and D_2O is given below :

	H_2O	D_2O
Melting point/K	373.0	374.4
Enthalpy of vaporisation at (373 K)/kJ mol^{-1}	40.66	41.61
Viscosity/centipoise	0.8903	1.107

On the basis of this data explain in which of these liquids intermolecular forces are stronger?

Solution. The values of melting point, enthalpy of vaporization and viscosity depend upon the intermolecular forces of attraction. Since, their values are higher for D_2O as compared to those of H_2O, therefore, intermolecular forces of attraction are stronger in D_2O than in H_2O.

Question 9. Dihydrogen reacts with dioxygen (O_2) to form water. Write the name and formula of the product when the isotope of hydrogen which has one proton and one neutron in its nucleus is treated with oxygen. Will the reactivity of both the isotopes be the same towards oxygen? Justify your answer.

Solution. The isotope of hydrogen which contains one proton and one neutron is deuterium (D).

$$2D_2(g) + O_2(g) \xrightarrow{\ Heat\ } 2D_2O$$

Dideuterium   Dioxygen   Deuterium oxide
(heavy water)

The reactivity of H_2 and D_2 towards oxygen will be different. Since, the D—D bond is stronger than H—H bond, therefore, H_2 is more reactive than D_2.

Question 10. Explain why HCl is a gas and HF is a liquid?

Solution. F is smaller and more electronegative than Cl, so it forms stronger H-bonds as compared to Cl. That's why HF is liquid and HCl is a gas.

Question 11. Rohan heard that instructions were given to the laboratory attendant to store a particular chemical, *i.e.*, keep it in the dark room, add some urea in it, and keep it away from dust. This chemical acts as an oxidising as well as a reducing agent in both acidic and alkaline media. This chemical is important for use in the pollution control treatment of domestic and industrial effluents.

(i) Write the name of this compound.

(ii) Explain why such precautions are taken for storing this chemical?

Solution.

(i) The name of the compound is hydrogen peroxide, H_2O_2. It acts as an oxidising agent as well as reducing agent in both acidic and basic medium.

(ii) H_2O_2 decomposes slowly on exposure to light and dust particles. In the presence of metal surfaces or traces of alkali present in glass containers, the decomposition of H_2O_2 is catalysed. It is, therefore, stored in wax lined glass or plastic vessels in dark. Urea is added as a negative catalyst to check its decomposition.

$$2H_2O_2(aq) \xrightarrow{hv} 2H_2O(l) + O_2(g)$$

Question 12. What is the importance of heavy water?

Solution. 1. It is extensively used as a moderator in nuclear reactors.
2. It is used as a tracer compound in the study of reaction mechanism.
3. It is used for the preparation of other deuterium compounds such as CD_4, D_2SO_4, etc.

Question 13. Write the Lewis structure of hydrogen peroxide.

Solution. The Lewis structure of hydrogen peroxide is

Hydrogen peroxide

Question 14. An acidic solution of hydrogen peroxide behaves as an oxidising as well as reducing agent. Illustrate it with the help of a chemical equation.

Solution. (i) H_2O_2 oxidises acidified KI to iodine.

$$2KI + H_2O_2 + H_2SO_4 \longrightarrow I_2 + K_2SO_4 + 2H_2O$$

(ii) H_2O_2 reduces $KMnO_4$ to MnO_2 in alkaline medium.

$$2KMnO_4 + 3H_2O_2 \longrightarrow 2MnO_2 + 2KOH + 3O_2 + 2H_2O$$

Question 15. Why can dilute solutions of hydrogen peroxide not be concentrated by heating. How can a concentrated solution of hydrogen peroxide be obtained?

Solution. Dilute solutions of H_2O_2 cannot be concentrated by heating because it decomposes much below its boiling point.

$$2H_2O_2 \longrightarrow 2H_2O + O_2$$

1% H_2O_2 is extracted with water and concentrated to ~ 30% (by mass) by distillation under reduced pressure. It can be further concentrated to ~ 85% by careful distillation under low pressure. The remaining water can be frozen out to obtain pure H_2O_2.

Question 16. Phosphoric acids is preferred over sulphuric acid in preparing hydrogen peroxide from peroxides. Why?

Solution. H_2SO_4 acts as a catalyst for decomposition of H_2O_2. Therefore, some weaker acids such as H_3PO_4, H_2CO_3 is preferred over H_2SO_4 for preparing H_2O_2 from peroxides.
$$3BaO_2 + 2H_3PO_4 \longrightarrow Ba_3(PO_4)_2 + 3H_2O_2$$
$$\text{(Insoluble)}$$

Question 17. Write redox reaction between fluorine and water.

Solution. Fluorine is a strong oxidising agent, it oxidises H_2O to O_2 or O_3.
$$2F_2(g) + 2H_2O(l) \longrightarrow O_2(g) + 4H^+(aq) + 4F^-(aq)$$
$$3F_2(g) + 3H_2O(l) \longrightarrow O_3(g) + 6H^+(aq) + 6F^-(aq)$$

Long Answer Type

Question 18. How can D_2O be prepared from water? Mention the physical properties in which D_2O differs from H_2O. Give at least three reactions of D_2O showing the exchange of hydrogen with deuterium.

Solution. (a) D_2O can be prepared by prolonged electrolysis of water.

(b) Physical properties
   (i) D_2O is colourless, odourless, tasteless liquid. It has maximum density – 1.1073 g mL^{-1} at 11.6°C (water at 4°C).
   (ii) Solubility of salts in heavy water is less than in ordinary water because it is more viscous than ordinary water.
   (iii) Nearly all physical constants of D_2O are higher than H_2O. It is due to the greater nuclear mass of deuterium atom than H-atom and stronger H-bonding in D_2O than H_2O.

(c) Exchange reactions of hydrogen with deuterium
$$NaOH + D_2O \longrightarrow NaOD + HOD$$
$$HCl + D_2O \longrightarrow DCl + HOD$$
$$NH_4Cl + D_2O \longrightarrow NH_3DCl + HOD$$

Question 19. What mass of hydrogen peroxide will be present in 2 L of a 5 molar solution? Calculate the mass of oxygen which will be liberated by the decomposition of 200 mL of this solution.

Solution. (i) Molar mass of $H_2O_2 = 34$ g mol^{-1}
1 L of 5 M solution of H_2O_2 will contain 34×5 g H_2O_2
2 L of 5 M solution of H_2O_2 will contain $34 \times 5 \times 2 = 340$ g H_2O_2
Mass of H_2O_2 present in 2 L of 5 molar solution $= 340$ g

(ii) 0.2 L (or 200 mL) of 5 M solution will contain

$$\frac{340 \times 0.2}{2} = 34 \text{ g } H_2O_2$$

$$\underset{2 \times 34 = 68 \text{ g}}{2H_2O_2} \longrightarrow 2H_2O + \underset{2 \times 16 = 32 \text{ g}}{O_2}$$

68 g H_2O_2 on decomposition will give 32 g O_2

$\therefore$ 34 g H_2O_2 on decomposition will give $\dfrac{32 \times 34}{68} = 16 \text{ g } O_2$

Question 20. An ionic hydride of an alkali metal has significant covalent character and is almost unreactive towards oxygen and chlorine. This is used in the synthesis of other useful hydrides. Write the formula of this hydride. Write its reaction with Al_2Cl_6.

Solution. It is LiH because it has significant covalent character due to the smallest alkali metal Li. LiH is very stable. It is almost unreactive towards oxygen and chlorine.

It reacts with Al_2Cl_6 to form lithium aluminium hydride.

$$8LiH + Al_2Cl_6 \longrightarrow 2LiAlH_4 + 6LiCl$$

Question 21. Sodium forms a crystalline ionic solid with dihydrogen. The solid is non-volatile and non-conducting in nature. It reacts violently with water to produce dihydrogen gas. Write the formula of this compound and its reaction with water. What will happen on electrolysis of the melt of this solid?

Solution. Sodium reacts with dihydrogen to form sodium hydride which is a crystalline ionic solid.

$$2Na + H_2 \longrightarrow 2Na^+H^-$$

It reacts violently with water to produce H_2 gas

$$2NaH + 2H_2O \longrightarrow 2NaOH + 2H_2$$

In solid state NaH does not conduct electricity. On electrolysis, in its molten state it gives H_2 at anode and Na at cathode.

Chapter 10

The s-Block Elements

Important Results

1. The s-block of the Periodic Table constitutes group-1 and group-2. Li, Na, K, Rb, Cs and Fr belong to group-1 (alkali metals) and have [inert gas] ns^1 configuration. Be, Mg, Ca, Sr, Ba and Ra belong to group-2 (alkaline earth metals) and have [inert gas] ns^2 configuration.

2. Alkali metals have low melting and boiling points and these decrease on moving down the group. Generally densities of alkali metals increase from Li to Cs. However, density of K < Na.

3. Hydration energy decreases on moving down the alkali metals and it increases in a period from left to right. Therefore, hydration energy of IInd group > hydration energy of corresponding I group element.

4. The order of mobility of alkali metal ions in aqueous solution is
$$Li^+ < Na^+ < K^+ < Rb^+ < Cs^+ < Fr^+.$$

5. Although lithium has the highest ionization potential, yet it is the strongest reducing agent due to its large heat of hydration.

6. In Bunsen flame, all alkali metals and alkaline earth metals (except Be and Mg) impart characteristic colours due to the excitation of outermost orbital electron to a higher energy level.

7. All alkali and alkaline earth metals form ionic compounds. The ionic character increases down the group. Alkaline earth metal compounds are less ionic than alkali metal compounds.

8. Solution of alkali metals in liquid ammonia is good conductor of electricity and is a good reducing agent. The blue colour of the solution is due to the ammoniated electrons. In concentrated solution, the blue colour changes to bronze colour.

9. Alkali metals form normal oxides, peroxides and superoxides. Order of stability – normal oxides > peroxides > superoxides. The normal oxides and peroxides are colourless when pure, but the superoxides are yellow or orange in colour.

10. Hydroxides of alkali metals are obtained by the reaction of the oxides with water. These are strongest of all bases and dissolve freely in water with evolution of much heat on account of intense hydration.

11. Due to very small size and high IE, lithium shows resemblance in properties with magnesium placed diagonally opposite.

12. Na_2CO_3 is soda ash and $Na_2CO_3 \cdot 10H_2O$ is called washing soda or salt soda. It is generally prepared by Solvay process.

13. An aqueous solution of 28% NaCl (by weight) is called brine.

14. Sodium hydroxide (caustic soda), NaOH is generally prepared commercially by the electrolysis of sodium chloride in Castner Kellner cell. A brine solution is electrolysed using a mercury cathode and a carbon anode. Na metal is discharged at the cathode forming Na-Hg and Cl_2 gas at the anode.

15. Sodium hydrogen carbonate is known as baking soda because it decomposes on heating to generate CO_2 bubbles.

16. The chemistry of alkaline earth metals is very much like that of alkali metals. However, some difference arise because of reduced atomic and ionic sizes and increased cationic charges in case of alkaline earth metals. Their oxides and hydroxides are less basic than the alkali metal oxides and hydroxides.

17. The order of solubility of metal hydroxides is
    CsOH > RbOH > KOH > NaOH > LiOH
    $Ba(OH)_2 > Sr(OH)_2 > Ca(OH)_2 > Mg(OH)_2$

18. The order of stability of metal carbonates is
    $Li_2CO_3 < Na_2CO_3 < K_2CO_3 < Rb_2CO_3$
    $BeCO_3 < MgCO_3 < CaCO_3 < SrCO_3$

19. The order of stability of metal halides is $MF > MCl > MBr > MI$

20. The order of solubility of metal sulphate is
    $BeSO_4 > MgSO_4 > CaSO_4 > SrSO_4 > BaSO_4$

21. Plaster of Paris $\left(CaSO_4 \cdot \frac{1}{2}H_2O\right)$ is obtained by heating the gypsum ($CaSO_4 \cdot 2H_2O$) at 120°C. However, gypsum on heating at 200°C gives dead burnt plaster ($CaSO_4$) and at 400°C gives CaO, SO_2 and O_2.

22. The general composition of Portland cement is 70%-CaO, 18%, SiO_2, 5%-Al_2O_3, 3%-Fe_2O_3 and 2%-MgO. Some gypsum is added to cement to slow down its setting process.

Exercises

Question 1. What are the common physical and chemical features of alkali metals?

Solution. **Physical Properties**

1. Alkali metals are silvery white, soft and light metals.

2. Their densities are quite low (because of the large size). It increases on moving down the group. However, potassium is lighter than sodium.

3. The melting and boiling points of alkali metals are low because of the weak metallic bonding due to the presence of one electron in their valence shell.

4. Alkali metals and their salts produce characteristic colour to the flame due to easy excitation of valence electron from lower to higher energy level.

Metal :	Li	Na	K	Rb	Cs
Colour :	Crimson red	Yellow	Violet	Red violet	Blue

Chemical Properties

Alkali metals are highly reactive due to their low ionization enthalpy. Their reactivity increases down the group.

1. **Reactivity towards air** The alkali metals tarnish in dry air due to the formation of their oxides. Lithium forms monoxide, sodium forms peroxide, and the other metals form superoxides.

$$4Li + O_2 \longrightarrow 2Li_2O \qquad \text{(oxide)}$$
$$2Na + O_2 \longrightarrow Na_2O_2 \qquad \text{(peroxide)}$$
$$M + O_2 \longrightarrow MO_2 \quad \text{(superoxide)} \; M = K, Rb, Cs.$$

Lithium reacts directly with nitrogen of air to form lithium nitride, Li_3N.

2. **Reactivity towards water** Alkali metals react with water to form hydroxide and dihydrogen.

$$2M + 2H_2O \longrightarrow 2M^+ + 2OH^- + H_2 \quad (M = \text{alkali metal})$$

Reaction of Li with water is less vigorous than that of sodium.

Alkali metals also react with proton donors such as alcohol, gaseous NH_3 and alkynes.

3. **Reactivity towards dihydrogen** Alkali metals react with hydrogen to form ionic or saline hydrides.

$$2M + H_2 \xrightarrow{\;673\text{ K}\;} 2M^+H^- \quad (M = \text{Li, Na, K, etc.})$$

4. **Reactivity towards halogens** Alkali metals readily react with halogens to form ionic halides.

$$2M + X_2 \longrightarrow \underset{\text{Metal halide}}{2MX} \qquad (M = \text{alkali metals})$$

5. **Reducing nature** The alkali metals are strong reducing agent as they lose their single valence electron easily.

$$Na \longrightarrow Na^+ + e^-$$

Lithium is the strongest and sodium is the least powerful reducing agent.

6. **Solubility in liquid NH_3** All alkali metals dissolve in liquid NH_3 and form deep blue solution which are conducting in nature.

$$M + (x + y)\,NH_3 \longrightarrow [M(NH_3)_x]^+ + [e\,(NH_3)_y]^-$$

(Ammoniated electron)

7. **Formation of alloys** Alkali metals form alloys amongst themselves and with other metals. With mercury they form amalgams and the reactions are highly exothermic.

Question 2. Discuss the general characteristics and gradation in properties of alkaline earth metals.

Solution. Element of group-2, Be, Mg, Ca, Sr, Ba and Ra are collectively known as alkaline earth metals (except beryllium).

General Characteristics

A. Atomic Properties

1. **Electronic configuration** Their general electronic configuration is represented as [noble gas]ns^2.

2. **Atomic and ionic radii** Atomic and ionic radii of these metals are smaller than those of alkali metals in the same period. Within the group the atomic and ionic radii increase with increase in atomic number.

3. **Ionization enthalpies** First ionization enthalpies of alkaline earth metals are higher than those of alkali metals due to their small size. $\left(IE \propto \dfrac{1}{atomic\ size}\right)$. Second ionization enthalpies of alkaline earth metals are smaller than those of the corresponding alkali metals.

4. **Hydration enthalpies** Like alkali metal ions, the hydration enthalpies of alkaline earth metal ions decrease with increase in ionic size on moving down the group.

$$Be^{2+} > Mg^{2+} > Ca^{2+} > Sr^{2+} > Ba^{2+}$$

The hydration enthalpies of these metal ions are larger than those of alkali metal ions.

B. Physical Properties

1. These metals are silvery white, lustrous and relatively soft but harder than the alkali metals.

2. The melting and boiling points of these metals are higher than the corresponding alkali metals due to their smaller size. The trend is, however, not regular.

3. **Flame colouration** Alkaline earth metals except Be and Mg impart a characteristic colour to the flame. The different colours arise due to different energies required for electronic excitation and de-excitation.

Metal	Be/Mg	Ca	Sr	Ba	Ra
Colour	No colour	Brick red	Crimson	Apple green	Crimson

4. **Densities** Densities of these metals decrease slightly from Be to Ca after which it increase. These metals are denser, heavier and harder than the alkali metals due to their smaller atomic size.

C. Chemical Properties

The alkaline earth metals are less reactive than the alkali metals. The reactivities of these metals increases on moving down the group.

1. **Reactivity towards air and water** Be and Mg are inert to oxygen and water due to the formation of a protective oxide layer on their surface. However, powdered Be burns brilliantly on ignition in air.

$$2Be + O_2 \xrightarrow{\text{Ignition}} BeO$$
$$\text{Air}$$

$$3Be + N_2 \longrightarrow Be_3N_2$$
$$\text{Air}$$

Similarly, magnesium is more electropositive and burns with dazzling brilliance in air to give MgO and Mg_3N_2. Ca, Sr and Ba are readily attacked by air to form oxide and nitride.

2. **Reactivity towards hydrogen** All these metals except Be combine with hydrogen upon heating to form their hydrides, MH_2 type $(M = Be, Mg, Ca, Sr, Ba)$

3. **Reactivity towards halogens** These metals react with halogens at elevated temperature forming MX_2 type halides.

$$M + X_2 \longrightarrow MX_2 \qquad\qquad (X = F, Cl, Br, I)$$

4. **Reactivity towards acids** These metals readily react with acids and liberate H_2 gas.

$$M + 2HCl \longrightarrow MCl_2 + H_2$$

5. **Reducing nature** Like alkali metals, alkaline earth metals are strong reducing agents. However, their reducing power is less than that of alkali metals. Their reducing power increases on moving down the group.

6. **Solutions in liquid NH_3** Like alkali metals, the alkaline earth metals dissolve in liquid ammonia to give deep blue black solutions.

$$M + (x + y) NH_3 \longrightarrow [M(NH_3)_x]^{2+} + 2 [e (NH_3)_y]^-$$

Question 3. Why are alkali metals not found in nature?

Alkali metals are highly reactive because of their very low ionisation energy.

Solution. Due to high chemical reactivity alkali metals do not occur free in nature. They are found in the earth's crust in the form of halide, sulphate, carbonate, silicate, borate, oxide ores, etc.

Question 4. Find out the oxidation state of sodium in Na_2O_2.

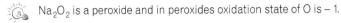
Na_2O_2 is a peroxide and in peroxides oxidation state of O is -1.

Solution. Let x be the oxidation state of Na in Na_2O_2.

Na_2O_2 contains a peroxide linkage in which O has an oxidation state of – 1.

$$\overset{x}{Na_2}\ \overset{-1}{O_2} \text{ or } 2x + 2\,(-1) = 0 \text{ or } x = +1.$$

Thus, the oxidation state of sodium in Na_2O_2 is + 1.

Question 5. Explain why is sodium less reactive than potassium?

Reactivity depends upon the ionization enthalpy and electrode potential ($E°$). As the size increases, ionization enthalpy decreases.

Solution. The ionization enthalpy (Δ_iH_1) of potassium (419 kJ mol^{-1}) is less than that of sodium (496 kJ mol^{-1}) and the standard electrode potential ($E°$) of potassium (– 2.925 V) is more negative than that of sodium (– 2.714 V) that's why potassium is more reactive than sodium.

Question 6. Compare the alkali metals and alkaline earth metals with respect to

   (i) ionization enthalpy   (ii) basicity of oxides

(iii) solubility of hydroxides.

Solution.

  (i) **Ionization enthalpies** The first ionization enthalpies of the alkaline earth metals are higher than those of the corresponding alkali metals. This is due to their small size as compared to the corresponding alkali metals. But second ionization enthalpies of the alkaline earth metals are smaller than those of the corresponding alkali metals.

 (ii) **Basicity of oxides** The oxides of the alkali and alkaline earth metals dissolves in water to form basic hydroxides. The alkaline earth metal hydroxides are however less basic and less stable than alkali metal hydroxides.

(iii) **Solubility of hydroxides** The solubility of hydroxides of alkaline earth metals is relatively less than their corresponding alkali metal hydroxides.

Question 7. In what ways lithium shows similarities to magnesium in its chemical behaviour?

Solution. Lithium resembles with magnesium due to their similar size [atomic radii, Li = 152 pm, Mg = 160 pm; ionic radii : Li^+ = 76 pm, Mg^{2+} = 72 pm,.] The important points of similarity are

  1. Both lithium and magnesium are harder and lighter than other elements in the respective groups.

  2. Both Li and Mg reacts slowly with water.

  3. Oxides and hydroxides of Li and Mg are much less soluble in water. Their hydroxides decompose on heating.

$$2LiOH \xrightarrow{\Delta} Li_2O + H_2O$$

$$Mg(OH)_2 \xrightarrow{\Delta} MgO + H_2O$$

4. Li and Mg both form nitrides (Li_3N and Mg_3N_2) by direct combination with nitrogen.
5. Both Li and Mg combine with carbon on heating.

$$2Li + 2C \longrightarrow Li_2C_2$$
$$Mg + 2C \longrightarrow MgC_2$$

6. Li and Mg both form monoxide on heating in oxygen.

$$4Li + O_2 \longrightarrow 2Li_2O$$
$$2Mg + O_2 \longrightarrow 2MgO$$

7. Li_2SO_4 like $MgSO_4$ does not form alums.
8. Both LiCl and $MgCl_2$ are deliquescent and crystallise from aqueous solution as hydrates, $LiCl \cdot 2H_2O$ and $MgCl_2 \cdot 6H_2O$.
9. Lithium and magnesium carbonates both decompose easily on heating to form the oxides and CO_2.

$$Li_2CO_3 \xrightarrow{\Delta} Li_2O + CO_2$$

$$MgCO_3 \xrightarrow{\Delta} MgO + CO_2$$

10. Solid hydrogen carbonates are not formed by lithium and magnesium.
11. Both lithium nitrate and magnesium nitrate decompose on heating producing nitrogen dioxide.

$$4 LiNO_3 \xrightarrow{\Delta} 2Li_2O + 4NO_2 + O_2$$

$$2Mg(NO_3)_2 \xrightarrow{\Delta} 2MgO + 4NO_2 + O_2$$

Question 8. Explain why can alkali and alkaline earth metals not be obtained by chemical reduction methods?

Solution.

1. Alkali and alkaline earth metals are themselves strong reducing agents. Therefore, these metals cannot be obtained by chemical reduction of their oxides and other compounds.

2. These metals are highly electropositive in nature. So, these cannot be displaced from the aqueous solutions of their salts by other metals.

Question 9. Why are potassium and caesium, rather than lithium used in photoelectric cells?

Metals having very high tendency to lose electrons are used in photoelectric cells. Lower the ionization energy, higher is the tendency to lose electrons.

Solution. Potassium and caesium have much lower ionization enthalpy than that of lithium. Therefore, these metals on exposure to light emit electrons easily but lithium does not. That's why K and Cs rather than Li are used in photoelectric cells.

Question 10. When an alkali metal dissolves in liquid ammonia, the solution can acquire different colours. Explain the reasons for this type of colour change.

Solution. The dilute solutions of alkali metals in liquid ammonia exhibit dark blue colour because ammoniated electrons absorb energy in the visible region of light.

$$M + (x + y) NH_3 \longrightarrow [M(NH_3)_x]^+ + \underset{\text{Ammoniated electron}}{[e^- (NH_3)_y]}$$

However, if the concentration increases above 3M, the colour changes to copper-bronze and it becomes diamagnetic.

Question 11. Beryllium and magnesium do not give colour to flame whereas other alkaline earth metals do so. Why?

The colour of the flame is due to the excitation of loosely bound electrons of the metal atom.

Solution. Be and Mg atoms due to their small size and high effective nuclear charge bind their electrons more strongly. Therefore, they required high excitation energy and are not excited by Bunsen flame. While other alkaline earth metals impart a characteristic colour to the flame, due to easy excitation of electrons to higher energy levels.

Question 12. Discuss the various reactions that occur in the Solvay process.

Solution. In Solvay ammonia process, CO_2 is passed through brine, (a concentrated solution of NaCl) saturated with ammonia. The process involves the formation of a sparingly soluble sodium bicarbonate.

$$NaCl + NH_3 + CO_2 + H_2O \longrightarrow NaHCO_3\downarrow + NH_4Cl$$

Sodium bicarbonate thus formed is filtered, dried and heated to obtain sodium carbonate.

$$2NaHCO_3 \xrightarrow{\Delta} Na_2CO_3 + CO_2 + H_2O$$

CO_2 used in carbonating tower is prepared by heating calcium carbonate and the quicklime, CaO thus formed is dissolved in water to form slaked lime, $Ca(OH)_2$.

$$CaCO_3 \xrightarrow{\Delta} CaO + CO_2$$
$$CaO + H_2O \longrightarrow Ca(OH)_2$$

In ammonia recovery tower, NH_3 is prepared by heating NH_4Cl with $Ca(OH)_2$.

$$2NH_4Cl + Ca(OH)_2 \longrightarrow 2NH_3 + \underset{\text{(by-product)}}{CaCl_2} + 2H_2O$$

Question 13. Potassium carbonate cannot be prepared by Solvay process. Why?

Potassium bicarbonate is highly soluble in water, so it cannot precipitate out.

Solution. Potassium carbonate cannot be prepared by Solvay process because potassium bicarbonate being highly soluble in water, would not be precipitated out.

Question 14. Why is Li_2CO_3 decomposed at a lower temperature whereas Na_2CO_3 at higher temperature?

Solution. Lithium being very small in size polarises a large CO_3^{2-} ion leading to the formation of more stable Li_2O and CO_2. All the carbonates of alkali metals (except lithium carbonate) are thermally quite stable. That's why Li_2CO_3 is decomposed at a lower temperature whereas Na_2CO_3 at higher temperature.

Question 15. Compare the solubility and thermal stability of the following compounds of the alkali metals with those of alkaline earth metals.

(a) Nitrates   (b) Carbonates   (c) Sulphates

Solution.

(a) **Nitrates of alkali metals and alkaline earth metals**

  (i) Alkali metal and alkaline earth metal nitrates are highly soluble in water.

  (ii) Alkali metal nitrates on strong heating decompose to nitrites (except $LiNO_3$).

    On heating further at higher temperature, the products are oxides.

$$2NaNO_3 \overset{500\,°C}{\rightleftharpoons} 2NaNO_2 + O_2$$

$$4\,NaNO_3 \overset{800\,°C}{\rightleftharpoons} 2Na_2O + 5\,O_2 + 2N_2$$

$$2LiNO_3 \overset{\Delta}{\longrightarrow} Li_2O + 2NO_2 + \frac{1}{2}O_2$$

Alkaline earth metal nitrates on heating decompose into their corresponding oxide with the evolution of mixture of NO_2 and O_2 (except $(Be(NO_3)_2)$).

$$2Mg(NO_3)_2 \overset{\Delta}{\longrightarrow} 2MgO + 4NO_2 + O_2$$

(b) **Carbonates of alkali metals and alkaline earth metals**

  (i) Alkali metal carbonates are thermally quite stable upto 1273 K; above which they melt and then are converted into oxides.

$$Na_2CO_3 \overset{\Delta,\,>1273\ K}{\longrightarrow} Na_2O + CO_2$$

Li_2CO_3 is considerably less stable and decompose readily.

$$Li_2CO_3 \overset{\Delta}{\longrightarrow} Li_2O + CO_2$$

All alkaline earth metal carbonates decomposes on heating to give CO_2 and metal oxide.

$$CaCO_3 \xrightarrow{\Delta} CaO + CO_2$$

Thermal stability of alkaline earth metal carbonates increases down the group. $BeCO_3$ is least stable.

(ii) All the alkali metal carbonates are generally soluble in water and their solubility increases down the group because their lattice energy decreases more readily than the hydration energy.

Alkaline earth metal carbonates are sparingly soluble in water and their solubility decreases down the group. However, these are more soluble in the presence of CO_2.

(c) **Sulphates of alkali and alkaline earth metals**

(i) Sulphates of alkali metals are thermally quite stable except Li_2SO_4 while sulphates of alkaline earth metals are decomposed on heating. Their thermal stability increases down the group.

$$Li_2SO_4 \longrightarrow Li_2O + SO_2 + \frac{1}{2}O_2$$
$$2MgSO_4 \xrightarrow{\Delta} 2MgO + 2SO_2 + O_2$$

(ii) The alkali metal sulphates are soluble in water (except Li_2SO_4). The solubility of alkaline earth metal sulphates in water decreases down the group. $BeSO_4$ and $MgSO_4$ are fairly soluble while $BaSO_4$ is completely insoluble.

Question 16. Starting with sodium chloride how would you proceed to prepare

(i) sodium metal   (ii) sodium hydroxide
(iii) sodium peroxide   (iv) sodium carbonate?

Solution.

(i) **Sodium metal** It is manufactured by electrolysis of a fused mixture of NaCl (40%) and $CaCl_2$ (60%) in Down's cell at 873 K. Na, liberated at the cathode is collected, in kerosene oil while Cl_2 is evolved at the anode.

$$NaCl(l) \xrightarrow{\text{Electrolysis}} Na^+ + Cl^-$$

At cathode $\quad Na^+ + e^- \longrightarrow Na(l)$
At anode $\quad\quad 2Cl^- \longrightarrow Cl_2(g) + 2e^-$

(ii) **Sodium hydroxide** It is manufactured by electrolysis of an aqueous solution of NaCl (brine) in Castner-Kellner cell using mercury cathode and carbon anode. Sodium metal which is discharged at the cathode combines with mercury to form sodium amalgam. Cl_2 gas is evolved at the anode.

At cathode $\quad Na^+ + e^- \xrightarrow{Hg} Na\text{-amalgam}$
At anode $\quad\quad 2Cl^- \longrightarrow Cl_2 + 2e^-$

The sodium amalgam thus obtained is treated with water to form sodium hydroxide and hydrogen gas.

$$2\text{Na-amalgam} + 2H_2O \longrightarrow 2NaOH + 2Hg + H_2$$

(iii) **Sodium peroxide** It is obtained by heating sodium metal (which is obtained by the electrolysis of molten NaCl), in excess of air. The initially formed sodium oxide reacts with more O_2 to form Na_2O_2.

$$4Na + O_2 \xrightarrow{\Delta} 2Na_2O$$

$$2Na_2O + O_2 \xrightarrow{\Delta} 2Na_2O_2$$

(iv) **Sodium carbonate** It is obtained by Solvay ammonia process.

When CO_2 is passed through a concentrated solution of brine (aqueous solution of NaCl) saturated with ammonia, $NaHCO_3$ gets precipitated. $NaHCO_3$ on subsequent heating gives Na_2CO_3.

$$NaCl + NH_3 + CO_2 + H_2O \longrightarrow NaHCO_3 \downarrow + NH_4Cl$$

$$2NaHCO_3 \xrightarrow{\Delta} Na_2CO_3 + CO_2 + H_2O$$

Question 17. What happens when

(i) magnesium is burnt in air   (ii) quicklime is heated with silica

(iii) chlorine reacts with slaked lime (iv) calcium nitrate is heated?

  (i) Air contains nitrogen and oxygen, so when Mg burns in air, addition of these elements takes place.

  (ii) Addition reaction occurs between CaO and SiO_2.

  (iii) It is the method of preparation of bleaching powder.

  (iv) On heating, alkaline earth metal nitrate decompose into oxide with the evolution of NO_2 and O_2 gases.

Solution.

(i) $2Mg(s) + O_2(g) \xrightarrow{\Delta} 2MgO(s)$

and $\quad\quad 3Mg(s) + N_2(g) \xrightarrow{\Delta} Mg_3N_2(s)$

(ii) $\underset{\text{Quicklime}}{CaO(s)} + \underset{\text{Silica}}{SiO_2(s)} \xrightarrow{\Delta} \underset{\text{Calcium silicate}}{CaSiO_3(s)}$

(iii) It reacts with Cl_2 to form calcium hypochlorite, $Ca(OCl)_2$

$$\underset{\text{Slaked lime}}{2Ca(OH)_2} + 2Cl_2 \longrightarrow \underbrace{CaCl_2 + Ca(OCl)_2}_{\text{Bleaching powder}} + 2H_2O$$

(iv) $2Ca(NO_3)_2(s) \xrightarrow{\Delta} 2CaO(s) + 4NO_2(g) + O_2(g)$

Question 18. Describe two important uses of each of the following :
(i) caustic soda, (ii) sodium carbonate (iii) quicklime.

Solution. **1. Caustic soda**

  (i) It is used in the manufacture of soap, paper, artificial silk, etc.

  (ii) It is used in the textile industries for mercerising cotton fabrics.

2. Sodium carbonate

(i) It is used in water softening, laundering and cleaning.

(ii) It is used in the manufacture of glass, soap, borax, caustic soda, etc.

3. Quicklime

(i) It is used in the manufacture of sodium carbonate from caustic soda.

(ii) It is employed in the purification of sugar and in the manufacture of dyestuffs.

Question 19. Draw the structure of
(i) $BeCl_2$ (vapour)　　　　　　　(ii) $BeCl_2$ (solid).

Solution.

(i) In the vapour state, it exists as a chlorine bridged dimer.

$$Cl-Be\underset{Cl}{\overset{Cl}{\diamond}}Be-Cl$$
(Vapour state)

(ii) In the solid state, $BeCl_2$ has polymeric chain structure with chlorine bridges.

$$\underset{}{\text{Be}}\underset{Cl}{\overset{Cl}{\diamond}}\text{Be}\underset{Cl}{\overset{Cl}{\diamond}}\text{Be}\underset{Cl}{\overset{Cl}{\diamond}}$$
(Solid state)

Question 20. The hydroxides and carbonates of sodium and potassium are easily soluble in water while the corresponding salts of magnesium and calcium are sparingly soluble in water. Explain.

High hydration energy and low lattice energy are the favourable conditions for a salt to be soluble in water.

Solution. The solubility of a salt in water depends upon the lattice energy and hydration energy.

$$\Delta H_{solution} = \Delta H_{lattice\ energy} + \Delta H_{hydration\ energy}$$

More negative is $\Delta H_{solution}$, more is the solubility of compounds.
For sodium and potassium hydroxides and carbonates hydration energy is more than that of their lattice energy. Therefore, they are soluble in water. For magnesium and calcium hydroxides and carbonates lattice energy is greater than that of their hydration energy. Therefore, these are sparingly soluble in water.

Question 21. Describe the importance of the following :
(i) limestone　　(ii) cement　　(iii) plaster of Paris.

Solution.

(i) **Limestone**

　　1. Calcium carbonate along with magnesium carbonate is used as a flux in the extraction of metals such as iron.

2. It is also used as an antacid, mild abrasive in toothpaste, a constituent of chewing gum and as a filler in cosmetics.

(ii) **Cement**
   1. It is an important building material.
   2. It is used in concrete and reinforced concrete, in plastering and in the construction of bridges, dams and buildings.

(iii) **Plaster of Paris**
   1. It is extensively used in the building industry as well as plasters.
   2. It is used in dentistry, in ornamental work and for making casts of statues and busts.
   3. It is also used for immoblising the affected part of organ where there is bone facture or sprain.

Question 22. Why are lithium salts commonly hydrated and those of the other alkali metal ions usually anhydrous?

Smaller the size, higher is the hydration enthalpy and size of alkali metal ions increases on moving down the group.

Solution. Because of its smallest size among alkali metals, Li^+ has the maximum degree of hydration. That's why lithium salts are commonly hydrated and those of other alkali metal ions usually anhydrous.

$$\underrightarrow{Li^+ > Na^+ > K^+ > Rb^+ > Cs^+}$$

$\Delta H_{hydration}$ in decreasing order

Question 23. Why is LiF almost insoluble in water whereas LiCl is soluble not only in water but also in acetone?

Solution. LiF is almost insoluble in water due to its high lattice energy. But LiCl is soluble in water due to high hydration energy of Li^+ ion. LiCl is also soluble in acetone due to its predominantly covalent nature. (Because covalent character increases with increase in the size of anion.

$$LiF < LiCl < LiBr < LiI$$

Question 24. Explain the significance of sodium, potassium, magnesium and calcium in biological fluids.

Solution. Sodium and potassium ions play a very important role in biological fluids. These ions participate in the transmission of nerve signals. Potassium ions are the most abundant cations within cell fluids, where they activate many enzymes, participate in the oxidation of glucose to produce ATP.

In plants, chlorophyll is a main pigment for absorption of light. Chlorophyll contains magnesium.

About 99% of body calcium is present in bones and teeth. Calcium plays important roles in neuromuscular function, interneuronal transmission, cell membrane integrity and blood coagulation.

Question 25. What happens when
(i) sodium metal is dropped in water?
(ii) sodium metal is heated in free supply of air?
(iii) sodium peroxide dissolves in water?

    (i) Sodium being highly reactive metal, reacts with water and evolve H_2 gas.
    (ii) Sodium reacts with O_2 of air to give oxide and peroxide.
    (iii) Any true peroxide gives H_2O_2 when dissolves in water/acid.

Solution.
(i) H_2 gas is evolved which catches fire due to the liberation of extreme heat in the reaction.

$$2Na(s) + 2H_2O(l) \longrightarrow 2NaOH(aq) + H_2(g)$$

(ii) Na_2O_2 along with a small amount of Na_2O is formed.

$$4Na(s) + O_2(g) \longrightarrow \underset{\text{(Minor)}}{2Na_2O(s)}$$

$$Na_2O(s) + \frac{1}{2}O_2(s) \longrightarrow \underset{\text{(Major)}}{Na_2O_2(s)}$$

(iii) H_2O_2 is formed when sodium peroxide is dissolved in water.

$$Na_2O_2(s) + 2H_2O(l) \longrightarrow 2NaOH(aq) + H_2O_2(l)$$

Question 26. Comment on each of the following observations
(a) The mobilities of the alkali metal ions in aqueous solution are $Li^+ < Na^+ < K^+ < Rb^+ < Cs^+$.
(b) Lithium is the only alkali metal which forms nitride directly.
(c) E° for $M^{2+}(aq) + 2e^- \longrightarrow M(s)$
(where, M = Ca, Sr or Ba) is nearly constant.

    (a) (i) Smaller the size, higher is the hydration energy.
        (ii) A small ion moves faster.
    (b) Li shows resemblance in properties with Mg.
    (c) E° depends upon the ionisation enthalpy, hydration enthalpy and enthalpy of vaporisation.

Solution.
(a) Smaller the size of the ion, more highly it is hydrated and greater the hydration of the ion, lower is its ionic mobility. Since, the extent of hydration decreases in the order

$$Li^+ > Na^+ > K^+ > Rb^+ > Cs^+$$

Therefore, ionic mobility increases in the reverse order :

$$Li^+ < Na^+ < K^+ < Rb^+ < Cs^+$$

(b) Because of its smaller size lithium like magnesium forms a nitride while other alkali metals do not.

$$6Li(s) + N_2(g) \xrightarrow{\Delta} 2Li_3N(s)$$

(c) $E°$ for $M^{2+} + 2e^- \longrightarrow M(s)$

where, $M = Ca, Sr, Ba$ is almost same because, $E°$ of any M^{2+}/M electrode depends upon three factors : (i) enthalpy of vaporization, (ii) ionization enthalpy (iii) enthalpy of hydration. Since, the combined effect of these factors is approximately the same for Ca, Sr and Ba, therefore, their electrode potentials are nearly constant.

Question 27. State as to why
(a) a solution of Na_2CO_3 is alkaline?
(b) alkali metals are prepared by electrolysis of their fused chlorides?
(c) sodium is found to be more useful than potassium?

 (i) It is due to anionic hydrolysis, so describe on this basis.
(ii) $E°$ of hydrogen is lesser than that of Na, so H_2 will liberate, instead of Na if aqueous sodium chloride is used.
(iii) Sodium is a highly reactive metal but less reactive than potassium.

Solution.
(a) Na_2CO_3 is a salt of a weak acid (H_2CO_3) and a strong base (NaOH) therefore, it undergoes hydrolysis to produce strong base, NaOH and hence, its aqueous solution is alkaline in nature.

$$Na_2CO_3(s) + H_2O(l) \longrightarrow \underset{\text{(Strong base)}}{2NaOH(aq)} + \underset{\text{(Weak acid)}}{H_2CO_3(aq)}$$

(b) (i) Alkali metals are strong reducing agents, hence cannot be extracted by reduction of their oxides and other compounds.

(ii) Being highly positive in nature it is not possible to displace them from their salt solutions by any other element.

(iii) Alkali metals cannot be obtained by the electrolysis of the aqueous solution of their salts because H_2 is liberated at cathode instead of alkali metal. That's why alkali metals are prepared by electrolysis of their fused chloride,

$$NaCl \xrightarrow{\text{Fusion}} Na^+ + Cl^-$$

During electrolysis;
At anode :

$$2Cl^- \longrightarrow Cl_2 + 2e^-$$

At cathode : $2Na^+ + 2e^- \longrightarrow 2Na$

(c) Sodium is found to be more useful than potassium as it is highly reactive but not as reactive as potassium. Sodium is used
(i) As a coolant in nuclear reactor.
(ii) In the manufacture of tetraethyl lead–an anti-knock additive for petrol.

$$4C_2H_5Cl + 4Na - Pb \longrightarrow (C_2H_5)_4Pb + 3Pb + 4NaCl$$

(iii) In sodium vapour discharge lamps.
(iv) As a laboratory reagent for organic analysis.

Question 28. Write the balanced equations for the reactions between
(a) Na_2O_2 and water   (b) KO_2 and water   (c) Na_2O and CO_2.

Solution.   (a) $Na_2O_2(s) + 2H_2O(l) \longrightarrow 2NaOH(aq) + H_2O_2(aq)$

(b) $2KO_2(s) + 2H_2O(l) \longrightarrow 2KOH(aq) + H_2O_2(aq) + O_2(g)$
or $4KO_2(s) + 2H_2O(l) \longrightarrow 4KOH(aq) + 3O_2(g)$

(c) $Na_2O + CO_2 \longrightarrow Na_2CO_3$

Question 29. How would you explain
(i) BeO is insoluble but $BeSO_4$ is soluble in water?
(ii) BaO is soluble but $BaSO_4$ is insoluble in water?
(iii) LiI is more soluble than KI in ethanol?

Solution.

(i) Lattice energy of BeO is greater than its hydration energy so, it is insoluble in water while in case of $BeSO_4$, hydration energy is greater than lattice energy, so it is readily soluble in water.

(ii) Lattice energy of BaO is much smaller than that of its hydration energy, so it is soluble in water. In $BaSO_4$, lattice energy predominates over hydration energy, so it is insoluble in water.

(iii) LiI is more covalent because Li^+ is smallest and polarised anion (I^-) to maximum extent, so it is more soluble than KI in ethanol.

Question 30. Which of the alkali metal is having least melting point?
(a) Na   (b) K   (c) Rb   (d) Cs

Solution. (d), As the size of the metal increases, the strength of metallic bonding decreases and hence, its melting point decreases. Therefore, Cs has the least melting point.

Question 31. Which one of the following alkali metals gives hydrated salts?
(a) Li   (b) Na   (c) K   (d) Cs

Solution. (a), Among alkali metal ions, Li^+ is the smallest. Therefore, it has the maximum degree of hydration than any other alkali metal cation.

Question 32. Which one of the following alkaline earth metal carbonates is thermally the most stable?
(a) $MgCO_3$ (b) $CaCO_3$ (c) $SrCO_3$ (d) $BaCO_3$

Solution. (d), As the electropositive character of the metal increases or the basicity of their hydroxides increases on moving down the group, their thermal stability increases. Thus, $BaCO_3$ is the most stable.

Selected NCERT Exemplar Problems

Short Answer Type

Question 1. How do you account for the strong reducing power of lithium in aqueous solution?

Solution. Electrode potential is a measure of the tendency of an element to lose electrons in the aqueous solution. It mainly depends upon the following three factors, *i.e.*,

(i) $Li(s) \xrightarrow{\text{Sublimation enthalpy}} Li(g)$;

(ii) $Li(g) \xrightarrow{\text{Ionization enthalpy}} Li^+(g) + e^-$

(iii) $Li^+(g) + aq \longrightarrow Li^+(aq) +$ enthalpy of hydration

> With the small size of its ion, lithium has the highest hydration enthalpy. However, ionization enthalpy of Li is highest among alkali metals but hydration enthalpy predominates over ionization enthalpy. Therefore, lithium is the strongest reducing agent in aqueous solution mainly because of its high enthalpy of hydration.

Question 2. When heated in air, the alkali metals form various oxides. Mention the oxides formed by Li, Na and K.

Solution. The reactivity of alkali metals towards oxygen increases on moving down the group with the increase in atomic size. Thus, Li forms only lithium oxide (Li_2O), sodium forms mainly sodium peroxide (Na_2O_2) along with a small amount of sodium oxide while potassium forms only potassium superoxide (KO_2).

$$4Li + O_2 \xrightarrow{\Delta} 2Li_2O$$

$$2Na + O_2 \xrightarrow{\Delta} \underset{\text{Peroxide (major)}}{Na_2O_2} + \underset{\text{Monoxide (minor)}}{Na_2O}$$

$$K + O_2 \xrightarrow{\Delta} \underset{\text{superoxide}}{KO_2}$$

The superoxide O_2^- ion is stable only in the presence of large cations such as K, Rb, etc.

Question 3. Complete the following reactions,
(i) $O_2^{2-} + H_2O \longrightarrow$ (ii) $O_2^- + H_2O \longrightarrow$
Solution.
(i) Peroxide ions react with water to form H_2O_2.
$$O_2^{2-} + 2H_2O \longrightarrow 2OH^- + H_2O_2$$
(ii) Superoxides react with water to form H_2O_2 and O_2.
$$2O_2^- + 2H_2O \longrightarrow 2OH^- + H_2O_2 + O_2$$

Question 4. Why are $BeSO_4$ and $MgSO_4$ readily soluble in water while $CaSO_4$, $SrSO_4$ and $BaSO_4$ are insoluble?

Solution. The lattice energy of alkaline earth metal sulphates is almost constant due to large size of sulphate ion. Thus, their solubility is decided by hydration energy which decreases on moving down the group. The greater hydration enthalpies of Be^{2+} and Mg^{2+} ions overcome the lattice enthalpy factor and therefore, their sulphates are soluble in water. However hydration enthalpy is low for Ca^{2+}, Sr^{2+}, ions, and cannot overcome the lattice energy factor. Hence, these are insoluble.

Question 5. All compounds of alkali metals are easily soluble in water but lithium compounds are more soluble in organic solvents. Explain.

Solution. Exceptionally small size of Li^+ ion and high polarising power, these are the two factors which develops covalent character in the lithium compounds (Fajan's rule). Compounds of other alkali metals are ionic in nature. So, they are soluble in water, while lithium compounds being relatively covalent are soluble in alcohol and other organic solvents.

Question 6. In the Solvay process, can we obtain sodium carbonate directly by treating the solution containing $(NH_4)_2CO_3$ with sodium chloride? Explain.

Solution. No, $(NH_4)_2CO_3$ reacts with NaCl as

$$(NH_4)_2CO_3 + 2NaCl \rightleftharpoons Na_2CO_3 + 2NH_4Cl$$

Because the products obtained Na_2CO_3 and NH_4Cl are highly soluble and the equilibrium will not shift in forward direction. That's why in the Solvay process, we cannot obtain sodium carbonate directly by treating the solution containing $(NH_4)_2CO_3$ with sodium chloride.

Question 7. Write Lewis structure of O_2^- ion and find out oxidation state of each oxygen atom? What is the average oxidation state of oxygen in this ion?

Solution. The Lewis structure of O_2^- is $:\overset{\bullet}{O}—\overset{\bullet\bullet}{\underset{\bullet\bullet}{O}}:^-$.

Oxygen atom carrying no charge has six electrons, so its oxidation number is zero. But oxygen atom carrying – 1 charge has 7 electrons, so its oxidation number is – 1.

Average oxidation number of each oxygen atom $= -\dfrac{1}{2}$.

$$O_2^- = 2x = -1$$
$$x = -\dfrac{1}{2}$$

Long Answer Type

Question 8. When a metal of group 1 was dissolved in liquid ammonia, the following observations were obtained:
   (i) Blue solution was obtained initially.
   (ii) On concentrating the solution, blue colour changed to bronze colour.
How do you account for the blue colour of the solution? Give the name of the product formed on keeping the solution for sometime.
Solution.
   (i) The following reaction takes place when group 1 metal is dissolved in liquid ammonia, $M + (x + y) NH_3 \longrightarrow [M(NH_3)_x]^+ + [e (NH_3)_y]^-$

   The blue colour of the solution is due to the presence of ammoniated electrons which absorb energy in the visible region of light and thus impart blue colour to the solution.
   (ii) In concentrated solution, the blue colour changes to bronze colour due to the formation of metal ion clusters. The blue solution on keeping for some time liberate hydrogen slowly with the formation of amide.

$$M^+(am) + e^- + NH_3 \longrightarrow \underset{\text{(amide)}}{MNH_2(am)} + \frac{1}{2}H_2$$

$$(am = \text{solution in ammonia})$$

Question 9. The stability of peroxide and superoxide of alkali metals increase as we go down the group. Explain giving reason.
Solution. The stability of peroxides or superoxides increases as the size of metal ion increases, *i.e.*, $KO_2 < RbO_2 < CsO_2$.
The reactivity of alkali metals towards oxygen to form different oxides is due to strong positive field around each alkali metal cation. Li^+ is smallest, it does not allow O^{2-} ion to react with O_2 further. Na^+ is larger than Li, its positive field is weaker than Li^+. It cannot prevent the conversion of O^{2-} into O_2^{2-}. The larger K^+, Rb^+ and Cs^+ ions permit O_2^{2-} ion to react with O_2 further forming superoxide ion (O_2^-).

$$\underset{\text{Oxide}}{O^{2-}} \xrightarrow{\frac{1}{2}O_2} \underset{\text{Peroxide}}{O_2^{2-}} \xrightarrow{O_2} \underset{\text{Superoxide}}{2O_2^-}$$

Further more, increased stability of the peroxide or superoxide with increase in the size of metal ion is due to the stabilisation of large anions by larger cations through lattice energy effect.

Question 10. When water is added to compound (*A*) of calcium, solution of compound (*B*) is formed. When carbon dioxide is passed into the solution, it turns milky due to the formation of compound (*C*). If excess of carbon dioxide is passed into the solution, milkiness disappears due to the formation of compound (*D*). Identify the compound *A*, *B*, *C* and *D*. Explain why the milkiness disappears in the last step?

Solution. Appearance of milkiness on passing CO_2 in the solution of compound B indicates that compound B is lime water and compound C is $CaCO_3$. Since, compound B is obtained by adding H_2O to compound A, therefore compound A is quicklime, CaO. The reactions are as follows:

(i) $\underset{\substack{\text{Calcium oxide} \\ (A)}}{CaO} + H_2O \longrightarrow \underset{\text{Lime water } (B)}{Ca(OH)_2}$

(ii) $Ca(OH)_2 + CO_2 \longrightarrow \underset{\substack{\text{Calcium} \\ \text{carbonate } (C) \\ \text{(milkiness)}}}{CaCO_3} + H_2O$
$\quad\quad (B)$

(iii) When excess of CO_2 is passed, milkiness disappears due to the formation of soluble calcium bicarbonate (D)

$\underset{\text{Milkiness } (C)}{CaCO_3} + CO_2 + H_2O \longrightarrow \underset{\substack{\text{Calcium bicarbonate} \\ \text{(soluble in } H_2O) \\ (D)}}{Ca(HCO_3)_2}$

Question 11. Lithium hydride can be used to prepare other useful hydrides. Beryllium hydride is one of them. Suggest a route for the preparation of beryllium hydride starting from lithium hydride. Write chemical equations involved in the process.

Solution. BeH_2 can be prepared from the corresponding halides by the reduction with complex alkali metal hydrides such as lithium aluminum hydride, $LiAlH_4$.

$$8\,LiH + Al_2Cl_6 \longrightarrow 2\,LiAlH_4 + 6\,LiCl$$
$$2\,BeCl_2 + LiAlH_4 \longrightarrow 2\,BeH_2 + LiCl + AlCl_3$$

Question 12. Ions of an element of group 1 participate in the transmission of nerve signals and transport of sugars and amino acids into cells. This element imparts yellow colour to the flame in flame test and forms an oxide and a peroxide with oxygen. Identify the element and write chemical reaction to show the formation of its peroxide. Why does the element impart colour to the flame?

Solution. Yellow colour flame in flame test indicates that the alkali metal must be sodium. It reacts with O_2 to form a mixture of sodium peroxide, Na_2O_2 and sodium oxide, Na_2O.

$$4Na + O_2 \xrightarrow{\Delta} 2Na_2O$$
$$\text{(Minor)}$$
$$2Na_2O + O_2 \xrightarrow{\Delta} 2Na_2O_2$$
$$\text{(Major)}$$
$$2Na + O_2 \xrightarrow{\Delta} Na_2O_2$$

Ionization enthalpy of sodium is low. When sodium metal or its salt is heated in Bunsen flame, the flame energy causes an excitation of the outermost electron which on reverting back to its initial position gives out the absorbed energy as visible light. That's why sodium imparts yellow colour to the flame.

Chapter 11

The *p*-Block Elements

Important Results

1. In *p*-block elements, the last electron enters in the outermost *p*-orbital. There are six groups of *p*-block elements in the Periodic Table numbering from 13 to 18. Their valence shell electronic configuration is ns^2np^{1-6} (except for helium).

2. Group-13 consists of boron (B), aluminium (Al), gallium (Ga), indium (In) and thallium (Tl). Except boron (non-metal), all other elements are metals. Their general electronic configuration is [inert gas] ns^2np^1.

3. Atomic radii of elements of boron family increases on moving down the group. However, atomic radius of Ga is less than that of Al. This is because, the presence of additional $10\,d$-electrons offer only poor shielding effect for the outer electrons from the increased nuclear charge in Ga.

4. Ionization enthalpy $\propto \dfrac{1}{\text{atomic size}}$; the order of ionization enthalpies as expected is $\Delta_iH_1 < \Delta_iH_2 < \Delta_iH_3$.

5. Due to small size of boron, the sum of its first three ionization enthalpies is very high. This prevents it to form +3 ions, so it forms only covalent compounds. The elements of group-13 show + 3 and + 1 oxidation states. The stability of lower oxidation state increases on moving down the group due to inert pair effect.

6. Since, halides of this group can accept electrons, they act as Lewis acid. The order of acidity is $BCl_3 < AlCl_3 < GaCl_3 < InCl_3$. The relative acid strength of the boron trihalides is $BF_3 < BCl_3 < BBr_3 < BI_3$.

7. Aluminium chloride exists in the form of dimer Al_2Cl_6. Among the chlorides of 13 group elements, only $AlCl_3$ sublimes on heating.

8. Boranes are the compounds of boron with hydrogen. These are of B_nH_{n+4} and B_nH_{n+6} type.

9. $B_3N_3H_6$ is called borazole or inorganic benzene.

10. Boron carbide (B_4C_3) is one of the hardest known substance. It is an artificial substance and is called norbia.

11. Borax is $Na_2B_4O_7 \cdot 10H_2O$ and its important application is borax bead test.

12. H_3BO_3 (orthoboric acid) is a weak monobasic acid and acts as a Lewis acid.

13. Group-14 includes carbon (C), silicon (Si), germanium (Ge), tin (Sn) and lead (Pb). The general electronic configuration is [inert gas] ns^2np^2.

14. Carbon is a non-metal. Silicon and germanium are metalloids while tin and lead are metals. In this group, IE of Pb > Sn. However, other elements follow the general trend of IE.

15. Carbon has maximum tendency of catenation. Diamond, graphite and fullerenes are the crystalline allotropic forms of carbon. Out of these forms, diamond is the hardest substance and graphite is a conductor of electricity. Anthracite is the purest form of coal while lamp black is the softest form.

16. Carbon forms $p\pi$-$p\pi$ bond while silicon and other form $p\pi$-$d\pi$ bond.

17. The members of the carbon family mainly exhibit $+4$ and $+2$ oxidation states. Compounds in $+4$ oxidation states are generally covalent in nature. The tendency to show $+2$ oxidation state increases among the heavier elements. Lead in $+2$ state is stable whereas in $+4$ oxidation state it is a strong oxidising agent. Carbon also exhibits negative oxidation states.

18. CO_2 is acidic while CO is neutral. Solid CO_2 is called dry ice or drikold (commercial name). SiC, known as carborundum, is extremely hard substance.

19. The mixture of CO and H_2 is known as water gas and the mixture of CO and nitrogen is known as producer gas.

20. CO_2 is a gaseous oxide while other dioxides of this group, *e.g.,* SiO_2 GeO_2, etc., are network solids.

21. Silicones are a group of organosilicon polymers which have (R_2SiO—) repeating units. These have high thermal stability, high dielectric strength and resistance to oxidation and chemicals.

22. Feldspar, zeolites, mica and asbestos are the examples of silicate minerals. The basic structural unit of silicates is SiO_4^{4-} in which silicon atom is bonded to four oxygen atoms in tetrahedron fashion. Two important man-made silicates are glass and cement.

23. Zeolites are aluminosilicates. These are widely used as a catalyst in petrochemical industries for cracking of hydrocarbons and isomerisation. Hydrated zeolites are used as an ion exchangers in softening of hard water.

Exercises

Question 1. Discuss the pattern of variation in the oxidation states of
(i) B to Tl (ii) C to Pb.
Solution.

(i)

Element	B	Al	Ga	In	Tl
Oxidation state	+3	+3	+3, +1	+3, +1	+1

Boron and aluminium show an oxidation state of +3 only because
they do not exhibit inert pair effect due to the absence of *d*- or
f-electrons. Elements from Ga to Tl show two oxidation states, *i.e.*,
+1 and +3. The tendency to show +1 oxidation state increases down
the group due to the inability of ns^2 electrons of valence shell to
participate in bonding which is called inert pair effect. Therefore,
Tl^+ is more stable than Tl^{3+}.

(ii)

Element	C	Si	Ge	Sn	Pb
Oxidation state	+4	+4	+4,+2	+4, +2	+4, +2

Carbon and silicon show an oxidation state of +4 only. In heavier
members the tendency to show +2 oxidation state increases in the
sequence Ge < Sn < Pb. It is due to the inability of ns^2 electrons of
valence shell to participate in bonding (inert pair effect). Ge forms
stable compounds in +4 state and only few compounds in +2 state.
Sn forms compounds in both the oxidation states and lead
compounds in +2 state is more stable than +4 oxidation state.

Question 2. How can you explain higher stability of BCl_3 as compared
to $TlCl_3$?
Solution.   Boron exhibits only +3 oxidation state. So, it forms BCl_3, a
stable compound. On moving down the group, the inert pair effect
becomes more and more pronounced therefore, in thallium +1 oxidation
state is more stable than +3 oxidation state. That's why BCl_3 is more
stable than $TlCl_3$.

Question 3. Why does boron trifluoride behave as a Lewis acid?
  Lewis acids have a tendency to accept electrons, *i.e.*, they are electron
  deficient.
Solution. BF_3 being electron deficient, is a strong Lewis acid. It reacts
with Lewis bases easily to complete the octet around boron.

$$\underset{\text{Lewis acid}}{F_3B} \ + \ \underset{\text{Lewis base}}{:NH_3} \ \longrightarrow \ F_3B \leftarrow NH_3$$

Question 4. Consider the compounds, BCl_3 and CCl_4. How will they
behave with water? Justify.
Solution. BCl_3 is an electron deficient molecule. It easily accepts a pair
of electrons from water and hence BCl_3 undergoes hydrolysis to form
boric acid (H_3BO_3) and HCl.

$$BCl_3 + 3H_2O \longrightarrow H_3BO_3 + 3HCl$$

CCl_4 is an **electron precise molecule** having absence of d orbitals in C atom, and hence it neither accepts nor donates a pair of electrons. Thus, CCl_4 does not undergo hydrolysis in water.

Question 5. **Is boric acid a protic acid? Explain.**

 Protic acids give proton in water.

Solution. It is not a protic acid because it does not ionize in H_2O to give a proton. It acts as a Lewis acid by accepting electrons from a hydroxyl ion of water and in turn releases H^+ ions.

$$B(OH)_3 + HOH \longrightarrow [B(OH)_4]^- + H^+$$

Question 6. **Explain what happens when boric acid is heated?**

Solution. Boric acid, on heating loses water in three different stages at different temperatures ultimately giving boron trioxide.

$$\underset{\text{Boric acid}}{H_3BO_3} \xrightarrow{\text{370 K}} \underset{\text{Metaboric acid}}{HBO_2} + H_2O$$

$$\underset{\text{Metaboric acid}}{4HBO_2} \xrightarrow[-H_2O]{\text{410 K}} \underset{\text{Tetraboric acid}}{H_2B_4O_7} \xrightarrow{\text{Red heat}} \underset{\text{Boron trioxide}}{2B_2O_3} + H_2O$$

Question 7. **Describe the shapes of BF_3 and $[BH_4]^-$. Assign the hybridization of boron in these species.**

1. In boron only 3 electrons are present in the valence shell. It has one empty p-orbital, in which it can accept electrons.
2. Count the number of bonds (or bond pairs) to find structure and hybridization because if number of bond pairs are 3, hybridization is sp^2 and structure is trigonal planar, and if number of bond pairs are 4, hybridization is sp^3 with tetrahedral structure.

Solution. In BF_3, boron is sp^2-hybridized as it contains three bond pairs and, therefore, BF_3 molecule is trigonal planar in shape. On the other hand, in $[BH_4]^-$ boron is sp^3-hybridized because of the presence of four bond pairs and hence $[BH_4]^-$ species is tetrahedral in shape.

BF_3 sp^2-hybridized
Trigonal planar shape

$[BH_4]^-$, sp^3-hybridized
Tetrahedral shape

Question 8. **Write the reactions to justify amphoteric nature of aluminium.**

Amphoteric means reacts with acids as well as bases. So give the reactions of Al with acid and base.

Solution. Al dissolves both in acids and alkalies evolving dihydrogen and thus, shows amphoteric nature.

$$2Al(s) + 3H_2SO_4(aq) \longrightarrow Al_2(SO_4)_3(aq) + 3H_2(g)$$

$$2Al(s) + 2NaOH(aq) + 6H_2O(l) \longrightarrow$$

$$\underset{\text{Sod. tetrahydroxoaluminate(III)}}{2Na^+[Al(OH)_4]^-(aq)} \quad + \quad 3H_2(g)$$

Question 9. What are electron deficient compounds? Are BCl_3 and $SiCl_4$ electron deficient species? Explain.

Solution. Electron deficient compounds are those in which the octet of all the atoms is not complete *i.e.*, all the element present in the compound do not have 8 e^- in their outer shell.

In trivalent state, the number of electrons around the central atom B in BCl_3 is six.

$$Cl \overset{\cdot\cdot}{\underset{}{B}} Cl \qquad Cl-B\overset{\displaystyle Cl}{\underset{\displaystyle Cl}{\Big\langle}}$$

Such (electron deficient) molecules have a tendency to accept a pair of electrons to achieve stability and hence, behave as Lewis acids.

In $SiCl_4$, the number of electrons around the central atom Si is eight so, it is electron precise molecule.

$$:\overset{\cdot\cdot}{\underset{\cdot\cdot}{Cl}}:\overset{\cdot\cdot}{\underset{\cdot\cdot}{Si}}:\overset{\cdot\cdot}{\underset{\cdot\cdot}{Cl}}: \qquad Cl\overset{\displaystyle Cl}{\underset{\displaystyle Cl}{\overset{|}{-Si-}}}Cl$$

Question 10. Write the resonance structures of CO_3^{2-} and HCO_3^-.

Draw all the possible structures which differ only in the arrangement of electrons.

Solution. Resonance structures of CO_3^{2-} ion :

Resonance structures of HCO_3^- ion :

Question 11. What is the state of hybridization of carbon in
(a) CO_3^{2-} (b) diamond   (c) graphite?

Hybridization depends upon the number of σ bonds, so count the number of σ bonds formed by C. If number of bonds is 4, the hybridization is sp^3, if σ bonds are 3, hybridization is sp^2 and if σ bonds are 2, hybridization is sp.

Solution. The state of hybridization of carbon in CO_3^{2-}, diamond and in graphite is sp^2, sp^3 and sp^2 respectively.

CO_3^{2-}

Diamond

Graphite

Question 12. Explain the difference in properties of diamond and graphite on the basis of their structures.

Solution.

S. No.	Diamond	Graphite
1.	C is sp^3 hybridized.	C is sp^2 hybridized.
2.	Three dimensional, tetrahedral structure.	Two dimensional, sheet like (layer like structure).
3.	Crystalline, transparent with extra brilliance (due to high refractive index).	Crystalline, opaque and shiny substance.
4.	Hardest substance with high density and high melting point.	Soft having soapy touch with low density and high melting point.
5.	Bad conductor of heat and electricity (no free electron).	Good conductor of heat and electricity (fourth electron is free).
6.	It is used in glass cutting and jewellery and as abrasive.	It is used as a lubricating agent, in making electrodes, in pencils, crucibles (due to high melting point).

Question 13. Rationalise the given statements and give chemical reactions :

(i) lead (II) chloride reacts with Cl_2 to give $PbCl_4$.
(ii) lead (IV) chloride is highly unstable towards heat.
(iii) lead is known not to form an iodide, PbI_4.

☀ Pb^{2+} is more stable than Pb^{4+} due to inert pair effect.

Solution.

(i) Due to inert pair effect, Pb is more stable in + 2 state than in + 4 oxidation state. Therefore, lead (II) chloride does not react with Cl_2 to give lead (IV) chloride.

(ii) Lead (IV) chloride on heating decomposes to give lead (II) chloride and Cl_2 because lead in + 2 oxidation state is more stable than in + 4 oxidation state.

$$PbCl_4(l) \longrightarrow PbCl_2(s) + Cl_2(g)$$

(iii) Due to strong oxidising power of Pb^{4+} ion and reducing power of I^- ion, PbI_4 does not exist.

Question 14. Suggest reason why the B—F bond lengths in BF_3 (130 pm) and BF_4^- (143 pm) differ?

Solution. In BF_3, boron is sp^2 hybridized. It has a vacant $2p$-orbital. Each fluorine in BF_3 has completely filled unutilized $2p$-orbitals. Since, both of these orbitals belong to same energy level so $p\pi$-$p\pi$ back bonding occurs in which a lone pair of electrons is transferred from unutilized completely filled $2p$-orbital of F to vacant $2p$-orbital of B. This type of bond formation is known as back bonding. Therefore, B—F bond has some double bond character. That's why all the three boron-fluorine bonds are shorter than the usual single boron-fluorine bond.

In $[BF_4]^-$ ion, boron is sp^3 hybridized. It does not have empty $2p$-orbital, so there is no back bonding. In $[BF_4]^-$ ion all the four B—F bonds are purely single bonds. Double bonds are shorter than single bonds. Therefore, B—F bond length in BF_3 is shorter (130 pm) than B—F bond length (143 pm) in $[BF_4]^-$.

Back bonding in BF_3 molecule

Question 15. If B—Cl bond has a dipole moment, explain why BCl_3 molecule has zero dipole moment?

Solution. Boron in BCl_3 is sp^2 hybridized due to this the shape of BCl_3 molecule is trigonal planar. It is symmetrical in shape. The net dipole moment for symmetrical molecule is zero (because individual dipole moments cancel out due to the symmetry of the molecule.)

$$\mu = 0$$

Thus, dipole moment of BCl_3 is zero.

Question 16. Aluminium trifluoride is insoluble in anhydrous HF but dissolves on addition of NaF. Aluminium trifluoride precipitates out of the resulting solution when gaseous BF_3 is bubbled through. Give reasons.

Solution.

(i) Anhydrous HF is a covalent compound and is strongly H-bonded. Therefore, it does not give F^- ions and hence AlF_3 does not dissolve in HF. NaF is an ionic compound. It contains F^- ions which combine with electron deficient AlF_3 to form the soluble complex.

$$3NaF + AlF_3 \longrightarrow Na_3[AlF_6]$$
Sod. hexafluoroaluminate (III)
(soluble complex)

(ii) Boron due to its small size and higher electronegativity has greater tendency to form complexes than aluminium. Hence, precipitation of AlF_3 takes place when BF_3 is passed through $Na_3[AlF_6]$ solution.

$$Na_3[AlF_6] + 3BF_3 \longrightarrow 3Na[BF_4] + AlF_3(s)$$
Sod. tetrafluoroborate (III)
(soluble complex)

Question 17. Suggest a reason as to why CO is poisonous?

Solution. Carbon monoxide reacts with haemoglobin and form a stable compound carboxyhaemoglobin. Carboxyhaemoglobin is 300 times more stable than oxyhaemoglobin. Formation of carboxyhaemoglobin reduces the oxygen carrying capacity of the blood, as a result of this suffocation takes place. Low level poisoning results in headache and drowsiness, high level poisoning may cause death.

Question 18. How is excessive content of CO_2 responsible for global warming?

Solution. CO_2 is a green house gas. About 75% of the solar energy reaching the earth is absorbed by the earth's surface. The rest of the heat radiates back to the atmosphere. But the heat radiated by the heated surface cannot pass freely into the space because excessive CO_2 in the atmosphere absorb more heat. This results in increase in the average temperature of the atmosphere. This is known as global warming.

Question 19. Explain the structures of diborane and boric acid.

Solution. **Structure of diborane** In diborane, the four terminal hydrogen atoms and the two boron atoms lie in one plane. Above and below this plane, there are two bridging hydrogen atoms. The four terminal B—H bonds are regular bonds while the two bridge (B—H—B) bonds are different and known as banana bonds (3-centre-2-electron bridge bonds).

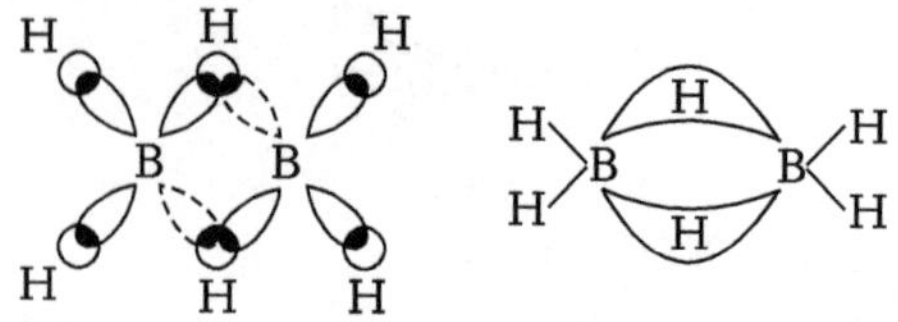

Bonding in diborane

Structure of boric acid Boric acid has a layer structure in which H_3BO_3 units are joined by hydrogen bonds.

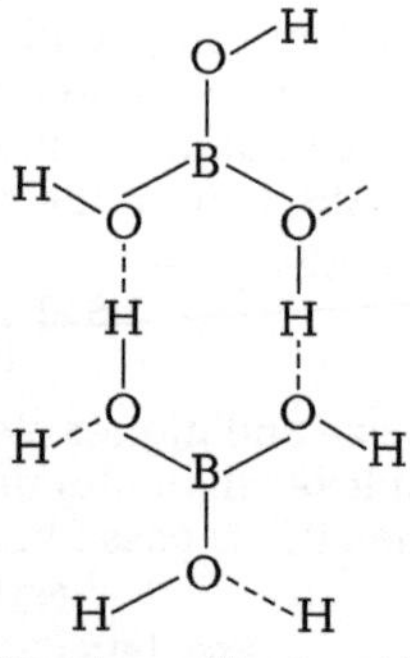

Structure of boric acid

Question 20. What happens when
(a) borax is heated strongly,
(b) boric acid is added to water,
(c) aluminium is treated with dilute NaOH,
(d) BF_3 is reacted with ammonia?

Solution.

(a) When borax is heated strongly, a transparent glassy bead which consists of sodium metaborate and boric anhydride is formed.

$$\underset{\text{Borax}}{Na_2B_4O_7 \cdot 10H_2O} \xrightarrow{\text{Heat}} \underset{\substack{\text{Anhydrous swollen} \\ \text{white mass}}}{Na_2B_4O_7} + 10H_2O$$

$$Na_2B_4O_7 \xrightarrow{\text{Heat}} \underset{\text{Sod. metaborate}}{2NaBO_2} + \underset{\text{Boric anhydride}}{B_2O_3}$$

$$\underbrace{}_{\text{Transparent glassy bead}}$$

(b) Boric acid is sparingly soluble in cold water, but fairly soluble in hot water. It acts as a weak monobasic acid. It is not a protonic acid but it acts as a Lewis acid by accepting a hydroxide ion of water and releasing a proton into the solution.

$$H—OH + B(OH)_3 \longrightarrow [B(OH)_4]^- + H^+$$

(c) When aluminium is treated with dilute NaOH, dihydrogen is evolved.

$$2Al(s) + 2NaOH(aq) + 6H_2O(l) \longrightarrow 2Na^+[Al(OH)_4]^-(aq) + 3H_2(g)$$

(d) BF_3 being a Lewis acid accepts a pair of electrons from NH_3 to form the corresponding complex.

$$\underset{\text{Lewis acid}}{F_3B} + \underset{\text{Lewis base}}{:NH_3} \longrightarrow \underset{\text{Complex}}{F_3B \leftarrow NH_3}$$

Question 21. Explain the following reactions.
(a) Silicon is heated with methyl chloride at high temperature in the presence of copper.
(b) Silicon dioxide is treated with hydrogen fluoride.
(c) CO is heated with ZnO.
(d) Hydrated alumina is treated with aqueous NaOH solution.

Solution.

(a) When Si is heated with CH_3Cl at high temperature in the presence of Cu as a catalyst, a mixture of mono-, di- and trimethylchlorosilanes along with a small amount of tetramethylsilane is formed.

$$\underset{\text{Methyl chloride}}{CH_3Cl} + Si \xrightarrow[\text{570 K}]{\text{Cu powder}} CH_3SiCl_3$$

$$+ (CH_3)_2SiCl_2 + (CH_3)_3SiCl + (CH_3)_4Si$$

(b) When SiO_2 reacts with HF, silicon tetrafluoride is formed which dissolves in HF to from hydrofluorosilicic acid.

$$SiO_2 + 4HF \longrightarrow SiF_4 + 2H_2O;$$
$$SiF_4 + 2HF \longrightarrow H_2SiF_6$$

(c) CO is a strong reducing agent but it cannot reduce ZnO as for $CO \rightarrow CO_2$ $\Delta_rG°$ is always higher than that of ZnO. Thus, no reaction takes place.

(d) Alumina dissolves to form sodium meta-aluminate.

$$\underset{\substack{\text{Hydrated alumina} \\ \text{or bauxite}}}{Al_2O_3 \cdot 2H_2O \,(s)} + 2NaOH(aq) \xrightarrow{\text{Heat}} \underset{\text{Sod. meta aluminate}}{2NaAlO_2} + 3H_2O$$

Question 22. Give reasons.
  (i) Conc. HNO_3 can be transported in aluminium container.
  (ii) A mixture of dilute NaOH and aluminium pieces is used to open drain.
  (iii) Graphite is used as lubricant.
  (iv) Diamond is used as an abrasive.
  (v) Aluminium alloys are used to make aircraft body.
  (vi) Aluminium utensils should not be kept in water overnight.
  (vii) Aluminium wire is used to make transmission cables.

Solution.
  (i) Al reacts with conc. HNO_3 to form a protective layer of aluminium oxide on its surface which prevents it from further reaction.

$$2Al(s) + 6HNO_3 \,(\text{conc.}) \longrightarrow \underset{\substack{\text{Alumina} \\ \text{(a passive protective layer)}}}{Al_2O_3(s)} + 6NO_2(g) + 3H_2O(l)$$

Therefore, Al becomes passive that's why aluminium containers can be used to transport conc. HNO_3.

  (ii) NaOH reacts with Al to evolve dihydrogen gas. The pressure of the hydrogen gas can be used to open drains.

$$2Al(s) + 2NaOH(aq) + 2H_2O(l) \longrightarrow 2NaAlO_2(aq) + 3H_2(g)$$

  (iii) Graphite has layered structure. Layers are held together by weak van der Waals' forces and hence can be made to slip over one another. Therefore, graphite acts as a dry lubricant.

  (iv) In diamond, each sp^3 hybridised carbon atom is linked to four other carbon atoms. It has three dimensional network of carbon atoms. It is very difficult to break extended covalent bonding and therefore diamond is a hardest substance on the earth. That's why it is used as an abrasive.

  (v) Aluminium alloys such as duralumin is light, tough and resistant to corrosion and hence, it is used in making aircraft body.

(vi) Because aluminium reacts with water and oxygen (dissolved in to form a thin layer of toxic aluminium oxide on the surface of utensils.

$$2\,Al(s) + O_2(g) + H_2O(l) \longrightarrow Al_2O_3(s) + H_2(g)$$

(vii) Aluminium possesses high electrical conductivity. Therefore, it is used in making transmission cables. Further on weight to weight basis conductivity of aluminium is twice as Cu.

Question 23. Explain why is there a phenomenal decrease in ionization enthalpy from carbon to silicon?

Solution. As we move from carbon to silicon atomic size increases, *i.e.*, the distance between the outermost electron and nucleus increases. Thus, this electron experience very small attraction from the nucleus and hence, easy to remove. Since, the size of Si atom is larger, the outer electron experience lesser attraction and hence, its ionization enthalpy (energy required to remove an electron) is smaller.

Question 24. How would you explain the lower atomic radius of Ga as compared to aluminium?

Solution. Electronic configuration of Al and Ga are as $_{13}Al = 1s^2 2s^2 2p^6 3s^2 3p^1$; $_{31}Ga = 1s^2 2s^2 2p^6 3s^2 3p^6 3d^{10} 4s^2 4p^1$

The screening tendency of *d*-electrons is poor. Thus, on moving from Al to Ga, shielding effect of 10 *d*-electrons is unable to compensate increased nuclear charge. Therefore, atomic radius of Ga is smaller than that of aluminium due to effective nuclear charge.

Question 25. What are allotropes? Sketch the structure of two allotropes of carbon namely diamond and graphite. What is the impact of structure on physical properties of two allotropes?

Solution. The phenomenon of existence of an element in two or more forms which differ in physical properties but have almost same chemical nature is known as allotropy and the different forms of the element are known as allotropes.

Crystalline carbon occurs mainly in two allotropic forms (i) graphite and (ii) diamond. A third allotropic form of carbon called fullerene was discovered in 1985 by H.W. Kroto, E. Smalley and R.F. Curl.

In diamond, each carbon is sp^3 hybridised and is linked to other four atoms tetrahedrally. There is three dimensional network of carbon atoms in diamond.

In graphite, each carbon is sp^2 hybridised and makes three sigma bonds with three neighbouring carbon atoms. It has layered structure and the layers are held by weak van der Waals' forces.

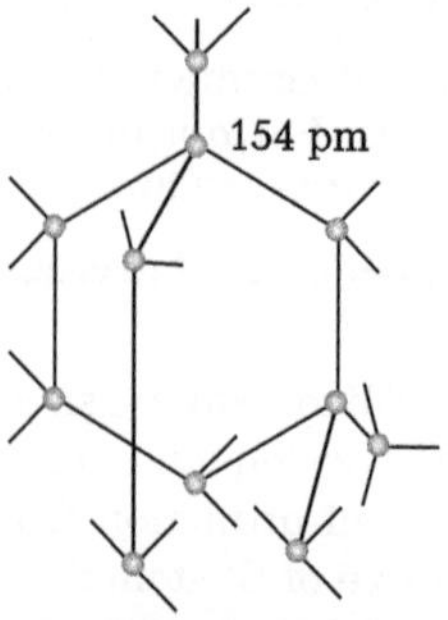

142pm

340 pm

154 pm

Structure of diamond 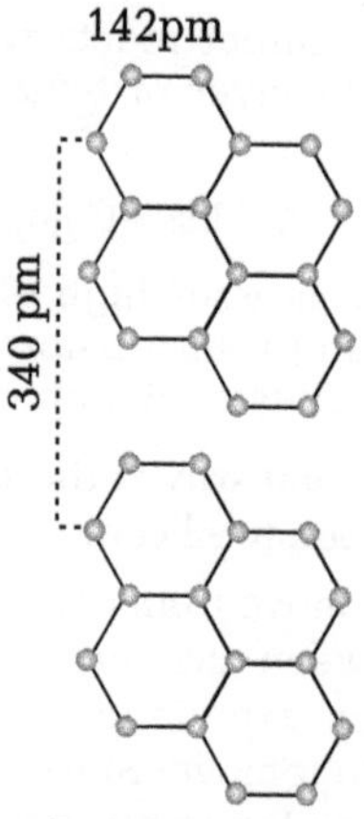   Structure of graphite

Impact of the structures of diamond and graphite on physical properties of the two allotropes

1. Diamond because of its hardness, is used as an abrasive and in making dyes while graphite is so soft that it marks paper and it is used as a dry lubricant in machines.
2. Diamond does not conduct electricity whereas graphite is a good conductor of electricity because of the presence of one free electron in each carbon atom.
3. Diamond is transparent while graphite is opaque.

Question 26. (a) Classify the following oxides as neutral, acidic, basic or amphoteric : $CO, B_2O_3, SiO_2, CO_2, Al_2O_3, PbO_2, Tl_2O_3$.
(b) Write suitable chemical equations to show their nature.
Solution.

(a) **Neutral oxides :** CO; **Acidic oxides :** B_2O_3, SiO_2, CO_2

Basic oxide : Tl_2O_3; **Amphoteric oxides :** Al_2O_3, PbO_2

(b) (i) Being acidic B_2O_3, SiO_2 and CO_2 react with alkalis to form salts.

$$\underset{\substack{\text{Boric}\\\text{anhydride}}}{B_2O_3} + 2NaOH \longrightarrow \underset{\text{Sodium metaborate}}{2NaBO_2} + H_2O;$$

$$\underset{\text{Silica}}{SiO_2} + 2NaOH \xrightarrow{\Delta} \underset{\text{Sodium silicate}}{Na_2SiO_3} + H_2O$$

$$\underset{\text{Carbon dioxide}}{CO_2} + 2NaOH \longrightarrow \underset{\text{Sodium carbonate}}{Na_2CO_3} + H_2O$$

(ii) Being amphoteric, Al_2O_3 and PbO_2 react with both acids and bases.

$$Al_2O_3 + 3H_2SO_4 \longrightarrow Al_2(SO_4)_3 + 3H_2O$$

$$\underset{\text{Alumina}}{Al_2O_3} + 2NaOH \xrightarrow{\text{Fuse}} \underset{\text{Sodium meta aluminate}}{NaAlO_2} + H_2O$$

$$2PbO_2 + 2H_2SO_4 \longrightarrow 2PbSO_4 + 2H_2O + O_2$$

$$\underset{\text{Lead dioxide}}{PbO_2} + 2NaOH \longrightarrow \underset{\text{Sodium plumbate}}{Na_2PbO_3} + H_2O$$

(iii) Being basic, Tl_2O_3 reacts with acid.

$$Tl_2O_3 + 6HCl \longrightarrow 2TlCl_3 + 3H_2O$$

Question 27. In some of the reactions, thallium resembles aluminium, whereas in others it resembles with group I metals. Support this statement by giving some evidences.

Solution. Thallium and aluminium both the elements belong to group-13. Their general electronic configuration for the valence shell is ns^2np^1. Aluminium shows only $+ 3$ oxidation state. Like Al, thallium also shows $+3$ oxidation state in some compounds like Tl_2O_3, $TlCl_3$, etc. Like aluminium, thallium also forms octahedral ions like $[AlF_6]^{3-}$ and $[TlF_6]^{3-}$. Like group-I alkali metals, thallium shows $+1$ oxidation state due to inert pair effect in some compounds like $TlCl$, Tl_2O, etc. Like alkali metal hydroxides, $TlOH$ is water soluble and its aqueous solution is strongly alkaline. Tl_2SO_4 also forms alums like alkali metal sulphates. Tl_2CO_3 is soluble in water like alkali metal carbonates.

Question 28. When metal X is treated with sodium hydroxide, a white precipitate (A) is obtained, which is soluble in excess of NaOH to give soluble complex (B). Compound (A) is soluble in dilute HCl to form compound (C). The compound (A) when heated strongly gives (D), which is used to extract metal. Identify (X), (A), (B), (C) and (D). Write suitable equations to support their identities.

Solution. Since, metal X on treatment with sodium hydroxide gives white precipitate which dissolves in excess of NaOH to give soluble complex (B), therefore, the metal X is Al.

$$\underset{(X)}{Al} + 3NaOH \longrightarrow \underset{\substack{\text{white ppt.} \\ (A)}}{Al(OH)_3\downarrow} + 3Na^+$$

$$\underset{(A)}{Al(OH)_3} + \underset{\text{(excess)}}{NaOH} \longrightarrow \underset{\substack{\text{Sodium tetra hydroxoaluminate (III)} \\ (B)}}{2Na^+[Al(OH)_4]^-}$$

$$\underset{(A)}{Al(OH)_3} + 3HCl(aq) \longrightarrow \underset{(C)}{AlCl_3} + 3H_2O$$

$$\underset{(A)}{2Al(OH)_3} \xrightarrow{\Delta} \underset{(D)}{Al_2O_3} + 3H_2O$$

Question 29. What do you understand by
 (a) inert pair effect   (b) allotropy   (c) catenation?
Solution.

(a) **Inert pair effect** It is defined as the tendency of s-electrons to remain together or the reluctance of s-electrons to participate in a reaction, because the energy required to unpair the ns^2 electrons is not compensated by energy released in forming two additional bonds. Heavier members of group 13, 14 and 15 exhibit an oxidation state two less than the number of valence shell electrons they possess, *e.g.*, Tl in + 1 oxidation state is more stable than that of + 3 oxidation state.

(b) **Allotropy** The phenomenon of existence of a chemical element in two or more forms differing in physical properties but having same chemical nature is known as allotropy. This phenomenon is due to the difference either in the number of atoms in the molecules, *e.g.*, in O_2 and O_3 or arrangement of atoms in the molecules in graphite, diamond and fullerenes (crystalline allotropic forms of carbon).

(c) **Catenation** The tendency of formation of long open or closed chains by the combination of same atoms is known as catenation. It is maximum in carbon and decreases down the group, *e.g.*, C >>Si > Ge $\approx$ Sn > > Pb.

Question 30. A certain salt X, gives the following results.
 (i) Its aqueous solution is alkaline to litmus.
 (ii) It swells up to a glassy material Y on strong heating.
 (iii) When conc. H_2SO_4 is added to a hot solution of X, white crystals of an acid Z separate out.
 Write equations for all the above reactions and identify X, Y and Z.

 Borax swells upto a glassy mass on strong heating.

Solution.

(i) Aqueous solution of salt X is alkaline. It indicates that 'X' is the salt of a strong base and a weak acid.

(ii) On strong heating, the salt 'X' swells up to a glassy material Y. It indicates that the salt 'X' is borax.

(iii) Hot aqueous solution of borax on reaction with conc. H_2SO_4 gives crystals of orthoboric acid. The equations for the reactions involved in the question are as follows :

(a) $\underset{\text{Borax }(X)}{Na_2B_4O_7 \cdot 10H_2O} \xrightarrow{\text{Water}} \underset{\text{Strong base}}{2NaOH} + \underset{\text{Weak acid}}{H_2B_4O_7} + 8H_2O$

(b) $\underset{(X)}{Na_2B_4O_7 \cdot 10H_2O} \xrightarrow{\Delta} \underset{\substack{\text{Anhydrous (swollen}\\\text{white mass)}}}{Na_2B_4O_7} + 10H_2O$

$$Na_2B_4O_7 \xrightarrow{\Delta} \underbrace{2NaBO_2 + B_2O_3}_{\text{Glassy bead, Y}}$$

Glassy material 'Y' consists of sodium metaborate and boric anhydride.

(iii) $\underset{(X)}{Na_2B_4O_7 \cdot 10H_2O} + H_2SO_4 \longrightarrow \underset{\substack{\text{Orthoboric acid} \\ (Z)}}{4H_3BO_3} + Na_2SO_4 + 5H_2O$

Question 31. Write balanced equations for

(i) $BF_3 + LiH \longrightarrow$ (ii) $B_2H_6 + H_2O \longrightarrow$

(iii) $NaH + B_2H_6 \longrightarrow$ (iv) $H_3BO_3 \xrightarrow{\Delta}$

(v) $Al + NaOH \longrightarrow$ (vi) $B_2H_6 + NH_3 \longrightarrow$

Solution.

(i) $2BF_3 + 6LiH \longrightarrow \underset{\text{Diborane}}{B_2H_6} + 6LiF$

(ii) $B_2H_6 + 6H_2O \longrightarrow \underset{\text{Orthoboric acid}}{2H_3BO_3} + 6H_2$

(iii) $2NaH + B_2H_6 \longrightarrow \underset{\text{Sodium borohydride}}{2Na^+[BH_4]^-}$

(iv) $\underset{\substack{\text{Orthoboric acid}}}{H_3BO_3} \xrightarrow[\text{370 K}]{\Delta} \underset{\text{Metaboric acid}}{HBO_2} + H_2O$

$\quad \underset{\text{Metaboric acid}}{4HBO_2} \xrightarrow[-H_2O]{\Delta} \underset{\text{Tetraboric acid}}{H_2B_4O_7} \xrightarrow{\Delta} \underset{\text{Boron trioxide}}{2B_2O_3} + H_2O$

(v) $2Al + 2NaOH + 6H_2O \longrightarrow \underset{\text{Sodium tetrahydroxoaluminate (III)}}{2Na^+[Al(OH)_4]^-} + 3H_2$

(vi) (a) $B_2H_6 + 2NH_3 \longrightarrow \underset{\text{Borane-ammonia complex (adduct)}}{2BH_3 \cdot NH_3}$

$\qquad\qquad\qquad\qquad\qquad\qquad \text{or } [BH_2(NH_3)_2]^+ [BH_4]^-$

(b) $3B_2H_6 + 6NH_3 \longrightarrow 3[BH_2(NH_3)_2]^+[BH_4]^- \xrightarrow{\Delta}$

$\qquad\qquad\qquad\qquad\qquad \underset{\substack{\text{Borazine} \\ \text{(inorganic benzene)}}}{2B_3N_3H_6} + 12H_2$

Question 32. Give one method for industrial preparation and one for laboratory preparation of CO and CO_2 each.

Solution.   **Carbon monoxide**

Industrial preparation By the passage of steam over hot coke.

$$C(s) + H_2O(g) \xrightarrow[473 \text{ K} - 1273 \text{ K}]{\text{Limited air}} CO(g) + H_2(g)$$

Laboratory preparation By dehydration of formic acid in the presence of conc. H_2SO_4.

$$HCOOH \xrightarrow{\ H_2SO_4\ } CO + H_2O$$
$$\text{Formic acid}$$

Carbon dioxide

Industrial preparation By heating limestone.

$$CaCO_3 \xrightarrow{\ \Delta\ } CaO + CO_2$$

Laboratory preparation By the action of dil. HCl on $CaCO_3$.

$$CaCO_3(s) + 2HCl(aq) \longrightarrow CaCl_2(aq) + CO_2(g) + H_2O(l)$$

Question 33. An aqueous solution of borax is
(a) neutral   (b) amphoteric   (c) basic   (d) acidic

Solution.   (c) Borax is a salt of strong base (NaOH) and weak acid (H_3BO_3), therefore, its aqueous solution is basic in nature.

Question 34. Boric acid is polymeric due to
 (a) its acidic nature
 (b) the presence of hydrogen bonds
 (c) its monobasic nature
 (d) its geometry

Solution.   (b) Boric acid is polymeric due to the presence of H-bonds. (as it has polar O—H bonds)

Question 35. The type of hybridisation of boron in diborane is
(a) *sp*   (b) *sp*^{2} (c) *sp*^{3} (d) *dsp*^{2}

Solution.   (c) In B_2H_6, each boron atom is *sp*^{3}-hybridized.

Question 36. Thermodynamically the most stable form of carbon is
 (a) diamond   (b) graphite   (c) fullerenes   (d) coal

Solution.   (b) Thermodynamically the most stable form of carbon is graphite.

Question 37. Elements of group 14
 (a) exhibit oxidation state of + 4 only
 (b) exhibit oxidation state of + 2 and + 4
 (c) form M^{2-} and M^{4+} ions
 (d) form M^{2+} and M^{4+} ions

Solution.   (b) Due to inert pair effect, elements of group 14 exhibit oxidation states of + 2 and + 4.

Question 38. If the starting material for the manufacture of silicones is $RSiCl_3$, write the structure of the product formed.

Solution.   Hydrolysis of alkyltrichlorosilanes followed by condensation polymerisation gives cross-linked silicones.

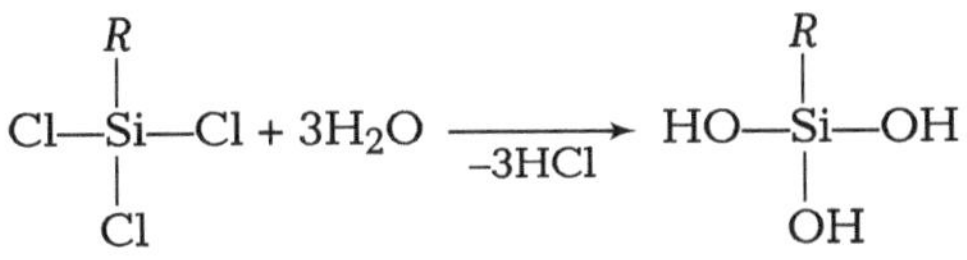

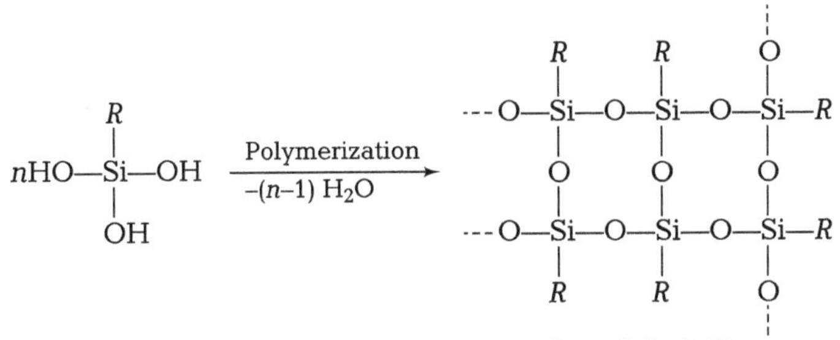

R
|
Cl—Si—Cl + 3H$_2$O $\xrightarrow[-3HCl]{}$ HO—Si—OH
| |
Cl   OH

R
|
R $\cdots$O—Si—O—Si—O—Si—R
| Polymerization | | |
nHO—Si—OH $\xrightarrow[-(n-1)\,H_2O]{}$ O   O   O
| | | |
OH $\cdots$O—Si—O—Si—O—Si—R
                                | | |
                                R   R   O
                                          $\vdots$

Cross-linked silicone

Selected NCERT Exemplar Problems

Short Answer Type

Question 1. Draw the structures of $BCl_3 \cdot NH_3$ and $AlCl_3$ (dimer).

Solution. (i) $H_3N{:} + BCl_3 \longrightarrow H_3N \rightarrow BCl_3$ Or $BCl_3 \cdot NH_3$

(ii)

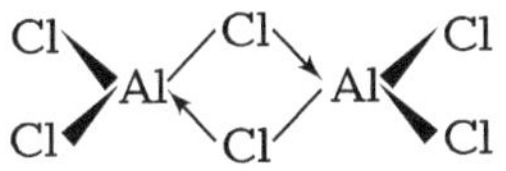

Al_2Cl_6 (dimer)

Question 2. Give reasons for the following.
(i) CCl_4 is immiscible in water, whereas $SiCl_4$ is easily hydrolysed.
(ii) Carbon has a strong tendency for catenation as compared to silicon.

Solution.
(i) Carbon tetrachloride (CCl_4) is a covalent compound while H_2O is a polar compound and CCl_4 does not form H-bond with water molecule. Hence, it is immiscible in water. Further more CCl_4 does not hydrolysed by water because of the absence of *d*-orbitals in carbon. While $SiCl_4$ is readily hydrolysed by water.

$$SiCl_4 + 4H_2O \longrightarrow \underset{\text{Silicic acid}}{Si(OH)_4} + 4HCl$$

The hydrolysis of $SiCl_4$ occurs due to coordination of OH^- with empty $3d$-orbitals in silicon atom of $SiCl_4$ molecule.

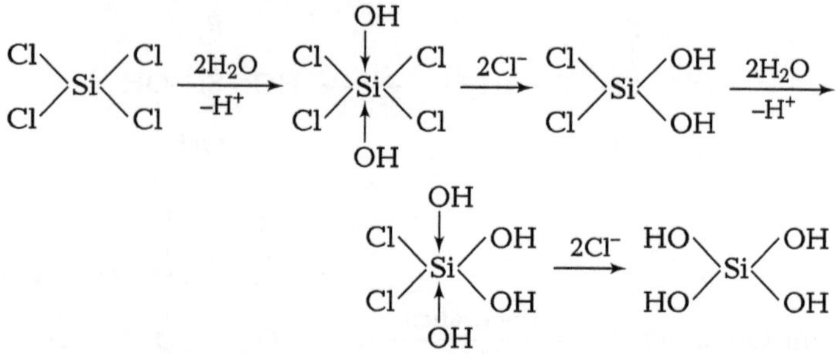

$$\underset{Cl}{\overset{Cl}{>}}Si\underset{Cl}{\overset{Cl}{<}} \xrightarrow[-H^+]{2H_2O} \underset{Cl}{\overset{Cl}{>}}\underset{\underset{OH}{\uparrow}}{\overset{\overset{OH}{\downarrow}}{Si}}\underset{Cl}{\overset{Cl}{<}} \xrightarrow{2Cl^-} \underset{Cl}{\overset{Cl}{>}}Si\underset{OH}{\overset{OH}{<}} \xrightarrow[-H^+]{2H_2O}$$

$$\underset{Cl}{\overset{Cl}{>}}\underset{\underset{OH}{\uparrow}}{\overset{\overset{OH}{\downarrow}}{Si}}\underset{OH}{\overset{OH}{<}} \xrightarrow{2Cl^-} \underset{HO}{\overset{HO}{>}}Si\underset{OH}{\overset{OH}{<}}$$

(ii) The catenation is maximum in carbon and decreases down the group. With increase in atomic size, electronegativity decreases, and due to this, tendency to show catenation decreases. C—C bond enthalpy (348 kJ mol^{-1}) is greater than Si—Si bond enthalpy (297 kJ mol^{-1}). Therefore, C—C bond is stronger than Si—Si bond. That's why carbon has much higher tendency for catenation than silicon.

Question 3. Explain the following.
 (i) CO_2 is a gas whereas SiO_2 is a solid.
 (ii) Silicon forms SiF_6^{2-} ion whereas corresponding chloro compound of carbon is not known.

Solution.
 (i) CO_2 has a linear structure. Its dipole moment is zero. It is believed that CO_2 molecule is a resonance hybrid of following structures

$$O=C=O \longleftrightarrow \overset{-}{O}—C\equiv\overset{+}{O} \longleftrightarrow \overset{+}{O}\equiv C—O^-$$
$$sp \text{ hybridised}$$

The CO_2 molecules are held together by weak van der Waals' forces and thus, it exists as gas. In SiO_2, due to large electronegativity difference between Si and O, the Si—O bonds have considerable ionic nature. Therefore, silica has three dimensional network like structure in which Si atom is tetrahedrally bonded to four oxygen atoms and each oxygen atom is bonded to two silicon atoms by covalent bonds.

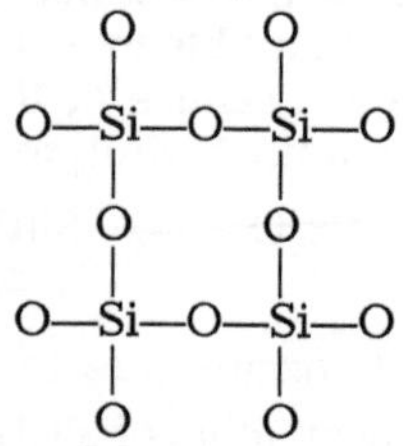

$$\begin{array}{c} O \quad\quad O \\ | \quad\quad\quad | \\ O—Si—O—Si—O \\ | \quad\quad\quad | \\ O \quad\quad O \\ | \quad\quad\quad | \\ O—Si—O—Si—O \\ | \quad\quad\quad | \\ O \quad\quad O \end{array}$$

There is no discrete SiO_2 molecule. It is a network solid with octahedral coordination.

(ii) SiF_6^{2-} is known whereas $SiCl_6^{2-}$ is not known because six large chloride ions cannot be accommodated around Si^{4+} due to limitation of its size. Further, interaction between lone pair of chloride ion and Si^{4+} is not very strong.

Question 4. If a trivalent atom replaces a few silicon atoms in three dimensional network of silicon dioxide, what would be the type of charge on overall structure?

Solution. The structure of SiO_2 crystal is as

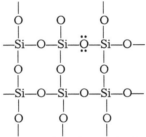

When some Si atoms are replaced by trivalent impurity, holes are created, which are equivalent to positive charge. These holes make the crystal conductor of electricity.

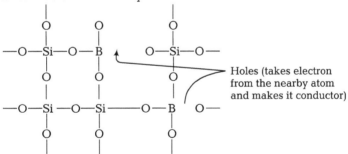

Holes (takes electron from the nearby atom and makes it conductor)

Since, the crystals on the whole are always electrically neutral, the obtained crystal is also electrically neutral.

Question 5. When BCl_3 is treated with water, it hydrolyses and forms $[B(OH)_4]^-$ only whereas $AlCl_3$ in acidified aqueous solution forms $[Al(H_2O)_6]^{3+}$ ion. Explain what is the hybridisation of boron and aluminium in these species?

Solution. In trivalent state, most of the compounds being covalent are hydrolysed in water, e.g., BCl_3 on hydrolysis in water form tetrahedral $[M(OH)_4]^-$ species; the hybridization state of B is sp^3.

$$BCl_3 + 3H_2O \longrightarrow B(OH)_3 + 3HCl$$
$$B(OH)_3 + H_2O \longrightarrow [B(OH)_4]^- + H^+$$

$AlCl_3$ in acidified aqueous solution forms octahedral $[Al(H_2O)_6]^{3+}$ ion. In this complex, the $3d$ orbitals of Al are involved and the hybridization state of Al is sp^3d^2.

$$AlCl_3 + water \xrightarrow{HCl} [Al(H_2O)_6]^{3+} + 3Cl^-(aq)$$

Electronic configuration of Al^{3+}	$1s$	$2s$	$2p$			$3s$	$3p$			$3d$				

Electronic configuration of Al^{3+}: $1s$ [1↓] $2s$ [1↓] $2p$ [1↓][1↓][1↓] $3s$ [ ] $3p$ [ ][ ][ ] $3d$ [ ][ ][ ][ ][ ]

Formation of $[Al(H_2O)_6]^{3+}$: $1s$ [1↓] $2s$ [1↓] $2p$ [1↓][1↓][1↓] [×][×][×][×] [×][×] [ ][ ][ ]

sp^3d^2 hybridization

Question 6. Aluminium dissolves in mineral acids and aqueous alkalies and thus shows amphoteric character. A piece of aluminium foil is treated with dilute hydrochloric acid or dilute sodium hydroxide solution in a test tube and on bringing a burning matchstick near the mouth of the test tube, a pop sound indicates the evolution of hydrogen gas. The same activity when performed with concentrated nitric acid, reaction doesn't proceed. Explain the reason.

Solution. Aluminium being amphoteric in nature dissolves both in acids and alkalies evolving H_2 gas which burns with a pop sound.

$$2Al + 6HCl \longrightarrow 2AlCl_3 + 3H_2$$
$$2Al + 2NaOH + 2H_2O \longrightarrow \underset{\text{Sodium meta aluminate}}{2NaAlO_2} + 3H_2$$

When Al is treated with conc. HNO_3, a protective layer of Al_2O_3 is formed on its surface which prevents further action.

$$2Al + 6HNO_3 \longrightarrow Al_2O_3 + 6NO_2 + 3H_2O$$

Question 7. Explain the following.
  (i) Gallium has higher ionisation enthalpy than aluminium.
 (ii) Boron does not exist as B^{3+} ion.
(iii) Aluminium forms $[AlF_6]^{3-}$ ion but boron does not form $[BF_6]^{3-}$ ion.
 (iv) PbX_2 is more stable than PbX_4.
  (v) Pb^{4+} acts as an oxidising agent but Sn^{2+} acts as a reducing agent.
 (vi) Electron gain enthalpy of chlorine is more negative as compared to fluorine.
(vii) $Tl(NO_3)_3$ acts as an oxidising agent.
(viii) Carbon shows catenation property but lead does not.
 (ix) BF_3 does not hydrolyse completely (modified).
  (x) Why does the element silicon, not form a graphite like structure whereas carbon does?

Solution.
  (i) In gallium due to poor shielding of valence electrons by the intervening $3d$-electrons, the nuclear charge becomes effective,

thus, atomic radius decreases and hence, the ionisation enthalpy of gallium is higher than that of aluminium.

(ii) Due to small size of boron, the sum of its first three ionization enthalpies is very high. This prevents it to form + 3 ions and forces it to form only covalent compound. That's why boron does not exist as B^{3+} ion.

(iii) Aluminium forms $[AlF_6]^{3-}$ ion because of the presence of vacant *d*-orbitals so it can expand its coordination number from 4 to 6. In this complex Al undergoes sp^3d^2 hybridization. On the other hand, boron does not form $[BF_6]^{3-}$ ion, because of the unavailability of *d*-orbitals as it cannot expand its coordination number beyond four. Hence, it can form $[BF_4]^-$ ion (boron in $[BF_4]^-$ ion is sp^3 hybridised).

(iv) Due to inert pair effect, Pb in + 2 oxidation state is more stable than in + 4 oxidation state, hence, PbX_2 is more stable than PbX_4.

(v) Due to inert pair effect tendency to form + 2 ions increases down the group hence Pb^{2+} is more stable than Pb^{4+}. That's why Pb^{4+} acts as an oxidising agent while Sn^{2+} is less stable than Sn^{4+} and hence Sn^{2+} acts as a reducing agent.

$$\underset{\text{R.A.}}{Sn^{2+}} \longrightarrow Sn^{4+} + 2e^-; \qquad \underset{\text{O.A.}}{Pb^{4+}} + 2e^- \longrightarrow Pb^{2+}$$

(vi) Electron gain enthalpy of Cl is more negative than electron gain enthalpy of fluorine because when an electron is added to F, the added electron goes to the smaller $n = 2$ quantum level and suffers significant repulsions from other electrons present in this level. For $n = 3$ quantum level (in Cl), the added electron occupies a larger region of space and the electron-electron repulsion is much less.

(vii) Due to inert pair effect Tl in + 1 oxidation state is more stable than that of + 3 oxidation state. Therefore, $Tl(NO_3)_3$ acts as an oxidising agent.

(viii) Property of catenation depends upon the atomic size of the element. Down the group size increases and the tendency to show catenation decreases. That's why carbon show property of catenation but lead does not show catenation.

(ix) Unlike other boron halides, BF_3 does not hydrolyse. However it forms an addition product with water.

$$BF_3 + H_2O \overset{H_2O}{\longrightarrow} H^+ [BF_3OH^-] \rightleftharpoons H_3O^+ [BF_3OH]^-$$

(x) In graphite, C is sp^2 hybridised. Carbon due to its smallest size and highest electronegativity among group 14 elements has strong tendency to form $p\pi$-$p\pi$ multiple bonds. While silicon due to its larger size and less electronegativity has poor ability to form $p\pi$-$p\pi$ multiple bonds. That's why the element silicon does not form a graphite like structure.

Question 8. Identify the compounds A, X and Z in the following reactions :

(i) $A + 2HCl + 5H_2O \longrightarrow 2NaCl + X$

$$X \xrightarrow[370 \text{ K}]{\Delta} HBO_2 \xrightarrow[>370 \text{ K}]{\Delta} Z$$

Solution.

(i) $\underset{\text{Borax }(A)}{Na_2B_4O_7} + 2HCl + 5H_2O \longrightarrow 2NaCl + \underset{\text{Orthoboric acid }(X)}{4H_3BO_3}$

(ii) $\underset{(X)}{H_3BO_3} \xrightarrow{\Delta,\ 370 \text{ K}} \underset{\text{Metaboric acid}}{HBO_2} + H_2O$

$4HBO_2 \xrightarrow[-H_2O]{\Delta,\ >370 \text{ K}} \underset{\text{Tetraboric acid}}{[H_2B_4O_7]} \xrightarrow{\text{Red heat}} \underset{\substack{\text{Boron trioxide} \\ (Z)}}{2B_2O_3} + H_2O$

Question 9. Complete the following chemical equations :

$$Z + 3LiAlH_4 \longrightarrow X + 3LiF + 3AlF_3$$
$$X + 6H_2O \longrightarrow Y + 6H_2$$
$$X + 3O_2 \xrightarrow{\Delta} B_2O_3 + 3H_2O$$

Solution. $4BF_3 + 3LiAlH_4 \longrightarrow \underset{\text{Diborane }(X)}{2B_2H_6} + 3LiF + 3AlF_3$

$\underset{(X)}{B_2H_6} + 6H_2O \longrightarrow \underset{\text{Orthoboric acid}}{2H_3BO_3} + 6H_2$

$\underset{(X)}{B_2H_6} + 3O_2 \xrightarrow{\Delta} B_2O_3 + 3H_2O$

Long Answer Type

Question 10. Account for the following observations :

(i) $AlCl_3$ is a Lewis acid.

(ii) Though fluorine is more electronegative than chlorine yet BF_3 is weaker Lewis acid than BCl_3.

(iii) PbO_2 is stronger oxidising agent than SnO_2.

(iv) The $+1$ oxidation state of thallium is more stable than its $+3$ state.

Solution.

(i) In $AlCl_3$, Al has only six electrons in its valence shell. It is an electron deficient species. Therefore, it acts as a Lewis acid (electron acceptor).

(ii) In BF_3, boron has a vacant 2p-orbital and fluorine has one 2p completely filled unutilized orbital. Both of these orbitals belong to same energy level therefore, they can overlap effectively and form $p\pi$-$p\pi$ bond. This type of bond formation is known as back bonding. While back bonding is not possible in BCl_3 because there is no effective overlapping between the 2p-orbital of boron and

3p-orbital of chlorine. Therefore, electron deficiency of B is higher in BCl_3 than that of BF_3. That's why BF_3 is a weaker Lewis acid than BCl_3.

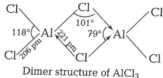

2p   2p
(vacant) (completely filled)

(iii) Pb^{4+} is less stable than Pb^{2+}, due to inert pair effect therefore, Pb^{4+} salts act as strong oxidising agents. Sn^{2+} is also less stable than Sn^{4+}, thus Sn^{4+} can also act as an oxidising agent. But Pb^{4+} is a stronger oxidising agent than Sn^{4+} because inert pair effect increases down the group.

(iv) Tl^+ is more stable than Tl^{3+} because of inert pair effect.

Question 11. When aqueous solution of borax is acidified with hydrochloric acid, a white crystalline solid is formed which is soapy to touch. Is this solid acidic or basic in nature? Explain.

Solution. When an aqueous solution of borax is acidified with HCl, boric acid is formed.

$$Na_2B_4O_7 + 2HCl + 5H_2O \longrightarrow 2NaCl + 4H_3BO_3$$
$$\text{Borax} \qquad\qquad\qquad\qquad\qquad\qquad \text{Boric acid}$$

Boric acid is a white crystalline solid. It is soapy to touch because of its planar layered structure. Boric acid is a weak monobasic acid. It is not a protonic acid but acts as a Lewis acid by accepting electrons from a hydroxyl ion.

$$B(OH)_3 + 2HOH \longrightarrow [B(OH)_4]^- + H_3O^+$$

Question 12. BCl_3 exists as monomer whereas $AlCl_3$ is dimerised through halogen bridging. Give reason. Explain the structure of the dimer of $AlCl_3$ also.

Solution. Boron halides do not exist as dimer due to small size of boron atom which makes it unable to coordinate four large sized halide ions. $AlCl_3$ exists as dimer. Al makes use of vacant 3p-orbitals by coordinate bond, i.e., Al atoms complete their octet by forming dimers.

Dimer structure of $AlCl_3$

Question 13. Boron fluoride exists as BF_3 but boron hydride doesn't exist as BH_3. Give reason. In which form does it exist? Explain its structure.

Solution. Boron fluoride exists as BF_3. Due to its small size, B atom cannot coordinate to 4 larger fluoride ions and hence, cannot form the

neric molecule. On the other hand boron hydride exist as B_2H_6. This is
.e to the fact that hydrogen atom in BH_3 has no electron to form $p\pi$-$p\pi$
ick bonding. Thus, boron possesses incomplete octet and BH_3 is
imerised to form B_2H_6 molecule with covalent and three centre bond.

Structure of diborane, B_2H_6

In B_2H_6, the four terminal hydrogen atoms and the two boron atoms lie
in one plane. Above and below this plane there are two bridging
H-atoms. The four terminal B—H bonds are regular while the two
bridge (B—H—B) bonds are three centre-two electron bonds.

Question 14. (i) What are silicones? State the uses of silicones.

(ii) What are boranes? Give chemical equation for the preparation of
diborane.

Solution.

(i) Silicones are a group of organosilicon polymers, which have
(R_2SiO) as a repeating unit. These may be linear silicones, cyclic
silicones and cross-linked silicones. These are prepared by the
hydrolysis of alkyl or aryl derivatives of $SiCl_4$ like $RSiCl_3$, R_2SiCl_2
and R_3SiCl and polymerization of alkyl or aryl hydroxy derivatives
obtained by hydrolysis.

$$2CH_3Cl + Si \xrightarrow[570\text{ K}]{\text{Cu powder}} (CH_3)_2SiCl_2 \xrightarrow{\text{Hydrolysis}}$$

$$(CH_3)_2Si(OH)_2 \xrightarrow[-H_2O]{\text{Polymerisation}}$$

Silicone

Uses These are used as sealant, greases, electrical insulators and
for water proofing of fabrics. These are also used in surgical and
cosmetic plants.

(ii) Boron forms a number of covalent hydrides with general formulae
B_nH_{n+4} and B_nH_{n+6}. These are called boranes. B_2H_6 and B_4H_{10} are
the representative compounds of the two series respectively.

Preparation of diborane It is prepared by treating boron trifluoride
with $LiAlH_4$ in diethyl ether.

$$4BF_3 + 3LiAlH_4 \longrightarrow 2B_2H_6 + 3LiF + 3AlF_3$$

On industrial scale it is prepared by the reaction of BF_3 with sodium
hydride.

$$2BF_3 + 6NaH \xrightarrow{450\text{ K}} B_2H_6 + 6NaF$$

Question 15. A compound (A) of boron reacts with NMe_3 to give an adduct (B) which on hydrolysis gives a compound (C) and hydrogen gas. Compound (C) is an acid. Identify the compounds A, B and C. Give the reactions involved.

Solution. Since, compound 'A' of boron reacts with NMe_3 to form an adduct 'B'. Thus, compound 'A' is a Lewis acid. Since, adduct 'B' on hydrolysis gives an acid 'C' and hydrogen gas, therefore, 'A' is B_2H_6 and 'C' is boric acid.

$$\underset{\text{Diborane }(A)}{B_2H_6} + 2NMe_3 \longrightarrow \underset{\text{Adduct }(B)}{2BH_3NMe_3}$$

$$BH_3 \cdot NMe_3 + 3H_2O \longrightarrow \underset{\text{Boric acid }(C)}{H_3BO_3} + NMe_3 + 6H_2$$

Question 16. A tetravalent element forms monoxide and dioxide with oxygen. When air is passed over heated element (1273 K), producer gas is obtained. Monoxide of the element is a powerful reducing agent and reduces ferric oxide to iron. Identify the element and write formulas of its monoxide and dioxide. Write chemical equations for the formation of producer gas and reduction of ferric oxide with the monoxide.

Solution. Producer gas is a mixture of CO and N_2, therefore, the tetravalent element is carbon and its monoxide and dioxide are CO and CO_2 respectively.

$$\underbrace{2C(s) + O_2(s) + 4N_2(g)}_{\text{Air}} \xrightarrow{1273 \text{ K}} \underbrace{2CO(g) + 4N_2(g)}_{\text{Producer gas}}$$

The carbon monoxide is a strong reducing agent and reduces ferric oxide to iron.

$$Fe_2O_3(s) + 3COg) \xrightarrow{\Delta} 2Fe(s) + 3CO_2(g)$$

Chapter **12**

Some Basic Principles and **Techniques**

Important Results

1. Berzelius, a Swedish chemist, proposed that a 'vital force' was responsible for the formation of organic compounds. However, this notion was rejected in 1828 when F. Wohler synthesised an organic compound, urea from an inorganic compound ammonium cyanate.

$$\underset{\text{Ammonium cyanate}}{NH_4CNO} \xrightarrow{\Delta} \underset{\text{Urea}}{NH_2CONH_2}$$

2. Organic compounds are formed due to covalent bonding. The nature of the covalent bonding in organic compounds can be described in terms of **orbitals hybridization** concept, according to which carbon can have sp^3, sp^2 and sp hybridized orbitals. The sp^3, sp^2 and sp hybridized carbons are found in compounds like methane, ethene and ethyne respectively.

3. Hybridization influences the bond length and bond enthalpy in organic compounds. The change in hybridization affects the electronegativity of carbon. The greater the s-character of the hybrid orbitals, the greater is the electronegativity, *i.e.*, sp hybridized carbon atom is more electronegative than that of sp^2 or sp^3 hybridized carbon.

4. Organic compounds can be represented by various structural formulae. The three dimensional representation of organic compounds on paper can be drawn by **wedge** and **dash** formula.

5. Organic compounds can be classified on the basis of their structure or the functional groups they contain. A **functional group** is an atom or group of atoms bonded together in a unique fashion and which determines the physical and chemical properties of the compounds.

6. **IUPAC system of nomenclature**

    (i) Locate the longest chain with as many possible secondary functional groups along with multiple bonds.

(ii) Select rootword corresponding to the length of longest possible chain.

(iii) Number the longest possible chain according to the rules to give an identification number to each C-atom of longest possible chain.

(iv) Add suitable prefixes and suffixes along with numerals to indicate the number and position of each side chain substituent or functional group present in the compound.

Hence, according to these rules, the IUPAC name of a compound can be written as,

Prefix	Root word	Suffix
Tells us about the branches or substituents except in the case of multiple bonds.	Tells us about the length of longest possible chain.	Tells us about the principle functional groups and multiple bonds mostly except in case of halogens.

7. **Isomerism** Those compounds which have the same molecular formula but differ in their chemical and physical properties are called isomers and the phenomenon is called isomerism. Types of isomerism—(i) structural isomerism and stereoisomerism.

8. **Structural isomerism** is due to the difference in the arrangement of atoms within the molecules. Chain isomerism, position isomerism, functional isomerism, metamerism are the types of structural isomerism.

9. The compounds that have the same constitution and sequence of covalent bonds but differ in relative positions of their atoms or groups in space are called stereoisomers. This special type of isomerism is called **stereoisomerism** and can be classified as geometrical and optical isomerism.

10. The organic reaction begins with the breakage of covalent bond and this breakage or fission are of two types;

(a) Homolytic fission produces free radicals.

$$A—B \longrightarrow \overset{\bullet}{A} + \overset{\bullet}{B}$$
$$\text{Free radicals}$$

(b) Heterolytic fission produces ions (*i.e.,* anion and cation)

$$A—B \longrightarrow \underset{\text{Electrophile}}{A^+} + \underset{\text{Nucleophile}}{B^-}$$

11. An ion containing a positively charged carbon centre is known as carbocation or carbonium ion. Order of stability of carbocations is $3° > 2° > 1° > CH_3^+$.

e.g., $\qquad (CH_3)_3C^+ > (CH_3)_2CH^+ > CH_3CH_2^+ > CH_3^+$

12. Allylic and benzylic carbocations are more stable due to resonance. Electron withdrawing groups decreases the stability of carbocation.

13. An ion containing a negatively charged carbon centre is known as carbanion.

    Order of stability of carbanion is $CH_3^- > 1° > 2° > 3°$

    e.g., $\quad CH_3^- > CH_3CH_2^- > (CH_3)_2CH^- > (CH_3)_3C^-$

14. Allylic and benzylic carbanions are more stable due to resonance.

15. Order of stability of free radicals, $(CH_3)_3C^• > (CH_3)_2CH^• > CH_3^•$

16. **Electron displacement effects in covalent bonds**

    (i) **Inductive effect** is observed when a group having different electronegativity is attached to carbon chain. Groups showing negative inductive effect increase the acidic character while that shows positive, *i.e.*, electron releasing inductive effect decrease the acidic character.

    (ii) **Electromeric effect** is a temporary effect and observed only in the presence of attacking reagent. It involves the complete transfer of the electrons of a multiple bond to atom.

    (iii) **Resonance or mesomeric effect** In case of conjugated systems (having alternate σ- and π-bonds), the electron can flow from one part of the system to other due to resonance. The flow of electrons from one part of the conjugated system to the other creating centres of low and high electron density due to phenomenon of resonance is called resonance (R-) or mesomeric (M-) effect.

      (a) Groups which donate electrons to the conjugated system: —OH, —OR, —SH, —SR, —NH₂, —NHR, —NR₂, —Cl, —Br, —I, etc.

      (b) Groups which withdraw electrons from a conjugated system towards themselves : $\Large\rangle$C=O, —CHO, —COOR, —CN, —NO₂, etc.

    (iv) **Hyperconjugation effect** When an alkyl group is attached to an unsaturated system, the delocalisation of electrons due to overlapping between a π-orbital and a σ-bond orbital of the alkyl group takes place. Such effect is also called no bond resonance or Baker-Nathan effect.

17. Attacking reagents are of three types

    (i) **Electrophiles** are positively charged atom or contain an electron deficient atom.

    (ii) **Nucleophiles** are negatively charged or electron rich atom.

    (iii) **Ambiphiles** have both electrophilic and nucleophilic sites, hence have dual (amphoteric) nature.

18. Electrophiles are electron deficient molecules, so also called Lewis acids while nucleophiles are electron rich species, so also called Lewis bases.

19. **Methods of purification of organic compounds**
    (i) Solid substances, soluble in a suitable solvent are purified by crystallisation.
    (ii) Naphthalene, camphor and benzoic acid are purified by sublimation. However, a mixture of benzoic acid and naphthalene is separated by chemical methods.
    (iii) In case of organic compounds which are decomposed by heat, sublimation is done at reduced pressure.
    (iv) Distillation is used to separate volatile substance from a non-volatile impurity.
    (v) Compounds having nearly equal boiling point (within the limit of 10 K to 15 K) are separated by fractional distillation.
    (vi) Substances which decompose at their boiling points are separated by distillation under reduced pressure.
    (vi) Chromatography is used for separation, isolation, purification and identification of the constituents of a mixture.

20. **Qualitative analysis of organic compounds :**
    (i) **Detection of carbon and hydrogen** The presence of C and H in an organic compound is detected by heating with dry CuO in a test tube.

    $$C + 2CuO \xrightarrow{\Delta} CO_2 + 2Cu$$

    $$2H + CuO \xrightarrow{\Delta} H_2O + Cu$$

    CO_2 turns lime water milky while water turns anhydrous $CuSO_4$ blue.

    $$\underset{\text{Lime water}}{Ca(OH)_2} + CO_2 \longrightarrow \underset{\text{Milkyness}}{CaCO_3} + H_2O$$

    $$\underset{\text{White}}{CuSO_4} + 5H_2O \longrightarrow \underset{\text{Blue}}{CuSO_4 \cdot 5H_2O}$$

    (ii) Presence of extra elements (such as N, S and halogens) is detected by Lassaigne's test.
    (iii) In Lassaigne's test, organic compound is fused with sodium and the extract so obtained is called Lassaigne's extract or sodium extract.
    (iv) Sodium extract $+ FeSO_4 + NaOH + H_2SO_4 \longrightarrow$ Prussian blue colour
    $\Rightarrow$ N is present.
    (v) Sodium extract $+ FeSO_4 + NaOH + H_2SO_4 \longrightarrow$ Red ppt.
    $\Rightarrow$ N and S are present.
    (vi) Sodium extract $+$ sodium nitroprusside $\longrightarrow$ Blue or violet colour or ppt.
    $\Rightarrow$ S is present.

(vii) Sodium extract + HNO_3 + $AgNO_3$ $\longrightarrow$

$\longrightarrow$ white ppt. $\Rightarrow$ Cl present (AgCl)

$\longrightarrow$ pale yellow ppt $\Rightarrow$ Br is present

$\longrightarrow$ yellow ppt $\Rightarrow$ I is present.

21. Quantitative analysis of organic compound :

(i) % of C = $\dfrac{12}{44} \times \dfrac{\text{wt. of } CO_2}{w} \times 100$

where, w = weight of the compound

(ii) % of H = $\dfrac{2}{18} \times \dfrac{\text{wt. of } H_2O}{w} \times 100$

(iii) % of Cl = $\dfrac{35.5}{143.5} \times \dfrac{\text{wt. of AgCl}}{w} \times 100$

(iv) % of Br = $\dfrac{80}{188} \times \dfrac{\text{wt. of AgBr}}{w} \times 100$

(v) % of I = $\dfrac{127}{235} \times \dfrac{\text{wt. of AgI}}{w} \times 100$

(vi) % of S = $\dfrac{32}{233} \times \dfrac{\text{wt. of } BaSO_4}{w} \times 100$

(vii) % of N = $\dfrac{28}{22400} \times \dfrac{\text{volume of } N_2 \text{ at NTP}}{w} \times 100$

(Duma's method)

(viii) % of N = $\dfrac{1.4\ NV}{w}$ **(Kjeldahl's method)**

(ix) % of O = 100 − (% of rest elements)

Exercises

Question 1. What are hybridization states of each carbon atom in the following compounds?

$$CH_2{=}C{=}O,\ CH_3CH{=}CH_2,\ (CH_3)_2CO,$$
$$CH_2{=}CHCN,\ C_6H_6$$

 Hybridization depends upon the number of σ bond formed by an atom. If number of σ bonds is 2, hybridization is sp, if 3, sp^2, if 4, sp^3 and so on. So count the number of σ bonds and find the hybridization.

Solution.

$$H{-}\overset{sp^2}{\underset{|}{C}}{=}\overset{sp}{C}{=}O, \quad H{-}\overset{sp^3}{\underset{|}{C}}{-}\overset{sp^2}{C}{=}\overset{sp^2}{C}{-}H, \quad H{-}\overset{sp^3}{\underset{|}{C}}{-}\overset{sp^2}{\underset{||}{C}}{-}\overset{sp^3}{\underset{|}{C}}{-}H$$

$$H{-}\overset{sp^2}{\underset{|}{C}}{=}\overset{sp^2}{\underset{|}{C}}{-}\overset{sp}{C}{\equiv}N, \qquad \text{In benzene each C is } sp^2\text{-hybridized}$$

Question 2. Indicate the σ- and π-bonds in the following molecules. C_6H_6, C_6H_{12}, CH_2Cl_2, $CH_2{=}C{=}CH_2$, CH_3NO_2, HCONHCH$_3$

Single bonds are only σ bonds, double bond contains one σ and one π bond and triple bond contains one σ and two π bonds. Mark σ and π bonds on this basis.

Solution.

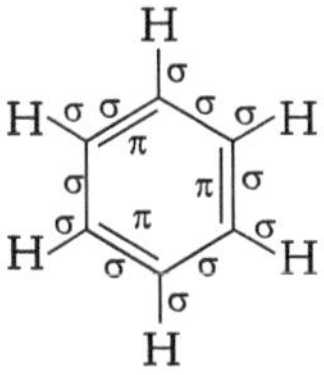

$\begin{pmatrix} 12\sigma \\ 3\pi \end{pmatrix}$ (18σ) 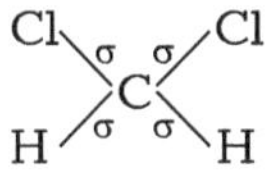 (4σ)

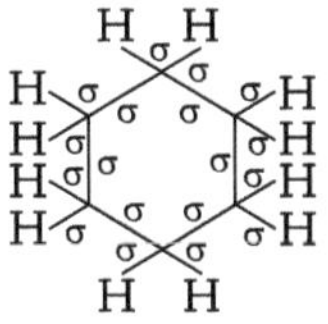

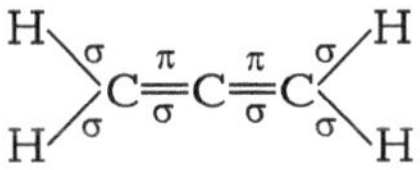

(6σ, 2π) 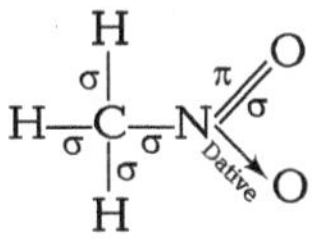 (6σ, 1π) 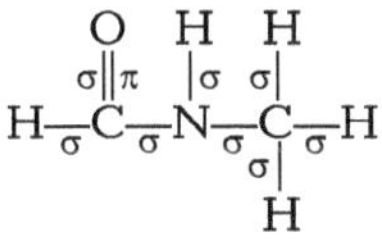 (8σ, 1π)

Question 3. Write bond-line formulas for : Isopropyl alcohol, 2,3-dimethylbutanal, heptan-4-one.

To draw the bond line formulae of the given compounds, first draw the complete structure of each compound and then convert it into bond line formula in which joint represent the carbon atoms. In such a structure, H-atoms remain hidden.

Solution.

$\underset{\text{Complete structure}}{CH_3\overset{OH}{\underset{|}{C}}HCH_3} = \underset{\text{Isopropyl alcohol}}{\overset{OH}{\wedge}}$

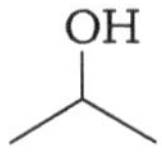

$\underset{4}{CH_3}{-}\underset{3}{\overset{\overset{CH_3}{|}}{CH}}{-}\underset{2}{\overset{\underset{|}{CH}}{CH}}{-}\underset{1}{CHO} = $ 2,3-dimethylbutanal

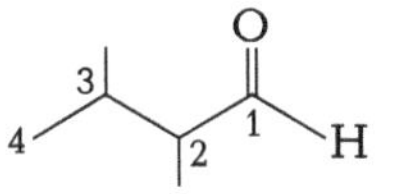

$\underset{7}{CH_3}\,\underset{6}{CH_2}\,\underset{5}{CH_2}\,\overset{O}{\underset{4}{C}}\,\underset{3}{CH_2}\underset{2}{CH_2}\underset{1}{CH_3} = $ Heptan-4-one

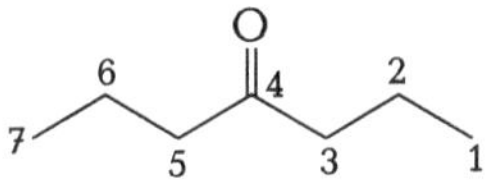

Question 4. Give the IUPAC names of the following compounds :

(a)   (b)   CN

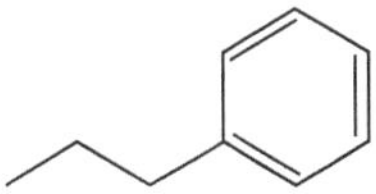

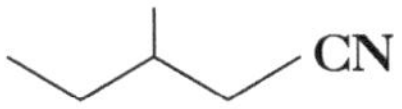

(c) 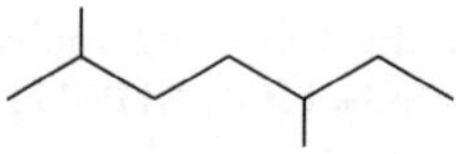 [structure]

(d) 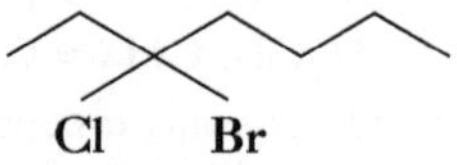 [structure]
Cl Br

(e) 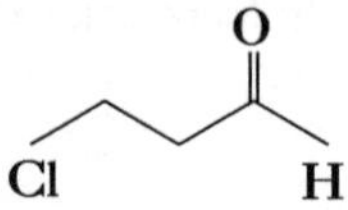 [structure]
Cl   H

(f) Cl_2CHCH_2OH

Solution.

(a) 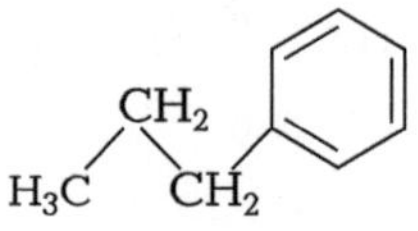
CH₂/H₃C CH₂ [benzene ring]
Propylbenzene

(b) 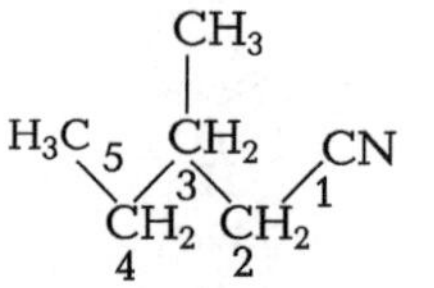
CH_3
$H_3C\ 5\ CH_2\ CN$
$CH_2\ CH_2$
 4   2
3-methylpentanenitrile

(c) 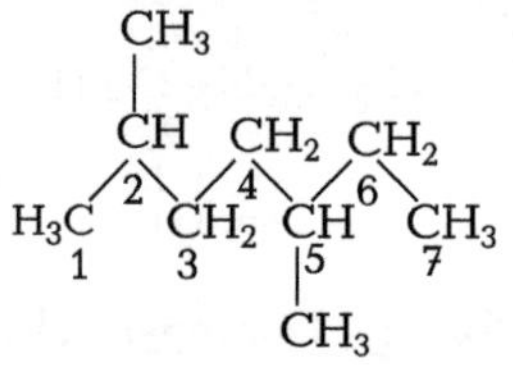
CH_3
$CH\ CH_2\ CH_2$
$H_3C\ CH_2\ CH\ CH_3$
 1   3   5   7
CH_3
2,5-dimethylheptane

(d) 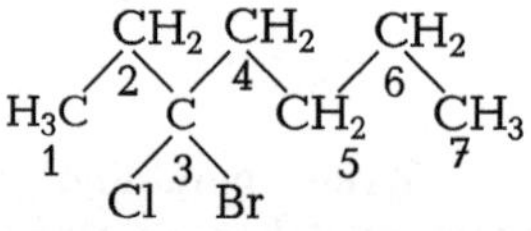
$CH_2\ CH_2\ CH_2$
$H_3C\ C\ CH_2\ CH_3$
 1   3   5   7
Cl Br
3-bromo-3-chloroheptane

(e) 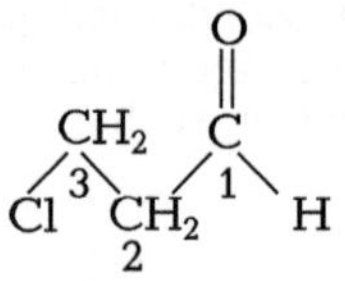
$CH_2\ C$ (O)
$Cl\ CH_2\ H$
 2
3-chloropropanal

(f) 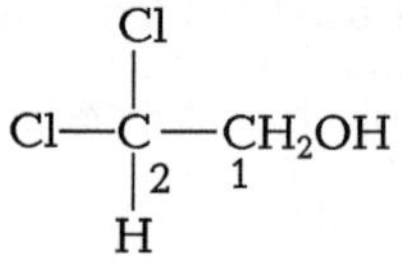
Cl
$Cl—C—CH_2OH$
 2   1
H
2,2-dichloroethanol

Question 5. Which of the following represents the correct IUPAC name for the compounds concerned?
(a) 2, 2-dimethylpentane or 2-dimethylpentane
(b) 2, 4, 7-trimethyloctane or 2, 5, 7-trimethyloctane
(c) 2-chloro-4-methylpentane or 4-chloro-2 methylpentane
(d) But-3-yn-1-ol or But-4-ol-1-yne.

Solution.
(a) 2,2-dimethylpentane (because for the two alkyl groups on the same carbon, its locant is repeated twice) (b) 2, 4, 7-trimethyloctane (because 2, 4, 7-locant set is lower than 2, 5, 7). (c) 2-chloro-4-methylpentane. (Alphabetical order of substituents) (d) But-3-yn-1-ol (because lower locant for the principal functional group, *i.e.*, alcohol).

Question 6. Draw formulas for the first five members of each homologous series beginning with the following compounds.
(a) H—COOH   (b) CH$_3$COCH$_3$ (c) H—CH=CH$_2$.

Solution.

Carboxylic acids	Ketones	Alkene
HCOOH Methanoic acid	CH$_3$COCH$_3$ Propanone	CH$_2$=CH$_2$ Ethene
CH$_3$COOH Ethanoic acid	CH$_3$CH$_2$COCH$_3$ Butan-2-one	CH$_3$CH =CH$_2$ Propene
CH$_3$CH$_2$COOH Propanoic acid	CH$_3$CH$_2$COCH$_2$CH$_3$ Pentan-3-one	CH$_3$CH$_2$CH=CH$_2$ But-1-ene
CH$_3$CH$_2$CH$_2$COOH Butanoic acid	CH$_3$CH$_2$CH$_2$COCH$_3$ Pentan-2-one	CH$_3$CH$_2$CH$_2$CH=CH$_2$ Pent-1-ene
CH$_3$CH$_2$CH$_2$CH$_2$COOH Pentanoic acid	CH$_3$CH$_2$CH$_2$COCH$_2$CH$_3$ Hexan-3-one	CH$_3$CH$_2$CH$_2$CH$_2$CH=CH$_2$ Hex-1-ene
	CH$_3$CH$_2$CH$_2$CH$_2$COCH$_2$CH$_3$ Heptan-3-one	

Question 7. Give condensed and bond line structural formulas and identify the functional group(s) present, if any, for
(a) 2,2,4-trimethylpentane (b) 2-hydroxy-1,2,3-propanetricarboxylic acid
(c) Hexanedial.

To write condensed and bond line formulas first write the structural formula of the given compounds.

Solution.

(a) 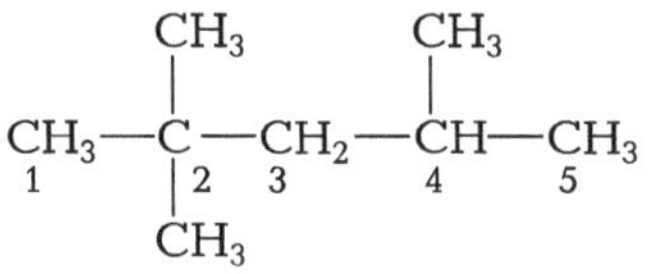
$$CH_3—\underset{\underset{\underset{2}{CH_3}}{|}}{\overset{\overset{CH_3}{|}}{C}}—CH_2—\overset{\overset{CH_3}{|}}{CH}—CH_3$$

2,2,4-trimethyl pentane

(b) 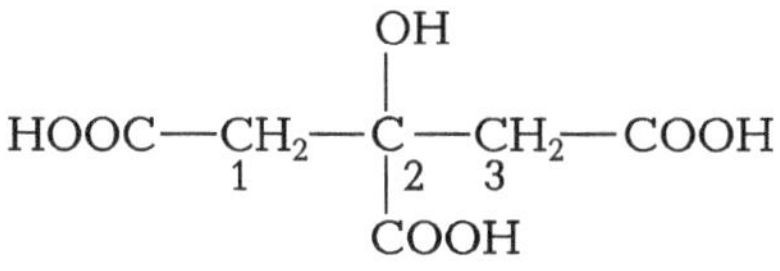
$$HOOC—CH_2—\underset{\underset{2}{\underset{COOH}{|}}}{\overset{\overset{OH}{|}}{C}}—CH_2—COOH$$

2-hydroxy-1,2,3,-propanetricarboxylic acid

(c) OHC—CH$_2$—CH$_2$—CH$_2$—CH$_2$—CHO
     1   2   3   4   5   6
Hexanedial

	Condensed formula	Bond line formula	Functional groups
(a)	$(CH_3)_3CCH_2CH(CH_3)_2$	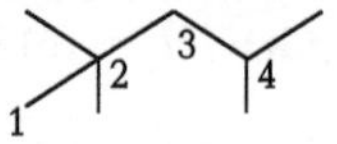	—
(b)	$HOOCCH_2C(OH)$ $(COOH)CH_2COOH$	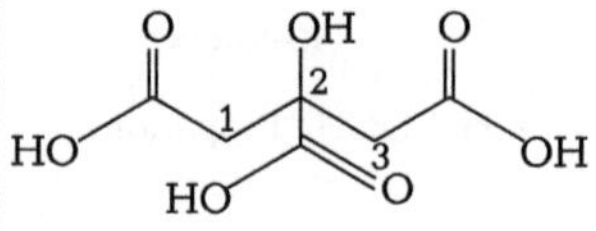	—C—OH (carboxyl) and —OH (hydroxyl)
(c)	$OHC(CH_2)_4CHO$	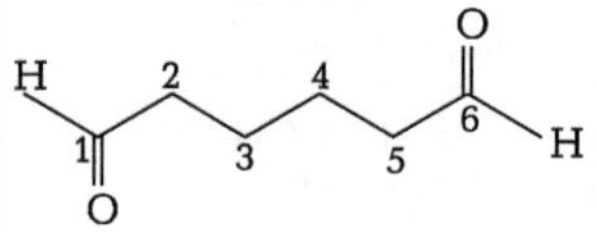	—C—H (aldehyde)

Question 8. Identify the functional groups in the following compounds.

(a)

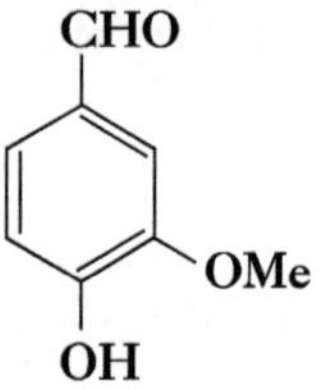

(b)

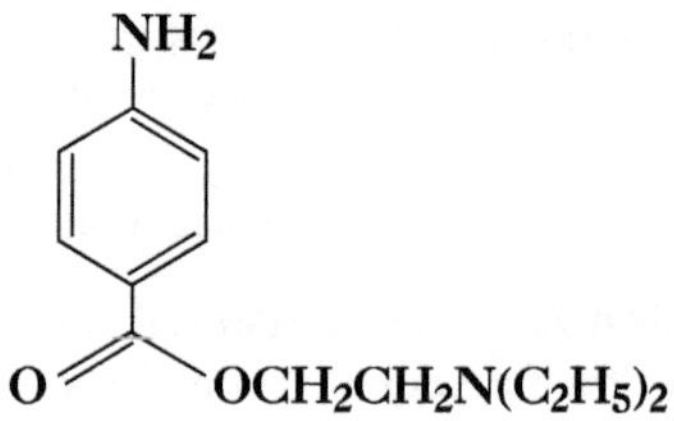

(c)

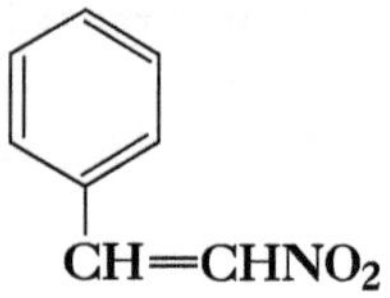

Solution.

(a)

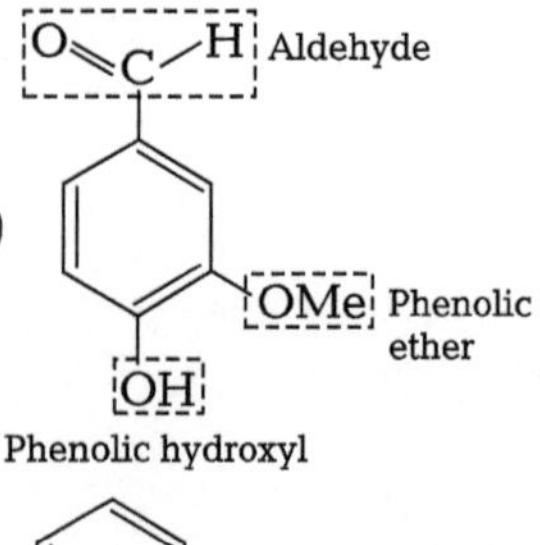

(b)

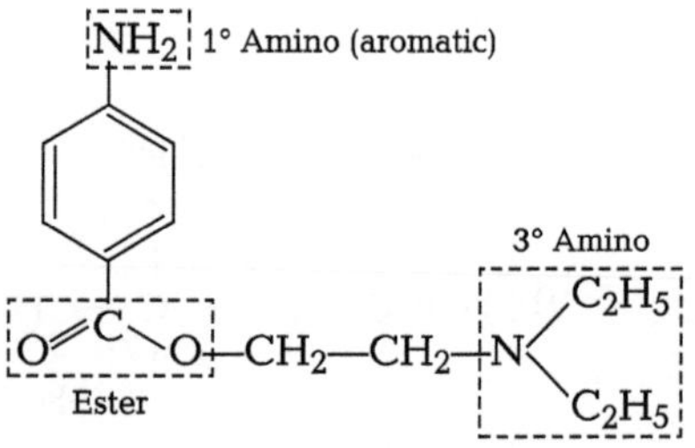

(c)

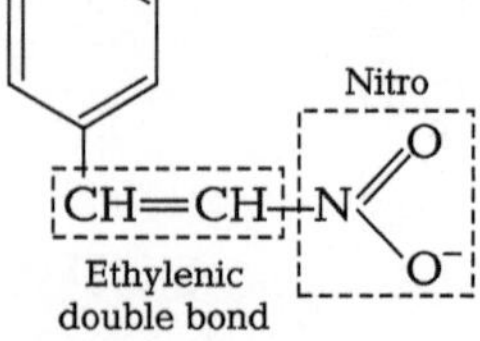

Question 9. Which of the two : $O_2NCH_2CH_2O^-$ or $CH_3CH_2O^-$ is expected to be more stable and why?

Stability of a carbanion increases in the presence of electron withdrawing group but decreases in the presence of electron releasing group.

Solution. $O_2N-CH_2-CH_2O^-$ is expected to be more stable than $CH_3-CH_2O^-$ because $-NO_2$ group has $-I$ effect, this leads to the dispersal of negative charge. On the other hand $-CH_3$ group has $+I$ effect, this leads to the intensification of the negative charge. Dispersal of the charge leads to the stability of ion while intensification of negative charge leads to the unstability of ion.

$$O_2N \leftarrow CH_2 \leftarrow CH_2 \leftarrow O^- \qquad CH_3 \rightarrow CH_2 \rightarrow O^-$$
$$\text{More stable} \qquad\qquad \text{Less stable}$$

Question 10. Explain why alkyl groups act as electron donors when attached to a π-system?

Solution. Due to hyperconjugation, alkyl groups act as electron donors when attached to a π-system as shown below.

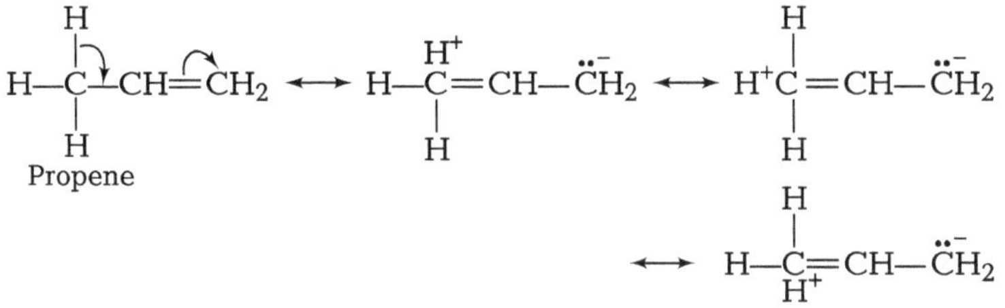

Propene

Question 11. Draw the resonance structures for the following compounds. Show the electron shift using curved arrow notation.
(a) C_6H_5OH
(b) $C_6H_5NO_2$
(c) $CH_3CH=CHCHO$
(d) C_6H_5-CHO
(e) $C_6H_5-\overset{+}{C}H_2$
(f) $CH_3CH=CH\overset{+}{C}H_2$

Resonance structures differ only in the arrangement of electrons but not in the positions of atoms.

Solution. (a)

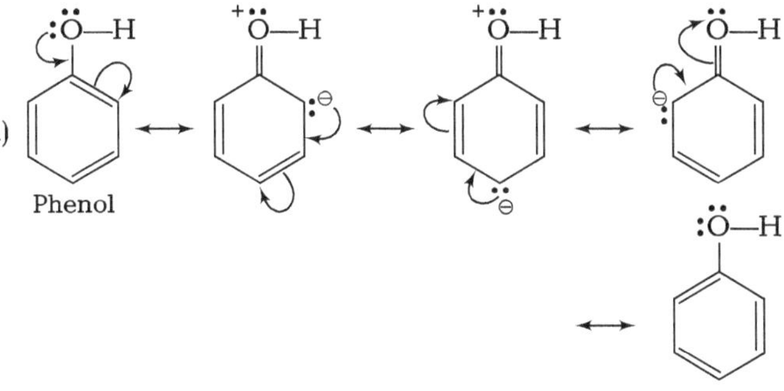

Phenol

(b)

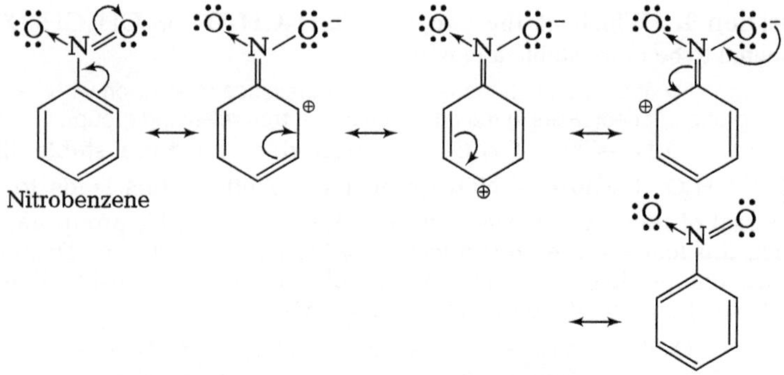

Nitrobenzene

(c) $CH_3—CH=CH—CH=\overset{..}{\underset{..}{O}}:$ ⟷ $CH_3—CH=CH—\overset{+}{CH}—\overset{..}{\underset{..}{O}}:^-$

But-2-en-1-al

⟷ $CH_3—\overset{+}{CH}—CH=CH—\overset{..}{\underset{..}{O}}:^-$

(d)

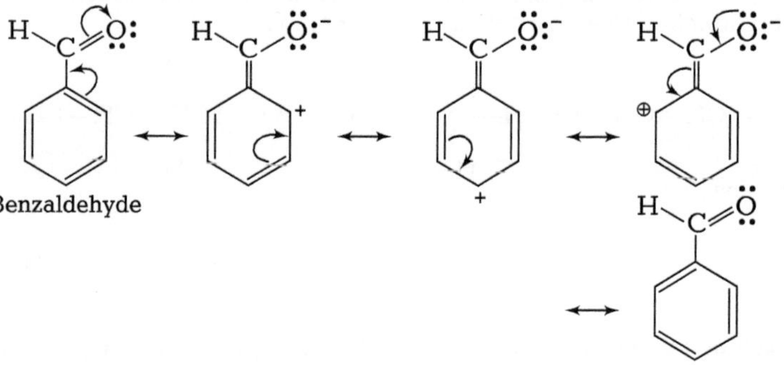

Benzaldehyde

(e)

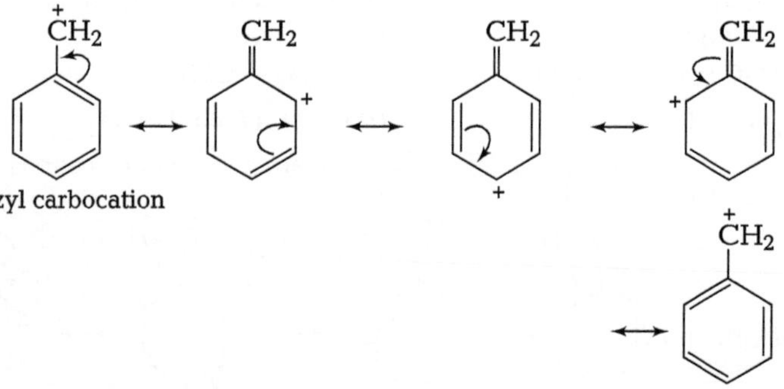

Benzyl carbocation

(f) $CH_3—CH=CH—\overset{+}{C}H_2$ ⟷ $CH_3—\overset{+}{C}H—CH=CH_2$

But-2-en-1-yl carbocation

Question 12. What are electrophiles and nucleophiles? Explain with examples.

Solution.

1. **Electrophiles** The neutral or positively charged species with deficiency of electrons and capability of accepting a pair of electrons (Lewis acid) are called electrophiles.

   Some examples are,

   Neutral electrophiles BF_3, $AlCl_3$, SO_3, $FeCl_3$, $SiCl_4$, $\overset{..}{:}CH_2$ (carbenes),

   $\overset{..}{:}NR$ (nitrenes)

   Charged electrophiles H^+, Cl^+, Br^+, NO^+, NO_2^+, $R\overset{+}{\underset{\parallel}{C}}$,
   $\qquad\qquad\qquad\qquad\qquad\qquad\qquad\qquad\qquad\quad O$

2. **Nucleophiles** The neutral or negatively charged species which are capable of acting as donor of electron pair (Lewis base) are called nucleophiles. Some examples are,

   Neutral nucleophiles $\overset{..}{N}H_3$, $R\overset{..}{N}H_2$, $R_2\overset{..}{N}H$, $R_3\overset{..}{N}$, $H_2\overset{..}{\underset{..}{O}}{:}$, $R\overset{..}{\underset{..}{O}}H$, $R\overset{..}{\underset{..}{O}}R$

   Charged nucleophiles CN^-, OH^-, X^-, $\overset{..}{:}OR^-$, $\overset{..}{:}SH^-$, $RCOO^-$, $HC{\equiv}\overset{-}{C}{:}$

Question 13. Identify the underlined reagents in the following equations as nucleophiles or electrophiles.

(a) $CH_3COOH + \underline{HO^-} \longrightarrow CH_3COO^- + H_2O$

(b) $CH_3COCH_3 + \underline{{}^-CN} \longrightarrow (CH_3)_2C(CN)(OH)$

(c) $C_6H_6 + \underline{CH_3\overset{+}{C}O} \longrightarrow C_6H_5COCH_3$

> Electrophiles are electron deficient species, *i.e.*, carry positive charge and nucleophiles are electron rich species *i.e.*, carry negative charge.

Solution.   (a) HO^- is a nucleophile   (b) $\overset{-}{C}N$ is a nucleophile

             (c) $CH_3\overset{+}{C}O$ is an electrophile

Question 14.   Classify the following reactions in one of the reaction type studied in this unit.

(a) $CH_3CH_2Br + HS^- \longrightarrow CH_3CH_2SH + Br^-$

(b) $(CH_3)_2C{=}CH_2 + HCl \longrightarrow (CH_3)_2CCl{-}CH_3$

(c) $CH_3CH_2Br + HO^- \longrightarrow CH_2{=}CH_2 + H_2O + Br^-$

(d) $(CH_3)_3C{-}CH_2OH + HBr \longrightarrow (CH_3)_2CBrCH_2CH_3 + H_2O$

> (a) A nucleophile (Br^-) is substituted by other nucleophile (HS^-)
> (b) HCl is added to the double bond ($C{=}C$)
> (c) H and Br are eliminated from successive carbon atoms.
> (d) Nucleophile (OH^-) is substituted by Br^-.

Solution.
 (a) Nucleophilic substitution reaction
 (b) Electrophilic addition reaction
 (c) β-elimination reaction
 (d) Nucleophilic substitution reaction with rearrangement.

Question 15. What is the relationship between the members of following pairs of structures? Are they structural or geometrical isomers or resonance contributors?

(a)

(b)

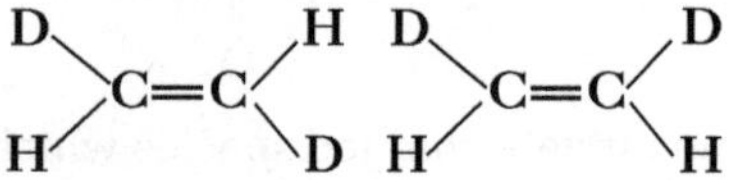

(c) 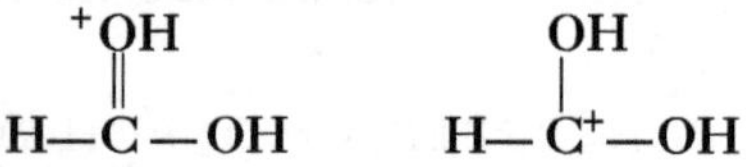 H—C—OH   H—C⁺—OH
    (with ⁺OH above and OH above respectively)

Solution.
 (a) Structural isomers (differ in position of the functional group)
 (b) Geometrical isomers

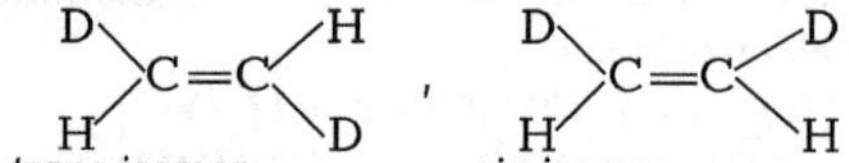

trans isomer
(as similar groups
are on opposite side
of double bond)

cis-isomer
(as similar groups are
on same side
of double bond)

 (c) Resonance contributors (differ in the position of electrons but not atoms.)

Question 16. For the following bond cleavages, use curved-arrows to show the electron flow and classify each as homolysis or heterolysis. Identify reactive intermediate produced as free radical, carbocation and carbanion.

(a) $CH_3O—OCH_3 \longrightarrow CH_3\dot{O} + \dot{O}CH_3$

(b)  $=O + {}^-OH \longrightarrow =O + H_2O$

(c) 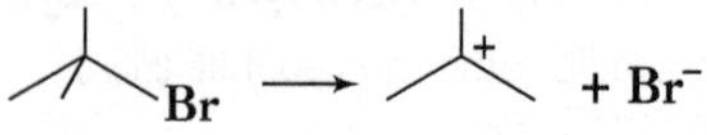 $\longrightarrow$ + Br⁻

(d) 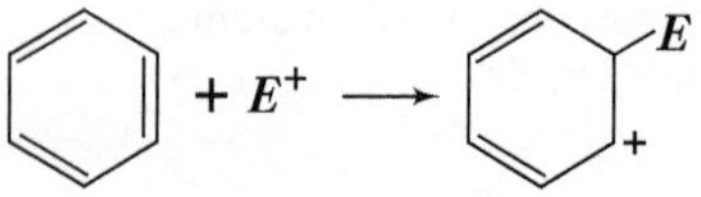 + E⁺ $\longrightarrow$

Free radicals are the result of homolysis while ions (carbanion or carbocation) are formed when reactant undergoes heterolysis.

Solution. (a) $CH_3\overset{\frown\frown}{O-O}CH_3 \xrightarrow{\text{Homolysis}} CH_3\dot{O} + \dot{O}CH_3$
Free radicals

(b) $HO^- + H\!-\!\!<\!\!=\!\!O$ $\xrightarrow{\text{Heterolysis}}$ $>\!\!=\!\!O + H_2O$
Carbanion

(c) $\xrightarrow{\text{Heterolysis}}$ $+ Br^-$
Carbocation

(d) $+ \overset{+}{E}$ $\xrightarrow{\text{Heterolysis}}$ E
Carbocation

Question 17. Explain the terms inductive and electromeric effects. Which electron displacement effect explains the following correct orders of acidity of the carboxylic acids?

(a) $Cl_3CCOOH > Cl_2CHCOOH > ClCH_2COOH$

(b) $CH_3CH_2COOH > (CH_3)_2CHCOOH > (CH_3)_3C \cdot COOH$

Solution. **Inductive effect** It is the permanent displacement of shared pair of electrons along the chain of carbon atoms due to the presence of polar covalent bond at one end of the chain, *e.g.,*

$$C\!-\!C\rightarrow\!C\twoheadrightarrow \overset{\delta+}{C}\Rrightarrow X^{\delta-} \; (X = \text{electronegative group or atom})$$

Inductive effect decreases with increase in the distance from the electronegative atom.

The effect is said to be $-I$ if a group pulls the electrons from the carbon chain. Such a group is called electron withdrawing group or $-I$ showing group.

The effect is said to be $+I$ if a group pushes the electrons towards the carbon chain. Such a group is called electron releasing group or $+I$ showing group.

The $+I$ effect of some of the atoms or groups in the decreasing order is

$$-O^- > -COO^- > (CH_3)_3C- > (CH_3)_2CH-$$
$$> CH_3CH_2CH_2- > CH_3CH_2- > CH_3-$$

The $-I$ effect of some of the atoms or groups in the decreasing order is

$$\overset{+}{R_3N}- > -NO_2 > -CN > -COOH$$
$$> -F > -Cl > -Br > -I > -OCH_3 > -OH > -C_6H_5$$

Inductive effect is a permanent effect. It explains greater reactivity of alkyl halides as compared to alkanes, relative acidic strength of carboxylic acids, basic strength of amines and relative reactivity of carbonyl compounds towards nucleophilic attack.

Electromeric effect It is a temporary displacement of π-electrons in a multiple bond towards one of the bonded atom at the call of attacking species.

+ E effect The effect is known as + E effect if transfer of π-electrons takes place towards the atom where attacking group attacks *e.g.,*

– E effect The effect is known as – E if transfer of electrons takes place away from the atom where the attacking group attacks.

(a) **– I effect** As the number of halogen atoms decreases, the overall – I-effect decreases and the acidic strength of carboxylic acids decreases accordingly.

(b) **+ I effect** As the number of alkyl group increases, the + I effect increases and the acidic strength of carboxylic acids decreases accordingly.

Question 18. Give a brief description of the principles of the following techniques taking an example in each case:

(a) Crystallisation   (b) Distillation   (c) Chromatography.

Solution. **Crystallisation** It involves conversion of an impure compound into its pure crystals. It is based on the difference in the solubilities of the compound and the impurities in a suitable solvent. The impure compound is dissolved in a solvent in which it is sparingly soluble at room temperature but appreciably soluble at higher temperature. The solution is concentrated to get a nearly saturated solution at higher temperature. On cooling the solution, pure compound in the form of crystals separate out, *e.g.*, iodoform is crystallised with alcohol, benzoic acid mixed with naphthalene can be purified by hot water.

Distillation It involves the process of heating a liquid to convert it into the vapours and condensing the vapours to get back the liquid. It is applied only for the purification of liquids which boil without decomposition at atmospheric pressure and contain non-volatile impurities. A mixture of two liquids having sufficient difference in their boiling point can be separated and purified by distillation, *e.g.*, chloroform (b.p. 334 K) and aniline (b.p. 457 K) are easily separated by the distillation. On boiling, the vapours of lower boiling component are formed first so it is collected first in the receiver.

Chromatography It is a technique for the separation, purification and identification of the constituents of the mixture. It is based on the principle of selective adsorption of components of a mixture between two phases, a stationary phase and a moving phase. The stationary phase can be a solid or a liquid while a moving phase is a liquid or gas.

Types of adsorption chromatography

(a) Column chromatography
(b) Thin layer chromatography
(c) Partition chromatography

   In column chromatography, the stationary phase is solid and mobile phase is a mixture of solvents of different polarities. The solid adsorbent with a suitable non-polar solvent is packed into a vertical glass tube of suitable length. A small amount of concentrated solution of organic mixture to be separated and purified is added from the top of the column. Separation of the components of the mixture takes place as a result of differential adsorption. The components of a mixture are separated into a number of individual layers called bands (chromatogram).

Question 19. Describe the method, which can be used to separate two compounds with different solubilities in a solvent *S*.

Solution. Two compounds with different solubilities in a solvent *S* can be separated by fractional crystallisation. When a hot saturated solution of these two compounds is allowed to cool, the less soluble compound crystallises out earlier than the more soluble compound. The crystals are separated from the mother liquor and the mother liquor is again concentrated and allowed to cool when the crystals of the second compound are obtained.

Question 20. What is the difference between distillation, distillation under reduced pressure and steam distillation?

   Discuss on the basis of boiling points of different substances.

Solution. Distillation involves the process of heating a liquid to convert it into the vapours and the condensation of the vapours to get back the liquid. Simple distillation is applied only for the purification of those liquids which boil without decomposition and contain non-volatile impurities.

Distillation under reduced pressure is applicable for those organic liquids which decompose at a temperature below their boiling point. A liquid boils when its vapour pressure is equal to the atmospheric pressure. Such liquids are made to boil at a temperature lower than their normal boiling point by reducing the pressure on their surface. The pressure is reduced with the help of a water pump or vaccum pump. Glycerol can be separated from spent-lye in soap industry by using this technique.

Steam distillation is codistillation with water. This technique is used to separate substances which are steam volatile and are immiscible with water. Aniline is separated by this technique from aniline-water mixture. In steam distillation, the liquid boils when the sum of vapour pressures due to the organic liquid (p_1) and due to the water (p_2) becomes equal to the atmospheric pressure (p), *i.e.*, $p = p_1 + p_2$. Since, p_1 is lower than p, the organic liquid vaporises at lower temperature than its boiling point.

Question 21. Discuss the chemistry of Lassaigne's test.

Solution. **Preparation of Lassaigne's extract** Organic compound is fused with sodium metal in a fusion tube. The red hot tube is broken in distilled water, boiled and filtered. The filtrate is called Lassaigne's extract. It is used for testing the elements N, S and halogens in the given organic compound.

Test for nitrogen

$$\underset{\substack{\text{From organic}\\\text{compound}}}{Na + \quad C + N} \xrightarrow{\text{Fuse}} NaCN$$

When Lassaigne's extract is boiled with ferrous sulphate solution and then acidified with conc. H_2SO_4 following reaction takes place

$$FeSO_4 + 2NaOH \longrightarrow \underset{\substack{\text{Ferrous hydroxide}\\\text{(green)}}}{Fe(OH)_2} + Na_2SO_4$$

$$Fe(OH)_2 + 6NaCN \longrightarrow \underset{\text{Sodium ferrocyanide}}{Na_4[Fe(CN)_6]} + 2NaOH$$

On heating some of the Fe^{2+} ions are oxidised to Fe^{3+} ions.

$$4Fe^{3+} + 3Na_4[Fe(CN)_6] \longrightarrow \underset{\substack{\text{Ferric ferrocyanide}\\\text{(Prussian blue)}}}{Fe_4[Fe(CN)_6]_3} + 12Na^+$$

Appearance of Prussian blue colour confirms the presence of nitrogen in the compound.

Test for nitrogen and sulphur if present together

$$Na + C + N + S \xrightarrow{\Delta} \underset{\text{Sod. thiocyanate}}{NaSCN}$$

Sodium thiocyanate gives blood red colour and no Prussian blue in the test of nitrogen since there are no free cyanide ions.

$$Fe^{3+} + NaSCN \longrightarrow \underset{\text{Blood red colour}}{Fe(SCN)_3} + 3Na^+$$

Test for sulphur

$$2Na + S \xrightarrow{\Delta} Na_2S$$

(i) When lead acetate is added to Lassaigne's extract and acidified with acetic acid, a black ppt. of PbS is obtained.

$$Na_2S + (CH_3COO)_2Pb \longrightarrow PbS + 2CH_3COONa$$

(ii) When sodium nitroprusside solution is added to Lassaigne's extract, a violet colour is appeared due to the formation of sodium thionitroprusside.

$$Na_2S + \underset{\text{Sodium nitroprusside}}{Na_2[Fe(NO)(CN)_5]} \longrightarrow \underset{\substack{\text{Sodium thionitroprusside} \\ \text{(violet or purple colour)}}}{Na_4[Fe(CN)_5NOS]}$$

Tests for halogens

A part of Lassaigne's extract is boiled with some conc. HNO_3 to decompose sodium cyanide or sodium sulphide in the extract if compound contains N and S. Otherwise these ions would interfere with silver nitrate test for halogens.

$$NaCN + HNO_3 \longrightarrow NaNO_3 + HCN \uparrow$$

$$Na_2S + 2HNO_3 \longrightarrow 2NaNO_3 + H_2S \uparrow$$

The solution is cooled and a small amount of $AgNO_3$ solution is added.

(i) If a white ppt. (AgCl) is obtained which is soluble in NH_3 (*aq*) but insoluble in HNO_3, the organic compound contains chlorine.

$$NaCl + AgNO_3 \longrightarrow \underset{\text{White ppt.}}{AgCl \downarrow} + NaNO_3$$

(ii) A pale yellow ppt. (AgBr) sparingly soluble in ammonium hydroxide indicates the presence of bromine in organic compound.

$$NaBr + AgNO_3 \longrightarrow \underset{\text{Pale yellow ppt.}}{AgBr} + NaNO_3$$

(iii) A yellow ppt. (AgI), insoluble in ammonium hydroxide indicates iodine in organic compound.

$$NaI + AgNO_3 \longrightarrow \underset{\text{Yellow ppt.}}{AgI} + NaNO_3$$

Question 22. Differentiate between the principle of estimation of nitrogen in an organic compound by (i) Duma's method (ii) Kjeldahl's method.

Solution.

(i) **In Duma's method** when a known mass of the nitrogen containing organic compound is heated with excess of CuO in an atmosphere of CO_2, nitrogen of the organic compound is converted into N_2 gas. The volume of N_2 thus obtained is converted into STP and the percentage of nitrogen is determined.

$$\%N = \frac{28}{22400} \times \frac{\text{Vol. of } N_2 \text{ at STP}}{\text{mass of the substance taken}} \times 100$$

(ii) **In Kjeldahl's method**, a known mass of the nitrogen containing organic substance is digested (heated) with conc. H_2SO_4 and $CuSO_4$ (in little amount) in **Kjeldahl's flask**. Nitrogen present in the organic compound is quantitatively converted into $(NH_4)_2SO_4 \cdot (NH_4)_2SO_4$ thus obtained is boiled with excess of NaOH solution to liberate NH_3 gas which is absorbed in a known excess of a standard solution of H_2SO_4 or HCl.

The volume of acid left after absorption of NH_3 is estimated by titration against a standard alkali solution. From the volume of the acid used, the percentage of nitrogen is determined by applying the equation,

$$\%N = \frac{1.4 \times (\text{molarity of the acid} \times \text{basicity of the acid}) \times \text{volume of the acid used}}{\text{mass of the substance taken}}$$

Question 23. Discuss the principle of estimation of halogens, sulphur and phosphorus present in an organic compound.

Solution. Halogens, sulphur and phosphorus present in an organic compound are estimated by Carius method.

Estimation of halogens

A known mass of an organic compound is heated with fuming nitric acid in the presence of silver nitrate in Carius tube in a furnace. Carbon and hydrogen present in the organic compound are oxidised to CO_2 and H_2O respectively and halogen forms the ppt. of silver halide. It is filtered, washed, dried and weighed.

Let the mass of organic compound taken = m g

Mass of AgX formed = m_1 g; % of halogen = $\dfrac{\text{atomic mass of } X \times m_1 \times 100}{\text{molecular mass of AgX} \times m}$

Estimation of sulphur

A known mass of an organic compound is heated in a Carius tube with sodium peroxide or fuming nitric acid. Sulphur is oxidised to H_2SO_4. It is precipitated as $BaSO_4$ by adding excess of $BaCl_2$ solution in water. The ppt. is filtered, washed, dried and weighed.

Let the mass of organic compound taken = m g

Mass of $BaSO_4$ formed = m_1 g

$$\% \text{ of sulphur} = \frac{32 \times m_1 \times 100}{233 \times m}$$

Estimation of phosphorus

A known mass of an organic compound is heated with fuming HNO_3, phosphorus is oxidised to phosphoric acid. It is precipitated as ammonium phosphomolybdate $(NH_4)_3PO_4 \cdot 12MoO_3$ by adding NH_3 and ammonium molybdate (molar mass of ammonium phosphomolybdate = 1877).

Let the mass of organic compound taken = m g

Mass of ammonium phosphomolybdate = m_1 g

$$\% \text{ of phosphorus} = \frac{31 \times m_1 \times 100}{1877 \times m}$$

Alternatively, phosphoric acid may be precipitated as $MgNH_4PO_4$ by adding magnesia mixture which on ignition produces magnesium pyrophosphate (molar mass of $Mg_2P_2O_7 = 222$).

$$\% \text{ of phosphorus} = \frac{62 \times m_1 \times 100}{222 \times m}$$

Question 24. Explain the principle of paper chromatography.

Solution. Paper chromatography is a type of partition chromatography. It is based on the principle of partition, *i.e.*, it is based upon continuous differential partitioning or distribution of the various components of the mixture between the stationary and the mobile phases.

In it, the solution of the mixture to be separated is applied as a small spot at the base of chromatography paper (about 2 cm above one end of the paper strip). It is suspended in a suitable solvent. This solvent acts as mobile phase. Solvent rises up the paper. After some time the spots of the separated colored compounds are visible at different heights from the position of initial spot on the chromatogram. The coloured components of a mixture are identified by their R_f value, which can be given as,

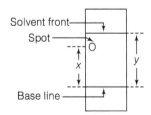

Developed chromatogram

Retardation factor, R_f value

$$= \frac{\text{Distance travelled by the compound, x}}{\text{Distance travelled by the solvent, y}}$$

In case of colourless compound, the spot is observed by the use of an appropriate spray reagent.

Question 25. Why is nitric acid added to sodium extract before adding silver nitrate for testing halogens?

Solution. Sodium extract is boiled with nitric acid to decompose NaCN and Na_2S, if present.

$$NaCN + HNO_3 \longrightarrow NaNO_3 + HCN \uparrow$$

$$Na_2S + 2HNO_3 \longrightarrow 2NaNO_3 + H_2S \uparrow$$

If cyanide and sulphide are not removed, they will react with $AgNO_3$ and hence, will interfere with the silver nitrate test for halogens.

$$NaCN + AgNO_3 \longrightarrow \underset{\text{(White ppt.)}}{AgCN} + NaNO_3$$

$$Na_2S + 2AgNO_3 \longrightarrow \underset{\text{(Black ppt.)}}{Ag_2S} + 2NaNO_3$$

Question 26. Explain the reason for the fusion of an organic compound with metallic sodium for testing nitrogen, sulphur and halogens.

Solution. Nitrogen, sulphur and halogens are present in an organic compound in covalent form so their detection is not easy. By fusing with Na metal these elements are converted into NaCN or Na_2S or NaX, *i.e.,* in an ionic form. In ionic form, these can be easily detected by ionic reactions.

Question 27. Name a suitable technique of separation of the components from a mixture of calcium sulphate and camphor.

Camphor is a sublimate while $CaSO_4$ is not. A sublimate from a non-sublimate is separated by sublimation.

Solution. A mixture of $CaSO_4$ and camphor can be separated by sublimation. Because camphor is sublimable but $CaSO_4$ is not therefore, sublimation of the mixture gives camphor on the sides of funnel while $CaSO_4$ is left in the china dish.

Question 28. Explain, why an organic liquid vapourises at a temperature below its boiling point in its steam distillation?

Solution. In steam distillation, the mixture consisting of the organic liquid and water boils when the sum of the vapour pressures of the organic liquid (p_1) and that of water (p_2) becomes equal to the atmospheric pressure (p), *i.e.,* $p = p_1 + p_2$.

Since, p_1 is lower than p, the organic liquid vaporises at lower temperature than its boiling point.

Some Basic Principles and Techniques 313

Question 29. Will CCl_4 give white precipitate of AgCl on heating it with silver nitrate? Give reason for your answer.

CCl_4 is a covalent compound and does not give Cl^-ions.

Solution. CCl_4 will not give a white ppt of AgCl with $AgNO_3$ solution because CCl_4 is a covalent compound. It does not ionize to give Cl^- ions required for the formation of AgCl precipitate.

Question 30. Why is a solution of potassium hydroxide used to absorb carbon dioxide evolved during the estimation of carbon present in an organic compound?

Solution. CO_2 is slightly acidic in nature, therefore, it reacts with the strong base KOH to form K_2CO_3 and from the weight of the CO_2 obtained, percentage of carbon in the organic compound is calculated.

$$2KOH + CO_2 \longrightarrow K_2CO_3 + H_2O$$

The increase in the weight of U-tube containing KOH gives the weight of CO_2 produced and from the weight of the CO_2 obtained, percentange of carbon in the organic compound is calculated as,

$$\%C = \frac{12}{44} \times \frac{\text{weight of } CO_2 \text{ formed}}{\text{weight of substance taken}} \times 100$$

Question 31. Why is it necessary to use acetic acid and not sulphuric acid for acidification of sodium extract for testing sulphur by lead acetate test?

Solution. If H_2SO_4 is used, lead acetate itself will react with H_2SO_4 to form white ppt. of lead sulphate.

$$\underset{\text{Lead acetate}}{Pb(OCOCH_3)_2} + H_2SO_4 \longrightarrow \underset{\text{White ppt.}}{PbSO_4\downarrow} + 2CH_3COOH$$

Hence, white precipitate of $PbSO_4$ will interfere with the following test of sulphur.

$$Pb(CH_3COO)_2 + Na_2S \longrightarrow \underset{\text{Black ppt.}}{PbS\downarrow} + 2CH_3COONa$$

However, if acetic acid is used, it does not react with lead acetate, so does not interfere in the test.

Question 32. An organic compound contains 69% carbon and 4.8% hydrogen, the remainder being oxygen. Calculate the masses of carbon dioxide and water produced when 0.20 g of this substance is subjected to complete combustion.

Solution. $\%C = \frac{12}{44} \times \frac{\text{mass of } CO_2 \text{ formed}}{\text{mass of substance taken}} \times 100$

$$69 = \frac{12}{44} \times \frac{\text{Mass of } CO_2 \text{ formed}}{0.2} \times 100$$

$$\therefore \text{ Mass of } CO_2 \text{ formed} = \frac{69 \times 44 \times 0.2}{12 \times 100} = 0.506 \text{ g}$$

$$\%H = \frac{2}{18} \times \frac{\text{mass of } H_2O \text{ formed}}{\text{mass of substance taken}} \times 100$$

$$4.8 = \frac{2}{18} \times \frac{\text{Mass of } H_2O \text{ formed}}{0.2} \times 100$$

$$\therefore \quad \text{Mass of } H_2O \text{ formed} = \frac{4.8 \times 18 \times 0.2}{2 \times 100} = 0.0864 \text{ g}$$

Question 33. A sample of 0.50 g of an organic compound was treated according to Kjeldahl's method. The ammonia evolved was absorbed in 50 mL of 0.5 M H_2SO_4. The residual acid required 60 mL of 0.5 M solution of NaOH for neutralisation. Find the percentage composition of nitrogen in the compound.

(i) Calculate the volume of the H_2SO_4 used to neutralize NaOH.

(ii) Calculate percentage of nitrogen by using the formula $N\% = \dfrac{1.4 \times NV}{w}$

Solution.   Volume of the acid taken = 50 mL of 0.5 MH_2SO_4

$$= 25 \text{ mL of } 1.0 \text{ } MH_2SO_4$$

Volume of alkali used for neutralization of excess acid

$$= 60 \text{ mL of } 0.5 \text{ M NaOH}$$
$$= 30 \text{ mL of } 1.0 \text{ M NaOH}$$

$$H_2SO_4 + 2NaOH \longrightarrow Na_2SO_4 + 2H_2O$$

1 mole of H_2SO_4 = 2 moles of NaOH

Hence, 30 mL of 1.0 M NaOH = 15 mL of 1.0 M H_2SO_4

∴ Volume of acid used by ammonia = 25 – 15 = 10 mL

$$\% \text{ of nitrogen} = \frac{1.4 \times N_1 \times \text{vol. of acid used}}{w}$$

(where, N_1 = normality of acid and w = mass of the organic compound taken)

$$\% \text{ of nitrogen} = \frac{1.4 \times 2 \times 10}{0.5} = 56.0$$

Question 34. 0.3780 g of an organic chloro compound gave 0.5740 g of silver chloride in Carius estimation. Calculate the percentage of chlorine present in the compound.

Solution.   The mass of the organic compound taken = 0.3780 g

Mass of AgCl formed = 0.5740 g

$$\text{Percentage of chlorine} = \frac{35.5}{143.5} \times \frac{\text{mass of AgCl formed}}{\text{mass of substance taken}} \times 100$$

$$= \frac{35.5}{143.5} \times \frac{0.5740}{0.3780} \times 100 = 37.566\%$$

Question 35. In the estimation of sulphur by Carius method, 0.468 g of an organic sulphur compound afforded 0.668 g of barium sulphate. Find the percentage of sulphur in the given compound.

Solution.   The mass of organic compound taken = 0.468 g

Mass of $BaSO_4$ formed = 0.668 g

Percentage of sulphur $= \dfrac{32}{233} \times \dfrac{\text{mass of BaSO}_4 \text{ formed}}{\text{mass of substance taken}} \times 100$

$= \dfrac{32}{233} \times \dfrac{0.668}{0.468} \times 100 = 19.60\%$

Question 36. In the organic compound $CH_2 = CH - CH_2 - CH_2 - C \equiv CH$, the pair of hybridised orbitals involved in the formation of $C_2 - C_3$ bond is

(a) $sp - sp^2$ (b) $sp - sp^3$ (c) $sp^2 - sp^3$ (d) $sp^3 - sp^3$

Solution.   (c), When double and triple bonds are present at equivalent positions, then preference is given to double bond while numbering the carbon chain. Thus,

$$\overset{1}{CH_2} = \overset{2}{CH} - \overset{3}{CH_2} - \overset{4}{CH_2} - \overset{5}{C} \equiv \overset{6}{CH}$$
$$\underset{sp^2}{} \quad \underset{sp^2}{} \quad \underset{sp^3}{} \quad \underset{sp^3}{} \quad \underset{sp}{} \quad \underset{sp}{}$$

$\therefore C_2 - C_3$ bond is formed by overlap of sp^2 and sp^3 orbitals.

Question 37. In the Lassaigne's test for nitrogen in an organic compound, the Prussian blue colour is obtained due to the formation of

(a) $Na_4[Fe(CN)_6]$ (b) $Fe_4[Fe(CN)_6]_3$
(c) $Fe_2[Fe(CN)_6]$ (d) $Fe_3[Fe(CN)_6]_4$

Solution.   (b) The Prussian blue colour is due to the formation of ferric ferro cyanide, $Fe_4[Fe(CN)_6]_3$.

Question 38. Which of the following carbocation is most stable?

(a) $(CH_3)_3C\overset{+}{C}H_2$ (b) $(CH_3)_3\overset{+}{C}$

(c) $CH_3CH_2\overset{+}{C}H_2$ (d) $CH_3\overset{+}{C}HCH_2CH_3$

Solution.   (b) The order of stability of carbocation is $3° > 2° > 1°$

(a) $(CH_3)_3C - \overset{+}{C}H_2$ (b) $(CH_3)_3\overset{+}{C}$
    $1°$ carbocation $3°$ carbocation

(c) $CH_3CH_2\overset{+}{C}H_2$ (d) $CH_3\overset{+}{C}HCH_2CH_3$
    $1°$ carbocation $2°$ carbocation

$3°$ carbocation, *i.e.*, $(CH_3)_3\overset{+}{C}$ is the most stable carbocation.

Question 39. The best and latest technique for isolation, purification and separation of organic compounds is

(a) Crystallisation   (b) Distillation
(c) Sublimation   (d) Chromatography

Solution.   (d) Chromatography is the best and latest technique for isolation, purification and separation of organic compounds.

Question 40. The reaction,

$$CH_3CH_2I + KOH(aq) \longrightarrow CH_3CH_2OH + KI$$

is classified as

(a) electrophilic substitution   (b) nucleophilic substitution
(c) elimination   (d) addition

Solution. (b) This is an example of nucleophilic substitution reaction because the nucleophile I^- is replaced by the nucleophile OH^-.

Selected NCERT Exemplar Problems

Short Answer Type

Question 1. For testing halogens in an organic compound with $AgNO_3$ solution, sodium extract (Lassaigne's test) is acidified with dilute HNO_3. What will happen if a student acidifies the extract with dilute H_2SO_4 in place of dilute HNO_3 ?

Solution. On adding dilute H_2SO_4, white precipitate of Ag_2SO_4 is obtained. It will interfere with the test of chlorine.

Question 2. What is the hybridization of each carbon in $H_2C{=}C{=}CH_2$?

Solution.

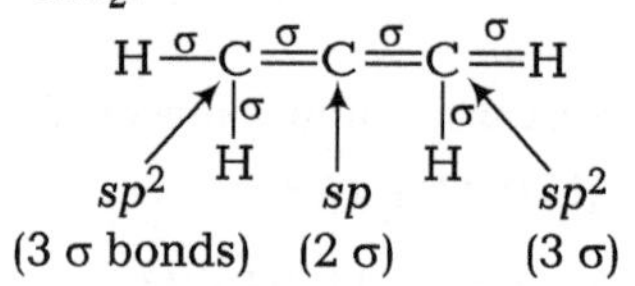

$$H\overset{\sigma}{-}C\overset{\sigma}{=}C\overset{\sigma}{=}C\overset{\sigma}{=}H$$

$$sp^2 \quad H \quad sp \quad H \quad sp^2$$
$$(3\ \sigma\ \text{bonds})\quad (2\ \sigma)\quad (3\ \sigma)$$

Question 3. Explain, how is the electronegativity of carbon atoms related to their state of hybridization in an organic compound?

Solution. Electronegativity of carbon atoms increases with increase in s-character of the hybridized carbon.

$$sp^3 \quad < \quad sp^2 \quad < \quad sp$$
$$25\% \text{ } s\text{-character} \quad 33.3\% \text{ } s\text{-character} \quad 50\ \% \text{ } s\text{-character}$$

Thus, sp hybridized carbon is most electronegative.

Question 4. Show the polarisation of carbon-magnesium bond in the following structure.

$$CH_3{-}CH_2{-}CH_2{-}CH_2{-}Mg{-}X$$

Solution. Carbon is more electronegative than magnesium therefore, Mg acquires a partial positive charge and carbon acquires a partial negative charge.

$$CH_3{-}CH_2{-}CH_2{-}\overset{-\delta}{C}H_2{-}\overset{+\delta}{Mg}{-}X$$

Question 5. Compounds with same molecular formula but differing in their structures are said to be structural isomers. What type of structural isomerism is shown by

$$CH_3—S—CH_2—CH_2—CH_3 \text{ and } CH_3—S—CH\begin{smallmatrix}CH_3\\\\CH_3\end{smallmatrix}?$$

Solution. The two compounds differ in the position of the functional group on the carbon skeleton. So, they should be called position isomers and this phenomenon as position isomerism.

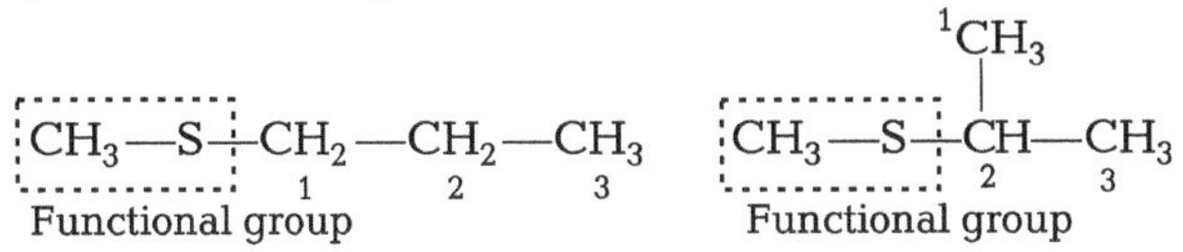

$$\underset{\text{Functional group}}{\boxed{CH_3—S}}\underset{1}{—CH_2}\underset{2}{—CH_2}\underset{3}{—CH_3} \qquad \overset{^1CH_3}{\underset{\text{Functional group}}{\boxed{CH_3—S}}\underset{2}{—CH}\underset{3}{—CH_3}}$$

But in case of polyvalent functional group, it is called metamerism.

Question 6. In DNA and RNA, nitrogen atom is present in the ring system. Can Kjeldahl method be used for the estimation of nitrogen present in these? Give reason.

Solution. DNA and RNA have nitrogen in the heterocyclic rings. Nitrogen present in rings, azo and nitro groups cannot be converted into $(NH_4)_2SO_4$. That's why Kjeldahl method cannot be used for the estimation of nitrogen present in these.

Question 7. Draw the possible resonance structures for $CH_3—\overset{..}{\underset{..}{O}}—\overset{+}{C}H_2$ and predict which of the structures is more stable. Give reason for your answer.

Solution. The given carbocation has two resonance structures,

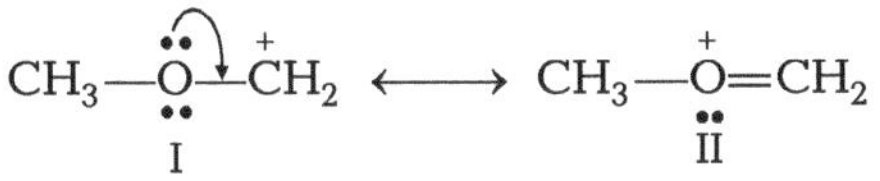

$$\underset{I}{CH_3—\overset{..}{\underset{..}{O}}\overset{+}{—}CH_2} \longleftrightarrow \underset{II}{CH_3—\overset{+}{\underset{..}{O}}=CH_2}$$

Structure (II) is more stable because both the carbon atoms and the oxygen atom have an octet of electrons.

Question 8. Which of the following ions is more stable? Use resonance to explain your answer.

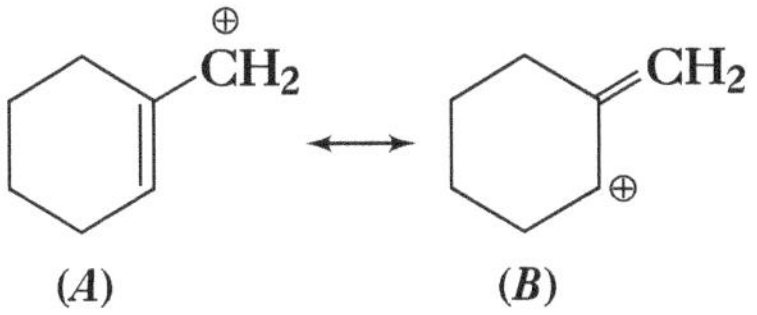

$$(A) \qquad\qquad (B)$$

Solution. Carbocation (*A*) is more stable than carbocation (*B*) due to resonance. Further more, double bond is more stable within the ring in comparison to outside the ring.

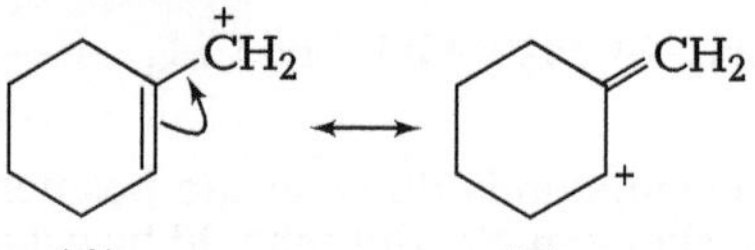

(*A*)   (*B*)

Question 9. The structure of triphenylmethyl cation is given below. This is very stable and some of its salts can be stored for months. Explain the cause of high stability of this cation.

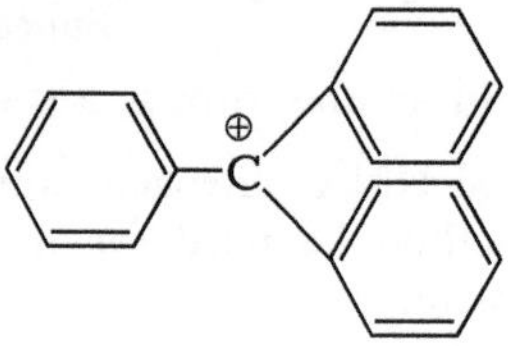

Solution. Triphenylmethyl cation is highly stable due to following nine possible resonance structures.

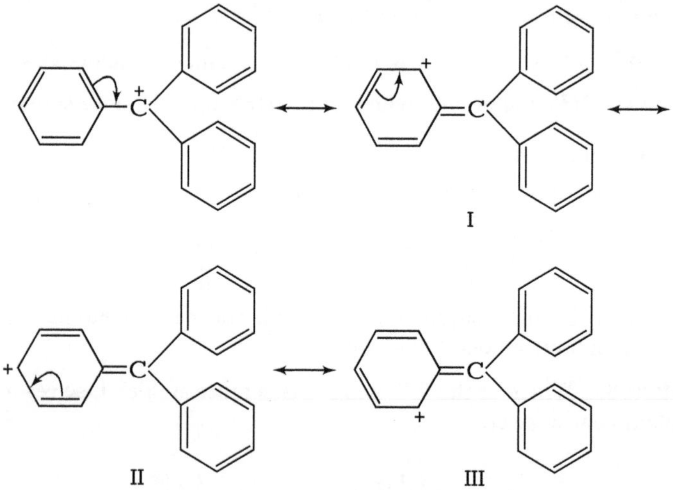

I

II   III

+

Six more such structures are
possible due to resonance in the
other two benzene rings.

Question 10. Name the compounds whose bond line formulae are given below.

(i)

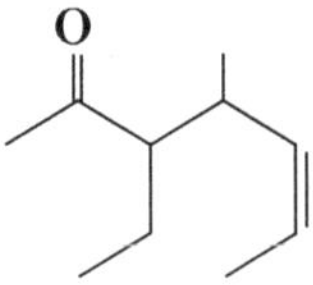

(ii) 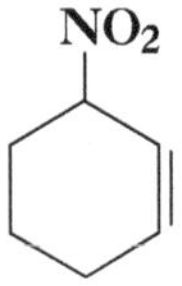 NO$_2$

Solution.

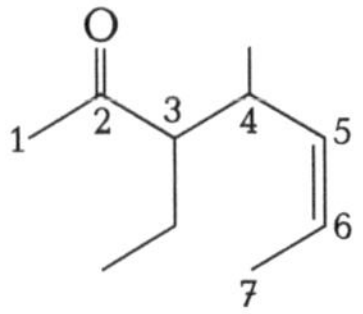

3-ethyl-4-methylhept-5-en-2-one 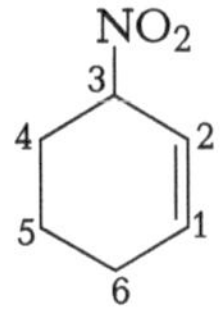   3-nitrocyclohex-1-ene

Question 11. Write the structural formulae for compounds named as
(a) 1-bromoheptane   (b) 5-bromoheptanoic acid

Solution. (a) $\overset{7}{C}H_3-\overset{6}{C}H_2-\overset{5}{C}H_2-\overset{4}{C}H_2-\overset{3}{C}H_2-\overset{2}{C}H_2-\overset{1}{C}H_2Br$
1-bromoheptane

(b) $\overset{7}{C}H_3-\overset{6}{C}H_2-\overset{5}{C}H-\overset{4}{C}H_2-\overset{3}{C}H_2-\overset{2}{C}H_2-\overset{1}{C}-OH$
                 | ||
                Br   O
5-bromoheptanoic acid

Question 12. Identify the most stable species in the following set of ions giving reasons :

(i) $\overset{+}{C}H_3, \overset{+}{C}H_2Br, \overset{+}{C}HBr_2, \overset{+}{C}Br_3$ (ii) $\overset{\ominus}{C}H_3, \overset{\ominus}{C}H_2Cl, \overset{\ominus}{C}HCl_2, \overset{\ominus}{C}Cl_3$

Solution.

(i) $\overset{\oplus}{C}H_3$ is the most stable species because the replacement of H by Br increases positive charge on carbon atom and destabilises the species.

(ii) $\overset{\ominus}{C}Cl_3$ is the most stable species because on replacing H by Cl, negative charge on carbon is reduced and species is stabilised.

Question 13. Why does SO_3 act as an electrophile?
Solution. Three highly electronegative oxygen atoms are attached to sulphur atom. It makes sulphur atom electron deficient. Further, due to resonance, sulphur acquires positive charge. Both these factors, make SO_3 an electrophile.

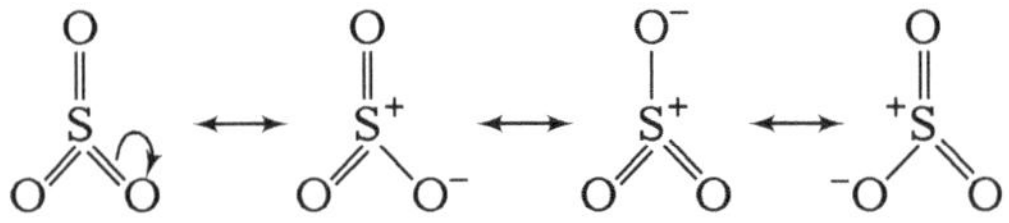

Long Answer Type

Question 14. Benzoic acid is an organic compound. Its crude sample can be purified by crystallisation from hot water. What characteristic differences in the properties of benzoic acid and the impurity make this process of purification suitable?

Solution. Benzoic acid can be purified by hot water because of the following characteristics:

(i) Benzoic acid is more soluble in hot water and less soluble in cold water.

(ii) Impurities present in benzoic acid are either insoluble in water or are more soluble in water to such an extent that they remain in solution as the mother liquor upon crystallisation.

Question 15. Two liquids (*A*) and (*B*) can be separated by the method of fractional distillation. The boiling point of liquid (*A*) is less than boiling point of liquid (*B*). Which of the liquids do you expect to come out first in the distillate? Explain.

Solution. If the difference in boiling points of two liquids is not much, fractional distillation is used to separate them. In this technique, fractionating column is fitted over the mouth of the round bottom flask. When vapours of a liquid mixture are passed through a fractionating column, the vapours of the low boiling liquid (*A*) will move up while those of the high boiling liquid will condense and fall back into the flask. Therefore, liquid (*A*) with low boiling point will distill first.

Question 16. A liquid with high boiling point decomposes on simple distillation but it can be steam distilled for its purification. Explain how is it possible?

Solution. In steam distillation, the distilling mixture consists of steam and the vapour of organic substance. Therefore, the sum of the vapour pressure of the organic substance (p_1) and that of steam (p_2) becomes equal to the atmospheric pressure (p) at the temperature of distillation. $p = p_1 + p_2$ or $p_1 = p - p_2$.

Since, the vapour pressure of the organic substance is lower than p, it distills below its normal boiling point without decomposition, *e.g.*, aniline which normally boils at 457 K can be distilled at 371.5 K by this process.

Chapter 13

Hydrocarbons

Important Results

1. Hydrocarbons are the compounds of carbon and hydrogen only. Hydrocarbons are mainly obtained from coal and petroleum, which are the major sources of energy.

2. Petrochemicals are the prominent starting materials used for the manufacture of a large number of commercially important products.

3. Liquefied petroleum gas (LPG) and compressed natural gas (CNG), the main sources of energy for domestic fuels and the automobile industry, are obtained from petroleum.

4. Hydrocarbons are classified as open chain saturated compounds (alkanes) and unsaturated compounds (alkenes and alkynes), cyclic (alicyclic) and aromatic, according to their structure.

5. Alkanes are obtained by the following reactions.

   (i) By the hydrogenation of unsaturated hydrocarbons in the presence of Pt or Pd or Ni.

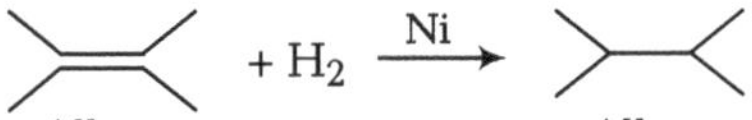

$$\diagdown\!\!=\!\!\diagup \; + \, H_2 \xrightarrow{\;Ni\;} \diagup\!\!\diagdown\!\!-\!\!\diagup\!\!\diagdown$$

   Alkene   Alkane

   (ii) From alkyl halides, $RX \xrightarrow{Zn + dil. HCl} R\!-\!H$

   $\xrightarrow[\text{Na, dry ether}]{\text{Wurtz reaction}} R\!-\!R$

   (iii) From sodium salts of carboxylic acids

   (a) $RCOONa \xrightarrow[\text{decarboxylation}]{NaOH/CaO} R\!-\!H$

   (b) $RCOONa \xrightarrow[\text{method}]{\text{Kolbe's electrolytic}} R\!-\!R$

6. Alkanes react with halogens in the presence of sunlight and give alkyl halides. Alkanes having six or more carbon atoms on heating at 773 K and 20-30 atm pressure in the presence of catalyst get dehydrogenated and cyclized to benzene and its homologues. The process is known as **aromatization.**

7. In **pyrolysis,** higher alkanes on heating to higher temperature decompose into lower alkanes, alkenes, etc. Preparation of oil gas or petrol gas from kerosene oil or petrol involves the principle of pyrolysis.

8. Alkanes show **conformational isomerism** due to free rotation along C—C sigma bonds. Out of staggered and eclipsed conformations of ethane, staggered conformation is more stable as hydrogen atoms are farthest apart.

9. Alkenes exhibit **geometrical** (*cis-trans*) **isomerism** due to restricted rotation around the carbon-carbon double bond.

10. **Preparation and properties of alkenes** may be summarized as

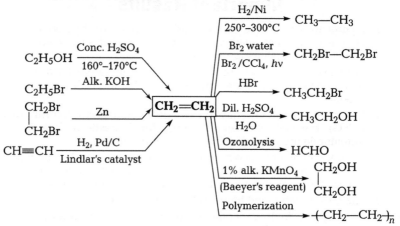

11. **Preparation and properties of alkynes** may be summarized as

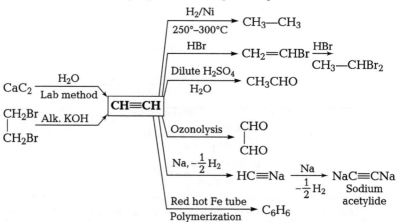

12. Preparation and properties of benzene can be summarized as

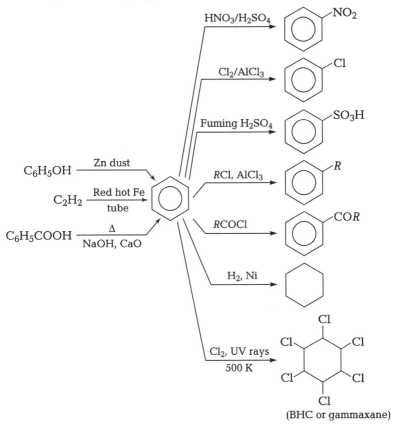

(BHC or gammaxane)

13. Aromaticity Aromatic compounds possess following characteristics:

(i) Planarity

(ii) Complete delocalization of the π-electrons in the ring system.

(iii) Presence of $(4n + 2)$ π-electrons in the ring (where, $n = 0$, 1, 2 ...).

This is often referred to as Huckel rule.

14. Ortho and para directing groups The groups which direct the incoming groups to *ortho* and *para* positions are called *ortho* and *para* directing groups, *e.g.*, —OH, —NH$_2$, —NHR, —NHCOCH$_3$, —OCH$_3$, —CH$_3$, —C$_2$H$_5$, etc. These are also known as activating groups because these group activate the benzene ring for further substitution.

15. *Meta* **directing groups** The groups which direct the incoming group to *meta* position are called *meta* directing groups, *e.g.,* $-NO_2$, $-CN$, $-CHO$, $-COR$, $-COOH$, $-COOR$, $-SO_3H$, etc. These groups are also called deactivating groups because presence of these groups in the benzene ring decreases the electron density in the ring and makes further substitution difficult.

Exercises

Question 1. How do you account for the formation of ethane during chlorination of methane?

Solution. Free radical chain mechanism for the chlorination of methane.

(i) **Initiation**

$$Cl\overset{\frown}{\underset{}{-}}Cl \xrightarrow{h\nu, \text{ homolysis}} \overset{\bullet}{Cl} + \overset{\bullet}{Cl}$$
$$\text{Chlorine free radicals}$$

(ii) **Propagation**

(a) $CH_4 + \overset{\bullet}{Cl} \xrightarrow{h\nu} \overset{\bullet}{CH_3} + H-Cl$

(b) $\overset{\bullet}{CH_3} + Cl\overset{\frown}{-}Cl \xrightarrow{h\nu} CH_3-Cl + \overset{\bullet}{Cl}$

(iii) **Termination**

(a) $\overset{\bullet}{Cl} + \overset{\bullet}{Cl} \longrightarrow Cl-Cl$ (b) $H_3\overset{\bullet}{C} + \overset{\bullet}{CH_3} \longrightarrow CH_3-CH_3$
$$\text{ethane}$$

(c) $H_3\overset{\bullet}{C} + \overset{\bullet}{Cl} \longrightarrow H_3C-Cl$
$$\text{Chloro methane}$$

From the above mechanism, it is evident that methyl free radicals are produced during propagation step. If two methyl free radicals combine with each other [as in termination step –(b)], *a* molecule of ethane is formed.

Question 2. Write IUPAC names of the following compounds :

(a) $CH_3CH=C(CH_3)_2$ (b) $CH_2=CH-C\equiv C-CH_3$

(c)

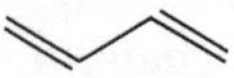

(d) 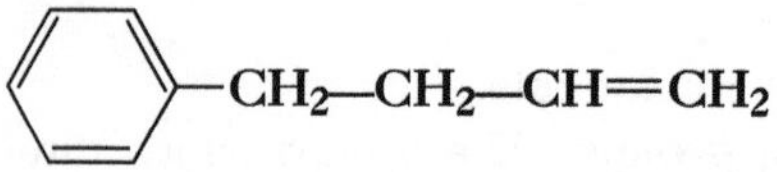 $-CH_2-CH_2-CH=CH_2$

(e) 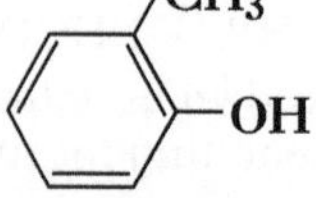 $-OH$ (f) $CH_3(CH_2)_4\underset{\underset{CH_2-CH(CH_3)_2}{|}}{CH}(CH_2)_3CH_3$

(g) $CH_3CH=CH-CH_2-CH=CH-\underset{\underset{C_2H_5}{|}}{CH}-CH_2-CH=CH_2$

    (i) Find the longest chain including functional group and write the root word.
    (ii) Write suffix of the functional group with its position.
    (iii) Write the name of the substituents with their positions before the root word, in alphabetical order.

Solution.

(a) $\overset{4}{C}H_3-\overset{3}{C}H=\overset{2}{\underset{\underset{CH_3}{|}}{C}}-\overset{1}{C}H_3$
2-methylbut-2-ene

(b) $\overset{1}{C}H_2=\overset{2}{C}H-\overset{3}{C}\equiv\overset{4}{C}-\overset{5}{C}H_3$
Pent-1-ene-3-yne

(c) 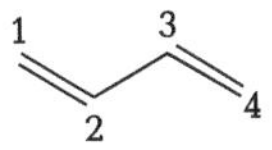 Buta-1,3-diene

(d) 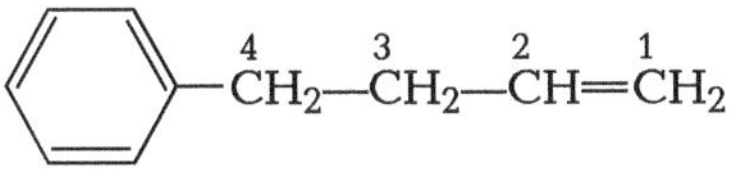 $-\overset{4}{C}H_2-\overset{3}{C}H_2-\overset{2}{C}H=\overset{1}{C}H_2$
4-phenylbut-1-ene

(e) 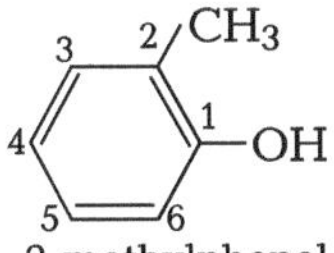 $\overset{2}{C}H_3$ ... $-OH$
2-methylphenol

(f) $\overset{10}{C}H_3-\overset{6-9}{(CH_2)_4}-\overset{5}{C}H-\overset{2-4}{(CH_2)_3}-\overset{1}{C}H_3$
                           $\underset{\overset{1}{CH_2}\ \overset{2\ 3}{CHCH_3}}{|}$
                                $\underset{CH_3}{|}$
5-(2-methylpropyl)decane

(g) $\overset{10}{C}H_3-\overset{9}{C}H=\overset{8}{C}H-\overset{7}{C}H_2-\overset{6}{C}H=\overset{5}{C}H-\overset{4}{\underset{\underset{C_2H_5}{|}}{C}H}-\overset{3}{C}H_2-\overset{2}{C}H=\overset{1}{C}H_2$
4-ethyldeca-1,5,8-triene

Note *Numbering is done from the side which gives lowest locant to the principle functional group.*

Question 3. For the following compounds, write structural formulae and IUPAC names for all possible isomers having the number of double or triple bond as indicated :
(a) C_4H_8 (one double bond)
(b) C_5H_8 (one triple bond)

     (i) Isomers have the same molecular formula but different structure, so draw all the possible structures for $C_4H_8(C_nH_{2n})$ and C_5H_8 (*i.e.*, C_nH_{2n-2})
     (ii) Write their IUPAC name (as in the previous Q.).

Solution.
(a) Isomers of C_4H_8 having one double bond are :

(i) $\overset{4}{C}H_3\overset{3}{C}H_2-\overset{2}{C}H=\overset{1}{C}H_2$
But-1-ene

(ii) $\overset{4}{C}H_3$ $\overset{3}{C}=\overset{2}{C}$ $\overset{1}{C}H_3$ (H below)
Cis-but-2-ene

(iii) CH_3 $C=C$ H ... H ... CH_3
Trans-but-2-ene

(iv) $CH_3-\underset{|}{\overset{CH_3}{C}}=CH_2$
2-methylprop-1-ene

(b) (i) $\overset{5}{C}H_3\overset{4}{C}H_2\overset{3}{C}H_2\overset{2}{C}\equiv\overset{1}{C}H$
Pent-1-yne

(ii) $\overset{5}{C}H_3\overset{4}{C}H_2-\overset{3}{C}\equiv\overset{2}{C}-\overset{1}{C}H_3$
Pent-2-yne

(iii) $\overset{4}{C}H_3-\overset{3}{C}H-\overset{2}{C}\equiv\overset{1}{C}H$ with $\overset{CH_3}{|}$ on C3
3-methylbut-1-yne

Question 4. Write IUPAC names of the products obtained by the ozonolysis of the following compounds :
(i) Pent-2-ene
(ii) 3,4-dimethylhept-3-ene
(iii) 2-ethylbut-1-ene
(iv) 1-phenylbut-1-ene

     (i) To find the product of ozonolysis, break the double bond and add two O atoms, one with each double bonded C atom.
     (ii) Give the IUPAC name of product obtained.

Solution.

(i) $\overset{5}{C}H_3-\overset{4}{C}H_2-\overset{3}{C}H=\overset{2}{C}H-\overset{1}{C}H_3$
Pent-2-ene $\xrightarrow[\text{(ii) } Zn/H_2O]{\text{(i) } O_3/CH_2Cl_2, 196\ K}$

$\overset{3}{C}H_3-\overset{2}{C}H_2-\overset{1}{C}H=O + O=\overset{1}{C}H-\overset{2}{C}H_3$
Propanal   Ethanal

(ii) $\overset{7}{C}H_3 - \overset{6}{C}H_2 - \overset{5}{C}H_2 - \overset{4}{C} \doteq \overset{3}{C} - \overset{2}{C}H_2 - \overset{1}{C}H_3$ $\xrightarrow[\text{(ii) Zn/H}_2\text{O}]{\text{(i) O}_3/\text{CH}_2\text{Cl}_2,\ 195\ \text{K}}$

$\underset{CH_3}{|}\quad\underset{CH_3}{|}$

3,4-dimethylhept-3-ene

$\overset{5}{C}H_3 - \overset{4}{C}H_2 - \overset{3}{C}H_2 - \overset{O}{\overset{||}{C}} - \overset{1}{C}H_3 + \overset{4}{C}H_3 - \overset{3}{C}H_2 - \overset{O}{\overset{||}{C}} - \overset{1}{C}H_3$

Pentan-2-one   Butan-2-one

(iii) $\overset{4}{C}H_3 - \overset{3}{C}H_2 - \overset{2}{C} = \overset{1}{C}H_2$ $\xrightarrow[\text{(ii) Zn/H}_2\text{O}]{\text{(i) O}_3/\text{CH}_2\text{Cl}_2,\ 195\ \text{K}}$

$\underset{CH_2 - CH_3}{|}$

2-ethylbut-1-ene

$\overset{1}{C}H_3\overset{2}{C}H_2 - \overset{O}{\overset{||}{\underset{3}{C}}} - \overset{4}{C}H_2\overset{5}{C}H_3 + HCHO$

Pentan-3-one   Methanal

(iv) $\overset{4}{C}H_3 - \overset{3}{C}H_2 - \overset{2}{C}H \doteq \overset{1}{C}H - C_6H_5$ $\xrightarrow[\text{(ii) Zn/H}_2\text{O}]{\text{(i) O}_3/\text{CH}_2\text{Cl}_2,\ 195\ \text{K}}$

1-phenylbut-1-ene

$CH_3 - CH_2CHO + C_6H_5CHO$

Propanal   Benzaldehyde

Question 5. An alkene '*A*' on ozonolysis gives a mixture of ethanal and pentan-3-one. Write structure and IUPAC name of '*A*'.

 (i) Write the structures of the products of ozonolysis in such a way that their oxygen atoms pointing towards each other. Join the two ends through a double bond after removal of oxygen atoms to obtain structure of alkene A.

     (ii) Write the IUPAC name of A.

Solution.

$\begin{matrix} \overset{1}{C}H_3 - \overset{2}{C}H_2 \\ \\ \overset{5}{C}H_3 - \overset{4}{C}H_2 \end{matrix}\Big\rangle\overset{3}{C} \doteq O + O \doteq CH - CH_3$

Ethanal

Pentan-3-one

$\begin{matrix} \overset{5}{C}H_3 - \overset{4}{C}H_2 \\ \\ CH_3 - CH_2 \end{matrix}\Big\rangle\overset{3}{C} = \overset{2}{C}H - \overset{1}{C}H_3$

3-ethylpent-2-ene

(A)

Question 6. An alkene '*A*' contains three C—C, eight C—H σ-bonds and one C—C π-bond. '*A*' on ozonolysis gives two moles of an aldehyde of molar mass 44 u. Write IUPAC name of '*A*'.

 (i) Identify the structure of aldehyde, RCHO from the molar mass (44 u) to find the structure of A.

     (ii) Join two molecules of aldehyde to find the structure of A.

     (iii) Count the number of σ and π-bonds in A. Are they satisfy the given data.

Solution. An aldehyde having molar mass 44 u is ethanal, CH_3CHO. Write the structures of two molecules of ethanal in such a way that their oxygen atoms pointing towards each other. Join the two ends through the double bond with the removal of both of the oxygen atoms to obtain alkene *A*.

$$CH_3CH\overset{......}{=}O + O\overset{......}{=}CHCH_3 \longleftarrow CH_3—CH=CH—CH_3$$
Ethanal   Ethanal   (*A*) But-2-ene

$$H\overset{\sigma}{—}\underset{\underset{H}{|\sigma}}{\overset{\overset{H}{|\sigma}}{C}}\overset{\sigma}{—}\underset{}{\overset{\overset{H}{|\sigma}}{C}}\overset{\sigma}{\underset{\pi}{=}}\underset{}{\overset{\overset{H}{|\sigma}}{C}}\overset{\sigma}{—}\underset{\underset{H}{|\sigma}}{\overset{\overset{H}{|\sigma}}{C}}\overset{\sigma}{—}H$$

Hence, alkene (*A*), *i.e.*, but-2-ene contains three C—C, eight C—H, σ-bonds and one C—C π-bond (as given in the question).

Question 7. Propanal and pentan-3-one are the ozonolysis products of an alkene? What is the structural formula of the alkene?

  Write the structures of the products of ozonolysis in such a way that their oxygen atoms pointing towards each other. Join the two ends through a double bond after removal of oxygen atoms to obtain structure of alkene *A*.

Solution. $\overset{3}{C}H_3 \overset{2}{C}H_2\overset{1}{C}H\overset{......}{=}O + O\overset{......}{=}\overset{3}{C}\overset{\overset{2}{C}H_2 \overset{1}{C}H_3}{\underset{\overset{4}{C}H_2 \overset{5}{C}H_3}{<}}$
       Propanal   Pentan-3-one

$$\longleftarrow \overset{6}{C}H_3\overset{5}{C}H_2\overset{4}{C}H=\overset{3}{C}\overset{\overset{2}{C}H_2\overset{1}{C}H_3}{\underset{CH_2CH_3}{<}}$$
                        3-ethylhex-3-ene

Question 8. Write chemical equations for combustion reaction of the following hydrocarbons :

  (i) Butane   (ii) Pentene   (iii) Hexyne   (iv) Toluene

  All hydrocarbons on complete combustion give CO_2 and H_2O.

Solution.

(i) $C_4H_{10}(g) + \dfrac{13}{2}O_2(g) \xrightarrow{\Delta} 4CO_2(g) + 5H_2O(g)$
   Butane

(ii) $C_5H_{10}(g) + \dfrac{15}{2}O_2(g) \xrightarrow{\Delta} 5CO_2(g) + 5H_2O(g)$
   Pentene

(iii) $C_6H_{10}(g) + \dfrac{17}{2}O_2(g) \xrightarrow{\Delta} 6CO_2(g) + 5H_2O(g)$
   Hexyne

(iv) [Toluene structure: benzene ring with CH_3 group] (g) or $C_7H_8(g) + 9O_2(g) \xrightarrow{\Delta} 7CO_2 + 4H_2O(g)$

Toluene

Question 9. Draw the *cis-* and *trans-* structures of hex-2-ene. Which isomer will have higher boiling point and why?

Solution. Hex-2-ene is $CH_3-CH_2-CH_2-CH=CH-CH_3$. The structures of *cis-* and *trans-* isomers of hex-2-ene are

[Cis-form structure: H_3C and H on one carbon, $CH_2CH_2CH_3$ and H on the other, double bond $C=C$]   [Trans-form structure: H_3C and H on one carbon, H and $CH_2CH_2CH_3$ on the other, double bond $C=C$]

      Cis-form   *Trans*-form

Cis- form is more polar than *trans*-form. Due to this *cis*-form has higher dipole moment than *trans*-form. Thus, the boiling point of *cis*-isomer is greater than that of *trans*-isomer because of the greater dipole-dipole interactions between the molecules in it. Further more *trans*-isomer of hex-2-ene is almost non-polar.

Question 10. Why is benzene extra ordinarily stable though it contains three double bonds?

Solution. Resonance and delocalization of electrons generally leads to the stability of benzene molecule.

[Resonance structures of benzene with hybrid structure showing dotted circle]

Hybrid structure

The dotted circle in the hybrid structure represents the six electrons which are delocalized between the six carbon atoms of the benzene ring. Therefore, presence of delocalised π-electrons in benzene makes it more stable than the hypothetical cyclohexatriene.

Question 11. What are the necessary conditions for any system to be aromatic?

Solution. The necessary conditions for any system to be aromatic are
  (i) The molecule should be planar.
 (ii) The molecule should be cyclic with alternate single and double bonds *i.e.*, there is complete delocalisation of the π-electrons in the ring.
(iii) The molecule should contain $(4n + 2)$ π-electrons, where, $n = 0, 1, 2, 3$, etc. (Huckel rule).

     A molecule which does not satisfy any one or more of the above mentioned conditions is said to be non-aromatic.

Question 12.   Explain why the following systems are not aromatic?

(i) 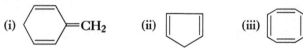   (ii)   (iii)

For a molecule to be aromatic, it should satisfy the following conditions.
(i) It should be planar *i.e.*, all the carbons are sp^2 hybridized.
(ii) It contains $(4n + 2)\ \pi\ e^-$.

Solution.

(i) sp^3  $=CH_2$

Non-aromatic
The molecule is not planar because of the presence of sp^3 hybridized carbon atom. It contains six π-electrons but its π-electron cloud does not surround all the carbon atoms of the ring. Therefore, it is not an aromatic compound.

(ii)

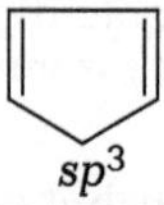

sp^3
Non-aromatic

The molecule is not planar because of the presence of sp^3 hybridized carbon atom. Moreover, it contains only 4π-electrons. Thus, the molecule is not aromatic as it does not contain planar cyclic electron cloud, having $(4n + 2)\ \pi$-electrons.

(iii)

Non-aromatic
Cyclo octatetraene is non-planar with 8π-electrons and hence, it is not aromatic.

Question 13.   How will you convert benzene into
(i) *p*-nitrobromobenzene   (ii) *m*-nitrochlorobenzene
(iii) *p*-nitrotoluene   (iv) acetophenone?

(i) Bromo is *o/p*-directing while NO_2 is *m*-directing, so to obtain *p*-nitrobromobenzene, do bromination, followed by nitration.
(ii) Chloro is *o/p*-directing while NO_2 is *m*-directing, so to obtain *m*-nitrochlorobenzene, do nitration followed by chlorination.
(iii) —CH_3 is *o/p*-directing while NO_2 is *m*-directing, so to obtion *p*-nitro toluene do Friedel Craft's alkylation followed by nitration.
(vi) Friedel Craft's acylation introduces a—COR group.

Solution.

(i) Since, the two substituents in the benzene ring are present at *p*-position, therefore, the first substituent in the benzene ring should be a *o, p*-directing group.

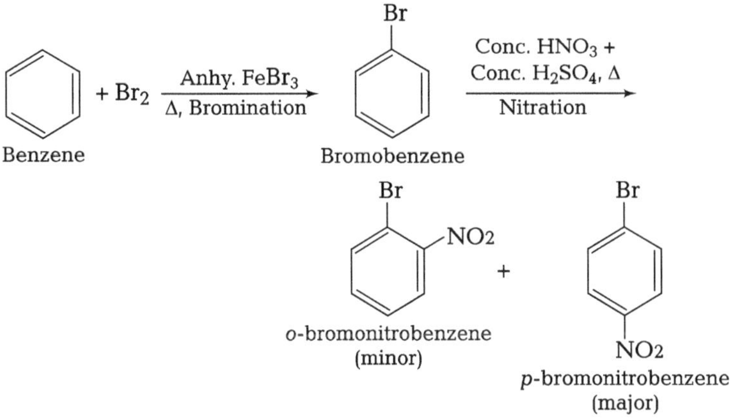

Benzene $+ Br_2$ $\xrightarrow[\Delta, \text{Bromination}]{\text{Anhy. FeBr}_3}$ Bromobenzene $\xrightarrow[\text{Nitration}]{\text{Conc. HNO}_3 + \text{Conc. H}_2\text{SO}_4, \Delta}$

o-bromonitrobenzene (minor)

+

p-bromonitrobenzene (major)

(ii) Since, the two substituents in the benzene ring are present at *m*-positions, therefore, the first substituent in the benzene ring should be *m*-directing.

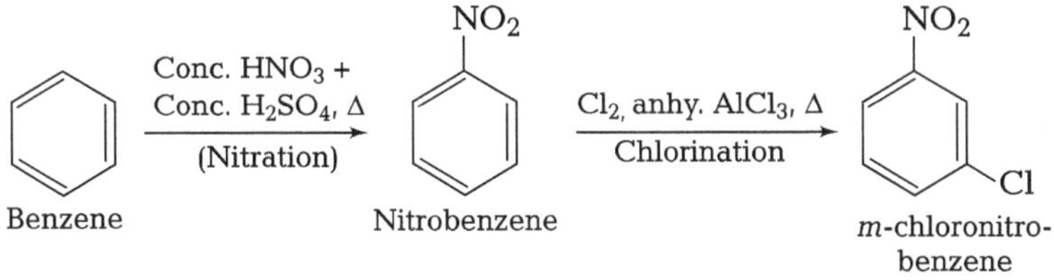

Benzene $\xrightarrow[\text{(Nitration)}]{\text{Conc. HNO}_3 + \text{Conc. H}_2\text{SO}_4, \Delta}$ Nitrobenzene $\xrightarrow[\text{Chlorination}]{\text{Cl}_2, \text{anhy. AlCl}_3, \Delta}$ *m*-chloronitro-benzene

(iii) Benzene $\xrightarrow[\text{anhy. AlCl}_3]{\text{CH}_3\text{Cl,}}$ Toluene $\xrightarrow[\Delta, \text{Nitration}]{\text{Dil. HNO}_3 + \text{Dil. H}_2\text{SO}_4}$

o-nitrotoluene (minor)

+

p-nitrotoluene (major)

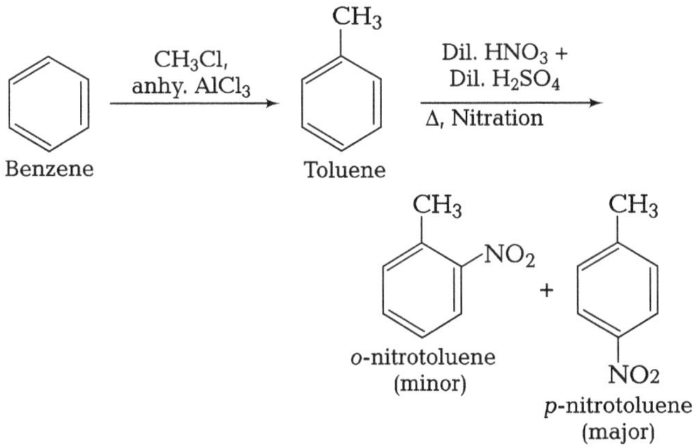

(iv) Acetophenone can be prepared by Friedel Crafts acylation.

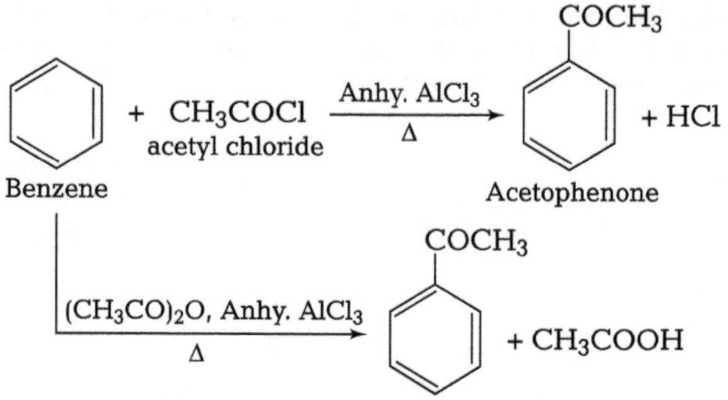

Question 14. In the alkane $H_3CCH_2-C(CH_3)_2-CH_2CH(CH_3)_2$, identify $1°, 2°, 3°$ carbon atoms and give the number of H-atoms bonded to each one of these.

The carbon which is attached with only 1 or no other carbon atom, is called 1° carbon. Similarly, carbon attached with 2, 3 or 4 other carbon atoms is called 2°, 3°, or 4° carbon atom respectively. Similarly, hydrogens attached with 1°, 2°, 3° or 4° carbon atoms are called 1°, 2°, 3° or 4° hydrogens respectively.

Solution.

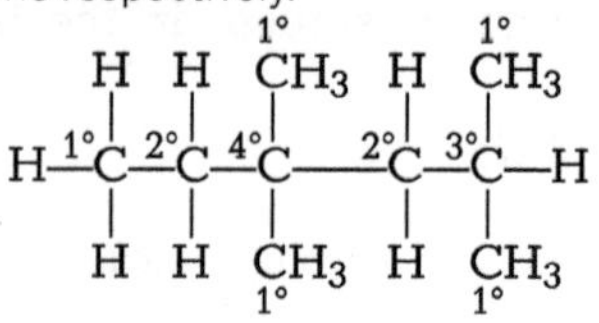

$$H-\overset{1°}{\underset{}{C}}-\overset{2°}{\underset{}{C}}-\overset{4°}{\underset{}{C}}-\overset{2°}{\underset{}{C}}-\overset{3°}{\underset{}{C}}-H$$

15 H-bonded to five 1°C-atoms
4 H-bonded to two 2°C-atoms
1 H-bonded to one 3°C-atom

Question 15. What effect does branching of an alkane chain has on its boiling point?

Boiling point depends upon the forces of attraction and as the size of chain increases van der waals' forces increases.

Solution. van der Waals' force of attractions ∝ surface area. Surface area decreases with increase in branching. Hence, boiling point of an alkane decreases with increase in branching due to decrease in van der Waals' forces of attractions.

Question 16. Addition of HBr to propene yields 2-bromopropane, while in the presence of benzoyl peroxide, the same reaction yields 1-bromopropane. Explain and give mechanism.

In the absence of peroxide, the reaction occurs by cationic mechanism while in the presence of peroxide, it follows free radical mechanism.

Solution. Addition of HBr to propene (uneven alkene) occurs through **Markownikoff's rule.**

Mechanism HBr provides an electrophile, H^+ which attacks double bond to form carbocation.

(i) $H\overset{\frown}{-}Br \longrightarrow H^+ + Br^-$

(ii) $CH_3—CH{=}CH_2 + H^+ \longrightarrow \underset{\text{1° carbocation (less stable)}}{CH_3—CH_2—\overset{+}{C}H_2}$

$\downarrow$ 1,2-hydride shift

$\underset{\text{2° carbocation (more stable)}}{CH_3—\overset{+}{C}H—CH_3}$

The 2° carbocation is attacked by Br^- ion to form the product as follows

(iii) $\overset{\frown}{Br^-} + CH_3—\overset{+}{C}H—CH_3 \longrightarrow CH_3—\underset{\underset{\text{Br}}{|}}{C}H—CH_3$

2-bromopropane
(major product)

In the presence of benzoyl peroxide, addition of HBr to propene (unsymmetrical alkene) takes place against Markownikoff's rule.

(This happens only with HBr but not with HCl or HI). This reaction is known as peroxide or Kharash effect or addition reaction anti to Markownikoff's rule.

Mechanism

(i) $C_6H_5—\overset{\overset{O}{||}}{C}—O—O—\overset{\overset{O}{||}}{C}—C_6H_5 \xrightarrow{\text{Homolysis}}$

$2C_6H_5—\overset{\overset{O}{||}}{C}—\overset{\cdot\cdot}{\underset{\cdot\cdot}{O}}{:} \longrightarrow 2\overset{\cdot}{C}_6H_5 + 2CO_2$

(ii) $\overset{\cdot}{C}_6H_5 + H—Br \xrightarrow{\text{Homolysis}} C_6H_6 + Br^{\cdot}$

(iii) $CH_3—CH{=}CH_2 + \overset{\cdot}{Br} \longrightarrow CH_3—\underset{\underset{\text{Br}}{|}}{C}H—\overset{\cdot}{C}H_2 +$

1° free radical (less stable)

$CH_3—\overset{\cdot}{C}H—CH_2—Br$
2° free radical (more stable)

(iv) $CH_3—\overset{\cdot}{C}H—CH_2Br + H—Br \xrightarrow{\text{Homolysis}} CH_3—CH_2—CH_2Br + \overset{\cdot}{Br}$

1-bromo propane
(major product)

(v) $CH_3-\overset{|}{\underset{Br}{CH}}-\overset{\bullet}{CH_2} + H-Br \xrightarrow{\text{Homolysis}} CH_3-\overset{|}{\underset{Br}{CH}}-CH_3 + \overset{\bullet}{Br}$

2-bromo propane
(minor product)

Question 17. Write down the products of ozonolysis of 1,2-dimethyl benzene (o-xylene). How does the result support Kekule structure of benzene?

Solution.

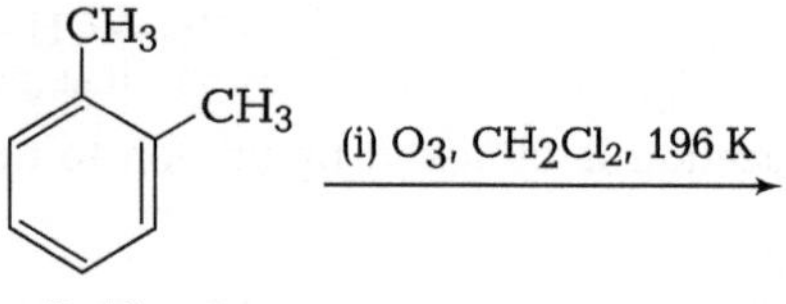

1,2-dimethyl benzene

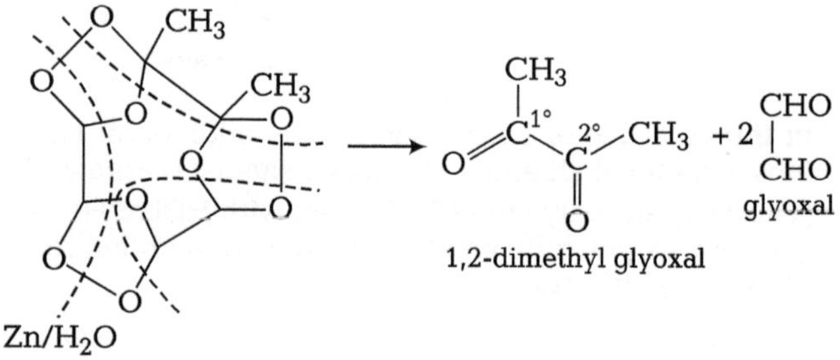

(i) O_3, CH_2Cl_2, 196 K

$+2 \begin{array}{l} CHO \\ | \\ CHO \end{array}$ glyoxal

1,2-dimethyl glyoxal

Similarly,

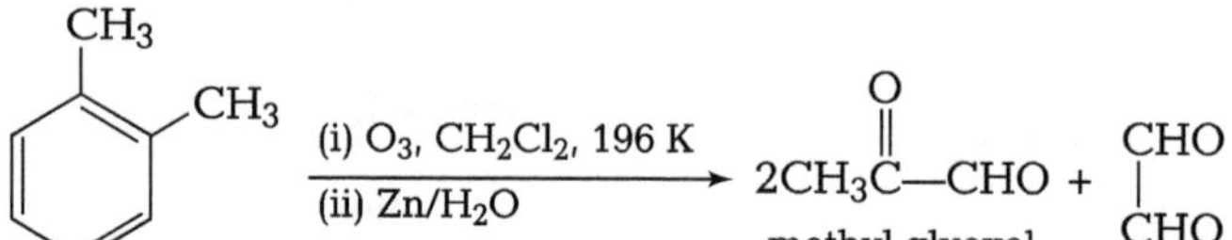

(i) O_3, CH_2Cl_2, 196 K
(ii) Zn/H_2O

$2CH_3\overset{O}{\overset{||}{C}}-CHO +$ methyl glyoxal

$\begin{array}{l} CHO \\ | \\ CHO \end{array}$ glyoxal

All the three products can not be obtained from any one of the two Kekule structures. This indicates that o-xylene is a resonance hybrid of two Kekule structures I and II.

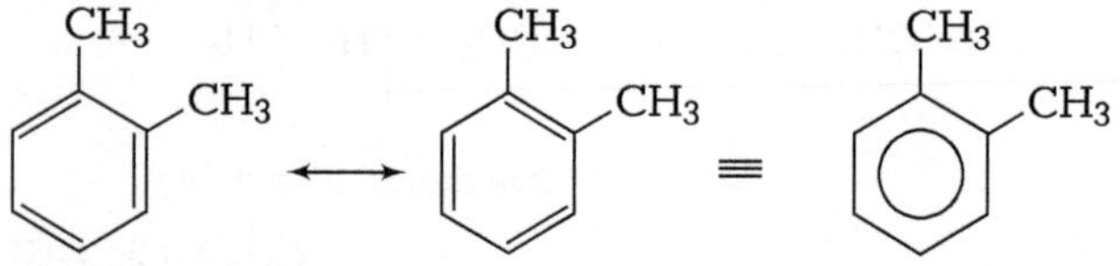

I   II   Resonance hybrid

Question 18. Arrange benzene, n-hexane and ethyne in decreasing order of acidic behaviour. Also give reason for this behaviour.

Higher the s-character, higher is the acidity, so first find hybridization of all the given compounds and then compare their acidity.

Solution. The hybridization state of carbon in the given compounds is

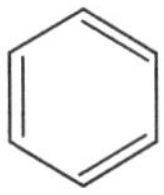

		$CH_3—(CH_2)_4—CH_3$	$H—C\equiv C—H$
	Benzene	Hexane	Ethyne
Type of hybridization	sp^2	sp^3	sp
s-character	33.33%	25%	50%

Acidic character increases with increase in s-character of the orbital. Hence, decreasing order of acidic behaviour of benzene, n-hexane and ethyne is as follows

Ethyne > Benzene > Hexane

Question 19. Why does benzene undergo electrophilic substitution reactions easily and nucleophilic substitutions with difficulty?

Solution. Due to the presence of delocalized 6π-electrons, benzene acts as a rich source of electrons. So, it attracts the electrophilic reagent (electron deficient species) towards itself but repels the nucleophilic reagents. That's why benzene gives electrophilic substitution reactions easily and nucleophilic substitution reactions with difficulty.

Question 20. How would you convert the following compounds into benzene?

(i) Ethyne (ii) Ethene (iii) Hexane

Solution (i) $3HC\equiv CH \xrightarrow[873\ K]{\text{Red hot iron tube}}$
Ethyne — Benzene

(ii) $CH_2=CH_2 \xrightarrow{Br_2/CCl_4} CH_2(Br)—CH_2(Br) \xrightarrow[\text{dehydrobromination}]{\text{Alc. KOH, }\Delta}$
Ethene

$CH_2=CHBr \xrightarrow[196\ K,\ \text{dehydrobromination}]{NaNH_2/\text{liq. }NH_3}$
Vinyl bromide

$HC\equiv CH \xrightarrow[873\ K]{\text{Red hot Fe tube}}$
Ethyne — Benzene

(iii)

$\xrightarrow[Mo_2O_3\text{-}Al_2O_3\ \text{cyclization}]{Cr_2O_3/V_2O_5,\ (-H_2)}$ $\xrightarrow[(-3H_2)]{\text{Aromatisation}}$
Cyclohexane — Benzene

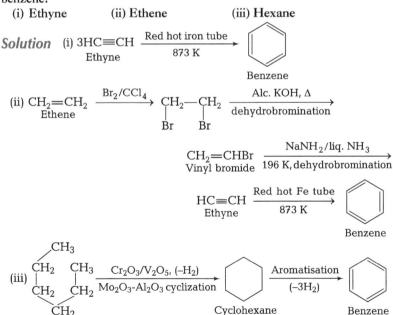

Question 21. Write structures of all the alkenes which on hydrogenation give 2-methyl butane.

Solution. Structure of 2-methyl butane is

$$\overset{1}{C}H_3 - \overset{2}{C}H - \overset{3}{C}H_2 - \overset{4}{C}H_3$$
$$\overset{|}{CH_3}$$
2-methyl butane

Put the double bonds at different positions and also satisfy the tetravalency of each carbon atom in the molecule.

$$CH_2=C-CH_2-CH_3, \quad CH_3-C=CH-CH_3, \quad CH_3-CH-CH=CH_2$$
$$\qquad \overset{|}{CH_3} \qquad\qquad\qquad \overset{|}{CH_3} \qquad\qquad\qquad \overset{|}{CH_3}$$
2-methylbut-1-ene   2-methylbut-2-ene   3-methylbut-1-ene

Question 22. Arrange the following set of compounds in order of their decreasing relative reactivity with an electrophile, E^+

(a) Chlorobenzene, 2,4-dinitrochlorobenzene, *p*-nitrochlorobenzene

(b) Toluene, $p\text{-}H_3C-C_6H_4-NO_2$, $p\text{-}O_2N-C_6H_4-NO_2$

(i) As the number of electron withdrawing groups increases, reactivity of benzene nucleus towards E^+ decreases.

(ii) An electron releasing group activates the nucleus for electrophilic substitution while an electron withdrawing group deactivates it towards E^+.

Solution. Presence of electron releasing group (or activating group) increases the electron density in benzene nucleus. Therefore, electrophile will attack benzene nucleus easily. But the presence of electron withdrawing group like $-NO_2$ decreases the electron density in benzene ring. Therefore, electrophile will attack benzene nucleus with difficulty.

The order of reactivity towards electrophile, E^+ in order of their decreasing relative reactivity is

(a) Chlorobenzene > *p*-nitrochlorobenzene > 2,4-dinitrochlorobenzene

(b) Toluene > $p\text{-}CH_3-C_6H_4-NO_2$ > $p\text{-}O_2N-C_6H_4-NO_2$

Question 23. Out of benzene, *m*-dinitrobenzene and toluene which will undergo nitration most easily and why?

Nitration is an electrophilic substitution reaction and reactivity of benzene nucleus towards E^+ decreases in the presence of electron withdrawing group while increases in the presence of electron releasing group.

Solution. Nitration of benzene is an electrophilic substitution reaction. Presence of electron releasing group such as $-CH_3$ activates the benzene nucleus towards electrophilic substitution while presence of electron withdrawing group such as $-NO_2$ deactivates the benzene nucleus towards electrophilic substitution.

Therefore, the ease of nitration decreases in the order

Toluene > benzene > *m*-dinitrobenzene

Thus, toluene will undergo nitration most easily.

Question 24. Suggest the name of a Lewis acid other than anhydrous aluminium chloride which can be used during ethylation of benzene.

Solution.

$$\text{Benzene} + C_2H_5Cl \xrightarrow{\text{Anhy. } AlCl_3} \text{Ethylbenzene} \; (C_2H_5)$$

In ethylation of benzene, ethyl group is introduced in the benzene ring. This is carried out by Friedel Crafts alkylation reaction of benzene. Anhydrous $FeCl_3$ or $SnCl_4$ can be used in place of anhydrous $AlCl_3$ as a catalyst.

Question 25. Why is Wurtz reaction not preferred for the preparation of alkanes containing odd number of carbon atoms? Illustrate your answer by taking one example.

Solution. For the preparation of alkanes containing odd number of carbon atoms, two different alkyl halides are taken and two different alkyl halides can react in three different ways. Therefore, a mixture of alkanes is produced, e.g.,

$$3CH_3I + 6Na + 3C_2H_5I \xrightarrow{\text{Dry ether}} CH_3-CH_3 \;(\text{Ethane}) + CH_3CH_2CH_3 \;(\text{Propane})$$
$$+ CH_3CH_2CH_2CH_3 \;(\text{Butane}) + 6NaI$$

That's why this method (Wurtz reaction) is not suitable for the preparation of odd number alkanes.

Selected NCERT Exemplar Problems

Short Answer Type

Question 1. Why do alkenes prefer to undergo electrophilic addition reaction while arenes prefer electrophilic substitution reactions? Explain.

Solution. Alkenes are rich source of loosely held pi(π) electrons, due to which they show electrophilic addition reaction. Electrophilic addition reactions of alkenes are accompanied by large energy changes so these are energetically favourable than that of electrophilic substitution reactions.

In special conditions alkenes also undergo free radical substitution reactions.

In arenes during electrophilic addition reactions aromatic character of benzene ring is destroyed while during electrophilic substitution reactions it remains intact. Electrophilic substitution reactions of arenes are energetically more favourable than that of electrophilic addition reaction.

That's why alkenes prefer to undergo electrophilic addition reaction while arenes prefer electrophilic substitution reactions.

Question 2. Alkynes on reduction with sodium in liquid ammonia form *trans*-alkenes. Will the butene thus formed on reduction of 2-butyne show geometrical isomerism?

Solution. $\overset{4}{C}H_3 - \overset{3}{C} \equiv \overset{2}{C} - \overset{1}{C}H_3$ $\xrightarrow[\text{196}-\text{200 K}]{\text{Na, liquid NH}_3}$

$$\underset{H}{\overset{CH_3}{>}}C=C\underset{CH_3}{\overset{H}{<}}$$

2-butyne   *Trans*-2-butene

Trans-2-butene formed by the reduction of 2-butyne is capable of showing geometrical isomerism.

Question 3. Draw Newman and Sawhorse projections for the eclipsed and staggered conformations of ethane. Which of these conformations is more stable and why?

Angle of rotation or angle of torsional or dihedral angle

Solution

(i) Eclipsed   (i) Staggered   (i) Eclipsed   (i) Staggered

Sawhorse projections of ethane   Newman projections of ethane

Staggered form of ethane is more stable than the eclipsed conformation, by about 12.5 kJ mol^{-1}. This is because any two hydrogen atoms on adjacent carbon atoms of staggered conformation are maximum apart while in eclipsed conformation, they cover or eclipse each other in space. Thus, in staggered form, there is minimum repulsive forces, minimum energy and maximum stability of the molecule.

Question 4. The intermediate carbocation formed in the reactions of HI, HBr and HCl with propene is the same and the bond energy of HCl, HBr and HI is 430.5 kJ mol^{-1}, 363.7 kJ mol^{-1} and 296.8 kJ mol^{-1} respectively. What will be the order of reactivity of these halogen acids?

Solution. Addition of halogen acids to an alkene is a electrophilic addition reaction.

$$CH_3 - CH = CH_2 + H^+ \xrightarrow[\text{Ist step}]{\text{Slow}} CH_3 - \overset{+}{C}H - CH_3$$

$$\xrightarrow[\text{IInd step}]{X^-, \text{ fast}} CH_3 - \underset{X}{\overset{|}{C}H} - CH_3$$

Ist step is slow so, it is rate determining step. The rate of this step depends upon the availability of proton. This in turn depends upon the bond dissociation enthalpy of the H—X molecule. Lower the bond dissociation enthalpy of H—X molecule, greater the reactivity of halogen halide.

HI(296.8 kJ) > HBr (363.7 kJ) > HCl (430.5 kJ)

(Reactivity in decreasing order)

Question 5. What will be the product obtained as a result of the following reaction and why?

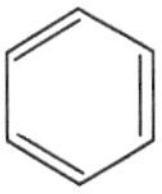

Solution. $CH_3-CH_2-CH_2-Cl + AlCl_3 \xrightarrow[-AlCl_4^-]{}$

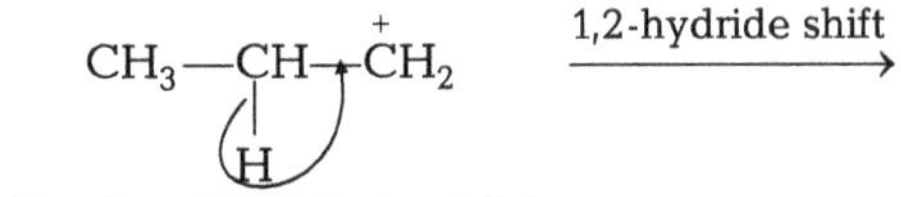

$CH_3-\overset{+}{CH}-CH_2$ (with H)   1,2-hydride shift $\longrightarrow$

1° carbocation (electrophile)
(less stable)

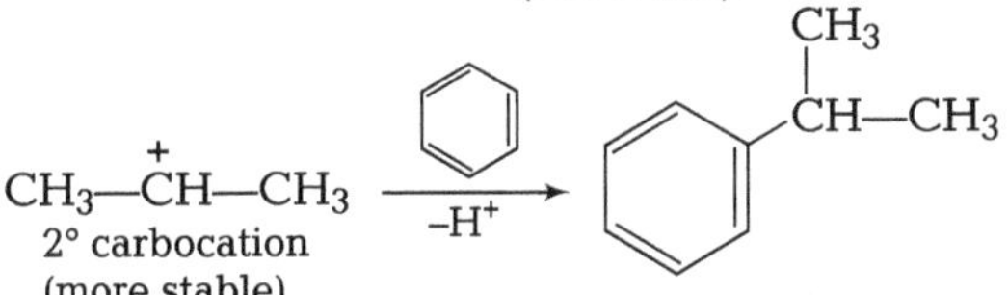

$CH_3-\overset{+}{CH}-CH_3$
2° carbocation
(more stable)

$\xrightarrow[-H^+]{}$

Iso-propyl benzene

When Friedel Crafts alkylation is carried out with higher alkyl halide, e.g., n-propyl chloride, then the electrophile, n-propyl carbocation (1° carbocation) rearranges to form more stable iso-propyl carbocation (2° carbocation) and the main product formed will be iso-propyl benzene.

Question 7. Arrange the following set of compounds in the order of their decreasing relative reactivity with an electrophile. Give reason.

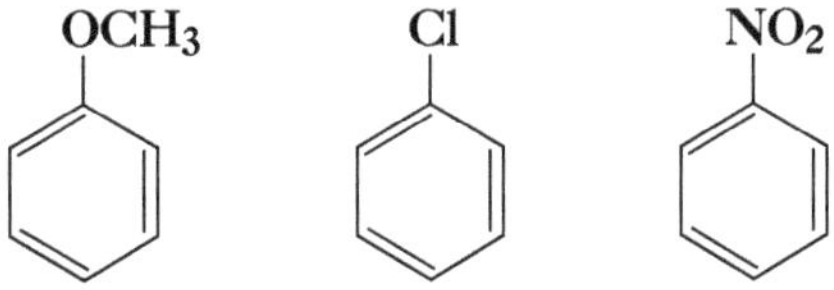

OCH₃   Cl   NO₂

Solution. —OCH_3 (methoxy group) is electron releasing group. It increases the electron density in benzene nucleus due to resonance effect (+ R effect). Hence, makes anisole more reactive than benzene towards electrophiles.

In case of aryl halides, halogens are moderately deactivating because of their strong – I effect, thus, overall electron density on benzene ring decreases. It makes further substitution difficult. —NO_2 group is electron withdrawing group. It decrease the electron density in benzene nucleus due to strong $-I$ effect. Hence, makes nitrobenzene less reactive. Therefore, overall reactivity of these three compounds towards electrophiles decreases in the following order

Anisol   Chlorobenzene   Nitrobenzene

Question 8. Despite their $-I$ effect, halogens are *o*- and *p*-directing in haloarenes. Explain.

Solution. Halogens are moderately deactivating group. Because of their strong $-I$ effect, overall electron density on benzene ring decreases. However, due to resonance the electron density on *o*- and *p*-positions is greater than that at *m*-position. Hence, they are also *o*- and *p*-directing groups.

Question 9. Suggest a route for the preparation of nitrobenzene starting from acetylene?

Solution $3CH{\equiv}CH \xrightarrow[\substack{873\ K \\ (\text{Cyclic polymerization})}]{\text{Red hot Fe tube}}$

Acetylene

Benzene

$\xrightarrow[\substack{333\ K\ (\text{nitration})}]{\text{Conc. } HNO_3 + \text{Conc. } H_2SO_4}$

Nitrobenzene

Question 10. Nucleophiles and electrophiles are reaction intermediates having electron rich and electron deficient centres respectively. Hence, they tend to attack electron deficient and electron rich centres respectively. Classify the following species as electrophiles and nucleophiles.

(i) H_3CO^- (ii) $H_3C{-}\overset{\overset{\displaystyle O}{\|}}{C}{-}O^-$ (iii) $\overset{\bullet}{Cl}$ (iv) $Cl_2C\!:$

(v) $(H_3C)_3C^+$ (vi) Br^- (vii) H_3COH

(viii) $R{-}NH{-}R$

Solution. Electrophiles are electron deficient species. These may be neutral or positively charged.

$$\underset{\text{(iii)}}{\overset{\bullet}{Cl}}, \underset{\text{(iv)}}{Cl_2C\!:}, \underset{\text{(v)}}{(H_3C)_3C^+}$$

Nucleophiles are electron rich species. These may be neutral or negatively charged.

$$H_3CO^-, H_3C-\overset{\overset{O}{\|}}{C}-O^-, Br^-, H_3C-\overset{..}{\underset{..}{O}}-H, R\overset{..}{N}HR$$

(i)   (ii)   (vi)   (vii)   (viii)

Question 11. The relative reactivity of 1°, 2°, 3° hydrogen's towards chlorination is 1 : 3.8 : 5. Calculate the percentages of all monochlorinated products obtained from 2-methylbutane.

Solution.

$$\underset{(1°)}{CH_3}-\underset{(3°)}{\overset{\overset{(1°)}{CH_3}}{CH}}-\underset{(2°)}{CH_2}-\underset{(1°)}{CH_3}$$

Relative amount of monochlorinated product

= Number of hydrogen × relative reactivity

For (1°) monochlorinated product = 9 × 1 = 9

(2°) monochlorinated product = 2 × 3.8 = 7.6

(3°) monochlorinated product = 1 × 5 = 5

Total amount of monochlorinated compounds = 9 + 7.6 + 5 = 21.6

% of 1° monochlorinated product = $\dfrac{9 \times 100}{21.6}$ = 41.67

% of 2° monochlorinated product = $\dfrac{7.6 \times 100}{21.6}$ = 35.18

% of 3° monochlorinated product = $\dfrac{5 \times 100}{21.6}$ = 23.15

Question 12. Write hydrocarbon radicals that can be formed as intermediates during monochlorination of 2-methylpropane. Which of them is more stable? Give reasons.

Solution. 2-methylpropane gives two types of radicals.

$$\underset{(2\text{-methylpropane})}{CH_3-\overset{\overset{CH_3}{|}}{CH}-CH_3} \longrightarrow \underset{(I)}{CH_3-\overset{\overset{CH_3}{|}}{\underset{\bullet}{C}}-CH_3} \text{ and } \underset{(II)}{CH_3-\overset{\overset{CH_3}{|}}{CH}-\overset{\bullet}{CH_2}}$$

Radical (I) is more stable because it is 3° and stabilized by nine hyperconjugative structures (as it has 9 α-hydrogens).

Radical (II) is less stable because it is 1° and stabilized by only one hyperconjugative structure (as it has only 1 α-hydrogen).

Question 13. An alkane C_8H_{18} is obtained as the only product on subjecting a primary alkyl halide to Wurtz reaction. On monobromination this alkane yields a single isomer of a tertiary bromide. Write the structure of alkane and the tertiary bromide.

Solution. Since, alkane C_8H_{18} on monobromination yields a single isomer of a tertiary bromide, therefore alkane must contain tertiary hydrogen. This is possible if primary alkyl halide (which undergoes Wurtz reaction) has a tertiary hydrogen.

$$\underset{\text{1-halo-2-methylpropane}}{CH_3-\overset{\overset{\displaystyle CH_3}{|}}{CH}-CH_2-X} + 2Na + X-CH_2-\overset{\overset{\displaystyle CH_3}{|}}{CH}-CH_3$$

$$\xrightarrow[\text{Wurtz reaction}]{\Delta,\ -2NaX} \underset{\text{2,5-dimethylhexane (alkane)}}{\overset{6}{CH_3}-\overset{5}{\overset{\overset{\displaystyle CH_3}{|}}{CH}}-\overset{4}{CH_2}-\overset{3}{CH_2}-\overset{2}{\overset{\overset{\displaystyle CH_3}{|}}{CH}}-\overset{1}{CH_3}}$$

$$\xrightarrow[-HBr]{Br_2,\ h\nu} \underset{\substack{\text{Br} \\ \text{2-bromo-2,5-dimethylhexane} \\ (3^\circ \text{ bromide})}}{\overset{1}{CH_3}-\overset{2}{\underset{|}{\overset{\overset{\displaystyle CH_3}{|}}{C}}}-\overset{3}{CH_2}-\overset{4}{CH_2}-\overset{5}{\overset{\overset{\displaystyle CH_3}{|}}{CH}}-\overset{6}{CH_3}}$$

Question 14. Suggest a route to prepare ethyl hydrogen sulphate $(CH_3-CH_2-OSO_2-OH)$ starting from ethanol (C_2H_5OH).

Solution. **Step I: Protonation of alcohol**

$$H_2SO_4 \longrightarrow H^+ + \bar{O}SO_2OH$$

$$CH_3CH_2-\overset{..}{\underset{..}{O}}H + H^+ \rightleftharpoons CH_3-CH_2\overset{+}{\overset{..}{\underset{..}{O}}}\begin{smallmatrix}H\\H\end{smallmatrix}$$

Ethanol   Protonated ethanol

Step II: Attack of nucleophile

$$\underset{\text{Hydrogen sulphate ion}}{HO-SO_2-O^-} + CH_3-CH_2-\overset{+}{\overset{..}{O}}\begin{smallmatrix}H\\H\end{smallmatrix} \xrightarrow{383\ K}$$

$$\underset{\text{Ethyl hydrogen sulphate}}{CH_3-CH_2-OSO_2OH} + H_2O$$

Temperature should not be allowed to rise above 383 K, otherwise diethyl ether will be produced at 413 K or ethene at 433 K.

Long Answer Type

Question 15. An alkyl halide $C_5H_{11}Br(A)$ reacts with ethanolic KOH to give an alkene 'B', which reacts with Br_2 to give a compound 'C', which on dehydrobromination gives an alkyne 'D'. On treatment with sodium metal in liquid ammonia, one mole of 'D' gives one mole of the sodium salt of 'D' and half a mole of hydrogen gas. Complete hydrogenation of 'D' yields a straight chain alkane. Identify A, B, C and D. Give the reactions involved.

Solution. 1 mole of alkyne D gives 1 mole of sodium-alkynide and $\frac{1}{2}$ mole of H$_2$. Further more D gives straight chain alkane on hydrogenation, and is obtained from five membered compound therefore, D must be five membered straight chain terminal alkyne, *i.e.,*

1-pentyne. Since, alkene B on reaction with Br_2 forms a compound 'C' which on dehydrohalogenation, gives 1-pentyne, therefore, 'C' must be 1,2-dibromopentane and alkene 'B' must be 1-pentene.

Since, alkene 'B' is obtained by dehydrohalogenation of alkyl halide, therefore, alkyl halide A must be 1-bromopentane.

Reactions are as follows :

$$\underset{\text{1-bromopentane }(A)}{CH_3CH_2CH_2CH_2CH_2Br} \xrightarrow[-\text{ HBr}]{\text{Alc. KOH, } \Delta} \underset{\text{1-pentene }(B)}{CH_3CH_2CH_2CH=CH_2} \xrightarrow{Br_2 \text{ in } CS_2}$$

$$\underset{\text{1, 2-dibromopentane }(C)}{CH_3CH_2CH_2\overset{2}{-}\overset{}{CHBr}\overset{1}{-}CH_2Br} \xrightarrow[-\text{ 2HBr}]{\text{Alc. KOH, } \Delta} \underset{\text{1-pentyne }(D)}{CH_3CH_2CH_2C\equiv CH}$$

$$\xrightarrow{\text{Na in liq. } NH_3} \underset{\text{Sodium 1-pentynide}}{CH_3CH_2CH_2C\equiv CNa} + \frac{1}{2}H_2$$

Question 16. 896 mL vapour of a hydrocarbon 'A' having carbon 87.80% and hydrogen 12.19% weighs 3.28 g at STP. Hydrogenation of 'A' gives 2-methylpentane. Also 'A' on hydration in the presence of H_2SO_4 and $HgSO_4$ gives a ketone 'B' having molecular formula $C_6H_{12}O$. The ketone 'B' gives a positive iodoform test. Find the structure of 'A' and give the reactions involved.

Solution.

(i) Determination of empirical formula of hydrocarbon A

Element	% age	Atomic mass	Relative ratio	Relative no.of atoms	Simplest ratio
C	87.8	12	$\dfrac{87.8}{12} = 7.31$	$\dfrac{7.31}{7.31} = 1$	$1 \times 3 = 3$
H	12.19	1	$\dfrac{12.19}{1} = 12.19$	$\dfrac{12.19}{7.31} = 1.66$	$1.66 \times 3 = 5$

∴ Empirical formula of hydrocarbon $(A) = C_3H_5$

Empirical formula mass $= 12 \times 3 + 5 \times 1 = 41$ u

(ii) Determination of molecular mass of hydrocarbon (A)

896 mL vapours of hydrocarbon (A) weigh at STP $= 3.28$ g

∴ 22400 mL vapours of A will weigh at STP

$$= \frac{3.28 \times 22400}{896} \text{ g mol}^{-1} = 82 \text{ g}$$

∴ Molecular mass of hydrocarbon $(A) = 82$ g mol^{-1}

(iii) Determination of molecular formula of hydrocarbon A.

$$n = \frac{\text{Molecular mass}}{\text{Empirical formula mass}} = \frac{82}{41} = 2$$

Therefore, molecular formula of hydrocarbon

$(A) = n \times$ Empirical formula $= 2 \times C_3H_5 = C_6H_{10}$

Since, hydrogenation of *A* gives 2-methyl pentane therefore compound '*A*' have 5 carbon atoms in straight chain. It should be an alkyne because compound '*A*' adds a molecule of H_2O in the presence of Hg^{2+} and H^+ to give a ketone '*B*'. Ketone '*B*' gives iodoform test so it should be a methyl ketone. Therefore, the structures of compound *A* and compound *B* are as follows :

$$CH_3—\overset{\overset{\displaystyle CH_3}{|}}{C}H—CH_2—C{\equiv}CH \quad \xrightarrow[Hg^{2+}]{H_2O/H^+}$$

4-methylpent-1-yne
(*A*)

$$CH_3—\overset{\overset{\displaystyle CH_3}{|}}{C}H—CH_2—\overset{\overset{\displaystyle O}{||}}{C}—CH_3$$

4-methylpentan-2-one
(*B*)

Question 17. An unsaturated hydrocarbon '*A*' adds two molecules of H_2 and on reductive ozonolysis gives butane-1,4-dial, ethanal and propanone. Give the structure of '*A*', write its IUPAC name and explain the reactions involved.

Solution. Hydrocarbon '*A*' adds two molecules of H_2, therefore '*A*' is either an alkadiene or an alkyne. On reductive ozonolysis '*A*' gives three fragments one of which is dialdehyde. It means molecule has broken down at two sites, therefore, '*A*' has two double bonds. It gives the following three fragments.

$$\underset{\text{(Butane-1,4-dial)}}{OHC—CH_2—CH_2—CHO}, \quad \underset{\text{(Ethanal)}}{CH_3CHO} \text{ and } \underset{\text{(Propanone)}}{CH_3COCH_3}$$

Hence, the structure of compound *A* is

$$CH_3\overset{\overset{\displaystyle H}{|}}{C}{=}O + O{=}\overset{\overset{\displaystyle H}{|}}{C}—CH_2—CH_2—\overset{\overset{\displaystyle H}{|}}{C}{=}O + O{=}\overset{\overset{\displaystyle CH_3}{|}}{C}—CH_3$$

$$\underset{8}{CH_3}\underset{7}{CH}{=}\underset{6}{CH}—\underset{5}{CH_2}—\underset{4}{CH_2}—\underset{3}{CH}{=}\underset{2}{\overset{\overset{\displaystyle CH_3}{|}}{C}}—\underset{1}{CH_3}$$

(*A*) 2-methylocta-2,6-diene

$$A \xrightarrow{O_3} CH_3{-}CH \quad CH{-}CH_2{-}CH_2{-}CH \quad C{\overset{\diagup CH_3}{\diagdown CH_3}} \xrightarrow{Zn/H_2O}$$

Diozonide

$$\underset{\text{Ethanal}}{CH_3CHO} + \underset{\text{Butane-1, 2-dial}}{CHO{-}CH_2{-}CH_2{-}CHO} + \underset{\text{Propanone}}{CH_3COCH_3}$$

$$\underset{\text{(A)}}{CH_3CH{=}CHCH_2{-}CH_2{-}CH{=}C(CH_3)_2} \xrightarrow[Ni]{2H_2} \underset{\text{2-methyloctane}}{CH_3(CH_2)_5C(CH_3)_2}$$

Question 18. In the presence of peroxide, addition of HBr to propene takes place according to anti-Markownikoff's rule but peroxide effect is not seen in the case of HCl and HI. Explain.

Solution. Peroxide effect in not observed in addition of HCl and HI. This is due to the fact that the H—Cl bond being stronger $(430.5 \text{ kJ mol}^{-1})$ than H—Br bond $(363.7 \text{ kJ mol}^{-1})$ is not cleaved by the free radical whereas the H—I bond is weaker $(296.8 \text{ kJ mol}^{-1})$ and iodine free radicals combine to form iodine molecules instead of adding to the double bond.

It can also be explained on the basis of thermodynamic data. The enthalpy change for the steps involved in the free radical addition reactions of hydrogen halides are

HX	ΔH_1 $X^\circ + CH_2{=}CH_2 \rightarrow XCH_2\overset{\bullet}{C}H_2$	ΔH_2 $X\,CH_2\overset{\bullet}{C}H_2 + HX \rightarrow CH_3CH_2X$
HCl	− 67 kJ/mol	+ 12.6 kJ/mol
HBr	− 25 kJ/mol	− 50.2 kJ/mol
HI	+ 46 kJ/mol	− 117 kJ/mol

It is evident from the above mentioned data that both steps in the addition of HBr are exothermic, a favourable condition for reaction whereas in case of HCl and HI, one of the step is endothermic which is thermodynamically not favourable for a chemical reaction.

Chapter **14**

Environmental Chemistry

Important Results

1. Environmental chemistry deals with the study of the origin, transport, reactions, effects and fates of chemical species in the environment. Chemical species present in the environment are either naturally occurring or generated by human activities.

2. Pollution is defined as a deviation from the natural composition of a part of the environment, resulting in adverse effects on life.

3. Pollutant is a harmful solid, liquid or gaseous substance present in such concentration in the environment which leads to be injurious for the whole living biota.

    (i) Primary pollutants are emitted directly from an identifiable source.

    (ii) Secondary pollutants are derived from primary pollutants by chemical reactions.

4. **Tropospheric pollution** It occurs due to the presence of undesirable solid or gaseous particles in the air. Gaseous air pollutants are oxides of sulphur, nitrogen, and carbon, hydrogen sulphide, hydrocarbons, ozone and other oxidants. Particulate pollutants are dust, mist, fumes, smoke, smog, etc.

5. The vaporised matter with suspended particles of carbon, that arises as a result of burning or combustion of something is called **smoke**. The visible moisture present in atmosphere is called **fog**. Thin vapour of fog, smoke or dust in the air is called **haze**.

6. A cloud of dust, gas or a large mass of water vapour like a light fog is called **mist**. It is formed when a finely divided liquid is suspended in the atmosphere.

7. Smog is a harmful mixture of smoke and fog.

    (i) **Classical smog** It occurs in cool humid climate. It is a mixture of smoke, fog and SO_2. Chemically it is reducing smog.

    (ii) **Photochemical smog** It occurs in warm, dry and sunny climate. It has high concentration of oxidizing agents, so it is called oxidizing smog. Its common components are O_3, NO, acrolein, formaldehyde and peroxyacetyl nitrate (PAN). Photochemical smog causes serious health problems.

8. Air borne particles of solid arising from the condensation of vapours or from chemical reactions are called **fumes**.
9. The air borne solid particles having size 0.1 μ-25 μ are called **dust**.
10. A black substance consisting mainly of carbon particles formed as a result of incomplete combustion of burning matter is called **soot**.
11. The upper layer of the atmosphere, enveloped by ozone (16km-40km) is commonly known as **ozonosphere**, ozone layer, stratospheric ozone layer, protective layer or ozone umbrella. Ozone layer acts as a protective shield in the biospheric ecosystem against their exposure to harmful ultraviolet (UV) radiations.
12. The main cause of ozone depletion is the wide spread use of chlorofluorocarbons (CFCs). Ozone depletion is also taking place due to NO_x, SO_2, CH_4, photochemical smog and green house effect.
13. A **green house** is that body which allows the short wavelength incoming solar radiation to come in, but does not allow the long wave outgoing terrestrial infrared radiation to escape. **Green house effect** is the presence of green house gases blocked in the IR radiation from the earth's surface to the atmosphere. The major green house gases are CO_2, CH_4, N_2O and CFCs.
14. Acid rain means the presence of excessive acids in rain waters. Its main components are H_2SO_4 and HNO_3.
15. Detergents, toxic metals, pesticides, acids, alkalies, salts, sediments, medical wastages, etc, are the main source of water and soil pollution.
16. BOD is the amount of O_2 used up during oxidation of oxygen demanding waste when a sample of water is incubated for five days at 20°C with DO measured before and after.

$$BOD = \frac{\text{Number of mg of } O_2 \text{ required}}{\text{Number of litres of samples}} = \frac{\text{Parts } O_2}{\text{Million parts of sample}}$$

For clean water, the BOD value is less than 5 ppm while highly polluted water could have a BOD value of 17 ppm or more.
17. The process in which nutrient enriched water bodies support a dense plant population, which kills animal life by depriving it of oxygen and results in subsequent loss of biodiversity is known as eutrophication.
18. Soil pollutants are chemicals used as fertilizers, pesticides, and industrial wastage, etc.
19. Pollution may be prevented by using
   (i) zoning
   (ii) installation of controlling devices and equipments.
   (iii) by providing means of equipments to discharge pollutants at higher altitudes.

(iv) by planting trees and growing vegetation.

(v) by public awareness.

20. Green chemistry utilizes the existing knowledge and practices so as to bring about reduction in the production of pollutants.

Exercises

Question 1. Define environmental chemistry.

Solution. Environmental chemistry deals with the chemical interrelations with our surroundings, *i.e.*, study of the origin, transport, reactions, effects and fates of chemical species in the environment.

Question 2. Explain tropospheric pollution in 100 words.

Solution. Tropospheric pollution occurs due to the presence of undesirable solid or gaseous particles in the air. The major gaseous and particulate pollutants present in the troposphere are :

(i) **Gaseous air pollutants** These are oxides of sulphur, nitrogen and carbon, hydrogen sulphide, hydrocarbons, ozone and other oxidants.

(ii) **Particulate pollutants** These are dust, mist, fumes, smoke, smog, etc.

Gaseous air pollutants

(a) **Oxides of sulphur** These are produced when sulphur containing fossil fuel is burnt. SO_2 gas is poisonous to both animals and plants.

(b) **Oxides of nitrogen** These are produced by the reaction of nitrogen and oxygen at high altitudes when lightning strikes.

$$N_2(g) + O_2(g) \xrightarrow{1483 \text{ K}} 2NO(g)$$
$$2NO(g) + O_2(g) \longrightarrow 2NO_2(g)$$
$$NO(g) + O_3(g) \longrightarrow NO_2(g) + O_2(g)$$

(c) **Hydrocarbons** Incomplete combustion of fuel used in automobiles is the major source for the release of hydrocarbon. These are carcinogenic and cause cancer. They also harm plants.

(d) **Oxides of carbon** Carbon monoxide is one of the most serious air pollutants. It is highly poisonous to living beings because it blocks the supply of oxygen to the organs and tissues. It is produced due to the incomplete combustion of carbon.

Carbon dioxide is the main contributor towards green house effect and global warming. It is released into the atmosphere by respiration, burning of fossil fuels and by decomposition of limestone during cement manufacturing.

Question 3. Carbon monoxide gas is more dangerous than carbon dioxide gas, why?

Solution. Carbon monoxide gas is a poisonous gas. It binds to haemoglobin of the blood to form carboxyhaemoglobin. It is 300 times

Environmental Chemistry

349

more stable than oxyhaemoglobin complex. When concentration of carboxyhaemoglobin reaches about 3-4%, the oxygen carrying capacity of blood is greatly reduced. This results into headache, nervousness and cardiovascular disorder.

CO_2 gas does not combine with haemoglobin so it is less harmful as a pollutant. Its increased amount in air is mainly responsible for global warming.

Question 4. Which gases are responsible for green house effect? List some of them.

Solution. CO_2 gas is the major contributor to green house effect. Besides CO_2, other green house gases are methane, water vapour, nitrous oxide, CFCs and ozone (CFC's = chlorofluorocarbons).

Question 5. Statues and monuments in India are affected by acid rain. How?

Statues and monuments are made up of marble *i.e.,* $CaCO_3$ and acid rain contains H_2SO_4. Metal carbonates release CO_2 gas with mineral acids.

Solution. The air around the statues and monuments in India contains fairly high levels of oxides of sulphur and nitrogen. It is mainly due to a large number of industries and power plants around areas. Oxides of nitrogen and sulphur are acidic in nature. SO_2 and NO_2 after oxidation and reaction with water are major contributors to acid rain.

$$2SO_2(g) + O_2(g) + 2H_2O(l) \longrightarrow 2H_2SO_4(aq)$$
$$4NO_2(g) + O_2(g) + 2H_2O(l) \longrightarrow 4HNO_3(aq)$$

This acid rain reacts with marble of statues and monuments causing damage to these.

$$CaCO_3 + H_2SO_4 \longrightarrow CaSO_4 + H_2O + CO_2$$

Question 6. What are smogs? How are classical and photochemical smogs different?

Solution. The word smog is derived from 'smoke' and 'fog'. It is the most common example of air pollution that occurs in many cities throughout the world. There are two types of smog:

(i) **Classical smog** It occurs in cool humid climate. It is a mixture of smoke, fog and SO_2. Chemically, it is a reducing mixture, so it is called reducing smog.

(ii) **Photochemical smog** It occurs in warm, dry and sunny climate. Its main components ozone, formaldehyde, acrolein and peroxy acetyl nitrate are produced by the action of sunlight on unsaturated hydrocarbons and nitrogen oxides produced by automobiles and factories. Chemically, it is oxidizing smog because it has high concentration of oxidizing agents.

Question 7. Write down the reactions involved during the formation of photochemical smog.

Solution. When fossil fuels are burnt, the pollutants unburnt hydrocarbons and nitric oxide are emitted. In the presence of sunlight,

NO is converted to nitrogen dioxide, NO_2. This NO_2 absorbs energy from sunlight and breaks up into nitric oxide and free oxygen atom.

$$NO_2(g) \xrightarrow{hv} NO(g) + O(g)$$

Oxygen atoms are very reactive and combine with O_2 in air to produce ozone.

$$O(g) + O_2(g) \rightleftharpoons O_3(g)$$

The ozone reacts rapidly with nitric oxide (NO) to regenerate NO_2.

$$NO(g) + O_3(g) \longrightarrow \underset{\text{Brown gas}}{NO_2(g)} + O_2(g)$$

NO_2 and O_3 are strong oxidizing agents and can react with unburnt hydrocabrons to produce formaldehyde (HCHO), acrolein

$(CH_2{=}CHCH{=}O)$ and peroxyacetyl nitrate (PAN), $CH_3\overset{\overset{O}{\|}}{C}OONO_2$.

$$3CH_4 + 2O_3 \longrightarrow \underset{\text{Formaldehyde}}{3HCHO} + 3H_2O$$

Question 8. What are the harmful effects of photochemical smog and how can they be controlled?

Recall the constituents of photochemical smog and give their harmful effects.

Solution. Photochemical smog consists of O_3, NO, acrolein, formaldehyde and PAN. O_3 and NO irritate the nose and throat and their high concentration causes headache, chest pain, dryness of throat, cough, difficulty in breathing. Aldehydes and PAN cause irritation in eyes. PAN is highly toxic substance to plants and causes bronzing of tender leaves. Ozone also affects the rubber articles and causes cracking and ageing.

Control of photochemical smog If primary precursors of photochemical smog such as hydrocarbon and NO_2 are controlled, the secondary precursors such as O_3 and PAN will automatically be reduced. In automobiles, catalytic converters are used to prevent the release of nitrogen oxide and hydrocarbons to the atmosphere. Certain plants such as pinus, juniparus, etc., can metabolise nitrogen oxide and can help in reducing photochemical smog.

Question 9. What are the reactions involved for ozone layer depletion in the stratosphere?

Solution. The main reason of ozone layer depletion is the release of chlorofluoro carbon compounds (CFCs), also known as freons. CF_2Cl_2 and $CFCl_3$ are examples of the deadly CFCs. These destroy the ozone layer in the following manner.

(i) In stratosphere, chlorofluorocarbons are broken down by UV rays to produce chlorine free radicals.

$$CF_2Cl_2(g) \xrightarrow{\text{UV rays}} \overset{\bullet}{Cl}(g) + \overset{\bullet}{C}F_2Cl(g)$$

(ii) Chlorine free radicals react with ozone to form chlorine monoxide radicals and molecular oxygen.

$$\overset{\bullet}{Cl}(g) + O_3(g) \longrightarrow \overset{\bullet}{ClO}(g) + O_2(g)$$

(iii) Chlorine monoxide radical reacts with atomic oxygen to produce more chlorine radicals.

$$\overset{\bullet}{ClO}(g) + O(g) \longrightarrow \overset{\bullet}{Cl}(g) + O_2(g)$$

These chlorine free radicals are continuously regenerated to destroy ozone. It has been calculated that one molecule of CFCs can destroy more than thousand molecules of O_3.

Question 10. What do you mean by ozone hole? What are its consequences?

Solution. In stratosphere, ozone is continuously created and destroyed by the sun's radiations. This results in an equilibrium concentration of ozone. In 1980s atmospheric scientists working in Antarctica reported about the depletion of ozone layer commonly known as ozone hole over the south pole.

Effects of depletion of the ozone layer Ozone layer shields the earth from the harmful ultraviolet radiations of the sun. With the depletion of ozone layer, more UV radiation will freely enter earth's atmosphere. These radiations possess high energy and are harmful to man's life. They cause skin cancer, ageing of skin, cataract, sun burn, killing of many phytoplanktons, damage to fish productivity, etc. UV radiation leads to the harmful mutation of cells.

These harmful mutations may cause more severe problems. It also increases evaporation of surface water through the stomata of the leaves and decreases the moisture content of the soil.

Question 11. What are the major causes of water pollution? Explain.

Solution. Pollution of water originates from human activities. Causes of water pollution are :

(i) **Pathogens** Pathogens are disease causing agents such as bacteria and other microorganisms. These pathogens enter in water from domestic sewage and animal excreta.

(ii) **Organic wastes** Organic matter such as discharge from food processing factories, leaves, grass, etc. pollute water. These wastes are biodegradable. The large population of bacterias decomposes organic matter present in water. These bacteria consume oxygen dissolved in water. If too much of organic matter is added to water, all the available oxygen is used up. This causes oxygen dependent aquatic life to die. Anaerobic bacteria also decompose the organic wastes and produce chemicals that have a foul smell and are harmful to human health.

(iii) **Chemical pollutants** Water is an excellent solvent. It dissolves inorganic chemicals that include heavy metals such as cadmium, mercury, nickel which are harmful to humans because our body cannot excrete them. These metals can damage kidneys, central nervous system, liver, etc. Organic chemicals present in the petroleum products pollute many sources of water, *e.g.*, major oil spills in oceans. Various industrial chemicals such as cleansing solvent, detergents and fertilizers also pollute water.

Eutrophication is another source of water pollution. It is the process that results when large quantities of phosphates and nitrates are released into aquatic ecosystems. This pollution causes the amount of oxygen in water to decrease and many organisms die because there is not enough oxygen present for respiration.

Question 12. Have you ever observed any water pollution in your area? What measures would you suggest to control it?

Solution. Yes, polluted water is the water whose quality has been degraded by the addition of substances such as chemical effluents, metal residues, sewage, oil, fertilizers, detergents, etc. It can be controlled by the following methods :

1. Industrial waste discharge from paper, fertilizers, pesticides, detergents, drugs industries and refineries should not be allowed to get mixed in water bodies such as river, lakes, etc.
2. Non-biodegradable detergents should be avoided and only biodegradable detergents should be used for cleansing of clothes.
3. The pH of water should be checked.
4. Excessive use of fertilizers should be prevented.
5. Oil spills should be avoided as much as possible.
6. Domestic waste water should be properly discharged and treated.
7. Avoid the use of DDT, malathion at home.
8. Waste water should be treated in sewage treatment plant.

Question 13. What do you mean by biochemical oxygen demand (BOD)?

Solution. The amount of oxygen required by bacteria to break down the organic matter present in a certain volume of a sample of water is called biochemical oxygen demand (BOD). The amount of BOD in the water is a measure of the amount of organic matter in water, in terms of how much oxygen will be required to break it down biologically. Clean water would have BOD value of less than 5 ppm.

Question 14. Do you observe any soil pollution in your neighbourhood? What efforts will you make for controlling the soil pollution?

Solution. Yes, it can be controlled by the following methods :

1. Insecticides, pesticides which are used for the protection of our crops cause soil pollution. Herbicides (weed killers) also cause soil pollution. Therefore, there is a need for their judicious use.

Environmental Chemistry 353

2. After the World War-II DDT was put to use in agriculture to control the damages caused by insects, rodents, weeds and various crop diseases. However due to adverse effects, its use has been banned in India. Pesticides such as aldrin and dieldrin are organic toxins. These are water insoluble and non-biodegradable. These causes serious metabolic and physiological disorders in animals. Now a days organophosphates and carbamates are also used as pesticides. These are more biodegradable but these chemicals are severe nerve toxins and hence, more harmful to humans.

Therefore, chemicals like fertilizers, detergents, pesticides, polymers, should be used only when necessary.

3. Biodegradable domestic waste should be deposited in land fills.
4. Non-biodegradable waste should be recycled.
5. Use of polythene should be avoided.
6. Household waste, biological waste and chemical waste is often incinerated. Incineration greatly reduces the waste volume.

Question 15. What are pesticides and herbicides? Explain giving examples.

Solution. **Pesticides** These are the substances that are used to kill or block the reproductive processes of pests. These are basically synthetic toxic chemicals with ecological repercussions. Their accumulation in higher animals (through food chain) causes serious metabolic and physiological disorders. DDT, aldrin, dieldrin, organophosphates and carbamates are some examples of pesticides.

Herbicides These are weed killers, *e.g.,* sodium chlorate and sodium arsenite ($NaClO_3$ and Na_3AsO_3). These are toxic to mammals. Some herbicides cause birth defects. Now a days triazines, better herbicides are used for the corn fields.

Question 16. What do you mean by green chemistry? How will it help to decrease environmental pollution?

Solution. Green chemistry is a method of utilizing the existing knowledge and principles of chemistry and other sciences to reduce the adverse impact on environment. Green chemistry is a production process that would bring about minimum pollution or deterioration to the environment. The by-products generated during a process, if not used gainfully, increases the environmental pollution. Such processes are not only environmental unfriendly but also cost-ineffective. The waste generation and its disposal both are economically unsound. Utilization of existing knowledge base to reduce the chemical hazards along with the developmental activities is the foundation of green chemistry.

Question 17. What would have happened if the green house gases were totally missing in the earth's atmosphere? Discuss.

 Green house gases maintain the temperature of the earth.

Solution. Carbon dioxide, methane, water vapour, nitrous oxide, CFCs and ozone are green house gases. These gases trap some of the heat radiated by the earth's object near the earth's surface and keep it warm.

This is called natural green house effect because it maintains the temperature and makes the earth perfect for life. If there were no green house gases, there would have no vegetation and life on our earth (because the earth would convert into a cold planet).

Question 18. A large number of fish are suddenly found floating dead on a lake. There is no evidence of toxic dumping but you find an abundance of phytoplankton. Suggest a reason for the fish kill.

Solution. Large quantities of phosphates and nitrates increases the growth of phytoplankton. These phytoplankton use so much oxygen that it is not enough available for other organisms to use in respiration. Moreover a large population of bacteria decomposes organic matter such as leaves, grass, etc., in water. During this process, they consume the oxygen dissolved in water. Microorganisms may become so abundant that they form a mat covering on the water surface and preventing sunlight from penetrating the surface and thereby preventing photosynthesis. In all these processes concentration of dissolved oxygen in water decreases. When the concentration of dissolved oxygen of water is below 6 ppm, the growth of fish gets inhibited and they cannot survive.

Question 19. How can domestic waste be used as manure?

Solution. Domestic wastes are collected in small bins and carried to the disposable site. At the site garbage is sorted out and separated into biodegradable and non-biodegradable wastes. Biodegradable wastes such as vegetable and fruits waste, animal waste, etc. are deposited in land fills and are converted into manure.

Question 20. For your agricultural field or garden, you have developed a compost producing pit. Discuss the process in the light of bad odour, flies and recycling of wastes for a good produce.

Solution. The compost producing pit should be set up at a suitable place to protect ourselves from bad odour and flies. Biodegradable domestic wastes e.g., used tea leaves, vegetable and fruits waste are put in the compost pit and it is covered with a little sand. After some time, it is converted into compost by the action of heat and bacteria. Compost pit should be kept covered so that flies cannot make entry into it and the foul odour is minimize.

Non-biodegradable domestic waste such as plastic, glass, metal scraps, polythene bags, etc are sent for recycling. Recycling converts waste into wealth.

Selected NCERT Exemplar Problems

Short Answer Type

Question 1. Green house effect leads to global warming. Which substances are responsbile for green house effect?

Solution. Green house gases namely carbon dioxide, methane, nitrous oxide (N_2O), ozone and chlorofluorocarbons (CFC's) are responsible for green house effect, *i.e.*, for maintaining temperature of the earth as these absorb the outgoing radiations from the earth 's surface.

Question 2. Acid rain is known to contain some acids. Name these acids and where from they come in rain?

Solution. Acid rain contains H_2CO_3, HNO_3 and H_2SO_4.

H_2CO_3 is formed by the dissolution of CO_2 of the air in the water.

$$CO_2 + H_2O \longrightarrow H_2CO_3$$

Forest fire and lightning are the natural source of nitric oxide (NO). Nitrogen oxides are also produced by combustion engines, aircraft, furnaces, incinerators, industrial plants.

Nitric oxide slowly reacts with atmospheric air and produce $NO_2 \cdot NO_2$ dissolves in water to form HNO_3.

$$3NO_2 + H_2O \rightleftharpoons 2HNO_3 + NO$$

Sulphur oxides are produced by the burning of fossil fuels and in extraction of metals from their sulphide ores, etc. Sulphur dioxide also produces sulphuric acid in the similar way.

$$SO_2 + O_2 + H_2O \xrightarrow[\text{metal oxide}]{\text{Soot particles}} H_2SO_4$$

Question 3. Ozone is a toxic gas and is a strong oxidizing agent even then its presence in the stratosphere is very important. Explain what would happen if ozone from this region is completely removed?

Solution. Ozone prevents harmful UV radiations of the Sun from reaching to the earth's surface, thereby it protects life from bad effects of UV radiations. If ozone is removed completely from the stratosphere, the UV rays will reach to the earth and leads to several diseases like sun burn, skin infection etc.

Question 4. Dissolved oxygen in water is very important for aquatic life. What processes are responsible for the reduction of dissolved oxygen in water?

Solution. The processes which are responsible for the reduction of dissolved oxygen in water are excessive use of phosphatic and nitrate fertilizers, detergents, the discharge of human sewage and organic waste from food, paper and pulp industries. The microorganisms which oxidize organic matter also used oxygen dissolved in water. Moreover, during night, photosynthesis stops but the aquatic plants continue to respire, resulting in reduction of dissolved oxygen.

Question 5. On the basis of chemical reactions involved, explain how do chlorofluorocarbons cause thinning of ozone layer in stratosphere?
Solution. CFC's are stable compounds. These undergo decomposition in the presence of sunlight, as shown below :
Reactions :

$$CF_2Cl_2(g) \xrightarrow{\ \text{UV}\ } \overset{\bullet}{C}l(g) + \overset{\bullet}{C}F_2Cl(g)$$

$$\overset{\bullet}{C}l(g) + O_3(g) \longrightarrow Cl\overset{\bullet}{O}(g) + O_2(g)$$

$$Cl\overset{\bullet}{O}(g) + O(g) \longrightarrow \overset{\bullet}{C}l(g) + O_2(g)$$

Chain reactions continue in which ozone layer is depleted.

Question 6. What are biodegradable and non-biodegradable pollutants?
Solution. Biodegradable pollutants are those which are decomposed by bacteria, *e.g.*, sewage, cow-dung, fruit, vegetable, etc.
Non-biodegradable pollutants are those which cannot be decomposed by bacteria, *e.g.*, mercury, aluminium, lead, copper, DDT, etc.

Question 7. What are the sources of dissolved oxygen in water?
Solution. Sources of dissolved oxygen in water are (i) photosynthesis (ii) natural aeration and (iii) mechanical aeration.

Question 8. What is the importance of measuring BOD of a water body?
Solution. BOD is a measure of level of pollution caused by organic biodegradable material present in the sample of given water. Low value of BOD indicates that water contains less organic matter.

Question 9. A factory was started near a village. Suddenly villagers started feeling the presence of irritating vapours in the village and cases of headache, chest pain, cough, dryness of throat and breathing problems increased. Villagers blamed the emissions from the chimney of the factory for such problems. Explain what could have happened? Give chemical reactions for the support of your explanation.
Solution. The symptoms observed in villagers indicates that nitrogen oxides and sulphur oxides are released from the chimney of the factory. These are produced by the burning of fossil fuels such as gasoline, coal, natural gas, etc. In an automobile engine, at high temperature when fossil fuel is burnt, dinitrogen and dioxygen combine to yield NO, nitric oxide.

$$N_2(g) + O_2(g) \xrightarrow{\ 1483\ K\ } 2NO$$

$$2NO + O_2 \xrightarrow{\ 1100\ C\ } 2NO_2$$

SO_2 is produced by burning of sulphur containing fossil fuel or by roasting of sulphide ores such as iron pyrites, copper pyrites, etc.

$$Cu_2S + O_2 \longrightarrow 2Cu + SO_2$$

Question 10. Oxidation of sulphur dioxide into sulphur trioxide in the absence of a catalyst is a slow process but this oxidation occurs easily in the atmosphere. Explain how does this happen? Given chemical reactions for the conversion of SO_2 into SO_3.

Solution. The presence of particulate matter in polluted air catalyses the oxidation of SO_2 to SO_3.

$$2SO_2 + O_2 \xrightarrow{\text{Particulates}} 2SO_3$$

Question 11. How is ozone produced in stratosphere?

Solution. Ozone in stratosphere is a product of action of UV radiations on dioxygen (O_2) molecules. The UV radiations split apart molecular oxygen into free oxygen atoms. These oxygen atoms combine with the molecular oxygen to form ozone.

$$O_2(g) \xrightarrow{\text{UV radiations}} O(g) + O(g)$$

$$O_2(g) + O(g) \underset{\text{radiations}}{\overset{\text{UV}}{\rightleftharpoons}} O_3(g)$$

Question 12. Some time ago formation of polar stratospheric clouds was reported over Antarctica. Why were these formed? What happens when such clouds break up by warmth of sunlight?

Solution. In summer season, nitrogen dioxide and methane react with chlorine monoxide and chlorine atoms forming chlorine sinks, preventing much ozone depletion, whereas in winter, special type of clouds called polar stratospheric clouds are formed over Antarctica. These polar stratospheric clouds provide surface on which chlorine nitrate gets hydrolysed to form hypochlorous acid. It also reacts with hydrogen chloride to give molecular chlorine.

$$\overset{\bullet}{Cl}O(g) + NO_2(g) \longrightarrow ClONO_2(g)$$

$$\overset{\bullet}{Cl}(g) + CH_4(g) \longrightarrow \overset{\bullet}{C}H_3(g) + HCl(g)$$

$$ClONO_2(g) + H_2O(g) \longrightarrow HOCl(g) + HNO_3(g)$$

$$ClONO_2(g) + HCl(g) \longrightarrow Cl_2(g) + HNO_3(g)$$

When sunlight returns to the Antarctica in the spring, the sun's warmth breaks up the clouds and HOCl and Cl_2 are photolysed by sunlight.

$$HOCl(g) \xrightarrow{hv} \overset{\bullet}{O}H(g) + \overset{\bullet}{C}l(g)$$

$$Cl_2(g) \xrightarrow{hv} 2\overset{\bullet}{C}l(g)$$

The chlorine radicals thus formed, initiate the chain reaction for ozone depletion.

Question 13. A person was using water supplied by Municipality. Due to shortage of water he started using underground water. He felt laxative effect. What could be the cause?
Solution. The laxative effect is observed only when the sulphates present in water have concentration greater than 500 ppm. Otherwise at moderate levels it is harmless.

Long Answer Type

Question 14. How can you apply green chemistry for the following :
  (i) to control photochemical smog.
  (ii) to avoid use of halogenated solvents in dry cleaning and that of chlorine in bleaching.
  (iii) to reduce use of synthetic detergents.
  (iv) to reduce the consumption of petrol and diesel.
Solution.
  (i) Certain plants, *e.g.*, Pinus, Juniparus, Quercus, Pyrus and Vitis can metabolize nitrogen oxide (NO) and therefore, their plantation could help in reducing photochemical smog.

  (ii) Liquefied CO_2 with a suitable detergent is used for dry cleaning and H_2O_2 (hydrogen peroxide) is used for the purpose of bleaching clothes in the process of laundary which gives better results and makes use of lesser amount of water.

  (iii) Soaps are 100% biodegradable so they should be used in place of detergents. Now a days biodegradable detergents are available. Therefore, they should be used in place of non-biodegradable hard detergents.

  (iv) CNG (compressed natural gas) should be used as it causes much less pollution. Moreover, electrical vehicles should be used to reduce the consumption of petrol and diesel.

Question 15. A farmer was using pesticides on his farm. He used the product of his farm as food for rearing fishes. He was told that fishes were not fit for human consumption because large amount of pesticides had accumulated in the tissues of fishes. Explain how did this happen?
Solution. Pesticides from the soil are transferred into the crops and from the crops these are transferred into fish food. Pesticides entered into water through fish food and finally entered into the bodies of the fishes. Therefore, pesticides are transferred from lower trophic level to higher trophic level through food chain. Over the time, the concentration of pesticides in fishes reach a level which causes serious metabolic and physiological disorders.

Question 16. For dry cleaning, in the place of tetrachloroethene, liquefied carbon dioxide with suitable detergent is an alternative solvent. What type of harm to the environment will be prevented by stopping use of tetrachloroethene? Will use of liquefied carbon dioxide with detergent be completely safe from the point of view of pollution. Explain.

Solution.

   (i) Tetrachloroethene, $Cl_2C=CCl_2$ is suspected to be carcinogenic and also contaminates the ground water. This harmful effect will be prevented by using liquefied CO_2 along with suitable detergent.

  (ii) Use of liquefied CO_2 along with detergent will not be completely safe because most of the detergents are non-biodegradable and they cause water pollution. Moreover, liquefied CO_2 will ultimately enter into the atmosphere and contribute to the green house effect.

Ingram Content Group UK Ltd.
Milton Keynes UK
UKHW021358250423
420747UK00015B/665